THE CULTURE

OF MAKE

BELIEVE

Also by Derrick Jensen

Railroads and Clearcuts

Listening to the Land

A Language Older Than Words

Standup Tragedy (live CD)

THE

DERRICK JENSEN

CULTURE OF MAKE BELIEVE

CONTEXT BOOKS　　　NEW YORK　　　2002

www.contextbooks.com

Designer: Julie Burke
Jacket design: Julie Burke
Cover Photograph: Jerry N. Uelsmann
Typeface: Janson

Context Books
368 Broadway
Suite 314
New York, NY 10013

Library of Congress Cataloging-in-Publication Data

Jensen, Derrick, 1960-
  The culture of make believe / Derrick Jensen.
      p. cm.
Includes bibliographical references.
  ISBN 1-893956-28-8 (pbk. : alk. paper)
1. Racism. 2. Racism—Economic aspects. 3. Race relations—
Economic aspects. 4. International economic relations—Social
aspects. I. Title.
  HT1523 .J46 2002
  305.8—dc21

2002000045

  ISBN 1-893956-28-8

Parts of this book have previously appeared in somewhat
different form in *The Sun*.

9   8   7   6   5   4   3   2   1

Manufactured in the United States of America

CONTENTS

ix   Preface

4   Uncovering

16   Utility

34   Invisibility

66   Contempt

74   Power

86   Property

98   Philanthropy

110   Giving Back the Land

136   Beginning to See

156   Redemption and Failure

188   Flesh

206   Seeing Things

232   The Other Side of Darkness

252   Criminals

276   Killers

298   The Cost of Power

308   Tranquillity and Felicity

316   Assimilation

338   The Impossibility of Forgetting

350   Production

376   False Contracts

388   Competition

408   Distance

426   Corporations, Cops, and Hungry Ghosts

446   War

464   Resistance

484   Expanding the Frontier

512   The View From Inside

532   The Closing of the Iron Cage

554   Holocausts

600   Coming Home

607   Acknowledgments

610   Notes

671   Bibliography

PREFACE

 IN 1918, the husband of Mary Turner, a black woman from Valdosta, Georgia, was killed by a mob of white men, not for any offense he had committed, but rather because another black man had killed a white farmer. I do not know precisely how Turner's husband died. I do not even know his name. I know only that in retaliation for the killing of the white farmer, many white citizens of Valdosta lynched eleven black men—who were simply in the wrong place at the wrong time with the wrong color skin—before they shot and killed the man they were after.

In the wake of her husband's murder, Mary, who was eight months pregnant, vowed to avenge those who killed her husband. An Associated Press article later commented on her "unwise remarks," noting that "the people, in their indignant mood, took exception to her remarks, as well as her attitude." If you dig beneath the delicate language, it is easy to see what was coming. A mob of several hundred white men and women determined they would "teach her a lesson," or, perhaps more precisely, they would teach a lesson to those others who might be tempted to act as she did. They tied her ankles together and hung her upside down from a tree. Then they doused her clothes with gasoline and burned them off of her. They used a hog-splitting knife to open her belly. Her infant fell to the ground, and cried briefly, until someone crushed its head with his heel. The mob then shot her, not once or twice, but hundreds of times.

Now, let's remove ourselves from the emotionally safe dustbin of history to another death that happened in 2001. This person who died—I do not know her name, or very much about her except that she was seventeen years old—was one of about forty people killed over Easter weekend in Alto Naya, in Colombia. Her killers were what these days we call a death squad. I do not know what the members of the death squad said to her or the other people from her village, before they killed her, any more than I know what the members of the mob said to the husband of Mary Turner. I do not know what they were thinking, or feeling, nor do I know the set of their faces. I do not know whether they laughed, or spat, or whether they were simply doing what they felt needed to be done. I know only that when her body was later exhumed, it was discovered that members of the death squad had cut off her hands with a chainsaw, and used that also to open her belly and throat.

It is as easy as it is unwise to simply throw up our hands in the face of these acts, declare them incomprehensible or, just as safely, having nothing whatsoever to do with any of us. *I've never stuck anyone with a knife, nor even* aimed *a chainsaw at a human being. I just don't understand how someone could do this. Maybe they're just evil.*

But are the actions really so difficult to understand, and do they really have nothing to do with us? What do we make of the fact that in the aftermath of the killing of Mary Turner and the others, five hundred black people quietly and quickly left Valdosta for greener (or, at least, safer, pastures) leaving plenty of fine farmland ripe for new tenants, including those who never held a rope, gun, or knife? Similarly, is it significant that in Colombia, U.S. oil companies— including a company for which George W. Bush was a board member before becoming president of the United States—operate in the regions where these death squads kill, routinely?

The texture and direction of this book was deeply informed by the deaths—the killings—of these four human beings, and by a desire to understand not only the meanings of these deaths, but the threads that tie them together. What is the precise relationship between our economic system and hate? Is there a relationship between economics and race? If so, what is it? And as long as we're delving into the destructive activities of our culture, what about our seeming antipathy toward women? Why, also, I wanted to know, the shift in the frontier where the most grotesque of these atrocities are committed? Thousands of black men and women were lynched in this country in the first twenty years of the twentieth century. Not so often, now, though, do we see black men hanging long-necked from lamp posts. Is this country now color-blind, as much mainstream discourse would have us believe? For that matter, is color-blindness a good thing? Or are there certain economic and social conditions that facilitate, even call forth, certain forms of atrocity, and are there other economic and

THE CULTURE OF MAKE BELIEVE

social conditions that require other forms of making certain that people's attitudes do not become too "unwise"?

There is something else I have wanted to explore while writing this book, having to do with perception, or rather the lack of it. Let's be honest. The activities of our economic and social system are killing the planet. Even if we confine ourselves merely to humans, these activities are causing unprecedented privation, as hundreds of millions of people—and more today than yesterday, with probably more tomorrow—go their entire lives with never enough to eat. Yet curiously, none of this seems to stir us to significant action. And when someone does too stridently point out these obvious injustices, the response by the mass of people seems so often to be that which was meted out to Mary Turner, a figurative if not physical blow to the gut, leading inevitably to a destruction of our common future. Witness the enthusiasm with which those native nations that resisted their conquest by our culture have been subdued, and the eagerness with which this same end is today brought to those—native or not— who continue to resist too strongly. How does this come to happen, in both personal and social ways?

My book, *A Language Older Than Words*, was a deeply intimate exploration of, among many other things, the complex relationship between domestic violence and how this violence tricks out on a grander social scale. This book you hold in your hands is not quite so personal, in great measure because, while I suffered directly from violence within my family—my father raped my mother, my sister, and me, and beat everyone in my family but me—I have not suffered from, but rather, at least indirectly, benefited by, whatever racism exists in our society. So in some senses this book is more about racism—and, far more broadly, hate as it manifests in our Western world—from the inside. I have no interest in reproducing *Black Like Me*. I leave it to black people to interpret their experience of living in our culture, and to Indians their experience, and women theirs. Instead it falls to me—and others of my race and gender—to explore and articulate—and thus, I hope, help to halt—the white male experience of this hatred: How did we come to enslave one continent, significantly depopulate another, and work our will on all of the others? How, in short, have we come to conquer the world? Why have

Preface

we wanted to do this in the first place? And can we stop wanting it?

Although the tectonic psychosocial movements of history can be interesting, in and of themselves they are meaningless. Any exploration of them must return to the personal, to the particular, because that's all we've got. There is a sense in which the entire history of white enslavement of Africans was of no importance whatsoever to Mary Turner in her last moments. What probably mattered to her most in her last seconds of consciousness was that her skin hurt terribly from the flames, her belly hurt—more than I can imagine—from its gaping wound, her heart was broken, having witnessed, first, her husband's death, and then her child's head being crushed under a man's boot, and that she knew in a few moments she too would be dead. But it is as dangerous as it is tempting to discuss her death without discussing the larger social context that led to it, far more surely than her "unwise remarks," and, I would say, just as surely as the gasoline, knife, and bullets. This is where I hope this book will be of some use. If we wish to stop the atrocities, we will need to understand and change the social and economic conditions that cause them.

There was another person killed in Alta Naya, Colombia, whose death deeply informed this book. I've written it partly in homage to him, even though I do not know his name. But I know that when a member of the death squad came to shoot him, he wrested the gun from the man's hands. Unfortunately for him, he did not know how to use it. Presumably, he had never before fired a gun. He was overpowered, tied to a tree, and killed with a chainsaw.

This book is a weapon. It is a gun to be put into the hands of all of us who wish to oppose these atrocities, and a manual on how to use it. It is a knife to cut the ropes that bind us to our ways of perceiving and being in the world. It is a match to light a fuse.

THE CULTURE OF MAKE BELIEVE

THE CULTURE

OF MAKE

BELIEVE

MONSTERS EXIST, BUT THEY ARE TOO FEW
IN NUMBER TO BE TRULY DANGEROUS.
MORE DANGEROUS ARE THE COMMON MEN,
THE FUNCTIONARIES READY TO BELIEVE AND
TO ACT WITHOUT ASKING QUESTIONS.

PRIMO LEVI

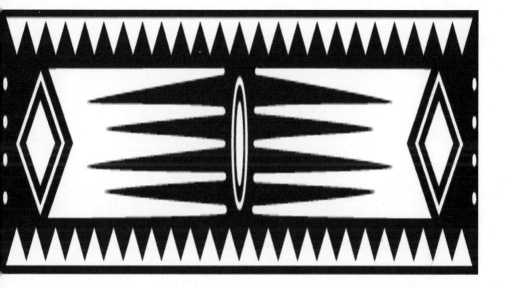

UnCOVeRiNG

AT FIRST GLANCE, hate groups may seem to have little in common with the culture at large. We're told that hate groups, while on the rise, remain an aberration and stand in opposition to everything we hold dear. This line of thought holds that while racism may at one time have reigned supreme in this country, we're well on our way to being color-blind and widely tolerant, with the exception of a few white-robed buffoons who chant "White Power" in mush-mouthed accents. No longer, for example, do we allow black men to be lynched with impunity. When a black man was recently dragged to his death behind a pickup, those guilty faced not only lethal injection, but the disgust of an entire nation.

But the gulf between hate groups and the mainstream isn't so vast as that first glance would lead us to suspect. To attempt to really understand hate groups is to begin to burrow into the culture's soft, white, underbelly, and to confront painful truths about who we are, what we believe, and how we act.

■   ■   ■

How, exactly, would you define a hate group? The obvious answer is slippery. For example, most people would agree that the Ku Klux Klan (KKK) is a hate group, the granddaddy of American racist organizations. But literature from the Knights of the Ku Klux Klan states explicitly that the KKK "is not a hate group, but we are a LOVE group. We are a love group because we LOVE America and we LOVE our people." The literature continues, "We don't want those who are only looking for an outlet for their hatred. Hatred never accomplishes anything. We feel terrible for those who have been victims of non-white crime and anti-white discrimination, but turning your life over to hatred isn't the answer. It will only cause self destruction. On the other hand if you have a deep sense of love for your white brothers and sisters and truly desire for them to have a better life, then your efforts to awaken them to the plot to destroy western Christian civilization will be fruitful. God will bless your efforts which are based on love."

The point seems elementary, but bears being stated explicitly: Either we accept that the KKK isn't a hate group, or we shouldn't blindly rely on a group's self-description. Choosing the former means devaluing the definition of a hate group to mean only those groups whose members aren't sophisticated enough to mask their messages of hate behind claims to virtue. Choosing the latter leads to another question: On what *should* we rely? The group's actions? If so, then which actions? Murder? If so, are some murders more despicable than others? Does the race, gender, or sexual preference of the victim play into the discussion? Or is the simple number of murders more important? How about the motivation of the killers?

UnCOVERinG

The man in Texas who was dragged to death behind a pickup was killed because he was black. This seems a hate crime, pure and simple. But what if the killers had been more sophisticated than these happened to be, and their rhetoric was not then to be trusted? Had these killers masked their motives with a robbery, would it still be a hate crime? What if they honestly believed their motivation was fiscal, yet simply chose, for whatever reason, to rob only or primarily black people, or only or primarily poor people? And say, then, that most of these robbery victims just happened to end up dying? Would these be hate crimes? Of course you could also say it doesn't really matter: Economics or hate, the victim is dead either way.

■　　　■　　　■

Most of the people convicted of Crimes Against Humanity at the main Nuremberg trials for major war criminals in 1946 were those we would have expected: Hermann Göring, director of the Luftwaffe and founder of the Gestapo; Ernst Kaltenbrunner, head of the Reich Security Office and second in command of the SS after Himmler; Hans Frank, governor of occupied Poland; and so on. But one person—Julius Streicher—was convicted and hanged for the crime of running a newspaper.

"It may be that this defendant is less directly involved in the physical commission of crimes against Jews," one of the prosecutors told the court. "The submission of the Prosecution is that his crime is no less the worse for that reason. No government in the world . . . could have embarked upon and put into effect a policy of mass extermination . . . without having a people who would back them and support them. . . . It was to the task of educating the people, of producing murderers, educating and poisoning them with hate, that Streicher set himself. . . . In the early days he was preaching persecution. As persecution took place he preached extermination and annihilation. . . . [T]hese crimes . . . could never have happened had it not been for him and for those like him. . . . Without him, the

Kaltenbrunners, the Himmlers . . . would have had nobody to carry out their orders."

■   ■   ■

Perhaps it's not murder as such that defines a hate group, but the attempt to inspire terror in a specific category of victim. That was one purpose, to choose an obvious example, of the Night Riders of the KKK's nineteenth-century incarnation. They visited the homes of black people with the intent of, among many other things, terrorizing them into not using their recently gained right to vote.

Yet here, once again, the definition slips from our grasp. If the definition of a terrorist is anyone who wishes to create terror in a specific category of victim, with the purpose of altering the behavior of the members of that category, does this then mean that anyone who supports imprisonment and especially the death penalty as deterrents to crime is by definition a terrorist? (The same question could be asked, then, of anyone who spanks or threatens to spank a child.) Clearly the stated purpose is to terrify a specific group of people into changing their behavior. That's what deterrence is. And given the rates at which blacks, Latinos, and American Indians, are imprisoned (and on death row), it could be argued that a good part of the judicial and penal systems in the United States constitutes a giant racist, terrorist organization. Simply looking at the numbers it becomes clear that the judicial and penal systems have achieved the segregation of black males—into prisons—on a scale of which the KKK and their puny brethren could only dream.

■   ■   ■

The purpose here is not to blur distinctions between the KKK and the U.S. government. Clearly there are differences. But what *are* the differences, and what are the similarities?

There are many important distinctions; for one thing, if the KKK

UnCOVERiNG

had the full resources of the state, it would presumably work hard to lock up the other two out of three young black males who've thus far been able to avoid the judicial system.

Another important distinction: The judicial system is part of the government—*our* government—and when we speak of hate groups, we're normally referring to groups acting in opposition to the government, and in opposition to the will of the ultimate governors, the people.

Or are we? To state that governments, and in fact entire peoples, cannot be hate groups pushes us into an absurdity: It would mean that while the American Nazi Party, with its paltry membership is a hate group, the Third Reich, with its death camps, military aggression, slavery, race-based murder, and other crimes against humanity, was not. Given the awesome power of the state to inflict violence and terror on its own and other citizens (remember the Soviet Union?), it seems unwise to arbitrarily exclude nations from consideration as hate groups.

Here is another argument: The judicial and penal systems are imprisoning only *criminals*, people who've done something to deserve imprisonment. Ostensibly they're not targeting specific races or classes, but statistics as well as racial-profiling policies—such as routinely stopping motorists for the crime of Driving While Black— put the lie to this. All that said, we need to admit that the judicial and penal systems exist to protect all of society. But this argument leads us just as quickly into difficulty. Most extralegal lynchings were precipitated by some offense—real or imagined—on the part of the victim, and even the modern KKK states that it, too, is protecting society, in this case, against "the plot to destroy western Christian civilization." Don't forget that the Nazi government stated it acted defensively when with due process of law it ordered Jews segregated into concentration camps, or prisons.

Nothing is so simple as, at first glance, it seems.

■　　　　■　　　　■

In the Violent Crime Control and Law Enforcement Act of 1994, Congress defined a hate crime as "a crime in which the defendant intentionally selects a victim . . . because of the actual or perceived race, color, national origin, ethnicity, gender, disability, or sexual orientation of any person."

Each year the Federal Bureau of Investigation is required by law to compile statistics on the prevalence of hate crimes in the United States. In 1998, 7,755 "bias-motivated criminal incidents" were reported by forty-six states and the District of Columbia. Of these, 4,321 were motivated by racial bias, 1,390 by religious bias, 1,260 by sexual-orientation bias, 754 by ethnicity/national origin bias, twenty-five by disability bias, and the remaining five were the result of multiple biases. The thing that interested me about all this is that none of these were explicitly and solely gender-based. I called my local district attorney and asked, If a hate crime is defined as "a crime in which the defendant intentionally selects a victim . . . because of the actual or perceived . . . gender," why isn't rape, or, at least, most rape, considered a hate crime? Just as James Byrd, Jr., was chosen to be dragged behind a pickup for no meaningful reason other than his race, so, too, a good percentage of rape victims are chosen for no meaningful reason other than their gender. The D.A. replied that rape is covered under its own law, and needn't be covered separately as a hate crime. I told him the same logic would be true for murder.

"That's my point," he said. "There are as many reasons for rape as there are for murder." He then explained to me that if a man rapes a woman specifically because she's black, it counts as a hate crime. If he rapes her because she's white and dating a black man, it counts as a hate crime. If he rapes her because she's a lesbian, it counts as a hate crime.

"What if," I asked, "he rapes her because she's a woman?"

"Rape by itself isn't a hate crime," he said. "It's a sex crime."

"But if the victim is chosen because she's a woman. . . ?"

"If you don't like it," he said, with unwarranted testiness, "take it up with the legislature."

UNCOVERING

Instead, I took it up with the FBI. This time I spoke with a woman. Same question.

She said, "The reason rape isn't included is that the motivation is obviously different. The motivation is not to violate their civil rights, but from a desire to hurt, or from a desire to just have sex."

I asked for the FBI's definition of civil rights.

She looked it up and said: "The rights belonging to a person by virtue of his or her status as a citizen or as a member of civil society."

I asked for the FBI's definition of a hate crime.

She was very patient. She quoted from the FBI uniform crime report: "A hate crime is a criminal offense committed against person, property, or society, which is motivated in whole or in part by the offender's bias against a race, religion, disability, sexual orientation, or ethnicity."

No gender this time. One more definition. Rape.

"Carnal knowledge of a female forcibly and against her will."

"The definition doesn't include males," I said.

"Interesting, isn't it?"

"Okay," I said. "Let me get this straight. A woman's, or any person's, civil rights do not include freedom from unwanted carnal knowledge."

"Gender isn't included as one of the protected classes in federal statute."

"What about the inclusion of gender in the Violent Crime Control and Law Enforcement Act of 1994?"

"There's confusion about what is and isn't included. Legislation is pending to include gender as a protected class."

"Okay," I said. "Let's say gender *were* a protected class. Would rape then be included?"

"Again, the motivation is obviously different. It's not a hate crime."

The difference wasn't obvious to me. My brain hurt. I hung up, and went to a maximum security prison, where I teach creative writing.

THE CULTURE OF MAKE BELIEVE

•   •   •

The woman at the FBI had said something that piqued my interest, which was that involuntary servitude, even based on race, does not constitute a hate crime.

I called another FBI spokesperson a few days later. I wanted to know if I understood correctly. "If someone beats a man because he's black, that can be a hate crime."

"Correct."

"If someone rapes a woman because she's Asian, that can be a hate crime."

"Correct."

"If someone rapes a woman because she's a woman, that cannot be a hate crime."

"Correct."

"If someone enslaves a man or otherwise forces him to work because he's black, that cannot count as a hate crime."

"Correct."

I thanked him.

•   •   •

In 1823, U.S. Supreme Court chief justice John Marshall wrote a decision remarkable for its candor about a subject we would all generally prefer not to acknowledge: The means by which the United States government, and more broadly EuroAmerican culture, took possession of this continent. By now there can be few who still believe the continent was empty when the Pilgrims and other colonists landed here, or that, for whatever reason, the original inhabitants—the Indians—held no prior claim to the land. To this day, the federal government admits that 33 percent of the land mass of the continental United States was never ceded by treaty, and, therefore, is held illegally. How, then, does the government, and, once, again more broadly, do we nonnatives, justify possession of this land?

uNCOVERiNG

Here's what Marshall had to say about it. In a case called Johnson v. M'Intosh, Marshall declared that "discovery gave title . . . which title might be consummated by possession." He reasoned, "However extravagant the pretension of converting the discovery of an inhabited country into conquest may appear; if the principle has been asserted in the first instance, and afterwards sustained; if a country has been acquired and held under it; if the property of the great mass of the community originates in it, it becomes the law of the land, and cannot be questioned." Translation: If conquest forms the basis for your community—if your community would simply not exist without it—*conquest cannot be questioned.*

He was explicit: "However this . . . may be opposed to natural rights, and to the usages of civilized nations, yet, if it be indispensable to that system under which the country has been settled, and be adapted to the actual condition of the two people, it may, perhaps, be supported by reason, and certainly cannot be rejected by Courts of justice." He also said, "Conquest gives a title which the Courts of the conqueror cannot deny, whatever the private and speculative opinions of individuals may be." Let us translate this as well: If an entire system is based upon an injustice, the Supreme Court can do no other than to codify this injustice into law. To translate it further, and perform a perhaps forgivable anachronism: To kill one Indian may or may not be a "hate crime"; to dispossess an entire culture may "be supported by reason, and certainly cannot be rejected by Courts of justice."

■   ■   ■

What is a hate crime? What is hatred? What, for that matter, is a crime? When discussing hate groups, why do we so often constrict our vision to include only the most absurd, the most grotesque, the most individual or small-scale of crimes? Why not go after larger targets? What about hatred or exploitation that is systematic, that is codified, that hides behind the screen of law, religion, philosophy, science? Certainly the Nazis cloaked their hatred of those they de-

THE CULTURE OF MAKE BELIEVE

creed *untermenschen*—less than human—in the language of science: eugenics, crazed biological determinism cohabiting with social Darwinism. And what about hatred masquerading as economics? What about, to take an obvious example, apartheid?

UNCOVERING

WHAT AN ABUNDANCE OF
RAIN AND GRASS WAS
TO NEW ZEALAND
MUTTON, WHAT A PLENTY
OF CHEAP GRAZING
WAS TO AUSTRALIAN
WOOL, WHAT THE
FERTILE PRAIRIE
ACRES WERE TO
CANADIAN WHEAT,
CHEAP NATIVE LABOR
WAS TO SOUTH AFRICAN
MINING AND
INDUSTRIAL ENTERPRISE.

C. W. DE KIEWIET

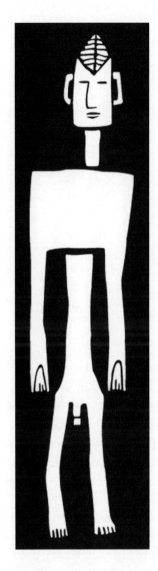

UTILITY

CONSIDER A DIAMOND. The majority of people in the United States own at least one. Few of them realize that nearly all these stones were supplied by one company—DeBeers. Even fewer are aware that the laws of apartheid were drafted and implemented at the request of, and explicitly to serve, DeBeers and related mining companies.

Prior to the arrival of Europeans, southern Africa was home to stable, functioning, ancient human communities. These included the San, who, along with their evolutionary predecessors, had probably been in the region for nearly two million years, the longest any human culture has existed in one place; the Khoikhoi, pejoratively labeled Hottentots by Dutch settlers; and a wide-ranging and inter-mingled group of cultures united by their use of the Bantu family of languages.

It's hard to say whether the actions of European explorers and settlers read more like a bad dream or like a replay of European explorers and settlers everywhere. Probably both. They came, they saw, they conquered, and they did not question their right to do so. The Dutch East India Company established a post near modern Cape Town, then expanded it year by year. When displaced Khoikhoi asked, according to the post's commander, Jan Van Riebeeck, "whether, if they were to come into Holland, they would be permitted to act in a similar manner," Van Riebeeck stated, presaging Marshall by some hundred and sixty years, that the country had been "justly won by the sword in defensive warfare, and that it was now our intention to retain it." If the Khoikhoi continued to complain, he said, "they would lose still more of their land by the right of conquest, unless indeed they had the courage to expel us." The Khoikhoi were driven off their land, enslaved, and, ultimately, exterminated. The San, too, were driven off their land. The Bantu? That's where diamonds come into play.

But before we get to diamonds, we need to be clear about one thing. From the perspective of the perpetrators—from inside the system of thought that gave rise to apartheid—nothing that's been done to these people has been motivated primarily by hatred or racism. None of it would be understood as a hate crime perpetrated by a hate group. Indeed, apartheid wasn't a crime: it was *the law.*

Instead of hate, the motivation for the treatment of the Africans could have been been territorial expansion. It could have been progress. It most certainly could have been economic production. It could have been that the laws of apartheid were actually implemented to help the natives: as Governor Harry Smith told native chiefs, whom he routinely forced to kiss his feet at bayonet point, "You may no longer be naked and wicked barbarians, which you will ever be unless you labour and become industrious. . . . You must learn it is money that makes people rich by work."

Or it could be that the laws of apartheid were simply deemed necessary, no questions asked. So long as vision remains constricted, hatred can often remain invisible from the inside.

vTiLiTY

Now, to diamonds. Diamonds were discovered in South Africa in 1867, precipitating a rush that by 1871 made South Africa the world's largest supplier. Mines could only be owned by whites, and were worked almost exclusively by blacks. Because labor was by far the greatest expense of owning a mine, a free market in labor could have driven up wages—catastrophe for mineowners—which meant workers needed to be restricted. Thus were enacted the first of the infamous Pass Laws of apartheid, these prohibiting native movement after 8:00 PM, and requiring, under threat of flogging, all native workers to carry signed passes to be shown at any time "to anyone who may demand it." The laws were passed not from any overt hatred, but for reasons of economy. We'll find that this was true at each step of apartheid's implementation.

Employers were concerned about theft of diamonds, and in any case, the Pass Laws didn't suffice to prevent a free market in labor, so African workers began to be confined to company "compounds" for the duration of their employment, a practice originating with the use of convict labor that continues to this day. Workers were separated from their families, and from all other outsiders, for the yearlong duration of their contract. Exceptions to the rule of noncontact were made for missionaries, who were "enjoined to impress upon the native mind two simple Christian precepts—the virtue of obedience and the dignity of labour."

Gold has been at least as important as diamonds to the South African economy, and to the creation of apartheid. Gold deposits were found in South Africa in 1868, but modern South African gold mining really began with the discovery of the main gold-bearing formation at Witwatersrand in 1886. The monopolistic mineowners, who also owned the diamond mines, faced the same need in both sectors: cheap labor.

A South African mining official asked, "Is there any way short of compulsion to make him [an African] go to a mine?—Not one that I know of. He would have to be compelled?—We might achieve it by paying a very high rate, but that would . . . defeat the object we have in view." Not only that, but according to the Director of Native

Labour, "To make him an entirely free agent as a labouror . . . would certainly cause industrial dislocation and jeopardise the economic prosperity of the country."

If your community is founded on an injustice, that injustice cannot be questioned.

Most natives lived off the land, and thus did not need to sell their labor. To force them off the land and into the mines, the government (made up of the mineowners and others like them) passed poll, hut, and even dog, taxes. Because the natives had not previously been part of a cash economy, they had to go into mines to earn money to pay taxes.

More laws followed, passed, still and always, of course, not out of hatred, but compassion. The purpose of the laws, according to Cecil Rhodes, prime minister of South Africa and owner of DeBeers and other mining concerns, was to "remove these poor children out of their state of sloth and laziness, and give them some gentle stimulants to go forth and find out something of the dignity of labour." To this end he introduced a Masters and Servants Bill, giving white employers the right to beat their nonwhite employees. The bill became popularly known as the Every-Man-to-Wallop-His-Own-Nigger Bill. He later passed the Glen Grey Act in the Cape, which imposed taxes, replaced communal with individual land ownership, and forced Africans to follow rules of inheritance guaranteeing that all but one member of every family would be made landless. Additional Masters and Servants Laws prohibited Africans from breaking their contracts, no matter how harsh the working conditions. Nothing in the Masters and Servants Laws, however, prohibited death from breaking the contracts: Death rates in the mines ran between 8 and 10 percent per year, translating to 8,000–10,000 human beings killed in the mines just in 1899 (around twenty-five per day).

Thus the final pieces of the apartheid puzzle fell into place during the first two decades of the twentieth century: dispossession, decimation of communal social structures, and racial segregation on a national scale. What the mines needed at this point, according to the president of the Chamber of Mines, was "a policy that would

UTILITY

establish once and for all that outside special reserves, the ownership of the land must be in the hands of the white race, and that the
surplus of young men, instead of squatting on the land in idleness
and spreading out over unlimited areas, must earn their living by
working for a wage, as every white man who is not a land-owner
must do."

The mines got the workers they needed.

■   ■   ■

I have to admit I'm glad I was born white. Very rarely have I received
stares of hatred due to my race. When I was a teenager, I spent a
summer at the University of Southern California, and often wandered off-campus into Watts, where I'd see black men playing basketball. At first I was scared to join them. I was white, they were
black, and I'd been told by television that these men could be dangerous. Finally I asked someone in my dorm—a black man—if he
thought it would be okay. I will never forget the pained look he gave
me before he said, "You grew up in a white community, didn't you?
You don't know anything." Then he turned my insult into a joke. He
started laughing and said, "So long as they're holding a basketball,
they can't pull a gun on you." After that we began running early
mornings through Watts. He cautioned me, playfully poking fun at
my racist fears, "Make sure you don't lag behind me. A white man
chasing a black man just won't fly here."

I went to play basketball many nights. We had fun. The only
night I got worried was during a marathon one-on-one game (to one
hundred) with a guy who kept dashing to his bag to grab what he
called "pep pills." I got scared. I'd been warned on TV, after all,
about black youths and drugs. He could become violent at any moment. He might try to hook me on something. Finally, he asked if I
wanted any, and held out his hand. They were jelly beans.

But there have been times I've been hated for my race. Not
often, but a few times, playing basketball with black men, the sport
has failed to erase the racial tension, and I've been elbowed a bit

harder than necessary, been cursed when I've done nothing to deserve it. A few times among Indians I've received hard stares a propos of nothing I've said. Other times I've blundered and received stares for insulting them as ignorantly as I insulted my friend at U.S.C.

But the most hateful stares I've received because of my race have been from whites. I was in New Zealand with my friend Jeannette Armstrong, an Okanagan Indian. She was doing some work with Maori friends, and I was there to help. At least one of the Maori disliked me intensely for my race, but on the main they were among the most welcoming people I've ever met. As I went to leave, a couple of them gave me a beautiful black shirt with a Maori flag on the front, with the caption *Maori Rangotiritanga—Maori Independence*. I was as proud to wear it as they were to give it to me.

I had never before understood the phrase *nigger lover*, nor the contempt with which such race traitors are regarded. But now at least, to some small degree, I did. White men and women looked at my face, stared at my shirt, then moved their gaze back up to meet mine, their lips set and downturned, jaws tight, cheeks hard, eyes angry. I knew if given the opportunity, a few of them would have been eager to hurt me.

I was on my way out of the country. I experienced the hatred only for the few hours it took to get to the airport and fly across New Zealand. After that, on the international flight, and now, at home, the shirt is no affront to those who don't know what it means.

It's a cliché to say one *cannot imagine* something, but the truth is that it's impossible for me to fathom what it would be like to receive those stares not for a shirt I can shed but for skin I cannot. I don't know what it would do to my heart to always be so noticed, and so unwelcome, no matter where I went, to be met with contempt or worse every day of the year. I think it wouldn't be very difficult for me to internalize those stares, and to begin even to hate myself.

There's another reason I'm glad I'm white. I enjoy going into the prison to teach, but I enjoy even more the fact that I get to come home when I'm done. My students don't have that luxury.

UTILITY

Although blacks make up only 12 $\frac{1}{2}$ percent of the population of this country, they account for more than 45 percent of prison inmates sentenced to more than one year. The United States imprisons black men nine times more frequently than it does whites, and four times more than South Africa did during apartheid. Over 30 percent of this nation's African-American males between the ages of twenty and twenty-nine are under criminal justice supervision—awaiting trial, in jails or prisons, or on probation or parole. In some areas the figures are even worse: in Washington, D.C., 42 percent of black men between the ages of eighteen and thirty-five are under criminal justice supervision, and in Baltimore it's 56 percent. More than half. During the first two years California's three-strikes law was in effect, 43 percent of those sentenced for a third strike were black, even though blacks account for only 7 percent of the population and 20 percent of those arrested. Hispanics, Asian-Americans, and Native Americans are also grossly overrepresented in the prison system.

I teach four classes at the prison. Three of them are in "level four," or maximum security. One is in "level one," or minimum security. Out of about sixty level-four students, six are white. Of six students in level one, only one isn't.

I'm glad I was born white.

■   ■   ■

How, precisely, do you define a police state? Is it the number of police per capita? How about the number of prisons? Police use of machine guns or armored personnel carriers? The use of the police or the military to put down strikes, or to otherwise "keep the trains running on time," as was Mussolini's specialty? Perhaps it's the use of the police or the military to halt civil unrest. Or maybe the widespread use of curfews. Arbitrary confiscation of private property. How about this? Could a police state be defined, as in Nazi Germany, by the use of force to segregate members of a specific race into concentration camps or prisons?

■   ■   ■

The best estimates are that every day in the United States, at least four to six people die because they encountered police. These deaths are the result of shootings, beatings, high-speed pursuits, and medical neglect in jails and prisons. The vast majority of those killed are members of racial or ethnic minorities. The vast majority of police are white.

The numbers could be slightly lower, or they could be substantially higher. No reliable national database exists on the use of excessive force by police. Since the passage of the Crime Control Act of 1994, the federal government has been legally required to collect national data on police use of excessive force—similar to its collection of data on hate crimes—but each year Congress fails to provide funding. Not having data makes it that much harder to recognize and analyze the problem, and that much harder to take effective action to stop it.

This means that all information is anecdotal. Yet the anecdotes continue to roll in, each one so much more, to those involved, than just an anecdote or a statistic. Each one a life ended.

■   ■   ■

Each of the following died unarmed, unresisting:

> Edward Anthony Anderson, January 15, 1996, shot while handcuffed and on the ground. Frankie Arzuega, fifteen years old, January 12, 1996, shot in the back of the head; the following Mother's Day, his family received taunting phone calls from anonymous sources: they dialed *69 (call back) and the police answered. Anthony Baez, December 22, 1994, choked to death for playing football on the streets of New York City. Rene Campos, whom police said committed suicide in cus-

UTILITY

tody by stuffing more than half his T-shirt down his
own throat, reaching three-quarters of the way down to
his lungs. Garland Carter, seventeen years old, January
8, 1996, shot in the back by police who earlier that day
had driven by his home, making their fingers into the
shape of a gun and "firing." Angel Castro, fifteen years
old, October 23, 1996. Having already moved out of a
neighborhood because of death threats from police,
Castro rode his bike back to the neighborhood to a
friend's birthday party: He accidentally ran into a police
cruiser, breaking his teeth, and as he rose from the
ground a cop shot him. Sherly Colon, April 24, 1997,
pushed off the roof of a housing project, after which police removed the cuffs which had held her hands behind
her back. Moises DeJesus, April 11, 1994, beaten to
death after his family called 911 because he was having
a seizure. Amadou Diallo, February 4, 1999, shot forty-
one times as he reached for his wallet in the vestibule of
his own building in New York City. Arthur Díaz,
September 10, 1994, who ran when police caught him
Dumpster-diving (he had outstanding traffic violations), after which they ran over him with their police
cruiser, then backed up and ran over him again.
Kenneth Brian Fennell, August 30, 1993, shot four
times at close range after having been stopped for al-
legedly driving 70 mph in a 65 mph zone, but in reality
for Driving While Black. Ramón Gallardo, Sr., sixty-
four-year-old retired farmworker and father of thirteen,
July 11, 1997, shot fifteen times by a SWAT team that
had gone to the wrong address. Jonny Gammage,
October 12, 1995, beaten with a flashlight, then choked
to death, because he was a successful black businessman
driving through a white neighborhood. Ralph Garrison,
sixty-nine years old, December 16, 1996, shot, after
calling 911 and walking to his porch carrying a gun, by

a black-clad SWAT team he thought was burglarizing rental property next door (for good measure, they shot his dog, too). Wayne Garrison, shot by police while hiding naked in his closet. Malice Green, beaten to death with a flashlight because he refused to open his hand, which contained a piece of paper (the convictions of the officers who killed him were overturned in part because the jury watched the movie *Malcolm X* during a break in deliberations). LaTanya Haggerty, June 4, 1999, the first of her working-class family to go to college, shot to death because she held a cell phone. Esequiel Hernandez, Jr., eighteen years old, May 20, 1997, shot in the back of the head while herding his family's goats after school (he did, admittedly, have a gun, but it was to protect the goats, and he never even knew he was being stalked by the cops). Salomon Arambula Hernandez, February 15, 1997, forgot to pay for gas after pumping, then drove back, paid the five dollars, and was told by the clerk that the police had already been called: He waited there for them, and the police promptly shot him three times. Nicholas Heyward, Jr., eleven, September 27, 1994, had been threatened by police that he would not live to be fifteen: At thirteen he was playing cops and robbers with friends, using an orange toy gun, when a policeman arrived in his building. Nicholas dropped the gun and said, "We're only playing, we're only play—" before he was shot to death. Daryl Howerton, September 8, 1994, shot six times because he was feeding someone's guard dog; Yong Xin Huang, March 24, 1995, ninth-grade honors student, shot in the head by a police officer who first threw him into a glass door. Felix Jorge, Jr., July 28, 1994, beaten by prison guards, who then stuffed fifteen yards of toilet paper into his mouth and nose, causing him to suffocate. Tyisha Miller, December 28, 1998, shot twelve times after being startled awake while sleeping in a disabled car. Jason Nichols, October 17, 1994, pinned facedown on the ground and shot in the head because police thought he was someone else. Robin Pratt, March 28, 1992, machine-gunned as she ran to shield her infant daughter from a SWAT team at the wrong house. Bobby Russ, June 5, 1999, two weeks from graduating from Northwestern University, shot and killed while driving to his parents' home. Henry Sanchez, October 19, 1996, beaten to death riding his bicycle near his home. Thomas Scheel, May 19, 1998, whose body was riddled with bullets because he was masturbating wearing black lace panties and a white apron in a parking lot. Dwight Stigons, shot in the back because he jaywalked, then reached for his Bible. Kenneth Michael Trentadue, August 21, 1995, arrested and thrown into a cell by police who, after sabotaging surveillance cameras, crushed his skull with a baton, kicked him in the face hard enough to leave boot marks, tasered him, slit his throat, moved his body to another room, and called it suicide. Hilton Vega and Anthony Rosario, cousins, January 12, 1995, suspected of nothing, shot, for no reason, in the back fourteen times while handcuffed and on the ground, leading New York mayor Giuliani that night to call the police who killed them for congratulations on a job well done. Antoin Keshawn Watson, June 13, 1996, shot eighteen times while sitting in his car with his hands in the air (after the first shot, one cop said, "You're a dead nigger"). Aaron Williams, June 4, 1995, asked by police, who suspected him of burglary, to come out of his home, and when he did, twelve cops swarmed him, hog-tied him, rammed his head against the wall, beat and pepper-sprayed him, kicking him hard enough in the face to leave a boot print, after which they placed a surgical mask over his

nose and mouth to keep in the pepper spray, threw him
into the back of the police van, drove past three hospitals on the way to the police station, and left him parked
in the van until he was dead.

The list is as long as you want to make it.

■   ■   ■

Imagine what it must be like to walk for the first time into prison, and
to know that this is where you will live for the next year, two years,
five years, ten years. Maybe for the rest of your life. Imagine hearing
the whistles, and walking shackled down the long row of cells, looking up the tiers and seeing the faces looking back at you. Imagine
wondering which of them will be the one to victimize you.

I was told by one of my students, "The real problem isn't so
much with the prisons as the county jails. There, the other prisoners
extort money from you, and if they like you they beat you with tennis shoes inside of socks, then force you to sleep on the floor under
the toilet."

"And if they don't like you?"

"You don't want to know."

So often when a man thinks about what it would be like to enter
prison, one of the first things that comes to mind is the possibility
that he will be raped. That reality has entered public consciousness
enough that it has become a stock joke on sitcoms, in movies, and on
late-night television talk shows: the fear that the innocent man will
be locked in a cell with love-starved Bubba, who spends his days
pumping iron, and his nights alone with you.

That fear is not without merit. Estimates put out by the Federal
Bureau of Prisons suggest the rates for male rape inside prison run
between 9 and 20 percent. The best and most thorough statistical
survey of a prison—a medium-security institution in California in
1982—suggested that 14 percent of that prison's population had been
sexually assaulted there (9 percent of the heterosexuals and forty-one

uTiLiTY

percent of the homosexuals had been sexually assaulted). More recently a researcher conducted a survey of the entire Nebraska prison system: 22 percent of those who responded indicated they'd been forced to have sexual contact. These estimates are universally regarded as conservative. I need to add, however, that when I asked my level-one students at the prison about this (many of these students having been previously in higher-security prisons) they all stated that they had rarely seen or heard of incidents of prison rape, and I believe them.

As well as suffusing public awareness and becoming fodder for throwaway jokes, the extreme level of rape inside prison (presuming that my students are exceptions to what seems to be a statistical rule) has generated no small amount of outrage. The level is high enough to have caused a court of appeals in 1988 to label it a "national disgrace." Perhaps even more damning, Vermont's commissioner of corrections called it a "fact of life for those behind bars," and then went on to elaborate that "few aspects of incarceration are more horrifying than the prospect of sexual exploitation and forcible rape within jail and prison walls. It is a subject to which society reacts with a combination of fear, disgust, and denial. We don't want to believe that our criminal justice system tolerates such a cruel and unusual form of punishment. However, this is a brutal reality faced daily by inmates in crowded prisons and jails throughout the country, including bucolic Vermont. . . . The issue of coerced sex will not simply go away."

■   ■   ■

Most people acknowledge that at least on the inside, rape is not a sex crime, but a crime of power. In an all-male prison, the absence of women forces men to create women, that is, to create a subordinate class, the feminine to their masculine, the submissive to their aggressive, the penetrated to their penetration, to create a class of the fucked. Gender roles are socially re-created in this crucible of powerlessness, this place where nearly everyone has been deprived of

most of his power—power of movement, power of eating when and what you want, sleeping when you want or with whom you want, power to choose one's associates—which makes every remaining act fraught with meaning, a flashpoint for personal power. One of my students had his throat slit ear to ear because he stole someone's shoes, then bragged about it. When shoes are invested with this much meaning, how much more so the integrity of one's body? It is no wonder that in a social setting where so many have been systematically deprived of so much power, that so many then strike out with what's left to them.

Rape in prison breaks down strongly along racial lines. In a 1968 benchmark study, a prison-rape researcher found that 15 percent of the cases involved white aggressors and white victims, 29 percent involved black aggressors and black victims, and 56 percent involved black aggressors and white victims. No cases involving white aggressors and black victims were reported. At first these results didn't seem so meaningful as they would later, because the vast majority of the inmate population in question was black: The number alone would have skewed the statistics. But more recent studies have confirmed similar ratios at prisons where as few as 22 percent of the inmates are black.

Most of the people who've studied this pattern concur that patterns of racial domination in prison often become mirror images of social dynamics on the outside. Now white people, and especially the white middle class, are victimized in a not-so-subtle revenge for what goes on in "the real world."

■   ■   ■

I'm glad I was born male.

There's something interesting about the rate at which men in prison are raped: it's lower than the rate at which women are raped in the culture at large. Most studies suggest that 25 percent of women in the United States are raped during their lifetimes, and another 19 percent have to fend off rape attempts. I suppose you could

UTILITY

say that for women—and not just those in prison—rape is "a fact of life." When a man goes to prison, everyone seems to think: "Oh, shit, he's going to get raped." But every day, women walk down the streets, or stay in their homes, and face that same possibility.

■   ■   ■

I don't know what to make of the fact that when I do a quick Alta Vista search of the Internet using the keyword "rape," I get far more pornography sites than any other category (rape crisis hot lines, support groups, scholarly analyses, histories, news, and so on). Pornography makes up more than a third of the total sites. And remember, the keyword here was *rape*, not *sex*, *body*, *nude*, or even *vagina*, *penis*, *dick*, or *pussy*; we're talking action, not anatomy.

I visited some of these sites. Leaving aside the more obvious and routine treatment of women as objects to be invaded ("Feeling a little sneaky? Take a tour through a house with live hidden cams. Watch unsuspecting victims get caught! Shower cam. Inside her toilet cam!") I was struck by the sheer number of depictions of outright violence against women accompanied by a correspondingly violent—and (sorry to be naïve) disrespectful—ambience. "Nasty little breeders." "You command the action of these young sluts. Your wish is there [*sic*] command." "Look at those dirty little asian sluts." "Fuck this asian teen in every hole." And there were images of women tied, being struck, with jars or feet or things I couldn't quite figure out in their vaginas.

The point here is not to express outrage at the depictions—though that would be easy enough to do—but to point out once again how slippery is our notion of hate. I strongly suspect that if the photos were not of women but instead of members of a "protected class"—imagine sites with tens of thousands of pictures of black men bound because they're black, with captions like "You command the action of these young bucks," or white men gagged because they're white, with captions labeling them "dirty little breeders"—the sites would be recognized as promoting hate. The organizations that

monitor hate groups would watch closely. But even the most comprehensive hate-watch sites—for example, the extraordinary "Hate Directory," which monitors even such obscure sites as American Christian Nationalists CyberMinistries Sodomy Information Center, Grendel's White Power Video Games, and Why Christians Suck—do not count these as hate sites. Truth be told, I've yet to encounter at any of the racist sites 1/100th the crudity or overt violence manifest at these. This is not to say the racist sites aren't hateful, but rather to point out an obvious blind spot.

This all leads to a slew of questions. The first and most obvious is, Why are materials depicting (and even reveling in) violence against women not counted as hate propaganda? The "protected class" argument doesn't actually work in the case of the Hate Directory, because the Directory's "Criterion Statement" reads: "Included are Internet sites of individuals and groups that, in the opinion of the author, advocate violence against, separation from, defamation of, deception about, or hostility toward others based upon race, religion, ethnicity, gender or sexual orientation." The second and, in many ways more important, and profound, question is, Why are some forms of hate so transparent to us? The third and perhaps most troubling question is, How many more of these "invisible" forms of hate are there?

uTiLiTY

THE TRUTH IS REPLACED

BY SILENCE, AND

THE SILENCE

IS A LIE.

YEVGENY YEVTESHENKO

iNViSiBiLiTY

THE "INVISIBLE EMPIRE" of the Ku Klux Klan sprang into being almost overnight after the Civil War, spreading, according to the Klan version of the story, "with inconceivable rapidity, until its 'dens' largely dominated the States of Mississippi, Alabama, Tennessee, Georgia, North Carolina, South Carolina, Florida, and parts of Arkansas and Louisiana. It . . . sent forth 100,000 armed men to do its bidding, passed laws without Legislatures, tried men without courts, and inflicted penalties, sometimes capital ones, without benefit of clergy; it was the most thoroughly organized, extensive, and effective vigilance committee the world has ever seen; or is likely to see." Even allowing for the puffery that accompanies nearly any organization's autobiography, the pervasiveness of the Klan was total enough and its level of activity high enough that even in Texas—not at the time one of the Klan's primary strongholds—the commanding officer of the federal troops reported, "Murders of Negroes are so common as to render it impossible to keep accurate accounts of them." In the weeks preceding the presidential election of 1868, at least 2,000 people were killed or wounded by Klan violence in Louisiana alone.

President Woodrow Wilson later gave a reason for the killings: "The white men of the South were aroused by the very instinct of self-preservation to rid themselves, by fair means or foul, of the intolerable burden of government sustained by the votes of ignorant negroes. . . . There was no place of open action or of constitutional agitation, under the terms of reconstruction, for the men who were the real leaders of the Southern communities."

The popularity of the Klan—and the fact that it was often made up of "the real leaders of the Southern communities"—in some ways makes irrelevant its precise origins; it doesn't really matter whether it was founded by former Confederate general Nathan Bedford Forrest, as common mythology has it, or whether a half-dozen young men got together in the winter of 1865, as one of the KKK's founders put it, and as is these days generally accepted, "to start something to break this monotony, and to cheer up our mothers and the girls."

At first the purpose of the Klan was nothing more than "purely social" and for its members' "amusement," as the KKK's first Grand Turk stated, a bunch of kids back from the war putting on ridiculous robes and scaring each other. But something about the Klan sparked the imagination of the community at large, giving voice and form— at first in small ways, later in decidedly larger and more overtly violent ways—to resentment and racism felt by many, if not most, white Southerners. It acted as a lens to focus the ambient energy of the community onto a target deemed detrimental to the community's well-being.

And so the pranks took on an edge of purpose. African-Americans increasingly became the butt of practical jokes meant to intimidate. Then the activities moved beyond pranks. Prayer meetings and political gatherings of African-Americans were broken up. Guns were confiscated from blacks by spectral figures carrying skulls under their arms and claiming to be the ghosts of Confederate dead. "Insolent" blacks were terrorized into moving from their homes. And if they refused to move? As a Klan history drolly puts it, "Notice to leave the country was frequently extended and rarely declined, and, if declined, the results were likely to be serious."

Lynching, rape, torture, castration. The Klan—this invisible empire of hooded men—became the perfect vehicle for an incipient hatred toward blacks and others who threatened traditional economic, social, and political structures. Anonymous, nocturnal, its members were the white shadows of the community leaders they were by day. Throughout the South, ministers, newspaper editors, former Confederate officers, local politicans—all these banded together in local Klans joined only loosely in a national organization. As brevet lieutenant Joseph W. Gelray, sent by the Freedmen's Bureau to investigate the violence of the KKK in Tennessee, stated, "[T]here is *no intention or desire on the part of the civil authorities or the community at large to bring the murderers to justice.* Those who could will not, and those who would are afraid. Perhaps all are more or less afraid; but the most shocking part of this whole matter is that some of those who are considered good citizens, and actual leaders of good society and moulders of public opinion, are active with both tongue and pen in defending and justifying the Ku-Klux Klan in their most horrible outrages against law and nature." A writer for the *Cincinatti Gazette* observed, "Were all the Ku-Klux arrested and brought to trial, among them would be found sheriffs, magistrates, jurors, and legislators, and it may be clerks and judges. In some counties it would be found that the Ku-Klux and their friends comprise more than half of the influential and voting population."

The first point to be made about this is that even then the stereotype of Klan members as mere buffoons was almost entirely false, sleight of mind that, to this day, allows all of us to acknowledge the existence of racism while pretending it is equal to unsophistication and stupidity. Perhaps more importantly, it allows us to isolate racism in some Other who, though we might find him frightening on a personal level (I would hate to be caught with a bunch of New Zealand racists in an alley containing just enough light for them to see my *Maori Rangatiratanga* shirt), we can comfortably deem him socially insignificant. Our maintenance of this stereotype facilitates the maintenance of our personal and social self-image as nonracists. A second point buttresses the first. The Klan's explosion across the entire South, combined with its true grassroots nature, makes clear that it was no splinter group, no slender Other we can place into ideological quarantine. It was, and is, something much closer to our own hearts.

■　　　　■　　　　■

I just got off the phone with my friend John Keeble. He is an extraordinary novelist and thinker, and the author of an excellent novel about the murky and unacknowledged relationship between transnational corporations and hate groups. "It's not that corporations always funnel money to hate groups," he said, "although that does happen." His voice was thoughtful and slow, resonant, with always a slight hesitation before speaking, as though checking his sentence one last time before sending it into the world. He continued, "The connection between Henry Ford and fascism is well known. I think the same is true of Joe Coors. Rupert Murdoch. And of course in the Third World—in the colonies—transnationals routinely support death squads and vice versa."

I thought of the words of Ogoni activist Ken Saro-Wiwa in 1994: *They are going to arrest us all and execute us for Shell.* Saro-Wiwa said this after reading a leaked Nigerian military memo that stated, "Shell operations still impossible unless ruthless military operations are undertaken for smooth economic activities to commence." It went on to recommend that soldiers begin "wasting" Ogoni leaders, "especially vocal individuals," and concluded by recommending pressure on oil companies for "prompt, regular" payments to support the cost of military operations. Four days after this memo was written, four traditional Ogoni leaders were murdered by a mob at a rally, and al-

invisibility

though Saro-Wiwa was in military custody at the time, nine months later he was charged with inciting the riot. He was executed. After this, I thought of another memo, this one written by a spokesperson for Shell Nigeria: "For a commercial company trying to make investments, you need a stable environment; dictatorships can give you that." And I thought also of something else Ken Saro-Wiwa had said. "Human life does not mean much to those who have benefited from the oil."

I thought of Weyerhaeuser, the first company to sign contracts with the military dictatorship in Indonesia, and of the use of the Indonesian military to support Freeport McMoRan. Occidental Petroleum in Columbia, where, as I write this, 5,000 U.S.-backed troops are marching into U'Wa territory to force the U'Was to accept more oil wells on their homeland. Dictatorships and transnationals. Hand in glove.

"But that's not the connection that interests me the most," John said.

There was that hesitation, and, had I not known him so well, I would have asked what he meant. But I knew to wait.

He said, "They're cousins."

I just listened.

"Nobody talks about this," he said, "but they're branches from the same tree, different forms of the same cultural imperative. . . ."

"Which is?"

"To rob the world of its subjectivity."

"Wait—" I said.

"Or to put this another way," he continued, "to turn everyone and everything into objects."

Again he paused, before he said, "The methodology used by each is different. Corporations are carriers of ruin, turning everything they touch to money. They are culturally sanctified, supported, and protected in their role of turning the living—forests, oceans, mountains, rivers, human lives—into the dead: money. And because they are culturally sanctified they get to act aboveground."

"And hate groups?"

"Beneath, hidden, hated. But serving that same function of objectifying. Their entire self-definition is based on this objectification." He paused. "Of course that's true for corporations as well, in a different way."

Neither of us spoke, until finally he returned to the subject of hate groups. "I can hate another person *because* of who he is without denying his individuality. In fact it's possible to hate him *because* of who he is. But if I hate a person because she's black, or an Indian, or a Jew, or a woman, or a homosexual, I'm not even giving her the honor of hating her in particular. I'm hating a stereotype that I'm projecting onto her."

That movement toward depriving others of their subjectivity, I thought, is *the* central movement of our culture. Many Indians have told me that the most basic difference between Western and indigenous ways of being is that Westerners view the world as dead, and not as filled with speaking, thinking, feeling subjects as worthy and valuable as themselves.

I asked him why he's spent so long—a decade, nearly 20 percent of his life—studying both hate groups and big oil. He said, "They provide fingerholds by which we can pry our way in, gain access to the hidden workings of our culture. The way big oil provides the fingerhold should be pretty clear. Each individual member of an oil company may not intend to commit a hate crime. They are merely attempting to maximize profits, and in so doing they talk themselves into committing the most horrible of atrocities. That brings us to hate groups. Hate groups state openly that they're racist and afraid. We're all racist, and we're all afraid. It's just that most of us are afraid to admit it. This means we all get to hate the hate groups, for their heavy-handed, comic-book propaganda, and especially for the hatred that is there in the culture, but which we cannot acknowledge." He paused, then continued, "And that's too bad, because a threat unacknowledged is ultimately—on a bone level—far more disturbing than an acknowledged and understood threat. Of course it's also more

iNVISIBILITY

dangerous. This is true whether we're talking about something as simple, and as easy to fix, as a broken stairstep, or something as convoluted and confusing as an abusive family, or an abusive culture."

■   ■   ■

The psychiatrist R. D. Laing once formulated three rules by which a pathological family—one plagued by alcoholism or severe abuse—can keep its pathology hidden even from the family members themselves. Adherence to these rules allow perpetrators, victims, and bystanders alike to maintain the delusion that they're one big happy family.

"Rule A: Don't.

"Rule A.1: Rule A does not exist.

"Rule A.2: Do not discuss the existence or non-existence of Rules A, A.1, or A.2."

It should be obvious that these rules apply not only to social systems as small as nuclear families, but equally to those as large as cultures.

■   ■   ■

It really isn't possible to talk about hate without talking about children as objects of hatred. I know that age isn't a protected class under the Violent Crime Control and Law Enforcement Act of 1994, but, bear with me.

Each year an estimated 20,000 Mexican children disappear, many for use as mules, to transport drugs inside their bodies, others taken for the harvest of their organs, to be transplanted into children in the United States. This is according to a study performed by the Institute for Law Research at the Autonomous National University of Mexico and presented at a conference on "International Traffic in Children."

Worldwide, entire economies have been founded specifically on the sexual trade in children. One hundred to eight hundred thousand Thai girls and boys work as prostitutes (A brochure distributed in

THE CULTURE OF MAKE BELIEVE

England advertising a Thai resort reads, "If you can suck it, use it, eat it, feel it, taste it, abuse it or see it, then it's available in this resort that truly never sleeps"). Nearly all of them are enslaved or indentured. A good portion have received death sentences from HIV. There are 1.5 to 2 million child prostitutes in India (those in Bombay, for example, are often held in cages; fifty cents buys half an hour of sex with a twelve-year-old). Five hundred thousand child prostitutes work in Brazil (a child of thirty-five pounds is considered a prime size in many mining towns). There are 200,000 child prostitutes in or from Nepal (most of these girls are kidnapped, sold for between forty and a thousand dollars, "broken in" through a process of rapes and beatings, and then rented out up to thirty-five times per night for one to two dollars per man). Between 100,000 and 300,000 children work the sex trade in the United States (one study of U.S. survivors of prostitution found that 78 percent were victims of rape by pimps and buyers an average of forty-nine times per year; 84 percent were the victims of aggravated assault; 49 percent had been kidnapped and transported across state lines; 53 percent were victims of sexual abuse and torture; and 27 percent had been mutilated). On average, a child prostitute services more than 2,000 men per year. At least a million new girls per year are forced into prostitution.

Kids are not, of course, injured only through sexual exploitation. A half-million children die every year of starvation or other direct results of so-called debt payment from Third World countries—from the colonies—to those countries which lend them money while holding their resources and infrastructures as collateral—colonialism in the twenty-first century—and eleven million children die annually from easily treatable diseases. This latter has been called by the World Health Organization director-general "a silent genocide."

This is not counting the children who are simply beaten. According to the U.S. Centers for Disease Control, in 1993, 614,000 American children were physically abused, 300,000 were sexually abused, 532,000 were emotionally abused, 507,000 were physically neglected, and 585,000 were emotionally neglected. 565,000 of these children were killed or seriously injured. That's just in the United States.

iNViSiDiLiTY

So here's the question: Do all these numbers—or, more precisely, the reality behind these numbers—imply that we hate children? Perhaps the answer would be more evident if we simply invert the question: "Do we value children?"

The answer, of course, is yes. One to two dollars per fuck, unless we happen to be in the Philippines, in which case it will cost us six dollars to have sex with a six-year-old.

So let me put the question another way: Was slavery in the United States based on hatred of the Africans, or was it based on economics? Is hate even the right word?

The problem we have in answering (or even asking) these questions comes from the fact that hatred, felt long enough and deeply enough, no longer feels like hatred. It feels like economics, or religion, or tradition, or simply the way things are. Rape is not a hate crime because our hatred of women is transparent. Child prostitution is not a hate crime for the same reason that beating a child is not a hate crime, because our hatred of children is transparent. The economic murder of children (or creating the economic conditions for their slavery as prostitutes) is not a hate crime because we've held this hatred long enough to enshrine it into our macroeconomic policies.

If we did not hate children, we would not cause or even allow them to be destroyed by any of these means. And if we do not love even our children, what, precisely, can we truly say we love?

■   ■   ■

I took a walk this afternoon on a beach near my home. The beach is beautiful—gray sand with pockets of baby-fist–sized pebbles—and nearly always devoid of people. Today was no exception. I shared the beach only with an acquaintance I met last year at the prison. No, not an inmate who climbed the fence (multiple fences, actually: one concrete wall under clear view of the gunner, followed by a dead zone that offers an open field of fire and then electrified razor wire, followed by still more razor wire) so that he could glimpse the ocean and hear the hollow gurgling of waves receding over and through the pebbles (and, of course, to have a scintillating conversation with me), but one of the prison psychologists.

We've gotten together a couple of times, and I don't believe we'll get together again. I've been troubled by some of the things he's said in the past, and today he pushed me too far. About six months ago he got on this big kick where he began trying to talk me into taking a full-time job at the prison, teaching basic education. I told him I enjoy teaching there once or twice a week, but that any more would bite into my writing time.

He shook his head. "You could always write when the prisoners are locked down."

"And when they're not?"

"That's easy," he said. "Go to Thomas and say, 'You wouldn't believe the shit Hollingshead is saying about you.' Then go to Hollingshead and say, 'Thomas says you're a woman, and says he wants to fuck you.' Next time they're on the yard, one of them sticks the other, and there you go: instant lockdown."

I'd tried to pass that off as a feeble and offensive attempt at humor, hoping it was out of character. Tonight I decided it wasn't. Here's how it happened: I started to tell him about this book. He bristled at my suggestion that the judicial and penal systems are racist (I believe it was Upton Sinclair who stated, "It's difficult to get a man to understand something when his salary depends on his not understanding it"), but his real objection came when I mentioned the sections about rape. He said, "Rape is a really loaded word."

"It's not the word that's loaded," I replied. I gave him the incidence statistics.

He shook his head. "There are so many forms of sexual expression—heterosexual, homosexual, older people with younger people—and when we talk about rape we're really talking about people entering a zone of discomfort. We don't like to talk about those zones, much less enter them. But if you're going to grow you have to enter the discomfort."

I didn't know how to respond.

He continued, "It's like me. Lately I've been making a lot more money, and I've grown to realize that I'm not comfortable with my own success. Does that mean I have to be afraid of it? No, of course not."

"I don't think," I said, "that you really want to compare making more money to getting raped."

"Come on," he responded. "Don't be so serious. I heard a great joke the other day. Want to hear it?"

I told him *No*, but he continued anyway.

"What's the difference between rape and ecstasy?"

I'd heard the "joke" before, only with the alliterative "rape and rapture." I didn't want him to continue, but didn't know how to stop him.

"Salesmanship," he said. And then he burst out laughing.

By this time we were no longer on the beach. We were sitting in his car, outside my home. It was dark. I told him I needed to get to work, and began to open the door. The interior light came on.

He said, "We're leaving some issues up in the air. Don't you want to talk them through?"

"I really need to get to work."

I got out of the car and walked into my home. I wished I would have told him the version of this "joke," told by a woman from Mexico: "There is no difference between being raped and being hit by a truck, except that after rape men ask if you liked it." I was disappointed in myself. I should have said something.

■   ■   ■

Years ago I stayed for a few days at the house of a friend who runs a battered-women's shelter. One of the remarkable things about this woman is that whenever she meets a new man, whether he drives her in a taxi, sits next to her on the subway, or crashes in her spare room, she asks him what it will take for men to stop beating on women.

She has her own theory. She believes that violence against women will stop—and presumably the same is true for violence against blacks, Jews, children, homosexuals, or other targeted classes—only when other men refuse to socially reward those who are violent. "Women can't do it by ourselves. If a man hits his girlfriend, the man's friends need to stop playing basketball with him, and they need to tell him why. They need to confront him about it, and they need to socially isolate the men who have shown themselves incapable of mature relationships. And they need to do it every time. The bottom line is that members of the class of people who are doing the violence—in this case, men—need to take responsibility for the violence done by their class, and they need to work to stop it. Until that happens, not very much will change."

■   ■   ■

I just got back from the prison. I did not teach. Instead, when I arrived, I was told the place was in "a state of emergency." There had been a terrible riot that morning, and shots were fired.

I asked, "Is everything okay now?"

"Yes," was the response I got. "No staff was injured."

I turned to go home.

I stopped when I heard him say, almost as an afterthought, "One more thing. Nine inmates were shot. At least one is dead. Another is on a ventilator. Four more were shot in the head or chest."

"That's terrible," I said.

"That's prison," he replied.

■   ■   ■

A few days ago, a jury of eight whites and four blacks found four police officers not guilty of murdering Amadou Diallo. That is, they found them not guilty of intentional first-degree manslaughter, intentional second-degree murder, second-degree murder with depraved indifference, criminally negligent homicide, or reckless endangerment.

Amadou Diallo, an African immigrant, was a devout Muslim who neither smoked nor drank. He worked twelve hours a day selling

invisibility

scarves, hats, and videos on street corners around Manhattan. Each month he sent a check to relatives in Guinea.

Here is how he died. He left his apartment a little after midnight, and was approached by four plainclothes policemen in the lighted vestibule of his building. The officers later claimed that Diallo "behaved in a threatening manner," but were unable or unwilling to elaborate on this statement. A *defense* witness at the subsequent trial stated that the police never identified themselves, and that they approached with their guns already drawn. The police opened fire, with two officers firing all sixteen rounds from their nine-millimeter Glock handguns, another firing five times, and the fourth firing four, for forty-one shots in all. The same defense witness testified that Diallo fell in the first shots, and yet the police continued to fire into him. He eventually was hit nineteen times, including through the bottom of his foot. He died in the vestibule.

Immediately after the killing, a neighbor overheard one officer telling the others that they had to get their stories straight: "Okay, okay, we'll say this." After that, police ransacked Diallo's apartment and detained his roommate in a desperate attempt to discover drugs, weapons, or anything that might justify their shooting. They found nothing.

The response by defenders of the police was as predictable as the incident itself. Lawyer Stephen Worth of the Patrolmen's Benevolent Association made a statement that accurately describes not only the actions of the police officers that night, but, also, ultimately provides a key, perhaps *the* key, to understanding the behavior of our culture as a whole: "The idea is for them to use all the firepower available until the threat is removed." Remember this sentence, and its context, the next time the United States invades a Third World nation. As I edit this book, the United States has nearly finished bombing Afghanistan, and is gearing up to do the same to Somalia. My understanding is that the Sudan is next on the list. In each case, all available firepower has been used.

New York mayor Rudolph Giuliani's response to the killing of Diallo was to state at a press conference that the New York police would now begin to use hollow-point rounds for their Glock nine millimeters. This ammunition, illegal, according to international rules of warfare, because it expands upon impact and thus explodes huge holes in the flesh of the victim, is not, evidently, illegal for use on the home front.

It's important, I think, to not demonize the individual cops and their protectors. Even though three of the four defendants had already had multiple charges *filed against them for abuse of authority, excessive force, or racial* insensitivity, and even though one of them had already shot to death another black man, the problem is larger, and more slippery. We have in place in this country a system of courts that exists ostensibly to determine innocence or guilt in these cases, and to determine appropriate punishment. In this instance, charges were brought, and the jurors found the officers not guilty of all charges, because, as one juror later stated, "Based on the case before us and the instructions given to us, we had no choice. We were told to see the shooting from the officers' point of view, not Mr. Diallo's. The judge said to the jury they should put themselves in the shoes of the officers." One of the jurors, the wife of a former FBI agent, found the prosecutors' case—that an unarmed man was shot nineteen times at close range, many of those shots coming after he was down—to be "weak," and wondered publicly why charges had been brought in the first place.

It may or may not be appropriate to remark that within a few days of the verdict, another unarmed black man in the same neighborhood was shot to death by a police officer.

I need to say also that on the day I wrote these words, I opened the newspaper to read of yet another unarmed man shot dead by New York police. This man was an ex-convict who no longer used drugs. An undercover cop tried repeatedly to get the man to set up a deal for him. The man refused. The cop insisted. The man grew upset at what he thought was a drug dealer, and he pushed the guy away. Of course, the guy was a cop, and pulled out a gun and shot the man dead.

It is a safe bet that the policeman will not be found guilty of any crime.

iNVISIBILITY

■   ■   ■

The KKK didn't cause the violence against blacks and those who supported them; the violence was already happening. In May of 1866, to provide one example among many, long before the KKK expanded its range beyond Pulaski County, Tennessee, and long before the Klan's avowed purpose became anything other than to "have fun, make mischief, and play pranks on the public," mass violence broke out hundreds of miles away in Memphis. The violence began when a group of black men protested the arrest of two of their friends by six white policemen. Police fired into the crowd, wounding one. Someone in the crowd fired back, wounding a police officer. I don't know whether the fact that any crowd members survived that immediate engagement is testimony to the restraint of nineteenth-century police, compared to their modern-day counterparts, or to the relative ineffectiveness of their weapons. In any case, the restraint was short-lived. The entire police force—along with a good percentage of the white citizenry—soon gathered in the town's center. John Creighton, the city's recorder, called out, "Let us prepare to clear every negro son of a bitch out of town!" According to a later congressional report, the mob proceeded to "shoot, beat, and threaten every negro met within that portion of the city." The final casualty count was two whites and forty-six blacks dead (one white accidentally shot by his own), and two whites and eighty blacks wounded. Scores of black churches, schools, and homes were burned.

Another "race riot" (as the massacres are often called) took place in New Orleans on July 30, 1867. Angered by the state legislature's failure to allow black men the vote, twenty-five white Republican delegates and two hundred black supporters, primarily veterans from the Civil War, reconvened the constitutional convention. It didn't take long for former Confederates, aided by New Orleans police, to gather outside and begin their attack, which continued long after delegates and their supporters raised white flags, and didn't stop until thirty-four black and three (Republican) white men lay dead.

All through the South, even prior to the rise of the Klan, black preachers were being killed for preaching, black women were being killed for resisting the sexual advances of whites (some were merely scalped or had their ears cut off), and black men and women were being killed, as a military attaché reported, "just out of wanton cruelty, for no reason at all that one can imagine." One planter in Georgia argued that a former slave had shown himself "certainly unfit for freedom" because, "impudently," he didn't allow himself to be whipped. In South Carolina, a man was murdered and his stepdaughter whipped because she'd had the insolence to "embarrass" a white family by bearing the child of one of its members. Southern whites did not need the Klan in order to kill blacks.

I'm not suggesting the KKK didn't make the violence worse, for it did: As historian Wyn Craig Wade has stated, "The number of outrages committed upon blacks between 1868 and 1871 still defies reasonable estimation. The multitude who were murdered left no accounts. And most who survived were too frightened to report attacks on them to the law." Conservative figures put the number of Klan murders for those years at twenty thousand, in addition to tens of thousands of other acts of violence committed by the Klan. But to simply blame the KKK for the violence would be to miss a deeper point, akin to blaming McDonald's for high blood pressure or Weyerhaeuser for global deforestation. The Ku Klux Klan, like McDonald's, like Weyerhaeuser, like the United States government, is a fiction created or adapted to accomplish some set of social purposes. It exists only insofar as we believe it does.

This doesn't mean that violence committed by people who called, or call themselves Klan members isn't real, nor that membership in the Klan doesn't encourage certain behaviors on the parts of its members, because, clearly, it does, as membership in any social organization does. I don't know of many people who, for example, deforest hillsides simply for the hell of it; they do so because they're socially rewarded—in this case, paid—for doing so, Weyerhaeuser being just one of the social forms created to facilitate this social reward.

What this means is that on one hand it's pointless and misleading—and thus harmful—to demonize the KKK (or McDonald's,

iNViSiÐiLiTY

Weyerhaeuser, or the United States government), because the impulse to commit atrocities doesn't so much originate with the organization as pass through and become amplified by it. To merely eliminate the KKK—no matter how tempting a thought—would not stop the atrocities.

On the other hand the KKK *is* worth demonizing (or, rather, perceiving accurately, which is itself a pretty appalling perception), and perhaps eliminating, not only for this amplification, but also for its institutional inertia, by which I mean that once the original impulse to commit atrocities has been institutionalized—reified—it can become in a sense self-perpetuating, and certainly self-reinforcing. Perception creates behavior. Perception encourages behavior. And because this institution—this artifice—continues to socially reinforce patterns of perception and behavior, if this behavior is destructive, it may not be a bad idea to eliminate or curtail the institution.

In October 1871, because white violence against blacks had become so extreme, and because so much of this violence was associated with the Ku Klux Klan, and because local governments were so inculpated in the violence as to render any relief impossible, President Ulysses S. Grant suspended the writ of habeus corpus—becoming the first president to do so in peacetime—in parts of South Carolina, and sent in federal soldiers (including three troops of the 7th Cavalry, withdrawn from the West, where they'd been fighting Indians). Klan leaders not arrested by the soldiers fled, and within months the Klan had been broken in South Carolina. Trials followed in which enough details of Klan violence became public that even *defense* attorney Reverdy Johnson told a jury, "I have listened with unmixed horror to some of the testimony which has been brought before you. The outrages proved are shocking to humanity. They admit of neither excuse nor justification. They violate every obligation which law and nature impose upon men." The examples of mass arrests in South Carolina, and, to a lesser extent, Mississippi, in combination with a national revulsion—even in some parts of the South—at the bloody details, put a stop to the violence originating with the KKK. Blacks and their supporters could breathe more easily.

Or could they? While the KKK had been broken, left intact were the impulses that led to its original explosion. Left intact also were the social conditions that gave rise to the violence, that a group whose privilege was based on the exploitation of others was threatened with the loss of some of that privilege.

Contrary to popular belief, and contrary, really, to the statement of the military attaché whose imagination could not encompass the reasons for white violence against blacks, the vast majority of this violence in the years following the Civil War was neither random nor simply aimed at beating down the insolent. Much of it had a specific political purpose. President Grant put this purpose as succinctly as may be possible: The purpose of Klan violence was "by force and terror to prevent all political action not in accord with the views of the members, to deprive colored citizens of the right to bear arms and the right of a free ballot, to suppress schools in which colored children were taught, and to reduce the colored people to a condition closely akin to that of slavery." The Klansmen stated as much: The Klan had been organized for the "killing and whipping and crowding out men from the ballot boxes . . . to advance the Conservative party and put down the Republican party." The general rule in many states was, "One vote, one life."

Federal prosecution of the KKK essentially ceased by 1874, primarily because the KKK had ceased to exist. What that meant on the ground was that whites no longer put on robes before whipping, castrating, or killing blacks. It meant also that instead of calling themselves members of the Ku Klux Klan, they called themselves members of the White League, or the Red Shirts, or the Rifle Club.

The killings and intimidation worked. Democrats were voted back into office in Georgia in 1871, in Texas in 1873, in Alabama and Arkansas in 1874, and in Mississippi in 1875. Once white control of the legislatures had been reestablished through violence ("Go to the polls tomorrow," a "Call to Arms" in North Carolina commanded, "and if you find the Negro voting tell him to leave the polls, and if he refuses, kill him, shoot him down in his tracks. We will win tomorrow if we have to do it with guns"), these legislators—as demo-

iNVISiBiLiTY

cratically elected as legislators before or since—began passing laws that legitimized black disenfranchisement. Lawmakers in many states used voting tests (whereby, before blacks could vote, they had to answer such questions as, "How many windows in the White House?"), poll taxes (which, though sold to whites as an antiblack measure, had the added benefit of disenfranchising poor whites), and property qualifications (having already passed laws barring blacks from owning land) to maintain the desired social order. A constitutional convention in Mississippi in 1890 eliminated almost 123,000 blacks from voter rolls, the number of black voters in Louisiana dropped from 130,334 in 1896 to 1,342 by 1904, and in five counties of Florida (where the registrar told black applicants, "Go ahead and register if you can take what comes afterwards!") only 110 out of 16,533 potential black voters had dared to sign up.

The KKK was both necessary and unnecessary to the violence. Whites were killing blacks before the creation (and perversion) of the KKK. The KKK amplified already extant violence. The elimination of the KKK reduced that violence, but in no way eradicated it. And, in any case, the political aims of the KKK were eventually achieved, legally, with no help from the now-defunct Ku Klux Klan. Of course, a little violence now and then was necessary to maintain the social order, but what's a few dead niggers compared to the maintenance of a way of life?

■　　　　■　　　　■

Nigger is one of the most offensive and inflammatory racial slurs in English. My *Webster's* calls it a "vulgar, offensive term of hostility and contempt, as used by Negrophobes." It comes from the French *nègre*, which came from the Spanish *negro*, for the color black. This in turn comes from the Latin *niger*, which also means the color black.

The Romans, however, did not call Africans *nigers*, or *negroes*. They called them *Afer* or *Maurus* (as in Moors). This raises the question: Where did the Latin *niger* come from, and how did it come to be associated with Africans? Does the name derive, as Martin Bernal suggested, from the "beautiful blackness" of the Nigretai or Nigretes, nomadic tribes who lived some three thousand years ago in what is now Libya? Or does the name derive from the River Niger, home to at least some of the Afer people?

It's possible the river got its name from the Semitic root <(n)gr (water to flow into sand), because it flows east away from the Atlantic, apparently into the desert. The root, however, is found all over North Africa and southwest Asia, and means "spring forth," "flow," "oasis," or "river in the desert." Another possibility, this from the *Dictionary of Word Origins*, is that the river's name derives from the native *gher n-gherea*, river among rivers. I guess what this means is that the beautiful Nigretai—whose name has long since been turned into a slur—may simply have been at first the people of the oasis.

The first use of the word *negro* to describe neither the color black nor the river among rivers but, African people, occurred around 1443, when Portuguese explorers made their way down the coast of Africa, past the Senegal River to Guinea, where they soon began capturing Africans to sell as slaves ("How fair a thing it would be," stated a Portuguese commander, "if we . . . were to meet with the good luck to bring the first captives before the face of our prince"). By 1555, shortly after the first slaves were brought to London, *negro* was adopted by the English as their term for Africans and other people of color.

By then, the term was also in use in the Americas, as African slaves had been brought over with Cortes, Balboa, and other con-quistadores. Just between 1576 and 1591, forty to fifty thousand "ne-gros" were brought to Brazil, where they were used roughly enough to cause a Jesuit priest to comment that the "expenditure in human life . . . in these past twenty years is a thing that is hard to believe; for no one could believe that so great a supply could ever be exhausted, much less in so short a time." The spelling and pronunciation of *negro* and *nigger* varied widely, from the description of "neager maides," included in a North American estate inventory, to the casual observation in the preamble to a 1652 act of the Warwick and Providence colonies that it is "a common course practiced amongst

iNViSiDiLiTY

Englishmen to buy negers." Variants notwithstanding, by the late seventeenth century, *negro* was firmly established as the designation in North America for African people who had been enslaved. Firmly established also was the act of enslavement itself: By 1808, when the United States made illegal the importation of any "negro, mulatto, or person of colour, as a slave," (neglecting, however, to devise any mechanism for enforcement) more than a half-million black men, women, and children had made the Middle Passage to this country (a mere 6 percent of the "whole migration," as one historian puts it, because the United States, he states, seemingly ruefully, was "a late customer and a minor purchaser" of this commodity). Within another hundred years, the words *nigger, negro,* and *slave* were interchangeable.

■　　　■　　　■

By now I think most of us take as self-evident that the race-based slavery of the antebellum South was hate-bound in its conceptualization and implementation. FBI definitions aside, forcing a race or class of people into involuntary servitude would seem to require at the very least a fair amount of disdain for those so enslaved.

That said, it's interesting to look at the rationales for slavery put forward before the Civil War, which were full of common sense—in its root meaning of *sensus communus*, the sense we hold in common—more often than they were of hatred, or at least of hatred unmasked. The proslavery arguments fell basically into five categories: religious, historical, scientific, economic, and philanthropic.

The religious argument was straightforward: If slavery was good enough for Noah, Abraham, Moses, Jesus, Peter, Paul, and, most of all, God, it was good enough for the humble tobacco, rice, and cotton farmers who made up the southern aristocracy.

Their logic was, if you believe the Bible is the infallible, unchanging word of God, then you have to accept that God meant for some people to be slaves, and for others to own them. This was true in the time of Noah, who, because his son Ham saw him naked, cursed Ham and his descendants, enslaving them forever to the descendants of Noah's other two sons, Shem and Japheth (Africans were, and in some quarters still are, considered to be the descendants of Ham: I leave it to readers to guess who are then considered descendants of Shem or Japheth). Abraham, that beloved of God, soon followed, accumulating, often by conquest, sheep, oxen, asses, camels, silver, gold, and slaves no matter where he went. When Abraham impregnated Hagar, one of his wife's slaves—with his wife's permission, though the Bible remains silent on Hagar's thoughts on the subject—Hagar became in time insolent, and so suffered the fate of insolent inferiors in more recent times: She was beaten, or as Genesis puts it, "Sarai [Abraham's wife, who was also, by the way, his half-sister] dealt harshly with her." Hagar ran away, and in the desert encountered an angel of God. The commentary of Thornton Stringfellow, whose works were commonly considered "vastly the best" of the religious defenses of slavery, is worth reading: "If God had commissioned this angel to improve this opportunity of teaching the world how much he abhorred slavery, he took a very bad plan to accomplish it. For instead of repeating a homily upon doing to others as we 'would they should do unto us,' and heaping reproach upon Sarah, as a hypocrite, and Abraham as a tyrant, and giving Hagar direction how she might get into Egypt, from whence (according to Abolitionism) she had been unrighteously sold into bondage," the angel told her, "Return to thy mistress, and submit thyself under her hands."

Moses, David, Solomon: They all owned slaves or made clear the distinction between "freemen" and those who were not free. Much was made by abolitionists that the King James version of the Bible didn't use the word *slaves*, but, instead, *servants*. This meant, in their minds, that God didn't *really* approve of slavery. But that argument was linguistic at best. Slavery was codified and even sanctified in the tenth commandment, throwing slaves (and wives) in with other property belonging to one's neighbor that one must not covet. The Bible even regulated—as opposed to banning outright—the killing of slaves, stating that if a slave were beaten to death, the slave owner should be punished (though not killed himself, as would be his fate

iNVisiDiLiTY

were he to kill a freeman), but if the slave didn't die until a day or two after the beating, the slave owner "shall not be punished, for he [the slave] *is* his money." Stringfellow had something to say about this: "If the death did not take place for a day or two, then it is to be *presumed* that the master only aimed to use the rod, so far as was necessary to produce subordination, and for this, the law which allowed him to lay out his money in the slave, would protect him against all punishment. This is the common-sense principle which has been adopted substantially in all civilized countries, where involuntary slavery has been instituted, from that day till this." The commonsense principle to which Stringfellow referred presumably is that acts of violence committed to produce subordination should not be punished. And because God himself laid out these rules, Stringfellow concludes, those who disagree with slavery "must hold God in abhorrence."

Abolitionists who conceded Old Testament support of slavery generally argued that slavery's moral rectitude—imperative would be a better word—got tossed when Jesus brought the New Covenant. Stringfellow replied, reasonably enough, that "it is passing strange, that . . . Jesus should fail to prohibit its further existence, if it was his intention to abolish it. Such an omission or oversight cannot be charged upon any other legislator the world has ever seen." Nor did Jesus' apostles attempt to do away with slavery. Quite the opposite. Peter devoted the better part of a chapter to exhorting slaves to "be subject to *your* masters with all fear; not only to the good and gentle, but also to the froward" (or, as the Living Bible translates it, "tough and cruel"). He goes so far as to tell them to praise the Lord when they're punished for doing right ("When ye do well, and suffer *for it*, yet take it patiently, this is acceptable with God"). First Peter is quite an extraordinary document, calling for complete political and personal subjection to authority structures of every form. Stringfellow brings the implications home: "It is worthy of remark, that he [Peter] says much to secure civil subordination to the State, and hearty and cheerful obedience to the masters, on the part of servants; yet he says nothing to masters in the whole letter. It would seem from this, that danger to the cause of Christ was on the side of *insubordination among*

the servants, and *a want of humility with inferiors,* rather than *haughtiness among superiors. . . .*" If Peter was hard on slaves, Paul was worse. In addition to making obligatory calls for obedience, "with fear and trembling," Paul went so far as to return a runaway slave to his master.

To believe Christianity stands in opposition to slavery is at best to think anachronistically and at worst to not understand Christianity. As Samuel Francis noted in 1998 in *Southern Partisan,* a magazine that, according to attorney general John Ashcroft, "helps set the record straight": "Neither Jesus nor the apostles nor the early church condemned slavery, despite countless opportunities to do so, and there is no indication that slavery is contrary to Christian ethics or that any serious theologian before modern times ever thought it was."

If one believes God speaks through the Bible, then it's easy to conclude, as did pre–Civil War politician John Henry Hammond, that "American slavery is not only not a sin, but especially commanded by God, through Moses, and approved by Christ through his apostles." If, as even a cursory reading of the Bible would suggest, it is true that slavery was commanded by God and approved by Christ, then more questions immediately arise: What sort of God is this? What sort of people would follow (or create) this God?

■   ■   ■

I've been thinking about Ham getting cursed by Noah, and I've been thinking about how it happened. Here's the story: Noah got drunk and passed out naked in his tent. Ham came in, saw "the nakedness of his father," and went outside to tell his brothers. His brothers picked up a garment, walked backward into the tent, covered their father, and made their way out, the whole time keeping eyes averted from the sight of Noah's naked body.

I can picture the brothers, and the scene. Though the sun has slid only partway up the morning sky, the air is already hot. A dry wind brings with it the smell of goat and cedar smoke. Shem and Japheth open the flap to their father's tent. They know without speaking,

iNVISIBILITY

without thinking, that they must keep their attention on everything—anything—but their father's body. Their father's body—the nakedness of their father's body—ceases to exist. They have a task, which is to cover something they cannot acknowledge, to cover something that is not there. They walk backward, never stumbling, because even though they have never done this before, never covered their father's nakedness that does not exist—or have they? they have no idea—their feet know where to step. They smell but do not smell the sourness of Noah's breath—the sharp bitterness of the rank wine—and hear but do not hear the rumbles and catches of his snoring. They do not touch his body as they cover him with cloth, but the garment fits perfectly over the parts they must never see. They walk quickly, purposefully, yet also absently, to the front of the tent, and emerge into the morning that is already hot, and smell the dry wind that brings with it the scent of goat and cedar smoke.

I picture also Ham, as he walked in earlier, saw his father's body, the upturned head, gaping mouth, exposed throat, splayed arms, hairy chest, with hair dwindling down his belly, then becoming coarser, thicker, near his exposed genitals. Ham steps closer, looks at his father's legs, belly, neck, parts of his father he has never seen like this.

These images have stuck with me since I was a child. Even then, reading the story, which takes only a few short verses in the Bible, I was able to feel the oppressive heat of the tent and smell its rancid air. I always wondered what was so wrong with what Ham did. What was he supposed to not look at, and why was he supposed to not talk? Why did his brothers go to such great lengths to not see?

In my mind, Ham's first impulse in the tent is to simply keep staring as he realizes, perhaps for the first time, that his father is merely human. His next impulse is to cover his father, then leave and pretend he did not see what he now knows he saw. Then he has a third impulse, which is to leave without covering his father, and to tell his brothers of his newfound understanding. As he considers, he looks away to the flap of the tent, looks back to his father's body,

THE CULTURE OF MAKE BELIEVE

looks more and more closely still, then finally turns and walks outside, into the daylight.

■   ■   ■

The historical arguments in support of slavery were as straightforward as the religious. Slavery and other forced labor, the argument asserted, have always been the bedrock upon which civilization is assembled. In 1837, William Harper wrote a carefully reasoned analysis of the role of slavery in our society. He said, "President Dew [another speaker at the conference where he first delivered this message] has shown that the institution of Slavery is a principal cause of civilization. Perhaps nothing can be more evident than that it is the sole cause. If any thing can be predicated as universally true of uncultivated man, it is that he will not labour beyond what is absolutely necessary to maintain his existence. Labour is pain to those who are unaccustomed to it, and the nature of man is averse to pain. Even with all the training, the helps and motives of civilization, we find that this aversion cannot be overcome in many individuals of the most cultivated societies. The coercion of Slavery alone is adequate to form man to habits of labour. Without it, there can be no accumulation of property, no providence for the future, no taste for comforts or elegancies, which are the characteristics and essentials of civilization. He who has obtained the command of another's labour, first begins to accumulate and provide for the future, and the foundations of civilization are laid. . . . Since the existence of man upon the earth, with no exception whatever, either of ancient or modern times, every society which has attained civilization has advanced to it through this process." Friedrich Engels, no fan of slavery, said much the same thing. "It was slavery that first made possible the division of labour between agriculture and industry on a considerable scale, and along with this, the flower of the ancient world, Hellenism. Without slavery, no Greek state, no Greek art and science; without slavery, no Roman Empire. But without Hellenism and the Roman Empire as

iNViSiDiLiTY

the base, also no modern Europe. We should never forget that our whole economic, political and intellectual development has as its pre-supposition a state of things in which slavery was as necessary as it is universally recognized."

They're right. The evidence to support the historical necessity of slavery is just as solid, the logic as inescapable, as that supporting slavery's divine ordination. Slaves built the levees, canals, and grana-ries vital to the agricultural revolution. They built the pyramids of Egypt and the great hydraulic systems of China. Every great ancient city was built by slave laborers. "Let it be remembered," Harper noted, "that all the great and enduring monuments of human art and industry—the wonders of Egypt—the everlasting works of Rome—were created by the labor of slaves." Indeed, without slave labor there would have been neither Bronze nor Iron Ages: until modern times, no sane person ever uncoerced became a mine worker (and even today it often takes either coercion or relatively high wages in de-pressed communities). The work is simply too hard, too dangerous, the conditions too dismal. Only prisoners, captives, and slaves—three branches from the same tree—ever entered the underworld, and even then did so only under the lash, or at the point of a sword.

Slavery was a central concern of governance from the time of the first nation-state. The Code of Hammurabi, the earliest known set of laws for governing an empire, prescribed death for anyone who har-bored a fugitive or otherwise helped a slave to escape. The relation-ship between the law and bondage goes back even farther: Indeed, the oldest extant legal documents don't concern the sale of land, houses, or even animals, but slaves.

Slavery's use was so central to the foundation of civilization that it dictated the design of early cities, for example Mohenjo-Daro, where the great food storehouse was located within the citadel's heavy walls, protected, by armed soldiers, not against foreign marauders but against the citizenry itself. Social critic Lewis Mumford noted with charac-teristic understatement the placement of this storehouse. "Planned scarcity and the recurrent threat of starvation played a part from the beginning in the effective regimentation of the urban labor force."

Slavery was just as necessary to the Greeks as it had been to earlier civilizations. At the height of Greek democracy, Athens contained more slaves—about sixty thousand—than citizens. Until a slave revolt in 103 BCE, more than ten thousand slaves worked the famous silver mines at Laurium. It was commonly presumed that the labor of slaves allowed citizens the leisure to conduct their democracy. An equal presumption was that democracy predicated on slavery not only *was* democracy, but the way democracy (and the world) should be. As Aristotle firmly stated, "Humanity is divided into two: the masters and the slaves; or, if one prefers it, the Greeks and the Barbarians, those who have the right to command; and those who are born to obey."

Rome, too, was built on centuries of slavery. Slaves quarried stone for cities, and they built the cities themselves. They built the aqueducts that brought water to the cities. And they built the fortunes of the rich: the use of slaves was *the* customary way in which prosperity was created. By the end of the Republic, there were probably two million slaves in Italy, accounting, during the next couple of generations, for probably one-third of the total population of the nascent Roman Empire. A half-million new captives were required every year.

"Servitude," Harper noted, "is the condition of civilization." It seems pretty clear, then, that if you want civilization, you've got to have slavery, or at least servitude. To undo slavery—if this argument holds—would be to undo the civilization we—at least those of us who might be considered slaveholders—all enjoy.

■   ■   ■

In 1967, R. D. Laing wrote, "In order to rationalize our military-industrial complex, we have to destroy our capacity to see clearly any more what is in front of, and to imagine what is beyond, our noses. Long before a thermonuclear war can come about, we have had to lay waste our own sanity. We begin with the children. It is imperative to catch them in time. Without the most thorough and rapid brain-

iNViSiÐiLiTY

washing their dirty minds would see through our dirty tricks. Children are not yet fools, but we shall turn them into imbeciles like ourselves, with high I.Q.'s if possible."

I understand now what was wrong with what Ham did, and why Noah had no choice but to curse and enslave him, because I now understand that it's not so important to this story what happened—if it happened at all—thousands of years ago in what has since become a godforsaken desert. What's more important is the lesson that can be pulled from this cautionary tale, which is that in order for a system of domination to be maintained (remember, Noah had the power and will to enslave one of his sons and all of that son's descendants to his two others and theirs) rigid protocols must be maintained, which include first and foremost that one must never see those in power as they are—in this case, naked—nor especially to perceive them as vulnerable—in this case, passed out. To see them at the same time naked and vulnerable is to find oneself no longer susceptible to any power of theirs save physical force.

In order for a slave—or, for that matter, a slaveholder—to become free, a series of successive perceptions must be realized. First, the person must perceive that the owners (and slaves) are merely human, that is, putting all rhetoric aside, that there exists a dichotomy of privilege and exploitation, and that the privilege is a result of the exploitation. The Greek form of democracy was made possible through the labor of slaves. The wealth of Romans was lifted from the same source. Aristocratic culture in the antebellum South—with its clichés of mint juleps, formal balls, and beautiful Southern belles saying "fiddle-dee-dee" in the face of trouble—was based on the sweat and blood of black slaves (as well as land taken from its original inhabitants).

The second realization is, once again, that the owners and slaves are merely human, meaning, this time, that the exploitation and consequent privilege are not inevitable, but the result of social arrangements and force (as well as a huge dollop of bad luck on the part of those enslaved). The citizens of Mohenjo-Daro obeyed not because they were inferior but because they would starve if they did not.

Likewise, many Greek or Roman slaves were kidnapped in *razzias*, or full-fledged military assaults. Black slaves in the American South were either captured or born into slavery. Although damn bad luck often determined which individuals would become slaves and which would remain free, the existence of a class of slaves has *always* been the result of political, economic, and military decisions.

The third realization is yet again that the owners are merely human, by which I now mean they are vulnerable. Wealth does not protect them. I was going to qualify this by saying it doesn't protect them from death, nor even from direct violence from the slaves (a knife in the throat kills the rich as surely and quickly as it kills the poor), but the truth is that wealth doesn't protect them in any but an illusory sense from much of anything. The wealthy are still susceptible to disease, sorrow, loneliness, pain, and, of course, death.

The difficulty comes—and here is the real beauty of the story of Noah and his sons—when, like Ham (or at least my vision of Ham), you find your way through these shifts in perception and see the patriarch naked and vulnerable. What do you do then? Do you, like Ham, talk about what you have seen? As the story makes clear, there are grave strictures against doing so, with severe consequences.

Or do you follow the lead of Ham's brothers, and reap the privilege that comes from averting your eyes?

There is another question, however, that I really want to understand. If Ham was enslaved not simply because Shem and Japheth needed the extra labor (in other words, not simply for purely economic reasons), and if this story works as a metaphor to help us understand the relationship between perception and exploitation, and if a class of people today still exists whose exploitation leads to the privilege of others, then what, precisely, is it that those who are exploited see (or have seen) about those in power? What is it that their relationship reveals that so frightens those who enslave and control these others?

iɴⱱisiᴅiʟiᴛⱱ

"EVEN A WOMAN

IS GOOD

AND SO

IS A SLAVE,

ALTHOUGH IT

MAY BE SAID

THAT A

WOMAN IS

AN INFERIOR

THING AND A

SLAVE BENEATH

CONSIDERATION."

ARISTOTLE

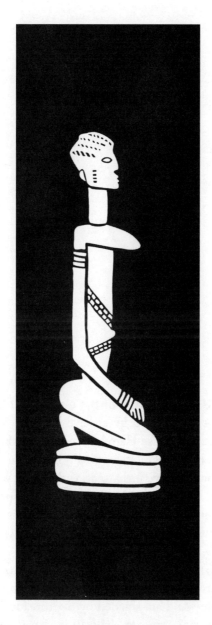

CONTEMPT

THIS ALL LEADS US BACK to the question of hate. Did Noah hate Ham? If not, how could he enslave him and his descendants? Did Noah fear Ham because Ham had seen him naked—for what he was? What, then, is the relationship (if any) between fear and hatred? Or did fear and hatred have little to do with it, and was Noah simply exercising power he felt was his due? Or, even more impersonally, was Noah just enacting a cultural norm? Was his enslavement of Ham nothing but the right and accepted—perhaps, even, morally correct—thing to do?

I'm trying to tease my way through a tangle of relationships I don't quite understand. I tug on one thread—the notion of enslavement, for example—and am startled by the threads that move in response—as much as I criticize civilization, I was surprised that so many people articulate a one-to-one relationship between civilization and servitude. (I chose only a couple of the best quotes, but they're everywhere: Just yesterday I read in Kevin Bales's book, *Disposable People: New Slavery in the Global Economy*, that "Slavery as we know it began when human beings started to settle and farm instead of wandering as hunters and gatherers. What we often call the beginnings of human history are also the beginnings of bondage.") I was equally surprised at how intransigent certain threads are. No matter how I tug on the thread of slavery, the thread representing hatred remains unmoving. What—I'm trying to understand—are the relationships between hate and fear, hate and power, power and fear? What are the relationships between any of these and the desire or need to control? And what are the relationships between all of *these* and a desire or need to perceive others as objects? It seems obvious to me that enslaving another requires that the other be, at least to some degree, objectified: Does objectification imply hatred? I used to think so, but I'm beginning to think the relationship is more complex.

Just yesterday I went to teach my creative writing class at the prison. I passed through checkpoints, walked past the lethal electric fence, past more checkpoints, through steel gates in concrete walls. I passed a waiting room, and glanced inside, where I saw prisoners— no need for me to objectify them, so the truth is that I saw people— standing or sitting in metal cages the shape of—and about twice the size of—high school lockers, with openings in the mesh just large enough for them to put their hands through to be cuffed and uncuffed. They were waiting for their counselor (for all I know the same counselor who joked about pitting them against each other). Now, when I wait for my therapist, I sit in a stuffed chair, watch the fish in the aquarium, and read *Sports Illustrated*.

Their conversations with the guards in these circumstances are nothing like we've seen in movies. Often they chat about the weather, about sports, about nothing much in particular. Within the larger social context that requires prisoners wait confined to

CONTEMPT

metal lockers for their therapists, everybody just kind of gets along. Do the guards hate the prisoners? Do the prisoners hate the guards? I don't think so, at least not in the way we normally think about hate.

I arrived at my classroom. One of my students is a former pimp, and a former soldier. Thus his name: Pimp Soldier. He has written many stories about his life on the streets. One stands out in my mind. A girl moved from rural South Carolina to southern California, where she met one of Soldier's ho's, and through her, Soldier. Soldier fell hard for the new girl, in part because of her trombone ass (I've asked, but I'm still not sure what this means: To my questions, my students always reply by laughing and making the sound of a trombone), in part because her legs went from here to forever, in part because she'd freak (push the boundaries of sex) whenever he wanted, and mainly because she made him a ton of money. She became one of his special whores. He didn't hit her. They had a lot of sex. But one night he went to her apartment, and found her and the ho who had brought them together in bed, cold, dead, overdosed. He'd never before felt so down and out, he said. I asked why, presuming the obvious. I was wrong. Without hesitation, he said it was because they'd been two of his best moneymakers. He left the apartment quickly, but not before he went through their purses, to remove whatever money they had.

Part of my problem in teasing these threads apart, I think, is that I've been confusing categories: the personal and the social. When I think of hatred I usually think of anger, red faces, and of somebody doing me wrong. The guards don't have red faces, and I'd imagine most of them would in all honesty disavow any personal hatred for most of the prisoners, even those confined in lockers. Pimp Soldier would similarly say he didn't hate the women he used. When he read his stories aloud, other students laughed and said, "That's cold, man, but that's a pimp." Many stated it was clear from the way he wrote about the woman from South Carolina that he'd held a special affection for her, an affection that was dangerous to his profession, his lifestyle, and though they didn't say this, his worldview.

To switch metaphors for a moment, away from the tangled web of cause and effect, I'm now seeing hate—on a social level—as a river. Pimp Soldier's cold attitude and appalling actions take place within the confines of a social river of hate. Pimp Soldier didn't *particularly* hate women: His actions in fact make a sort of economic sense: He got a lot of money and a lot of sex from a lot of what he said were beautiful women. It sounds like James Bond's wet dream, and probably the wet dream of many more men than that. Pimp Soldier merely went with the flow.

I am in this same river. I can't much help it. I admit it: I'm racist. The other night I saw a group (or maybe a pack?) of white teenagers standing in a vacant lot, clustered around a 4x4, and I crossed the street to avoid them; had they been black, I probably would have taken another street entirely. And I'm misogynistic. I admit that, too. I'm a shitty cook, and a worse housecleaner, probably in great measure because I've internalized the notion that these are women's work. Of course, I never admit that's why I don't do them: I always say I just don't much enjoy those activities (which is true enough; and it's true enough also that many women don't enjoy them either), and in any case, I've got better things to do, like write books and teach classes where I can feel morally superior to pimps. And naturally I value money over life. Why else would I own a computer with a hard drive put together in Thailand by women dying of job-induced cancer? Why else would I own shirts made in a sweatshop in Bangladesh, and shoes put together in Mexico? The truth is that, although many of my best friends are people of color (as the cliché goes), and other of my best friends are women, I am part of this river: I benefit from the exploitation of others, and I do not much want to sacrifice this privilege. I am, after all, civilized, and have gained a taste for "comforts and elegancies" which can be gained only through the coercion of slavery. The truth is that like most others who benefit from this deep and broad river, I would probably rather die (and maybe even kill, or better, have someone kill for me) than trade places with the men, women, and children who made my computer, my shirt, my shoes.

CONTEMPT

■   ■   ■

My publisher, who is also my editor, is quitting smoking. He's miserable. Two nights ago, in a restaurant, he asked the server if she had a hammer.

"Why?"

"So you can hit me over the head and kill me. At least that would stop the cravings."

I haven't shown him any of this book. I did tell him, in a telephone conversation, about the tangle I'm trying to puzzle out, and he said, "You should talk about contempt."

I asked why.

"It fits," he said. "I don't know whether the tobacco executives hate me, but I'm pretty sure they feel contempt for me—not so much me in particular, but as a target. They'd have to feel contempt for me in order to make money from my slow suicide."

Tobacco, I thought? Contempt? Growing tobacco a hate crime? I just don't know. But he's got a point. To intentionally addict people to something you know will kill them would take, as I said earlier of slavery, a fair amount of disdain. The tangle of threads just keeps getting thicker.

I sighed.

He said he'd tried to quit several times before, but this time he was going to make it.

I asked why.

"Because I understand now why I was killing myself. It's not just that the tobacco executives feel contempt for me, but that I felt contempt for myself."

Though he couldn't see me, I nodded.

"If I really valued myself," he said evenly, "could I hurt myself in this way?"

I shook my head. Silence on the line.

"I think this is one reason, too, that we're killing the planet." He paused, and almost unconsciously I listened for the slight puffing that in previous times would have indicated he was taking a drag, followed by a long, slow exhalation, but I heard nothing. "I think deep inside we don't believe we deserve clean rivers, clean air, ponds full of frogs, intact ecosystems, a livable world."

I told him I agreed.

"If we loved ourselves," he said, before correcting himself and speaking so quickly the words ran into each other, "or even if we just didn't hate ourselves"—a long pause, and again I listened in vain for the puff—"would we be able to destroy our home?"

CONTEMPT

WAS THERE EVER ANY DOMINATION WHICH DID

NOT APPEAR NATURAL TO THOSE WHO

POSSESSED IT?

JOHN STUART MILL

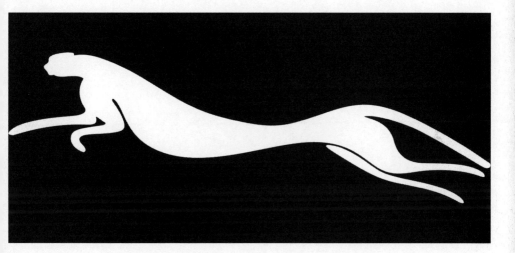

POWER

SLAVES CAPTURED IN AFRICA for eventual use in the Americas were transported in ships across the Atlantic Ocean in what is called the Middle Passage. Between nine and sixteen million human beings survived the voyage. Yearly mortality rates varied from 3 to 10 percent, meaning that maybe an additional million people died on board. The length of the journeys varied, depending on where the people were eventually to be sold. The shortest journeys lasted thirty to fifty days, from Angola to Brazil, while some trips lasted much longer. The longest was 284 days.

Conditions for the "migration," as most scholars call it, were inhuman. I mean this not hyperbolically, but precisely. Conditions were fitted to maximize revenue, and suggested scant interest in promoting life. This meant packing the most niggers—I use this word to emphasize that the enslaved were property, and thus objects, as opposed to subjects—into the smallest space while causing the least loss of product viability (much like in modern factory farms). Thus we can read that on at least one ship, the *Brookes*, that if every adult male slave was allotted six feet by one foot four inches of platform space (with a ceiling space of three to four feet), every adult female slave was allotted five feet ten by one foot, four, every boy was allotted five feet by one foot two, and every girl four feet six by one foot, the ship could hold 451 slaves. We can read also that the ship carried upward of six hundred slaves.

Because fresh air was required for product viability, five to six air ports were provided on each side of the ship, each being about four by six inches. It was necessary to close these whenever it rained, or when the seas grew rough. One ship's doctor noted, "The confined air, rendered noxious by the effluvia exhaled from their bodies and by being repeatedly breathed, soon produces fevers and fluxes which generally carry off great numbers of them. . . . I frequently went down among them till at length their rooms became so extremely hot as to be only bearable for a very short time. But the excessive heat was not the only thing that rendered their situation intolerable. The deck, that is, the floor of their rooms, was so covered with the blood and mucus which had proceeded from them in consequence of the flux [i.e., diarrhea], that it resembled a slaughter-house."

The constant motion of the ship frequently rubbed the skin and even the flesh off the shoulders, elbows, and hips of the slaves, revealing bones and reducing the ultimate value of the cargo.

Those slaves who could, often threw themselves overboard, preferring to drown or be eaten by sharks rather than continue the migration. Shipowners tried their hardest to prevent this, because insurance sometimes did not pay for losses due to suicide. Those slaves who found no opportunity to jump ship often tried to kill themselves by not eating, and because this too cost their owners money, those who refused to eat had their mouths forcibly opened, or, failing that, had their lips burned with hot coals.

■   ■   ■

POWER

Those who say that seeing is believing have it all wrong. Only when we believe do we begin to see (what we are supposed to see). An example of this is the scientific defense of slavery, which, while it had the same inescapability and internal consistency as the Biblical and historical defenses, had as well the same tautology manifested in Justice Marshall's decision: "If the principle has been asserted in the first instance, and afterwards sustained . . . it becomes the law of the land." It seems clear that the scientific defenders of racism—and I wonder how much of the rest of our science is similarly selective—went looking for physical differences between themselves and those they enslaved to justify exploitation. "There is a marked difference between the heads of the Caucasian and the Negro," wrote the physician and scholar Josiah C. Nott in 1844, "and there is a corresponding difference no less marked in their intellectual and moral qualities." He was saying by this, I suppose, that the enslavers were morally superior to the enslaved. So far as the physical difference, Nott wrote, "The head of the Negro is smaller by a full tenth—the forehead is narrower and more receding, in consequence of which the anterior or intellectual portion of the brain is defective." He continued, "There is in the animal kingdom, a regular gradation in the form of the brain, from the Caucasian down to the lowest order of animals, and the intellectual faculties and instincts are commensurate with size and form." He compares the teeth of the Negro with "those of carnivorous animals," and their "nerves coming off the brain" with "animals, where the senses and sensual faculties predominate."

He's driving at three points. The first is that Caucasians and Negroes are not merely different races but different species ("Now it will be seen from this hasty sketch, how many points of resemblance Anatomists have established between the Negro and Ape"). The second is that, based on anatomy and history, one can deduce that the species of Caucasians are intellectually and morally superior to the species of "the Mongol, the Malay, the Indian and Negro." The third and most crucial point is that the intellectual and moral superiority of the Caucasians gives them just as much a right—and duty—to enslave (domesticate would now probably be a better word) members of these other species (Mongols, Malays, Indians, and Negroes) as it does *other* nonhumans, for example, horses, oxen, and pigs.

Ultimately, though, as with Marshall's legal commentary, Nott stresses that it doesn't much matter what case he or anybody makes in defense of (or, for that matter, against) slavery, because the bottom line was, as he quoted the poet Alexander Pope in glorious all to end his argument: "One truth is clear, WHATEVER IS, IS RIGHT."

■   ■   ■

The notion that whatever is, is right, by the way, applied only to social structures for which Nott and others like him wanted to provide scientific support. Presumably the possibility that the aboriginal social structures they encountered were right did not occur to them, any more than it occurred to them that the natural world, too, needed no civilizing.

■   ■   ■

Nott, of course, was not alone in his belief that black people are inferior to white people. Voltaire considered blacks midway between whites and apes. David Hume allowed that black people might be able to develop certain attributes of human beings in much the same way that a parrot picks up a few words. The anatomist Etienne Serres stated that black people are of necessity "primitive" because of the short distance between the navel and the penis. Zoologist Louis Aggasiz determined that the brain of the black adult is equivalent to that of a seven-month-old white fetus.

■   ■   ■

Science aside, it's simply not true that Africans were enslaved because they were inferior. A good portion of the whites who came to North America before the nineteenth century were slaves as well.

POWER

A few years ago I stumbled across an extraordinary book entitled *They Were White And They Were Slaves: The Untold Story of the Enslavement of Whites in Early America*. The author, Michael A Hoffman II, is overtly racist, and attempts to make the case that the enslavement of whites by commercial interests in Britain and the Americas was worse than the enslavement and genocide of Africans (and, though he doesn't really mention them, Indians) perpetrated by those same interests. It's an odd case for him to try to make, as though the suffering of poor whites somehow negates or diminishes the suffering of members of other cultures and other races. Unfortunately, showing that one group was made miserable in no way lessens the misery of any other. It can, however, point out that the rationale for exploiting one or another group is just that: rationale.

While Hoffman's analysis is seriously flawed, his book cites a bitter cornucopia of original sources for the particular series of atrocities he sets out to describe. At first, I must admit, I expected his scholarship to be as shoddy as his analysis, but I was, in a sense, being a bigot: Just because he believes whites to be superior to blacks doesn't mean he can't read. In fact, his scholarship is impressive, and the story he tells is both interesting and horrifying. I realized as I read through his material that given the culture in which we live—a culture that in the name of commerce, religion, history, science, or to simply serve "what is" (or rather, "WHAT IS") has subjugated, exploited, and/or destroyed every other culture it has encountered—it is absurdly selective to single out Hoffman for his manifest racism: Because to acquiesce is to participate, it's simply true that all of us who one way or another defend or participate in our economic or social system are merely less direct in our racism.

It's all part of being in that river.

When England claimed North America, no pretense was made for the most part to parcel out land in anything resembling an egalitarian manner. Having claimed title to what is now Virginia, for example, King James I turned it into "basically a large estate" by granting it to the Virginia Company of London. To profit from the land, the company's shareholders then found slaves to raise crops, and financed transoceanic voyages for potential settlers, who on arrival became indentured servants to the company. After a specified time—sometimes seven years, sometimes ten or longer; sometimes never (as when tenants were to "belong to the said office for ever")—the servants were to claim a hundred acres; until then most servants functioned explicitly as slaves, the remainder being sharecroppers, giving the company their entire crop, minus an allowance of "just enough money to live on." The Englishman William Eddis described the condition of these "servants," often called "slaves" in parliamentary debate, by writing, "Generally speaking, they groan beneath a burden worse than Egyptian bondage." As was true as well of black and Indian slaves, white slaves were regularly subjected to whippings, rape, dismemberment, and murder. In 1688 a member of the British nobility stated that the slaves "are used with more barbarous cruelty than if in Algiers. Their bodies and souls are used as if hell commenced here and only continued in the world to come." The period of servitude was often extended by owners beyond the original contract. The owners used fictitious debts or such crimes as becoming pregnant, stealing food, "indolence," being absent from the plantation (one year added for every two hours' absence), or missing church to maintain permanent control over the lives of their servants. In some colonies, one-third to one-half of even the most healthy indentured servants—those in their late teens—did not live to see their freedom. In others, 80 percent of the indentured servants died their first year.

The middle and southern colonies of Pennsylvania, New Jersey, Maryland, Virginia, the Carolinas, and Georgia used the "headright" system, in which land (typically fifty acres per head) was granted to those who paid their own and/or others' transport from Europe. Thus ship captains acquired would-be indentured servants from taverns and fairs, and bribed judges and debtors' prison jailers to secure prisoners who could be indentured. Political prisoners

POWER

"were sold at auction . . . for various terms of years, sometimes for life, as slaves." In 1701, citizens in England protested, according to the Calendar of State Papers, against the "encouragement to the spiriting away of Englishmen without their consent and selling them for slaves, which hath been a practice very frequent and known by the name of kidnapping." At the request of the Virginia Company, a bill passed in 1618 permitted the capture of children of eight years or older to be transported as slaves to America, where the boys were to be owned by the company for up to sixteen years, the girls up to fourteen. Officials were paid a bounty by the company for each kid they nabbed, and judges received up to 50 percent of the profits from the sale of children, so constables roamed the streets looking for children while aldermen entered the homes of the poor to look for more. The historian John Van der Zee commented, "Press gangs in the hire of local merchants roamed the streets seizing 'by force such boys as seemed proper subjects for the slave trade.' Children were driven in flocks through the town and confined for shipment in barns. . . . So flagrant was the practice that people about Aberdeen [for example] avoided bringing children into the city for fear they might be stolen. . . . The stealing of children became so notorious in Scotland that the Scottish term for the practice entered the English language: 'kid-nabbing.'" In the colonies, mortality rates for these children often reached 90 to 95 percent within five years.

Hundreds of thousands of political dissidents were enslaved by the British Crown and transported to the colonies. The definition of dissidents included prisoners of war, actual dissidents, Jacobites, the Irish (one hundred thousand Irish, including religious leaders, boys, girls, and even women up to the age of eighty), and so on.

At least in the case of the Irish, the enslavement was done for the slaves' own good, and out of the goodness of the slavers' hearts: In 1655, Henry Cromwell of the Puritan Protectorate in London issued the decree that "Concerning the younge [Irish] women, although we must use force in takinge them up, yet it beinge so much for their owne goode, and likely to be of soe great advantage to the publique, it is not the least doubted, that you may have such number of them as you thinke fitt to make uppon this account [i.e., capture, enslavement, and transport to the colonies]."

Criminals, as well, were sent as company slaves to the Americas, people being transported for such crimes as begging, vagrancy, fishing in enclosed ponds, bigamy, solemnizing marriage vows in secret, "wand'ring," stealing a bowl of soup, poaching deer, destroying shrubbery, or stealing apples from the trees in an aristocrat's garden. In 1655, four teenagers were whipped through the streets of Edinburgh, burned behind the ears, and sent to slavery in America because they had interrupted the sermon of a minister.

Ten thousand poor people are estimated to have been sold into slavery each year in Great Britain. Between 1609 and the early 1800s, as many as two-thirds of the white colonists are estimated to have been forced to come over as slaves.

■   ■   ■

I just got off the phone again. This damn tangle keeps getting bigger every time I open my mouth. An old friend just added a few more threads, and knotted them tight.

I told her about the tangle, and about what my publisher said, and she commented, "I don't think it's contempt so much as it is disregard."

"How about at least disdain?" I offered weakly.

"I think the people getting killed by the tobacco executives simply don't exist in the executives' minds, any more than trees and forests exist for their own sake in the minds of timber executives, or cows and chickens exist for their own sake in the minds of agricorporation CEOs. Do you remember that HBO special a few years ago on the treatment of animals?"

Unfortunately, I did.

"Do you remember the scenes about how they get cat and dog fur for trimming on coats?

POWER

Unfortunately, I did.

"There's that scene of the guy skinning the cat while it's still alive."

I work with a lot of difficult material. I've spent hours among the stacks at libraries stifling sobs at this or that new horror I've uncovered—the children in cages in Bombay; the African who so wanted freedom from his Portuguese slavers that he dove into the ocean like a cormorant, and as one of his captors put it, was "so valiant that two men, strong as they were, could not drag him into the boat until they took a boathook and caught him above one eye, and the pain of this made him abate his courage, and allow himself to be put inside the boat"; the frontispiece of a book which is a military photograph of smiling white soldiers (in the hire of diamond mining corporations) standing around a tree from whose limbs hang the broken and contorted bodies of Africans. But the one image among all these that I wish I had never seen was that of the cat. Normally I double-check all of my sources to verify their accuracy, but I could not bring myself to watch this scene again. So this is what I remember. The cat is in a vat of hot water, and is trying to swim. It is a small cat. A man stands, with a large paddle, and with another implement I do not recognize, to stir the water. But I see immediately what it is for. He uses it to peel back the fur from the cat's body. It comes off smoothly in one piece. The cat—the skinned cat—is still trying to swim, and I can see that it is trying to meow. I said, "I remember that scene."

"Do you remember his face?"

I didn't look at the man's face.

"He's smiling," she said. "He's not thinking about the cat. He's thinking about something else entirely. But he's torturing this animal. I don't think he hates cats. He probably doesn't care about cats at all. But that's his job. That's what I've read about most torturers of humans, too. They don't necessarily hate the people they're torturing. It's just what they do. They may even like the people. But—"

I cut her off. "It's not about hate, is it?"

THE CULTURE OF MAKE BELIEVE

"No," she said.
"It's all about power."
"Yes," she said. "Yes, it is."

POWER

"GOVERNMENT HAS NO OTHER END BUT THE PRESERVATION OF PROPERTY."

JOHN LOCKE

PROPERTY

GEORGE FITZHUGH WAS THE AUTHOR of the two best-known books in support of slavery: *Sociology for the South; or the Failure of Free Society* and *Cannibals All! or Slaves Without Masters.* He professed support for white as well as black slavery. In 1857, he wrote, "The South is fulfilling her destiny and coming up to her work beautifully. She is multiplying her academies, her colleges, and her universities, and they are all well patronised [*sic*] and conducted by able professors." He continued, "Cotton is king; and rice, sugar, Indian corn, wheat, and tobacco are his chief ministers. It is our great agricultural surplus that gives us power, commands respect, and secures independence. . . . [T]ake away our surplus from the world's supply, and famine and nakedness will be the consequence. . . . Our present pursuits are more honorable, lucrative, and more generative of power and independence than those we fondly aspire to." All of this power and independence were based on slavery. Religion, the comforts and elegancies of life, the cultivation of arts and letters, the development of moral and intellectual excellence (for the masters): all of these were not seen as possible without forced labor.

And unless abolitionists were also anticapitalist, the proslavery argument went, they were hypocrites. "What," William Harper asks, "is the essential character of *Slavery*, and in what does it differ from the *servitude* of other countries?" He answers his own question: "Where a man is compelled to labor at the will of another, and to give him the greater portion of the product of his labor, there *Slavery* exists; and it is immaterial by what sort of compulsion the will of the laborer is subdued. . . . What difference does it make, if you can starve him, or alarm him for the subsistence of himself or his family? And is it not under this compulsion that the *freeman* labors?" So what, Harper argues, if the laborer can change employers? One capitalist will be as willing and ready to exploit the worker as the next, and in any case, most laborers would prefer a long term, committed relationship, precisely the sort of relationship provided by chattel slavery. He asks, "Is not the condition of the laboring poor . . . too often that of masterless slaves?"

He takes his case even further, arguing that calling laborers under a capitalist system free merely adds to their misery. If you're a slave, at least you know you're not free. But if everyone tells you that you *are* free, if you still feel exploited it must be your own fault: free laborers "feel indignity more acutely, and more of discontent and evil passion is excited; they feel that it is mockery that calls them free." To switch to modern parlance, even though Harper would, I'm sure, never have used the *f* word, calling industrial laborers free is really just mind-fucking them. If you're going to use them as slaves, why not just make them chattel?

The answer, according to the consensus of slave owners, and many capitalists (including, as we shall eventually see, many modern capitalists), is that it's cheaper to call laborers free than it is to own

PROPERTY

them outright. It is in the capitalist's best interest to not own workers. "It is a fallacy to suppose that ours is *unpaid labor*," wrote John Henry Hammond. "The slave himself must be paid for, and thus his labor is all purchased at once, and for no trifling sum." In 1850, an average field laborer cost between $1000 and $1800, three to six times the annual wage of an American worker, the equivalent of $50,000 to $100,000 today. "Besides the first cost of the slave," Hammond continued, "he must be fed and clothed, well fed and well clothed, if not for humanity's sake, that he may do good work, retain health and life, and rear a family to supply his place. When old or sick, he is a clear expense, and so is the helpless portion of his family. No poor law provides for him when unable to work, or brings up his children for our service when we need them. These are all heavy charges on slave labor," charges that are avoided by nonslave-owning capitalists.

But if slavery is so unprofitable (and modern studies suggest that slavery was, in fact, not all that profitable, with an average annual return of about 5 percent on the investment in each slave), why, then, own slaves? It ends up that from the standpoint of production, slave owning is the rational choice when there is a lot of land, and not many people to work it. When there is less land and more people to work it ("a pool of excess labor," as the phrase goes), it's in the producer's best interest not to own his slaves, and to thereby relieve himself of responsibility for their care and upkeep. Here's the logic. Access to land leads to self-sufficiency. Land is the source of food, clothing, and shelter. If someone (or a community) has access to land, and requisite skills (which nearly all people have had throughout human existence until recently) there has been no reason for that person (or members of that community) to sell labor to another. Remember the difficulty white South Africans encountered trying to generate a supply of workers for their diamond and gold mines. Remember, for that matter, that the builders of Mohenjo-Daro found it expedient (if not crucial) to separate the city's populace—its potential workforce—from their food supply. When land is plenty and labor scarce, I've either got to pay wages high enough to induce others to work for me—to overcome their natural aversion to work, as slaveholders would have put it—or, and this is usually the option of choice, I've got to *force* these others to work for me. If I can set up the military, philosophical, and legal framework to force these others to go to work, it becomes in my economic self-interest to enslave them: There is simply no other way to get them to work at reasonable rates, and to keep them working. Unfortunately for me in this case, enslavement carries with it a few legal, moral, ethical, and, most especially, practical obligations. I need to provide food, shelter, and clothing for my slaves, or at least enough to maintain worker productivity. Remember, if workers are scarce, they're expensive, and I don't want to starve to death a worker who cost me as much as a house.

If, on the other hand, there's not much land, or if a few people own most of the land and so can deprive the majority of the people of its use, and if, at the same time, the population has increased such that a lot of people need to find a way to provide themselves the necessities of life, it becomes no longer in my best interest to own or in any way constrain these workers. I hire them for as little as I can, and if they don't like the wages I pay, I hire someone else who is just the tiniest bit more desperate. Hammond put it well: "In all countries where the denseness of the population has reduced it to a matter of perfect certainty, that labor can be obtained, whenever wanted, and that the laborer can be forced, by sheer necessity, to hire for the smallest pittance that will keep soul and body together, and rags upon his back while in actual employment—dependent at all other times on alms or poor rates—in all such countries it is found cheaper to pay this pittance, than to clothe, feed, nurse, support through childhood, and pension in old age, a race of slaves." It's simple self-interest. Under the rubric of this economics, slaveholders are nothing if not rational (no hatred here, no matter how I tug at the tangle; or at least no personal hatred—yet), and, Hammond concedes, "If I could cultivate my lands on these terms, I would, without a word, resign my slaves, provided they could be properly disposed of."

PROPERTY

■　　　■　　　■

Like many children of my generation, my introduction to chimney sweeps was the lucky lads in *Mary Poppins*, who smiled through the soot as they danced across the rooftops with Dick Van Dyke: "Good luck will rub off," they sang, "if you shakes hands with me." The movie came out in 1964, when I was three, by which age—had I been born in a different time and place—I would nearly have been old enough to begin work as a "human broom," as sweeps were sometimes called. I didn't actually see the movie, though, until I was nine or ten, and even though I was a child, I would, by this time, have been nearly too old for the trade.

Real chimney sweeps did not dance. They climbed the insides of flues twelve by fourteen inches or smaller, and scrubbed or brushed away the soot by hand. Young and tiny children were especially useful because they could get into smaller places, leading to the popular advertising slogan "Little boys for small flues."

England abolished slavery in 1808, which means that the children who were chimney sweeps were not chattel slaves, as such. But an early-nineteenth-century investigation could not discover even a single child who had voluntarily entered the trade. They were all either orphans or indigents sold by parish workhouses to masters of sweeps, children of famished parents sold to same, or kidnap victims. Because land was dear and children cheap, the going rate to purchase a child ranged from a few shillings to two guineas—"the smaller the child, the better the price," for obvious reasons. One field hand in the American South cost as much as several hundred of the "climber boys."

It wasn't merely that sweeps did not dance, but most of them could not, even if they'd wanted to. Employers kept them malnourished so they could fit inside the chimneys (and, in any case, were not responsible for the boys' food—these children not being chattel— meaning the boys had to beg). Enough boys developed malignant tumors on their scrotums—from malnutrition and constant exposure to so much soot that it lodged in significant quantities in the folds of

THE CULTURE OF MAKE BELIEVE

skin covering the scrotum—for the tumors to gain the name "chimney sweep's cancer." Crippling injuries and deformities were common. Because the children were expendable—I mean this word precisely—they were often sent to clean even hot flues: The children's safety and well-being were worth even less than heated meals served at the proper time. Climber boys who hesitated to ascend hot chimneys were beaten, or if they ascended partway and started back down, had straw lit beneath them to force them up. These practices were routine. As historian Georgina Battiscombe wrote, "Forced screaming and sobbing up dark, narrow chimneys, their skin scorched and lacerated, their eyes and throats filled with soot, these small children—Ashley found a child of four-and-a-half working as a climbing boy—faced suffocation in the blackness of a chimney or perhaps a slow and painful death from cancer of the scrotum, the climbing-boys' occupational disease."

In 1828, Joseph Glass improved the design of a chimney-cleaning machine invented some years earlier. The machine could cheaply and efficiently clean flues of any size or design, and cost only four pounds. But boys were cheaper, so for many years they continued in common use.

■　　　■　　　■

Property is the central organizing feature of our culture. The protection or sanctity of private property—or at least the private property of those in power—informs nearly every decision made by the rulers, and certainly informs the great moral debates of recent history. The question of property was central, of course, to the slave debates of the 1840s and 1850s. In his classic study, *Abolition of Negro Slavery*, Professor of Political Law Thomas Roderick Dew used as his first argument against emancipation, "We take it for granted that the right of the owner to his slave is to be respected, and consequently that he is not required to emancipate him, unless his full value is paid by the state." In *his* defense of slavery, William Harper begins a description of a hypothetical utopia with the phrase, "Let us suppose a

PROPERTY

state of society in which all shall have property. . . ." The point is that slaves were property—no more and certainly no less—and a nearly insurmountable philosophical, political, and practical difficulty in even *talking* about their emancipation was the enormous cost of compensating the traffickers in humans for their property. Dew threw out a figure of $100 million in 1832 dollars for the slaves in just Virginia, which compares far too closely with the assessed value of all of the houses and lands in that state at the time: $206 million. In all of the debate, even the most fervent abolitionists objected merely to *humans* as property: It was as unthinkable then as it is now to discuss the morality of property itself.

Property has *always* been the central consideration of the United States government, but it has become even more so over time. Between the signing of the Declaration of Independence in 1776, to provide just one obvious, and, in some ways, silly, example (silly because all of the terms are seemingly obvious, yet in fact nearly impossible to adequately define) and the passage of the Fourteenth Amendment to the U.S. Constitution in 1868, the inalienable rights with which men [*sic*] are self-evidently endowed by their Creator, and which may not be abridged by the State, changed from "Life, Liberty, and the pursuit of Happiness," to life, liberty, and property. The Fourteenth Amendment, passed during the KKK's maiden reign of terror, ostensibly to protect the rights of blacks from racist state governments, has been used far more often to protect the rights to property: Of the Fourteenth Amendment cases brought before the Supreme Court between 1890 and 1910, only nineteen dealt with the rights of blacks, while two hundred and eighty-eight dealt with the rights of corporations.

On the other side of the Atlantic, private property even informed something so open-and-shut as the debates about the safety of chimney sweeps in England: Attempts to mandate larger flues to facilitate their cleaning by adults or machines were rejected for decades on the grounds that, in the words of Lord Sydney Smith, one of those opposing the mandate, they "could not be carried into execution without great injury to property." Smith said this after listing five pages

THE CULTURE OF MAKE BELIEVE

of horrors inflicted upon climber boys, and was explicit that the essential reason for opposing the mandate was that property is worth more than life, stating that "it was quite right to throw out the bill for prohibiting the sweeping of chimneys by boys—because humanity is a modern invention; and there are many chimneys in old houses which cannot possibly be swept in any other manner." Influential economist David Ricardo consistently and steadfastly refused to speak out in favor of the climbing boys (although he spoke out on nearly every subject related to the economy); the reason can be inferred from the premise constant in his writings, which is that legislature (including that which was charged with protecting child laborers) must not be allowed to infringe on the rights of property owners.

I have two questions. The first has to do with David Ricardo. In graduate school I studied economics. My macroeconomics textbook listed Ricardo as one of the three most important classical economists (his work, along with Adam Smith's and John Stuart Mills's, "dominated" the period). Here's the first question: What sort of a culture would value the thoughts of someone who perceives property rights as more important than the health and safety of children (or of anyone, for that matter), and most especially, what sort of a culture would value this person's thoughts highly enough to continue to teach them (with no mention of their inhumanity) a couple of hundred years later? And what sort of culture would enact policies that produce this sort of inhumanity?

Here's the other question. Why am I exploring the notion of private property? What is the relationship, if any, between the sanctity of private property and hate, contempt, disregard? For simplicity's sake, let's call it hate. I keep asking myself why this discussion of hate seems to lead me toward property. On one hand, it seems absurd. Hate is an emotion. The sanctity of private property is a belief system. End of discussion. No connection. But there is something there. The flayed cat. The chimney sweeps. The Middle Passage. Each of these horrors occurs because people—the owners and their employees—value money, value property, over living beings. But that still

PROPERTY

doesn't quite explain the relationship between these atrocities and hate. doesn't quite explain the relationship between these atrocities and hate.

Or does it? Is this a case of hatred—hatred of life itself, perhaps?—having been felt long enough that it no longer feels like hate, but tradition—in this case the sanctity of private property?

So far I've held a straight face while writing about democracy—and the good things in life—as they are made possible for the owning class through the efforts of the enslaved, and I've been quoting without disagreement defenders of this politics of luxury. But maybe now it's time to begin asking some more fundamental questions. What sort of democracy can be based explicitly on the misery of others? And what sort of people would desire and claim a luxury which has as its cost the hopes and lives of a race of slaves? I include myself in this question, as I sit now in front of my computer made in Thailand, wearing a sweatshirt and a sweater made in sweatshops in Korea (at least the shirt I'm wearing today was made in the United States by a company that does not overly exploit its workers). I don't *feel* like I hate the workers in Thailand and Korea. Truth be told, I feel nothing toward them. I don't even know who they are. How, then, do I support their suffering, and, in the case of the workers in Thailand, their deaths? It's too easy for me to simply blame it all on our economic system, or to call that system one current in the cultural river of hate. It's too sanctimonious to invoke the defense of the good Germans: I did not know, and to the degree that I did, I was merely following orders. Or just getting along.

The problem isn't property and ownership as such. You don't have to own people to misuse them. All you have to do is see them as means to ends, to see the world through the lens of utilitarianism, or instrumentality, as John Keeble averred when he said that corporations and hate groups are branches from the same tree, different forms of the same cultural imperative: to rob the world of its subjectivity, to turn everyone and everything into objects.

Here's one last question in this chapter of many questions. Does someone who objectifies, one who perceives the living planet and its members as objects to be used, hate the world, and hate life? Or is it more true that for these people the world (or children, or blacks, or women, or whatever category they or we wish to objectify) simply doesn't exist? I have to admit that it seems like a stretch to say that those who objectify the world hate life, but given that our culture clearly objectifies the world, and given that it is rapidly destroying life on the planet, maybe it's time to stretch.

PROPERTY

LOVE AND VIOLENCE, PROPERLY SPEAKING,
ARE POLAR OPPOSITES. LOVE LETS THE OTHER
BE, BUT WITH AFFECTION AND CONCERN.
VIOLENCE ATTEMPTS TO CONSTRAIN THE OHER'S
FREEDOM, TO FORCE HIM TO ACT IN THE WAY
WE DESIRE, BUT WITH ULTIMATE LACK OF
CONCERN, WITH INDIFFERENCE TO THE
OTHER'S OWN EXISTENCE OR DESTINY. WE
ARE EFFECTIVELY DESTROYING OURSELVES
BY VIOLENCE MASQUERADING AS LOVE.

R. D. LAING

PHILANTHROPY

I LEARNED ABOUT THE WOMEN in Thailand from my friend and fellow activist George Draffan. We were talking about global trade. Years ago I asked him what he thought it would take for life on Earth to survive, and he answered without hesitation, "Democracy." I asked him again recently, and he said, "Stopping international trade."

I asked him about that seeming contradiction.

He responded that maybe it was the same answer looked at from different levels. "On the economic level," he said, "international trade is the mechanism or engine for a lot of social and environmental destruction. But what would it take to stop international trade? We won't run out of oil for a long time. The politicians of the world aren't about to ban international trade. So what would make a difference in the global economy?" He stopped awhile to think, then started up again. "On the political level it would take a certain amount of democracy, defined perhaps as everybody having equal access to resources. You can't have a huge difference in wealth or power—as we have now—and have a democracy."

I told him I thought slaveholders would have disagreed. I told him Democrats and Republicans would probably also disagree.

He shrugged. An appropriate response.

I pushed him. "We keep hearing international trade is good, and we want it to keep expanding." He frowned, and I asked, "What's wrong with people being able to get cheap cassettes from Taiwan?"

He answered, "Only a very small elite of the world's population can afford the latest electronics equipment. The U.S. has five percent of the population, and consumes the majority of the world's resources, so the breadth of your perspective determines your answer. Most people in the world don't benefit from international trade. The people at the top of the pyramid benefit (if you equate benefit with consumption), and seem to assume that everyone enjoys the same. But the rest of the world gets a lot of sacrifice and deprivation and destruction, even if you're just looking at humans. If you're also looking at nonhuman species and the ecological capacity of the Earth, it's even more lopsided. The people who tell you international trade is good are the people who benefit from it. But they're a very small minority."

I thought of two questions asked by proslavery philosopher William Harper. The first was, "How are we to weigh the pains and enjoyments of one man highly cultivated and of great sensibility against those of many men of blunter capacity for enjoyment or suffering?" The second was similar: "If there are sordid, servile, and laborious offices to be performed, is it not better that there should be sordid, servile, and laborious beings to perform them?" Both seemed to apply to the present conversation.

"It's maybe not so obvious to those of us on the top of the global heap," George continued, "but the statistics on the gap between the

PHILANTHROPY

rich and the poor are sobering. In 1960, U.S. corporate CEOs received forty times the average worker's salary; today they receive over three hundred times what the average worker does. The economic 'boom' the politicians talk about has benefited the already-wealthy at the expense of everyone else: Between 1983 and 1995, the bottom forty percent of U.S. households lost eighty percent of their wealth; the top one percent of U.S. households now owns forty percent of all wealth. The optimist points out that most Americans now own some stock, but the fact remains that most households are in debt. Ten percent of the U.S. population owns more than three-fourths of all real estate, corporate stock, and bonds. If you want to know what's wrong with that, ask a poor person."

I asked him about the argument we always hear that international trade is good for nonindustrialized nations. The only way they can "join us," we're told, is if we "liberalize" trade.

He shook his head. "That's what we hear, but the more international trade there is, the higher the Third World debt," he said, speaking very fast now. "Mexico, Brazil, and Indonesia have been paying off hundreds of billions of dollars of debt over the last couple of generations, yet they're farther in debt all the time. The wealth gap between the First and Third Worlds is even worse than the U.S. wealth gap. And wherever there's been economic 'restructuring' to join the new world order, unemployment and income disparity *increases*. Once again, it's good for the elite at the top— that is, if you consider consuming more than your share a good thing!"

He continued, "We hear over and over that development—industrialization, whatever you want to call it—and trade are good, but I see them as destruction. *Development* is a euphemism, much like the word *efficiency*. Efficiency within the current system is really about how fast you can turn forests and mountains into wastepaper and soda-pop cans. Is that good? If the purpose of life is to consume and destroy, then international trade and industrial civilization are definitely proven ways to speed that up. International trade is the ultimate institutional and economic tool for leveraging our ability to consume, destroy, and work our will on the world."

The tape recorder hummed between us. I wondered where this fit into the question of hate, and the question of objectification.

Before I could say anything, though, he started up again: "International trade and the whole corporate state are based on a set of delusions that have been institutionalizing and hemming us in for six thousand years. We weren't always so destructive. But for some reason maybe six thousand years ago we began to see ourselves as separate from the world, separate from—and set against—other tribes, other cultures, other species: *others*. How you behave depends on how you see and feel your *self*. Once we see ourselves as separate from the rest of the world, we start to see every other being as a mere thing, and we begin to believe that we can get away with working our will on the world, that there wouldn't be negative consequences for attempting to do so, for pretending we're separate. But as you once wrote, Derrick, ignorance or denial of ecological law in no way exempts us from the consequences of our actions."

I'd forgotten that I'd written that. It was many years ago. He didn't give me time to try to recall exactly where it was.

He said, "Our power to work our will upon the world has far outstripped our ability to distinguish what's sustainable. The international trade system is clearly beyond our capacity to control or use in a sustainable or democratic way. Any economy that's beyond the community level, where there's immediate and face-to-face feedback about what you do, is going to cause problems. How can I still be a citizen yet be in an international economy? I can't even know what injustice or ecological destruction the purchase of my computer has had. I had no contact with the women in Thailand who've gotten cancer from putting hard drives and computer chips together. Even if my intent is 'good,' I can have only the slightest understanding of the impacts of my consumption. It is impossible to understand all the social and environmental impacts of a com-

PHILANTHROPY

puter or a car made in a dozen different countries. That's why consumers and industry are so enamored with the idea of certifying products so that the consumer can just walk into the store and buy the computer with a green star on the box. No thinking, no feeling, just confident consuming. 'More of everything,' says the motto at Eagle Hardware."

I nodded and thought. I reminded him of something he'd said many years before, that one of the problems is that our economy fragments us into many parts, two of which would be, for example, consumer and citizen, and these fragments are pitted against each other. I said, "It's clearly in your best interest as a consumer. . . ."

He finished my thought, ". . . to have my computer made by a woman who doesn't get paid enough, and who isn't protected by health and safety regulations. And who is thousands of miles away, and I will never meet. It's nearly irresistible to me as a consumer to buy the cheapest products."

I thought that, given the system of rewards central to our economic system, in which profit maximization is valued above all else, and specifically above life, it is probably just as irresistible to the owners of capital (human or otherwise) to exploit workers (and the land): "Nothing personal," they can say as they load their property onto the ship bound for the Middle Passage, "but a man's gotta turn a dime."

George said, "Even as someone who spends the majority of his working life examining the impacts and trying to change the system, I still drive a car, and I still buy computers assembled by underpaid people in the Third World. No matter how clear my perception or how pure my intent, as a consumer in the global economy I'm still drawn into situations that as a human I find abhorrent. It's an impossible situation. Look. I live a mile downwind from a Boeing airplane plant that produces toxic waste. The fact that I know about it, and that I have certain feelings and motivations around toxics, wasn't a strong enough deterrent to keep me from living here. I can live with those contradictions, and I may well die from the cancer that results. Polls indicate that most of us consider ourselves environmentalists—yet we're killing ourselves and destroying the ability of ecosystems to function. We're eating ourselves to death. Is anybody home?"

I wondered about that question, and I wondered how this fit into my exploration of slavery, hatred, objectification, and what we're going to do about it all.

■   ■   ■

The final primary argument in favor of chattel slavery was philanthropic: Far from being something to be abolished, the argument went, slavery was a positive good, beneficial not only to the masters but most especially to the slaves. Not only did contact (albeit unwanted) with EuroAmericans raise Africans (Indians, Chinese, and so on) out of their squalid life of savagery, but because slaves were expensive, they were generally treated better than their free counterparts, the wage slaves.

Early European accounts of their contact with Africans often reveals revulsion on the part of the Europeans (who are strangely silent on what the Africans thought of them). For example, Pyard de Laval wrote in 1610, "The people along this coast . . . are very brutish and savage, as stupid as can be and without intelligence, black and mis-shapen. . . . They live without law or religion, like animals." In 1616 the Reverend Terry disparagingly commented on the fact that the Khoikhoi of southern Africa dressed in skins, calling them, "Beasts in the skins of men rather than men in the skins of beasts." Frederick Andersen Bolling called them "the most hideous folk that can be found in the world," and Wouter Schouten got right to the point when he said, "Truly they more resemble the unreasoning beasts than reasonable man, living on

PHILANTHROPY

earth such a miserable and pitiful life, having no knowledge of GOD nor of what leads to their salvation."

Fortunately for the Africans, the Europeans were more than willing to provide salvation, in the form of slavery, which, as William Harper pointed out, "has done more to elevate a degraded race in the scale of humanity; to tame the savage; to civilize the barbarous; to soften the ferocious; to enlighten the ignorant, and to spread the blessings of christianity [*sic*] among the heathen, than all the missionaries that philanthropy and religion have ever sent forth." Harper asked rhetorically, "Can there be a doubt of the immense benefit which has been conferred on the race, by transplanting them from their native, dark, and barbarous regions, to the American Continent and Islands?"

I thought of the argument put forward now about how global trade is supposed to benefit members of nonindustrialized nations, and wondered how much things have really changed in the last one hundred and seventy years. Substitute the words *capitalism, industrialization,* or *free markets* for *slavery* and I could find these quotes tomorrow in the newspaper. I wondered also how many of the things I am told are good for me actually are, and how many are nothing more than rationales for exploitation: sweet words to keep me from perceiving my own predicament. It made me wonder also something even worse: What things are done to me and to others in ways I cannot even begin to perceive? Do those in power have my best interests at heart? Did the enslavers really believe their own rhetoric? I'm not sure I want to know the answers.

Although "slavery educates, refines, and moralizes the masses," according to George Fitzhugh, by "bringing them into continual intercourse with masters of superior minds, information, and morality," there was only so much—because of the raw material with which the masters had to work—that slave owners could hope to accomplish. Without more or less constant supervision, Africans almost always reverted to their prior or natural state of shiftlessness: "We have already seen that the principle of idleness triumphed over the desire for accumulation among the savages of North and South America, among the African nations, among the blacks of St. Domingo, &c, and nothing but the strong arm of authority could overcome its operation," wrote Thomas Roderick Dew. The reason for the triumph of idleness was that, according to Dew, "In dealing with a negro we must remember that we are dealing with a being possessing the form and strength of a man, but the intellect only of a child."

I derive a different lesson from all of this, that it takes a hell of a lot of force to ruin the lives of people who were happy not working for you.

Harper, too, noted that "Slaves are perpetual children," who needed protection, and Fitzhugh provided the answer as to how this protection should be accomplished: "To protect the weak, we must first enslave them, and this slavery must be either political and legal, or social; the latter, including the condition of wives, apprentices, inmates of poor houses, idiots, lunatics, children, sailors, soldiers and domestic slaves. Those latter classes . . . require masters of some kind, whose will and discretion shall stand as a law to them, who shall be entitled to their labor, and bound to provide for them."

I have spent the past several hours now thinking about the notion that masters "shall be entitled to their labor," and at the risk of overstating, it seems to me that entitlement is key to nearly all atrocities, and that any threat to perceived entitlement will provoke hatred.

The man who flayed the cat presumably felt that his employers were entitled to the cat's skin. Europeans felt that they were (and are) entitled to the land of North and South America. Slave owners clearly felt they were entitled to the labor (and the lives) of their slaves, not only in partial payment for protecting slaves from their own idleness, but also simply as a return on their capital investment. Owners of nonhuman capital today feel they, too, are entitled to the "surplus return on labor," as economists put it, as part of their reward for furnishing jobs, and to provide a return on *their* investment in

PHILANTHROPY

capital. Rapists act on the belief that they are entitled to their victims' bodies, and entitled to inflict cruelty upon them. Americans act as though we are entitled to consume the majority of the world's resources, and to change the world's climate. All industrialized humans act like they're entitled to anything they want on this planet.

Nietzsche wrote, "One does not hate so long as one despises." There seems to me a pretty clear relationship between feeling entitled to exploit someone and despising her or him. My dictionary defines *entitle* as "to qualify (a person) to do something: to give a claim to; to give a right to demand or receive." It comes from the Latin *intitulus*, to give a title, meaning to honor or dignify with a title. By right of my title as a white man, I have a claim to a black man's labor. Any black man's. By right of my title as a man, I have a claim to a woman's body. Any woman's. By right of having enough money to invest in capital, I have a claim to "surplus" of other people's labor. By right of having enough money to buy the rights to land, I have a claim to all of the resources it holds. My dictionary defines *despise* as "to look down upon, to scorn; to disdain; to have a low opinion of; to regard as contemptible." It comes from the Latin *de-specere*, to look down. If I am above, I have claims upon those I look down upon. I am entitled to take from those I despise.

From the perspective of those who are entitled, the problems begin when those they despise do not go along with—and have the power and wherewithal to not go along with—the perceived entitlement. That's where Nietzsche's statement comes in, and that's where hatred of the sort I'm trying to get at in this book becomes manifest. Several times I have commented that hatred, felt long and deeply enough, no longer feels like hatred, but more like tradition, economics, religion, what have you. It is when those traditions are challenged, when the entitlement is threatened, when the masks of religion, economics, and so on are pulled away that hate transforms from its more seemingly sophisticated, "normal," chronic state— where those exploited are looked down upon, or despised—to a more acute and obvious manifestation. Hate becomes more perceptible when it is no longer normalized. Another way to say all of this is that if the rhetoric of superiority works to maintain the entitlement, hatred and direct physical force remain underground. But when that rhetoric begins to fail, force and hatred waits in the wings, ready to explode.

PHILANTHROPY

"ASK OF ME, AND i SHALL GiVE THEE,
THE HEATHEN FOR THINE iNHERITANCE,
AND THE UTTERMOST PARTS OF THE
EARTH FOR THY POSSESSION."

PSALMS 2:8

GIVING BACK THE LAND

LET ME PUT THIS ANOTHER WAY. Pretend that you were raised to believe that blacks—niggers would be more precise in this formulation—really are like children, but strong. And pretend that niggers working for whites is simply part of the day-to-day experience of living. You do not question it any more than you question breathing, eating, or sleeping. It is simply a fact of life: Whites own niggers, niggers work for whites.

Now pretend that someone from the outside begins to tell you that what you are doing is wrong. This outsider knows nothing of the life you live and that your father and his father have lived. To your knowledge, this outsider has never walked the fields and actually watched the slaves work, has never gone over the figures to see that your farm wouldn't be viable without these slaves, and doesn't know the slaves well enough to know that they, too, could not survive without the things you provide for them. Pretend that your slaves listen to this outsider, and because of this, your relationship with them begins to deteriorate, even to the point that you begin to lose money.

If it were me—had I been raised under these circumstances and with those beliefs—I think it possible that, once I got over my initial shock at the temerity of this outsider meddling in something that is none of his or her business, I would have become angry, and perhaps, eventually, felt outrage toward this interloper who was threatening to ruin my way of life. Raised in those circumstances, it would have taken more courage than most of us have, I think, to admit that one's way of life is based on exploitation, and to gracefully begin to live a different way.

It's easy enough at this remove to simply say that slaveholders were immoral, and that members of the KKK and other hate groups were a bunch of stupid bigots with whom we have nothing in common.

But are you sure? Try this. What if, instead of owning people, we're talking about owning land. Someone tells you that no matter how much you paid to purchase title to some piece of land, the land itself does not belong to you. No longer may you do whatever you wish with it. You may not cut the trees on it. You may not build on it. You may not run a bulldozer over it to put in a driveway. All of those activities are immoral, because they're based on your exploitation of a living thing: in this case, the land. Did you ask the land if it wants you to build on it? Do you care what the land thinks? But the land can't think, you say. Ah, but that's just what *you* think. It is how you were taught to think. Let's say, further, that your livelihood and your way of life are based on working this land—the outsiders call it exploiting—and that if the outsiders have their way, you'll be out of business. Again and again they tell you that you are a bad person, a stupid bigot, because you refuse to see that your way of life is based on the exploitation of something you don't perceive as having any rights—or sentience—to begin with.

Angry yet?

Then how about this? Outsiders take away your computer because the process of manufacturing the hard drive killed women in

GiViNG DACK THE LAND

Thailand. They take your clothes because they were made in sweat-shops, your meat because it was factory-farmed, your cheap vegetables because the agricorporations that provided them drove family farmers out of business (or maybe because lettuce doesn't like to be factory-farmed: "lettuce prefers diversity," say the outsiders), and your coffee because its production destroys rain forests, decimates migratory songbird populations, and drives African, Asian, and South and Central American subsistence farmers off their land. They take your car because of global warming, and your wedding ring because mining exploits workers and destroys landscapes and communities. They take your TV, microwave, and refrigerator because, hell, they take the whole damn electrical grid because the generation of electricity is, they say, so environmentally expensive (dams kill salmon, coal plants strip the tops off mountains and generate acid rain, wind generators kill birds, and let's not *even talk* about nukes). Imagine if outsiders wanted to take away all these things—without your consent—because they had determined, without your input, that all of these things are exploitative and immoral. Imagine that these outsiders actually began to succeed in taking away these parts of your life which you see as fundamental. I'd imagine you'd be pretty pissed. Maybe you'd start to hate the assholes doing this to you, and maybe if enough other people who were pissed off had already formed an organization to fight these people who were trying to destroy your life—I could easily see you asking, "What do these people have against me anyway?"—maybe you'd even put on white robes and funny hats, and maybe you'd even get a little rough with a few of them, if that was what it took to stop them from destroying your way of life.

■ ■ ■

What if, even without outside agitation, the slaves began to revolt? They began to upset—to violate—the natural order of things. Would you find it incomprehensible that slaves could be so ungrateful as to not appreciate your providing them food, clothing, and shelter? Would

THE CULTURE OF MAKE BELIEVE

you try to teach them, at first with words, and then through other means, that their thinking was in error? Would you try to put your life back in order through any means possible? Would you find it hard to hear what your slaves—or rather (though not from your perspective) the people whom you had enslaved—were trying to tell you?

Now, what if the land itself were speaking to you? What if creatures opted for extinction rather than submit to the type of world you're trying to order around you? What if the planet were changing its climate in an attempt to get you to stop enslaving it? What if the planet and its inhabitants were doing everything they could to tell you that they do not like what you're doing, that they do not want to live this way? Would you be able to hear them?

I didn't think so.

■　　　■　　　■

No matter where any of us walk, there we tread on the bones of slaughtered indigenous peoples. Today I went to Yontocket—a nearby site that is sacred to the Tolowa, the local Indians—with my two dogs, and with a friend, Karen Rath, an extraordinary environmental activist who knows the place's history.

She stopped at my home, and we drove north about ten miles, passing on the way the prison where I teach. We saw tall, blue, empty watchtowers, made irrelevant by the lethal electric fence that runs the perimeter, and we saw the parking lot full of cars belonging to guards and administrators. We saw huge slabs of concrete assembled to hold people inside. We saw all this through the thick screen of redwoods that separates the prison from the rest of the world.

After the prison we traversed farm roads. We saw a huge flock of geese. Karen said, "This is a little early for the Aleutians to be back." Each spring the world's population of Aleutian geese—smaller cousins to Canada geese—stages near Crescent City on their way from their wintering grounds in central California to the Aleutian Islands, and each spring they stage here on their way back north. Their population dropped as low as eight hundred in 1967, but by

GiViNG DACK THE LAND

now they've recovered to more than thirty thousand. They stay a month or more, fattening themselves for their transoceanic flight—two thousand miles nonstop—to their nesting grounds.

The extreme concentration of birds here—and their heavy feeding—means the costs of recovery of this species have been carried largely by eleven ranchers and farmers, on whose pastures these geese feed in early spring. The farmers are not always pleased to see the geese's arrival, perceiving the grass disappearing into the birds' gullets not so much as fuel for an extraordinary journey as calories that could fatten their own calves.

"It's interesting," Karen said, "many of these farmers—not just those affected by the geese, but a lot of the region's large landowners—are direct descendants of settlers who killed Tolowa Indians and took their land. Today some of them talk about rapprochement, and I've even heard a few apologies, but no one ever talks about giving back the land."

We stopped the car and got out. I let the dogs out of the back. They touched their noses to my hands in greeting, ran past a gate erected to keep cars away from the cemetery, and dashed down the dirt road in front of us. But the dogs pulled up short when they saw cows standing in a pasture on the opposite side of a triple-strand electric fence. Both dogs stood, stiff-legged and jumpy, not sure what to make of these huge creatures, the likes of which they'd never encountered. A cow lumbered toward them, curious. Narcissus, a springer spaniel/black lab mix who somehow ended up smaller than either, began to retreat toward the car, then changed his mind and returned. The other stood stock-still. Narcissus reared on hind legs, presumably to get a better view. He hopped a couple of times, fell back to all fours, then reared up again. He whined interestedly. By now the other dog, Amaru, a solidly-built border collie cross, had evidently become convinced the cows were no threat. Equally convinced of their fundamental dullness, Amaru lost interest and padded down the path.

We caught up to the dogs, and walked with them along the road that split two pastures. We started up a hill. At the top was a small

THE CULTURE OF MAKE BELIEVE

cemetery ringed by a wooden fence. Plastic flowers, crosses, feathers, and prayer flags hung from the slats.

"This is where some of them were buried," she said.

I nodded, but didn't say anything.

"It wasn't the only time the settlers here massacred Indians." She stopped, then added emphatically, "It wasn't even the only time they massacred them that year."

I asked her when it happened.

"In 1853, settlers attacked and burned the northernmost Tolowa village of Howonquet. They killed about seventy people, maybe more. I've heard that many Indians ran to the far side of a rock, next to the ocean, and hid there. When the tide began to rise, they had a choice: the cold ocean on one side or whites with guns and clubs on the other. Many drowned."

I closed my eyes.

She continued. "That sort of thing happened all across California. Groups of white men formed 'volunteer armies'—with the government paying all expenses, including guns and ammo, so that these militias could, as a commissioner of Indian affairs put it, 'rid the state of this population'—and periodically swept down on Indian villages, killing them, enslaving them, forcing them into prostitution. The turn of the Tolowas at Yontocket came that year during a winter dance—probably their annual ten-day dance of world renewal."

Karen stopped, looked at me for a moment, then abruptly looked to the far side of the valley. She didn't say anything for a time, until finally she began again: "Do you remember that scene in the movie *The Empire Strikes Back* where the main characters carry on a running battle with the Empire, with the forces of darkness, flying fast through an ancient redwood forest?"

"Yes," I said.

She pointed with her chin to a hill across the valley. "It was filmed over there."

I didn't say anything.

"In exchange for being allowed to film there, part of the deal the

GIVING BACK THE LAND

producers struck with the corporate owners was that they wouldn't publicize that the area was going to be clear-cut, and that they wouldn't oppose the felling of the trees."

I wondered where she was going with this.

"A good friend of mine was standing here during the cutting, and all the way over here, across the valley"—it must have been two miles—"he could feel the thuds in his feet as they felled the old ones."

I didn't say anything.

She said, "In 1853, over four hundred and fifty Indians were murdered here. Afterward the whites built a huge fire and threw in the Indian's sacred ceremonial dresses, their regalia, their feathers."

She stopped again.

I didn't think I wanted her to continue; she did. "Then they threw in the babies, many still alive. Some whites tied weights around the necks of the dead and threw them into some nearby water."

"Were all of the Indians killed here?"

"I read an account, by an Indian who survived—and this account is where I learned most of this—who said many were killed at the ponds." She pointed, again with her chin, down a road leading south.

We followed this road for maybe a mile and a half. The day was deceptively hot, and as I walked I peeled off layers—first a jacket, then a sweater, finally a sweatshirt, leaving only a short-sleeved button-down—and dropped them beside the path. We would come back this way. Karen gave me an apple from a friend's tree up in the mountains to the east. It was juicy, sweet, and just a little sour. Perfect. The dogs ran ahead, dashing into the woods to chase squirrels, then returning to dance in circles around our feet. To the west, we heard waves falling on sand: The beach was just over a wooded ridge and past a few grassy hillocks.

We came to the ponds, large shallow spaces far below the road. At this time of year, October, nearing the end of the the dry season, the ponds are little more than mudflats, but I'd seen them before— knowing nothing of their history—on a walk I took here a couple of years ago from a different direction. They'd been full, covered with broad-leaf water plants, and large with the sounds of frogs.

THE CULTURE OF MAKE BELIEVE

Karen said, "Two men who escaped hid under lily pads, and breathed through reeds. They said that the next morning blood had stained the ponds red."

I didn't know how much more I could take in right then, but Karen continued. "The next year whites attacked again. The excuse was that an Indian had stolen a horse. Whites gathered outside the homes of the Indians, and began shooting. They killed men, women, and children as fast as they could reload their guns. A few of the Indians were able to make it to Lake Earl, but the whites followed, and shot at every head that appeared above the water."

I looked away from her, down to the ponds. I tried to look beyond the trees and grasses around the pond and into the past, to see and feel and hear the Indians running, hiding, being found, bludgeoned, shot, killed with axes. I tried to see into the souls of their attackers, and to understand what made them do this, what perceptions and beliefs would lead them to these actions. But I saw nothing except mud and water and trees and reeds, the latter two moving slightly in the hot afternoon's hesitant breeze.

I'd like to say I did something special to mark the slaughter, but I didn't. We turned and walked back toward the car. I threw the apple core into the woods. As we walked, I put back on the layers. We didn't talk much. There wasn't much to say.

■   ■   ■

As we walked, it began to come clear to me why so often we do not commemorate the slaughters of indigenous peoples: There are too many sites from too many massacres, and to commemorate them all—even with an action so simple as that of a Catholic who reflexively makes the sign of the cross each time she encounters a cemetery—would afford little time for us to enjoy the comforts and elegancies civilization affords. I would wager every county in the United States has hosted at least one massacre, recorded or forgotten. Del Norte, where I live in the far north of California, has at least three, and it was far from any of the major Indian "wars." Tecumseh,

GIVING BACK THE LAND

of the Shawnees, wrote, "Where today are the Pequot? Where are the Narragansett, the Mohican, the Pokanoket, and many other once powerful tribes of our people? They have vanished before the avarice and the oppression of the White Man, as snow before a summer sun." Tecumseh's list was of course far shorter than it could have been, even counting only his extended neighborhood. There were the Wampanoags, the Chesapeakes, the Chickahominys, the Potomacs (of whom only Pocahontas is remembered): all exterminated. There were the Montauks, Nanticokes, Machapungas, Catawbas, Cheraws, Miamis, Hurons, Eries, Senecas: all scattered or reduced to remnants, clinging tight to their cultural existence.

The pattern has been repeated on all continents. In southern Africa in 1812, for example, the commissioner for the frontier, Lieutenant-Colonel Graham, stated: "My intention is now to attack the savages in a way which I confidently hope will leave a lasting impression on their memories, and show them our vast superiority in all situations. I have ordered 500 men to enter the wood on foot . . . with orders to stay there so long as a kaffir [a colonial term for an African, with the rough connotation of *nigger*] remains alive. . . ." As he drove more than twenty thousand Xhosa peoples out of that region, Graham told a reporter, "The only way of getting rid of them is by depriving them of the means of subsistence and continually harassing them, for which purpose the whole force is constantly employed in destroying prodigious quantities of Indian corn and millet which they have planted . . . taking from them the few cattle which they conceal in the woods with great address, and shooting every man who can be found. This is detestable work. . . . We are forced to hunt them like wild beasts." The "detestable work" paid off for Graham: the governor directed that the spot where Graham was headquartered "shall in future be called . . . Graham's Town . . . in respect for the services of Lieutenant-Colonel Graham, through whose spirited exertions the kaffir hordes have been driven from that valuable district."

The nightmare goes on, even, once again, in that same neighborhood. On August 25, 1828, an expedition under Henry Somerset attacked a sleeping Ngwane encampment "with great guns, and small guns, and sabres and assegais, and made . . . indiscriminate havoc before the savages were awake or knew what had come upon them. . . ." The survivors, "gaunt and emaciated by hunger and age, crawled out of their miserable sheds, but with pitiable apathy sat or lay down again, as if heedless of their fate. . . . The field presented a scene indescribably shocking: old decrepit men, with their bodies pierced, and heads almost cut off; pregnant females ripped open, legs broken, and hands severed from the arms for . . . the armlets, or some trifling ornament; little children mutilated and horribly mangled. . . ." And again: Colonel Harry Smith, who later became Cape governor, described his normal military activities to his wife: "You gallop in, and half by force, half by stratagem, pounce upon them wherever you can find them; frighten their wives, burn their homes, lift their cattle, and return home quite *triumphant.*"

These triumphs have been replicated everywhere, although in some places, for example, much of Europe, many of the massacres, the conquerings, the burned villages, the wasted crops, have by now been almost fully erased from memory, by time, by a belief system that excuses the slaughters as necessary or desirable, and, perhaps, most importantly, by a deep need to forget the atrocities—and underlying hatred—upon which our system is based.

■   ■   ■

It's a month later, and finally I returned to Yontocket. This time I went with another friend, John Osborn. I met him when I lived in Spokane, where he's the heart of the regional environmental community. He introduced me to activism more than a decade ago. I'd told John a little about what happened at Yontocket, and when he came to visit me over Thanksgiving, he wanted to see the cemetery.

I've eaten Thanksgiving dinner with John nearly every year for the past decade. Each year we meet at my mother's, give thanks (mainly to the animals and plants we're about to eat), eat, give more thanks (this time to my mom and to everyone else who prepared and brought food), then do what we always do when we get together (and

GIVING BACK THE LAND

admittedly what we each do separately most of the time we're apart), which is to try to understand the dominant culture's widespread destructiveness, and try to figure out what to do about it. After dinner one year we watched a long documentary on the Nuremberg trials, and talked about the necessity now of putting CEOs and politicians on trial for crimes against humanity. Another year we watched a documentary on how the big four timber companies in the Pacific Northwest got their land illegally from the public domain (the subject of a book John and I cowrote with George Draffan). A third year we talked about the world AIDS epidemic: By night, John's an environmentalist, and by day he's a doctor at the Spokane Veterans Administration Hospital, where he runs the AIDS clinic. As you could probably surmise, neither of us has what could be deemed an active social life. But I have to say that one year, before the serious talk, we listened to an impromptu Chopin concert by the elderly father of another friend of ours who had been a guest at dinner (I must admit, though, that I fell asleep during the performance, lying on the floor with my stomach simply too full of turkey, potatoes, pumpkin pie, and the best fruit salad known to humans).

This year we went to Yontocket. We didn't bring the dogs. The cows were still there, though noticeably bigger: They looked to be teenagers. The day was once again nice, though not quite warm enough for me to begin removing clothes.

As we walked, John asked, "Do you know what the main instrument of genocide is these days?"

I shook my head. There are too many instruments to choose quickly.

"A hint," he said. "It's no longer the church, the military, not even corporations or other institutions."

I looked at him out of the corner of my eye, and saw he wore a wry smile.

He said, "Television."

I nodded. One way or another, he and I had been talking about the role of television in the perpetuation of our culture and the perpetration of atrocities for the entire decade of our friendship.

THE CULTURE OF MAKE BELIEVE

"It's the great homogenizer," he said.

I thought not about television but about genocide. The word so often carries with it—rightly so—images of greasy smoke pouring from the stacks at Treblinka, or broken treaties and broken bodies of Indians killed at Wounded Knee (or, for that matter, Yontocket). But something we too often forget is that genocide in no way equals mass murder. A person, or more likely a culture or an institution, like a nation-state or corporation, can commit mass murder without committing genocide, and can just as surely commit genocide without killing a single individual. Genocide consists, according to the 1948 United Nations Convention on the Prevention and Punishment of the Crime of Genocide (which, by the way, the United States refused to endorse until 1988, and to this day explicitly refuses to comply with), of any one or more of a set of specific "acts committed with intent to destroy, in whole or in part, a national, ethnical, racial or religious group as such." Mass murder committed without the intent to destroy (in whole or in part) one of these groups would not be considered genocide. Thus familial child abuse, which cuts across national, religious (some more so than others), ethnical (though not all), and class lines, would not be considered genocidal, even though it results in widespread deaths. A case could be made, on the other hand, that child prostitution has genocidal implications—setting aside for a moment the question of intent on the part of pimps and johns—because so many of the victims are poor children of color belonging to impoverished ethnic groups from impoverished regions of impoverished nations, meaning that, in great enough numbers, child prostitution tears at the fabric of these communities, which is the essence of genocide.

The 1948 Convention lists five acts as possibly constituting genocide. One consists of killing the members of a group outright. This is the act that most of us are most familiar with, and leads to the images of Treblinka and Wounded Knee. Another consists of deliberately inflicting on a group conditions calculated to bring about its physical destruction in whole or in part. One example would be the intentional slaughter of bison in order to bring the Plains Indians to

GIVING BACK THE LAND

terms. Another would be the destruction of the great runs of salmon in the Pacific Northwest in order to break the cultural backs of the region's Indians. A third act considered genocidal is to impose measures intended to prevent births within a group, through involuntary sterilization or forced abortion (the words *involuntary* and *forced* being crucial here). When the state imposes birth control as a matter of policy on targeted groups so they cannot conceive and/or reproduce, with the ultimate intent that the group disappears, that is genocide. An example of this would be the approximately three thousand per year involuntary or coerced sterilizations performed at Indian Health Services hospitals on American Indian women of childbearing age during the early 1970s (given the small American Indian population, this would have been the equivalent of sterilizing about four hundred thousand non-Indian American women per year). The fourth act covered by the Convention is that of forcibly transferring children of one group to another group, and training them to see themselves as something other than part of the cultural context into which they were born. When that happens, the culture cannot, for obvious reasons, perpetuate itself. During much of the nineteenth century and into the twentieth (at least until this most recent generation) upward of 80 percent of American Indian children were forcibly removed from their homes and sent to boarding schools, or adopted into white families, where the children were denied the right to speak their language, to practice their religion, to dress in a manner representative of the culture of their birth. They were, in short, raised to be brown-skinned, black-haired, dark-eyed white kids. This is a form of genocide under the law. The final act covered by the 1948 Convention consists of causing serious bodily or mental harm to members of some group, so that members "voluntarily" separate themselves from the group, dissolving the community to spare themselves this discomfort. An obvious example of this would be the choice of Christianity or death offered so often for so many centuries to so many indigenous peoples worldwide. A less obvious but perhaps ultimately even more damaging example, John said, might be television, which causes mental harm, and causes the dissolution of com-

THE CULTURE OF MAKE BELIEVE

munities. He mentioned also that television trains children to be part of a social context other than the one in which they were born.

"But what about intent?" I asked. "The U.N. Convention emphasizes intent."

He looked at me sharply. "You don't think there's intent?"

I shook my head, then said quickly, "Now that I say this, I'm not sure intent matters." My thoughts hurried. I hoped I could catch them. Things get tricky when we start talking about motivation. As I hope is clear by now, only the most unsophisticated take their hate pure. Most of the time we mix ourselves a brew of self-interest, tradition, economics, and old-time religion. Even the Nazis had their claims to virtue, keeping their focus on nothing so indelicate as mass murder or genocide but instead always on the need to purify and protect the their Prussian culture.

If intent is crucial, I thought, we need to make clear whether we're talking about conscious and stated intent, or intent unspoken, intent hidden, even, or especially, from those who find themselves swept up—whether by sudden fury at the insolence of those they would prefer to despise than to hate, or by the inexorable logic of economics, science, or religion, or by the deep, smooth, swift-flowing current of tradition—into committing reprehensible actions. As the doctors at Indian Health Services hospitals opened specula inside Indian women's vaginas, as they pierced vaginal walls, as they tied fallopian tubes, did they intend—consciously—to rub these races out? Or did they assemble each time a logic that led them, each time, to make decisions that at the time seemed to them appropriate? *This woman*, a doctor may have thought, *cannot without government hand-outs support the children she has, so am I not doing her and her children—born and unborn—a favor by preventing her from conceiving?*

To put the question of intent into another context; If race-based slavery makes economic sense (for the enslaver)—by which I mean that the *conscious intent* is not explicitly to destroy that other race as a group or community, but instead merely to exploit it (even at the cost of extinguishment)—does that mean race-based slavery is not an act of genocide?

GiViNG BaCK THE LaNd

To switch contexts again, what are we to make of the 1991 internal memo (leaked to environmentalists) by World Bank chief economist Lawrence Summers: "Just between you and me, shouldn't the World Bank be encouraging MORE migration of the dirty industries to the LDCs [Less Developed Countries]? . . . . The measurements of the costs of health impairing pollution depends on the foregone earnings from increased morbidity and mortality. From this point of view a given amount of health impairing pollution should be done in the country with the lowest cost, which will be the country with the lowest wages. I think the economic logic behind dumping a load of toxic waste in the lowest wage country is impeccable and we should face up to that. . . . I've always thought that under-populated countries in Africa are vastly *under*-polluted. . . . Only the lamentable facts that so much pollution is generated by non-tradable industries (transport, electrical generation) and that the unit transport costs of solid waste are so high prevent world welfare enhancing trade in air pollution and waste." Is killing people in impoverished countries by polluting their homeland not genocidal because the economic logic is impeccable? It should be noted that Lawrence Summers was not censured for his articulation, which in fact guides World Bank policies to this day (Summers also noted in that same memo that "The problem with the arguments against all of these proposals for more pollution in LDCs (intrinsic rights to certain goods, moral reasons, social concerns, lack of adequate markets, etc.) could be turned around and used more or less effectively against every Bank proposal for liberalization.") When Summers's memo became public in February 1992, Brazil's then-secretary of the environment Jose Lutzenburger wrote to Summers: "Your reasoning is perfectly logical but totally insane. . . . Your thoughts [provide] a concrete example of the unbelievable alienation, reductionist thinking, social ruthlessness and the arrogant ignorance of many conventional 'economists' concerning the nature of the world we live in. . . . If the World Bank keeps you as vice president it will lose all credibility. To me it would confirm what I often said . . . the best thing that could happen would be for the Bank to disappear." Unfortunately for members of the underpolluted regions of the world, neither the World Bank nor Summers disappeared. Lutzenberger, on the other hand, was fired shortly after writing this letter. Summers remained with the World Bank until joining the Clinton administration, where he eventually became secretary of the treasury, and, more recently, president of Harvard.

I told John all of this.

He said, "I still think we can make a case for intent. Say, for example, a group of people live in a community that values relationships more highly than material objects."

He was, of course, describing the vast majority of communities through human existence.

He continued. "Now, introduce television. TV is based on creating dissatisfaction. It cannot exist without dissatisfaction. Happy people make bad consumers."

I remembered a conversation I'd had earlier this year with Kalle Lasn, an anticorporate, anticonsumeristic culture-jamming activist who runs *Adbusters Magazine* out of Vancouver, British Columbia. He'd told me, "The first agenda of the commercial media is to sell fear, because it breeds insecurity, and then consumer culture offers us any number of ways to buy our way back to feeling secure, however temporarily. We're fed these images of what we're supposed to look like: pouting lips, pert breasts, buns of steel, everlasting youth."

"White," I added.

He continued, "It's not possible to internalize again and again these images of what's beautiful and what's desirable without having that affect your self-perception. And it alters the very foundations of your personality. It distorts your sexuality. What does it mean that so many of us are willing to give up so much of our power, voluntarily and systematically, to strangers? What does it mean that the most private parts of ourselves—how we are in relationship to ourselves and to those we love—have been designed in great measure by those who have no interest in us other than that we feel insecure enough to buy their products?"

I told John this, then told him that I think the problem with television is even more fundamental than just causing insecurity. The

GIVING BACK THE LAND

problem is existential. We all know what happens when you introduce television into indigenous communities. In her book, *Ancient Futures: Learning From Ladakh*, Helena Norberg-Hodge commented that the "incredible vitality and joy that I experienced in the villages [in Ladakh, part of the trans-Himalayan region of Kashmir] was almost certainly connected to the fact that the excitement in life was here and now, with you and *in* you. People did not feel that they were on the periphery; the center was where they were." The arrival of television changed all this, she said, because "idealized stars make people feel inferior and passive, and the here and now pales in comparison with the colorful excitement of faraway places."

The effects of TV on indigenous communities are both immediate and insidious, I said. In the 1980s, television was introduced into Dene and Inuit villages in the far north of Canada. Jerry Mander interviewed members of these communities. "People weren't visiting each other anymore," a Dene woman said. "It was hard to get the kids to do anything. The women weren't sewing anymore, either, and the woodpiles were too low." Another said, "The social relationships of the people and the language and learning of the kids changed overnight. What they started learning best was all the stuff that's in those commercials from white society." She continued, "I would really like to know what it is about TV that causes the addiction. . . . I get glued to it, even if it's something like soap operas with those kinds of values."

I thought about all this as John and I walked, and I told him why I don't have a TV: Life is short enough the way it is. I don't need to shorten it further by looking at a television, then suddenly looking away and realizing several hours of my life are gone forever. I told him what a Dene man said: "The type of learning we get in school and also on TV is the type of learning where we just sit and absorb. But in family life it's a different kind of learning. Children learn directly from their parents. That is the native way of teaching. Learning has to come from doing, not intellectualizing. A long time ago they only taught people by doing things, but now they just sit and watch TV." Another Dene woman said: "Those stereotypes on TV really twist people. The way they show what a terrific thing it is to have a drink. Their lifestyles are so different. How does that make you feel about yourself? . . . . I try to get people to talk, but they don't want to anymore. They just sit and watch." Finally, I told John about a Dene woman who said, "Legends are tools that help people grow in certain ways. A lot of what matters is the power and the feeling of the experience. It's like when you're tanning hides, it's not only important to learn how to do the scraping and the cutting. In the old way, the process was also a kind of meditation, a prayer to help put power into it. There used to be prayers for how to grind the corn. It wasn't just grinding corn, it was also the feeling in it. But when you put something . . . on TV, you can see it all right, but you're really looking only at the shell."

John and I walked in silence, except for the sound of our feet on the gravel and dirt of the two-track road. At last I said, "It's not just our sex lives, and it's not just indigenous peoples."

"TV is everywhere," he responded. "It's everything to so many people."

I told him of the line by the Scottish patriot Andrew Fletcher: "If I were permitted to write all the ballads I need not care who makes the laws of the nation."

He nodded. We began to talk of the way that stories socialize us into our roles as men and women, and to talk of the great transformation that has taken place over the last fifty years, as children have been decreasingly socialized by stories told by parents, schools, communities, churches, and even nations, and more by stories produced by marketing conglomerates who are simply trying to sell us something.

This reminded me of a conversation I'd had years before with television critic George Gerbner, who'd said to me, "Because most scripts are written by and for men, they project a world in which men rule, and in which men play most of the roles. Television and movies project the power structure of our society, and by projecting it, perpetuate it, make it seem normal, make it seem the only thing to do, to talk about, to think about. Once viewers have become habituated to a certain type of story, they experience great consternation if you

GIVING BACK THE LAND

try to change it. Let's say you try to countercast, or change the typical casting in a typical story. A woman, now, is going to wield power. She is going to use violence. Suddenly, you can't tell any story other than the one that describes why this is so. The story has to revolve around why a woman is doing things that seem scandalous for her, yet seem normal for a man. By telling a story that is different from what the audience has come to expect, you disturb public sensibilities."

I'd asked George if that means television is representative of our culture.

He'd responded, "No, it's representative of the power structure. Not the culture. This means those in power are overrepresented, they're more likely to be successful, and they're more likely to inflict violence than to suffer it."

"This means," I'd said, "that it's not *really* even representative of the power structure, but instead the *fantasies* of those in power."

"Exactly. Television is an agency of the power structure by which those in power represent their fantasies. By doing so they contribute to those fantasies becoming real, becoming a part of the consciousness of each of us."

He'd continued. "In culture, it's the supply that determines the demand, never the other way around. Just imagine a group of writers talking about a story, and someone says, 'Why is it that most of the time the victim is a woman? Why don't we equalize the scales?' The answer would be, 'A violent woman is distasteful.'"

Although Gerbner is best known for his studies conducted through the Cultural Indicators Project, a nonprofit group formed to study violence on television (and the relationship between the stories we tell and the society at large), he told me he doesn't believe that either frequency or explicitness of violence are the primary issues. "Violence," he said, "is a demonstration of power, and the real issue, once again, is who is doing what to whom. If time and again you hear and see stories in which people like you—white males in the prime of life—are more likely to prevail in a conflict situation, you become more aggressive, and if you are in the same culture, and a member of a group or a gender that is more likely to be victimized, you grow up more insecure, more dependent, more afraid of getting into a conflict, because you feel your calculus of risk is higher.

"That," he continued, "is the way we train minorities. People aren't born a minority, they are are trained to act like a minority through that kind of cultural conditioning. And women, who are a numerical majority of humankind, still are trained to act like a minority. The sense of potential victimization and vulnerability is the key."

We'd been talking in the small lunchroom at the Fort Mason Center, in San Francisco. Although George talks confidently, I'd sometimes had to strain to hear him over the sounds of other people talking and eating. I remember specifically having to strain to hear over one fellow who for some reason kept crumpling and uncrumpling the paper sack in which he'd brought his lunch.

George had said, "Of course not all people react the same way to anything." Women of color may react differently to their sense of potential victimization than do men of color. We have to ask, again, how have they been socialized to behave?

"Most of the time people talk about violence as if it were a simple act. Well, it's a complicated scenario, a social relationship between violators and victims. The question we need to always ask ourselves is, who takes what role? What power relationship is being demonstrated? For every ten violent characters, there are ten victims. For every ten women who are written into scripts to express the kind of power that white males express with relative impunity, there are nineteen women who become victimized. For every ten women of color who are written into scripts to act in an aggressive way, there are twenty-two women of color who are victimized. Your chances of victimization double if you are not a member of the group for whom it is accepted to be a victimizer, who are more likely to be aggressors and less likely to be victims."

I'd asked him whether that just represents reality. Although in domestic violence women sometimes beat men, the violence runs overwhelmingly in the other direction.

His response was central to everything I've been trying to talk about in this book: "Children are not born into these roles. Stories

GiViNG BACK THE LAND

teach them how to act, whether they are to act the victim or victimizer, how and toward whom they may or may not express their aggression. Both men and women learn that women are legitimate victims, receptacles for aggression. White males are not acceptable victims. And now having shaped reality, these stories then of course reflect it back."

He'd told me to remember that a mirror is not a passive instrument. "It is a kind of exchange in which you see—your tie perhaps, or your makeup—and then you either change what you see, or you don't change what you see. The same is true with television. You look into it and see yourself, and then you either conform, or you don't conform. But it takes a conscious decision to not conform, and even then your decision to rebel is based on what you have seen: Even rebellion depends on having something to rebel against, and that is provided in the culture, in the stories."

I told John about all this, sparing him such details as the man crumpling and uncrumpling his sack. John's response to our conversation—this conversation so familiar between us—surprised me not in the slightest. He is an activist, and he is a doctor. One of his favorite sayings is, "The first step toward treatment is correct diagnosis." Now that we had a diagnosis—that television serves the interests of those in power by distorting our psyches and diminishing our communities—I knew he was itching for a treatment. He asked, and I could have mouthed the words of his question, "What should we do about it?"

I'm sure he could just as easily have mouthed my response: "Smash the televisions."

He laughed, as he had each time we'd had this exchange. Then he began, "Apart from blowing up television stations—"

"—Or maybe in addition—"

"—what do you think we should do?"

"When I showed Frankie the beginning of this book"—Frankie is Frances Moore Lappé, a dear friend, and author of *Diet For A Small Planet*—"she read the bit about putting Julius Streicher on trial at Nuremberg, and said we should put media executives on trial for crimes against humanity, because their programming—that word is no accident—and advertising make us hate ourselves."

Frankie hadn't been joking when she said this. I wasn't joking either. John didn't laugh. He nodded his head. He said, "That might work."

"And if it doesn't," I responded, "there's always dynamite. . . ."

We got to the cemetery. John asked again what happened here, and I told him what little I knew. I noticed for the first time that no sign marked the massacre. For all any visitor might know, those buried here could have died in their sleep, lying in their lovers' arms, happy and aged.

"There should be a marker," I said.

John didn't respond.

"To commemorate," I added.

He still didn't say anything.

"To tell the truth."

Still nothing.

"To let us know."

He wasn't looking at me. I started to say something else, and finally just shut up. We stood next to each other for a long time. Finally he said, "You know about the Names Project, right?"

"What?"

"The AIDS quilt. Same thing."

I nodded once, and looked at him, waiting.

"That's what we need," he said.

"A quilt?"

"More than almost anything else, the Names Project brought AIDS before the public. I don't know how strong awareness about AIDS would have been in the late 1980s—or even now—without it. Thousands more people die from cancer than AIDS—"

"—A thousand Americans die of cancer every day," I said.

"Yet we talk about AIDS. We care about it. We cry about it. The Names Project has been enormously successful at getting the word out. That's a good thing."

"And. . ."

GIVING BACK THE LAND

"We need to remember these massacres. All of us."

"I get it," I said.

"We need memorial services. Ceremonies. Here. A walk from here to Crescent City. Every year. Again and again. Until we cannot forget. Until we do not forget. You remember that Santayana quote, don't you, about how people who do not remember the past are condemned to repeat it? Well, people could start learning the real history of their own backyards. They could remember the massacres that took place in their own counties. They could begin talking about them. All starting right at home."

I liked the idea.

"I could see this happening everywhere."

I nodded, then stopped suddenly and said, "We'd have to be sensitive to the tribes. . . ."

"Of course."

"The last thing they need is a bunch of whites co-opting their grief. We've taken their land, their traditions, and now we even want their grief, too. . . ."

Neither of us said anything for a moment.

I continued, "What if Nazis were still in power and sympathetic Germans wanted to commemorate. . . ."

"You're asking, what if members of the German resistance wanted to join in the mourning? Would that be so bad for them to acknowledge the atrocities committed by their race? How can that be wrong? *Of course* we'd have to follow the tribes' lead, but there are also things we can—and must—do that they cannot. Our culture was the one that did this, and we must be the ones who begin to take responsibility for it."

"By marking it."

"By remembering," he said. "And that would be a good start."

"Toward. . . ."

"Toward giving back the land," he said.

"Of course," I responded.

■   ■   ■

THE CULTURE OF MAKE BELIEVE

Near evening John and I walked by the ocean, down a long rocky spit that at high tide becomes an island. The waves were high, and though we stood far from where they rolled and crashed and sprayed against the jumbled rocks at the frontier between land and sea, we often found ourselves scrambling away from walls of water that always came faster and harder than we had anticipated. The waves seemed to come in series of large and small. During one of the lulls John pointed out a cormorant sunning atop a seastack, motionless, wings spread to catch the heat. During another he returned the conversation to Yontocket.

I asked whether he thought even a single treaty existed that was signed between Indians and whites that had been honored absolutely—or even reasonably—by whites.

"I'm sure there has to have been one or two that worked exclusively to white economic advantage."

A large wave came in, but it was a false alarm, not so big as it seemed, and the spray stayed far away.

John said, "The question we have to ask ourselves in each case is, what incentive was there—"

"—is there," I interrupted.

"—is there for whites to uphold treaties?"

"And. . . ."

"Yes," he said, knowing what I was going to say.

I said, "When you rule by conquest, by force—"

It was his turn to interrupt, "—and by an ideology that causes you to feel good about using that force. . . ."

"Yes," I said.

"Then you have to ask—"

I finished his sentence, "what you can do to undermine that ideology?"

"Yes," he said.

We each smiled, and looked to the ocean before us.

GIVING BACK THE LAND

CHRISTOPHE WAS GROWING A NEW SKIN.

CHRISTOPHE WAS GROWING A NEW SOUL. AND SEEING

THE WORN OUT AND ROTTEN SOUL OF HIS CHILDHOOD

FALL AWAY HE NEVER DREAMED THAT HE WAS TAKING ON

A NEW ONE, YOUNGER AND STRONGER. AS THROUGH

LIFE WE CHANGE OUR BODIES, SO ALSO DO WE

CHANGE OUR SOULS; AND THE METAMORPHOSIS

DOES NOT ALWAYS TAKE PLACE OVER SEVERAL DAYS;

THERE ARE TIMES OF CRISIS WHEN THE WHOLE IS

SUDDENLY RENEWED. THE ADULT CHANGES HIS

SOUL. THE OLD SOUL IS CAST OFF AND DIES. IN

THOSE HOURS OF ANGUISH WE THINK THAT ALL IS

AT AN END. AND THE WHOLE THING BEGINS AGAIN.

A LIFE DIES. ANOTHER ONE HAS ALREADY

COME INTO BEING.

ROMAIN ROLLAND

Beginning To See

PRETEND FOR A MOMENT that you grew up in a deeply racist society—I know, this is a stretch—one in which advantages accrue disproportionately to members of one race—say, for example, whites, or to a lesser degree those nonwhites who embrace the values of white culture—and that this race has a long and disturbing (when noticed) yet often underinvestigated history of exploiting other races. Pretend that the rich—those who have the means to control, through force or economic exigency, the behavior of others—are entitled to the benefits their wealth brings to them, even when it comes at the expense of the vast majority. Pretend also that in this society men subjugate women—I know, I know, I'm pushing the bounds of believability, but bear with me—both officially, through casting males (and once again, to a lesser degree females, who, like those mentioned above, have embraced the values of white male culture) as primary decision makers and by undervaluing or undercompensating the contributions of women (as well as by creating a philosophy, theology, and politics to undergird this subjugation); and unofficially, through an oftentimes officially disavowed yet omnipresent campaign of terrorism: rape and other forms of violence to keep women in their place. Pretend, finally, that this society perceives the natural world not to be replete with other beings with whom one can and should enter into respectful and mutually beneficial relationships (as do indigenous peoples worldwide) but is instead composed of objects to be exploited.

If you're a fully socialized white male within this group, that is, if you've been taught to believe on some level that whites are superior to nonwhites, that the rich somehow deserve their monetary and political wealth, that men are superior to women, that humans are superior to nonhumans, your default perspective will, naturally, conform to those beliefs. If your socialization is sophisticated enough, the beliefs may quite possibly be invisible to you. *Of course humans are more intelligent than rocks. This is a joke, right?* Simply substitute blacks, Jews, women, Indians, apes, rats, rivers, or whatever other group you want to exploit (and if you object to mixing humans and nonhumans in this example, you might consider the invisibility of your own socialization). Or the invisibility may manifest another way: *Whites superior to Indians? Preposterous. We live in a color-blind society*, we can say with all righteous truthfulness in this place taken by massacre from these same people. If your socialization has been thorough enough, you will probably not feel tremendously torn as you take your due, however directly or circuitously, from the labor of nonwhites and the poor, from the activities or bodies of women, from the rending of the fabric of the natural world. (These areas of perceived superiority are, by the way, somewhat separable, such that it's possible for someone to believe in the superiority of men but not whites, whites but not men, humanity but not white males.) Avoidance of inner conflict will require you to deny that those to be exploited have lives that are precious to them. You will, in short, have to live in a state of denial. You will also have to split off your own empathies for these others, which

BEGINNING TO SEE

means walling off, numbing, denying the existence of, or otherwise diverting attention from those parts of your own humanity which would normally have connected you to them. The white who whips his black slave must also enchain that part of himself which would recoil at causing this pain, numb it through any of the arguments for slavery already elucidated. The man who would, once again, through force or economic exigency, benefit from the slavery (wage or otherwise) of another, must likewise deaden his own empathies. The man who would beat a woman must step away from the part of himself who wants, expects, or hopes for her love. The human who would exploit the nonhuman must reject his own embeddedness in the sensual animal world he would so use. The man—the white man—who is fully enculturated into this exploitative society will be unaware that he has split off or rejected these parts of himself. The parts will have simply ceased to exist, or, more accurately, from his perspective, they never existed at all. That is one of the powers and beauties of denial—we don't (consciously) know what we are missing.

■   ■   ■

In the 1960s, Lestor Luborsky conducted an experiment in which he used a special camera to track the eye movements of people whom he'd asked to look at a set of pictures. This tracking allowed him to tell precisely where they looked. What he discovered was that if a photograph contained images that the people found morally objectionable, or that threatened their worldview, their eyes oftentimes wouldn't stray even once to those images. For example, one of the photos showed, in the background, an image of someone reading a newspaper, while the foreground contained the outline of a woman's breast. Many of those who found nudity morally objectionable did not look even once at the breast, and when asked about it later, could not remember that there had been a breast in the photograph. It seems reasonable to suppose that some part of their minds must have known—they must have seen out of the corners of their eyes—that something there would disturb them, and so, like Shem and Japheth, they chose not to look. I cannot say whether the decision not to look was made consciously or unconsciously by Shem and Japheth, but it seems pretty clear from the reactions of those who did not—could not—look at all parts of the photograph that their decision to not see were made on an entirely pre- or unconscious level. The point is that in nearly all circumstances we each know precisely where not to look in order to have our worldview remain unthreatened and intact.

.   .   .

It is possible, however, for someone raised in this imagined society where white males—especially rich white males—perceive themselves superior, to begin to feel the first faint stirrings of dissonance, to sense that he may be missing some element of connection, to begin untangling these knotted threads of hate and exploitation. It may be that he is able to think his way through the tautologies and absurdities that mark the logic supporting exploitation, or it may be that he begins to feel in his body some absence, which he may at some point be able to name as the disconnection necessary in order to exploit. Not all are able to begin to bring this dissonance to an articulable level, maybe not many. But it can happen. If it does, then questions may arise: Why do the arguments not hold up? What am I not understanding? What is wrong with me, that I no longer feel secure within the social nexus that spawned me? He may begin to question his perceptions—*Did I really see the outline of a breast in that photograph?*—or his sanity—*What is wrong with me, that I would project a breast into an innocuous picture of a man reading a newspaper? I must be sick.*

Something along these lines happened to me during the late 1980s. I thought I was insane. Then, as now, so much of what I saw around me made no sense. Our culture is killing the planet, yet most of us don't seem to care. Certainly our public (and most of our private) discourse falls short of the magnitude of the damage we are causing. Two days ago I watched wild coho salmon trying to spawn in waters clogged with sediment from the logging operations up-

BEGINNING TO SEE

stream. The fish—these were two and a half to three and a half feet of muscle, beautiful gray sides and white bellies, fins frayed from their journeys home—survived for tens of thousands, hundreds of thousands of years, swimming out to the ocean, gliding on deep cold currents, smelling the faintest traces of the places where they were born, then following these traces home to spawn and die. They will almost undoubtedly be extinct in the continental United States within the next decade or two. Mine will be the last generation of humans ever to witness them cleaning algae off rocks of their redd—the spawning bed—scooping out spaces for eggs, cleaning away sediment with their powerful tails. And yesterday I learned, through environmentalist channels, that the West African monkey called the Miss Waldron's red colobus has been declared extinct. This primate, which inhabited the rain forest canopy of Ghana and the Ivory Coast, has been wiped out by logging, road building, and hunting. Rather than this being a "one-off species extinction," as the communique read, which would be bad enough, this is probably the beginning of an extinction pattern which could claim the lives of most of the other primate species. Jane Goodall, the world's most well-respected expert on primates, has suggested that all of the great apes could be extinct within twenty years: At the start of the twentieth century, for example, more than two million chimpanzees lived in the forests of Africa; now there are maybe two hundred thousand. The final gasps of the Miss Waldron's red colobus, with all of its history, its adaptations, its potential, its beingness, did not make the newspapers. I searched in vain. But something so final is not news. Each day the newspaper devotes a dozen uncritical pages to the writhings of the stock market, and a dozen more to the drama of sports teams (as glorious as baseball may be, it's a game), yet fails to present similarly in-depth coverage of the murder of the planet. What coverage exists is near-uniformly skeptical (contrast the level of proof required in the following three headlines from three consecutive days: "Record temperatures add fuel to global warming debate;" "Tiger Woods' performance in U.S. Open silences all critics"; and "The jury is in: Americans love reality-based TV.") As this dawning dissonance

THE CULTURE OF MAKE BELIEVE

began to tear at my insides, again and again I considered that the confusion must come from within, that I must be missing some simple point: No one could be so stupid as to kill their own planet, all the while chatting breezily about golf, "reality-based TV" (whatever that means), bulging stock portfolios, and *How 'bout them Cubbies?* What seemed profoundly important to me seemed of no importance whatsoever to most people, and what seemed important to so many people seemed trivial to me. I couldn't wrap my mind around it. Lawrence Summers promotes the poisoning of poor people, and is elevated to secretary of the treasury. People profess concern over child prostitution as they continue to promulgate the economic and familial conditions that lead to it. The United States bombs Vietnam to save the Vietnamese people, it arms death squads through Latin America to save the people there, it bombs Iraq to save the people there. I kept thinking: *Is there something I'm missing?*

My fears for my own sanity began to abate when I discovered that there exists a long and powerful (though sometimes hidden) tradition of protest against and resistance to the injustices, illogicalities, and craziness of our culture. This tradition has manifested intellectually and artistically, as through the Cynics, Jesus, Jean-Jacques Rousseau, Henry David Thoreau, Walt Whitman, Emma Goldman, Petr Kropotkin, Berthold Brecht, Lewis Mumford, Erich Fromm, R. D. Laing, Neil Evernden, Howard Zinn, Noam Chomsky, Ward Churchill, Daniel Quinn, Frances Moore Lappé, Eduardo Galeano, John Zerzan, among many others, and it has manifested through direct physical resistance, as through slave rebellions, Indians fighting for their land, anarchists, Wobblies, resistance movements against the Nazis, resistance movements against the corporate/governmental rulership of the people and the land of the United States. To suddenly discover that there has always been a rich and vibrant community of resistance to the insanity of normalcy was to suddenly be able to breathe: It no longer felt like I stood alone against our culture.

Earlier this year, David Edwards, the author of *Burning All Illusions*, said to me, "If the first rule of a dysfunctional system is 'Don't talk about it,' then our primary goal should be to tell the truth,

to be as honest as we can manage to be. When I read something truthful, something real, I breathe a deep sigh and say, 'Fantastic—I wasn't mad or alone in thinking that, after all!' So often we are left to our own devices, struggling in the dark with this external and internal propaganda system. At that point, for someone to tell us the truth is a gift. In a world where people all around us are lying and confusing us, to be honest is a great kindness."

The primary point is this: I now understand that the dissonance I felt for so long is a natural step in rejecting one's socialization—a less refined term would be *brainwashing*. It is not possible—at least in my own case—to move from one way of perceiving the world to another without a transition of confusion, loss, even hopelessness. Had I known this earlier—had I an understanding of how transitions occur—my period of questioning my sanity may have been shorter, my desperation less deep. This may have been a good thing. Or it may not have been a good thing: My search for a community of like hearts and minds (in books and in person) may then have been less intense, less immediate.

I don't suppose that at this point it much matters. That particular transition is over for me, and so far as the other transitions and transformations that take place now, more or less routinely, I have come to accept dissonance—confusion, contradictory impulses, fear—as something not to be feared in and of itself, but in a sense to be welcomed and entered into as a necessary doorway to new understanding.

■   ■   ■

Our astounding ability to avoid reality works not only on the physical level of not perceiving the shape of a woman's breast when it is in front of our faces. I asked David Edwards how this plays out in our day-to-day lives. He told me, "We build our lives on certain beliefs, then spend much of our time protecting ourselves from conflicting facts, experiences, and ideas. This self-deception is made easier for us by our society's cult of specialization, whereby people are convinced that they're primarily journalists or arms salespeople or oil executives. Our jobs define our lives, and our job in the vast majority of cases is to make money for business. Any concern that goes beyond our profession is rejected as having 'nothing to do with me' or being 'outside my field.'"

This is true, I thought, whether we're talking about captains of slave ships, politicians, or dam-building engineers.

He continued. "This attitude is drilled into us all the way through school and into our career. We see being professional and talented and knowledgeable as a matter of being specialized. And the first thing you lose when you become specialized is your humanity. To paraphrase Jean-Jacques Rousseau: We've got plenty of chemists, physicists, and bankers, but there isn't a citizen among us.

"Say a corporate executive is convinced of his own fundamental goodness, as most people are. That person would have a terribly difficult time entertaining the notion that the corporation for which he's worked over a lifetime—indeed, the entire corporate system of which he's a part—is responsible for terrible loss of life and destruction of nature. To acknowledge that reality would be to acknowledge that he has lent his talents to genocide and ecocide. And he can't do that. He's spent years building up a career. His prestige and sense of self-worth are closely tied to his success—in other words, to how much oil he has discovered, or how many cars he has produced. Given all this, serious consideration of the moral status of his work would create a profound conflict between his morality and his financial—not to mention his emotional and social—needs."

David hesitated a moment, then said, "The money, by the way, is no small matter." He stopped again, as though considering changing the subject, then started again. "It may seem that he has everything to lose and nothing to gain from that sort of serious examination, and so his unconscious will protect his sense of self from a very painful conflict by dismissing or ignoring any evidence that he participates in these atrocities. And it will do so in such a way that it never even occurs to him—even with the evidence staring him in the face—that there's the slightest thing wrong with what he's doing. The same is

true of journalists, for example, or politicians, whose livelihoods and social esteem are based on serving corporate power; under no circumstances can they allow themselves to comprehend the true nature of the role they're playing."

·   ·   ·

Far more interesting, I think, than the racist fantasies that slavery benefits the enslaved—fantasies that happily coincide with the desire for the luxuries provided by slave labor—is the more reasoned, and reasonably well-supported, argument that because slave owners had a financial interest in their slaves, they were much less likely than their capitalist brethren to mistreat, underfeed, or overwork the laborers.

In his *Letter to an Abolitionist*, John Henry Hammond commented that in Great Britain (where the abolitionist to whom he was writing lived), "the poor and laboring classes of your own race and color . . . are more miserable and degraded, morally and physically, than our slaves." He quoted Reports of Commissioners appointed by Parliament and published by order of the House of Commons. On collieries, he cites, "The seams are so thin that several of them have only two feet headway to all the working. They are worked altogether by boys from eight to twelve years of age, on all-fours, with a dog belt and chain. The passages being neither ironed nor wooded, and often an inch or two of mud. . . . These poor boys have to drag the barrows with one hundred weight of coal or slack sixty times a day sixty yards, and the empty barrows back, without once straightening their back." Another: "Went into the pit at seven years of age. . . . When I drew by the girdle and chain my skin was broken, and the blood ran down. I durst not say anything. If we said anything, the butty, and the reeve, who works under him, would take a stick and beat us." And another: "Instances occur in which children are taken into these mines to work as early as four years of age, sometimes at five, not infrequently at six and seven, while from eight to nine is the ordinary age at which these employments commence." His point with all this was that no rational slave owner would work his slaves so hard, or so young.

The reports suggested British women and children worked twelve to sixteen hours per day, with men sometimes being worked twenty hours per day. Children often commenced work at five or six years of age, and in some fields, such as lace-making, they began work at two.

Of course the same thing happened here in the States. In 1900 the government estimated that more than 750,000 children between the ages of ten and fifteen worked under conditions described by a labor association president as "dragging out a life of slavery and wretchedness." The figure of 750,000 probably underestimated the total by as many as three and a half million, and in any case failed to include the scores of thousands of children between four and ten who worked sixty or more hours per week in textile and steel mills, in coal breaker rooms, in cotton fields. As Asa Chandler, founder of Coca-Cola, said, "The most beautiful sight that we see is the child at labor; as early as he may get at labor the more beautiful, the more useful does his life get to be." *The Washington Post* commented, about children as young as five in cotton mills, "The average life of the children after they go into the mills is four years. It would be less cruel for a state to have children painlessly put to death than it is to permit them to be ground to death by this awful process." Their mothers and older sisters fared no better, as is made clear by a woman who made $4.50 per week— as much as, to provide just one example, the banker J. P. Morgan made every hundred seconds: "The machines go like mad all day, because the faster you work the more money you get. Sometimes in my haste I get my finger caught and the needle goes right through it. It goes so quick, though, that it does not hurt much. I bind the finger up with a piece of cotton and go on working. We all have accidents like that. Where the needle goes through the nail it makes a sore finger, or where it splinters a bone it does much

BEGINNING TO SEE

harm. Sometimes a finger has to come off." In the mills, "The air of the room is white with cotton. . . . These little particles are breathed into the nose, drawn into the lungs. Lung disease and pneumonia—consumption—are the constant, never-absent scourge of the mill village. The girls expectorate to such an extent that the floor is nauseous with it."

There is no doubt that chattel slavery is a terrible thing, but I have begun to wonder whether there exist conditions of employment—conditions of ownership—that might be at least as bad.

■   ■   ■

Dissonance does not always lead to action, nor even to understanding. It is just as possible—if not more likely—to resist the understanding itself than it is to resist the injustice. Not only is it feasible, and for many, tempting, to retreat from the dissonance back into denial, it is just as possible to turn one's anger inward as it is to turn it where it belongs.

I see this a lot at the periphery (and only at the periphery) of, for example, the environmental movement, as many people whose sympathies run toward environmental protection find themselves unable to actively oppose ecological degradation, in great measure because their sense of self-loathing at being part of the industrial culture that's destroying the planet paralyzes them. The same dynamic tricks out in race, class, or gender issues, too, whenever people personalize the problem. Because they own a car, it becomes *their* fault the climate is changing. Because they live in a house or apartment (or a yurt, for that matter), they're somehow primarily culpable for deforestation, as culpable, I've heard them say, as even the CEO of Weyerhaeuser. They need, they say, to eradicate their own hatred or anger before they can act. They need, themselves, to be pure in thought, action, emotion, before they can begin to do *anything* constructive. Of course this is silly, and of course they never get around to doing anything at all. They hang paralyzed at the edge of constructive action for years, never quite falling back into dissonance, but never moving on.

It is always possible—at every step of burgeoning awareness of and resistance to the horrifying depth and breadth of the destructiveness and exploitation—and hatred—that undergirds civilization, with its comforts and elegancies based always on slavery, based always on misery—to suffer a failure of nerve, a failure of courage, a failure of imagination. It is remarkable, then, inspirational, even a miracle, that faced with civilization's size and momentum there exist so many who devote their lives to its opposition, to its opposite, to the eradication of coercion, to the flowering of potential (even among the enslaved), to intact natural human and nonhuman communities, and in fact, to love.

■　　　■　　　■

It is June. I just flew into New York City. I feel like shit. I don't know why the hell I write. I don't know why the hell I'm here in the city. Ten thousand eyes passed me by today, passed over me and abraded my skin. Ten thousand sharp corners of concrete and granite and marble. Straight lines everywhere, and a swirl of humanity, crammed in tighter than a being can bear. Pack any other mammal in such tight quarters, and the sewers would run red every night.

I got off the plane at LaGuardia, and caught a bus to Grand Central Station. My seatmate was a man, a male with a capital M. We got along great so long as we talked about him, and so long as I agreed with everything he said. Since his specialty is nineteenth-century archeobiological monographs, about which I, like (I presume) most people, know next to nothing, I had neither basis nor reason to disagree with him. And even if I had, why bother?

We got stuck in traffic. It probably only seemed like hours. Eventually he tired of speaking of himself, and tired even of hearing me speak about him, and so ventured to ask what I do.

"I write."

BEGINNING TO SEE

"About?"

I told him.

He embarked on a pattern easy to recognize and even easier to grow tired of: His first response to everything I said was, "No. Here's what you don't understand. . . ." Indians, I learned from him, were just as destructive of the natural world as we are.

"This street right here," I said, "used to be old growth forest. And salmon ran up the Hudson so thick they'd carry away your net."

"No," he replied. "There's something you don't understand." He went on like this. All cultures commit genocide, he told me, because humans are biologically driven to enslave the weak. "This explains race relations," he continued, "and also explains men's domination of women."

I raised my eyebrows, by now having been cowed into near-submission myself.

"Not that I would use the word *domination*," he said, "but that does seem the sort of word you'd use."

There were no empty seats on the bus. I checked. The first chance I got I changed the subject to the New York Mets. He was eager to tell me about them, and since I offered no opinions, there was no need for him to tell me what I didn't understand.

We arrived at Grand Central. I fled the bus as quickly as I could, yanking my luggage behind me as if I were running from a hotel fire.

The man on the bus annoyed me, and disturbed me some, but this man did not single-handedly cause me to question the relevance of my work. A woman did that, though we exchanged not a single word, and though I am sure we will never see each other again.

I caught a train to Mt. Kisko, north of New York City, where I would spend the night at the house of a friend. The train was nearly empty. I sat alone, staring out the window and rocking with the rhythm of the springs. I was tired. I'd crossed the continent that day, catching my first flight in the settled gray of dawn. Buildings topped with razor wire floated by outside, as did tall tenements. Puerto Rican flags hung from windows. I saw a few rooftop gardens. And then I saw the woman. She was on a balcony. She was black. She was not too far from the train. I could not tell for sure in the light, but it seemed that just for the briefest second our eyes locked. We met each other, and then the train pulled me away, and brought me to another tenement, and then another, and then street after darkened street of parked cars, more tenements, more razor wire, more asphalt, concrete, more and more people. But the woman stayed with me, and I asked myself what use my work—exploring and articulating the deep roots of our culture's destructiveness—is to her. I knew, or projected, from just that one moment of connection, or pseudo-connection, that she didn't so much need to know the land ownership conditions that determine whether it's in the capitalist's interest to own slaves or hire them; she just needed a job. She didn't so much care whether television leads to self-hatred; she just wished her brother would quit taking drugs. And the relationship between threats to perceived entitlement and hatred was far less important to her than the fact that she'd been raped three times before she was twenty.

It's also true that I was projecting. Maybe she had a job. Maybe she didn't want one. Maybe she didn't have a brother, or, if she did, he was clean and sober, and had never taken a drug in his life. Maybe she'd never experienced sexual or any other type of violence. I realize that in making these projections I'm stereotyping. But the stereotypes really aren't the point, because I have known this woman, and I have known her brothers. I have taught her brothers in prison. They do not come from Harlem, but Compton, Sacramento, or Oakland, California, or Pittstown, West Virginia, or some little town I've never heard of in Oklahoma. They may not be black. They may be white, Hispanic, or Indian. They might be Vietnamese. Their drug of choice might not be crack. It might be crank. It might be heroin. Her brother might be a former student of mine who sold drugs to pay the rent, and to buy clothes for his two children: "Try raising two kids," he once said to me, "on six bucks an hour. Dealing put food on the table." Her brother might be another former student of mine, put out to prostitution by his father when he was five. Or another, in prison for the rest of his life, who wrote a letter to his wife's sister, now raising his children, "to let you know what my

grandfather did—how he beat me almost to death so many times—so you might understand why I turned out so mean." And I have known her sisters. They live in Oldtown, Idaho, and Phoenix, Arizona. They live in Brooklyn and they live in Boulder, Colorado. They live in Washington state and Washington, D.C. They live in North Carolina. They're white, they're Asian, and they're black. They're Hispanic. They've been raped by fathers, by brothers, by uncles, by husbands, by acquaintances, and by strangers. They're frightened of sex. They're promiscuous. They're celibate. They only have sex with men they don't love. They only get aroused by anger. They only get aroused by fear. They don't love their bodies. They don't know their bodies. They hate their bodies. They want their bodies to disappear. They stay in relationships with men they don't want, and destroy relationships with men they do want.

I know these men, and I know these women, and I don't know what good my work does for any of them.

■　　　　■　　　　■

I just came across the transcript of a nationally syndicated commercial radio talk show hosted by Tom Leykis. The program began with Leykis reading letters from male listeners who said that women who've been sexually molested "put out" more. He commented, "If you believe that what guys are saying is true—they've had this experience that they're with these chicks who're all messed up in the head because they were abused, molested, whatever—and their [the men's] experience has been that the sex is really good—is there something unethical, is there something wrong with trying to determine that? I mean, as it is, you'll try to determine if a woman is easy, right? You'll try to determine if she'll put out for other reasons. You'll try to determine if you can, you know, give a woman some booze and see if she'll put out, or smoke pot to get her to put out, or buy her dinner or buy her drinks or buy whatever to get her to put out. . . . So that makes you wonder is everything fair game? If you think that a woman's more likely to put out or more likely to be good in bed because she has a history of abuse, is it wrong to try to find that out and then to go for the gold?"

Following this came a commercial consisting of music with a recorded female voiceover: "Roll me over and do me. Do me. Turn me over and do me. Do me. Throw me down and do me. Do me." A female caller said, "I agree with you . . . about women who've been molested. I was molested. . . . And the reason women put out like that when they've been molested is because they have a fear that men won't accept them any other way because that was basically how they were taught or how they were brought up—that this is what you do."

"So it's easier to get lucky with a woman who's been molested."

"It is . . . because their self-esteem is destroyed and so they don't have any more respect for themselves than that. I went through years of it."

"So," he replied, "it might be a good idea for a guy to try to find out if a woman's been molested."

Later, Leykis had male and female callers on at the same time. The man said, "If she's grown up consenting with it and it's turned her into some nymphomaniac, then who am I not—you know, what am I gonna do?"

The woman responded that she thought it was wrong to target women who'd been abused.

Leykis asked why.

"Because I think if you're targeting that and the girl has low self-esteem and the reason that she's going to perform for you in that way is because she's looking for some kind of healing—"

Leykis interrupted to say that most women have low self-esteem. The two argued this point for a while, before he said, "The woman who is the most insecure is the one you target. We, on this show, have talked about a theory and I've taught a class on the air called 'Leykis 101.' It's a ratio. It's a mathematical formula and you express it in the form of a fraction and the way it works is this: . . . the number on top you want to be as high as possible. You want a woman who's the most

BEGINNING TO SEE

attractive you can find. That's the top half of the equation. Bottom half of the equation? The lowest possible self-esteem. And that produces a ratio. The higher the ratio, the more you should go for it."

A little later in the show, another woman said that playing on a woman's weakness in order to get laid is the "same thing as going out and playing on a kid's innocence when you molest them."

Leykis responded, "I don't think it is and you want to know something? All men do that. All men do it. Now, we find different weaknesses. . . . We find out all kinds of weaknesses you have and that's how we get in."

"Don't you think it's a little cruel?"

"It's not cruel," he said. "It's reality. This is how you do it. Men want to get laid. We're not here to get to know you."

■   ■   ■

It took me a long time to understand why so many people hate, or at the very least are repulsed by, homosexuals. It's always seemed to me that the most reasonable action for someone disturbed by homosexuals is simply not to date one. But I realized several years ago a reason for the vehemence. The realization came, oddly enough, when I was listening to a military spokesperson outlining reasons gays should not be allowed into the military (I've always believed, by the way, that homosexuals *should* be prohibited from the military, but then again, I've always believed so should hetero- and bisexuals, and the transgendered, for that matter). His main reason was that it would destroy the chain of command. "Can you imagine what would happen," he asked, obviously rhetorically, "if a private had sex with a captain? The captain would no longer have any authority." It was clear from the context his point was not intimacy, but rather penetration. If the inferior penetrated the superior, the superior would no longer be such. I suddenly understood what a lot of feminists have been saying for many years, that within our system, sexuality is an act of power, with a *fucker*, and a *fucked*. And in a culture where men consider themselves superior to women, men fucking women is a sign that all is well with the world. Feminist author Catharine MacKinnon put this as succinctly as possible: "Man fucks woman, subject verb object." Any deviation from that behavior—and homosexuality is certainly not the only way to deviate—chips away at the illusions that it's natural for men to rule women and that it's also natural to manifest this rule through sex (as opposed to "using" sex for pleasure and communication, if I may venture a wild and crazy idea). Recognizing that our most intimate relationships need not be based on power points toward an even more dangerous possibility, that *all* of our relationships can have as their basis pleasure and communication: that they can consist of communion.

BEGINNING TO SEE

THERE ARE THREE THOUSAND MILES OF WILDERNESS BEHIND THESE INDIANS, ENOUGH SOLID LAND TO DROWN THE SEA FROM HERE TO ENGLAND. WE MUST FREE OUR LAND OF STRANGERS, EVEN IF EACH MILE IS A MARSH OF BLOOD!

ELDER PARFREY

REDEMPTION
aND FAiLURE

OUR CULTURE'S LAST CHANCE FOR REDEMPTION came when European explorers encountered North America. The Middle East—cradle of civilization—had been deforested, its people had been enslaved. So, too, in Europe, where "those who were born to obey," as Aristotle put it, were killed or enslaved first by the Greeks, then the Romans, then by their former indigenous brothers who had themselves donned the iron armor—both physical and emotional—of civilization. The people, forests, and wildlife of France, Germany, the British Isles—all fell to sword and ax.

North America presented a chance for a fresh start. Here was the chance to do it right this time (or better, to take the lessons back home and attempt to integrate them there). The continent was lush, redolent, ludicrously rich in life. Fish: "Cods are so thick by the shore that we hardly have been able to row a boat through them."

Mammals: Martens, now endangered, and a once-in-a-lifetime sight even for those who love the wild, were "a creature with which the whole country abounds, and is of all others most easily entrapped by the furrier." Birds: In the sixteenth-century, a fisherman making a raid on an island rookery (to use the bird flesh for bait to catch fish), found "so great an abundance of all kinds [of seabirds] so that all my crew and myself having cut clubs for ourselves, killed so great a number . . . that we were unable to carry them away. And aside from these the number of those which were spared and which rose into the air, made a cloud so thick that the rays of the sun could scarcely penetrate it." Unbroken forests stretched from the Atlantic to the Mississippi. Trees five hundred or a thousand years old—members of the type of natural communities seen now only in tiny remnants preserved essentially as museums, displays more sad than hopeful, small samples of what was and what could have been—covered what is now Manhattan, what is now Brooklyn, what is now Boston, what is now Washington, D.C., what is now Baltimore, what is now Richmond, Charleston, Atlanta, Knoxville, Cincinnati, Cleveland, Chicago, and everywhere in between.

A decade ago I drove from Fort Providence to Fort Simpson, along the Mackenzie River in the far north of Canada, one hundred and eighty miles of wild forest. The trees are small, because the summers are short, the winters long and sharp. But there were trees. There were no clear-cuts, no cities, nothing but one lonely gravel road cutting into the flesh of the forest. I was moved, both by the beauty of what I saw and by the idea of the beauty of long-gone forests that I will never see. I was moved also because I knew that the forests just to the south were already being clear-cut by transnational timber companies.

The Europeans could have learned from the generosity of the land, and from the generosity of the peoples who had lived here for millennia. The natives lived far differently from the Europeans. Central American and Caribbean expert Carl Sauer commented on the Arawak of that region: "The tropical idyll of the accounts of Columbus and Peter Martyr was largely true. The people suffered no want. They took care of their plantings, were dextrous at fishing and were bold canoeists and swimmers. They designed attractive houses and kept them clean. They found aesthetic expression in woodworking. They had leisure to enjoy diversion in ball games, dances, and music. They lived in peace and amity." Everywhere in the Americas, Europeans were met cordially by those they deemed savages (defined denotatively, removed from the word's pejorative connotations, these people were actually savages: "uncivilized, undomesticated, wild," coming from the Middle English *sauvage*, from the French *salvage*, from the medieval Latin *salvaticus*, alteration of Latin *silvaticus*, "of the woods, wild," from *silva*, "a wood." The savages of North America were as lush, rich with life, and generous as the forests that were their home). This fact has been mentioned by everyone from Amerigo Vespucci in South America in 1502 (the Indians "swam out to receive us . . . with as much confidence as if we had been friends for years") to Henri Cartier up in Canada in 1535 (the Indians "as freely and familiarly came to our boats without any fear, as if we had ever been brought up together").

William Brandon lays out an impressive list of possible reasons for the differences in attitudes between the indigenous and the civilized, in his book *New Worlds For Old: Reports from the New World and their effect on the development of social thought in Europe, 1500-1800*: "Religion rather than business being the principal business; living to live rather than to get; belonging rather than belongings as a reigning value; apparent rarity of enforced civil or military service; . . . group ownership of land and wealth, and consequent tendencies toward individual cooperation rather than competition, and apparent rarity of the police and lawsuits necessary to regulate individual possession."

In many cases the conquerors could not have survived to conquer had not the natives first been wildly generous, not only with their food but also in instruction on how to live on the land. Edmund S. Morgan commented that the Indians near Roanoke "welcomed the visitors, and the Indians gave freely of their supplies to the English, who had lost most of their own when the *Tyger* grounded. By the

THE CULTURE OF MAKE BELIEVE

time the colonists were settled, it was too late to plant corn, and they seem to have been helpless when it came to living off the land. They did not know the herbs and roots and berries of the country. They could not or would not catch fish in any quantity, because they did not know how to make weirs. And when the Indians showed them, they were slow learners: they were unable even to repair those that the Indians made for them. Nor did they show any disposition for agriculture. . . . The English, for lack of seed, lack of skill, or lack of will, grew nothing for themselves, even when the new planting season came round again." Had the Indians desired to kill the invaders—whom they thought at the time were merely visiting—they needn't have cut their throats, much as many of us may later have wished they had. All they would have had to do to avert the genocide perpetrated against them would have been to let the newcomers fend for themselves. Morgan states that "the Indians . . . could have done the English in simply by deserting them."

For ten years I lived in Spokane, Washington. The Spokane River runs through the center of the city. Often I walked to stand or sit by Spokane Falls—actually a number of falls in close succession—or what is left of them after the erection of a series of dams decades ago. The falls are still beautiful—liquid thunder in the swell of spring thaw, settling to a chatter come the hundred-degree days of late July and August—but often I wondered how much more beautiful they must have been before. I've seen photographs taken in the nineteenth century, but blurry washed-out sepia does not sufficiently replicate the experience of standing next to a rolling explosion of water, ice forming at the edges of liquid, cold spray finding its way into your mouth and onto the end of your nose, the force of the sound leaning into your belly like an open hand that pushes you back while beckoning you forward. A photograph cannot do that. I want to know what the old falls *felt* like. James Glover, one of the white founders of the city of Spokane, saw the falls and felt perhaps the same thing, but in him it turned over into something else. He said, and these words—words eerily similar to the words Tom Leykis said about getting laid—have stayed with me ever since I first read them on the wall of

REDEMPTION AND FAILURE

a museum in Spokane, "I was enchanted, overwhelmed with the beauty and grandeur of everything I saw. It lay just as nature had made it, with nothing to mar its virgin glory. I determined that I would possess it."

The Europeans did not come to North America to get to know the land, nor to get to know its inhabitants. They did not come to get to know themselves. They did not even come here to get laid. They came to possess, which I suppose was what Tom Leykis was really after as well (*possess*: "to have and hold as property; to enter into and control firmly; to insinuate one's gestalt into another, as in possession by a devil; to dominate; to have sexual intercourse with": from the Middle French *possesser*, to take possession of; from Latin *possessus*; from *potis*, having the power; more at potent: "having or wielding force, authority, or influence; able to copulate, usually said of a male: Middle English, from the Latin *potis*, having the power, akin to Gothic *brüfaths*, bridegroom; Greek *posis*, husband; Sanskrit *pati*, master). They came here, if we are bluntly honest, to enslave or exterminate the inhabitants—and we have to admit that they (or rather we) have done an extraordinary job. They came also to enslave the land, to yoke it to their own purpose, and ultimately to remove from it everything of monetary value. This behavior, of course, continues to this day.

Do Tom Leykis and his listeners hate women? If not, precisely what behavior would be considered hateful? I'm looking for a specific threshold at which it will finally be acceptable to use the word *hate*. Similarly, do Europeans—EuroAmericans, whites, nonsavages, members of the dominant culture, the civilized: whatever you want to call us—hate the continent and its original inhabitants? If not, why does it seem so? Once again if not, what threshold must be finally passed before we will begin to use that word?

If, on the other hand, we decide to use that heavily loaded word—*hate*—and to say that members of civilization as a whole hate this continent and its members, we are led immediately to many more questions, such as: Can we hate without even knowing it? If we can, what does that feel like? When I wrote earlier that hatred felt

THE CULTURE OF MAKE BELIEVE

long enough and deeply enough no longer feels like hatred, but like economics or religion or tradition, I was referring to someone else's hate, certainly not my own. What does it feel like—I now have to ask myself—to swim in this river of cultural hatred? Does it feel congruent, a simple unexamined life? Does it feel self-righteous? Does the feeling resemble pride, as you—or I—reap the social rewards of going with the flow? If we really are swimming in a river of hatred that extends to the land, to the inhabitants of the land, to women, what are we going to do about it?

■　　　■　　　■

For a couple of months now I've been trying to wrap my mind around the implications of the fact that the U.S. Seventh Cavalry, prior to going east to protect the civil rights of recently freed slaves, had been on the western frontier fighting Indians—hell, let's be honest about it, they were committing genocide—and as soon as the troops wrapped things up in South Carolina, off they went again to the West, to continue where they left off. I am not sure whether this irony speaks more to our culture's hatred of indigenous peoples or to the fact that soldiers are, in the end, little more than hired muscle, trained to follow orders, whether that order is to protect one person's rights or to violate another's. This training into a cult of obedience is of course a necessary precursor to the committing of any mass atrocities.

I'm not sure what the individual soldiers thought, or if they were at all struck by the irony of Indian-killing being one job and saving the lives of blacks another. I do, however, know what their leaders thought about the larger necessity of eradicating Indians. General William Tecumseh Sherman wrote in 1868 to his subordinate, General Phil Sheridan (famous for his response to an Indian who claimed to be "good," that, "The only good Indians I ever saw were dead"): "I will say nothing and do nothing to restrain our troops from doing what they deem proper on the spot, and will allow no mere vague general charges of cruelty and inhumanity to tie their hands,

REDEMPTION AND FAILURE

but will use all the powers confided to me that these Indians, the enemies of our race and of our civilization, shall not be able to begin and carry on their barbarous warfare on any kind of pretext that they may choose to allege. . . . You may now go ahead in your own way and I will back you with my whole authority, and stand between you and any efforts that may be attempted in your rear to restrain your purpose or check your troops."

The note from Sherman came not long before Sheridan's troops, specifically the Seventh Cavalry, attacked a Cheyenne village on the banks of the Washita River, in what is now Oklahoma. The chief of this village was Black Kettle, who had also been the chief of the village destroyed by Colonel John Chivington and his "Bloody Thirdsters" (the Third Cavalry of the Colorado militia) during the Sand Creek Massacre in 1864, after which more than a hundred Cheyenne scalps were displayed to rapturous applause in a performance by Chivington and the Thirdsters at Denver's Apollo Theater. For years prior to Sand Creek, Black Kettle had been trying to make peace with the whites, and for four years afterward—until whites killed him—he continued, to no avail. He seemed to believe that white and Indian cultures could coexist. The events of 1868 (and of course before and since) deny the tenability of his belief.

In November 1868, as Black Kettle negotiated with one white general, Hazen, another, namely Sheridan, marched on his village. His negotiations were doomed, of course, nothing more than a show to pass the time until government troops were in place. As historian Robert Utley put it, "While Sheridan made final arrangements to thrust south with the sword, Hazen repaired to Fort Cobb to hold forth the olive branch."

In the cold predawn of November 27, 1868, eight hundred soldiers of the Seventh Cavalry, led by George Armstrong Custer, under the command of Phil Sheridan, approached fifty-one Cheyenne lodges. The Indians were asleep. The white soldiers halted not far from the village to quietly gather the dogs that normally followed their camp. Most of these dogs were muzzled with ropes, then strangled or stabbed to keep them from barking and awakening the Indians. The soldiers drove a picket pin through the head of one of the dogs, named Bob. This dog survived, returned to the troop, and later died jumping off a train to get away from a soldier who was tormenting him.

The soldiers had, as always, brought a band, and when they were ready to begin their assault, the band "put their cold lips to the still colder metal," as Custer's wife (safe at home at the time) later described it, "and struck up 'Garryowen,'" Custer's famous theme song. Lieutenant Francis Gibson, a participant in the battle, wrote, "At last the inspiring strains of this rollicking tune broke forth, filling the early morning air with joyous music. . . . On rushed these surging cavalcades from all directions, a mass of Uncle Sam's cavalry thirsty for glory."

Indian warriors dashed from their lodges and frantically searched for cover—trees, fallen logs, the stream bank—behind which they could sell their lives dearly to gain time for their families to flee. The battle, such as it was, was over in maybe ten minutes, not long enough even for the band to play much more than three or four refrains of their rollicking tune. It took the rest of the morning to wipe out pockets of resistance, take scalps ("I dismounted," one Massachusetts private wrote, "turned the Indian over on his face, put my left foot on his neck and raised his scalp. I held it up . . . saying, 'John, here is the first scalp for M troop'"), count the dead, and begin adding up the loot. Custer later reported "a loss to the savages of 103 warriors," but he lied: only eleven could be categorized as combatants, with the other ninety-two being women, children, and old men. The soldiers captured a huge haul: according to Custer's report, "875 horses and mules were captured, 241 saddles (some of fine and costly workmanship), 573 buffalo robes, 390 buffalo skins for lodges, 160 untanned robes, 210 axes, 140 hatchets, 35 revolvers, 47 rifles, 535 pounds of powder, 1050 pounds of lead, 4000 arrows and arrow heads, 75 spears, 90 bullet moulds, 35 bows and quivers, 12 shields, 300 pounds of bullets, 775 lariats, 940 buckskin saddle bags, 470 blankets, 93

REDEMPTION AND FAILURE

coats, 700 pounds of tobacco; all the winter supply of dried buffalo meat, all the meal, flour, and other provisions; in fact, all they possessed was captured, as the warriors [sic] escaped with little or no clothing." They burned all this, as well as, according to a Lieutenant Godfrey, who'd been assigned the job of demolition, at least one bridal gown: "a 'one piece dress,' adorned all over with bead work and elks' teeth on antelope skins as soft as the finest broadcloth. I started to . . . ask to keep it, but as I passed a big fire, I thought, 'What's the use, "orders is orders" and threw it on the blaze."

The soldiers then turned to the Cheyenne's mules and ponies. Officers and scouts kept any they wanted, and the fifty-three captive women and children were instructed to choose mounts for their sixty- or seventy-mile ride to the soldiers' base camp. Custer told Godfrey to kill the rest. Godfrey and other soldiers tried to cut their throats, but had a hard time approaching them, because the animals could not abide the smell of white men, and so struggled desperately whenever a soldier came near. Eventually the soldiers tired of their task and requested reinforcements, who promptly shot the animals dead. The snow was red with their blood. This process of killing horses was routine (historian Evan S. Connell commented, not disapprovingly, "The strategy was merciless and effective. Let nothing survive") and, it seems, more traumatic for many soldiers than the killing of the Indians themselves: After another such slaughter of horses a soldier commented, "It was pathetic to hear the dismal trumpeting (I can find no other word to express my meaning) of the dying creatures, as the breath of life rushed through severed windpipes. The Indians in the bluffs recognized the cry, and were aware what we were doing."

In all my reading, I've rarely encountered such pathos in descriptions of the whites' killings of Indians, even women and children. Far more common are descriptions of "soldiers hearts . . . bursting with enthusiasm and joy at the glory that awaited them." I don't know what to make of this enthusiasm, or of a mythology that would lead to believing that killing noncombatants is glorious. Or maybe I do. Maybe we all comprehend the implications of this enthusiasm, and this definition of glory, but are afraid to speak of them.

For no particular reason, other than perhaps to show his marksmanship, Custer personally shot the Indians' dogs.

After the whites left, taking with them the women and children, the surviving Cheyenne returned to take care of their dead, including Black Kettle, who had been unfortunate enough to have arrived from his unsuccessful—and doomed—parlays before the white soldiers attacked. At first assault he had jumped on a pony, drew up his wife in front of him to shield her body with his own, and tried to flee. He'd been shot in the back. She died next to him. His people hid their bodies, which were not found by whites until 1934, when his bones were promptly donated by their finders to a local newspaper, which displayed them in a window.

The Cheyenne were terrified of being captured alive. A scout for the Seventh Cavalry, Ben Clark, later described the death of two of the Indians (two of the "warriors," according to Custer's report) at Washita: several Cheyenne were hiding behind a pile of dirt near the river. Soldiers killed all but one mother and her child. Clark said, "A squaw rose from behind the barricade holding a baby at arm's length. In the other hand was a long knife. The sharpshooters mistook the child for a white captive and yelled, 'Kill that squaw. She's murdering a white child.' Before a gun could be fired the mother with one stroke of the knife, disemboweled the child, drove the knife to the hilt in her own breast, and was dead. A trooper poked his carbine over the embankment and shot her through the head but it was a needless cruelty." This story quickly transmogrified into one not of mortal desperation on the part of a mother about to die, but of murderous rage on the part of a heartless savage: "In the midst of the conflict, the bullets falling around in a perfect shower, a squaw, with demoniac fury, knife in hand, as if looking for an object upon which to revenge the loss of the day,

fell upon an innocent captive child, and, with one terrible gash, completely disemboweled it—the warm, smoking entrails falling on the snow." Victim becomes perpetrator, and perpetrating race becomes victimized.

The truth, however, is that the Indians, especially the females, had reason to fear capture. Captain Frederick Benteen later described to another soldier what happened to the women: "Of course you have heard of an informal invitation from Custer for officers desiring to avail themselves of the services of a captured squaw, to come to the squaw round-up corral and select one! Custer took first choice," a seventeen-year-old Cheyenne woman named Me-o-tzi (alternatively Mo-nah-se-tah) whom Custer described as "an exceedingly comely squaw. . . . Her well-shaped head was crowned with a luxuriant growth of the most beautiful silken tresses, rivaling in color the blackness of the raven and extending, when allowed to fall loosely over her shoulders, to below her waist."

Even in the treatment of the Cheyenne women raped in or out of the "squaw round-up corral," victim and perpetrator get inverted. In his extraordinarily popular 1973 book on Custer, *Son of the Morning Star*, Evan S. Connell, highly-respected historian and overt racist, comments, on the rape of Cheyenne women, "Custer's *wasichus* [a Cheyenne name for whites] wiped out Black Kettle's village, but as often happens one way or another the victims get revenge. In this case, Fort Sill medical records show that during January and February of 1869 a number of Seventh Cavalry officers took the mercury cure for venereal disease."

I'm not sure, but I think Connell was trying to make a joke. I don't get it. I don't think I want to get it.

■   ■   ■

It is crucial for killers—more broadly perpetrators of any mass atrocities—to consider themselves the real victims. And in a sense they are. If you believe you're entitled to something that belongs to another—that person's land, that person's body, that person's labor—

and that person resists your appropriation, that is, threatens your potential enactment or realization of your perceived entitlement, it's easy to see how you could feel victimized.

Imagine a small child used to always getting his own way. Recall the shrieks you may have heard when such a spoiled child—somebody else's kid, of course—has a whim thwarted. He *deserves* the candy he sees at eye level in the grocery store, or his mother is an ogre. He *needs* the toy his little sister happens to be playing with, and if he doesn't get it, she'll pay. Always he must be right, always he must be the center of attention, the center of the universe. But even being the center of the universe can never be enough. In a finite world—especially one inhabited by other beings with needs, concerns, desires, and destinies all their own—to want everything is to bring on disappointment. And because being the center of the universe implies infallibility—if you are the standard, you must be right, except in those rare cases you deign to acknowledge some slight transgression (proving, with a wink, that real infallibility includes magnanimity)—this disappointment can never occur through any fault of your own. And further, because you *are* the center of the universe, the disappointment could never be the universe's fault (which would imply it was your fault), nor can it be bad luck. It must be someone else's fault. When anything goes wrong—when you receive less than everything that exists, or even that much but not more—it's because someone is stopping you. The point is that narcissism leads to disappointment. Ultimately, narcissism breeds paranoia.

Now, jump to a different level of narcissism: Imagine the Nazis. Far from Germans persecuting Jews, Jews victimized Germans. In the Nazi cosmology, Jews were responsible for nearly everything wrong in the world. They caused big problems, like despoiling the purity of the Aryan "race." Hitler wrote in *Mein Kampf,* "The black haired Jew-boy lurks for hours, his face set in a satanic leer, waiting for the blissfully ignorant girl whom he defiles with his blood, thus stealing her from her own people." (I've often thought Hitler should have been assassinated not merely for the atrocities he per-

REDEMPTION AND FAILURE

petrated on Europe and North Africa, but for writing such execrable prose.) Jews were also alleged to kidnap baby Aryans for sacrifice. And they also caused really big problems, like the invasion of Russia: "There must be a punitive expedition against the Jews in Russia," Julius Streicher published in his influential Nuremberg newspaper Der Stürming in 1939, "a punitive expedition which will provide the same fate for them that every murderer and criminal must expect: death sentence and execution." Not content with being the cause of *Fall Barbarossa*, Jews were the sole cause of World War II: Hanz Fritzsche, Germany's leading radio commentator (and a defendant at the main Nuremberg trials) wrote—and this sentiment was echoed by Nazis powerful and powerless during the war—"After the extension of the war instigated by Jews, this unpleasant fate [their extermination] may also spread to the New World, for you can hardly assume that the nations of the New World will pardon the Jews for the misery of which the nations of the *Old* World did not absolve them." Sometimes Fritzsche broadened the blame, as when he stated that "plutocrats, democrats, and Jews started this war. . . . [This] became evident when the Jewish National Council was stupid enough to send a telegram to Mr. Roosevelt expressing the congratulations of Jewry on the outbreak of the war." Jewish sins didn't stop here, though. Worse even than causing a world war, Jews were capable of destroying entire cultures. As early as 1925, Streicher wrote, "You must realize the Jews want our people to perish." That same year he told an audience in Nuremberg, the same town where later he would be hanged for his role in promulgating genocide, "For thousands of years Jews have been destroying peoples." He kept up that theme for many years. In 1937 he said, "The Jew always lives from the blood of other peoples, he needs such murders and such sacrifices."

Unfortunately for Germans, Jews weren't satisfied even with such large-scale havoc: They had to play the imp as well. A Jewish plot caused the explosion of the zeppelin *Hindenburg* in Lakehurst, New Jersey. Gold plates used by Jewish dentists disintegrated. Jewish doctors confined Nazis to lunatic asylums, where others made loud noises and pretended to be ghosts in order to drive them insane. The appearance in the 1920s of bobbed hair, called *Bubikof* in German, was part of a Jewish Bolshevist conspiracy to destroy German morals and the sensibility of the German *hausfrau*: "This is no matter of harmless style," one Nazi wrote, "It is a Jewish attack, an Oriental influence to make visible the Jewish victory over Christians. The *Bubikof* is Bolshevism." Fascists in America played the same game: Henry Ford claimed in the *Dearborn Independent* that Jews had caused the end of the horse-and-buggy age (I'm not sure where the inventor of the assembly-line Model T gets off blaming anyone but himself for destroying the horse-and-buggy age) as well as Marxism and Darwinism. They also started wars and were responsible for both short skirts and lipstick.

Now, imagine the United States, or, more broadly, American culture. Recall Woodrow Wilson—later *President* Woodrow Wilson—blaming blacks for the violence done to them, with "white men of the south" being "aroused by the very instinct of self-preservation to rid themselves, by fair means or foul, of the intolerable burden of government sustained by the votes of ignorant negroes." This was a common sentiment. In the late 1860s, the editor of Virginia's *Richmond Examiner* gave reasons for the explosion of Ku Klux Klan violence by stating that the organization "is rapidly organizing wherever the insolent negro, the malignant white traitor to his race, and the infamous squatter are plotting to make the South utterly unfit for the residence of the decent white man." No wonder decent white men of the South had to take up arms: Their homeland was being rendered unfit for residence! It's almost enough to make you want to grab a strong rope and a pocketknife (the rope, for obvious reasons, and the knife, to carve KKK into some wretch's skin, and, if his crime has been to insult—or look at—one of your women, to surgically remove his manhood).

Nearly half a century later, D.W. Griffith made one of the most influential moving pictures of all time, *The Birth of a Nation*, which has as its central theme the necessity of Klan violence—defensive violence only, mind you—against Negroes, who want nothing more

REDEMPTION AND FAILURE

than to ravish white women, and carpetbaggers, who want nothing more than to seize power from its rightful owners, the southern gentry. Near the film's climax an actor in blackface—Gus is the character's name—grabs a white woman named Little Sister, saying, "I'se a captain now, and I wants to git married." She flees. Gus follows, running low to the ground, shoulders back like an ape. The actor froths at the mouth, having been told by Griffith to swill hydrogen peroxide. Finally Gus catches her at the edge of a cliff, closes in. Little Sister falls to her death. Her brother summons the Klan. They lynch Gus. Meanwhile, another white woman has been captured by a mulatto (a person of mixed white and black ancestry, from the Spanish *mulato*, or *mulo:* mule), who is preparing another forced marriage. Never fear, though, because to the strains of "The Ride of the Valkyries" the Klan rides to the rescue, spawning, as we'll eventually see, the second incarnation of the KKK, as well as the climax of about three-quarters of the Westerns ever made, with blue coats substituting for white sheets, and red men replacing blacks as the devils to be vanquished.

As well as hating and fearing blacks, decent white men have always hated Indians, because the savages have always wanted nothing less than to destroy civilization. Unfortunately, it has not only been the directors of dime-a-dozen Westerns who have believed that whites were inevitably the victims in conflicts between the cultures. It has also been men with guns. Recall the reason William Tecumseh Sherman gave for telling his subordinates not to let "charges of cruelty and inhumanity" stop them from slaughtering Indian men, women, and children: so that the "Indians, the enemies of our race and of our civilization, shall not be able to begin and carry on their barbarous warfare." Sherman failed to ask the crucial question— whose land is being stolen?—because to ask that question would have been to question everything he'd built his life on. White men were— and are—entitled to the land. No questions asked. No questions allowed.

Killing redskins is as old as the European presence on the continent, and it is, as Supreme Court chief justice John Marshall made clear, "the law of the land, and must not be questioned." So Indians have been killed for reasons large and small. No reason is ever too small for those so entitled to feel victimized, no offense too slight to demand extermination of those they despise, those they look down upon. In July 1586, after months and years of relying on and mistreating the land's inhabitants, an anonymous European made the following revealing entries in his journal:

"The 13. we passed by water to Aquascococke.

"The 15. we came to Secotan and were well intertayned there of the Sauages.

"The 16. we returned thence, and one of our boates with the Admirall was sent to Aquascococke to demaund a silver cup which one of the Sauages had stolen from vs, and not receiuing it according to his promise, we burnt, and spoyled their corne, and Towne, all of the people being fledde."

Of course if someone steals your cup—presuming the cup was stolen, which *of course* it must have been—you destroy their home. It's natural. You must not allow them to victimize you, not in the slightest.

If Jews were hated for causing women to wear their hair short, Indians were hated for causing men to wear theirs long. In 1649, John Endicott, the governor of Massachusetts, declared, "Forasmuch as the wearing of long haire after the manner of Ruffians and barbarous Indians, hath begun to invade new England contrary to the rule of Gods word, which saith it is a shame for a man to wear long hair, as also the Commendable Custome generally of all the Godly of our nation until within this few yeares Wee the Magistrates who have subscribed this paper (for the clearing of our owne innocency in this behalfe) doe declare and manifest our dislike and detestation against the wearing of such long haire, as against a thing uncivil and unmanly whereby men doe deforme themselves, and offend sober and modest men, and doe corrupt good manners." Because the Pequot Indians, who so riled Endicott by their long hair, committed, according to the Pilgrim John Mason, many an often-unspecified "sin against God and man," and because the Pequots were especially "treacherous and

perfidious," making them, according to the most Reverend William Hubbard, "the Dregs and Lees of the Earth, and Dross of Mankind," whites killed those of the Pequots they could find. They burned their villages, burned alive the men, women, and children in these villages. One of the commanders in charge of killing the Indians, John Underhill, stated that those who escaped the fire, "our soldiers received and entertained with the point of the sword." God Himself, said John Mason, "laughed his Enemies and the Enemies of his People to Scorn, making them as a fiery Oven: Thus were the Stout Hearted spoiled, having slept their last Sleep, and none of their Men could find their Hands: Thus did the Lord Judge among the Heathen, filling the Place with dead Bodies!"

This nation's Founding Fathers were themselves victims of perfidious Indians, as can easily be seen in the present-day power balance between the two cultures. Indians control everything, right? They've got the land, they've got the resources. And of course they've got the casinos. But we don't even have to trust our own senses. We can take the Founding Fathers' words for it. John Quincy Adams said that "Indians are known to conduct their Wars . . . entirely without Faith and Humanity. . . . To let loose these blood Hounds to scalp Men and to butcher Women and Children is horrid." What's more, according to Adams, the Indians were ungrateful for the generosity and kindnesses shown them by decent white men: "What infinite pains have been taken and expenses incurred in treaties, presents, stipulated sums of money, instruments of agriculture, education, what dangerous and unwearied labors, to convert these poor ignorant savages to Christianity! And, alas! with how little success! The Indians are as bigoted to their religion as the Mahometans are to their Koran, the Hindoos to their Shaster, the Chinese to Confucious, the Romans to their saints and angels, or the Jews to Moses and the Prophets. It is a principle of religion, at bottom, which inspires the Indians with such an invincible aversion both to civilization and Christianity. The same principle has excited their perpetual hostilities against the colonists and the in-

THE CULTURE OF MAKE BELIEVE

dependent Americans." Because Indians will kill us if we don't kill them, the logic goes, and because Indians are as ungrateful and intransigent as Mahometans, we have no choice, it seems, but to exterminate them.

Thomas Paine argued that we—that is, I suppose, decent white men—needed to rebel against England because "that barbarous and hellish power . . . hath stirred up the Indians and Negroes to destroy us."

In 1779, George Washington sent instructions to Major General John Sullivan, in Alexander Hamilton's handwriting, that Sullivan was "to lay waste all the [Iroquois] settlements around, with instructions to do it in the most effectual manner, that the country may not be merely *overrun* but *destroyed*." He continued, "You will not by any means, listen to any overture of peace before the total ruin of their settlements is effected." The reason he gave, and we know it to be true and accurate because Washington could not tell a lie, was that the whites were scared of the Indians: "Our future security will be in their inability to injure us . . . and in the terror with which the severity of the chastizement they receive will inspire them. . . . When we have effectually chastized them we may then listen to peace and endeavor to draw further advantages from their fears." Evidently the "chastizement"—which included skinning the bodies of some Indians "from the hips downward, to make boot tops or leggings"—worked, because for this and many other actions George Washington earned the name "Town Destroyer" among the Indians, ten years later causing an Iroquois to tell Washington to his face that "to this day, when that name is heard, our women look behind them and turn pale, and our children cling close to the necks of their mothers."

Thomas Jefferson, considered by many historians a friend of the Indians, was another who spoke of their extermination as "necessary to secure ourselves against the future effects of their savage and ruthless warfare." He even at one point suggested invading Canada—much like Streicher suggested invading Russia, and for much the

same reason—only because "the possession of that country secures our women and children for ever from the tomahawk and scalping knife, by removing forever those who excite them."

This fear of Indians by the decent white men who were exterminating them is immortalized in the most sacred of United States documents: the Declaration of Independence. Thomas Jefferson carried language in his draft of the Virginia state constitution over to the "original Rough draught" of the Declaration. This language survived the edits of John Adams, Benjamin Franklin, and the rest of the Committee of Five in charge of the document, and with one minor addition and one slight cut survived the debates of the Continental Congress as a whole to enter the final draft we all know so well: that one of the reasons to rebel against the English is that King George III had "endeavored to bring on the inhabitants of our frontiers, the merciless Indian Savages, whose known rule of warfare, is an undistinguished destruction of all ages, sexes, and conditions."

■   ■   ■

This seems as good a time as any to debunk the notion that the "merciless Indian Savages . . . known rule of warfare is an undistinguished destruction of all ages, sexes, and conditions," which in the end is a falsehood no less absurd, indefensible, and self-serving—albeit more beautifully expressed—than the notion that black-haired Jew-boys lurk waiting around every corner for ignorant girls to defile. The only reason the former lie still has currency while the latter does not is that the Thousand Year Reich lost the war, while the decent white men have won all of theirs, at least so far.

And a primary—if not *the* primary—reason whites have consistently defeated Indians in war is because of the cultures' different understandings of war's purpose and conduct. The purpose of war for white culture is to conquer, to subdue, to take, to win (and one could argue that this is the purpose not merely of war within white culture but of white culture as a whole). Whites will do anything to

THE CULTURE OF MAKE BELIEVE

win. They will lie and cheat, and they will murder noncombatants. They will destroy foodstocks, and they will destroy the environment. They will pretend to be friendly, keeping in mind always the wisdom of John Hay, private secretary to Abraham Lincoln, later Secretary of State responsible for the treaty providing for construction of the Panama Canal, and poet laureate of the late nineteenth-century Republican party: "In reality, the White Man was not a philanthropist: he would treat the Black, Yellow, or Brown Man humanely if it was convenient, but if the dark-skinned resisted, the White Man would destroy him. Biology, according to the scientific cant of the day, required no less, in order that the Fittest might survive."

This notion of deceitful warfare is foreign to indigenous cultures. As Cortés advanced on the Aztec capital of Tenochtitlán, he repeatedly declared the peacefulness of his intentions. Montezuma, the Aztec leader, greeted him in friendship, as so many Indians had already greeted so many Europeans, and as so many more Indians would greet them in the future, all to their grief. Given the embeddedness of all of us in a culture that perceives war in monstrously utilitarian terms, and given our immersion in a river of deceit, a river where we take as accepted that one hand may hold forth an olive branch while another makes final arrangements to thrust with a sword, a river where treaties are abrogated at convenience, a culture in which lying to achieve one's goals is not only acceptable and expected, but routine, it is no surprise that most of us find it inconceivably naïve, foolish even, that Montezuma believed Cortés. He believed him enough to invite him and his armed entourage inside the city's gates, and to welcome them to a great feast in celebration of the god Huitzilopochtli. The Indians danced, played, and sang until on command the Spaniards drew their swords. According to sixteenth-century historian Bernardino de Sahagún, "The first Spaniards to start fighting suddenly attacked those who were playing the music for the singers and dancers. They chopped off their hands and their heads so that they fell down dead. Then all the other Spaniards began to cut off heads, arms, and legs and to disembowel

REDEMPTION AND FAILURE

the Indians. Some had their heads cut off, others were cut in half, and others had their bellies slit open, immediately to fall dead. Others dragged their entrails along until they collapsed. Those who reached the exits were slain by the Spaniards guarding them; and others jumped over the walls of the courtyard; while yet others climbed up the temple; and still others, seeing no escape, threw themselves down among the slaughtered and escaped by feigning death. So great was the bloodshed that rivulets ran through the courtyard like water in a heavy rain. So great was the slime of blood and entrails in the courtyard and so great was the stench that it was both terrifying and heartrending. Now that nearly all were fallen and dead, the Spaniards went searching for those who had climbed up the temple, and those who had hidden among the dead, killing all those they found alive."

To launch a deceitful surprise attack would have been unthinkable—obviously—to the Aztecs, as unthinkable to them as their traditions of sacred warfare would be to us, wherein it was sacrilegious to use treachery to gain advantage over an enemy. "So important was the notion of fair testing," wrote Inge Clendinnen, "that food and weapons were sent to the selected target city as part of the challenge, there being no virtue in defeating a weakened enemy."

Similar rules prevailed north of the Rio Grande, where, for example, in the seventeenth century a Lenape Indian explained the way war works to an undoubtedly incredulous British colonist: "We are minded to live at Peace: if we intend at any time to make War upon you, we will let you know of it, and the Reasons why we make War with you; and if you make us satisfaction for the Injury done us, for which the War is intended, then we will not make War on you. And if you intend at any time to make War on us, we would have you let us know of it, and the Reasons for which you make War on us, and then if we do not make satisfaction for the Injury done unto you, then you may make War on us, otherwise you ought not to do it." And of course similar rules of deceit prevailed on the side of the civilized, as when, to choose one example among many,

THE CULTURE OF MAKE BELIEVE

during the American Revolution a unit of the Continental militia approached the Delaware town of Gnadenhutten on the Muskingum River, where the Indians, pacifists who had been converted to Christianity, were harvesting corn in preparation to leave the war zone. The soldiers "assured them of sympathy in their great hunger and their intention to escort them to food and safety. Without suspicion, only thankful that they need not perish in Sandusky [where the main body of their tribe had gone for safety], the Christians agreed to go with them. . . . The militia relieved the Indians of their guns and knives, promising to restore them later. The Christians felt safe with these friendly men whose interest in their welfare seemed genuine." You can probably guess what happened next: "Once defenseless, they were bound and charged with being warriors, murderers, enemies and thieves, having in their possession horses, branding irons, tools, axes, dishes, all articles used by whites and not common to Indians. [These of course were purchased for them by their missionaries.] After a short night of prayer and hymns . . . twenty-nine men, twenty seven women, and thirty-four children were ruthlessly murdered. Pleas, in excellent English, from some of the kneeling Indians, failed to stop the massacre. Only two escaped by feigning death before the butchers had completed their work of scalping." The Continental militia, pleased with the ease of the massacre, declared their intent to move on to Sandusky for a repeat performance. But news traveled faster than did the whites, and the next village did not receive them so hospitably.

The early European conquerors often expressed scorn for the way the Indians fought, or, to their way of thinking, didn't fight. John Mason, whose God laughed as he burned the Pequot men, women, and children, and who caused the Pequot men to not be able to find their hands, despised the Indians because, among many other reasons, their "feeble manner . . . did hardly deserve the Name of *Fighting*." Another Englishman, Captain Henry Spelman, complained that when Indians fought, there was no great "slawter of nether side," but that ""having shott away most of ther arrows,"

REDEMPTION AND FAILURE

both sides "weare glad to retier." The Indian way of fighting was so undeserving of the name, commented a disgusted John Underhill, who had commanded his men to "entertain" fleeing Indians with the points of their swords, that "they might fight seven yeares and not kill seven men." The reason, he concluded, was that for Indians, "fight is more for pastime, than to conquer and subdue enemies." Roger Williams, founder of the Rhode Island colony, insisted that "Their Warres are farre lesse bloudy, and devouring than the cruell Warres of Europe; and seldome twenty slain in a pitcht field. . . . When they fight in a plaine, they fight with leaping and dancing, that seldome an Arrow hits, and when a man is wounded, unlesse he that shot followes upon the wounded, they soone retire and save the wounded." He noted also that as a point of honor Indians "ordinarily spared the women and children of their adversaries."

Many indigenous cultures, such as the Zuñi Pueblo, Semangs, and Mbutus were, to the best of our knowledge, unwarlike, or as Erich Fromm puts it, "the institution of war is absent." Yet even for most of the warlike indigenous cultures, war is nothing like we experience or for the most part can even conceptualize.

I've heard good things, for example, about how the Grand Valley Dani of New Guinea traditionally fought. They've long been considered, accurately enough, an extremely warlike people, yet their battles sound like great fun to me, with lots of leaping and dancing and a little bit of risk, but probably not much more actual damage than a good game of football, and a lot less than many rugby games I've heard of. In any case, on some level the Dani would rather not fight: as anthropologist Karl Heider pointed out in his classic, *Grand Valley Dani: Peaceful Warriors*, "The most common Dani way of coping with conflict is simple withdrawal. At a very early stage in conflict one party simply moves away from the situation. Individuals do it, and groups do it." Sometimes, however, serious troubles would arise, the major cause being the theft of pigs (Heider never encountered the theft of anything else). In common with indigenous peoples the world over, feuds or wars were never

THE CULTURE OF MAKE BELIEVE

fought for ideological reasons, but over tangible and/or personal insults. Among the Dani, if the conflict was not resolved through simple withdrawal, the next step was mediation and restitution. If the two sides were still aggrieved, yet were within the same social unit, involving *aguni juma-mege*, or "people from here," the conflict *may* have escalated to actual violence, yet very rarely did so, and even then the violence was short-lived. If, on the other hand, the enemy was *aguni dimege*, or "the foreigners," the conflict could escalate into a war that could last a half a generation, a war in which the ghosts of those slain often demanded vengeance. The length of these wars meant that nearly every Dani village was nearly always at war with one or another of its neighbors.

That sounds terrifying, but the battles were nothing like we Westerners would have expected, given the deadly and total nature of our own warfare. Instead, battles were more like giant games of capture the flag or paintball, with only potentially life-and-death consequences, and with deeper social significance. The battles were formal affairs involving hundreds of men on one of the regular battlefields in no-man's-land between warring confederations. Each battle would be sponsored by a Big Man, who took responsibility for what occurred. He had a claim on all trophies, but had to share blame if anyone got killed.

The night before the battle, the Big Man gathered men together to sharpen their spears and arrows, and to feast on a pig. They sent a messenger to the other village with their challenge. The challenge was usually accepted, and a battlefield was decided upon. On news of the acceptance the entire village erupted in a war whoop, making the sound of the cuckoo dove. This call was both an announcement and an invitation to join the next day's battle.

The men prepared for battle by covering themselves in pig grease, and arranging feathers in their hair. As Heider put it: "Everyone is attired differently, but all are elegant." The men carried spears, or bows and arrows, as well as tobacco to make cigarettes for their rest times during the battle.

REDEMPTION AND FAILURE

Participation was strictly voluntary, with no social pressure to join the fray, no epithets of *coward* or *nonpatriot* for those who'd rather stay home. Given the social freedoms and autonomy that characterize most indigenous cultures (leading, for example, two white colonists who defected to become Indians to say they did so because within the Indian community they experienced "the most perfect freedom, the ease of living, [and] the absence of those cares and corroding solicitudes which so often prevail with us") this should come as no surprise. It was not uncommon for Indian war parties to melt away before reaching their target as individual warriors changed their minds along the way. In the case of the Dani, most of the young men participated.

Once on the battlefield, the Dani fought as individuals. The Big Men often stood atop hills to the rear, shouting warnings and directions. Heider commented, "It was easy to imagine they were something like battlefield commanders, directing their troops. But it soon became apparent that this interpretation comes from the images of our own culture. In fact these men were hardly commanding, and whenever they tried, no one was obeying."

The battles themselves were relatively bloodless. The two sides shouted insults at each other, then charged back and forth. Archers shot off one arrow after another at their enemy, but since everyone watched every arrow, it was the rare arrow that found its mark. The men rushed to the front to show their courage, dodged arrows, then scampered back to safety. It's important to note that the arrows were unfletched, making them highly inaccurate, and that the Dani never shot arrows in volleys: If a dozen archers were to target a single man, they would surely have killed him. (American Indians followed similar patterns: John Underhill wrote with some disgust that the Indians "came not neere one another, but shot remote, and not point blanke, as we often doe with our bullets, but at rovers, and then they gaze up in the skie to see where the Arrow falls, and not untill it is fallen doe they shoot againe.") The Dani also didn't use guns in their battles, even though thanks to their encounters with the Dutch they were aware of their mortal effect. "If the sole aim of war was killing enemy

THE CULTURE OF MAKE BELIEVE

expeditiously," Heider noted dryly, "the Dani could not be considered very skillful. We need to consider war as having many functions, and killing is only one of them."

None of this means no one ever got hurt. Many men walked away with painful arrow wounds, and some were carried home to spend weeks recovering. But for the most part, the battles, Heider stated, were "exhilarating," and "full of excitement. There is a tremendous amount of shouting, whooping, and joking. Most men know the individuals on the other side, and the words which fly back and forth can be quite personal. One time, late in the afternoon, a battle had more or less run out of steam. No one was really interested in fighting anymore and some men began to head for home. Others sat on rocks and took turns shouting taunts and insults back and forth across the lines, and connoisseurs on both sides would laugh heartily when a particularly witty line hit home."

In the five and a half months that Heider observed Dani warfare in 1961, there were nine battles ("although two of them never really got going," he added) and nine raids. Six men and boys were killed in the raids. Nobody died in the battles, although he heard that two men died on the other side from wounds they'd suffered. Death rates from war were generally estimated to be at from a ½ to 1 percent of the population per year.

This is not to say that there are *never* terrible slaughters among indigenous peoples. In 1966 a group of Dani made a dawn attack on another village (not making a small raid, or declaring a battle, as normally happened, but making a more Western-style attack), burning an entire village, and killing one hundred and twenty-five people as they emerged from their burning huts, entertaining them, I suppose, with the tips of their spears, and the edges of a new weapon, the machete. This massacre was unprecedented among the Dani, and I do not know whether this massacre would have happened had the culture not already been stressed by contact with civilization. I do know that now the culture is under even more stress, as the Dani fight for their independence, and for their survival, against U.S.-backed Indonesian soldiers who kill them with U.S.-made guns, and against

REDEMPTION AND FAILURE

U.S.-corporations that kill them directly with bullets or indirectly through the 120,000 tons of mine tailings dumped each day from just one mine into just one river.

I also know that while massacres of one indigenous group by another do happen (for example, in the fourteenth century at least 486 men, women, and children were killed and mutilated on the plains of what is now South Dakota), such slaughters were extremely rare before these cultures encountered our own. As nineteenth-century historian and novelist William Simms said of the Indian: "His wars were seldom bloody until he encountered the Anglo-Norman, and then he paid the penalty of an inferior civilization."

Instead of being bloody, and full of great "slawter," warfare among traditional indigenous peoples was, as anthropologist Stanley Diamond noted, "a kind of play" in which "taking a life was an *occasion*." Simms concurred, stating that "The loss of a warrior was a serious event—the taking of a single scalp was a triumph. To gain but one shot at a foe, an Indian would crouch all day in a painful posture." Even at the expense of their way of life, many Indians could not comprehend the Western concept of total warfare. Long after whites had exterminated most of the Mission Indians of California, the anthropologist Ruth Benedict tried to talk of warfare to the remnants, but "it was impossible. Their misunderstanding of warfare was abysmal. They did not have the basis in their own culture upon which the idea could exist, and their attempts to reason it out reduced the great wars to which we are able to dedicate ourselves with moral fervor to the level of alley brawls."

A central feature of all indigenous warfare is its personal nature. The Dani shout insults at each other as they shoot their unfletched arrows, and because they are fighting their neighbors they know how to send insults more directly, and perhaps more on target, than the weapons that can actually kill. At least part of the point seems to be to show that in the ways of bravery—and of eloquence—one is a better man than one's enemy. What would be the point of killing someone if in that particular act I did not show myself to be a better man than he? Oftentimes, even in raids, to kill is not the

THE CULTURE OF MAKE BELIEVE

primary point: it is to have been able to get that close, to have snuck past the enemy's defenses, to have shown that I can do it. George Bird Grinnell spoke of the Indians of the plains, but his words apply to other warlike indigenous peoples as well: "Among the plains tribes with which I am well acquainted—and the same is true of all the others of which I know anything at all—coming in actual personal contact with the enemy by touching him with something held in the hand or with a part of the person was the bravest act that could be performed. . . . The bravest act that could be performed was to count coup on—to touch or strike—a living unhurt man and to leave him alive, and this was frequently done. . . . It was regarded as evidence of bravery for a man to go into battle carrying no weapon that would do any harm at a distance. It was more creditable to carry a lance than a bow and arrows; more creditable to carry a hatchet or war club than a lance; and the bravest thing was to go into a fight with nothing more than a whip, or a long twig—sometimes called a coup stick. I have never heard a stone-headed war club called coup stick."

The point is the particular. There are no masses of soldiers killing all males ten years and older. No mass destruction of crops. No mass *anything*. There are individuals who fight or not, as they wish. "No matter what the occasion for hostility," Diamond wrote, "it is particularized, personalized, ritualized." This is true not just of hostility but of everything. Diamond continues. "Conversely, civilization represses hostility in the particular, fails to use or structure it, even denies it."

This brings us to another distinction between the warfare of native North Americans and decent white men: until they were taught to do so by their civilized counterparts, Indians did not rape their women captives. In the West, the rape of captured women is a tradition long as literature, codified in the Bible, glorified in the *Iliad* (Chryseis, for example, was captured by the Spartans and given to Agamemnon, and when her father rescued her, with the aid of Apollo, Agamemnon sought solace by seizing another captured woman, Briseis, from fellow combatant—and fellow rapist—

REDEMPTION AND FAILURE

Achilles), central to the founding of Rome, common in the Crusades. It was well-nigh ubiquitous in the conquering and sub-duing of native peoples, whether we're talking about Custer's squaw corral, or "squaw chasing" in Oregon in the 1890s, a "popular local pastime" as historian Richard Drinnon called it, "that made all 'squaws' in the field, except the very old, fair sexual game for mounted ranchers." Drinnon retells a story told by his father, Jack, in which a "twist in the usual upshot of 'squaw chasing' came one day, it so happened, when one quick-thinking quarry squatted down and threw sand up into her 'privates,' as Jack always called them, before her ardent pursuer could haul her in with his lariat. The image of the thwarted rider of the purple sage and perhaps memo-ries of the old days always raised belly laughs from Sherm Wilcox and Jack's other homesteading cronies." Indians, on the other hand, simply didn't act this way. An anonymous narrator, describing the rape of a woman by British soldiers during the American Revolution, commented, "This is far Worse in this Respect than an Indian War, for I Never heard nor read of their Ravishing of Women Notwithstanding their cruelty to their captives." In 1799, General James Clinton, attacking the Iroquois at the time, noted, "Bad as the savages are, they never violate the chastity of any women, their prisoners." Another writer commented, "I don't re-member to have heard of an instance of these savages offering to violate the chastity of any of the fair sex who have fallen into their hands." Why? His answer: "This is principally owing to a natural inappetency in their constitution." All of this changed after the Indians' introduction to white ways, but at least at first even the women themselves who were captured by Indians were often clear in their statements that they'd never been raped: "I have been in the midst of those roaring Lyons and Salvage Bears that feared neither God, nor Man, nor the Devil, by night and day," wrote Mary Rowlandson, "alone and in company: sleeping all sorts together, and yet not one of them ever offered me the least abuse of un-chastity to me, in word or action." And the actions of many more captured women who'd been "rescued" by whites spoke louder than

their words ever could have: "Some women, who had been delivered up, afterwards found means to escape and run back to the
Indian towns," wrote Colonel Henry Bouquet in 1764. "Some, who
could not make their escape, clung to their savage acquaintance at
parting, and continued many days in bitter lamentation, even refusing sustenance."

What sort of war is this, we have to ask ourselves, in which there
is no great "slawter," not many deaths, no burning of entire towns,
no rape, no pillage? Faced with such different ways of being, we have
to ask: *What's wrong with these people?*

REDEMPTION AND FAILURE

WE NEED PRAY FOR NO HiGHER HEAVEN THAN
THE PURE SENSES CAN FURNISH,
A PURELY SENSUOUS LiFE.

HENRY DAViD THOREAU

FLESH

By saying that battles among indigenous people sound like great fun to me, I'm not meaning to take this form of warfare lightly. It's deadly serious, and *real*, and immediate, far more real in many significant ways than our own far more deadly—yet so often ideological and abstract—warfare.

And this, I think, brings us finally back to the notion of hate. Part of the Indians' problem—and I'm using that word in a sense ironically, even though their loss has been tangible as well as terrible—and part of the reason that indigenous peoples have been pushed everywhere out of their homes is that they didn't know how to hate. At least not the way we do.

In her novel *Last Standing Woman*, the Anishenaabeg writer and activist Winona LaDuke describes her culture's relationship to the

Lakota as that of "honored enemy." The two fight bitterly, over land, over hunting rights, over thefts, over insults. Yet to eradicate or subjugate the Lakota would be unthinkable: A universe without the Lakota would be incomplete. The Anishenaabig need the Lakota as much as—though in a different way than—they need their own. This is an entirely different notion of what constitutes an enemy than that articulated and enacted by Westerners from the beginnings of civilization through George Washington ("Town Destroyer") through Adolf Hitler through today.

I talked with Richard Drinnon about this continuity in Western civilization: what constitutes an enemy, how these enemies are chosen, what we do to them. In his crucial 1980 book Facing West: The Metaphysics of Indian-Hating and Empire-Building Drinnon clearly articulates at least part of the reason the civilized so hate the indigenous.

It was windy and a little rainy the day I drove to see him. It often is on this stretch of Oregon coast. Waves pounded rocks, and white foam rolled around the edges of sea stacks—small rocky islands—far out to sea. Hardly anyone was on the road, and the drive became a sort of meditation. I'd been thinking about Stanley Diamond, the anthropologist from the 1960s and before, who started his extraordinary book In Search of the Primitive: A Critique of Civilization with what is to my mind the best first line of any book: "Civilization originates in conquest abroad and repression at home." That is, he started his exploration by articulating the self-evident yet normally unspoken observations that the artifacts, impulses, and institutions of civilization—cities, libraries, chariots, tanks, guns, airplanes, the accumulation of wealth, increases in technology, city-states, nation-states, empires, corporations—are not realized out of thin air, but that they require that resources be funneled toward the creation of all of these, and that this funneling requires force, both against enemies exploited at the frontier, and against citizens exploited at home. The statement can also be read on the personal pyschological level, as the exploitation

FLESH

that marks this way of being requires that individuals perceive others as objects to conquer, and must repress their own feelings of empathy toward anyone or anything.

Central to Diamond's book is the understanding that primitive peoples—he uses the word *primitive* nonpejoratively to describe those I would call *indigenous*—live consistently and forcefully in the present, in the particular moment, the particular place, facing particular people. This is not a simple cliché of seizing the day, nor a spiritual *practice* as we—the civilized—would understand it of being here now. Indeed, the notion of spiritual practice implies a separation of the spiritual from the daily. Instead it is a way of living that affects every aspect of one's being, and that certainly ends up being central to our discussion of hatred, hate groups, racism, stereotyping, and our larger discussion of why we behave as we do. Diamond wrote about morality in a civilized world: "Our moral syntax has no predicate. Hence we speak of doing *good*, good for its own sake, or *evil*. We convert each to a pure substantive, beyond experience, abstract. That is what [anthropologist] Paul Radin meant when he observed that the subject (or object) to which love, remorse, sorrow, may be directed is regarded as secondary in our civilization. All have the rank of virtues as such: They are manifestations of God's if not of Man's way. But among primitives . . . the converse holds. Morality *is* behavior, values are not detached, not substantives; the good, the true, the beautiful or rather, the ideas of these things, do not exist. Therefore, one does not fall *in* love, one loves another; and that is an intricately learned experience, as hate, in a certain sense, also is."

So, I was thinking about hate as I drove from Crescent City, on the coast just south of the Oregon border, up to Port Orford about a hundred miles north, where Richard Drinnon lives. I was also attempting to wrap my mind around moral syntaxes with and without predicates. It's a difficult thing to be raised in a sea of abstractions and to attempt to find one's way back to a morality grounded in the particular, even when that is the only grounding that makes sense, that

THE CULTURE OF MAKE BELIEVE

connects with any of our senses. Our morality has somehow gotten unmoored from the here and now of life.

I got there early—maybe ninety minutes before the my appointed hour—and drove to the west side of the tiny town, to a trailhead leading to a promontory that hangs over the waves. I'd been there before. I parked in a small dirt lot, and started to walk. Almost immediately I saw a couple of newts standing, not near to each other, in the middle of the trail. Mine was the only car in the lot, and there didn't promise to be much foot traffic here on this drizzly early afternoon, but still I moved them to the side. I continued toward the ocean.

The coast of northern California and southern Oregon is the most beautiful I've ever seen. I was about to write that it is among the most beautiful in the world, but that would absent the statement from my own experience. I've *heard* it is among the most beautiful in the world, but this is what I know: When a wave rushes a cobblestone beach, it loses its momentum so quickly that though you've already leapt away, preparing to get drenched, the wave dies at your feet, then recedes with an alto gurgle that calls to your insides; even on clear days, heavy mists sometimes rise to hide distant stacks; I can walk for miles on sandy beaches, or pick my way over jumbled rocks at the base of staggered cliffs, and never see another human being. I *have* seen seals—sleek and gray, with intelligent eyes that follow you as you move, or lock on yours if you return their stare—surf big waves, then suddenly drop beneath, out of sight. And I've seen sea lions—tan and bulky, and rarely stopping to give you a glance—do the same. I've seen long lines of brown pelicans skating the fronts of waves, following troughs and never seeming to wet the tips of their wings.

This day I saw waves striking rocks already dark with rain, and I saw starfish, and I saw steep slopes held together by the roots of grasses. I sat and thought, and didn't think, then finally started back toward the car. I was still trying to understand how and why we loosed the tie between our ideas and ideals on the one hand,

FLESH

and our bodies on the other. I wondered how to retie them together, and thought of the consequences of that disconnect. I remembered another line by Stanley Diamond: "As soon as we become capable of analyzing values they have become . . . commodities, detached from ourselves, objects for the social scientist." I didn't know what to make of this. Having lived so much of my life in the world of ideas—I'm a writer, for crying out loud—the more I thought about the separation of value from being, the more confused I became.

I got to the car—I'd borrowed my mom's, since I wasn't sure mine would have made even the hundred miles—and followed the directions Drinnon had given me. His house was easy to find. He welcomed me warmly, and led me to his study. I turned on the tape recorder, and dove right in, asking him about a quote he'd used in *Facing West* by a turn-of-the-century American military officer in the Philippines: "We exterminated the American Indians, and I guess most of us are proud of it, or, at least, believe the end justified the means; and we must have no scruples about exterminating this other race standing in the way of progress and enlightenment, if it is necessary."

Most of us don't know this, but U.S. soldiers killed at least a million Filipinos in what is erroneously known as the Spanish-American War. Having taken the Philippines from the Spanish, the United States then had to take them from the Filipinos. This seizure was accomplished in the normal way. Filipinos were routinely tortured, as was discussed not disapprovingly by everyone from future president and Supreme Court justice William Howard Taft to officers who commanded and soldiers who did such dirty work as the "water cure," described thus to the American Senate by a participant: "A man is thrown down on his back and three or four men sit or stand on his arms and legs and hold him down, and either a gun barrel or a rifle barrel or a carbine barrel or a stick as big as a belaying pin . . . is simply thrust into his jaws and his jaws are thrust back, and if possible, a wooden log or stone is put under . . . his neck, so he can be held firmly. . . . In the case of very old men I

THE CULTURE OF MAKE BELIEVE

have seen their teeth fall out—I mean when it was done a little roughly. He is simply held down, and then water is poured onto his face, down his throat and nose from a jar, and that is kept up until the man gives some sign of giving in or becoming unconscious, and when he becomes unconscious he is simply rolled aside and he is allowed to come to. . . . Well, I know that in a great many cases, in almost every case, the men have been a little roughly handled; they were rolled aside rudely, so that water was expelled. A man suffers tremendously; there is no doubt about that. His suffering must be that of a man who is drowning, but who can not drown." Also central to military campaigning was of course the destruction of the Filipino landbase and foodstocks, or to put it another way, the adoption of, in the words of one of the generals, Jacob H Smith, "a policy that will create in the minds of all the people a burning desire for the War to cease; a desire or longing so intense, so personal . . . and so real that it will impel them to devote themselves in earnest to bringing about a state of real peace." This policy, called appreciatively by his soldiers the "Burn and kill the natives" campaign, neatly fits at least one of the five definitions of genocidal activities. The policy was accomplished, in the words of another American general, J. Franklin Bell (who had used similar tactics against the Lakota), by sending soldiers into the field "for the purpose of thoroughly searching each ravine, valley, and mountain peak for insurgents and for food, expecting to destroy everything I find outside of towns, all able-bodied men will be killed or captured. Old men, women, and children will be sent to towns." General Smith, who also had previously used these tactics against Indians, was even more to the point as regards the disposition of "able-bodied men." He gave orders: "I want no prisoners. I wish you to kill and burn; the more you kill and burn the better you will please me." When a subordinate requested clarification, Smith said he wanted all persons killed who were either in actual hostilities against the United States or who were capable of bearing arms. This latter category explicitly included children down to the age of ten.

FLESH

Drinnon thought for a moment before answering my question: "That quotation goes to the heart of a continuity in American history. Too many historians place too much emphasis on difference, and on specific events. This makes it more difficult to see patterns. For instance, we can analyze the massacre of the Pequots, or the massacres at Wounded Knee or My Lai, but what about the thread that connects them all?"

I asked what that thread is.

"It's the joined assumptions that there is only one way to understand reality, and that the carriers of Western civilization—the English, for example, and from them the Americans—are the sole possessers of that one way, and of virtue, and that their mission must be to spread that understanding—light and civilization—wherever they go. Those who don't understand the world in the one 'correct' way are expendable. Sometimes, as in the case of African slaves, they can instead be considered useful, but if their usefulness comes to an end, then they, too, can be dispensed with."

I didn't say anything, and considered the rates of incarceration of black males. I considered also that prisons—especially maximum-security prisons—are increasingly becoming little more than warehouses for the unwanted. Level four at Pelican Bay has been locked down for six months now, and there is talk of extending that lockdown indefinitely.

He continued, "This leads to a kind of mind-set about whom we can legitimately kill, who are legitimate targets for our aggressions. Racism is central to this mind-set. A central theme of American history is a conviction that nonwhites are human only under certain circumstances, and then only by way of toleration. There is, in short, a line running from the seventeenth century, and the settlements along the Atlantic seaboard, from the massacre of the Pequots (although one could just as easily start at Jamestown or any other early colony), to when President Clinton showed himself ready to distract attention from his difficulties by sending Tomahawk missiles to destroy a pharmaceutical factory in the

Sudan. It makes a huge difference that the Sudanese are African, and are thus not as fully human as somebody in France, say, or in Britain, or Germany. That officer in the Philippines was merely being perceptive, more perceptive than most of us like to be when we think about our history."

"Who is it okay to kill?" I asked.

Once again, he answered without hesitation. "Well, it's okay to kill the night watchman at the Al Shifa factory in Sudan. It's okay to kill people in camps in Afghanistan. It was okay to kill 150,000 Iraqis in 1991, during the so-called Gulf War. And now it's okay for us not to get too concerned that in the years since Operation Desert Storm, sanctions have killed perhaps five million Iraqis.

"Someone pointed out," he continued, "to our secretary of state, Madeline Albright, that about 500,000 children have been killed by the sanctions, and then asked, 'Is the price worth it?'"

I knew her answer.

"She responded, 'We think the price is worth it.' This response is the kind of quick writing off of people that we did in Vietnam, and before that in the Philippines, and before that in the genocidal destruction of the Indians in California, and before that. . . . We can work our way back across the country and back through time, with those in power delivering precisely the same sentiments in essentially the same words."

I thought even further back, to the words of Aristotle: "Humanity is divided into two: the masters and the slaves; or, if one prefers it, the Greeks and the Barbarians, those who have the right to command; and those who are born to obey." And I thought further back than that, to the words of the psalmist, projecting his urge to conquer into the voice of his God: "Ask of me, and I shall give thee, the heathen for thine inheritance, and the uttermost parts of the earth for thy possession."

"Normally these days the racism isn't so overt," Drinnon said, "although during the Gulf War we *did* see bumper stickers and T-shirts saying, 'I'd fly a thousand miles to smoke a camel jockey,' and

FLESH

in some parts of the country even now we encounter shirts saying, 'Save a fish, spear an Indian.' But whether the expression is evident or hidden, the underlying assumption remains, which is that it's much easier and more desirable to have a nonwhite enemy than, say, a German enemy.

"That doesn't mean whites never kill other whites. We did indeed bomb Germany in my war, in World War II, but we never developed toward the Germans the same kind of mercilessness we developed toward the Japanese. John W. Dower, in his good book, *Merciless War*, shows that our demonization of the Japanese far exceeded that of the Germans. I recall this from my own experience watching propaganda films in the Navy Air Corps. The Germans were sort of misguided. If they could only get rid of Hitler and his gang we could bring them around. Kind of a quarrel in the family. The Japanese? No."

He shook his head, then continued. "We also saw that in how we treated Japanese Americans. At Tule Lake, in California, just a couple of hundred miles from where we are now, there was a German prisoner of war camp and a Japanese American concentration camp. The Germans, who of course were not American citizens, were allowed out of the camp. They could bicycle into town. But the Japanese Americans, many of whom were American citizens, were kept behind barbed wire. At the same time, German and Italian nationals who lived in the United States—even those who were avid supporters of Hitler or Mussolini—were not picked up. Imagine the outcry if Vince and Dom and Joe Dimaggio had been placed in concentration camps based solely on their Italian heritage! Yet most people didn't disapprove when it came to these 'others.' Fears of the 'yellow peril' ran up and down the West Coast. When I was in high school in Salem, Oregon, I had some second-generation Japanese-American (*Nisei*) friends, yet it didn't seem unfair to me that after Pearl Harbor these friends were hauled off to horse stalls at the fairgrounds. The racism is embedded that close to home, and that deeply."

THE CULTURE OF MAKE BELIEVE

Something was bothering me. While I knew that, as early American Daniel Williams Harmon put it, "Savages pride themselves on being hospitable to strangers" (saying also that "in fact during several Days that we remained with those People, we met with more real politeness (in this way [of hospitality]) than is often shown to Strangers in the civilized part of the world"), I knew also that many indigenous cultures refer to themselves as *the people*, implying that everyone else is not *the people*. I asked whether, then, some form of xenophobia is inherent in all of us. I knew it was more complicated than this, but still I asked.

He thought a few moments before saying, "The name strikes you and me as xenophobic since a cardinal principle of our Western civilization has been what one anthropologist calls 'the negation of the other.' By contrast, tribal cultures affirmed 'the other who affirms you' and this principle of affirmation always carried with it the possibility of extending the people outward, beyond family and clan and tribe to all other beings and things in a universal embrace—adoption!—that would reflect the very antithesis of xenophobia, as I once ventured, namely 'humankind's unconscious yearnings for the unity of all people and lands.'"

This was helping me to make sense of something else I'd read in *In Search of the Primitive*. Diamond commented that the fact that many primitive peoples call themselves by the name representing *human being* implies nothing more than a "recognition of their uniqueness in a state of nature. Indeed, the dialectic between the uniqueness of the human being and the understanding of his commonality in nature, defines a dynamic perception in primitive culture. The primitive attitude towards the stranger, then is not a reflection of the latter's nonexistence as a human being, but of his *lack of status as a social person*. It follows that some way must be found to incorporate the stranger into a recognized system of statuses before one is able to relate to him specifically. . . . The point is that in primitive society a person must be socially located and named before his human potential is converted into a cultural identity."

FLESH

I was still pondering what Diamond was getting at, and not quite understanding it, when Drinnon said, "For those of us of European background, the principle of negation of the other has traditional ties to skin color. Over the centuries our reactions to degrees of melanin pigment in the skin and other identifiable hereditary characteristics have differentiated this racism from xenophobia and ethnocentrism and buried it far more deeply and explosively within the Western psyche."

He was on a roll. I had questions to ask, but didn't want to interrupt. He said, "The distinction between the victimizers and the victims—those who fall naturally into the role of master and those who fall just as naturally into hauling water and hewing wood—has been made primarily based on the difference of complexion, shading off into culture, language, and the like. This racism goes very far back. Some historians try to make the case that the first blacks the Europeans brought to this continent in the 1600s had it no worse than white indentured servants, but I don't think that's supportable. And we can follow the racism further back, and across the Atlantic. We know that before John Smith came to America, he served in Africa, and so had prior experience dealing with what the English used to call "the lesser breeds." We know that the Spanish and Portuguese had a considerable jump on the British so far as colonizing Africa and enslaving Africans. But we can take it even further back than this. We know that when the Roma, or Gypsies, started moving into Europe about 1000 C.E., the Europeans responded to them as vermin, as vile, brown creatures. Gypsy hunts in Europe presaged Indian hunts that took place later in America and Aborigine hunts in Tasmania. The response to these nonwhite outsiders was, and in many ways continues to be, similar to the response of white Europeans to other peoples they have encountered in the great eruption of Europe into the rest of the world."

He kept speaking, quickly. "The rationalizations for this racism have always kept pace with the times. In the nineteenth century, we had the scientific explosion surrounding the Darwinian notion of natural selection. This led inevitably to an ex-

THE CULTURE OF MAKE BELIEVE

plosion of scientific racism, which declared that nonwhites were genetically inferior and thus destined to be superseded by whites. Along these lines, Darwin noted that soon 'the civilised races of man will almost certainly exterminate, and replace, the savage races throughout the world.' Natural selection became the explicit justification for racism, and joined religion in furthering exploitation and genocide."

I asked Drinnon what he thought was the fundamental difference that racist whites perceive in their own minds between themselves and those they consider "the lesser breeds."

He said, "Apart from skin color, the difference was seen to be between those who could think, those who could plan, those who could control and dominate, and those who could not. Because blacks and Indians were seen to be like children, or like beasts, it was believed they couldn't control themselves, and so needed to be controlled. We can follow this thread back easily to the Age of Reason, where those in power came up with many reasons those who possessed reason distinguished themselves sharply from those who were creatures of their bodies, of the flesh."

I asked, "Do you think we destroy these others because we want their land, or do you think we want their land because we hate and want to destroy them?"

"I see it as a combination," he responded. "Sure, part of it is simple economics: We want what they've got. We see them running through the trees, and we perceive the trees as so many thousands of board feet which can be converted to so many dollars, so it doesn't take us long to convince ourselves that these forest-dwelling people need to be removed to the desert. When we later discover uranium under the desert, well, we need to kick them off again. All the fine words several hundred years ago about Christianizing the natives, and all the fine words today about 'the free market,' are simply cloaks for the same old drive to get Indian land and resources.

"But economics doesn't account for it all. In order for us not only to take their land, but feel good about doing it, we must per-

FLESH

ceive the land as empty. By far the dominant American fantasy has been that of an open continent, of unoccupied territory, not only *terra incognita* but also *terra vacuus*—empty. Americans are not the only ones to share this fantasy. It contributed to Hitler's *lebensraum* policy, which he explicitly stated was based on the Manifest Destiny policy of white Americans, and certainly it is shared by mainstream Israelis, with the assumption from Ben-Gurion on down that Palestinians really don't exist in any full sense."

I remembered Luborsky's experiments. If it would threaten our worldview—and our capacity to exploit—to perceive the land as already occupied, we simply do not perceive the inhabitants. Problem solved.

He continued. "But there's still a missing piece. Economics and feeling good about ourselves cannot account for the implacable hatred, and for the glee in destruction we have so often seen. Describing the slaughter of the Pequots, one old soldier reminisced that the killers were like men in a dream: 'then was our Mouth filled with Laughter, and our Tongues with Singing.'"

That corresponded with the enthusiasm that many whites felt when lynching blacks. I've encountered this often in my reading. "The execution of the negro was witnessed by hundreds of persons," the *Atlanta Journal* reported of one case in 1920, "and many thousands who were in the crowd literally fought to get close enough to see the actual details. Almost every person who had a firearm, and it seemed that every one carried a gun or pistol, emptied the weapon into the man's prostrate body. He was not shot until he had been mutilated [that is, according to the newspaper, "stabbed," and "treated to further surgical punishment below the belt"] and saturated with gasolene [*sic*] and a match touched. The infuriated mob could hold itself in check no longer. One shot was fired from a revolver and it was the signal for a thousand shots which made mincemeat of the body. Four young women from the crowd pushed their way through the outer rim of the circle and emptied rifles into the negro. They stood by while other men cut

THE CULTURE OF MAKE BELIEVE

off fingers, toes and other parts of the body and passed them around as souvenirs."

Drinnon was talking. "This too is part of the pattern that wends its way down till today. Why? The missing piece seems to be that of dominion over nature. We—Europeans, descendants of Europeans, civilized peoples—need to have dominion over what is 'out there.' These other people are *in* what is 'out there,' which means they *must* be dominated. These are deeply held convictions, not just rationalizations dreamed up to facilitate economic exploitation. This is an imperative that lies much deeper, that creates a bone-certainty among those committing genocide that we not only have the right to destroy these others, but that we must. Why? Because in the end our attempts to dominate nature can do no other than to reach around finally and catch ourselves in the same trap we've set for all others. Even the dominators are a part of nature, which means that those who set out to dominate nature must ultimately dominate themselves. Dominating ourselves means we're going to live ways we don't want to live, express things we don't want to express, and find out things about ourselves we don't want to find out."

■　　　■　　　■

I'm in New York, in a restaurant. It's the day after my conversation—using the word *conversation* loosely—with the capital M Male, the day after I saw the woman from the train. I feel better, or at least I would were it not for the woman sitting next to me. The restaurant's small, the space between tables nil. The woman holds a cigarette, yet evidently doesn't much care for the smell of smoke, because she keeps her hand at arm's length, not over her own table but over mine. At first I waved my hand feebly, then more vigorously. I stared. Finally I asked her to at least not rest her wrist on my table. She demurred. I've decided to hold my breath through the meal.

FLESH

Truth be told, though, smoke or no I *do* feel better. And here's why. Last night I talked with a friend till two or three in the morning. I told her what happened yesterday. After hearing of my experience with the Man, my friend asked, "If you could say one thing to him that he could hear, what would it be?"

I answered immediately. "I'd ask what he's afraid of. I'd ask what would happen if he began to listen, not necessarily to me, but to himself, and to other people. I'd ask what frightens him so much."

"Good," my friend said. "And the woman?"

That answer, too, came right away. "I'd tell her that things don't have to be the way they are."

"There's your answer," she said. "That's why you do this work."

■　　　■　　　■

I said to Richard Drinnon that it seems pretty clear to me that an urge to destroy underlies many of our activities, then mused, "I wonder how much of that urge is based on a need to eradicate those who represent other ways to be, and who thus remind us of what we're losing." I quoted him a line he'd used by Increase Mather: "People are ready to run wild into the woods again and to be as Heathenish as ever if you do not prevent it."

He responded, "There had to be strict laws in the New England colonies against fraternization with Indians, because so many Saints were so willing to throw off their Sainthood and live in the forest with the forest-dwellers, to throw off their rigid embrace of Puritanism and to embrace instead their bodies, to dance, as is so important to Indians, and to fall into relatedness, to allow themselves to be possessed by this shaggy New World instead of being mere possessors of it.

"We are of our bodies, and we cannot too long deny it. Our body always comes back to haunt us, to tempt us. And so it and all who remind us of it must be destroyed. This is of course one reason

for the widespread misogyny within our culture: One way of distinguishing across the genders is that she can bear children and I can't. But I *can* bear splendid theories, and in an attempt to define myself independently I must declare she cannot. And if she can give life, surely I can take it. Which of us then is the more potent?"

FLESH

IT IS DIFFICULT TO BELIEVE THAT SUCH WIDE-
SPREAD VIOLENCE [THAT GIRLS TWELVE YEARS
OLD IN THE UNITED STATES NOW STAND A
TWENTY TO THIRTY PERCENT CHANCE OF
BEING VIOLENTLY SEXUALLY ASSAULTED IN
THEIR LIFETIMES] IS THE RESPONSIBILITY OF A
SMALL LUNATIC FRINGE OF PSYCHOPATHIC
MEN. THAT SEXUAL VIOLENCE IS SO PERVASIVE
SUPPORTS THE VIEW THAT THE LOCUS OF VIO-
LENCE AGAINST WOMEN RESTS SQUARELY IN THE
MIDDLE OF WHAT OUR CULTURE DEFINES AS
"NORMAL" INTERACTIONS BETWEEN MEN AND
WOMEN. THE NUMBERS REITERATE A REALITY
THAT AMERICAN WOMEN HAVE LIVED WITH FOR
YEARS: SEXUAL VIOLENCE AGAINST WOMEN IS
PART OF THE EVERY-DAY FABRIC OF
AMERICAN LIFE.

ALLAN GRISWOLD JOHNSON

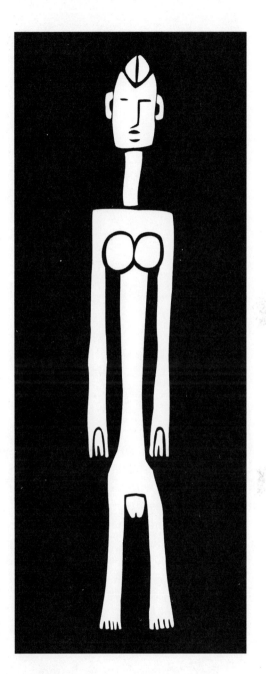

SEEING THINGS

OVER THE LAST COUPLE OF WEEKS I've taken to visiting some Internet porn sites, because there's something I'm trying to understand. I think it has to do with a couple of stories I've heard recently. The first story features a married couple—a friend's brother and sister-in-law—who sit simultaneously in opposite corners of a room, each at his or her computer, each on the Internet, each in a chat room, each masturbating while typing one-handed messages to strangers who type presumably one-handed messages in return. They sit, backs facing each other as they type, and as they touch themselves.

The second was told to me by a woman who used to live with a man who was paying her less and less attention. Often he left their bedroom to go to his study to work. Or so she thought, until one day she followed him, and saw that he was looking at pornography. The woman on the screen, she said, "Looked a lot like me. But there was no way I could compete with her, because she was silent." She ended the relationship, or what was left of it.

I'll tell you the part of each Internet page that most captivates my attention: the counters that reveal how many people have visited the site. I've had a (nonpornographic) site up on the Internet for a couple of years, and in that time have had maybe sixteen hundred visitors, half of them in the past four months. These days I get about fifty "hits," or visits, every week. I account for only four or five of those. But some of these porn sites have registered tens of millions of hits. The point here is not to complain that thousands of times more people (would it be *men?*) would rather look at photos of naked women than read my ever-startling and invigorating prose, but to point out that all of these men are looking at photographs: simulations of women. All week I've kept thinking of a line from the movie *The Ruling Class*, where a female stripper comments that she can't fathom the attraction of watching a man dance around in suspenders and a jockstrap. She says she'd rather have a steak than just smell one, and asks, reasonably enough, "Where's the fun?"

I remember reading in Randy Shilts's book *And the Band Played On* about the beginnings of the AIDS crisis in the 1980s, an analysis of anal fist-fucking and some of the other undoubtedly painful sexual practices from the San Francisco gay bathhouse scene. He said that sexuality requires a certain amount of stimulation, and when sex becomes abstracted from emotion, other forms of stimulation—in this case, painfully physical—rise to fill that gap. It seems to me, then, that an anonymous encounter in a bathhouse—a gay friend has told me of what he calls "glory holes": holes in the interior walls of bathhouses through which men put their penises, to be sucked by someone passing by—or elsewhere, is one step abstracted from relationship with that person. I am making no comment just quite yet on the desirability or nondesirability of relationship, or of abstraction. I am merely attempting to see clearly. And I'm thinking about a game played—or at least that used to be played—by Greenland Inuits stuck inside through the long Arctic winter. The game was called

SEEING THINGS

"doused lights." The rules were simple: Many people gathered, nude, in a house; the lights were doused, and silently everyone began to change places until on a signal each man "grabbed the nearest woman," as anthropologist Peter Freuchen put it. After a while, the lights were again lit, and everyone began to joke: "I knew it was you all the time, because. . ." Freuchen describes the practical purpose of the game: "The bleakness and utter loneliness of the Arctic when it shows its bad side can get on the nerves of even those people who know it and love it the most. Eskimos [Inuits] could go out of their minds, because bad weather always means uncertain fates. Then suddenly someone douses the light, and everybody runs around in the dark and ends up with a partner. Later the lamp is lit again, and the whole party is joking and in high spirits. A psychological explosion—with possible bloodshed—has been averted." I would add—or perhaps say the same thing in a slightly different way—that this sexual game, played within the context of an ongoing community, helps reform bonds of relationship—"I knew it was you all the time, because . . ."—that may very well be frayed by the stresses of this long period of confinement.

If anonymous sex is one step abstracted from relationship, then watching a stripper would seem to me to add another degree of abstraction. One of my students, married to a stripper, tells me he enjoys the fact that men look at his wife, want his wife, but when he's not in prison she comes home—and makes love—to him. Now, to look at a photograph, it seems to me, is to abstract once again: No longer can the woman even be smelled, or heard, and the perspective from which you watch has been limited to that chosen by the photographer.

This brings me partway to the question I've been trying to answer: Where's the fun? Or, more accurately, where's the attraction?

I could understand it with regard to my students in prison. Denied access to the possibility of interacting with flesh-and-blood women, they must relate to women in the abstract. My students don't have Internet access, anyway, although they *are* allowed porn. Rules exist for this sort of thing: Pictures of naked women are allowed (I've

THE CULTURE OF MAKE BELIEVE

heard that at least occasionally girlfriends or wives send pictures), while depictions of penetration are not. One student jokes that if he lets his *Playboy* out of his sight, it disappears almost immediately, "but I can leave my *Scientific American* out for weeks, and for some reason, nobody ever takes it." And just tonight, by the way, I learned some of the etiquette of masturbation behind bars: Don't talk to your celly while his blankets are "tented," or held up away from his midsection, and in minimum security (where showering is not so closely watched) it's bad manners to talk to someone who is showering with the lights off.

But what about those of us not cloistered? I'm reasonably certain that not all those millions of hits at porn sites come from monasteries, although for all I know the Brothers of the Immaculate Abstraction may have leapt headlong into the electronic information age. So what's going on? Where are the rest of them coming from? They can't all be coming from profeminist, anticivilizational authors doing research.

I look at a photograph. It is titled "Pussy10.jpg." It is of a woman on her back, legs slightly spread and held up against her breasts. Her head is at two o'clock, her hips at eight. She is blonde, though not bleach blonde. Her head is held slightly off the purple bedspread beneath her, and she is not looking at the camera, or to step further into the simulation (or do I mean stimulation?), she is not looking at me. She is wearing pink panties, which have been pushed onto the back of her right hip, exposing the outer and inner lips of her vagina.

Another photograph. This one, entitled "hot387.jpg," is of a woman sitting on a chair, facing the camera, facing me. Her lips are slightly parted. She is blonde, and her eyebrows and pubic hair are black. Her skin is very light. Her legs are spread. Behind her, at a desk, is a computer, two stuffed animals, and a couple of books, including *West's Business Law*, and another law book, the title of which I can't quite make out, no matter how much I magnify the photo.

And a third photograph. This woman's hair is brown. Her skin is darker than the others'. She's on her hands and knees, hips toward the camera, or, once again, toward me, ready, to fall deeper into the

SEEING THINGS

simulation, for me to enter her from behind. She looks at me, over her shoulder, her eyes meeting mine. She invites me.

I've found, these last few days, that if I look at pornography, it enters my dreams, in one form or another. This should surprise me less than it does, because a few months ago when I was writing about slavery, those images, too, permeated my sleep. Last night, I dreamt I was trying to start a relationship with a woman. I have never seen her in waking reality. I liked her. I could not tell if she liked me. We kissed, and were going, I thought, to make love. But she stopped suddenly and said she needed to go produce some porn. I did not know if this meant *making* porn, or *producing* films. In either case, I was sad. I did not think we would be in a relationship. I do not know what the dream means.

I guess the question I have is this: If sexuality normally creates, facilitates, magnifies, or manifests—engenders—some form of relationship between the two (or in the case of the Inuits, and I guess some others, more) participants, if I am attempting to interact with a photograph printed on a piece of glossy paper, or displayed on a computer monitor, what—or whom—precisely, am I entering into a relationship with? With Pussy10.jpg? With hot387.jpg? With the women these pictures simulate? Surely not. They have no idea I exist. I have no idea if these women are even still alive. And if they are, they may very well have been asleep when I saw their pictures, or sick in a hospital, or breastfeeding a first child, or making love with their newfound partners—with men who listen to them, who talk to them, who interact with them as human beings. Or they may not. And the point, I guess, insofar as there is one, is that I will never know.

There are other things I do not understand. Lost not only—obviously—is any question of relationship with the person who is Pussy10 or hot387, that is, lost is any chance of interacting with, or even *attempting* to understand the texture of, her personality, but lost also, even on the most basic level, is the texture of her skin, the smell and taste of her sweat and of her breath and of her sex. At least with the glory holes, those doing the sucking still get to smell and taste and feel those they're pleasuring, and those receiving the blow jobs still feel the tongue of the other person—this person they will never even see—still feel teeth behind soft lips.

It's important to note that I would certainly be the last person to attack masturbation, which I count only as a positive good (as well as, to steal a joke from Woody Allen, a hobby). I guess the real point I'm trying to get at is this: What disturbs me most about all of this— more than the fact that many photos cut the women into pieces (showing, for example, just a woman's labia, at twice or thrice life size); more than the fact that the poses are stereotypically submissive, reinforcing, à la Gerbner's casting and fate, the mythology of the dominant male and the submissive female; more, even, than the degrading prose attached not infrequently to the photographs—is that the photographs are so damn abstract. They are referents. They are signposts. But pointing to what? The photographs do not, in any real sense, exist. No matter how much I may wish to pretend I'm sitting across from a beautiful, intelligent (remember the law books) babe— not named hot387, by the way—who is opening her legs just for me, with whom I've just had a long, delicious, exhilarating conversation about the possibility and necessity of dismantling civilization—you would not *believe* how hot we both got when she said, "What do you think it will take to knock out the infrastructure of Las Vegas? Here's what I think. . . ."—the truth is that I'm sitting in a dark room, by myself, in a creaky, hard-backed, hard-cushioned chair, space heater running, CD of UFO playing *Rock Bottom* in the background, cats clustered around my feet, books and papers scattered about the floor, plastic bottle of hand lotion at the ready, sweats around my ankles, staring at a computer screen. No matter how I may fantasize, the truth is that I am still all alone. It's still my hand that will touch me, not any other's. No one's body but my own enters this picture (except when one of the cats decides to jump onto my lap, which I discourage with alacrity), and even *my* body enters only peripherally. But, looking at the pictures, I find myself rather more sad than aroused. Not only relationality but memory and imagination have been replaced in this scenario by flatness, by a photograph. I could foresee a day when we do away even with the hand lotion, and having already

SEEING THINGS

excised all senses save the visual (and, slightly, the tactile), we go ahead and do away with the senses altogether, simply hooking up the Internet directly to my brain, allowing me to think I've had an intense experience of relating to another human being, when I have no longer related even to my own body, much less to the body of another, and very much less so have I confronted any other as a whole.

■   ■   ■

Far better scholars and theoreticians than I have articulated the dangers of pornography, as it helps men to objectify women. I'm not sure that we—men—need that help. I just know that pornography is abstract. It has less to do with our actual bodies than it does representations: We're substituting imaginary experiences with the images of things for experiences with the things themselves, having already substituted the experience of *things* for the possibility of relationship with other *beings*. Danger aside, it also seems just plain silly and self-defeating.

This valuing of the abstract over the physical has *many* dangerous (as well as silly and self-defeating) consequences. Just today I saw an article from the British newspaper *The Independent* describing our culture's feeble response to global warming. The article states that according to the best estimates of the insurance industry (not exactly a hotbed of environmental extremism) within fifty years "the economic cost of global warming stands to surpass the value of the total world economic output." Note that this is *economic* cost, and does not speak to the disappearance of ice caps, oceans, forests, rivers, coastlines, cultures, or any other parts of reality to which our culture is insensate. The author of the article, Andrew Sims, recognizes this, stating, for example, that a "basic misunderstanding of our global governors in the IMF, World Trade Organisation and other still-emerging institutions, is to believe that abstract economic theory is more important than the real world."

This is a fundamental flaw of our culture, and is central to everything I've been writing about in this book. As I read through account

after account of lynchings, I see again and again descriptions of the murders of human beings not as particular people, but as members of a class: This is, I suppose, what lynching is all about. "Lynch the Wrong Negro in Texas: Little Mistake Made by a Mob in Madison County. . . . He was accused of riding his horse over a little white girl, inflicting serious injuries on her. Later developments go to show the mob got hold of the wrong negro." Or, "A mob willfully and knowingly hanged and burned an innocent man, as well as another who was probably innocent. . . ." (This was after one mob had already tortured one of them in an attempt to extract a confession, and finally determined he was innocent: Another mob, or maybe the same mob the next day, decided to go ahead and kill both him and another anyway.) A headline: "Two Blacks Strung Up; Grave Doubt of Their Guilt." Another: "Tennessee Colored Woman Lynched: Negro Charged With Theft Escaped From Mob, Which Wreaked Vengeance On His Sister." More text from another lynching: "The coroner is of the opinion that the wrong man was killed." And again: "It is possible that in the search for Richard Young, the negro wanted for the murder of Dower Fountain . . . a negro now unknown has been caught by a posse and burned in error."

Today the front page of the *San Francisco Chronicle* carried an article titled "Two Rookies Kill Fellow Cop Making Arrest." Evidently, the two police officers shot someone—a black man—whom they did not know was a cop. It is unclear what they thought, other than the obvious, that he was a black man in Oakland. The paper reported that the "uniformed officers were overcome with grief when they realized what they had done." And what they had done was not to kill a black man, but a cop. Evidently, there's a difference. A huge one. Of course.

I do not see a black man—*this* black man—standing in front of me: I see a nigger, or rather, I do not see anything at all, but I project into this space where a black man—*this* black man—would be standing were he to exist, what I want or need to see. I see a tool, a live tool, if I follow the logic of Aristotle. I see someone to pick my cotton, if I'm a Southern slave owner. I see someone standing in the

SEEING THINGS

way of oil exploration if I work for Shell. I see a scumbag criminal if I'm a cop. I see someone I must intimidate out of voting, if I'm an 1870s Democrat (or a 2000 Republican, if events in Florida are any indication). Or perhaps I see what I fear to see. I see sex, I see some-one who wants my woman, my women, who will steal them away from me if I do not stop him. I see someone who, if I try to play bas-ketball with him, will beat me up and steal my money to buy drugs.

I do not see my publisher as a friend and as a human being, I see him as a black-haired Jew-boy trying, too, to defile my women, trying, too, to steal my money, although he's clever enough to do this by trick-ery instead of by violence. This makes him all the more dangerous.

I do not see a woman—*this* woman—standing in front of me: I see a temptress, a slut, someone who will distract me from my work. I see a receptacle for my sex. I see an orifice. I see Pussy10 and hot387, and I see wet102 and shaved149. All waiting for me, legs open. Or maybe instead I see every woman who has ever hurt me. The ones who said they loved me, then ran away, or the ones who said they loved me, then tried to change me into someone else. But I do not see *her*. I never see her. Instead I see someone who will break my heart if I let her have it. So maybe I need to "let her have it" in another way, if you get my meaning. But my heart, never. Never. Never my heart. Not for her, not for my Jew-boy publisher, not for any of my students, nor for my nigger—*African-American, if you please*—friends. None of them will touch my heart. I'll make damn sure of that.

•   •   •

I subscribe to the *Anderson Valley Advertiser*, which is, I think, the best damn rag in the country. It's subhead is: *The Country Weekly That Tells It Like It Is!*, and below that are its slogans: "All Happy, none rich, none poor," and "Peace to the cottages! War on the Palaces!" It fea-tures local events for its geographical namesake, a couple hundred miles south of here, as well as analysis of national and international events, including by far the best coverage I've seen anywhere of the

Zapatista uprising in Chiapas and more recently the worldwide WTO protests. (And if this plug doesn't gain me a positive review in the mighty AVA, then I simply don't know what I'll do.)

A couple of weeks ago the AVA ran an article about a woman who'd gone to a strip bar, gotten falling-down drunk and taken some drugs, then at the urging of members of the volunteer fire department, had gone to their headquarters, where at least eight men had sex with her on the pool table, while others wandered in and out, watching. The men burned candles left over from their wives' charity candle sale. The melted wax damaged the table's felt. The point here is not to excoriate the men for what they later called consensual sex and what the woman called gang rape (the newspaper has done an extraordinary job of that), but to mention two letters to the editor attacking the AVA's coverage. One writer, a man named Michael Connelly, who lives in a town called Elk, wrote, "From what I read about the incident at the firehouse a good time was had by all. The only upset was the candles slightly damaging the pool table. So being a house painter, they should have put down a drop cloth first. I asked one of the Elk volunteer firefighters if an incident like this could have happened in Elk and we both agreed it could not—as the Elk Fire Department doesn't have a pool table." The paper received one other letter to the editor about the coverage, this from a Charles Moton (I include the men's names in case any women who read this book ever happen to meet them), who wrote, "I simply cannot understand the uproar. What did people think the red light on the firehouse meant anyway? . . . Bruce Anderson [the editor] . . . complained that the woman was . . . practically unconscious . . . when the alleged incidents took place. Of course, she was zonked. Did Anderson think she could have endured the incidents if she had been sober? . . . My sympathies, if sympathies are due, are for the much abused and maligned pool table. The underlying slate could take the physical pounding, but I fear for the green baize. Some stains simply will not come out."

It is no wonder that one out of four women in our culture are raped within their lifetimes, and that another 19 percent have to fend off rape attempts. They are objects, to be used, receptacles for our

SEEING THINGS

semen, willing or no, conscious or no, less worthy of our sympathy, empathy, or consideration, than the felt of a pool table.

•   •   •

I've been thinking some more about porn, and I fear I may have been a bit harsh. I think the truth is that we're all so lonely, so alienated, so scared, so disconnected from our own bodies and the bodies of others, that we can—have to, really—count these meager simulacrums of connection—connections with, if anything, flickering images of other human beings—as connections themselves. When you don't know how to connect, when connection frightens you so much, I suppose that this simulation is better than nothing.

Or maybe it isn't. Maybe this parody of connection feeds us just enough that we stay in stasis, too frightened to attempt to actually connect with another human being yet not quite miserable enough for us to attempt to relate differently (or, to be honest, to start to relate at all), not quite miserable enough for us to even begin to know that we are miserable, and lonely. How could I be lonely when each night I can choose from among thousands and tens of thousands and millions of women of all races, ages, and body types who are waiting, if the text at porn sites is accurate, to "suck down" my "goo"? And what about the women who seduce me from the television screen? Don't I want to double my pleasure, double my fun? What more could I want? Well, flesh would be nice, that of someone else other than my own, of someone who cares about me, and for whom I care. And how about love?

That said, I've got no problem with attempting to be intimate with a referent, insofar as that's not a contradiction. In some ways that's what art's about. That's what I'm doing right now as I write this book, and it's what you're doing as you read it. Last year I read *Anna Karenina*. The book moved me deeply. Leo Tolstoy is, of course, dead. Yet the referent left behind by him still changed my life. There are those who argue, I think most often rightly, that *all* symbolic representation by definition contributes to alienation. If I'm reading a

THE CULTURE OF MAKE BELIEVE

book, no matter how skillfully written it may be, I'm still "experiencing" only secondarily, and this "experience" is mediated by the author's choice of words and by the limitations of textual representation. Reading also presumes a false intimacy between the author and myself, an intimacy that might not be false were Leo and I sitting in front of his fireplace as he unfolds for me the story of Anna and her love, or better, the story of his own love.

I generally take a somewhat softer stand regarding "referents," and while I see the dangers of symbolic representation, I also see its beauty and utility. If stories can teach us to be "minorities," as Gerbner put it, if stories can acculturate us into perceiving that the owners of slaves hold title by divine right, or by dint of scientifically supported evolutionary superiority, or by any reason at all save naked (and well-dressed) force (which is one of the secrets of which we, like Ham, must never speak), can not stories also acculturate us in another direction? If so, what would those stories look like? What would stories look like that did not lead us toward the objectification of all others, but instead toward the acknowledgment of their subjectivity, and the realization of relationships with them?

I'm not suggesting by all of this that we simply do away with objectification. That's not existentially possible, because we're always surrounded by so many individuals, so many heartbeats, that to attempt to perceive every moment with any approximation of its real complexity would invite paralysis. For example—and please bear with me through this explication—today I got my hair cut. The person who cut my hair—Karen (not my environmentalist friend)—likes to talk as she works. Today I learned that her teenaged daughter used to play second-chair violin at her school orchestra, but now plays first. She's also good at tennis, but quit after much soul searching. Two other women work at the shop. One of them is out of town; what was she doing the precise instant Karen began to run warm water through my hair? Was she making love, using the toilet, eating, sleeping, acting out of anger, sorrow, joy? All of these at the same time? The third woman was handing out candy bars to the man in her chair (who works at the prison) and his adolescent daughter, who,

SEEING THINGS

for some reason, accompanied him to the salon. The woman was not eating candy, because she perceives herself (inaccurately) as over-weight.

"You don't like chocolate?" the man asked.

"I love it."

"Then why aren't you eating?"

"Look behind me."

Almost every day the guard goes to work at the prison. He comes home. I do not know if he is happy at home. He may be. He may not be. The prisoners stay behind. At Pelican Bay there are maybe 1,500 prisoners in the SHU, or Security Housing Units. It is solitary con-finement. Many will be in the SHU for the rest of their lives.

I leave the shop and get into my car, made fifteen years ago by people I will probably never know, even superficially. I see a man in a motorized wheelchair, on the back of which is a bumper sticker: *I'd rather be flying.* People drive by, in cars built by groups of individual humans. I pull out, and go home. On the way I see an elderly couple walking their dachshunds. One dog pulls hard on the woman's arm, while the other, evidently tired, has been picked up. The man is car-rying the dachshund for its walk. I used to do the same with an eld-erly dog I had years ago.

Attempting to maintain complete awareness of the fact that each person has a history, each one has preferences, each one has hobbies, causes me existentially to seize up, like an engine run too far in the red. I can feel my internal pistons begin to tap, then knock, and I know I've got to slow down. I can't always be aware of the fact that my postal carrier was once a child, nor that the bank teller might have bunions. All of this is one reason I live in a small town: To nav-igate within cities demands intense objectification in defense of one's sanity. I don't *even* want to consider what everyone's experiencing and thinking during a traffic jam on a hot Thursday afternoon in Los Angeles.

And we haven't yet begun to talk about the subjectivity of non-humans. Try getting through twenty-four hours considering that every fly, every spider, every moth that flutters at night into your

THE CULTURE OF MAKE BELIEVE

headlamps is an individual with preferences as strong as your own. I'm not talking specifically about not killing or harming them: I'm just saying that it's not possible—at least for me—to never objectify.

That said, I have also experienced moments of grace, when the world has opened up, or perhaps I have, and I have been able to perceive, take in, participate in, the beauty of the particular.

One day last fall I awoke early (for me) and looked out the window above the head of my bed. I saw the top of a cluster of redwood trees around an ancient stump. Above, I saw pale blue sky and long slender clouds, gray and dirty white. That's when the world—or I—opened. The clouds were unimaginably beautiful—*unimaginably* is the precise word—in design and color. More so than any painting I have ever seen. More so than it is *possible* to paint. I stared, fixing the patterns in my mind, then got up, moving slowly and carefully, as if one jarring movement could shake loose this feeling, take away this grace. I got dressed and went outside. I was still broken open. It was not merely the clouds that were beautiful, but everything I saw. The dappling of sunlight on downed redwood needles, the shape of bent grass, whorls of hair on the dogs' backs, my own fingers, the tangling of boughs from neighboring trees, the texture of bark on a cedar, one particular alder leaning against one particular redwood, the scent of panting dogs who've been running through redwoods, cedar, the sight of long-haired white mold on dog shit, the shape of a scar on my forearm, the sound of ravens' wings, the kittenlike mewing of tall trees in the slight wind. Each of these sensations was the most filling I had ever experienced, and I knew then for the first time what it is to be alive, to be an animal, to be awake in the world. I had lived my life to that point not half- but three-quarters asleep, and now I saw. I did not want to lose that feeling, but I knew also I could not always stay in that grace, so I took a risk and caused myself to no longer perceive, but to see the world as I always had, instrumentally, as this or that tree to be stepped around, or more precisely, as nothing at all, as I thought of something else. Only this time I caused myself to *intentionally* shut down. And then I opened up again. It worked, and I could again see the beauty of the particular. Shut and open. I prac-

SEEING THINGS

ticed all morning, so I would not forget the feeling of living fully in the present. I still carry it with me.

Martin Buber wrote, "One cannot live in the pure present: it would consume us if care were not taken that it is overcome quickly and thoroughly. But in pure past one can live; in fact, only there can a life be arranged. One only has to fill every moment with experiencing and using, and it ceases to burn." This is from Buber's extraordinary, and, at least for me, extraordinarily difficult, book, *I and Thou* (which really should be translated as *I and You*). Central to this book is the understanding that the way we participate in the world and with those in it falls sharply into two immiscible categories, that of I-It and that of I-You. The former is the world of experience, that of objectification. I encounter an It. I use an It. I exploit an It. An It does not have its own existence. The latter is the world of relationship. I meet a You. I consider a You. I affect and am affected by a You. "I contemplate a tree," Buber writes. "I can accept it as a picture: a rigid pillar in a flood of light, or splashes of green traversed by the gentleness of the blue silver ground. I can feel it as movement: the flowing veins around the sturdy, striving core, the sucking of the roots, the breathing of the leaves, the infinite commerce with earth and air—and the growing itself in darkness. I can assign it to a species and observe it as an instance, with an eye to its construction and its way of life. I can overcome its uniqueness and form so rigorously that I recognize it only as an expression of the law—those laws according to which a constant opposition of forces is continually adjusted, or those laws according to which the elements mix and separate. I can dissolve it into a number, into a pure relation between numbers, and eternalize it. Throughout all of this the tree remains my object and has its place and its time span, its kind and condition. But it can also happen, if will and grace are joined, that as I contemplate the tree, I am drawn into a relation, and the tree ceases to be an It. The power of exclusiveness has seized me. This does not require me to forego any of the modes of contemplation. There is nothing that I must not see in order to see, and there is no knowledge that I must forget. Rather is everything, picture and movement,

species and instance, law and number, included and inseparably fused. Whatever belongs to the tree is included: its form and its mechanics, its colors and its chemistry, its conversation with the elements and its conversation with the stars—all this in its entirety. The tree is no impression, no play of my imagination, no aspect of a mood; it confronts me bodily and has to deal with me as I must deal with it—only differently. One should not dilute the meaning of the relation: Relation is reciprocity. . . . What I encounter is neither the soul of a tree nor a dryad, but the tree itself."

Many of the implications of this bifurcation—between I-It and I-You—are obvious. My friend George Draffan once told me a quote from a Canadian lumberman: "When I look at trees I see dollar bills." Before we can deforest the planet, we have to change the way we perceive it. Up until five hundred years ago, the people in what we now call North America lived in basic equilibrium with the forests, as part of a complex web of relationships. Then another culture and the beginnings of the industrial system were brought in from "outside." Before the trees could be cut, they had to be redefined as private or public property. But even before that they had to be redefined as property at all. If I see a woman on the street, and I perceive her as another being with wants and desires all her own, I will treat her differently than if I perceive her as a worker or as property or as an object for my personal enjoyment. It is the same with trees, mountains, the hours of my own life. Are they alive, or are they mere objects for my consumption?

Buber digs even deeper. It's not merely that I see another as an object, it is that, as he puts it, "I-You can only be spoken with one's whole being," while the opposite is true of I-It, that it can *never* be spoken with one's whole being. In other words, to objectify another is to only partially exist oneself. But I knew this, from my brief experience with pornography, and my far longer experience with objectification in general.

A week or so ago I stopped visiting the Internet porn sites, in part because I was done writing about porn, and so there was no more reason for me to do the research, but, in greater measure, because I

SEEING THINGS

had to. The pornography was invading my dreams in a way I didn't like. I dreamt last week that I was in love with a chimera (no, not a "fire-breathing she-monster," as in dictionary definition number one, "with a lion's head, a goat's body, and a serpent's tail," but definition number two: "an unrealizable dream"). She was beautiful, yes, but unreal, and unrealizable. Each time I stepped forward to embrace her, she vanished—poof—leaving my arms empty. That dream was clear enough, but the next night was the kicker. In that dream, I needed a place to stay, and became a boarder at some man's house. I rarely saw him. I soon learned, however, that he regularly kidnapped women and forced them into rooms the size of appliance boxes. At night he would compel them to perform complicated dances with him in which they had to follow his every step. Afterward he would put them away, to bring them out another time, and another, until finally he would tire of them, rape them, and kill them. He tried to get me to help, by sending me to fetch two of the women. I went to their boxes, and let them out. Instead of bringing them to the room where he waited, however, I took them to the back door, and told them to run away as fast as they could, to run and bring back help. I awoke with a headache.

There was something else, too. I found that pornography was altering my spontaneous fantasy life, which historically has run to conversation: I'd see a woman I might be interested in, and wonder immediately, "How would she be to talk to?" I'd play out the creative and intense conversations we might have. But lately, after even this short time, sometimes when I see a woman, I've begun to wonder what is the color of her pubic hair, or the shape of her vulva. I do not like that at all. I want to go back to the way I was before. I hope I can, soon.

The "problem," of course, isn't pornography, any more than lynchings or other "hate crimes" are the "problem." Pornography is just an easy target, as are lynchings, as are white-robed buffoons. They're not even the most interesting targets, though, because, to return to porn, with pornography, at least it's obvious that the person is interacting sexually with an object, just as, with a lynching, it's ob-

vious that the mob is objectifying the person to be lynched. Yet the problem isn't objectification as such. Far more problematical is that we so often forget the difference between objectification and relationship. Perhaps more problematical even than this is the way that, through training and habit, objectification insinuates itself into what might have otherwise been relationships, and into those encounters that we *call* relationships. Witness the change in my fantasy life. Or how about this: If you've been told ten thousand times that the value of trees is in their wood, you may come to believe it, to *know* it, and it may happen that when you try to look at a tree you find yourself incapable of seeing anything but dollar bills. You may even devise an entire economic and governmental system to buttress and reify your constricted perceptions. If you have been told that women act in certain ways toward men, and only in those certain ways, you may believe it, and you may in subtle and not-so-subtle ways attempt to constrain (or provoke) them into behaving in the ways you expect. You may construct a theology that mirrors your belief. If you have been told what to expect when you encounter a black man, you may act appropriately to your expectations: If you are a policeman in Oakland (or any number of other cities), this may include fatally shooting him.

Having inured ourselves to the routine objectification of those around us, having long lost touch with the particular (*any* particular), when we encounter another, be it tree, woman, black man, or anything else under the sun, we too easily lose sight of that other, too easily lose our hold on the slender slip of possibility of actual encounter, that joining of will and grace, as Buber put it, and encounter instead little save our preconceptions, our projections already formed in a culture based on domination. It is not possible to overestimate the damage this does to the potential of relationship. Ask the Indians encountered by the colonists. Ask the Africans enslaved. As we enjoy the comforts and elegancies our way of life affords, and as we stand amidst the embers of a smoldering and dying planet, we should ask ourselves, too, what this systematic objectification costs—not only them, but us.

SEEING THINGS

We may no longer be able to provide an answer. Having been raised to see trees as dollar bills, we may, at this point, not be able to go back: We may never again be able to see another as a subject, not an object. From all evidence, most of us can no longer even tell the difference.

To become confused and to think that an object is a being is merely sad. This is why the pictures of naked and seemingly inviting women did not arouse so much yearning in me as sorrow. Those who become delusional enough in the direction of mistaking objects—to the degree that *anything* can truly be said to be an object—for subjects are sometimes put away. On the other hand, to become confused and think that a being is an object is more dangerous even than sad. I'll tell you what is even more dangerous, more sad, more pathetic than this. If you become so delusional that you no longer see trees, human beings, a living planet, but, instead, dollar bills, workers, resources—far from being put away, you may find yourself well-rewarded, perhaps the CEO of a corporation. If your name is Lawrence Summers, you may just become the secretary of the treasury or president of Harvard.

I am not the first to remark that our financial riches come at the expense of the planet, those we enslave, our capacity to engage in relationship, and our humanity. Time and again we make this wrong choice. We have created an entire society that rewards this wrong choice, that consistently cuts off realistic possibility of making the right choice, that consistently causes us to forget that we even have a choice to make in the first place. And we do have a choice: We can see others as objects, or we can open up to them as subjects. Neither is specifically and in all circumstances the only choice, or the right choice, to make. The decision is, as always, in the particular. Martin Buber put it succinctly. "And in all seriousness of truth, listen: without It a human being cannot live. But whoever lives only with that is not human."

■   ■   ■

I need to return for a moment to my conversation with Richard Drinnon. He told me, "Lurking in the deepest recesses of European and by extension American experience is the assumption that those who are closest to the body, those who run wild through the woods, those who aren't shut up, those who haven't denied themselves and channeled their energy into something else, into building an estate, into building a city on the hill, as one of our Puritan forefathers put it, must be tamed, and we will not rest, for truly we cannot, until they are."

"I'm thinking," I said, "about the constant references on the part of Europeans to tribal peoples the world over as 'lazy.' There's a great line by a Danish traveler in what is now South Africa, who said that the Khoikhoi, a group of people we've since eradicated, 'find it strange that we, the Christians, work, and they say, that we are all mortal, that we gain nothing from our toil, but at the end are thrown underground, so that all we have done is in vain.'"

Drinnon responded, "We can easily turn all the accusations of sloth on their head by arguing that happy, contented people, or those who have some sense of themselves, and who they are, and where they are, wouldn't constantly want to transcend themselves and what they want to do, and would instead simply stay more or less where they are, and not feel as though they have to go out as projectiles to conquer the rest of the world. Frederick Turner, in his very good book, *Beyond Geography*, argued that Western civilization has expanded as a wave of dissatisfaction spreading from a core. Now there are more and more peoples who have been moved by us to become dissatisfied, and who have gained the urge to go beyond their own geography, to go beyond who they are."

He stopped a moment, and we both looked outside. The slight rain was still falling. Everything outside was green.

He started up again, at first slowly, and then faster. "A sense of *place* is critical. For people who live *with* the land, the land becomes the center of their universe. It's a marriage. We are in a symbiotic relationship with the land where we live, and the notion that this rela-

SEEING THINGS

tionship should or even can be transcended is central to many of our problems, and to many of the problems we've created for others. Land is something to be respected, and this respect for land makes respect for self and others possible. When I taught in Pennsylvania I used to take my students to open pit mines. Some of the most effective teaching I ever did consisted of nothing more than sitting on the edge of these five-story-deep holes, looking across at a town under which fires still burned. Smoke still came up in the streets. What we do to the land says who we are, obviously. All I have to do is go back up the country road here two or three miles to see an area that is clear-cut, that is virtually destroyed. It's worse than something that's been paved over, because of the erosion. One look at a clear-cut is more compelling than any number of words."

Drinnon also wrote a biography of Emma Goldman. I asked him about a phrase that was very important to her: "Wenn Du es nicht fuhlst, wirst Du es nicht erraten"—If you do not feel a thing, you will never guess its meaning.

There was another pause, before he said, thoughtfully, "Although Emma Goldman had been an early supporter of the so-called Russian experiment in the new Soviet Union, she quickly became disillusioned with it, and was not afraid to express this disillusionment honestly. Up till reading about that, I had been an exponent of a kind of social scientism. 'Objectivity' was very important to me. But Emma Goldman helped me find my way to be able to say to my students, 'We're not looking for objectivity here. We're looking for honesty.' As much of it as we can come by.

"And this honesty is not about something we don't give a shit about: It's addressed to things we care about a lot. If I don't care for something, there is no problem with me telling you the truth. But if I do care, and there exists some evidence that makes my position awkward, it becomes a bit more tempting to try to cover it up or distract attention away from it. But that's no way to have discourse, and it's no way to live."

I nodded. Ham would have agreed. Noah would not.

He said, "If you can't feel a thing, you'll never guess its meaning.

That is the opposite of where we are. Where can an attempted dominion over nature and over self lead but to the eradication of feelings in any kind of fully human way? Where can it lead but to a
mind-set that creates people who can say, '500,000 Iraqi children is a
price we can afford to pay'? We can kill, but can we feel?"

I asked, "What is to be done?"

"I think one response we see too often is that in attempting to
comfort ourselves from the despair we constrain ourselves to 'feel-
good' messages, where the endings are always happy, the difficulties
easily surmountable. But those messages go nowhere, they don't even
comfort us, and are almost impossible to maintain against the evidence of our own senses. Much better, I believe, and more honest, is
to look our despair in the eye and be enheartened by an ongoing resistance that is our last best hope, however forlorn that hope sometimes seems."

Yet more silence before he started again. "It may be that we have
constructed for ourselves what Henry David Thoreau called an *atro-
pos*, a fate. We have a system that is self-propelled, largely, by virtue
of our not withholding our support from it, and not resisting it, not
fighting it as hard as we can. When he wrote that, he was talking
about the railroads. . . ."

I interrupted. "The prototypical modern corporation, by the
way. . . ."

He continued, ". . . and it's a hell of a lot more of a fate now than
it was then. How do you fight it?"

I looked away, then back to him.

He answered his own question. "Herman Melville wrote,
'Indian-hating still exists, and no doubt will continue to exist so long
as Indians do.' I think the single most important thing any of us can
do is lay bare the Indian-hating, make it known so we can deal with
it. I mean this both personally—because I come out of Indian-hating
circumstances . . ."

"As we all do," I said.

". . . and I mean it socially. I think that Melville, with his book
The Confidence-Man, did as much as anyone in the nineteenth century

SEEING THINGS

to expose Indian-hating for what it is. Across the decades, Melville spoke to me so directly it stunned me. But one of the problems we face, even in making the Indian-hating known, is that the more effectively and graphically we get our point across, the more potent and defensive is the reponse, and the more deeply embedded than ever is the hatred. An Indian man, Jerry Gamble, who used to be the editor of *Akwesasne Notes,* told one of my classes, 'Look, all of you have got this problem, which is that you've got to face your history, but if you face your history you can't live with it. What are you going to do?'

"This is a real dilemma. I used to see that all the time with my students. So many of them would march right up to the edge of a particularly difficult topic, and then they would walk away. I didn't want them to agree with any specific viewpoint; I just wanted them to confront the problem. But there were some who were able to bang their heads against the topic until they finally came to an understanding, to a response."

I thought again of Ham. All of us. I thought also, for some reason I didn't understand, of a streamer that hung above an anarchist school in Spain in the 1930s: "Children are the new world. And all dreamers are children; those who are moved by kindness and beauty. . . ." I mentioned the latter to Richard.

He responded, "If we look and listen we have stories to guide us, stories like that of the anarchist school, like the stories of resistance, like the stories of humans living comfortably and fully on this land. These stories are to be searched for and listened to, thought over. There are stories going back to the first people on this continent, and then all those thousands of years that we didn't have our system of government, our jails, our chainsaws. I'm not saying these people were perfect, because they weren't. They were limited. They were people who, so the Zuñi tell us, were so ill-advised as to have food fights, and who had to deal with that by coming up with a ceremony that would teach people to take care of their food. They were not people with answers to everything. But they were human. And if we were to listen to them, to their stories, and to pay attention to their dances—and maybe even in time join them in the dance—we might become a little more human ourselves."

I turned off the tape recorder. We talked a brief while longer, and then I left, to drive home in the light winter rain.

SEEING THINGS

FROM A CERTAIN

POINT ONWARD,

THERE IS NO

TURNING BACK.

THAT IS THE

POINT THAT

MUST BE

REACHED.

FRANZ KAFKA

THE OTHER SID

OF DARKNESS

A MONTH OR SO AGO I got a late-night E-mail from Karen (the activist, not the haircutter), saying she needed some help. The horrors were getting to her. She's been an activist now for a few years, and she's reaching a breaking point. I called. We talked. For the last several months she's been cataloguing poisons used in this region for agriculture, mainly pesticides applied to fields of flowers. The town of Smith River, just north of here, is the self-proclaimed Easter Lily capital of the world, which means that the Smith River itself, the estuary, the aquifer, and all who depend on it—human and nonhuman alike— are being killed for nothing more than frivolity, profits, and to send across the globe the beautiful and sweetly scented symbol of rebirth.

It was easy to see why she's been hit so hard. In the past year alone the growers used 170,120 pounds of dry chemicals and 32,652 gallons of liquid poisons on 1414 acres, for an average of one hundred and twenty pounds and twenty-three gallons per acre. This was not a typical year. The poisons used are deadly even at dilutions well-nigh inconceivable, and certainly immeasurable by standard means. The growers used 62,780 pounds of methyl bromide (also called Terro-gas), a chemical that was supposed to have been phased out worldwide by 2000, but has not, in great measure because of complaints (and dollars) from growers in California and Florida. One of the growers is from Belgium, a country where the chemical has already been banned; he moved his operation to Del Norte County because he knew that here he could use toxins banned elsewhere. Methyl bromide not only kills everything in the soil, but devastates the ozone layer at no extra charge: It destroys ozone molecules at fifty times the rate of the more infamous chlorofluorocarbons, or CFCs. During application, 80 to 95 percent of the methyl bromide escapes as a gas. Deadly if inhaled, methyl bromide is mixed with chloropicrin to make it stink, thus warning folks they're being poisoned. But chloropicrin, also used alone, has its own problems, primarily, that it kills at concentrations of four to ten parts per million. It was used as a nerve gas in World War I, though now, gas warfare generally being discouraged, it's used on the homefront. The growers used fourteen thousand pounds of disulfoton, which can kill at a dilution of one hundred and eighty parts per billion. They used 20,193 pounds of copper sulfate to poison the land, and considerably less for the chemical's not unheard-of alternative use: suicide (or rather, fast suicide, because when you get right down to it, application of any of this stuff constitutes not much more than a slightly slower form of murder-suicide), for which it takes only one or two grams. And they used 23,691 gallons of Metam Sodium, which has been shown to be toxic at levels of one part per trillion (yes, you read that correctly). An accidental spill on the Sacramento River in 1991 killed everything (yes, you read that correctly, too): old growth trees, fish, aquatic invertebrates, algae, you name it. The chemical kills so universally that the dead fish did not rot, because there were no living bacteria to cause them to decompose. The growers—it's ironic that we call them that, all things considered—also used many other

THE OTHER SiDE OF DARKNESS

chemicals: copper hydroxide, streptomycinsulfate, iprodine, glyphosate, polyethoxylated tallowamines, 2,4-D, bacillus thuringiensis, and penta-chloronitirobenzene (trade name Earthcide™, indicating whomever named it needs to take a few more courses in bureaucratic obfuscation).

Karen and I had talked weeks before about the concentrations that can kill; she'd wanted visuals to help her understand the levels of toxicity. For chloropicrin, lethal at dilutions down to four to ten parts per million, I suggested she picture a huge football stadium filled ten times over, and put in four to ten people representing the toxin (we spent a fair amount of time suggesting actual people who might be appropriate as manifestations of the poison (CEOs and politicians topped my list; growers, for obvious reasons, topped hers)): that concentration is enough to kill. It was harder for me to come up with a visual for Metam Sodium, with its lethality at one part per trillion (you're still reading that right). There are twelve inches in a foot, and 5,280 feet in a mile, so one part per trillion would be one inch in about 15,780,000 miles. For reference, the earth's circumference is about 24,000 miles, so this would be equivalent to going around the world 657 times. Another way to look at this is to consider that it's about 239,000 miles from the earth to the moon. So Metam Sodium would be toxic at concentrations representing one inch in the distance between the earth and the moon sixty-six times over. Or a third way to look at it is that the earth is a little over ninety million miles from the sun, meaning that Metam Sodium would be toxic at concentrations representing one inch to about one-sixth of the distance between the earth and the sun. Put yet another way, the volume of Metam Sodium used on these fields—23,691 gallons at 37.2 percent purity, for an effective dosage of 8813 gallons—would be enough to make poisonous eight or nine quadrillion gallons (what's another quadrillion gallons among friends?). To put this into slightly more manageable figures, this would be about 1.2 quadrillion cubic feet of water. Now, there are 147 billion cubic feet in a cubic mile. That's a lot. But there are still more than 8 cubic miles in 1.2 quadrillion cubic feet. This means that, evenly distributed, this amount of Metam Sodium would make toxic eight cubic miles of water. For comparison, and moving back to the more familiar unit of cubic feet, the flood-stage discharge of the Amazon River is about 6.2 million cubic feet per second, meaning, if these growers just put their minds to it, they could poison more than two days of the entire Amazon's flow. *During flood stage.* For the Mississippi it would be almost three weeks' worth. The Smith River—a river intentionally set aside as habitat from which embattled creatures can begin to recolonize their former range, presumably once the horror that is civilization has all but faded from memory, and one of the last bastions of the California and Oregon populations of salmon—generally has flows of between one and four thousand cubic feet per second during the winter season of rains, far less during the summer. Taking a figure of two thousand cubic feet per second as an extremely generous year-round average, using only a one-year supply of Metam Sodium (and remember, these are just a few entrepreneurs in a forgotten corner of the country) the growers could poison the entire output of the Smith for almost six hundred million seconds, or something over eighteen years.

Karen thanked me for telling her all this, although I'm not exactly sure why. I certainly don't think any of it reassured her, nor am I sure how much those figures helped her to picture it. So, science geek that I am, God help me, I gave her one more. If the population of the world is about 6,125,216,948 people (at 2:51:37 pm PST on February 18, 2001, according to the International Programs Center of the United States Bureau of the Census, although by the time I typed this sentence, the population had increased to 6,125,217,269) it would only take six one-thousandths of a person to make the whole world toxic. Poisonous as some people may be, this toxin is far more virulent.

Not only is the natural world being poisoned, but cases of non-Hodgkins lymphoma are up, and a representative of the Yurok tribe has mentioned new cases of this cancer, including a 2-year-old child. What began with guns and fire can now be completed chemically.

It's sometimes hard to believe that people manufacture this stuff on purpose. Perhaps even more unbelievable, other people pay to buy the stuff and to apply it, or more precisely, to pay migrant workers minimum wage to apply it.

THE OTHER SIDE OF DARKNESS

Not surprisingly, many of the growers have shown themselves willing not only to poison, but to exploit in other ways: Those they hire to work the poisoned fields do so twelve to fourteen hours per day, six days a week, with one ten-minute break and a twenty-minute lunch, no bathroom breaks, for minimum wage. They're allowed no days off for any reason. They have rashes that bleed chronically. They vomit. They have headaches. Doctors tell them not to go back, but they need the money. Sometimes they do not get even that. One grower has the habit of calling the Immigration and Naturalization Service each year at the end of the harvest so he won't have to pay back wages. The fine he receives for hiring undocumented workers (so-called illegal aliens) is less than the wages he no longer has to pay.

This is what Karen works on.

"I don't know how much more of this I can take in," she said. "It's all too awful, too absurd."

"Yeah," I said softly.

"It's so pointless."

I knew she meant the horrors, not the work.

"The sorrow gets so big that sometimes it feels like it will just swallow me whole."

"It's okay," I said. "It's okay if it does that."

I thought of all the activists I know who've passed over this same threshold, who've weathered this same painful transition. I thought of the woman I met once from a small town in Minnesota, a lawyer also fighting, nearly by herself, the poisoning of her county by agricorporations. She said to me, "Sometimes I think the only things that keep me going are sorrow and rage." And I thought of the woman who came up to me after I gave a talk, and said, quietly, so no one else could hear, "I'll tell you something I've never told anyone: I don't think our culture is salvageable. I think we're doomed." I'd told her I agreed. And I remembered the many times I've said in my public talks that although every cell in my body wants our culture to undergo a voluntary transition to a sane and sustainable way of living, I do not believe it will happen, and I remembered the nods of agreement I've seen—from at least half of the audience—and the lightening of their faces as they realize that someone has finally spoken the unspeakable. By coincidence, I had received that same night another E-mail on this same subject, from someone I did not know. She'd seen a talk I gave, and had been moved to write me: "I'm glad you said you don't believe we're going to turn it around. That thought actually felt good, a relief, because now there's no more waiting for the bad news. It reminded me of something I wrote ten years ago, in a bad poem, about the Worldwatch Institute saying we've got twenty years to turn it around, and I keep waiting for them to say it's just too late. It's oddly freeing to think of the state of the planet from the perspective of accepting that it's too late to turn our culture around. It frees us to ask, 'What do we do with that information?' And it opens us up in so many other ways." I know that for me, and for my activist friends, this understanding has freed us also to change our priorities, and paradoxically, to become more effective, whatever that means. Of course, as I alluded to earlier, it is also possible to become paralyzed by this realization, to use it as a fatalistic excuse for inaction: "If it's all going down, I'm free to do nothing." I have neither patience nor sympathy for this form of malaise, which reveals nothing less than an incapacity to love: No one who loves could consider inaction in the face of a threat as a form of freedom.

"I don't think we're going to make it," Karen said.

It took me a little while to decide to go ahead and say what I'd known all along was the right thing, "I've been waiting for you to say that."

■   ■   ■

By another coincidence, just today, the day after the late night in which I wrote the last section, I received an E-mail from someone who's been reading my previous book, *A Language Older Than Words*. He's a very good thinker and writer, named robert wolff. He'd written me a brief note yesterday thanking me for writing that book, and concluded his note: "Wishing you what rewards this world has to offer, but more than that, wishing you joy in the real world that is behind and often

THE OTHER SIDE OF DARKNESS

hidden by the veneer of what we think of as 'civilization' (which, I know, is nothing but the manifestation of . . . a planetary disease)."

I wrote him back, thanking him for his words, then added, "Yes, civilization has to end. I just hope there's something left when we do bring it down."

He responded, and this is from the note I got today. "I cannot imagine that 'we' will bring it down. It seems totally obvious that our civilization is already dead, and that it is just a matter of time until we and the rest of creation will get caught up in the last spasms of a dead body."

At least a few of my friends disagree with this. Certainly they understand that civilization is moribund, but they also think and most especially fear that it may limp along, continuing to consume everything in its path (and of course continuing to seek out new pathways for consumption) until there really is nothing left. Just this last weekend I had a long talk with one such friend, who could easily see civilization standing, albeit shakily—and on what?—for another five hundred years. I reminded her of a conversation we'd had a few years ago in which I'd asked if given the opportunity she'd want to travel one-way a couple hundred years into the future, just to see how things looked. She'd replied, "Only if I could take a gun to blow my brains out if it's as bad as I think it will be."

The man from Hawaii continued, "I suspect the earth will survive even humans. But it will be a different earth. Whether humans will survive is very doubtful. Certainly we cannot survive in our present state of non-awareness of What Is. My guess is that ten, twelve thousand years ago when we suddenly decided to invent agriculture (and territory, and domestication of animals as well as plants, followed by domestication of ourselves, and ownership and all that we now call 'civilization') we broke ourselves off from the earth, and so pushed ourselves into a dead end in evolution."

I am always surprised by how many people privately perceive civilization as a dead end—in more ways than one—yet how little that enters our public discourse. Call it the revenge of Noah.

He continued. "New Age people believe that somehow we will discover something and magically we will survive and everything will be

put aright. Some of my friends expect angels to come, others believe beings from the Pleiades will come to rescue us at the last moment."

In *Language* I explored, among many other things, the often-complex and just-as-often simple relationship between denial, domestic violence, and our culture's assault on the natural world and its members. I used my own childhood as a springboard into that exploration.

He wrote, "It never occurred to me to relate abuse to denial, but now it's obvious. Reading your book, I have looked back to my own childhood and have discovered the same mechanism operating: oppression, abuse, force, narrowing of perception, all leading to denial. Yet my childhood was very different from yours. I grew up at a time and a place where abuse and violence were literally unknown (there is no word in the Malay language for sexual abuse, for rape: beating a child, even forcing a child is unknown and unheard of). My parents were upper middle class Dutch intellectuals. I was raised with Freud in a Muslim country (Sumatra, Indonesia). I saw my parents for tea in the afternoon. Our (many) servants were my real family. They loved me unconditionally; my biological parents loved me conditionally."

I found his life story fascinating. I read on.

"Then, at age 17, after I finished high school, I was sent to Europe, 'to get culture,' very much against my wishes. . . . I arrived in Europe two weeks before the beginning of Word War II, and spent five years in Holland during the German Occupation. This is where I learned what violence and abuse meant. As it happened it was also the first time I lived in a completely Western, scientific environment among people who were convinced of science as the Truth with a capital T. What you experienced as a child, I experienced as an adolescent, as a young man. I also learned many things during that time, of course. For instance that I relate best with people of the underbelly of society—the whores, thieves, the 'underworld'—which later became the Resistance. Physically, I survived. It took me twenty-five years to re-discover 'myself,' and another ten or twenty to dig out from under all the crap and lies and falsehoods of modern life.

"But through all this I've known that there have existed people who were whole. I have known some. They went about almost naked,

THE OTHER SIDE OF DARKNESS

they did not have money, they were hunter/gatherers, gathering a lot more than hunting. They 'knew' things they could not possibly know. They slept in huddles, like cats do. They were nomads. They avoided confrontation and were appalled by (human) violence. Of course they were not civilized. A South African author, Laurens van der Post, said of another group of aboriginals he knew that 'they could not be tamed.' It is we 'tamed humans' who are lethal."

He concluded by asking, "Do you have friends who tell you not to be so 'negative'? I do."

Actually, I don't. My friends, to be honest, generally feel the same as I do on this. I cannot fight the culture and my friends as well, so I've found friends who are working to bring down civilization, or holding on by their/our fingernails so that grizzly bears or salmon may still be alive when the thing finally does come crashing down.

■   ■   ■

One of the curses of being even remotely aware of the effects and trajectory of our civilization is that it's increasingly difficult, especially for those who maintain touch with their capacity to spontaneously free associate, to feel unalloyed happiness, even in the presence of intense beauty. It is difficult to see salmon spawn without remembering the silt that clogs the stream, and without knowing that one day it was not two, nor three, nor even four fish that someone would see, but so many that the water would be white from the whipping of their tails and the cutting of their fins through the surface of the water. It is hard to listen to the frogs who sing outside my window—last year they were so loud I could not be heard, were I to talk in a normal voice near the pond—without being aware of the worldwide anthropogenic die-off of amphibians. It is early February, and only a few frogs are yet here. I feel tense, and wonder each day if this will be the year the frogs don't return, that I experience my own silent spring. I see clusters of newt or salamander eggs in the pond, and remember the tiger salamanders of my youth. They were everywhere, it seemed. Now my organic farmer friends in North Dakota tell me tiger salamanders are disappearing, victims of the same

and different pesticides that poison the Smith River delta. When I was a child, I caught a dolly varden trout, big, beautiful, and, we discovered when we cleaned her, gravid. Now dolly vardens—no longer called that, but instead bull trout—are endangered. I cannot tell you how many times I have stood deep in forests, and heard these forests speak, as birds call to each other, squirrels chatter, and as the trees themselves talk, groaning and creaking, or moaning like whales, and I cannot tell you how many times I have then heard far beyond these voices the throaty roar of log trucks, or the rasping whine of gunning chainsaws.

Tonight I had a visitor. I was working (okay, damnit, you caught me, I was playing a computer baseball game) and the dogs began to bark. I live in a forest. Many times I politely asked the dogs to be quiet. Each time, they looked at me, sort of nodded, walked in circles, and layed down. As soon as I returned inside, they started barking again. Finally, though, once, when I was outside, I heard branches creaking in a nearby tree. I lit a lantern and walked the three-eighths of a mile to my mom's to get a flashlight (lanterns cast a circle of light, yet I needed a beam), then walked back. My mom thought it might be a possum, but I had my doubts. I shined the light into the tree where I thought I'd heard the sound. Nothing. I moved closer. Still nothing. Closer still. Suddenly from a different direction, and from much lower in the tree than I'd expected, I heard a cough and heard branches striking each other. I'm not normally skittish, but I have to admit I skittered pretty damn quickly—using the least elegant of *skitter's* definitions—a half-dozen skittering steps away, and refocused the beam. It was a bear, probably a yearling.

I've seen bears plenty in my life. I like them. They don't scare me. (Okay, you got me again: I've been in griz country, and I have to admit *they* intimidate me just a tad, especially at night, when I'm in my sleeping bag, drifting off, and somewhere not so far away (not nearly far enough away) I hear a twig snap, and then another. . . .) When I was about twelve, I used to go bare-hands fishing with my sister's husband, Al, in a mountain stream. I'd crawl to streamside, then jump up suddenly and watch the trout scatter (perhaps the underwater equivalent of skitter) to hide in tiny caves beneath rocks. I'd wade in to find them.

THE OTHER SIDE OF DARKNESS

I didn't keep them but just looked at them closely and let them go. Once, I was standing thigh-deep in the stream, wearing cutoffs, no shirt, and no shoes, when I heard a sound on the far bank, maybe five feet away. I looked up to see a bear. Al said, "Run, Derrick!"

"I'm not going to run. I'm not wearing any shoes."

The bear was as surprised as we were. She turned and ran away, nothwithstanding the fact that she didn't have any shoes either.

On this land I've seen bear tracks quite a few times, including the biggest black bear track I've ever seen, and once lost deep in the woods I saw the place where this bear probably sleeps, in a hollow beneath a big downed redwood: The grass was flattened, and there were brownish-black hairs caught on nearby branches. Another time I left a big pile of apples out for the bears, and was rewarded in the same spot a few days later with an almost equally big pile of bear shit, apple skins, and other chunks clearly visible in the scat. I've seen the big bear once, ambling down the trail, away from me. My mom has seen it, too, in so doing solving a bit of a mystery at her house. Each night the dogs' food would be gone, even if the dogs were at my place. She figured opossums were eating it. But the first night she brought the food inside, she heard a noise on the porch, and when she went to investigate found herself nose-to-nose with the bear. Then another night she accidentally left her garage door open; the bear carried a garbage can of dog food into the driveway, dumped it, and feasted. Last week I got home from a tour to see my sliding glass door, normally open a foot or so to allow cats easy egress, wide open, and a bag of dog food outside. I knew immediately what had happened, and was thankful the bear hadn't made a mess. I much prefer dealing with polite and even meticulous bears over the messier ones.

The point is that no matter how many times I've seen bears, each time I encounter one anew it continues to be a gift and a joy, even when the bear causes me damage, as when I used to be a beekeeper and bears got to the bees. This meeting was no exception. I walked the dogs back to my mom's and put them in her garage, so they wouldn't scare the bear. Then I returned. I shined the light up in the branches but didn't see it. Moving the flashlight down the trunk, I saw the bear at the base,

just a few feet, actually, from where I had walked. I looked at it. It was cinammon. It looked back at me, though I'm not sure what it could see behind the beam. I thanked it for its politeness, and apologized for the dogs scaring it. I told it I would be glad to bring it some food, somewhere away from the house. It just stared at me. I stared at it. Then it started chuffing. I like bears, but I'm also fully aware that this bear, young as it is, still outweighs me, and has bigger teeth and claws than I. I'm also fully aware that I do not know its language: I don't know what the chuffing means. I decided to go inside. There, I read, in a book on bears, "If you hear one chuffing, Watch out! It means the bear is angry, or surly," or maybe, I thought, just sick of hearing first dogs and then a human yammering at it.

Here's the real point: I loved this encounter with a wild bear, with another being, with *this* particular bear in *this* particular tree on *this* particular night, but I could not keep myself from remembering—almost instantly, when I first saw the bear—something that happened when I lived in northeastern Nevada some fifteen years ago. There had been no bears in Elko County for decades, maybe a half-century. One wandered in from Idaho. It got scared and ran up a tree. You can probably guess what happened next. A rancher shot it. I don't know if another bear has wandered in. I would not blame them for avoiding the region.

■   ■   ■

For me, the tattered fragments of naïve hope that the movement of our culture as a whole—of our civilization, which originated in conquest abroad and repression at home—could be different than it has been from the beginning, could be toward something other than comforts and elegancies for the few, based on the sweat and blood of all others, could be reasonable, that our culture could respond to reason, could undergo the transition to a sane and humane way of living for which most of my friends devote most of their efforts, were finally stripped away by a story. I will tell you this story, but the story is not the point. The final trigger is never the point, because no naïve hope this strong,

THE OTHER SIDE OF DARKNESS

this large, this foundational, can ever be stolen away by a single incident, no matter how compelling the incident itself. Instead, this naïve hope is worn down, like a stone pillar in a desert sandstorm, by repeated betrayals read about or experienced, betrayals that characterize the progress of our culture. I read the words of Justice Marshall—"discovery gave title . . . which title might be consummated by possession"—and a portion of the pillar crumbled away. More of the pillar tumbled as I read the orders from Lord Amherst to Colonel Bouquet. "Could it not be contrived to send the *Small Pox* among those disaffected tribes of Indians? We must on this occasion use every stratagem in our power to reduce them." Even more of the pillar sloughed away as I read Bouquet's response, that he preferred "the Spanish method," a combination of hunting dogs, rangers, and light horsemen, to "effectively extirpate or remove that vermin." For years I filed timber sale appeals that stopped illegal federal timber sales on public lands. My friends shut down illegal logging on several national forests. The government response to our efforts across the country was to pass a law essentially exempting federal timber sales from environmental regulations. What happened to that pillar of naïve hope as every one of the upward of ten thousand acres I personally helped save in several years of activism was clear-cut over the next fifteen months? How much fell away with the felling of every ancient tree? What does it do to our naïve hope that even those who believe our political system has shreds of legitimacy take it for granted that those who run the country routinely lie to us? What happens when you take in the implications of the conceptualization and fabrication of neutron bombs, designed to kill humans (and all other living beings) yet leave edifices—nothing but concrete and glass and steel—standing?

Here was, for me, the final piece. I was reading Eduardo Galeano's *Century of the Wind*, from his *Memory of Fire* series, a stunning history of the Americas. I came across his story of the Black Admiral, of whom I had never heard. In 1910, Brazilian sailors mutinied against the practice of flogging, having one too many times watched one of their own whipped by an officer: "the last of the lashes," Galeano writes, "two hundred and forty-eight, two hundred and forty-nine, two hundred

and fifty—fall upon a flayed body, bathed in blood, unconscious or dead." An ordinary seaman, João Cándido, the Black Admiral, assumed command and sailed the ship into the harbor at Rio de Janeiro. The demand of the sailors was simple, and not unreasonable: Eliminate flogging and declare an amnesty for the mutineers, or they would blast the city into rubble. The government agreed immediately, and the sailors in good faith surrendered their swords. I'm sure you can see what's coming, as easily as you did with the murdered bear. Mutiny safely over and the previous order restored, the legislators condemned "with all severity the violence and barbarity" of the mutiny—which took the lives of precisely three officers—and stated that while they may personally have been opposed to flogging, the demand for its end could no longer be honored, because it had not been made, according to one of the legislators, "by constitutional means, using the proper channels within the framework of prevailing juridicial norms." The ink was still fresh, Galeano comments, on the law to end flogging, when the practice resumed, and the navy began killing the mutineers. The lucky among them were shot on the open ocean, while the less fortunate were buried alive in the catacombs of Cobra Island, also called the Isle of Despair, where they were thrown quicklimed water when they complained of thirst. As for the Black Admiral himself, he ended his days in a lunatic asylum.

A reasonable request met with betrayal: the story of resistance to civilization. Insane logic leading to inhumanity. That final piece could just as easily have been something else. It could have been President Thomas Jefferson—friend of the Indians—instructing his secretary of war that Indians who resist the theft of their land must be met with the hatchet, and furthermore, "if we are ever constrained to lift the hatchet against any tribe, we will never lay it down till that tribe is exterminated, or is driven beyond the Mississippi." He continued, in what is certainly the central theme of civilization, "in war, they will kill some of us; we shall destroy all of them." His words are reminiscent, if you recall, of those used by lawyer Stephen Worth of the New York Patrolmen's Benevolent Association, in his statement after the killing of Amadou Diallo by four police officers: "The idea is for them

THE OTHER SIDE OF DARKNESS

to use all the firepower available until the threat is removed." Perhaps Worth had been consciously mimicking the words of Jefferson. I doubt it, though. It's far more likely that this way of thinking, this way of entering into and confronting the world, has been inculcated into us deeply enough and for long enough that it has become a reflex. The final piece could have been President Andrew Jackson, who thankfully at least did not pretend to be anything other than what he was, boasting that "I have on all occasions preserved the sculps [sic] of my killed," and who personally supervised the mutilation of the bodies of about eight hundred Creek Indians—men, women, and children—that he and his men had massacred, cutting off their noses to preserve a record of their kills, and slicing off long strips of flesh to tan and turn into bridal reins. It could have been the phony treaties Jackson rammed down the throats of the Cherokees by imprisoning tribal leaders, shutting down their printing press, then, presaging a move oft-repeated since, negotiating with "cooperative" Indians to produce a treaty so ludicrous that even the military officer assigned to register the tribe's members to remove them in accordance with the treaty said, "that paper. . . called a treaty, is no treaty at all, because not sanctioned by the great body of the Cherokee and made without their participation or assent. I solemnly declare to you that upon its reference to the Cherokee people it would be instantly rejected by nine-tenths of them, and I believe by nineteen-twentieths of them. . . . The delegation taken to Washington . . . had no more authority to make a treaty than any other dozen Cherokee accidentally picked up for that purpose. . . . The Cherokee are a peacable, harmless people, but you may drive them to desperation, and this treaty can not be carried into effect except by the strong arm of force." It could have been the death march that was the implementation of this treaty, the Trail of Tears that killed eight thousand Cherokee men, women, and children, about half of what remained of that nation (and roughly equal, by the way, to the death rate of Jews in Germany, Hungary, and Rumania between 1939 and 1945). It could more recently have been the elevation to secretary of state by a unanimous vote in the U.S. Senate someone who had previously been found guilty by an international tribunal of war crimes and crimes against humanity—I'm talking about Colin Powell here—and someone who, when officially asked to investigate allegations of routine atrocities by American soldiers in Vietnam, including the rape, torture, and massacre of civilians at My Lai and elsewhere, concluded, "In direct refutation of this portrayal is the fact that relations between American soldiers and the Vietnamese people are excellent." It could have been the simple existence of ships like the *Atlantic Dawn*, a trawler capable of "handling" three hundred and forty-four tons of fish per day, spreading its nets more than a mile long, scraping the sea floor, destroying all life—fish, birds, other animals—in its path, and tossing much of it—called bycatch—back overboard, dead. It could have been the existence of Trident submarines, first-strike weapons capable of launching twenty-four missiles simultaneously, each missile containing up to seventeen independently targeted nuclear warheads, each warhead ten times more powerful than the bomb that incinerated Nagasaki, each warhead capable of traveling seven thousand miles, meaning that just one of these subs—and the United States has twenty-two—could effectively eliminate 408 cities across an entire hemisphere. It could have been, as was true for Karen, the ubiquity and stupidity of pesticides. Or it could have been, as happened recently, a straightforward conversation at a restaurant. I asked the server if she knew who won the Super Bowl. She looked at me as though I were a fool, and told me the answer. I then asked her, just out of curiosity, if she knew that wild salmon are on the verge of extinction through much of the Northwest. She said she wasn't aware of that. She was a senior in college, I soon learned, majoring in environmental studies.

The question becomes, I think, how do you incorporate—from the Latin *in corpor*, to take into the body—this understanding in a way that sustains rather than defeats you. I have no answer. I only know what sustained me through that transition.

The main thing that helped was the fact that I had many friends who had already gone over this threshold, and who were continuing to act as effectively as they could. The knowledge that our culture is not redeemable had not paralyzed but energized them. These people were

THE OTHER SIDE OF DARKNESS

my models, my inspirations. Most of them had not articulated this change in perspective—this stripping away of this particular false hope—but, far more importantly, they were living it, and living it beautifully and happily. They did not take the insanity of the culture personally. Oh, sure, many certainly cried about it, often, but they also recognized that by acting vigorously against the injustices and insanity they saw around them they could remove the shame of their participation in it—their participation by the mere fact of being in its center, in reaping some of its rewards. By an act of emotional and spiritual jiu jitsu, they could change their perception from that of living in the center of civilization—a place of unfair advantage where our way of life is based on the exploitation of all others—into having a different sort of advantage: access to the soft underbelly. Having grown up as the recipient of all of these comforts and elegancies gives us greater responsibility, and ability, to shut down the source of those unfair entitlements, and to fight against the contempt and ultimately the hatred on which they are based. Having been taught to read and write, for example, gives me tools denied to others. I can do more harm to civilization—which means I can do more good for humanity—from where I stand at its center, than someone—a starving child in Indonesia, to choose an obvious example, or the poor father or mother of several children in a Third World city, to choose a slightly less obvious one—who does not have that access. This does not mean I should court my privilege, or follow the slippery slope of increasing compromise to gain increasingly intimate yet ineffective access to the seats of power; it simply means that having been born into circumstances that give me certain privileges—based on my gender, the color of my skin, the country of my birth, my education—it becomes my duty to use those privileges to undermine or eradicate the basis for them.

I learned also at this time that it was not so much my sorrow nor even my pain at seeing the destruction on which our way of life is based that hurt me so much as it was my resistance to acknowledging and feeling it.

Through that time—and this was after I'd been an activist several years, and written my first two books, meaning either that Karen is a much quicker study than I, or the destructiveness of the culture has become that much more obvious in only these few years—I began to break down in sobs three or four times per week. Lynx, salmon, Port Orford cedar—all disappearing. The declarations of Lawrence Summers. The lies of politicans. The teaching of torturers and murderers at taxpayer expense at the School of the Americas (and it's only right, by the way, that it should be at taxpayer expense, since U.S. citizens benefit economically from the exploitation that necessitates the torture in the first place). Some of my friends, even those who'd already gone through this transition, told me to relax. "Take it easy," they said. "The problems will still be there when you come back to them." But I knew I had to keep pushing.

The person I think who helped me most through this transition—without whose help I could not be the activist and writer I am today—was Jeannette Armstrong. She is an Okanagan Indian, a writer and activist herself. I met her when I interviewed her for my first book, *Listening to the Land*, and we became friends. I called her the day I read the story of the Black Admiral. I said to her, "This culture hates everything, doesn't it?"

"Yes," she said. "Even itself."

"Unless it's stopped it will kill everything, won't it?"

"You know the answer to that one."

"And the culture's not going to change, is it?"

She said, invitingly yet firmly, "I've been waiting for you to say that."

That was the best thing she or anyone could have said to me. It helped me to understand that I need not fight despair, that despair is a normal and reasonable response to a desperate situation. It helped me to know that my response—breaking into sobs over the killing of so much beauty—is normal, and expected, and that to not feel these losses manifests another type of loss, that of one's own humanity, one's very heart. The moment I realized all of this was the moment, I think, that this culture of hate, the rule of Noah, lost its power over me. That was the moment I passed through, beyond, over to the other side of darkness.

THE OTHER SIDE OF DARKNESS

THE THIEF WHO IS IN PRISON IS NOT NECESSARILY MORE DISHONEST THAN HIS FELLOWS AT LARGE, BUT MOSTLY ONE WHO, THROUGH IGNORANCE OR STUPIDITY [OR, ADDS GEORGE DRAFFAN, RACISM OR POVERTY] STEALS IN A WAY THAT IS NOT CUSTOMARY. HE SNATCHES A LOAF FROM THE BAKER'S COUNTER AND IS PROMPTLY RUN INTO GAOL. ANOTHER MAN SNATCHES BREAD FROM THE TABLE OF HUNDREDS OF WIDOWS AND ORPHANS AND SIMILAR CREDULOUS SOULS WHO DO NOT KNOW THE WAYS OF COMPANY PROMOTERS; AND, AS LIKELY AS NOT, HE IS RUN INTO PARLIAMENT.

GEORGE BERNARD SHAW

CRIMINALS

I TAUGHT AT THE PRISON TONIGHT, in level one, or minimum security. For the foreseeable future I won't teach in level four. The maximum-security prisoners are still locked down from the riot I alluded to early in this book. Every time during the last eight months the administrators tried to "program," or let the prisoners back onto the yard; within a couple of weeks there would be an "incident," politespeak in this case for a sticking, or stabbing. Because Hispanics had originally attacked blacks, blacks now itched to get back at Hispanics. So a Hispanic might get stuck. And then of course the Hispanics would retaliate. And then. . . . Meanwhile, there was already bad blood, so to speak, between blacks and whites, based on incidents months prior (not to mention five hundred years of history). So even if the administration kept Hispanics locked down but let out the blacks and whites, well, the skin at the point of the shank's entry might look different, but the blood runs out the same color. Consequently, everyone has been locked down. I'm not sure what my former Asian, Mexican National, and American Indian students think about this: Had they known they were going to get locked down anyway, they might have broken some rules first, to at least feel like they deserved it.

I learned something about dedication tonight, and, to be honest, it creeped me out. My students were talking about the lengths to which some people will go to secrete weapons (I first accidentally typed excrete, which should give you a hint as to one of the standard hiding places: Putting something there is called "going to the hoop," or sometimes "putting it in the safe," or "packing the trunk"), and we found ourselves talking about a prisoner at Pelican Bay who has recently been in the news. He's in the SHU, Security Housing Unit (which, if you recall, is essentially solitary confinement) as a member of the Aryan Brotherhood, a prison gang.

Now, there are two ways to end up in the SHU. One is to violate prison rules: use drugs, have weapons, assault someone. One of my former students—an excellent writer whom I liked very much—should any day now be getting out of the SHU. After a riot in which, to my understanding, he did not participate, he was sitting on the yard along with other prisoners, hands cuffed behind his back, waiting to be taken to the (cold) showers to wash off pepper spray guards had fogged in to stop the fighting. A guard came to help him up, and my student said, "Don't touch me."

The guard responded, "Don't waste my time."

"I'll get up on my own."

The guard reached to help him up, and my former student put his shoulder into the man's belly. It was stupid, impotent, and, to my mind, a manifestation of misplaced rage. It was also, according to the California Department of Corrections, assaulting a staff officer. My student was sentenced to eighteen months in the SHU.

The other primary way a person can be sentenced to the SHU is to be "validated" by prison administrators as a member of a prison gang, that is, a gang that exists exclusively or almost exclusively in-

CRIMINALS

side prisons. The main prison gangs around here include the Mexican Mafia, commonly called the "Southern Structure," with members being called southerns, or sureños; La Nuestra Familia, or Northern Structure, with members called northerns, or norteños; the Black Guerrilla Family; the Aryan Brotherhood; and the Nazi Low-Riders. The first two are Hispanic, the third is African American, and the final two are white.

Relations between the groups don't break down strictly along racial lines, as one might expect. The greatest enmity is between the northerns and southerns, who are reported to have a "kill on sight" relationship. Other alliances spread out from there, as the Mexican Mafia and the Aryan Brotherhood work fairly closely together, and in opposition to this the northerns find themselves working with the Black Guerrilla Family, and, more broadly, with African Americans.

Race relations in prison are complicated. According to my students, most if not all of the prisoners are racists. One told me, "I wasn't racist when I came to prison, but I am now. It's almost impossible not to be a racist here." Another of my students calls prison a fractured mirror of society. They've told me that inmate rules exist to keep races separate. For example, a white shouldn't smoke after a black, meaning if a black offers a white his cigarette, the white shouldn't take it if the black man has already taken a puff. If you're white and like basketball, but blacks are often on the court, you're out of luck. You *can* play once in a while, but play too often and you'll be warned by fellow whites not to fraternize. Ignore the warning and you may be beaten. Card games, too, are segregated, if they're for fun. Playing for money, though, the only color that matters is green. The students who told me these rules are white; they said similar rules exist for blacks.

I also know that when a race riot takes place on the yard (and I have to say, they don't generally happen *that* often) if you're a prisoner, you participate. If you're a pacifist, and politicized, working for racial cooperation on the inside, you still participate: DeWayne Holmes, for example, framed for murder by the police because of his work making peace between Bloods and Crips, still had to "put in work" during riots, even when that meant fighting childhood friends. If you're almost ready to be paroled, you still participate: One former student had sixty days left till release when the big battle occurred last year. He had no choice but to fight. Consequently, he pulled a SHU term, with release similarly pushed back.

Within the confines of the arts-in-corrections classrooms, however, the prisoners all seem to get along great, no matter their race (or sexual orientation, for that matter: I've had a few openly homosexual students in classes, and, at least in the classroom, I've noticed significantly more acceptance and less homophobia than in mainstream culture). I've never seen even any latent hostility.

Although prison gangs are segregated along racial lines, they're not primarily racist organizations, but instead exist to serve a melange of mutual-protection and organized-crime purposes, with the question of race ever present but often secondary. The La Nuestra Familia, for example, was established in Soledad prison in California in the mid-1960s to protect younger rural Hispanic inmates from other prisoners, especially members of the Mexican Mafia. And in a microcosm of the realpolitik of nation-states, self-defense was soon redefined as control of resources, in this case, control over the introduction of contraband into prison. Thus the self-protection organization evolved into a criminal syndicate. Likewise, the Mexican Mafia works not only to instill ethnic solidarity and Latino pride ("Those six AM calisthenics would be too much for this old body," one nonmember told me, explaining why he never joined) but also to smuggle in narcotics. Similarly, although members of the Aryan Brotherhood often wear white supremacist tattoos and espouse a segregationist or supremacist ideology, central goals of the members in practice, according to a report by the Florida State Department of Corrections, include "getting high and getting over," in other words, making their stay in prison as comfortable as possible. This would include, as before and as always, the control of resources. Another couple of examples of the nebulous relationship between race and prison gangs include the fact that there are Jews in the Nazi Low Riders, and that 60 percent of the crimes committed by the NLR, including

CRIMINALS

murder, are perpetrated against other whites. A gang-unit cop in Los Angeles said, and this is probably true for other gangs, too (come to think of it, it's probably true all across the culture), "Business comes first for the NLR." The relationship between race and business was articulated well by another gang-unit cop: "They [Nazi Low Riders] hate blacks not just for being black but because blacks are a prison power group and a threat." Although the Black Guerrilla Family was founded by Black Panther member George Jackson with the explicit goals of struggling to maintain dignity in prison, eradicating racism, and overthrowing the United States government, its emphasis, too, has shifted away from the revolutionary and toward the more mundanely criminal.

Gang validation by prison administrators is a tricky thing. At least in California, validation requires three pieces of evidence, which can include everything from the obviously incriminating—confessions, gang tattoos, confiscated gang constitutions—to the arbitrary and dubious—testimony from "confidential informants" (whom the suspected gang member is not allowed to confront), anonymous "snitch notes," information in letters from home, association with known gang members (which, I've been told, can include your cellie, which seems unfair, since your cellmate is assigned to you by prison administrators).

Validation is an administrative decision, not a judicial one. Prisoners are given no trial, and they see neither their accusers nor the evidence. The decision is final. Even presuming that such nontrials are just and appropriate in the first place, it's easy to see how the rules of evidence could be twisted to punish those who find disfavor with prison administrators. Those validated could then include not only those who truly are a danger to other people but also those who are more precisely a danger to the established order or the administration's control, for example, revolutionaries and others whose politics the administrators don't like; jailhouse lawyers and others who, from the perspective of the prisoners, force administrators to obey the law, and from the perspective of the administration, file frivolous lawsuits merely to waste everybody's time; jailhouse doctors and oth-

THE CULTURE OF MAKE BELIEVE

ers who question the quality of care provided by prison doctors; others who agitate for better conditions; and gang truce organizers, because it's in the interests of guards and administrators for prisoners to be at odds with each other. A former prisoner told a reporter for the *Christian Science Monitor*, "Inmates dramatically outnumber guards, so [the prison] has a vested interest in keeping the inmate population divided against itself rather than [against] them. Guards need to channel any kind of unrest away from themselves and onto another group." Or ask an administrator: A San Francisco jail warden told National Public Radio, "If you're an officer and you've gotta supervise two hundred people on a tier, it's a lot easier for you if that tier is split up into five bickering factions rather than having two hundred people all looking at you as, 'Gee, why should we comply with the rules and regulations he's putting out?' So there is also that sort of staff encouragement of this kind of thing in many institutions."

Validated gang members are sent to the SHU. What it would be like to live inside there for any length of time would be unimaginable to most people. I have a hard enough time—looking now out my window at the wind playing with the tips of redwood branches, and thinking about walking outside to look at the pond, then maybe afterward wandering through the forest to my mom's house just to say hi and see what she's doing—imagining being confined to regular cells, with their arrow-slit windows (that don't open, for obvious reasons), their concrete walls and locked doors made of iron bars and Plexiglas, their stainless steel toilets next to bunks, their rigid schedules for eating, showering, socializing. In the SHU, prisoners are locked in to their cells (either by themselves or with one other person) for twenty-three or more hours per day. The cells have no windows, and all air is recycled. Their only access to the outside world is the door slot through which their meal trays are handed, and through which they extend their hands to be cuffed before they're escorted to their biweekly showers, or to the exercise yard, a concrete courtyard with no view of any horizon, no view of any living creature save guards and the occasional seagull that flies directly overhead. Their cells are monitored twenty-four hours per day by closed-circuit tele-

CRiMiNALS

vision. These prisoners have neither jobs nor educational programs, limited access to telephones, and noncontact visits with their family: separated by bulletproof glass, speaking through bugged and tinny intercoms. I have taught prisoners who were in the SHU or its predecessors for up to eighteen years. That's 6,574 days, including leap years, 157,776 hours, each hour not so very distinguishable from the hour before. Some former Black Panthers and other revolutionaries have been in solitary since the 1970s.

I asked one student how he spent his five years in the SHU, and he said, "Watching television."

"Did you do anything else?"

"I watched television."

Others write. In order to maintain discipline, some gangs assign essays—"By tomorrow I want 10,000 words on the topic of honor, on one page"—thereby accomplishing something I had thought heretofore impossible: making people dislike writing even more intensely than did their junior high and high school English teachers. Many people have a saddle-shaped callus near the tip of their index finger from writing so much. Others in SHU write on their own. And others practice martial arts, or do push-ups and burpees. A thousand burpees at a time. And still others go insane, covering themselves in shit, or wailing, or talking to themselves. Some hallucinate. Some kill themselves. Most merely put in time, day after day, year after year.

For those validated as gang members, there are precisely three ways out of the SHU: they can die, they can parole at the end of their term, or they can "debrief," or tell everything they know about the gang. Those who were validated inaccurately—those who, in fact, are not gang members—are in one type of impossible situation: With no secrets to reveal, they have no means to buy their freedom, and so should plan on spending a very long time alone. Those who are validated accurately are in an entirely different sort of impossible situation. Most of these gangs require members stay in for life. Attempting to leave—even without debriefing—is grounds to be killed. I talked to a former gang member who did not debrief, but left the gang because he found Jesus. "They knew I was telling the truth, so they wished me well," he said. "But if they would have thought I was faking it to get out, I wouldn't be standing here talking to you." For those who debrief, the stakes are even higher. Three former members of the Mexican Mafia provide a sobering case study, not because they debriefed, but because they acted as consultants to the Edward James Olmos film *American Me*, about the gang's rise. The film portrayed one of the Mexican Mafia's founders as having been raped in his youth. Because of this, the consultants were executed by the gang for treason. To name the names of other gang members, and to reveal secrets (give up game, as my students would say) such as how contraband is smuggled in or where weapons are hidden, would be to put a price on your own head. Tonight I learned a new bit of game, and no, this isn't the creepy thing I mentioned at the start of this section, and no, this isn't the sort of game that could get someone killed for revealing it (I hasten to add) because by now it's relatively old news. Here it is: A new sleight-of-hand trick had been developed by someone in SHU to enable inmates to hide knives during strip searches. Someone described this trick while debriefing, then, to demonstrate it, he smuggled a knife past two of the most diligent guards. Afterward, he showed them how to do it and what to look for. (Not, obviously, having been privy to their discussions myself, I have no idea what the trick is.) Once they've debriefed, former gang members take basic education classes as well as classes to help boost their self-esteem. When these classes are finished, the inmates are sent to special yards with other former gang members. To step foot onto the regular yard would be to die.

The whole situation, I think, is pretty nasty. I don't like prisons. I don't like gangs. I don't like violence. I don't like confining people in tiny cells. I don't like people hiding knives. I don't like people in uniforms holding clubs and pepper spray, then strip-searching people who are hiding knives because they want to stab other people in tiny cells or because they want to stab people in uniforms. I don't like people behind walls fighting over who gets to control the flow of drugs into the enclosed space. I don't like the walls. I don't like the drugs. I don't like the pointlessness of the whole thing. I do like the

CRIMINALS

people—my students, my supervisor—and I like the classes: basic education, self-esteem, art, and creative writing (especially the creative writing).

Finally we get to what I learned tonight. A couple of weeks ago a woman in San Francisco was killed by a dog as she stood in the hallway of her apartment building, just outside her door. The dog, it ends up, was owned by a guy here in the SHU. There are two versions as to why he owned the dog. His version was that because he was going to be stuck in this cell for the rest of his life, he wanted to at least be able to vicariously have a pet. Those who kept the dog for him sent him hundreds of pictures of the animal. Officials at the prison suggested instead that, in contravention of prison rules, he was running a business out of his cell. The business was that of supplying attack dogs—the breed is called presa canaria, and they look pretty damn big, with square heads and massive jaws—for use by the Mexican Mafia to guard their meth labs. An FBI investigation concurred with the inmate's, not the prison administration's, version of the story. The caretakers of the dog were the guy's attorneys, who also, as of the week of the killing, became his adopted parents.

The guy's name is Cornfed, and he's doing a life term in the SHU. He's about six feet four inches, and buff. From what I've heard he spends his time in the cell bodybuilding and practicing death kicks. Another thing I heard is that by practicing a very specific type of muscle control, he is able to hide a small knife in folds of muscle on the "wings" that spread under his arms at the side of his chest. Even when he has his hands raised during strip searches he's able to clench the knife in place. Administrators found this out when someone debriefed, and still the knife was hidden well enough that it took guards three tries to find it, even when they knew precisely where to look. Now to the dedication manifested by Cornfed. That wasn't the only knife he had hidden. He'd dug a hole into his leg, on the inside of his calf, and there he kept a shank, plastic, presumably, so it wouldn't set off metal detectors, embedded in his flesh. You couldn't see the slight bulge for the tattoos and muscles. Of course he had to keep the wound fresh so it wouldn't scar over, or he'd never have been able to

THE CULTURE OF MAKE BELIEVE

access the knife when he needed or wanted it. To maintain an open wound in your leg so you can hide a weapon there would, it seems to me, require a significant—and creepy—dedication to violence.

I guess all of this is yet another roundabout way of getting at the question of hate. By talking about the violence perpetrated by our economic, governmental, and social systems, I don't mean to ignore violence perpetrated by those not acting inside of this system, and by stating that our judicial and penal systems form a massive interlocking set of racist and terrorist organizations (a terrorist organization is defined, remember, as one that deters through terror) I don't mean to gloss over the violence perpetrated by those who are now, for example, in prison. There are some scary people in there. I don't deny that. From what little I've heard, I'm not sure I would like to have Cornfed angry at me: He seems a very resourceful person who might hurt people when he deems it necessary (I'm reasonably sure the knives weren't for buttering his bread), and it seems possible, once again, from what little I've read, that he might be the type who would follow the advice of Stephen Worth, modified to fit his circumstances, and use all the force available to him until whatever perceived threat to him was removed. (Note to any of Cornfed's friends who may be reading this: I recognize it's also possible that he's an extremely nice guy, perfectly swell, and no offense is meant by anything I've said. Really. I swear. And, heh, put down the knife, okay?)

Although I don't ask what my students are in for, I know from stories they've written and stories they've told me that I've worked with drug smugglers, and I've worked with murderers. I've worked with pimps. I've worked with rapists. I've worked with armed robbers, and I've worked with burglars. I've worked with Meth cooks with rotting teeth, and one fellow whose face was taken off in a meth lab explosion. One former student had been shot during a drug deal at a party; he grabbed the gun, pistol-whipped the man who shot him, put the barrel in the man's mouth, then counted the people in the room: six people, five bullets. He took the gun out of the man's mouth and said, "You're lucky this time." When he told me that story, I looked at him quizzically, and he said, simply, "Never leave a

CRiMiNALS

witness." One student put a screwdriver in his friend's neck because his gang demanded it of him. Another killed a couple of people in a drug deal gone bad.

Many of these people have obviously committed horrible crimes. Many of them I would not want as neighbors. The media call the inmates at this prison "the worst of the worst," and some of them have been to places and done things and hurt people in ways that are as unimaginable to me as are the conditions in their cells.

That's one way to look at them, and it's an important way to look at them. Another is to look at their faces, to enter into particular relationships with these particular men who have these particular backgrounds and have committed these particular crimes, for which they are paying their own particular prices: J.T., a white guy, a longtime junkie who's read more literature than I have. He said, "I tell my friends not to cry for me in here. At least I can get up in the morning. That's more than I can say for the person I murdered." I think about the pride on Charlie's face when he writes about volunteering to fight in Vietnam, and the eagerness that still rushes over him when he describes the drugs he got hooked on over there. He doesn't write much about his life after he got back. Then there's Hollins, the only man I've ever known who's actually read Joseph Conrad's *Nostromo*. His face betrayed no emotion when he wrote of watching his mother shoot his abusive father in the chest with a shotgun, or when he wrote about them living together afterward. He seemed more befuddled than anything when he wrote about the time he has spent inside institutions since he was eight. I just learned that another of my students—a young man now spending the rest of his life in prison—began living on the streets when he was six, sleeping in cardboard boxes, eating from Dumpsters. Or another student, since released, about twenty-two, who also had been inside since he was eight. He said to me, "I don't know how I'm going to survive out there. I don't know how to relate to people. I don't know anything but rage and fear." And, I thought, loneliness.

None of this excuses what they've done. Nothing does. But there are several reasons I write more about the hate that manifests

THE CULTURE OF MAKE BELIEVE

through our economy, government, and larger social systems than I do about the hate that manifests in the often vile acts that have been committed by prisoners or by others like them.

The first is that I can find no compelling reason to add my voice to the din condemning these men or their actions. Movies, television, magazines, newspapers, tinpot politicians left and right all make a buck off of demonizing these guys. The last time I checked, so-called nasty-ass motherfuckers already had a pretty bad reputation, with public relations currency running right around nil. And cop shows? You'll see a rogue cop once in a while, but always with the caveat that rogues are one in a hundred. Rarely do we see explorations of the systematic use of police and prisons to maintain the current social order.

And no matter how dangerous people in prison may seem, especially to those whose exposure to them has been primarily through *COPS*, *Dragnet*, *Key Largo*, *ConAir*, and *Natural Born Killers*, if we want to talk about real danger, we're talking about entirely the wrong group of people. The 1999 Uniform Crime Report put out by the Federal Bureau of Investigation reveals that there were 16,910 murders committed in the United States in 1998. Yet more people than that in the United States die every two weeks from cancer, which kills 450,000 Americans every year. Your odds of dying of cancer are roughly twenty-five times higher than your chances of getting murdered. But that's just life, right? Well, not exactly. Cancer rates are going up, even after adjusting for an aging population and for smoking (and let's not *even* talk about those nasty-ass motherfuckers in the tobacco industry). In other words, even nonsmokers are far more likely to get cancer now than one hundred years ago. Why? I asked Samuel Epstein, one of the world's foremost authorities on the carcinogenic effects of industrial pollutants in air, water, the workplace, and consumer products, and he said, "I think the answer is terribly simple. Parallel to the escalating incidence of cancer, there has been an explosive expansion of technologies—particularly in the petrochemical industry, which really took off in the early forties. Between 1940 and 1990, the total annual production of synthetic organic chemicals increased from one billion to more than six hundred bil-

CRIMINALS

lion pounds. Over the last few decades, our total environment has become pervasively contaminated with a wide range of toxic and carcinogenic chemicals, some of which are persistent—that is, long-lived. When I say 'total environment,' I mean our air, water, soil, consumer products, food, and workplace. Even our own body fats have become contaminated. This is true from the North Pole to the South, not only for humans but for a wide range of marine life and wildlife, as well." Of those 450,000 cancer deaths per year, Epstein says that far more than three hundred thousand are preventable. Asbestos, which has been known as a carcinogen at least since the 1920s, kills fifty thousand Americans per year, nearly three times as many as are murdered by those we call murderers.

We might be incarcerating the wrong people. Epstein has called for public health crimes trials, and testified before Congress that if for economic gain CEOs put in place practices that damage public health—in other words, that kill or injure innocent people—we should lock them up and throw away the keys.

What is true for murder is true as well for theft. The average armed robber nets about $250, and the average bank robber maybe several thousand. The average prison sentence for bank robbery is 9.4 years. The criminal collapse of the Savings and Loan industry in the 1980s—as of 1990, 50 percent of the failed S&Ls were considered criminal, having committed embezzlement, loan fraud, paper profit schemes involving subsidiaries and holding companies, and having acted out of conflicts-of-interest (as when, for example, owners lent money to themselves); in addition, money from union pension funds had been loaned to business partners, and then lost—cost American taxpayers $1.4 trillion, including interest. This amounts to $22,400 for every American family of four. Most of the crooks involved did not go to prison. Some didn't even lose their seats in the Senate or House of Representatives. George Bush Sr.'s son Neil cost taxpayers over a billion dollars with his failed S & L scheme, yet spent not a night in prison. Those few who were found guilty received average sentences of 1.9 years.

More generally, the Judiciary Subcommittee on Antitrust and

THE CULTURE OF MAKE BELIEVE

265

Monopoly has estimated that faulty goods, monopolistic practices, and other similar violations cost consumers around $200 billion per year. Of a paltry ninety-two people convicted of antitrust violations in 1993, ten were sentenced to prison, thirty-seven to probation, and forty-four received fines which were undoubtedly smaller than their profits. The median incarceration was six months, and the median probation was three years.

Rape. Politicians love to talk about locking up rapists. And, FBI definitions aside, what crime could be more hateful than rape? Some other forms of torture, I guess. Some types of murder. But rape is certainly an intimate manifestation of hatred. And who commits it? Well, first, a *lot* of men commit it: *one* out of four women in our culture are raped within their lifetimes. Second, the typical rapist is, Southern white male fantasies aside, not a strapping young black man with kinky hair, thick lips, and broad nose, nor is it, this time Hitler's fantasies aside, some black-haired Jew-boy. As Judith Herman, one of the world's foremost experts on the effects of psychological trauma, puts it, "The greater the degree of social relationship, the wider the latitude of permitted coercion, so that an act of forced sex committed by a stranger may be recognized as rape, while the same act committed by an acquaintance is not. Since most rapes are in fact committed by acquaintances and intimates, most rapes are not recognized by law. In marriage, many states grant a permanent and absolute prerogative for sexual access, and any degree of force is legally permitted." Once again, it is possible that the wrong people are in prison.

Not even prisoners like child molesters. For a prisoner to admit to having raped a child would be to sign his own death warrant, perhaps even more so than debriefing. Yet just as with the stereotypes we've been taught about who is a murderer and who is a rapist, the stereotype of child molesters as dirty old men with pasty faces and bad teeth haunting schoolyards, or, more recently, prowling the Internet, paints a picture that distracts us from the real points of danger. A child is far more likely to be molested by her own relatives than by anyone she meets on the Internet. The gold standard study

CRIMINALS

for prevalence of childhood sexual abuse suggests that 16 percent of all women have been sexually abused by a relative before they turn eighteen, with 4½ percent of all women having been abused by their fathers. Extrapolation implies maybe forty-four million women in the United States were molested as children by relatives, with twelve million of these having been molested by their fathers. This is not to speak of the little boys molested by relatives.

Nearly all of my students at the prison are there, one way or another, because of drugs. There have been songs written damning—*god*damning—the pusher man. But anybody who has been paying any attention at all for the last fifty years knows that the CIA has been up to its nostrils in the drug trade from the organization's inception (and, of course, Britain used force of arms—and corporate structures—to addict generations of Chinese to opium simply to make money). Because World War II interrupted global shipping, the number of heroin addicts in the United States dropped to twenty thousand in 1944–45, only a tenth of what it had been twenty years prior. But after World War II the CIA allied itself with the Corsican underground against the communists and unionists in Marseille (just as the Gestapo had done during the war), which turned that port into a major supplier of heroin to the States. The CIA ran drugs out of Asia's Golden Triangle, and then it ran them—or, at the *very* least, turned a blind eye as those it worked with ran them—into American inner cities. As Alfred McCoy concludes in his classic *The Politics of Heroin: CIA Complicity in the Global Drug Trade*, "Over the past twenty years, the CIA has moved from local transport of raw opium in the remote mountains of Laos to apparent complicity in the bulk transport of pure cocaine directly into the United States or the mass manufacture of heroin for the U.S. market. Finally, America's drug epidemics have been fueled by narcotics supplied from areas of major CIA operations, while periods of reduced heroin use coincide with the absence of CIA activity."

So, the first reason I've been emphasizing different purveyors of hate in this book more than perhaps people would normally expect is

THE CULTURE OF MAKE BELIEVE

that I think people have been looking in all too easy places, and thus blinding themselves to far greater dangers.

The second reason is that prison is just, as my student said, a fractured mirror of society anyway. A couple of years ago I talked to Luis Rodriguez, the author of *La Vida Loca: Always Running: Gang Days in L.A.*, and a former gang member who got out through the literature of revolution. He said, "One of the reasons these kids are so violent is that they pick up and distort many of the values of mainstream society. 'Survival of the fittest.' 'Kill or be killed.' Gang kids always say this. But where did they get it from? They got it from the larger society. That's capitalism in a nutshell. The whole social order. Now, most business people aren't actually going to kill somebody—"

I interrupted to say, "Not with their own hands. . . ."

He nodded, then continued, "but they'll find ways to step on people, undermine and manipulate them, crush them. Everybody does it. You go to the stock market, you go to the board room, and you see kill or be killed in action. People trying to oversell, undersell, trying to kill their opposition."

He stopped, then started again. "If you think about it, many of these gangs are creating capitalist worlds in their own little marginalized, impoverished ways. For example, drugs become their industry. And they literally kill and allow themselves to be killed just to have the drug sales. They become very good and adept capitalists. They learn accounting, they learn about money and what to do with it. But their business ventures aren't legitimatized by society as a whole, so they aren't able to invest or hold on to the money, which means they won't have much to show for it after all their years in business. But none of that really matters, because by becoming capitalists—illegitimate as their business may be—they've already bought into the whole system."

"Yet they're deprived," I responded, "of what they need most, which is larger social esteem."

He said, "They're not given any approval. They're not given college scholarships to further their business sense. So they stay in their

CRIMINALS

own destructive business making money. Of course they make nowhere near the money most people think. Instead they often end up with a bunch of other people who don't get approval, which is to say in prison. What this means is that prison is full of these entrepreneurs and others who know how to make money. They would be thriving capitalists in another environment. They're not. They're now sitting in prison because they bought into the system. And they're the first ones to tell you, 'I was just trying to make money.' There's a gangsta rap song called, 'If it don't make dollars it don't make sense.' I remember going to a juvenile hall and doing some poetry. Afterwards, this one guy got up and asked, 'Is there money in poetry?'

"'Actually there is, but that's not why I do it. I do it because I have the love and the calling.'

"He said, 'Forget that stuff. If it don't make dollars it don't make sense.'

"I looked at the kid and I thought, Who taught him that? The truth is that we all taught him that. Every commercial on TV, every Saturday morning cartoon, everything pushes him that direction. But instead of him being a thriving pillar of the community, he's in prison. This is how far 'If it don't make dollars it don't make sense' has taken him. But he's just trying to be part of what society says he should be."

The third reason for my focus is that I'm far more interested in, and frightened of, hate allied with power than I am of less potent hate. And by any real measure, these prisoners, to take an easy example of some group hated for their presupposed hatefulness, are pretty powerless. Most of them do not even have the power any longer of movement. My student who got the eighteen-month SHU term for putting his shoulder into the guard's belly had told me he wanted at some time to be transferred from level four to level three, because he wanted to have a night yard. He hadn't seen the stars since he'd been arrested, and wanted more than anything to see again the night sky.

The question of relative power is also one of the reasons I write more about hatred as it's manifested in mainstream white culture, and

THE CULTURE OF MAKE BELIEVE

more about atrocities committed by this culture, than I write about hatred manifested by, and atrocities committed by, say, black males. I'm not suggesting black men do not hate, nor that they do not commit atrocities. To do so would be absurd. I have seen hate in the faces of some of my students, and in some of my black friends. But by and large black culture does not wield the same sort of power as does white culture, making *on a social scale* white hatred far more dangerous. Put me by myself in a room with five black men who happen to be partial to violence, and who, for whatever reason, hate me (either personally or because of my race) and, balance of power shifted, I will be immediately and vitally interested in the dynamics of black male hatred, especially as manifested by these particular men who are too damn particularly close to me right now. But it's not black males who are enslaving the planet and its peoples. It is not the African cultures, nor African-American culture. It is white Western European civilization. I want to understand and disarm this more immediate threat. Just as, faced with these hateful and hypothetical black men, I would drop my concern for less immediate threats, to be picked up when the primary threat is gone, if we ever figure out how to get rid of our current hate-driven dominant culture, maybe I'll start to pick on someone else.

This leads to the fourth reason I focus on white culture. I'm no fan of Christianity, but I think Jesus was a pretty smart fellow, and I've tried to take to heart what he said about not worrying about the mote in my brother's eye while I've got a beam in my own. I'm white. I'm civilized. I was raised upper middle class. I was raised Christian. I'm not black. I'm not indigenous. I'm not Hispanic. I'm a man. I'm not going to write much about black traders in Africa who assisted white gatherers of slaves, nor black kings who conducted battles in order to procure these slaves for market (some contemporaries argued that the slavers were actually saving black lives because those captured would otherwise "be put to death [by their captors] if they had not the means of disposing of them," while others argued that this logic was backward, that the wars "owe their origin to the yearly number of slaves . . . the island traders, suppose will be wanted by the

CRIMINALS

vessels which arrive on the coast"). Nor am I going to write much about Indian scouts who assisted the (white) cavalry in their genocidal project against American Indians. Those are not the stories of my people. I want to understand my own people, and our shared history.

It is not blacks who have lynched whites, but whites who have lynched blacks. It was not blacks who enslaved whites, but whites who enslaved blacks, and other whites. It was not Indians who attempted to exterminate whites, but the other way around. I want to understand the social and cultural psychology that would lead to all of this.

I want to tell you two stories. The first is an account of a lynching. The second an account of a conversation. Before I started doing research for this book, I'd presumed, first, that lynchings were primarily a nineteenth-century phenomenon. Not so at all. Lynchings were an extremely popular form of entertainment, drawing crowds numbering into the several thousands—making them more a pastime or celebration than they were some more furtive pleasure on the part of a few perpetrators—from before the 1860s and at least into the 1920s, with sporadic encores into the 1930s. I'd presumed also that lynchings almost always consisted of black men, or occasionally women (and, rarely, a white man), being hanged by groups of white men, and, once again, occasionally women. The images that came to mind were from photographs I'd seen on the fronts of old picture postcards, a black man hanging from a lamppost or tall tree, his neck stretched perhaps twice its normal length, head cocked at that angle that lets you know the spine is severed, the life gone. What was once a person is now a sack of skin. In the background, the huge crowds, the smiling faces.

But I've since learned lynchings often involved fire. Sometimes the victims were burned after they were dead, and sometimes they were burned before. And sometimes when they were burned, nobody bothered to hang them. One of the latter is the story I want to tell now. Henry Lowry was a black man who died on January 26, 1921. It's pretty clear that prior to that he had murdered the man who owned the farm where he lived and worked, and that he had killed

THE CULTURE OF MAKE BELIEVE

that man's daughter as well. He was apprehended for this crime, and, while being transported, was taken from a train "by a mob of determined men." The men were comfortable enough with their plan of action—announced to everyone as taking Lowry to the scene of his crime and killing him at six that evening—to not wear masks, and to stop for lunch at a restaurant. They took Lowry inside with them while they ate. Although the scene drew some attention, a newspaper reported, "Nothing has occurred to mar the serenity of the party's journey. The party ate leisurely and after finishing went to E.A. Harrold's store, where a quantity of rope was purchased."

The men took Lowry to the scene of his crime, where six hundred people gathered to watch the man die. The crowd included Lowry's wife and children, clearly feeling something different than the rest of the people there. I do not think I can do better than the reporter for the *Memphis Press*, in describing what took place, who wrote, "The setting was a natural ampitheater between two bluffs, with the Mississippi River on one side and a huge lake, created by backwater, on the other. The negro was chained to a log. Members of the mob placed a small pile of dry leaves around his feet. Gasoline was then poured onto the leaves, and the carrying out of the death sentence was under way.

"Inch by inch the negro was fairly cooked to death. Lowry retained consciousness for forty minutes. Not once did he whimper or beg for mercy.

"As flesh began to drop away from his legs, and they were reduced to bones, once or twice he attempted to pick up hot coals and swallow them in order to hasten death. Each time the coals were kicked from his grasp by members of the mob.

"As the flames reached his abdomen, two men closed in on him and began to question him. . . . It resembled a courtroom scene, with prosecuting attorney and court reporter. . . . Words fail to describe the sufferings of the negro. Yet only once did he cry out. This was shortly before he lost consciousness as flames began to lick at his chest and face. He cried out some appeal to one of the many negro lodges of which he was a member.

CRIMINALS

"Then gasoline was poured over his head and it was only a few minutes until he had been reduced to ashes.

"After Lowry had been reduced to a charred mass, members of the mob headed in the direction of Osceola. It was whispered that they were planning to raid the jails at Marion and Blytheville in order to secure possession of five more negroes, in order to raise the total number lynched to an even half-dozen.

"The mob, after riding back and forth across the country for several hours, finally began to disperse and go home. It was evident that the leaders were practically exhausted after their long trip with Lowry."

That is why I want to focus on white hatred.

The other story I want to tell is of a conversation I had a few months ago, with a documentary film producer for WGBH, the big public television station in Boston. She called me at 6:30 one morning, introduced herself, said she was thinking of making a film about whether Ted Kaczynski was representative of a new breed of environmentalist willing to commit violence, and asked if it was a good time to talk. I told her I'd been writing till about 3:00 that morning, so perhaps. . . .

She said, "Why don't I give you ten minutes so you can have a cup of coffee, and I'll call you back."

Ten minutes wouldn't help, so I told her that I could talk about the possibility of violence against the system on a moment's notice. "Fire away," I said.

She told me a very little about the project, and then said, "The one thing I know for sure is that I wouldn't want to make a film that glorified a killer."

"I'm glad for that," I said. "I trust you'd hold other subjects to that same standard."

"What do you mean?" she asked.

"George Bush. Bill Clinton. Al Gore. George Bush the younger."

"I have no idea what you're talking about."

"Sanctions against Iraq kill eighteen thousand people every month," I said. "Half of them children under five. So far as Gore, his

THE CULTURE OF MAKE BELIEVE

family goes way back with Occidental Petroleum, which as we speak is committing genocide against the U'Wa in—"

She cut me off: "That has nothing to do with what we're talking about."

"It has everything to do with what we're talking about. What's the difference between sending mailbombs or sending missiles, except that the missiles kill a hell of a lot more people?"

"Violence is black and white," she said.

I've thought about her statement for months now, and I'm still not sure what she's talking about. I said, "Do you pay taxes?"

"Yes," she said, warily.

"Then you've killed tons of people, probably a lot more than Kaczynski. At least he didn't pay taxes."

"Don't be insulting," she said.

"I'm not. I'm just telling the truth, which is that your tax dollars have gone to the U.S. military. Just because you haven't pulled the trigger, doesn't mean you're off the hook."

"This is ridiculous," she said. She got off the phone soon after.

That conversation is precisely why I want to focus on the manifestations of hate at which we normally do not look.

CRIMINALS

THE GREATEST EVIL IS NOT NOW DONE IN THOSE SORDID "DENS OF CRIME" THAT DICKENS LOVED TO PAINT. IT IS NOT DONE EVEN IN CONCENTRATION CAMPS AND LABOUR CAMPS. IN THOSE WE SEE ITS FINAL RESULT. BUT IT IS CONCEIVED AND ORDERED (MOVED, SECONDED, CARRIED, AND MINUTED) IN CLEAN, CARPETED, WARMED AND WELL-LIGHTED OFFICES, BY QUIET MEN WITH WHITE COLLARS AND CUT FINGERNAILS AND SMOOTH-SHAVEN CHEEKS WHO DO NOT NEED TO RAISE THEIR VOICE. HENCE, NATURALLY ENOUGH, MY SYMBOL FOR HELL IS SOMETHING LIKE THE BUREAUCRACY OF A POLICE STATE OR THE OFFICES OF A THOROUGHLY NASTY BUSINESS CONCERN.

C.S. LEWIS

KiLLeRS

SURPRISINGLY ENOUGH—and this statement may dismay a lot of my liberal friends—I'm not 100 percent sold on the idea of abolishing prisons, or even of doing away with the death penalty. I believe that there are actions people can commit that cause them to forfeit their right to live in society, and even actions they can commit that cause them to forfeit their right to live.

That's not to say I don't want to abolish prisons as they presently exist, because I do. And it's also not to say I support the death penalty as it presently exists, because I don't.

The main argument I've heard to support the existence and expansion of prisons is public safety (I've seen the way prisoners are warehoused, so don't even *think* about bringing up the notion of rehabilitation): We've got to keep these dangerous people behind bars so that our streets are safe. It's ironic that prison proponents mention streets in this context: Last year I talked to anticar activist Jan Lundberg, who told me that more than five hundred thousand people worldwide die each year in road accidents: "Two-thirds of these deaths involve pedestrians," he said, "of which one-third are children. Just in the United States about forty-two thousand people die per year because of auto collisions, nearly as many as the total number of Americans killed in Vietnam. Everybody knows someone who has died or been seriously injured in a car crash, yet cars have insinuated themselves into our social life—and into our psyches—so thoroughly that we somehow accept these deaths as inevitable, or not shocking, as opposed to perceiving them for what they are: a direct and predictable result of choosing to base our economic and social systems on this particular piece of technology." What's worse is that even more people die each year from respiratory illness stemming from auto-related airborne toxins than die from traffic crashes.

Lundberg also said to me, "We have become slaves to these machines. If a group of aliens came to this planet and said they would bring us all sorts of goodies like jet skis, tomatoes in January, computers, and so on (or at least they would bring them to the richest of us), on the multiple conditions that we offer up to them a yearly sacrifice of a half-million human lives, change our planet's climate, individually spend increasing amounts of time serving them, and socially devote an ever-increasing amount of land and other resources to their service, we would rebel in a flash. Or at least I hope we would. But that's the reality we face. And that's the reality we accept. It's a reality we don't even talk about. More teenagers are killed by cars across the U.S. every afternoon than the fourteen high schoolers gunned down in Littleton. Everybody says that living in an inner city is dangerous, that you're going to get shot. But the truth is that because of car crashes, suburbs are statistically far more dangerous places to live. I've proven this to people, and they still refuse to walk with me in downtown Seattle, but they're perfectly happy to get in a car, just because it's normal. We don't talk about any of this because *this* violence—the violence of U.S. transportation policies—is so engrained into our psyches that we believe it is inevitable, and not the result of policy decisions and subsidies."

KILLERS

It seems also that if prisons were really about public safety, those responsible for the three hundred thousand preventable cancer deaths per year would be behind bars. And if prisons were about protecting property, those who looted the Savings and Loans would be serving terms commensurate with the amount they cost the public (exactly how many years would Neil Bush's billion dollars add up to?). Or, to combine the personal and the fiscal, if prisons were designed to both further public safety *and* protect our property, I can think of no better use than that they house those who have designed and put in place our nuclear weapons programs, for which every American man, woman, and child has been forced to pay more than twenty-one thousand dollars. We have received for this money not only the terror of living under the threat of nuclear annihilation, but, as a bonus (free with the purchase of a complete nuclear arsenal; some restrictions may apply), several major river systems that have been irradiated beyond any foreseeable eventual recovery, a generation of downwinders in eastern Washington, southern Nevada and Utah, Colorado, and several other states that have found themselves beset by leukemia and other cancers, and Rocky Flats, the Hanford Nuclear Reservations, Oak Ridge Reservation, and the Savannah River Site have all been hopelessly irradiated. But wait! There's more! For that same twenty-one thousand dollars we have received literally millions of tons of materials that will be dangerous in some cases for a quarter to half a million years. Under a just and reasonable judicial and penal system concerned with public safety and order, the nasty-ass motherfuckers—or, depending on your perspective, the decent white men—who put in place the policies leading to these programs would be attending my creative writing classes, that is, when level four prisoners aren't locked down. (Note to the friends of George Bush or any other president who may be reading this: I recognize it's also possible the presidents have been extremely nice guys, perfectly swell, and no offense is meant by anything I've said. Really. I swear. And, heh, put down the nuclear warhead, okay?)

Inhumane as SHU units across the country undoubtedly are, I'm not certain that I am unalterably opposed even to them. I've heard it said that approximately the same number of people control 95 percent of the world's economy as are in solitary confinement in the United States. There can be little doubt as to which group has killed the greater number of people. The same would hold true for which group has stolen the most, especially if we include resources, and which group has most damaged the planet. It is entirely possible that we have the wrong population in solitary. But, of course, so long as those in power decide who goes to prison, those in power will not go to prison.

Even if we just talk about street crime, the argument that prisons lend themselves to safe streets still doesn't work. In her book *The American Prison Business*, Jessica Mitford cited *The President's Commission on Causes and Prevention of Violence*: "Of 100 major crimes [felonies], 50 are reported to the police. For 50 incidents reported, 12 people are arrested. Of the 12 arrested, 6 are convicted of anything—not necessarily of the offense reported. Of the 6 who are convicted, 1.5 go to prison or jail." As Mitford says, "Does not the law-abiding citizen feel a twinge of self-satisfaction in these days of mounting terror of crime and criminals as he drives by the fastness of San Quentin or Sing Sing to think that behind these walls are locked away those ruffians who would rape his daughter, steal his television set, mug him on the street? His belief that the prison protects him is, it turns out, illusory. Only a miniscule fraction of lawbreakers are in prison, the vast majority are all around us in the community."

Short of imprisoning even greater numbers of Americans, if tough-on-crime politicians really want to make streets and homes safe, they might consider eliminating some of the causes of crime: the gap between rich and poor (don't hold your breath for this one to be addressed); child abuse (ditto for this one); glorification of violence (see above); and an oppressive reality that needs to be neutralized through the use of drugs.

My main problem with prisons—apart from their racism and inhumanity—is that damn blindness I've been trying to get at through this whole book: Why do we so severely punish some forms of violence while serenely ignoring, or worse, rewarding, far more egregious varieties? A couple more stories might help make this clear. The first has to do with another ex-student, who nearly always wrote stories of his

KILLERS

adventures on the street, most of which were, considering where he now lives, not all that horrific: drag races, getting stoned, chasing girls, minor burglaries. But one day he wrote the story of what he did that brought him to prison. He'd been at a party, high on crack (the smell, he'd said, sweet and smooth, was almost as good as that first hit) when someone approached him and said, "Are you down?"

I'd interrupted his reading of the story to ask what that meant. Another student laughed in a friendly way and used his index finger to paint a square in the air before him, indicating what I was. The first student—the writer—said, "It means, 'Are you ready?' or 'Are you tough?'"

He read the rest of his story. The two went into the backyard to fight. My student killed the other person. I do not know how. My student is in his early twenties. He will be in prison for a very long time. I've often wondered—surely not as often as he has—how his life would have been different had he stayed at home that night, or had he for whatever reason not fought the other man.

I sometimes contrast him in my mind with the lives that some of my other students lived on the street, which were often murders and other tragedies waiting to happen. When your gig is armed robbery, eventually you'll pull the trigger. I asked my students once to write from the prompt *panic*. One student, who normally wrote from any prompt I gave, sat and stared at his paper, then finally put down his pencil and stared across the room. Another student asked what was wrong. The first said, "I've never panicked."

"Not even when you saw those bodies on the floor?"

"They were dead. What was I going to do about them then?"

Here is a riddle for you, one that is not very funny. Question: What do you get when you cross a drug habit, guns, and a quick temper? Answer: Two consecutive life terms for murder, with an earliest release date of 2026.

That's the first story about prisons I want to tell you.

The other story has to do with someone I have never met, and it has to do with the murder of more people than have been killed by all of my students, combined. In fact, it has to do with the killing of more people than have been killed by everyone at this prison, combined,

THE CULTURE OF MAKE BELIEVE

more people than have been killed by all of the people who have been executed by state and federal governments, combined.

Because in this story the bodies were disposed of quickly—dumped into the Narbado River, burned, buried in mass graves, hauled off by the military—no one will ever know how many people were killed by the forty tons of methyl isocyanate (MIC) released from Union Carbide's Bhopal, India, plant on December 3, 1984. Crematorium and cemetery records suggest more than eight thousand human beings died soon after the leak. Other estimates run as high as fifteen thousand, and death rates among those poisoned remain twice normal, meaning death counts continue to rise. For political and economic reasons the Indian government and Union Carbide both placed the number of dead at less than four thousand (far more, by the way, than the number killed in the World Trade Center and Pentagon bombings). Politics and economics aside, however, so many people died that a doctor at a local hospital noted, "We didn't even have enough space to keep the corpses. We stacked them one on top of another like they were bags of wheat." To find Bhopal after the toxic release one had merely to look for vultures circling overhead. In addition to the deaths, approximately thirty-two thousand people suffered injuries to their eyes and between two hundred thousand and five hundred thousand were otherwise injured. More than a decade later, people still suffered throat irritation, choking, chest pain and extensive damage to the lungs, vomiting, diarrhea and other gastrointestinal distress, damage to livers and kidneys, muscular weakness, altered consciousness and brain damage, miscarriages, stillbirths, birth defects, including children born with second- and third-degree burns across their bodies, profuse vaginal discharges, cervical erosion, the suppression of lactation. An estimated sixty thousand are permanently disabled. Even more carry psychological scars from having witnessed death on such a mass scale.

Eight thousand dead. Two hundred thousand injured. Any mere accounting of the dead and injured, however, is too abstract for our purposes, and false to the degree that it fails to express the event as experienced by a living being. Contrast the economic language of Union Carbide officials, who stated in the company's 1984 Annual Report that

KILLERS

"victims of the Bhopal tragedy could be fairly and adequately compensated without a material adverse effect on Union Carbide's financial condition" with that of a victim of poisoning: "They were dead, every one of them, hundreds of them dead. They were all trying to get away from the gas. The dying were urinating, defecating, and vomiting. . . . In a few minutes I will be dead. What will happen to my body? It will rot here, or someone may burn my remains in this chamber of death. . . . If ever there is a hell, it must look like Bhopal on that gas day. It looked like the end of the world." Another victim: "I was rendered unconscious by the gas, and they put me in a truck with corpses destined for the cremation ground. I awoke with the impact, when I was thrown from the truck onto a heap of dead bodies. My wife died. I have a four-month-old daughter, who is not well at all." The stories build on one another, hundreds of thousands of them, one for each victim. There was Habib Ali, who was awakened at home by the smell of the gas. Having believed the words of his employer, Union Carbide, he thought, "Thanks to Allah that it was only MIC and not phosgene, which killed people'; he survived, but would never work again. There were people who ran toward the plant and toward their death, never having been told of MIC's danger. There was twelve-year-old Sunil Kumar Rajput, who ran with his mother, father, and six siblings across the prevailing wind, hoping to reach the edge of the cloud; the wind shifted and only Sunil survived. There were Munnibai Balkishensingh and V. K. Sharma, both of whom worked at the Bhopal railroad station. Munnibai tried to flee but passed out, to awaken only at the moment she was set on fire to be cremated. Instead of fleeing, Sharma and three other railway employees telephoned other stations to stop traffic from entering Bhopal, and before they collapsed were able to warn passengers on an arriving train to stay on board. There was Sajda Bano, whose husband had been poisoned by a Union Carbide gas leak three years earlier. Not having heard Sharma's warning, she and her two sons stepped off the train and collapsed on the platform. There was Ajeeza Bi, who has had three miscarriages since she was gassed: "They were all born dead. All with black skin like the color of coal and all shrunken in size. The doctors never told me why such things are happening to me."

THE CULTURE OF MAKE BELIEVE

I have heard the Bhopal disaster referred to as an accident. I do not see the deaths as any more accidental than the killing of the woman in San Francisco by a dog trained to kill, nor the filling of prisons built to be filled. Union Carbide makes bulk industrial chemicals, many of which are poisonous, and it does so to make a profit. MIC is a pesticide, and therefore by definition a poison. Just how accidental is it that people are poisoned by an intentionally fabricated poison? To minimize costs and thereby maximize profits, Union Carbide reduced safety features at the Bhopal plant: Human power was cut in half; training in how to safely handle MIC was reduced from one year to five days; technical manuals were never translated into Hindi, the workers' native language; safety features were unusable for months at a time (for example, on a different occasion there was a fire at the plant, during which the plant's fire truck was unusable, sitting on a jack with all four tires removed; Carbide's response to the fire was to remove outspoken union leaders and entertain government officials at luxury hotels); a Union Carbide operating manual stated, "If odor or eye irritation is not detected, the MIC is not present," although MIC can't be smelled until it reaches concentrations one hundred times higher than the threshold for safe human exposure.

A couple of years ago I got into an argument with an old scientist friend about risk assessment. This is the process whereby someone wishing to build, for example, a chemical refinery, analyzes risks associated with various processes, and produces a document stating that, say, rates of leukemia will go up by maybe one case per hundred thousand, and so on. The same is done for other risks. These assessments are comprised of much guesswork, and I can say from having dissected far more than my share that they're also filled with fudging and outright lies, and a healthy (or unhealthy) dose of good old-fashioned obfuscation. Often, the documents state that there will be no adverse impact at all. My friend was saying that at some point the risks start to become minimal and it's no longer feasible to attempt to reduce them anymore. It becomes a matter of diminishing returns: It may cost a certain amount to cut the increase in leukemia to "only" one additional per hundred thousand, but it may cost ten times that much to reduce

KILLERS

it again by half. The same would hold true, obviously, for other risks. The question of diminishing returns, I told him, is not as big a problem as accountability. And I guess accountability is really what I've been talking about through this whole discussion of prisons. My students have been held accountable for their crimes. The student at the party killed someone, and it cost him his freedom. Other students stole or harmed people or corporations (one of my students was an industrial burglar: "I would never steal from an individual—that would be immoral—but big companies were absolutely fair game"), and for that they're giving up parts of their lives. I told my scientist friend that I thought the authors of these risk assessments ought to be held accountable for their predictions.

"Oh, I've heard that one," he said. "Make the CEOs and engineers live just downwind of the plant."

"Wait," I said.

He talked over me. "The problem is that so often these engineers go job to job, and of course the CEO will be in charge of plants all over the world."

"No," I said.

He continued, "Which plant are you going to have the CEO live next to? It just won't work."

"That's not what I was going to say," I said. "I was going to simply suggest that if an engineer and a CEO say that the cancer rate won't go up if they build a certain type of manufacturing facility, and after the facility is operational it ends up they were lying, or simply wrong, and the rate does go up—"

"You're not going to suggest prison, are you?"

"No, not at all," I responded. "I'm going to suggest a life for a life. They kill, they die. Isn't that how capital punishment is supposed to work?"

"You're not serious."

"I'd think that would be a deterrent."

"You're crazy," he said. "If they had to put their lives on the line, none of these facilities would ever be built."

I looked at him and smiled.

THE CULTURE OF MAKE BELIEVE

Late in the evening of December 2, 1984, water used to clean pipes found its way into a tank of MIC, triggering a chemical reaction that dramatically increased the tank's temperature and pressure. The MIC began to escape, and by 12:40 AM the leak was out of control. A siren sounded at 1:00 AM. but was quickly turned off so it wouldn't panic the people living nearby. The alarm would have awakened people, but at that point many of them may still not have known what to do: Union Carbide never told those living around the plant what the alarms meant. It was not turned on again until 2:00, long after a poisonous fog had blanketed the area for miles. No one associated with the company had contacted the police; even when the magistrate called the Union Carbide works manager, J. Mukund, at home, Mukund said, "Our technology just can't go wrong. We just can't have such leaks." A company official finally arrived at the police station at 3:00 AM to say that there had in fact been a leak but it was now under control.

Although Union Carbide was aware that MIC is one of the deadliest chemicals the company fabricates—having commissioned confidential research in 1963 that concluded methyl isocyanate "is highly toxic by both the peroral and skin penetration routes and presents a definite hazard to life by inhalation" and additional research in 1970 confirming that MIC is "highly toxic by inhalation"—the company repeatedly stressed to workers and others that the chemical was harmless. Further, Union Carbide never developed an antidote, prompting Dr. Hireesh Chandra, head of the Department of Forensic Medicine and Toxicology at Gandhi Medical College, to later state—and this may be the most fundamentally sound (as well as the most fundamentally disregarded) statement anyone has ever made—that a company "shouldn't be permitted to make poison for which there is no antidote." (Readers should be aware, by the way, that far from having ready antidotes, nine out of ten chemicals used in pesticides haven't even been thoroughly tested for toxicity. The United States alone suffers at least 1400 toxic chemical accidents per year.) The company had told at least one doctor, N. P. Misra, dean of the Gandhi Medical College, of the dangers of MIC. But Misra, who was closely linked with Union Carbide, never told his colleagues of these dangers. When asked why, he replied,

KILLERS

"This is not the only compound about which you do not know. . . . There are thousands of other potentially dangerous compounds about which you do not know today, as you did not know about MIC."

Union Carbide clung tightly to the public fiction that MIC is harmless: When victims began streaming into a Bhopal hospital, doctors called Union Carbide's chief medical officer at the plant, Dr. L. S. Loya, who stated that MIC "is not poisonous" (Dr. Loya's mother later died from the effects of the gas); when at 4:30 AM newsmen arrived at the factory, Mukund assured them that "Our safety measures are the best in the country," and stressed that MIC was merely an irritant and not a poison; another Carbide official, whose name was not, surprisingly enough, Noah, standing within one hundred yards of dead bodies, told the press that "nothing has happened. Can't you see us alive?"

Later, Dr. Loya was candid about why Union Carbide had hidden the dangers of MIC from the community: "If I say that 'I'm carrying a deadly thing in my pocket,' people just turn you out of the town. [They] don't allow you to remain there, even though you aren't going to use it. . . . Here people are so emotional . . . if you tell them that, then the next day there will be a big procession and do-to-do and la-dee-da, 'will you please stop this factory, we don't want it,' even though it is not dangerous. Telling the truth is sometimes a difficult problem in our country."

The day of the leak, Dr. Chandra and a team of doctors from the Gandhi Medical Center began performing autopsies, and quickly discovered that many of the victims had been poisoned not only by MIC but cyanide as well; the reaction that led to the leak of MIC produced cyanide and several other toxic chemicals. That first day all one hundred and fifty-five autopsies revealed cyanide poisoning. Blood levels of cyanide were so high that many doctors began to suffer effects of cyanide poisoning from gases inhaled during autopsies. That afternoon, Chandra recommended injecting victims with sodium thiosulfate, a universally recognized antidote for cyanide poisoning. In response to a request from Bhopal, Dr. Bipin Avashia, Union Carbide's medical director at an MIC-producing plant in the United States, made the same recommendation.

THE CULTURE OF MAKE BELIEVE

This treatment, however, was not generally made available to victims. Since Union Carbide was facing what it already viewed as a nearly insurmountable public relations problem, and since cyanide carries powerful connotations among the general public—including its use in Nazi death camps—the company did not want people to associate cyanide either with Bhopal or Union Carbide's ongoing and worldwide use and storage of MIC. Consequently, the company denied cyanide was present, and Dr. Avashia backed away from his earlier recommendation. The corporate press in the United States went out of its way to support the company's denial, blacking out the cyanide story for more than three months after the disaster, only lifting it in April of the next year when both the *Wall Street Journal* and *The New York Times* published articles supportive of Union Carbide's position. The Indian government also denied cyanide's role in the disaster, keeping secret a study revealing that the air near Union Carbide's plant still contained cyanide even three days after the leak, as well as a study by the Indian Council of Medical Research verifying sodium thiosulfate's usefulness in treating victims. To further the fiction, the government quickly placed an effective ban on the drug's use, despite sodium thiosulfate's freedom from significant side effects and its verified utility.

Public pressure eventually caused the government to inject a few victims—mainly wealthy ones—at one hospital, on a pilot basis. When, by June of the next year, the government still refused to allow destitute victims to receive injections—at one point arguing victims were too ignorant to produce urine samples necessary for testing after treatment, prompting an angry demonstration of women holding beakers of urine—several groups of volunteer doctors occupied part of Union Carbide's plant and established there the People's Health Clinic. During the next three weeks the clinic treated about a thousand people with sodium thiosulfate.

Horrified government officials recognized the clinic had become a rallying point for victims and moved to shut it down. At 1:00 AM on June 25 police raided the clinic on the grounds of "illegal occupation," arresting and beating nine volunteers. They confiscated records and supplies, and turned them over to Union Carbide. Forty others associ-

KILLERS

ated with the clinic were awakened at their homes, taken to the police station "to prevent trouble," verbally abused, and locked up. Later that day, police used clubs to disperse a demonstration of three thousand gas victims, beating scores of men, women, and children and arresting twenty-one. This use of force against its own citizens was by no means unique; perhaps the most appalling use of force by police occurred when a group of women who had been made widows by the leak demonstrated for aid. Police beat sixty of them. The government defended its actions by claiming those running the clinic "were playing into the hands of the vested interests and had to be dealt with firmly before they caused needless and avoidable misery to the already suffering victims. They were cynically exploiting the people by organizing demonstrations. The government did not close down any voluntary clinic," and so on.

To step away from Bhopal for a moment to the larger discussion, I need to ask again whether the white people who captured Africans to sell as slaves hated Africans. How about the people who transported them: Did they hate Africans? How about those who passed laws legalizing the slave trade? And those who wrote editorials in support of it? Those who bought products created with slave labor? Did Pimp Soldier hate the women he called his ho's? Do those of us in North America who live on Indian land hate Indians? Did those who supported Union Carbide hate the people of Bhopal? By what right did the traffickers in human beings conduct their trade? By what right did those who own and run Union Carbide set up a factory to manufacture poisons in Bhopal? Who gave them that right? What entitled them to do this? None of these questions are rhetorical: I want answers. In order to fabricate these poisons, and ultimately poison these people, what contempt must those who own and run this company feel for those they may poison? Or do they feel even less than this? Do the people even exist? These particular people, living these particular lives. Are these living beings less important to them than abstractions, than numbers on ledgers. What is the relationship between these numbers and these people?

In the aftermath of the disaster, Union Carbide pursued a strategy of containment which had as its sole objective the protection of the company's assets. On the public relations front the company expressed concern for victims while simultaneously denying MIC's toxicity; denying cyanide's role in the deaths; blaming lung damage on preexisting tuberculosis; denying the leak's long-term health effects; acknowledging as victims only those who died in hospitals; blaming "the cultural background or the basic educational level" of Bhopal citizens; blaming "overregulation" by the Indian government; claiming that either a (nonexistent) group of "Indian extremists, which calls itself 'Black June'," or a disgruntled ex-employee sabotaged the plant; claiming that the effects of the gas leak, while regrettable, were more than counterbalanced by Union Carbide's positive role in India as a producer of pesticides and other bulk industrial chemicals; and blaming the company's Indian subsidiary; claiming, in the words of Carbide chief executive officer Warren Anderson, "You can't run a nine or ten billion dollar corporation all out of Danbury" Connecticut, headquarters of Union Carbide (this statement is, of course, a powerful though unintended indictment not only of Union Carbide but all transnational corporations, as well as the other large economic and political institutions that govern our lives). Within four months of the leak, Union Carbide's denial had progressed to the point that Anderson could say, "The company did nothing that either caused or contributed to the accident, and if it comes to litigation we will vigorously defend that position."

Financially, the company was no more forthcoming. Union Carbide's first settlement offer was for $100 million; the second was for $240 million. The latter corresponded precisely with Union Carbide's insurance coverage; had the offer been accepted by the Indian government, the disaster would have cost Union Carbide nothing, apart from the money it spent to hire Burson-Marsteller, the public relations firm that has also represented Nigeria during the Biafran war, Romania during the reign of Nicolae Ceausescu, the Argentinian military junta in the late 1970s, Babcock & Wilcox after Three Mile Island, A. H. Robbins during the Dalkon shield IUD controversy, Exxon after the

KILLERS

Valdez oil spill, and Hydro-Quebec. Union Carbide also spent an estimated $50 million on attorneys. The offer was rejected, however, and Union Carbide began selling or spinning off assets and distributing the cash from these sales to shareholders. Some of this restructuring came about because Carbide needed cash to fight a hostile takeover attempt, but much of it was done simply to place the company's assets beyond the reach of Bhopal victims.

The response of the Indian government was more closely aligned with the needs of Union Carbide than of its citizens. Soon after the leak the Indian ambassador to the United States said both governments were trying to "contain the damage," and continued, "I know the two governments are in close touch with each other trying to maintain an even atmosphere even though there is this enormous public sense of dismay and even outrage." The Indian poet and activist Ganesh War was more direct: "And besides the misinformation and misleading, the government is playing a nasty game, to save Union Carbide and companies like it in India."

An example of the government's game playing—and this forms a potent contrast to the treatment afforded my students at the prison—was its handling of Anderson's visit to India after the leak. Anderson—who was himself going to Bhopal to "contain the damage"—was arrested as he deplaned in Bhopal. But the arrest was a public relations move designed not only to protect Anderson from Bhopal residents clamoring for his execution but also to quell public outrage and mask governmental culpability. Anderson was "jailed" in Union Carbide's luxury guesthouse for six hours, after which he was released on $2,100 bail and flown out of Bhopal on a government plane. Later that day a government spokesperson said there "never was any intention of prosecuting him," but nonetheless used the arrest as an opportunity to put the kibosh on rumors that India had surrendered to American (or Union Carbide) imperialism.

Beginning the day of the disaster, when the Indian army carted off truckloads of dead bodies—bodies that were never accounted for—the Indian government kept secret from its citizens much information relevant to the disaster. The government sealed the factory, impounded

its records, and prohibited workers from talking to the media. It instituted a secret judicial inquiry, later abandoned, and refused efforts at cooperation and requests for information. It refused to make public the results of medical and epidemiological studies, victims' medical records, research on the long-term effects of MIC, and results of air, water, and other environmental studies, prompting a newspaper to note that while a gas leak may have been acceptable to the government, a news leak was not. The government even tried to destroy the remaining MIC and thus remove the possibility of testing. After the Indian High Court forced fifteen kilograms to be set aside, Union Carbide "destroyed" the rest by converting it into the pesticide Sevin and selling it for $200,000.

During the first months after the disaster, Union Carbide spent on relief about three cents per victim per day. The Indian government added about thirty-eight cents per victim per day. By mid-June of 1985, nine hundred and forty-six people had received an average of $118 each, 13,906 people had received an average of $16 each, and four thousand families had received $125 each.

Lawyers and activists working with people in Bhopal wanted to sue Union Carbide for all of its assets, about $10 billion. Since estimates of Bhopal's economic losses alone—including neither medical treatments for victims nor punitive damages against Union Carbide—ran to more than $4 billion, the idea of turning the company over to those it had poisoned was not economically unreasonable. But that's not what happened.

Because Union Carbide is chartered in the United States, the Indian government filed suit in New York. Union Carbide attempted to transfer the legal proceedings back to India, stating explicitly its fear that an American jury might value an Indian life as highly as it would an American life: "Indeed, the practical impossibility of American courts and juries, imbued with U.S. cultural values, living standards and expectations, to determine damages for people living in the slums or 'hutments' surrounding the UCIL [Union Carbide India, Limited] plant in Bhopal, India, by itself confirms that the Indian forum is overwhelmingly the most appropriate. Such abject poverty and the vastly different values, standards and expectations which accompany it are

KILLERS

commonplace in India and the third world. They are incomprehensible to Americans in the United States." Further, the company argued, trying the case in this country would set a bad precedent: Since many transnational corporations are based in the United States, "the courts of the United States would soon be overwhelmed by litigation from all parts of the globe." The company did not mention in its arguments that Indian courts do not allow punitive damages to be awarded. Nearly a year and a half later the judge agreed and the case was transferred to India.

Once in India, Union Carbide continued to drag out the proceedings. It dismissed victims' claims on whatever grounds it could find, stating, for example, that "the plaintiffs are illiterate and do not understand the contents of the affidavits on which they have placed their thumb prints. Therefore . . . the complaints must be thrown out." It appealed even minor procedural matters to the Indian Supreme Court.

Meanwhile, the meager relief efforts in Bhopal had stopped; even the people who were completely disabled received no compensation. That is how 1986 passed, and 1987, and 1988. Still, Union Carbide delayed. Finally, in 1989, at the order of the Indian Supreme Court, the Indian government and Union Carbide agreed to a settlement of $470 million: an average of $793 for each of the 592,000 people who filed claims. Groups representing victims challenged the settlement as too low, as did a new Indian administration elected later that year, but in 1991 the Indian Supreme Court upheld the amount. Still, the corporation stalled: Hundreds of thousands of survivors of Bhopal wait even today for compensation.

In 1984 Union Carbide had predicted that "victims of the Bhopal tragedy could be fairly and adequately compensated without a material adverse effect on Union Carbide's financial condition." The prediction was right, insofar as it concerned the company's financial condition: The terms of the settlement were so favorable to Union Carbide that when the settlement was announced, Carbide's stock rose two dollars on the New York Stock Exchange. But fair or adequate to those it poisoned? Listen again to a voice from Bhopal: "Since the gas I have not

THE CULTURE OF MAKE BELIEVE

been able to work a single day. The gas killed my daughter; she died in the morning after the gas leak. I am breathless all the time and I cough badly. My eyes have become weak, too. I have been admitted to the MIC ward more than five times since 1987. Last year, I was there for nine months at a stretch. This year, I have come home after eight months." Another voice, this of someone who was six on the day of the leak: "My father could not do any work after the gas disaster. He used to remain sick and in 1986 he died. My mother used to be sick also. . . . She used to get breathless and used to cough all the time. . . . My mother died in February 1988 in the hospital. . . . Carbide's official's must be punished. If these officials are let off easily, they will go on killing people and making them sick. What happened in Bhopal should not happen anywhere else." And yet one more voice, this of a woman whose husband was killed by the gas and who is herself too sick to work: "I believe that even if we have to starve, we must get the guilty officials of Union Carbide punished. They have killed someone's brother, someone's husband, someone's mother, someone's sister; how many tears can Union Carbide wipe? We will get Union Carbide punished. Till my last breath, I will not leave them."

Here's another riddle, this one perhaps even less funny than the first. Question: What do you get when you cross forty tons of poison, a major corporation, two national governments, and at least eight thousand dead human beings? Answer: Retirement with full pay and benefits.

If corporations and those who run them were held legally accountable for their actions, Union Carbide would have been convicted of murder thousands of times over, its corporate charter and the charters of its subsidiaries would have been revoked, and its officers and major stockholders would have been imprisoned or executed. Yet Union Carbide remains chartered and its officers and major shareholders remain free. Warren Anderson retired in November 1986.

The argument could be made that the officers and major shareholders of Union Carbide have not killed people directly (no one, of course, can make this claim for the corporation itself). The same, however, could be said of the eighteen defendants found guilty during the

KILLERS

main Nuremberg trials after World War II. None of those ten executed defendants were accused of killing people directly. Not even Hitler was accused of that.

This leads us, as always, back to the question of intent. One could say that the corporation and the people who run it never intended to kill anyone, that they were merely trying to make a profit. Presumably, that statement is true, and is also a central point of this book, because the same could be said for slave owners: Weren't they just trying to make a buck? If you kill someone while you're trying to earn what you perceive as an honest dollar, is the person you kill any less dead (is the murder any less complete?) than if you kill him in a drug deal gone bad, in a drug-induced backyard fight, if you drag him behind your pickup because you've been taught to hate members of his race, or if you hang him because you perceive him as a threat to the way of life to which you feel you are entitled? Does not the same contempt for the other, the same disregard, run like a silver thread through all of these scenarios?

It could be argued that the officers and shareholders of Union Carbide may themselves not be individually immoral, and thus are not deserving of punishment. But as Robert Jay Lifton, the world's foremost authority on the psychology of mass destruction, made clear in *The Nazi Doctors: Medical Killing and the Psychology of Genocide*, it is possible to participate in profoundly immoral activities even if one is not by oneself evil. Of those physicians whose work supported the Nazi genocidal project, he wrote, "Neither brilliant nor stupid, neither inherently evil nor particularly ethically sensitive, they were by no means the demonic figures—sadistic, fanatic, lusting to kill—people have often thought them to be." While writing the book, Lifton struggled with "the disturbing psychological truth that participation in mass murder need not require emotions as extreme or demonic as would seem appropriate for such a malignant project. Or, to put the matter another way, ordinary people can commit demonic acts." In the case of both the Nazis and those associated with Union Carbide, even those who may have been individually ethical lent their talents to destructive activities in order to further a perceived higher good. For some Nazis, this was the revitalization of Germany. For some associated with

Union Carbide, it was making money for the corporation. The perceived higher good leaves victims who are just as dead in either case.

Although some few Nazis were held accountable for their participation in destructive projects, a tremendous number escaped justice. It speaks to our inability or unwillingness to make the connection between economics and hatred that, as Robert E. Conot noted in *Justice at Nuremberg*, "the German industrialists who had robbed the populations of occupied lands, exploited the slave laborers, and built the factories to work concentration camp inmates to death were universally receiving light sentences—in most cases the men were released shortly after trial in consideration of the time they had been held in captivity."

It would be incorrect to say that Union Carbide "got away" with the killings at Bhopal simply because of the failure of judicial systems; this attribution implies, against all precedent, that courts, and, more broadly, governments, can be expected to hold corporations accountable. Instead the injustices need to be examined in the context of historical economics, and in the context of our long history of contempt for those who are exploited or killed, and hatred of those who stand in the way. No scheming cabal of judges could by themselves give Union Carbide the ability to poison people halfway around the globe: Technology, capital, and a whole economic and social way of life have combined to make that possible. This dynamic chain of relation has developed slowly, and over time (alchemically, in a crucible of consciousness and action), making Bhopal and tens of thousands of other tragedies inevitable. If we hope to stem the mass destruction that inevitably attends our economic system (and to alter the sense of entitlement—the sense of contempt, the hatred—on which it is based), fundamental historical, social, economic, and technological forces need to be pondered, understood, and redirected. Behavior won't change much without a fundamental change in consciousness. The question becomes: How do we change consciousness?

KILLERS

THOU SHALT HAVE

NO OTHER GODS

BEFORE ME.

EXODUS 20:3

THE COST OF
POWER

THE JOURNEY OF OUR CULTURE has been one of increasing abstraction from direct personal experience, manifesting in every aspect of our lives, from our pornography (and, more broadly, our intimate relationships) to our economics—which, time after tedious time, values abstractions such as ideology or money (what's a dollar worth, really?) over living beings—to our violence. Recall that, among the Plains Indians, the closer one got to one's enemy in battle, the more one was socially esteemed. Contrast that with modern warfare, in which the act of pushing a button, the mere movement of a finger, could destroy life on the planet. If I strangle someone, I must feel with my hands the other's life struggling not to end. If I stab someone, I must feel her or his blood, must watch it pulse or gurgle out, the last display of the rhythm of that person's heart, that person's life. Even shooting someone, I still must see the person whose life I am going to end.

But, you could ask, what about the blacks who've been tortured and killed by lynch mobs? Did the mob not take great pleasure in causing pain to this person? In a sense, no, because, even in the act of torture, they were not recognizing the uniqueness of their victim: He (or she) was killed for being of a class, as evidenced by all the lynchings of the "wrong person." What, then, of people, denied all individuality, killed, not for themselves, who are killed not merely at a psychic distance, but by a rainstorm of bombs—or poisons—sent to them from the other side of the planet?

Stanley Diamond commented that "Modern mass society creates the modern mass soldier, as a reflection of itself. The effort is made to train him as a deadly bureaucratic machine; in fact he may even shortly become obsolete to be replaced by machines. . . . He kills, whether by bombing at a distance or face to face—but he kills, it should be re-emphasized, at a psychic distance. 'We might as well be bombing New York,' said an Air Force officer in Vietnam. This distance is compounded, of course, by the ethnocentrism which the United States as an imperial power instills into its citizens. But the modern mass soldier [and I would add citizen] does not have to hate the specific enemy, which is an inverted way of saying that he does not necessarily recognize the humanity of the specific enemy. . . . Killing a 'gook,' or a Jew, remains killing at a distance, although physical proximity demands more of the psyche than bombing from the air; the total dissociation of the former is converted into the direct subjective distortion of the latter. The point remains that the people killed were insufficiently alive in the consciousness of the killers—and this mirrors the actors' inadequate sense of their own humanity. What we were facing at My Lai, then, is not an incident, not even a policy, but the tragic course of civilization."

POWER

■   ■   ■

I heard an extraordinary story at the prison, in class, today. Today's prompt was to write about the thing in their lives of which they are proudest. Most people wrote about quitting gangs, or seeing their children. I've had a few people over the years write about saving the lives of others (one freed a woman's hair from a hot-tub drain; another pulled a drowning child from a river, then dove in again to get her sister). Yesterday, the first sentence one of my students wrote was that he was proudest of the time he killed four people. His second sentence was: "Wait, I know what you're thinking, but hear me out." He was one of ten children. They were a close family. Farm workers. One day, when he was fifteen, he did not go to work, but instead went to town to purchase something for the family. When he returned, his sister told him through tears that their father had been stabbed. My student drove to the hospital, and spent the next two days by his father's bed. His father died. Afterward, the entire family gathered. He was the oldest of those who remained at home. His elder siblings had families of their own. He was ignored for much of this gathering, then, finally spoke. They argued with him for hours, but eventually it was agreed that he would be the one to kill those who had killed their father. He waited, for five years, until his father's killers came out on parole. And then he killed them. Having known for the intervening five years that he would spend the rest of his life in prison, he had worked extremely hard to set up a business that would take care of the rest of the family. And he had succeeded in doing so.

When he finished his story, the man sitting next to him asked him if he had any regrets. "No regrets at all."

I have thought about this a lot, and I will think about it a lot in the future. I am very moved by it. Even though I do not know the details (his father's behavior and relationship, if any, to the killers certainly makes a difference) I can understand this crime. There is a form of honor in it. It makes more sense to me for the son of someone who was murdered to kill the murderers than it does for a judge who is disconnected from all of those concerned to send the avenger to prison for the rest of his life, to be watched over by those who have no connection to the killing, and to be taught creative writing by someone else who is no way intimate with any of the participants. I would be able to understand were the relatives of those killed by my student to kill him in turn. I can understand a blood feud that goes on for decades. But I cannot understand an abstract, distanced retribution, morality removed from relationship.

I am not saying what my student did was acceptable. Nor am I saying it was unacceptable. It was human.

■　　　　■　　　　■

I wrote earlier that narcissistic individuals must ultimately be disappointed, and must then always displace onto others the blame for their disappointment. This is often, but not always, true. There is at least one condition—and, to be sure, this happens all the time—under which those who are narcissistic will accept blame, and in fact will act with all speed and diligence to correct their mistake.

The mistake, of course, is weakness, also known as empathy, compassion, communion, love, relationship, or humanity. More generally, the mistake that can be acknowledged and rectified is that of a failure to objectify. More generally, still, the mistake can be known as a failure to be narcissistic enough, the failure consisting of acknowledging the other's uniqueness and existence as a subject. In practice, this weakness finds its way into the world as a lack of will sufficient to annihilate one's enemies.

Failure to eradicate their enemies was, to go back to the cra-

POWER

dle of our civilization, a huge problem among the Israelites. God warned them time and again not to make covenants with those He delivered unto them: those they were supposed to exterminate and whose land they were to take. The deal was pretty clear, and it's just as clearly a deal we still adhere to: Give up your humanity and dissolve all interconnection with others, and you will receive power beyond your most insane dreams. Here's God's part of the bargain (and if you're an atheist or otherwise a humanist, just substitute for *God* the Market, Science, Technology, Capitalism, Free Enterprise, Democracy, the United States, Progress, Civilization, or whatever other abstraction you want, and the bargain still holds): "I will do marvels, such as have not been done in all the earth, nor in any nation. . . . Behold, I drive out before thee the Amorite, and the Canaanite, and the Hittite, and the Perizzite, and the Hivite, and the Jebusite." Our God having long since dispatched these peoples, we can make the list more current by substituting Khoikhoi, Arawak, Pequot, U'wa, or Aborigine. In order to benefit from these marvels, the Chosen People had to promise never to "make a covenant with the inhabitants of the land whither thou goest, lest it be for a snare in the midst of thee: But ye shall destroy their altars, break their images, and cut down their groves." The Israelites had to cut down the groves, just as today we have to deforest the planet, because otherwise it would be too tempting to enter into relationships with other gods, other humans, or the land where we live. And it simply won't do to form those other relationships, because "the LORD, whose name is Jealous, is a jealous God," and to enter into relationship with another is, as the book of Exodus so indelicately puts it, "whoring." To make sure the Chosen People deeply internalized this message, it was drilled into them. We read, again and again, "I will deliver the inhabitants of the land into your hand; and thou shalt drive them out before thee. Thou shalt make no covenant with them, nor with their gods." The reason? Always the same: If these oth-

THE CULTURE OF MAKE BELIEVE

ers live, it might be too tempting to gain their ways: "They shall not dwell in thy land, lest they make thee sin against me." The message is repeated in Deuteronomy, Joshua, indeed, the entire Old Testament. The message is acted out to this day.

The message is an extension of the lesson of Noah, the lesson of Lestor Luborsky, with his electrodes attached to eyeballs, letting us know where we dare not look, of R. D. Laing, with his three rules of a dysfunctional family or society. Don't. Don't look. Don't listen. Don't love. Don't let the other be. Don't. The best way to guarantee you won't be in a relationship with something is to not see it. The best way to make certain you won't see something is to destroy it. And, completing this awful circle, it is easiest to destroy something you refuse to see. This, in a nutshell, is the key to our civilization's ability to work its will on the world and on other cultures: Our power (individually and socially) derives from our steadfast refusal to enter into meaningful and mutual relationships.

This refusal—this key to power—was carried forward and used by slavers, Columbus, Pilgrims, the Founding Fathers, Hitler. It is put forward today by politicians who send soldiers to kill at a distance, and by soldiers who do the killing. It is pushed by CEOs and others who wish to reap the benefits of our economic system, and by purveyors of porn who tell us it's okay to represent women as objects to be "fucked in every hole" (or, judging by my Alta Vista search and the prevalence statistics, to be raped) but fail to mention any form of relationship at all. It is okay, we are told incessantly (for incessant repetition is necessary to make this painful and eventually numbing lesson stick) to utilize resources, whether the resources are trees, fish, gold, diamonds, land, labor, warm, wet vaginas, or oil. But one must never enter into relationship with this other who owns or is a resource. To do so would be to break the covenant with your God, whose name is Jealous, whose name is Power, because your power comes directly from

POWER

your unwillingness (or, perhaps, in time, inability) to maintain relationship: It is much easier to exploit someone you do not consider a living being—a You, as Buber would have put it—much less a friend, a lover, a member of your family. This is the key to understanding the difference between indigenous and civilized warfare: Even in warfare the indigenous maintain relationships with their honored enemy. This is the key to understanding the difference between indigenous and civilized ways of living. This is only one of many things those we enslave could tell us, if only we asked: They, too, are alive, and present another way of living, a way of living that is not—in contradistinction to our God and our Science and our Capitalism and everything else in our lives—jealous. It is an inclusive way of living. They could tell us that things don't have to be the way they are.

■　　　　■　　　　■

I just walked home from my mother's house. It's dark, but not so dark that I needed a lantern. I couldn't see my feet, but I know the path well enough to feel my way along. I know where the puddles are, and I know the places where I need to stretch my hands out to keep branches from my face. I walked in a canyon of redwoods, and at the midway point I finally looked up into the pale black sky to see the night's first stars: clusters already, and constellations. I don't know how I missed them before. Far before the opening where I live I could hear the singing of frogs. They're back again, and I'm happy. When I reached the opening I saw ahead of me the slender crescent moon splitting the space between two tall trees, a bright star hanging near its full side. I heard in the distance the calling of an unknown—to me—night bird. The dogs had run far ahead, and were waiting for me at the opening, tails wagging, mouths open in wide smiles. They pushed against me, one from each side. I was once again, and still happy. What more comforts

and elegancies could anyone want, I thought, than these relationships, to simply be in the world? The bargain offered to us by the
jealous God is not such a bargain; not for those whom the
covenant would have us ignore, and not for us.

POWER

THIS IS GOD'S COUNTRY. HE PEOPLED IT WITH RED MEN, AND PLANTED IT WITH WILD GRASSES, AND PERMITTED THE WHITE MAN TO GAIN A FOOTHOLD; AND AS THE WILD GRASSES DISAPPEAR WHEN THE WHITE CLOVER GAINS A FOOTING, SO THE INDIAN DISAPPEARS BEFORE THE ADVANCES OF THE WHITE MAN.

HUMANITARIANS MAY WEEP FOR POOR LO, AND TELL THE WRONGS HE HAS SUFFERED, BUT HE IS PASSING AWAY. THEIR PRAYERS, THEIR ENTREATIES, CAN NOT CHANGE THE LAW OF NATURE; CAN NOT ARREST THE CAUSES WHICH ARE CARRYING THEM ON TO THEIR ULTIMATE DESTINY—EXTINCTION.

THE AMERICAN PEOPLE NEED THE COUNTRY THE INDIANS NOW OCCUPY; MANY OF OUR PEOPLE ARE OUT OF EMPLOYMENT; THE MASSES NEED SOME NEW EXCITEMENT. THE WAR IS OVER, AND THE ERA OF RAILROAD BUILDING HAS BEEN BROUGHT TO A TERMINATION BY THE GREED OF CAPITALISTS AND THE FOLLY OF THE GRANGERS; AND DEPRESSION PREVAILS ON EVERY HAND. AN INDIAN WAR WOULD DO NO HARM, FOR IT MUST COME, SOONER OR LATER.

TRANQUILLITY
AND FELICITY

IN 1864, THE UNITED STATES CONGRESS created the Northern Pacific Railroad Company for the purpose of building and maintaining a rail line from Lake Superior to Puget Sound. To aid in the project, Congress conditionally granted Northern Pacific nearly forty million acres of land, which is more than 2 percent of the land mass of the contiguous forty-eight states, more land than this nation's nine smallest states put together.

There was a problem. Much of this granted land did not belong to the government, but to Indians. In order for the Northern Pacific to construct the railroad and receive the grant lands, Indians living on the granted lands had to be removed. This necessity had been recognized by the original grant's authors, who wrote that, "the United States shall extinguish, as rapidly as may be consistent with public policy and the welfare of the said Indians, the Indian titles to all lands falling under the operation of this act."

Unfortunately for the Indians, when public policy ran counter to the welfare of the said Indians, public policy won every time. The federal government soon began moving Indians off their land. Some Indians resisted, undoubtedly because they, in the words of a historian not particularly sympathetic to them, "rightly saw in [the railroad] a force that would bring about the destruction of the buffalo and an influx of whites, and that would consequently leave them little choice but to go to the reservation and live on the dole." General William Tecumseh Sherman saw this also, and it was reason enough for him use federal troops and federal tax dollars to support the railroad company. In Montana, the last native stronghold of the Great Plains, Sitting Bull and Crazy Horse began coordinating attacks against the surveyors and troops, first making clear to these intruders that they were not welcome, and then driving them away. Montana's superintendent of Indian affairs, J. A. Viall, who "could not abide Indians who wanted to live as Indians," called on the government to intervene more decisively: "Should those wandering Sioux . . . persist in their efforts to molest and interfere with the progress of the Northern Pacific Railroad, I sincerely trust that a sufficient military force will be sent against them to severely and sufficiently punish them, even to annihilation, should the same unfortunately be necessary. . . . [I]n the event of their continuing hostile, the interests of civilization and common humanity demand that they should be made powerless."

The government sent a force of fifteen hundred men to guard the surveyors. Among them were Custer and the Seventh Cavalry, fresh from putting down the Ku Klux Klan.

General Philip Sheridan ordered Custer to reconnoiter Pa Sapa, the Black Hills, in preparation for the construction of a fort to guard the railroad. Sheridan made plain the reason for the fort's location: "By holding an interior point in the heart of the Indian country we could threaten the villages and stock of the Indians."

TRANQUILLITY AND FELICITY

In clear violation of the Treaty of 1868 (which the Lakota had probably not even read) and acting as an agent of Northern Pacific, Custer led twelve hundred men—including his cavalry, two companies of infantry with Gatling guns and artillery, sixty Indian scouts, newspaper reporters, and scientists—to explore the Black Hills. One ostensible reason for the presence of federal troops was to protect Indians from the encroachment of miners, but, far from providing protection, the Seventh Cavalry brought miners with them. Further, in order to incite warfare, Custer (whom the Lakota called "the Chief of all Thieves") spread rumors of gold, and encouraged prospecting parties to enter the region. By the next summer, more than eight hundred miners searched for gold in the Black Hills.

The U.S. government made a ritual attempt to purchase the land. Red Cloud and other Chiefs asked for $600 million, and food and clothing for seven generations of Lakota people; the government countered with $6 million. The Lakota refused. Having fulfilled the ritual, negotiators stated to their superiors that negotiations would certainly be fruitless until the Indians had been taught a lesson.

President Grant ordered all "hostile" Indians (defined as anyone living in a traditional way), which they estimated at about three thousand, including a few hundred warriors, to come in to the Sioux agencies. It was hoped that the Indians could at that point be forced to give up the Black Hills and unceded land to the west of them, including the Big Horn Mountains and the Powder River country (where much of the coal claimed by Northern Pacific, and today by its corporate descendant, Great Northern Coal Properties, is located). Once the Indians arrived—primarily Red Cloud's "peaceful" Indians—Grant threatened to withhold their rations, thus forcing them to sign an agreement (which violated the 1868 Treaty provision that no new treaty could be made without the approval of three-fourths of adult Lakota males) giving up the Black Hills and all unceded land to the west.

Meanwhile, miners flowed into the region. Sherman stated the obvious: "If some [miners] go over the Boundary into the Black Hills,

I understand that the president and Interior Department will wink at it for the present." The president and the Interior Dept were soon winking like mad, because fifteen thousand miners moved in by the next winter.

Many of the Lakota resisted encroachment, which provided the government the excuse it had been waiting for. Indian bureau inspector E. C. Watkins laid out the plan: "The true policy, in my judgment, is to send troops against them in the winter, the sooner the better, and *whip* them into subjection." U.S. troops moved with far greater alacrity against the Indians defending their land than they ever had against those who were moving in. It would be satisfying to say the Indians repulsed the army, but the winter campaign failed primarily because of inclement weather.

By the summer of 1876, a thousand Lakota and Cheyenne warriors had gathered to fight the surveyors, troops, miners, and settlers who had by then irreversibly overrun their land. Custer returned to the campaign, and we are all familiar with what happened to him that year. It would be even more satisfying to be able to say that the victory of the Indians at the Little Bighorn was anything even approaching final—that it allowed them to maintain the territory which was by all rights—except that of force—theirs. But, as we all know, it did not.

Soon, Crazy Horse was in captivity, to be killed at Fort Robinson in 1877. Sitting Bull went into exile, not to return until 1881. Indians continued to lose land to the railroad: Thirty thousand square miles were taken from the Blackfoot, Arikaris, and Gros Ventre to allow Northern Pacific to pass, and land was taken as well from the Cheyenne, Crow, Flathead, Yakama, and so on.

The railroad was completed in 1883. Some of the owners thought it would be "unique and interesting" to have an Indian speak at Northern Pacific's Golden Spike ceremony, and so requested a soldier bring in Sitting Bull. Sitting Bull deviated from his ghost-written speech to say in his native tongue, "I hate you. I hate you. I hate all the white people. You are thieves and liars. You have taken away our land and made us outcasts, so I hate you." History does not record whether the translator hesitated before reciting instead the "friendly, courteous speech he had prepared."

I sometimes wish the atrocities of our culture were simply committed in bursts of the sort of hatred most of us are used to thinking about: a strong feeling, a passion. Such a motivation would at least still be human, and could be assuaged or accommodated or answered or defeated by other emotions or by reason. But our culture is implacable, inexorable, with atrocities committed willy-nilly with motivations—or at least surface motivations—as varied as the atrocities themselves. Sometimes the atrocities are committed out of a recognizable sense of hate. The lynchings. The dragging death of James Byrd, Jr. Rape—FBI definitions be damned. Or this, which I just read about yesterday, and which happened one hundred and fifty years ago here in northern California, just another step in the long journey toward one world culture. Some Mattole Indians—pejoratively called "diggers" by whites—killed a white trapper as he attempted to rape a Mattole woman. Local whites became incensed. One was recorded as saying, "I can't eat or sleep in peace til I kill a god-damned digger." Captain Geer, commander of militia in charge of exterminating the Mattole, later said of the ensuing slaughter, "We fought and killed quite a lot. There was no resistance; they simply hid as they always did." Sometimes the atrocities are committed with a sense of contempt: Andrew Jackson called Indians "savage dogs," and said attempts to eradicate or dispossess them would be futile until soldiers knew "where the Indian women were": Before that, their efforts would be like trying to kill a wolf "without knowing first where her den and whelps were." Sometimes the motivation is greed, as in a *San Francisco Argonaut* editorial. "We do not want the Filipinos. We want the Philippines. The islands are enormously rich, but unfortunately they are infested by Filipinos. There are many millions there and it is to be feared their extinction will be slow." Sometimes the motivation is simply business as usual, as in Bhopal, or the Northern Pacific Railroad. Sometimes the atrocities are committed out of a strong sense of benevolence, as in Andrew Jackson's second annual message to Congress. "Toward the aborigines of this country no one can indulge a more friendly feeling than myself, or would go further in attempting to reclaim them from their wandering habits and make them a happy, prosperous people." This benevolence is often tinged with a world-weary regret. Jackson continued, "Humanity has often wept over the fate of the aborigines of this country, and Philanthropy has been long busily employed in devising means to avert it, but its progress has never for a moment been arrested, and one by one have many powerful tribes disappeared from the earth. To follow to the tomb the last of his race and tread on the graves of extinct nations excite melancholy reflections. But true philanthropy reconciles the mind to these vicissitudes as it does to the extinction of one generation to make room for another." Jackson also wrote, immediately after the battle of Horseshoe Bend, or Tohopeka, one of the bloodiest slaughters of indigenous peoples by the U.S. Army (the dead numbered between five and eight hundred), "They have disappeared from the face of the earth. In their places a new generation will arise who know their duties better. . . . How lamentable it is that the path to peace should lead through blood, and over the carcasses of the slain!! But it is in the dispensation of that providence, which inflicts partial evil to produce general good." Most often, however, the atrocities are committed blithely, with a clean conscience and a deep sense of moral rightness. In 1831, Alexis de Tocqueville found it remarkable that whites were able to dispossess and exterminate Indians "with singular felicity, tranquilly, legally, philanthropically, without shedding blood [except, I would add, when the Indians resist], and without violating a single great principle of morality in the eyes of the world." I would emend his conclusion to read "in the eyes of those living in the civilized world."

TRANQUILLITY AND FELICITY

IF THE WORKER AND HIS BOSS ENJOY THE SAME TELEVISION PROGRAM AND VISIT THE SAME RESORT PLACES, IF THE TYPIST IS AS ATTRACTIVELY MADE UP AS THE DAUGHTER OF HER EMPLOYER, IF THE NEGRO OWNS A CADILLAC, IF THEY ALL READ THE SAME NEWSPAPER, THEN THIS ASSIMILATION INDICATES NOT THE DISAPPEARANCE OF CLASSES, BUT THE EXTENT TO WHICH THE NEEDS AND SATISFACTIONS THAT SERVE THE PRESERVATION OF THE ESTABLISHMENT ARE SHARED BY THE UNDERLYING POPULATION.

HERBERT MARCUSE

ASSIMILATION

THE ROLE OF HATE IN OUR CULTURE is not limited to the effects it has on women, children, and people of African or indigenous descent. Our culture originated in "conquest abroad and repression at home," as Stanley Diamond put it. It began in the Near East, and metastasized from there into the Mediterranean, Europe, and then across the globe. The spread of our culture by exploration (read, invasion) and bloody conquest is like the splayed water at the prow of a ship—taking out Dacians, Thracians, Gauls, Picts, Celts, and so on. Likewise, the ensuing repression is like a wake that expands outward to fill the "frontier," silencing or ignoring all voices of dissent, and expanding inward—psychologically—to silence the interior voices of dissent as well, capturing our motivations, thoughts, dreams, desires, making repression transparent so we no longer perceive ourselves as being repressed at all, and we can serenely, "tranquilly, legally, phil-anthropically," oppress all those we feel ourselves entitled to exploit, and all those who remind us of our own repression. Thus, just before American troops began giving the water cure, or worse, to Filipinos, and just before taking from them the Philippines, President William McKinley could proclaim, presumably with a clean conscience, "It should be the earnest and paramount aim of the military administration to win the confidence, respect, and affection of the inhabitants of the Philippines by assuring them, in every possible way, that full measure of individual rights which is the heritage of free peoples, and by proving to them that the mission of the United States is one of benevolent assimilation, substituting the mild sway of justice and right for arbitrary rule."

Even if we confine this exploration of hatred to the United States, we would have no problem finding victims aplenty. Chinese, Japanese, eastern Europeans, southern Europeans, Irish, Jews, Hispanics, Catholics, homosexuals, the poor, all these and many others have been cast with varying degrees of success in the role of *untermenschen* in the land of the free. They have been figuratively and physically tied to the whipping post.

Consider the Chinese, for just one example. The first Chinese arrived in North America long before Christopher Columbus, returning home with stories of a strange land, where people "have no arms or armor, nor do they make war," stories of villages with no walls, walls being unnecessary for peaceful people. Stranger, still, in this place women had choice in marriage: "If the woman does not accept [her suitor], he is sent away, but if he pleases her, the marriage is consummated." And strangest of all, this was a land with no taxes.

A few Chinese came to the Americas over the next couple thousand years (as was true also for Africans, and the indigenous of Europe) either returning home after their extended sojourn, or integrating themselves among the peoples already here. But the real influx of Chinese began around the time of the California Gold Rush, with the population of Chinese in California exploding from

ASSIMILATION

a few hundred in 1850 to twenty thousand just two years later. At first the Chinese were welcomed, desired, even feted, in great measure because the immigrants—nearly all men—were considered to be strong, highly competent, industrious, and taciturn. In short, they formed the perfect labor force for owners of capital. One newspaper enthused: "Chinamen are heavy in the pack. While the heathen is apparently physically deficient, he can carry a load that would disgust—not dismay, or astound, but disgust—the boss mule of a pack train. . . . It was a mystery how [the Chinese] managed to tote [this] weary load so gracefully, and not grunt or groan." This strength made some Southerners dream, after the Civil War, of the mass importation of Chinese to replace slaves: "Emancipation has spoiled the negro, and carried him away from the fields of agriculture," wrote the editor of the *Vicksburg Times* in 1869. "Our prosperity depends entirely upon the recovery of lost ground, and we therefore say let the Coolies come, and we will take the chance of Christianizing them." Also in 1869, a Southern planters' convention announced that it was "desirable and necessary to look to the teeming population of Asia for assistance in the cultivation of our soil and the development of industrial interests." The reason? "If God in His providence, has opened up the door for the introduction of the Mongolian race to our fields of labor, instead of repelling this class of population as heathens and idolaters, whose touch is contaminating, would we not exhibit more of the spirit of Christians by falling in with the apparent leadings of Providence, and whilst we avail ourselves of the physical assistance these pagans are capable of affording us, endeavor at the same time to bring to bear upon them the elevating and saving influence of our holy religion, so that when those coming among us shall return to their own country, they may carry back with them and disseminate the good seed which is here sown." It evidently never occurred to the planters to do the work themselves.

Much of the danger of our social system is that, in contradistinction to the majority of human societies for the majority of human existence, it is based not on cooperation but on competition, always on the victory of one at the expense of another. The arrival of the Chinese was a victory for capital, and a loss for labor.

To the consternation of American laborers, Chinese men were central to the construction of the transcontinental railroads. Tens of thousands of Chinese came to build the lines. The owners of the Central Pacific Railroad asked them to do the impossible—build a railroad through the Sierra Nevadas—and they did it, blasting and chipping away at seventy-five-degree inclines, or hanging hundreds of feet over cliff walls in baskets woven of reeds and vines, setting dynamite charges in rock faces, then swinging the baskets away with all their strength. They worked through the winter, month after month, living and building under the snow, with shafts to provide air and lanterns to give light. Avalanches carried away camps and crews. Frozen corpses, still standing upright with tools in their hands, were found the next spring. Because the company was paid by the mile, the owners forced crews to work from sunup to sundown, seven days a week. Chinese crews were paid less than white crews. In spring the Chinese laborers struck. The strike was immediately denounced in newspapers as a plot to destroy their "efficiency as laborers," and the Central Pacific began inquiries into the feasibility of bringing ten thousand black men up from the South to replace the Chinese. Most importantly, the company cut off their food supply. Stranded in the Sierra Nevadas, the Chinese men had no choice but to go back to work. They completed the railroad.

No one will ever know how many Chinese died building the Central Pacific (nor how many more, Chinese and otherwise, died building other rail lines: Consideration of the human costs of building these lines was perhaps best expressed by James Hill, the "Empire Builder," who said, "Give me enough Swedes and whiskey and I'll build a railroad through Hell"). By 1870 some twenty thousand pounds of bones had been gathered from shallow graves along the rights-of-way and returned to their homeland. But many thousands more of the dead remain in unmarked graves all through the West.

The reward on completion of the line was unemployment for the living, and although there had been fair resentment toward the

ASSIMILATION

Chinese by white Americans before, it now turned into hatred: Tens of thousands of workers—hard workers (or, as a Senator Miller from California put it, "inhabitants of another planet," a "degraded race" who were "machine-like . . . of obtuse nerve, but little affected by heat or cold, wiry, sinewy, with muscles of iron . . . automatic engines of flesh and blood . . . patient, stolid, unemotional . . . [herding] together like beasts")—were suddenly competing for jobs in an already tight market, a scenario familiar to nearly everyone in these postindustrial, free-trade days. The resentment became all the worse because the Chinese immigrants made themselves useful almost everywhere they went. In 1886, more than 85 percent of the farm workers in California were Chinese. The Chinese (for better or worse) built the levees that turned the San Joachin Valley into the breadbasket of the world. The Chinese (for better or worse) laid the foundations of the West Coast fishing industry. And because the vast majority of these Chinese workers were single males, and thus did not have to support families, they could afford to work for less (fortunate for them, since that's what they were consistently paid). Owners of capital inflamed resentment against the Chinese by using or threatening to use Chinese workers as strikebreakers—presaging today's overseas factories—which sent working conditions and wages to new lows. Even when the Chinese did not take jobs from white Americans, they still drove down wages and working conditions, as any landless people must of necessity do to survive in a wage economy.

In 1832, proslavery philosopher Thomas Roderick Dew stated that "Jack Cade, the English reformer, wished all mankind to be brought to one common level. We believe slavery, in the United States, has accomplished this, in regard to the whites. . . ." His point was that slavery acted in the American South as a great equalizer among members of the white race: "The menial and low offices all being performed by the blacks, there is at once taken away the greatest cause of distinction and separation of the ranks of society." So long as racial differences could be emphasized, poor whites would, the hope went, forget that rich whites exploited them as surely as

321

they exploited the blacks, and the poor whites might forget also that title to vast tracts of land by rich whites was based merely on social convention (as all titles to land is ultimately based), and not on anything else (except force, meaning the full might of the state).

The near ubiquity of this misperception—that of the poor perceiving others of their station in life to be the source of their misery, a misperception that continues unabated to this day—is not the product of mass stupidity on the part of members of those great sectors of the population who fall prey to it, nor is it part of a fiendishly clever plot by the rich to consistently keep the poor at each other's throats instead of their own (although the inculcation in this direction by those who own and thus control the media is literally mind numbing). It is a manifestation of the selective blindness that besets us all. We have been trained, from early on, to be able to perceive only certain threats, to perceive only certain forms of hatred, contempt, violence, and to perceive only certain sorts of people as even potential perpetrators of horrible crimes. We have been trained to perceive the world and those in it in very specific ways.

The other day I was thinking about pornography again, this time as I walked across a college campus. A woman approached me on the sidewalk. It was a warm day. She pulled off her sweatshirt. She smiled. I smiled back. We passed. End of story. But it caused me to reflect on how I perceived her, and *why* I perceived her as I did. Did I flash on a warm conversation concerning the rights of the poor? Did I instead see her remove next her shirt, then bra, then pants, then panties? Did I simply accept the brief moment of recognition for what it was and move on? How I perceived her was intimately and deeply determined by the ways I've learned (as a white, American male) to perceive women. That thought led me back to pornography: If something so obviously objectifying as pornography, and something I took into my body so briefly, could influence how I perceived those around me, how much more so are we all influenced—or beyond influenced: *formed*—by the myriad more subtle and more incessant messages we receive, and images we perceive? How are we affected by the unquestioned assumptions that make our schooling

ASSIMILATION

what it is, and that determine for us the words we choose, and that create the stories we take into our bodies via movies, books, newspapers, television. If these stories tell us that one kind of violence is violence, and another kind of violence is not (that it is "kinky," that it is "business," that it is "science," or that it is "defending national interest"), we will come to believe exactly that. Likewise, if these stories tell us that some people are meant to labor, and some others are meant to enjoy the comforts and elegancies that are the fruits of that labor, we may in time come to give our very lives (or dispatch others) to make certain that this seemingly divinely ordained social contract remains in place. It's no wonder, then, that so often members of those groups that share common interests end up scapegoating each other, instead of looking together at the people and organizations exploiting them both.

Several years ago, I was deep in the hills of northeastern Washington, collecting firewood from slash piles left over from clear-cuts, when I got a flat tire. I'd paid no attention to my spare for months (Oh, all right, if you must know, it had been years since I'd checked the spare), and discovered that it, too, was flat. There was no way I was going to walk all the way out, so I thumped along the backroads at about three miles per hour, until I came to a house. I asked the man who lived there if he had a pump. He said he didn't, and on I thumped. But a mile or two down the road he drove up behind me, and said he *did* have a spare. I put it on, and drove home. The next day I returned, with his spare, and with a cake. He thanked me, and asked me in. I met his wife. We shared cake. He told me he was a logger, then said if I wanted firewood, he had plenty, and he'd be glad to cut me some. I smiled and said thanks. We went outside to a big stack of tree trunks, cut in maybe eight-foot lengths. He held the chainsaw in his hand, and just as he was about to pull the cord to start it, he turned to me and asked, "So, what do you do?"

"I'm a writer," I said.

"What do you write?"

I'm in trouble, I thought. Shit. Loggers and environmentalists are supposed to hate each other. My mind spun quickly, and I wanted to

THE CULTURE OF MAKE BELIEVE

say, "Fantasy, science fiction. A little romance once in a while." But I've always been a terrible liar, so I told him about the book I was writing at the time, which was about how the big four timber companies in the Pacific Northwest—Plum Creek, Potlatch, Boise Cascade, and Weyerhaeuser—got their land illegally from the public domain.

He turned red in the face, and started swearing.

I looked for a break in the fence.

After the longest ten or fifteen seconds of my life, I realized he wasn't swearing at me, but at Plum Creek. It ended up that he was a gyppo—independent—logger who'd been put out of business by Plum Creek, and hated the company even more than I did. Till then I had not thought this possible. He knew at least as much as I did about the company. Within five minutes, we had our arms around each other's shoulders, swapping Plum Creek atrocities.

We agreed we should work together. I told him I was against all industrial forestry, but at least for now I wasn't worried about him. The task at hand was for us to take out Plum Creek and the other big timber companies. When they were gone, I said, maybe I'd come after him. We both laughed, knowing that our disagreements were in many ways theoretical, because the task ahead of us would take the rest of our lifetimes, and because for now we had a common enemy.

There is a point to be made here, about finding affinity with others with whom you share interests. But there's a larger point, too, which has to do with competition, and how our hyper-emphasis on competition in all aspects of our public life leads immediately and inevitably to insecurity and hatred. If you believe that the fundamental organizing principle of the world is competition (or if the fundamental organizing principle of your society *is* competition) you will perceive the world as full of ruthless competitors, all of whom will victimize you if they get the chance. The world as you perceive it will begin to devolve into consisting entirely or almost entirely of victims and perpetrators: those who do, and those who get done to; the fuckers, and the fucked. Your society will devolve—not in perception but

ASSIMILATION

in all truth—into these roles you have projected onto the world at large. You will begin to believe that everyone is out to get you. And why not? After all, you are certainly out to get them.

In 1790, John Philpot Curran wrote, "It is the common fate of the indolent to see their rights become a prey to the active. The condition upon which God hath given liberty to man is eternal vigilance, which condition if he break, servitude is at once the consequence of his crime, and the punishment of his guilt." We're probably more familiar with abolitionist Wendell Phillips's version of this sentiment, "Eternal vigilance is the price of liberty," which has been used to sell everything from increased military spending (already standing at 51.3 percent of the U.S. federal discretionary budget), to increased surveillance capabilities for the CIA and FBI, to a neat little hand-painted porcelain eagle night light I just saw in an ad ("perfect for den or office") that's available for only $15.95, plus $4.35 shipping and handling.

Nifty as this porcelain eagle may be, I think Curran and Phillips are wrong. In fact, eternal vigilance doesn't sound much like freedom to me, but just another form of slavery. It would be more accurate to say that the price of slaveholding is eternal vigilance: Not only must you always be on the lookout for more avenues of exploitation, but you must also be on guard against slave rebellions, and must be especially vigilant against all those others you presume to be as devoid of humanity as you are. Real freedom, it seems to me, as opposed to a nominal freedom that masks its opposite, would surely lead to a sense of peace.

An editorial cartoon from 1880 illustrates this point perfectly, and stands in contrast to the hospitality that is the hallmark of indigenous peoples the world over, who perceive the world as a place of cooperation instead of cutthroat competition. The cartoon is a panel of four drawings. The first shows a ragged white man dragging a blunderbuss, standing next to an Indian. The caption: "1620, Plymouth Rock: A weary traveler begs a little footing." The second shows a firm Uncle Sam pointing a rifle at an Indian: "1879, The 'weary travelers' Descendant: 'There, you infernal redskin. I've driven you from the Atlantic to the Pacific, now git.'" The third is of a pigtailed Chinese man in a supplicant posture before a rough and strong frontiersman: "1879, Chinese Immigrant: 'Mellican man, Lettee Chinaman Landee,—me washee, washee, and me workee cheapee.'" The final drawing shows a fat Chinese man holding a saber, and pointing at a skulking Uncle Sam: "1979: "Mellican man must git." The caption for the whole cartoon reveals a total lack of irony: "Will History Repeat Itself? Eastward the Star of China takes its way!—Population of the United States, 40,000,000; of China 400,000,000." No comment on white imperialism here.

The way this sentiment played out against Chinese immigrants is a story we've seen too often. First, the Chinese were demonized. The editor of a California newspaper claimed, "Every reason that exists against the toleration of free blacks in Illinois may be argued against that of the Chinese here." Chinese women were viewed, as were black women, as were women in general, as lustful and a threat to manhood, and Chinese men were viewed, as were black men, as threats to white women and children. "No matter how good a Chinaman may be," wrote Sarah E. Henshaw in *Scribner's Monthly*, "ladies never leave their children with them, especially little girls." Because, white men were told, Chinese immigrants competed for jobs, and drove wages down, white wives would be forced into prostitution, and compelled to sell their bodies to these selfsame Chinese, who were then likely to infect them with the "leprosy of the Chinese curse." (The truth was that 85 percent of the Chinese women in San Francisco in 1860 were prostitutes, the vast majority of whom had been tricked—"Even if I just peeled potatoes there, he told my mother I would earn seven or eight dollars a day, and if I was willing to do any work at all I would earn lots of money"—kidnapped, or sold—the famous Polly Bemis (born Lalu Nathoy) was sold by her parents for two bags of seed to bandits, then shipped to America, where she was auctioned off to a Chinese saloon keeper in an Idaho mining camp—into a life where many were confined to cribs four by six feet, spending the days and nights of their short, disease-ridden lives servicing men at cut rates: "*Lookee* two bits, *feelee*

ASSIMILATION

floor bits, *doee* six bits.") All of this demonization of the Chinese as destroyers of white morals, you may recall from history books, occurred well after whites—the United Kingdom—had used guns, warships, and economics to turn generations of Chinese nationals into opium addicts.

Next, Chinese immigrants were killed. They were hanged, burned alive, castrated, mutilated, branded, had their tongues cut out. They were scalped. Their homes were burned. The homes of those who employed them were burned. A Chinese laundryman was tied to a wagon wheel, and the buckboard was driven at high speeds until "the man's head fell off and rolled across the streets like a tumbleweed," revealing, if nothing else, that some things never change. On a single night in 1871 in Los Angeles, twenty Chinese men—not even accused of any crime—were hanged or burned alive. Four were crucified by being "spread eagled against the sides of 'sagebrush schooners' and executed with knife and gun." In 1885, twenty-eight Chinese men were massacred in Rock Springs, Wyoming: burned alive, mutilated. A half of a head would be found here, the bones of the lower half of someone else's body would be found there. Of one person they found only the sole and heel of the left foot. A memorial written by survivors noted that the bodies were strewn on the ground to be eaten by dogs and hogs. "It was a sad and painful sight to see the son crying for the father," the memorial said, "the brother for the brother, the uncle for the nephew, the friend for friend." Even women who had previously taught English to the Chinese "stood by, shouting loudly and laughing, and clapping their hands." The massacres were so commonplace that the editor of the *Montanian* wrote in 1873, "We don't mind hearing of a Chinaman being killed now and then, but it's been coming too thick of late. Don't kill them unless they deserve it, but when they do, why kill 'em lots." If only the Chinese threat could be removed, that same Senator Miller from California said, America could at last fulfill its destiny and become a land dotted with "the homes of a free, happy, people, resonant with the sweet voices of flaxen-haired children."

One of the fables we live by is that some day the killing will stop. If only we rid ourselves of Chinese, white men will have jobs and white women will have virtue, and then we can stop killing. If only we rid ourselves of Indians, we will fulfill our Manifest Destiny, and then we can stop killing. If only we rid ourselves of Canaanites, we will live in the Promised Land, and then we can stop killing. If only we rid ourselves of Jews, we can build and maintain a Thousand Year Reich, and then we can stop killing. If only we stop the Soviet Union, we can stop the killing (remember the Peace Dividend that never materialized?). If only we can take out the worldwide terrorist network of bin Laden and others like him. If only. But the killing never stops. Always a new enemy to be hated is found.

Another of our fables is that a primary purpose of the judicial system is to work for justice. But that's simply not true. Justice may be a secondary purpose, and one pursued at times with greater or lesser degrees of success, but the primary purpose is to justify the maintenance of the contract imposed upon society by those who make the rules, as Supreme Court justice John Marshall made clear in the case I've already mentioned. Nowhere perhaps was this stated more explicitly than in an 1854 California Supreme Court decision, regarding a case in which a white man assaulted a Chinese man, then killed another Chinese man who had come to the first victim's defense. The Supreme Court acquitted the killer on the grounds that there were no white witnesses, and cited Section 394 of the California State Civil Practice Act: "No black, or mulatto person, or Indian, shall be allowed to give evidence in favor of, or against, a white man." That the person testifying against him was Chinese (and not black, "mulatto," or Indian) did not matter, because the court held that the words, Indian, Negro, and mulatto are generic terms, and "must be taken as contradistinction from white," and were therefore included in the prohibition from being witnesses against whites. Whites (and corporations) are persons. All others are not. Because the killing of a nonperson is generally not a crime, the murders of Chinese men or women became nonmurders, and were almost invariably not prosecuted.

ASSIMILATION

Even though the Fourteenth Amendment to the U.S. constitution declared that all citizens of the United States had certain inalienable rights (rights which were quickly and most importantly extended to corporations) Chinese immigrants were denied these rights by the simple measure of making certain that they *could not* become citizens. Thus, they had no rights. In addition, white women who married Chinese men lost their citizenship, and, thus, even, their nominal rights.

In 1879, California rewrote its constitution. Article XIX, Section 4, of the new constitution explicitly and categorically declared that "foreigners ineligible to become citizens of the United States"—by which they meant Chinese—were "dangerous to the well-being of the State." Section 2 stated: "No corporation now existing or hereafter formed under the laws of this State, shall employ, directly or indirectly, any Chinese or Mongolian." And Section 3: "No Chinese shall be employed on any State, county or municipal or other public work, except in punishment for crime." And back to Section 4: "The legislature shall delegate all necessary power to the incorporated cities and towns of this State for the removal of Chinese. . . ." This is the state constitution.

In 1882, the U.S. Congress passed the Chinese Exclusion Act, which suspended Chinese immigration for ten years. In 1892, it extended this ban, and required all Chinese still in the United States to register. In 1902, the ban was extended yet again, in 1904 the ban was made indefinite, and in 1924, the ban was widened to include nearly all Asians. Chinese exclusion acts were repealed in 1943 (allowing a token hundred Chinese to enter per year), but the doors to Chinese immigration were not in reality opened again until 1965.

▪   ▪   ▪

The Chinese were hated, in part, simply because they looked different. I was going to say, "looked different than whites," but realized the last two words were unnecessary. They're implied. They're always implied. That's the problem. Whites are the standard against which all others are deemed similar or different, acceptable or unacceptable. Blacks fall outside this standard. Indians, too, whether from East or West. Difference, in this case, is a big disadvantage. Europeans have had it easier: Germans, Jews, Italians, and so on could and can anglicize their names, but the Chinese could not change the color of their skin. They were different, and thus feared.

It's not just color, though, and, in fact, color is only a small part of it. Another reason the Chinese were hated, and this is another way of getting at the same point, is that they did not so readily enter the "melting pot" like many European immigrants, but instead wanted to maintain a separate identity. They kept their queues, their dress, their "heathen" worship practices. They ate their own food. And, perhaps most horrifying to many Americans, they *bathed*.

The same hatred, once again, extended to the Indians who did not assimilate, and thus had to be eradicated. Once the cultures of the Indians had been decimated, that is, once the cultures and individuals no longer posed a serious threat to the ability of those in power to exploit anyone and anything around them, those in power—and by extension, all of us—no longer had to hate them. We were at leisure merely to despise them.

But the hatred goes beyond the maintenance of a simple power to exploit: These people were and are hated for their true difference, for reminding us that our way of living, which we have declared to be the One True Way, is not in fact the only way to live. It is possible to live without capitalism. It is possible to live without huge gaps between rich and poor, without the sweat of the many providing comforts for the few. It is possible to live without science. It is possible to live without destroying the planet. It is possible to live without penitentiaries. It is possible to live without slavery. It is possible to live without rape. It is possible to live without child abuse. There have existed cultures without any of these.

The Chinese (and I'm not suggesting the Chinese had no rape, child abuse, slavery, and so on; they have certainly had their problems) similarly were hated because they would not assimilate, or, to put this another way, they would not allow the process of consuming

ASSIMILATION

them to proceed to its bloody end: As a United States senator said of the Chinese, "These people are an indigestible element in our midst, a cold pebble in the public stomach that cannot be digested."

I've always been amazed that so many people continue to think of the notion of the melting pot as a good thing. Unless all parties act under conditions of equivalent power, and unless the melting is *purely* voluntary at every step of the process by everyone concerned, it seems by definition genocidal: whoever gets melted—assimilated—loses separate cultural identity. That's genocide.

But if you start making the claim that the melting pot is genocidal, you quickly find yourself alone (except for a few radicals, mainly people of color) in a room full of white supremacists, people like Professor Henry Pratt Fairchild, longtime director of the American Eugenics Society, and author of the 1926 book *The Melting Pot Mistake*; H. Millard, who argues that the melting pot is genocidal because nonwhites are going to make the United States "a slimy brown mass of glop"; and any number of others who argue passionately that whites are currently the victims of genocide, because they're being outbred by "Congoids" and others, and because "the habitat of the Nordish race is being invaded by competing life-forms or races."

I've got at least two problems with the argument that brown people (or any people, for that matter) are committing genocide against the "Nordish" culture (not race). The first is that the people who put forward this argument are at least a thousand years too late. The "Nordish" culture was enslaved a long time ago, and not by "Congoids" or others of their gloppy ilk, nor even by "competing life-forms," but by the civilized, and, ultimately, by civilization itself. When Aristotle spoke of the barbarians who were meant to be slaves, he was talking about the indigenous of northern Greece and further to the north. The word *slave* comes from the word *Slav*, as in "Slavic peoples," by way of the Latin *sclavus* or *sclava*, meaning "Slavonic (captive)" because the slaves in Rome were most often Slavs who'd been captured by German tribes and sold to the markets of Europe. It wasn't long before it was the turn of these German tribes, too, to find themselves brought into the fold. It's pointless to talk about anybody committing genocide against "Nordish" culture or cultures: The genocide happened when the Romans overtook the native peoples who stood in their way, and, later, when Rome fell but civilization continued, when those particular cultures rooted in those particular places were consumed, digested, and made part of civilization, a culture that ultimately—because it is groundless—is no culture at all.

The problem boils down to this: Who melts? Or, another way, who gets consumed? Think about this: What language is spoken by Indians assimilated into mainstream American culture? What core values have they had to internalize? Can they effectively remain animists? How many gods do they worship? I'm not talking about different names for power. What economic system must they struggle to fit into? Sure, the Spanish culture gave us the word buckaroo (from *vaquero*), and the Mexican culture gave us tacos and Carlos Santana, but the values and the ways of doing things in the dominant culture are the ones that must be adhered to. The same is true for patterns of land ownership. The belief that land can be bought and sold. The existence of the cash economy. The valuing of economic production over the process of living and over life itself. The existence of the wage economy: If immigrants were, as often happened, jailed, beaten, or killed for striking for better wages, just imagine what would have happened to them had they attempted to dismantle the wage economy, were they to question technological innovation, were they to live as nomadic hunter/gatherers? How could they, if the land base had been destroyed? Variation is allowed, but always and only within very specific constraints. Any true variation is made impossible by the myth-smaking and economic processes of our culture: the stories we are told, the words we use, and the things we are paid for.

When I spoke with David Edwards a year ago, we talked about how our culture coerces people to conform into specific molds. That we were talking about how this process forms politicians and CEOs—those who run the culture—and not immigrants, doesn't matter. The more general point was the way people are shaped by the reward sys-

ASSIMILATION

tems of our culture. Edwards had written, "To expect our leaders to adhere to basic standards of rationality and morality in their public lives is to indulge in a kind of anthropomorphism: they will not, indeed cannot."

I asked him about that.

He said, "The job of politicians and CEOs is to look very much like human beings. But they are peculiarly constrained by their public roles. It doesn't really matter whether leaders are personally moral or not, because in their public lives they're constrained from acting with the kind of compassion and reason we associate with the idea of being fully human. Their highest priority must at all times be the defense of profits, to which logic and morality are always without question subordinated. Where basic logic and reason threaten profits, leaders routinely resort to audacious extremes of illogic and unreason—often carefully wrapped in deliberate obfuscation—to hide the reality as far as possible. The same is true for morality: Where decency threatens profits, our leaders have no choice but to abandon their humanity as if it did not exist, or to risk disappearing from public view."

The same is true for every new person who enters our culture, whether by immigration or birth.

"What this means in practice," he continued, "is that while all but the most depraved individuals would agree that it is wrong to steal from children, to torture and kill them, our leaders are required in effect to disagree. They act accordingly. Profit can never be satisfied, and stealing food from dying children to give to the wealthy is institutionalized within the capitalist system. To expect humanity from our leaders—both political and corporate—is anthropomorphism. Time and again our hopes will be raised and then dashed. Indeed, the aim of much of politics is to raise our hopes and then let them drift off into nothingness, into 'business as usual.' It all comes back to an experiment I once saw on TV about how crystals are formed. If you put a square box on the floor, and you put a funnel over it, full of thousands of ping pong balls, and you tip the balls into the square frame, the balls automatically build a pyramid. Nobody's

THE CULTURE OF MAKE BELIEVE

consciously designing it. That's just the way the structure is built. I think it's vital to remember that politicians are little balls falling into that system."

I told him I thought that was true for all of us.

He said, "Most especially for those at the top, because those who make it there really fit the bill. The politician who succeeds represents the framing conditions. Politicians who don't fit into those framing conditions don't get to the top."

A few years ago I lived in Spokane, Washington, as overtly a racist town as any I've seen. My mother lived in a neighborhood that was all white, with the exception of a Japanese-American woman down the street (who, by the way (and entirely independent of her race) was crazy: She sometimes brandished pistols at her closest neighbors). In Spokane, this wasn't as strange as it sounded (the whiteness, not the brandishing, which *was* as strange as it sounded) since every neighborhood (including my own) was essentially all white. I was curious when a black man and a white woman moved in across the street and one door down from my mom. My mother had known them before they moved in (the woman cut my mom's hair), and their friendship grew in relation to their proximity. But the rest of the neighborhood accepted them as well. The man's color didn't seem to matter. I soon discovered the reason through conversations with a few of the neighbors. The black man had pleasantly surprised them with how *white* he seemed. He was a born-again Christian, a Promise Keeper. He worked a wage job at a Catholic college. He was a regular guy. The only thing that betrayed his race, apart from the color of his skin, was that occasionally when talking to a white man he would, unconsciously I presume, drop his eyes down and to the right in a signal of deference.

More and more lately I've heard the United States described approvingly as a salad bowl, not a melting pot. The idea seems to be this: Because lettuce leaves retain their color and at least some of their physical integrity in the salad bowl, so, too, people who come from other traditions into the United States are able to maintain some of their cultural integrity. This is all supposed to be a good

ASSIMILATION

thing, but I've got even more problems with this image—and the reality it describes—than I do with the melting pot. The salad bowl is far more dangerous because the melting pot metaphor makes no pretense at maintaining the original culture, while the metaphor of the salad bowl implies that culture is, first, independent of community—that a lone Grand Valley Dani in New York City is still a Grand Valley Dani, even if there are no other Danis around—and, second, the metaphor implies that cultures are transposable over space, which suggests, most critically, that culture can be separated from the land where it is native and has no deep relationship to the particular space from which it emerged. The metaphor suggests that we can move Chinese culture—or, more particularly, the culture that would emerge over time from the Estuary of Humen, from the mouth of the Pearl River, from the seasons of wind and rain and fog and the particular species of fish the people there catch each fall and the particular species of migrating birds who carry the spring season with them each year on their backs as they fly in—that all of this could be brought to the San Joaquin Valley without damaging both the culture and the valley (as well as the place from which the culture emerged). We can move Judeo-Christianity, this idea suggests, (or would suggest, if we were even conscious of it) from the Middle Eastern terrain that gave rise to it, over to North America, and it will still be a culture. For any culture to be sustainable in any particular place—and it seems self-evident that on a finite planet the only culture worth having is a sustainable one—it must have a deep and intimate relationship with that place. If the culture moves, it must adapt itself to the will of the locality, or it will consume the locality and the locality will die, which means, on a finite planet, that the culture will die as well.

The salad bowl metaphor conveniently leaves off what happens after we examine the beautiful salad in the bowl: The leaves get consumed and digested, along with the tomatoes, olives, mushrooms, Indians, Africans, Chinese, and so on. No matter how often he meditates, no matter if he has a Ph.D. in Japanese literature from the best university in Tokyo, a Japanese-American who lives in Silicon Valley,

THE CULTURE OF MAKE BELIEVE

dons blue jeans, and listens to World Beat music on his Hong Kong-made stereo system would still need to ask—as we all do—what are the conditions under which he is allowed to participate in American culture? Which of these conditions are negotiable, and which are not? What did his parents and grandparents have to give up in order to fit in here? What do all of us have to give away? And when we get digested, to push this metaphor to its logical conclusion, who, precisely, benefits from the metabolism of our bodies and of our souls?

ASSIMILATION

OBSERVANCE OF CUSTOMS AND LAWS CAN VERY EASILY BE A CLOAK FOR A LIE SO SUBTLE THAT OUR FELLOW HUMAN BEINGS ARE UNABLE TO DETECT IT. IT MAY HELP US TO ESCAPE ALL CRITICISM, WE MAY EVEN BE ABLE TO DECEIVE OURSELVES IN THE BELIEF OF OUR OBVIOUS RIGHTEOUSNESS. BUT DEEP DOWN, BELOW THE SURFACE OF THE AVERAGE MAN'S CONSCIENCE, HE HEARS A VOICE WHISPERING, "THERE IS SOMETHING NOT RIGHT," NO MATTER HOW MUCH HIS RIGHTNESS IS SUPPORTED BY PUBLIC OPINION OR BY THE MORAL CODE.

CARL JUNG

THE IMPOSSIBILITY
OF FORGETTING

WHEN I LISTED MODALITIES under which atrocities are commonly committed—hate, contempt, greed, a sense of moral rightness—I left out an important one: Sometimes the atrocities are perpetrated and perpetuated due to a strange sense of amnesia, one that reveals while it conceals. The salad bowl metaphor is an acknowledgement that the newcomers will be consumed, no matter what dressing we put on the act of assimilation. But this acknowledgment is almost accidental.

Just tonight I attended a local meeting sponsored by the California Department of Fish and Game about the development of a management plan for Lake Earl (and the conjoined body of water, Lake Tolowa), the lake into which Tolowa Indians were chased by the founders of Crescent City, the water where they were shot when they came up to breathe.

Lakes Earl and Tolowa (for ease I'll call it Lake Earl) is an extraordinarily interesting lake. Because it has no outlet—one dune separates it from the ocean—the water level varies dramatically, and, sometimes, quickly. All year-long, especially in the rainy season, water builds up until the lake stands ten or twelve feet above the ocean. Then, during a winter storm, on a spring tide, the waves might reach high enough to tear at the dune dividing salt water from fresh. The dune breaches, and the waters flow together. When the tide recedes, much of the lake recedes with it. Soon the breach closes, and water begins again to accumulate.

The creatures who live on the lake have long-since adapted themselves to this variation. The breach usually occurs in winter, well before the nests of marsh birds could be left dry by the falling lake. Because the birds normally move a little inland during heavy storms (and seem to know when some natural cataclysm is about to take place) and also because the breach occurs in the highest of high tides and pulls out slowly as the sea level falls, not many birds get sucked out to sea. Aquatic invertebrates love the variation in water level— "the wider the better," I heard one fisheries biologist testify tonight—and because aquatic invertebrates are within shouting distance of the bottom of the food chain, then, if it's good for invertebrates, it's probably good for lots of other creatures.

At least that's how it all worked, until the arrival of the dominant culture. After the whites killed many of the local Indians and took their land—the land was never ceded by treaty, but simply taken outright by the state of California and parceled out to ranchers for sometimes less than a dollar an acre; in the 1950s tribal members received one hundred and fifty dollars each in compensation—many began to raise dairy and beef cattle. Because the bottom of the lake made good pasture, and because it was inconvenient to have some of these pastures flooded part of each year, the county government authorized the lake to be breached whenever it went past the four foot level, that is, when the level of the lake was more than four feet above sea level. For decades the lake was breached with no consideration for its effect on the local critters, save cows and (some of the white) humans.

THE IMPOSSIBILITY OF FORGETTING

In the 1960s some people, looking to get rich—or more pre-cisely, some rich people looking to get richer—put in roads for a sub-division by the lake, called Pacific Shores, and began to sell parcels, many of which would be underwater were the lake to rise to normal levels. This didn't really matter, though, because even with the lake partially dewatered, the local geology makes the land unsuitable for building. Over the years the parcels have been sold and resold as ocean properties to unsuspecting owners all over the United States, in scenes perhaps reminiscent of the movie *Glengarry Glen Ross*. When the purchasers discover what they've bought, they often let the land go back to the county for taxes. The owners of Pacific Shores buy the land back from the county and start the process over.

Then, a few years ago, Fish and Game started making noise about restoring the lake to its natural variation. For the first time in a hundred years the water rose as high as it used to. The owners of Pacific Shores and the ranchers, with the full and eager support of a majority of the county commissioners, vigorously opposed this re-turn to nature, some of them going so far as taking a bulldozer out at night to try surreptitiously to breach the dune. Local environmental-ists started pulling all-night vigils to keep the vandals away.

What the ranchers were unable to accomplish illegally, however, they have been able to accomplish legally, getting Fish and Game, the Corps of Engineers, and other governmental organizations to grant interim permits for the dune to be breached until Fish and Game comes up with a long-term plan for how to deal with the lake. Thus the meeting.

I have been to Lake Earl when the water is high, and have seen water covering asphalt layed down in the sixties and buckled by time. I've seen families of plovers—babies tiny as mice—swim zigzags through inundated weeds by the side of the road, and I've seen fam-ilies of mergansers, grebes, pintails, coots, and teals. I've seen least bitterns standing stock-still, beaks pointed upward as they try to blend into reeds around them, and egrets standing still, too, then flashing their beaks down quickly to grab a frog or fish. I've seen

THE CULTURE OF MAKE BELIEVE

thousands of tiny fish swimming in the shallows, and seen the aquatic invertebrates so beloved of that biologist.

I have seen, too, the lake after it has been artificially breached, and I have seen the carcasses of waterbirds sucked out to sea and beaten to death in the waves. I have seen thousands of them scattered just above the high-water mark, white bills, feathers brown and black, green scales on the skin of their feet, with seagulls feasting on the soft parts. So many coots—who need to run across the water in order to take off, and so have no chance once the lake begins to move—so many birds, that the seagulls grow fat and leave them to rot.

Some of the people who were there tonight went this year to the place of the breaching, to run into the waves to grab the birds before they died, to carry them to the sand and dry them off, then to carry them back to the lowered lake. As they were drying the stunned birds, a man drove his off-road vehicle up the beach. Even after they asked him to stop, he roared his machine close to the frightened and dying birds (showing why the existence of off-road vehicles is generally considered one of the strongest arguments one can make in favor of unregistered handguns) and they had to chase him away with curses I hope one day come true.

The meeting tonight was packed, with ranchers in button-down shirts and belts above blue jeans or dress pants, and environmentalists in, well, I didn't notice what others were wearing, but I was wearing a sweater and blue jeans. The purpose of the meeting was for people to describe concerns they would like the management plan consider. Predictably, environmentalists primarily expressed concern for wildlife. Although the concerns of the ranchers were just as predictable, there was something about them that startled me.

The first concern of the ranchers was that the sanctity—a word I heard thrown around a lot—of their private property rights should not be violated: To allow the lake to rise and fall diminishes the fiscal value of their land. The second concern was that respect for cultural traditions be maintained: Because the families of many of these ranchers have been in this spot for up to one hundred and fifty years, having taken the land directly from the Tolowa Indians (who were here before them for at least ten times that long), they've established a cultural tradition that needs to be respected. Their third concern was for the preservation of the tradition of Tolowa Nation (note the lack of *the* word the preceding Tolowa: that's crucial to the story). The first person to testify tonight was a Tolowa woman who is, she said, of Tolowa Nation, which has land by the lake. She said the water level needs to be maintained at four feet—in agreement, coincidentally enough, with the ranchers and owners of Pacific Shores—because to allow the water level to rise would flood burial sites of her ancestors. The burial sites are at about the six-foot level, implying, if she is correct, that the Tolowa traditionally breached the lake, which means that it has been artificially breached not for a hundred years, but for either the two thousand years archaeologists suggest the Tolowa have been in the region, or, according to Tolowa creation stories, since the world began. She said she could not divulge the precise locations of these sites for fear that whites would desecrate them.

Here's the scoop. The Tolowa are a federally recognized tribe of Indians. Sometimes tribes are called nations. But "Tolowa Nation" is a corporation. Some of the land by the lake owned by Tolowa Nation was donated by some of the people who'd bought land in Pacific Shores. They discovered they'd been ripped off, and then received a letter suggesting they do their part to right the wrongs of their ancestors and return the land to its rightful owners, the Tolowa, or, rather, in this case, Tolowa Nation. The woman who is the representative of Tolowa Nation works closely with the ranchers and the masterminds of Pacific Shores, and is supportive of their positions. So far as the burial sites are concerned, she refuses to disclose their location not only to whites, but to Tolowas. Loren Bommelyn, a former chair of the Tolowa tribe (not Tolowa Nation) said he would be glad to lend his support to her position if she would show him where the bodies were buried. "They're my ancestors, too," he said. "I don't believe those sites exist," he went on. "Our ancestors weren't so stupid as to bury their dead underwater, and we can be pretty sure they never breached the lake: We know the lake wasn't an anadromous fishery, the elders never described ceremonies surrounding breaching, and what would we have breached the lake with anyway, clam-digging shovels?"

The disingenuous use of a "friendly" Indian purporting to represent a whole people forms an interesting bit of historical continuity, but I'm more interested in the ranchers' other two concerns: property rights and cultural traditions. Before we explore these concerns, however, there's another piece of the puzzle to bring in.

Scientists at the University of Oregon recently demonstrated in a laboratory what we have long known already, that if there is something we want to forget, we almost invariably succeed in doing so. The experimenters, Michael Anderson and Collin Green, asked college students to learn pairs of words that were loosely linked in meaning (such as 'ordeal' and 'roach'), so that when shown one, they'd remember the other. Then the students were told to try to remember some of the second words, and to attempt to forget the other second words. It took only a short while for the students to forget the words they were supposed to. They could not remember the words later, even when offered money. This means that even if something unpleasant passes the Luborsky test—in other words, if it is noticed in the first place—we still have another trick to make certain we follow Laing's Don't rule: We can push the memory out of awareness, and cause ourselves to forget.

"Amazingly," Anderson said, "this type of forgetting is more likely to occur when people are continuously confronted with reminders of the memory they are trying to avoid. This is contrary to intuition, which says that seeing reminders a lot ought to make your memory better."

He continued. "When reminders are inescapable, people must learn to adapt their internal thought patterns whenever they confront the reminder if they are to have any hope of avoiding the unwanted memory."

Ultimately, though, through all this talk of Luborsky, Laing, Noah, and selective blindness, there is something we have left out, which is that the truth will out. Anderson said that he didn't believe

THE IMPOSSIBILITY OF FORGETING

that the students "erased" their memories, but instead that they suppressed them. "I believe that the memories are still there," he said, "but they are difficult to access."

We can convince ourselves we've forgotten, but our bodies know better. This is a truth understood somatically by survivors of terror everywhere, from veterans of military wars to rape survivors—veterans of our culture's war on women—to survivors of child abuse—veterans of our culture's war on children—who can put the terror somewhere far behind, pretend the atrocities didn't happen, but who may remember each time they hear a chopper, or each time they sense a strange man (or more likely, a "friend" or family member) looking at them, or each time they close their eyes, to sleep.

I found it ironic—and, in a strange sense, exciting and hopeful—that the ranchers, who live on land that is stolen property, rely on, as the cornerstone of their argument the sanctity of property rights: What's mine is mine, and not only can you not take it outright, but you can't "take" any (fiscal) value from it. I found it even more ironic—and even more exciting and hopeful—that those whose wealth is directly based on genocidal (culture-destroying) actions speak of the importance of cultural preservation.

Why did they choose those specific arguments? Part of that can be explained by simple effectiveness: They are using arguments they believe work best. But the overwhelming cheekiness of it makes me think there's something else at play here.

The ranchers are impelled to talk about the crimes on which their wealth is founded, and they are bound to forget about them. As is true for survivors of trauma, their bodies know the truth, and want the story to be told. Try as the ranchers might, they won't be able to force their bodies to forget entirely. It was not by magic that Lestor Luborsky's experimental subjects avoided seeing the threatening images. They had known where to not look because they had seen the images. The images had first to be taken inside for their minds to be able to obtund them, and tell them to forget. The images cannot be completely forgotten. And like the beating of the telltale heart, they make their truths known.

THE CULTURE OF MAKE BELIEVE

What is true for ranchers is true for all of us. Although we pretend we don't know, we know, and because we know we try all the harder not to know, and to eradicate all of those who do, cursing and enslaving those who see us as we are, and who dare to speak of our nakedness, and cursing and enslaving especially those parts of ourselves which attempt to speak. But speak they will. And because we cannot normally allow them to directly speak these stories we do not want to hear, the stories must emerge roundabout, as in these ranchers accusing Fish and Game of committing their own crimes, as in Nazis accusing Jews of being a culture-destroying people, as in decent white men calling blacks lazy at the same time as they gain comforts and elegancies from their labor.

All of this—the selective blindness, perps claiming to be victims, the strange amnesiac dance of revealing and concealing—causes what passes for discourse to quickly become absurd, frantically so, as people say everything but the obvious. When the obvious is spoken, it is almost certain that no one will hear, and certain also that if anyone does hear, no one will be able to think, and if anyone does think, surely no one will be able to talk about it. And if anyone does talk, no one will listen. But if somebody does talk, and somebody else does listen, we can always kill them both. And then we won't talk about that killing, except when we do, and then we will be certain that no one will hear. And so on.

We were not meant for this. We were meant to live and love and play and work and even hate more simply and directly. It is only through outrageous violence that we come to see this absurdity as normal, or to not see it at all. Each new child has his eyes torn out so he will not see, his ears removed so he will not hear, his tongue ripped out so he will not speak, his mind juiced so he will not think, and his nerves scraped so he will not feel. Then he is released into a world broken in two: others, like himself, and those to be used. He will never realize that he still has all of his senses, if only he will use them. If you mention to him that he has ears, he will not hear you. If he hears, he will not think. Perhaps most dangerously of all, if he thinks he will not feel. And so on, again.

THE IMPOSSIBILITY OF FORGETTING

To maintain and propagate these nested systems of lies is expensive. We must fight our humanity at every step of the way—denying our senses, our thought processes, our emotions, our nature as social creatures. But it's worse than this. Not only must we keep our bodies and memories in check, we must convince others not to remind us, nor to notice when we remind them. Fortunately, or unfortunately, depending on your perspective, the dominant culture allocates resources sufficient to convince at least many of those it does not kill that it is not killing those it does, to convince those who benefit from exploitation that they are assisting those they enslave, and to convince those they enslave that they are being liberated.

Just yesterday I encountered a Web site that at first I thought was a clever parody. But I was wrong. It's dead serious. The title of the Web site is "Behavior Modification Operations: Achieving your organization's objectives in troubled areas worldwide."

Here is the text: "BMO (Behavior Modification Operations) is a unique international corporate advisory company ready to fulfill your specific behavior modification requirements in support of organizational objectives in unstable areas and nations of the world. BMO is staffed by psychological warfare and military operations professionals who specializes [sic] in developing regions of Africa, the Middle East, Asia and South America."

Then follows a picture of an oil refinery.

Then more text: "By means of specially designed crises communications programs, BMO personnel are thoroughly trained to facilitate local acceptance of your organization's objectives at all levels of a given society, from leaders of developing nations to hostile local groups and communities. Simply put, we will ensure your operations are sympathetically supported by both antagonistic and indifferent local populations groups [sic]. In our research and implementation programs, BMO will place at your organization's disposal only the most sophisticated, historically proven techniques developed and practiced by government agencies, armed forces and many diverse political/national movements. BMO operations combine historical precedence and trends with the strength of sciences such as cultural anthropology, social psychology, sociology, linguistics and mass communication including targeted public relation campaign communications to achieve your objectives. BMO will work with your organization to provide effective influence over a given local population's opinions, emotions and attitudes with the purpose of changing the conduct of human environment [*sic*] in the area of your operation, to fulfil [*sic*] your specific objectives. The truly unique and distinguishing feature of BMO services is our capability to implement behavioral change programs in the midst of situations such as low intensity conflict, tribal or ethnic warfare and collisions, social disturbances, riots and upheavals, insurgency and counterinsurgency contexts."

And so on.

THE iMPOSSiDiLiTY OF FORGETiNG

ARBEIT MACHT FREI

WORK WILL

MAKE YOU

FREE

(MOTTO OVER

THE GATES

AT AUSCHWITZ)

PRODUCTION

I USED TO THINK WE LIVE IN A DEMOCRACY. Every person has a vote, I'd been told, and every vote counts. I guess there are two senses in which I still believe we live in a democracy. The first is in a classical Greek sense, democracy for the few based on the exploitation of the many, better defined, really, as a plutocracy, rule by wealth (or, as corporate raider Charles Hurwitz says, government by the Golden Rule: The one with the gold makes the rules). We consider the Athenian democracy golden, although slavery was indispensable to the system—slaves were considered instrumental, and not having existences sufficient to themselves. Today our democracy continues that tradition, with workers, consumers, and the earth considered as only instrumental, and virtually nonexistent outside of their utility.

Even if we were to pretend that the votes of the poor count as much as the votes of the rich, the rich frame the terms of any given issue. So the poor can only voice their preferences as predicated by questions concocted by a wealthy minority. Imagine, for example, a national referendum to decharter all corporations, to hold corporate stockholders criminally and financially liable for deaths caused by these corporations, and to return all corporate-claimed lands to the poor. I believe the phrase is, *in your dreams.* In any case, even when the poor do get to vote, it's only after they've been bombarded by waves of propaganda: Imagine, to push the decorporatization example further, the sorts of editorials one could expect, were any such referendum to come to a vote.

The second way in which we participate in a democracy is similar to the way in which the early Ku Klux Klan was a popular grassroots organization. We have to admit that in many ways the government does give us what we want, or rather what we've been trained to want. Consider, although we do not rebel, when faced with the reality that we must pay for clean (bottled) water, or against the fact that we are being killed by myriad carcinogenic processes central to our industrial economic system, or against the government's interception of our communications, or the incarceration of significant portions of targeted populations (e.g., young black males), I strongly suspect that if the government were foolish enough to ban television entertainment, or cut off cell phone service, heads would roll within the week. The same would happen if prices in this country were raised to levels where they were no longer subsidized by: (a) the unsustainable use of nonrenewable resources; (b) the unsustainable use of renewable resources; (c) the expropriation of natural resources from the colonies; and (d) the exploitation of workers worldwide. You say you want a revolution? Pop the price of gasoline up to ten dollars a gallon and watch the fun begin. I once heard farmer, writer, and activist Wes Jackson say Wal-Mart is the main thing keeping Americans from rebelling: So long as we can get our diapers cheap, we'll stay in line. Although I enjoy complaining about the lack of

PRODUCTION

democracy in this country as much as the next person, the problem isn't an antidemocratic government, or rather, it's not *just* an antidemocratic government. The problem is our culture itself, of which the government and its form are only one inevitable manifestation, as are prisons, dams, corporations, the KKK, and so on.

If the problem were merely that our democracy was being corrupted by wealth, we could institute a functioning democracy in a flash. All we'd have to do is dump the notion of one vote per person, and give each person one vote divided by his or her net worth. A person with a net worth of a million dollars would get one-millionth of a vote, and a person with a net worth of one dollar would get one vote. This would effectively delink fiscal and political power. This won't happen, though, in part, for the same reason that those in power will never institute rules that cause those in power to go to jail for their crimes: When the health of the entire community (including the land base) is not a primary consideration of the culture, there's no compelling reason for those in power to create rules that, while they help the community as a whole, do not further their own power.

Of course, my suggestion is a joke, because ultimately we're not a democracy, nor even, really, a plutocracy. We're a theocracy, run by clerics, according to the unwavering dictates of a God who, like the God of the Old Testament, is jealous, and will allow no other gods to intrude.

I used to think the God of our culture is power, that all communities, people, landscapes, and relationships are sacrificed on that altar. I still think power is one part of our culture's holy trinity, and is too often unpleasantly central to our interpersonal relationships. But this central role played by power is questioned sometimes: People ask, even within the mainstream of our culture, whether our hyperemphasis on power serves us well. Yet there's another aspect of the culture's godhead that is even more invisible than power, and consequently less questioned. What, for example, was the motivating force behind slavery? What causes most of the world's environmental degra-

THE CULTURE OF MAKE BELIEVE

dation? In service of what is the full power of the U.S. military routinely employed?

Let me ask these questions another way: What value do communist, socialist, capitalist, and all other nation-states hold in common?

The answer is that they all value production and the economy over all else. Production is more important than profits: Essentially, all manufacturing would lose money without massive subsidies from the public by way of the state, which means that all industrial production is a losing gambit when the full costs are taken into account. Production is more important than communities. It is more important than ecological health or wealth. It is more important than happiness. It is more important than life.

■　　　■　　　■

Bhopal was not the first place Union Carbide caused death on a massive scale. The company is also responsible for the worst industrial disaster in the United States: the hundreds of deaths associated with the digging of the Hawk's Nest Tunnel in West Virginia in the 1930s.

Of the approximately 1,213 Union Carbide employees who worked at least two months digging the Hawk's Nest Tunnel, 764 (63 percent) died within seven years of silicosis.

Silicosis is considered the oldest occupational disease. Herodotus mentioned it after observing the premature deaths of miners. Agricola in the sixteenth century and Ramazzini in the eighteenth made the connection between certain types of dust and the onset of the disease. Seventeenth-century Spaniards noted that Indians forced to work in Peruvian mines died of silicosis within six to eighteen months.

By the late nineteenth century, the causal agent of silicosis had become even more clear. When tiny particles of silica—released when granite or sandstone are pulverized—are inhaled and absorbed deep in the lungs, the cells begin to digest themselves. The lungs be-

PRODUCTION

come scarred, lose their capacity to absorb oxygen, and become susceptible to infections such as pneumonia or tuberculosis. By 1911, twenty years before work commenced on the Hawk's Nest Tunnel, the connection between airborne silica and death by silicosis had been established well enough to cause even South Africa, with its cavalier attitude toward the deaths of black miners, to force its gold mines to use water to suppress dust when drilling. This means that while few South African miners who worked less than five years contracted silicosis, and while about 10 percent of those who worked ten years or more became ill, workers in the Hawk's Nest Tunnel had a greater than 60 percent death rate for less than two years of exposure. The point is that, to serve production, Union Carbide knowingly created conditions leading to the deaths of more than seven hundred and fifty human beings.

Here's how it happened.

In 1927 the Union Carbide and Carbon Corporation created the wholly-owned subsidiary New Kanawha Power Company. Later that year the subsidiary filed plans with the federal government to build a tunnel through the Hawk's Nest promontory in West Virginia, and to divert the flow of the New River through that tunnel. The entire river, large enough to be navigable one hundred and sixty-six miles above the Hawk's Nest site, would be diverted to generate electricity solely for the use of Union Carbide's metals plant at Boncar (now Alloy), West Virginia. The federal government did not oppose the plan. The next year, Union Carbide filed plans with the West Virginia State Public Service Commission. It was quickly approved. Martin Cherniak, author of *The Hawk's Nest Incident: America's Worst Industrial Disaster,* notes how remarkable it is "that a private corporation could buy parts of a major river system and effectively dewater more than five miles of riverbed without encountering significant objection from either state or federal government."

Construction on the three-mile tunnel began in 1930. Advancing at the breakneck pace of up to three hundred feet per week, the tunnel was completed by the end of 1931.

THE CULTURE OF MAKE BELIEVE

Since most of the workers were not local, having been attracted from all over the southern United States by the possibility of employment, Union Carbide's subcontractor, Rinehart and Dennis, built company camps. These camps were strictly segregated by race. Although the shanties in each camp were approximately the same size—one hundred to one hundred and fifty square feet divided into two rooms—those occupied by whites were wired for electricity and housed four men; those occupied by blacks (the majority of the workforce) were not wired and housed as many as twelve. No matter the occupancy, room and board for the shacks ran approximately six dollars a week, about half a laborer's salary.

Rinehart and Dennis routinely used violence against the black (though not the white) workers. A worker later recalled: "If a colored man was sick and really couldn't go to work in the morning, he had to hide out before the shack rouster came around. That fellow had two pistols and a blackjack to force men to go to work." The "shack rouster," employed by Rinehart and Dennis, had been deputized by the Fayette County sheriff. At least one of the white foremen routinely carried a baseball bat to assist him in overseeing the black workers, and a white engineer testified to the use of violence to force blacks to do the most dangerous work: "I have heard quite a few times that they used pick handles or a drillstead and knocked them in the head with it."

Typically, each shift of miners drilled three hundred and twenty holes into which they packed six to eight hundred pounds of dynamite. For the hour it took to detonate the charges, the men waited three to four hundred feet up the tunnel, after which they were forced—often at gunpoint and even before the dust had settled—to return to clear the debris. (They resisted returning because of the danger presented by silica dust.) Despite the tunnel being dug through rock, composed of 90 percent or more of silica (some estimates run to higher than 99 percent), and despite the well-understood relationship between exposure to airborne silica and death by silicosis, neither Union Carbide, New Kanawha Power Company,

PRODUCTION

nor Rinehart and Dennis ever measured dust levels in the tunnel. Worse, most of the drilling was "dry," that is, water was not used to suppress dust. Nor was water (or even ventilation) used to suppress dust from explosions. This led to dust in the tunnel "so thick that one could not identify anybody he met when the man was only a few feet away from him." At shift's end, dust concealed the complexion of the miners' faces as well as the color of their clothes, and dust marked their tracks for hundreds of feet as they returned to their camps.

Union Carbide responded to the rock's high silica content by requiring all New Kanawha employees, who were mainly engineers overseeing the project for Union Carbide, to wear respirators and receive warnings about the dangers of silica dust; the common laborers, on the other hand, received neither respirators nor warnings. After reports of the deaths of black workers reached Robert Lambie, director of the West Virginia Department of Mines, Lambie inspected the tunnel and wrote a letter to New Kanawha, warning of the hazards of silicosis and ordering that respirators be given to the laborers. His orders were ignored, at least in part because of the sentiment expressed by one company official: "I wouldn't give $2.50 for all the niggers on the job."

A 1931 article in the local paper, the *Fayette Tribune*, reveals another response by Union Carbide to the elevated silica content: "Like a tale from the story of Aladdin's lamp, boring of the tunnel has enriched the Union Carbide company with untold wealth. In the process of removing the rock, the workers came across a vast deposit of silica sandstone which assays 99.44 percent pure. . . . Discovery of this sandstone in the lower end of the tunnel, brought about a big change in the operations, for the excavations were immediately extended in size and the tunnel considerably enlarged." Union Carbide expanded the diameter of the tunnel from thirty-one to as many as forty-six feet and delivered three hundred thousand tons of silica ore to the site of its Boncar metals plant.

It was not long before workers began dying. To prevent public alarm or resentment against associated companies, Rinehart and

Dennis prohibited laborers from speaking to either the press or law officials (those who spoke out would get fired), and Union Carbide more firmly exerted its formidable influence over editorial policies of local newspapers.

The death toll grew too high to ignore, and, nearly a year after work began on the tunnel, the *Fayette Journal* finally noted "the great deal of comments about town regarding the unusually large number of deaths among colored laborers at tunnel works of the New Kanawha Power Company. The deaths total about 37 in the past two weeks." Cherniak comments on the paper's reluctance to forthrightly confront the disaster at Hawk's Nest: "A reader might wonder what height a local death toll must reach to merit mention in the newspapers of a rural town."

The physicians hired by Union Carbide and its associates were grossly inadequate for this wave of illness and death: Their prescription for what they called "tunnelitis" was that miners swallow "little black devils": tablets of baking soda coated with sugar. As the futility of this prescription became clear, Rinehart and Dennis surreptitiously, and at nearly twice the going rate, hired an undertaker from a neighboring county to quickly dispose of the bodies of workers who died on the job. The undertaker buried the bodies on his farm.

The company had no trouble replacing workers who died or fell ill. Material poverty and lack of other employment opportunities drove migrant workers to live in rotting shacks or fields, waiting for the rare chance at a job. Rinehart and Dennis were later to argue that since the laborers chose to work in the tunnel, presumably knowing those they replaced had fallen ill or died, no one but the workers themselves were culpable for the deaths. The judge in the first lawsuit against the companies made this claim as well. But were the workers in any meaningful sense making a choice? There is an important difference between making a choice and selecting an option from among artificially limited alternatives. In order for someone to make a choice, that person must also be free to not choose. In the 1982 film, *Sophie's Choice*, for example, on entry to a Nazi death camp the title character is forced to select one child to live,

PRODUCTION

and one to go immediately to the gas chamber. If she fails to select, they will both die. Using this definition, Sophie was not making a choice but selecting among bad alternatives. The same is true for workers hired by Union Carbide. Given the prevailing social conditions, laborers could select the option of working at this job, they could select the option of starving while they searched for another job in a depressed market, or they could select the option of working at no job and starving altogether. They did not have the freedom to not choose, that is, to not enter the wage economy, either by being self-sufficient or by relying upon an alternative community. As I hope was shown in the discussion of DeBeers and apartheid, and throughout this book, a primary function of government within our culture has been to disallow people the choice of remaining free of the "free-market" wage economy. Consider the taxes that were imposed by the South African government as a "gentle stimulus" to force workers into the mines, and consider the seventy million buffalo slaughtered as part of U.S. policy to bring Plains Indians to terms; these are only two of the many means by which people have been forced into the wage economy. Had it been possible, in a realistic sense, for the workers at the Hawk's Nest Tunnel to exit the wage economy and yet remain alive, they would have been making a choice. As it was, they were selecting one of many bad options. The systematic and ubiquitous replacement of choice with selection among inferior alternatives is a hallmark of our economics, and is one of the many ways people are forced to subsidize the business interests of those who govern.

In any case, once the new people were hired, room had to be made for them in the already crowded camps of the black laborers. One of the workers described how this was done: "When it got so a worker couldn't make it at all, when he got sick and simply couldn't go longer, the sheriff would come around and run him off the place, off the works. I have seen the sheriff and his men run the workers off their places when they were sick and weak, so weak that they could hardly walk. Some of them would have to stand up at the sides of trees to hold themselves up. And the sheriff and his men could plainly

THE CULTURE OF MAKE BELIEVE

see that the men were sick and unable to go, yet they kept making them keep on the move. . . . Many of the men died in the tunnel camps; they died in hospitals, under rocks, and every place else. . . . I can go right now and point to many graves only two blocks from where I live there now."

Soon after the tunnel's completion, in December 1931, workers and relatives of deceased workers began filing lawsuits against Rinehart and Dennis and/or Union Carbide's subsidiary, the New Kanawha Power Company.

At the first of these trials, some of the New Kanawha staff and many laborers testified to the high dust levels and to the use of dry drilling. In addition, five physicians also spoke in favor of the plaintiff, Raymond Johnson, including one who stated that 95 percent of the one hundred and seventy-five workers he had examined were suffering from acute silicosis. Others, however, testified that visibility in the tunnel had been excellent, better even than the air in the courtroom. A foreman for Rinehart and Dennis, who died, two years later, of silicosis, swore that all drilling had been wet. Robert Lambie, the director of the West Virginia Department of Mines, who earlier had ordered respirators for everyone in the tunnel, now testified on behalf of the companies. He stated visibility was seven hundred feet and that all drilling was wet. His previous letters and reports had been based, he said, on erroneous information received from his staff. Six days after his testimony, Lambie began a new business, that of private consultant to the largest industrial and mining corporations in the state. Near the end of the trial, one witness changed his testimony: The companies had threatened and bribed him to swear the air in the tunnel had been clean, he said, but his conscience now made him speak out. Nonetheless, the trial ended with a hung jury, and the judge dismissed the case. The judge later cited a jury member who had been driven to and from the court by Rinehart and Dennis employees. Referring to the corporations' purchase of witnesses and intimidation of jurors, a state investigator later said, "I think the payment of that money, the suspicious tampering with the jury system, was about the most damnable outrage

PRODUCTION

that had been perpetrated in any state up to that time." Raymond Johnson, the plaintiff, hired new attorneys to retry his suit, but died before the retrial.

By the spring of 1933, one hundred and fifty-seven lawsuits, seeking four million dollars, had been filed against the companies. In June, however, attorneys for both sides announced the cases were being settled for $130,000, half of which would go to the laborers' attorneys.

The attorneys ostensibly representing the workers secretly received an additional $20,000 in exchange for promising not to engage in further legal action and for handing their records over to the companies.

When knowledge of jury tampering and the attorneys' deal became public, an additional 202 victims filed suit. The court barred 142 of these as having been filed too late for consideration, and the West Virginia House of Delegates disallowed the rest by legislatively establishing impossible terms for the compensation of victims of silicosis. The House of Delegates retroactively placed a one-year statute of limitations on filing suits, despite (or, rather, because of) the potentially long latency period of silicosis, and despite (or, once again, because of) work having ceased on the Hawk's Nest Tunnel twenty-nine months earlier, and they also required victims to have been exposed to silica for a minimum of two years before they would be eligible for compensation. The latter requirement was added because work on the Hawk's Nest Tunnel lasted only eighteen months. After taking a test case to the Supreme Court and losing, the victims' attorneys settled out of court for $70,000.

As at Bhopal (and as these things nearly always go) Union Carbide interpreted the final settlement as a grand victory. The total compensation accruing to the 538 laborers—human beings—who filed suit was less than $130,000. Cherniak remarks that "the convergent acts or decisions of powerful corporate entities, state officials, and the courts had determined that less than four hundred dollars was the average worth of a tunnel worker's health or life."

THE CULTURE OF MAKE BELIEVE

The Hawk's Nest Tunnel was a successful investment for Union Carbide. It began to produce power for the company's Alloy plant in 1937, and to this day continues to generate electricity. In economic terms, the tunnel has paid for itself many times over—the costs of construction were repaid in less than a decade, only a few years after the 764th victim died of silicosis. As for the victims, well, the contractor put it best, when he said at later congressional hearings, "I knew I was going to kill these niggers, but I didn't know it was going to be this soon."

●　　　　　●　　　　　●

It would be a mistake, by the way, to think Bhopal and Hawk's Nest are the only places Carbide has killed people in the name of production. Take Oak Ridge, Tennessee, for example, where from the 1940s to 1984 Union Carbide ran nuclear weapons plants. The company insisted the plants were safe, and that workers were exposed to no more radiation than if they wore luminous-dial wristwatches. But the company was lying, as was revealed, in 1980, by one of the workers, Joe Harding, months before he died of radiation poisoning: "At the end of the day you could look back behind you and see your tracks in the uranium dust that had settled that day. You could look up at the lights and see a blue haze between you and the light. And we ate our lunch in this every day. We'd just find some place to sit down, brush away the dust, and eat lunch."

He described the company's safety testing: "We had these film badges we wore to indicate exposure. Every few days they'd take up the badges and send them off to the Oak Ridge National Laboratory [also run by Union Carbide] for analysis. One day a few of us men layed our badges on a smoking chunk of uranium for eight hours and turned it in. We never heard from it. They took urine samples from us every ten days. Once somebody dropped a small chunk of uranium in the urine sample. Nothing was ever said about it."

The supervisors told them to falsify records pertaining to radioactive contamination, and made clear that they were going to

PRODUCTION

lose their jobs if they didn't. Harding went along, and later described the company's disposal methods: "If we had tanks of contaminated liquid or gases that had to be disposed of, we'd just wait until a dark night when there was no moon and just shoot it right up the stack. Sometimes we didn't even wait for a dark night. Of course we were dumping it around on all these farms. . . ." As a result of these practices people who worked at an Oak Ridge factory for between five and ten years are nearly five times more at risk than normal for brain cancer and more than nine times more at risk for leukemia and aleukemia. None of those poisoned by radiation received disability compensation from the company. Even a partial cleanup of the chemical and radioactive pollution left at Oak Ridge by Union Carbide would cost U.S. taxpayers at least $838 million.

The problems are not confined to Tennessee. By the 1970s, the company's plant at Alloy, West Virginia, was the dirtiest plant in the United States, releasing seventy thousand tons of particulates per year, more than the total emitted in New York City in 1971. By the 1980s Union Carbide's pesticide, "Temik," had directly poisoned hundreds of people and contaminated ground and drinking water in twenty-two states. When a test of eight thousand wells on Long Island revealed that two thousand of them were contaminated with Temik, Union Carbide lobbied the New York Department of Health to raise the level considered safe. The Department of Health threshold was seven parts per billion. The wells tested as high as 515 parts per billion.

Union Carbide has typically denied the existence or minimized the severity of the harm it does to others. For example, after a cloud of gas escaped a Union Carbide plant, drifted into a mall, and left shoppers semiconscious, the company for two days denied it had been the source. Another example: After a leak of chemicals used to manufacture Temik sent 135 people to seek medical attention, Union Carbide chair Warren Anderson said, "I think that, if we had a release of [the perfume] Arpege, 135 of them would go to the hospital." This spill, and Anderson's comment, came after Bhopal, revealing that the

THE CULTURE OF MAKE BELIEVE

deaths of those eight thousand taught him nothing. And another: The company caused the worst mercury spill in U.S. history. Between 1953 and 1977, Union Carbide discharged 2.4 million pounds of mercury from one of its Oak Ridge facilities, at least 475,000 pounds of which entered just one stream. The company's response was threefold, and by now I'm sure you can predict it: to classify the information and not warn those exposed; to reprimand for insubordination the scientist who, in 1983, working on his own time, uncovered the extent of the pollution; and to claim that since Oak Ridge was a "relatively affluent city for East Tennessee, populated by scientists and engineers who have other life pursuits than habitual sports fishing," fish consumption should not be a problem. This last statement ignored the fifteen hundred African Americans who lived along the stream and ate its fish. And of course it ignored the fish. Yet again: In Indonesia, after mercury from a Union Carbide plant contaminated rice fields and groundwater and caused kidney disease in 402 employees, company officials told doctors not to tell workers about the problem, and workers who struck against dangerous factory conditions were fired. While beside the point, it's worth noting that female workers who married or became pregnant were fired as well. The list of releases and denials goes on, with spills or explosions in New York, Texas, South Carolina, California, Louisiana, Virginia, Puerto Rico, Belgium, Australia, and Mexico, among many others. Between 1987 and mid-1994, Union Carbide reported more than five hundred toxic spills from its U.S. operations alone. That's more than one per week.

■　　　■　　　■

It would be just as much of a mistake to think Carbide is the only company that has killed people in the name of production. I could just as easily write about Freeport-McMoRan, an American-based mining company committing genocide in southeastern Asia by destroying the environment of native cultures, dispossessing natives of their land, and mowing down with machine-gun fire those who re-

PRODUCTION

sist. Or I could write about RTZ committing genocide in South America by destroying the environment of native cultures, dispossessing natives of their land, and mowing down with machine-gun fire those who resist. Or I could write about Shell, a Dutch-based oil company committing genocide in Africa by destroying the environment of native cultures, dispossessing natives of their land, and having hanged those who resist. Or I could write about the routine atrocities committed in the insatiable pursuit of profits by Cargill, Exxon, Monsanto, Weyerhaeuser, RJ Reynolds, General Electric, Tyson, Maxxam, or any other large corporation.

Corporations, like pieces of art, religions, or other human artifacts, beliefs, or institutions, are manifestations of cultural desire. Any human construct arises in its precise form only within the specific culture that creates it. The music of Jimi Hendrix could not have happened in the 1920s, and the art of Picasso could not have been created and nourished by twelfth-century Normans. Christianity arose within the specific historical-geographical context of the Judeo-Roman Middle East; Taoism at the ancient boundary between civilized and indigenous China; Christianity could not have arisen two thousand years ago in what is now the Pacific Northwest of the United States; nor could primal Taoism originate in modern Asia. American Indians did not create corporations. Only our culture has done that.

Corporations such as DeBeers, Union Carbide, Freeport McMoRan, and any others you care to name are fruits of our modern, civilized, industrialized society. What cultural desires manifest themselves in these institutions?

It's not just corporations. Think about a number I mentioned in passing a few pages ago. More than half of the U.S. government's discretionary spending goes to the military, to war. This country is the largest exporter of weapons, including weapons of mass destruction. The United States is the largest user of weapons, including, once again, weapons of mass destruction. It is also the largest producer of instruments of torture.

Consider the B-2 bomber. We can conservatively estimate that

each B-2 bomber costs $2.4 billion. Since each plane weighs between 130 and 135 tons, these planes cost the American public over $500 an ounce, more than the price of gold or platinum and one hundred times the price of silver. The bombers cost considerably more to those whose lives are most intimately affected by them: their targets, the people of Iraq, Serbia, and anywhere else the United States decides to flex its muscles, in support of industrial production.

In a finite world, every resource expended for one purpose is unavailable for any other purpose. If you eat a salmon, I cannot eat that particular salmon. If one eats or otherwise kills all of the salmon, no one will ever eat salmon again. The same principle works in economics. Every dollar spent building a B-2 bomber is unavailable to pay for immunization and food that a child needs to survive. Every human-hour used is unavailable to rehabilitate damaged streams, to create music or poetry, to play with children, or to teach people how to read. Every gigawatt of electricity consumed is unavailable to run hospitals or schools, or to take down the ecologically destructive dams that may have generated the electricity (although the wattage more likely came from fossil fuels). Since no one in her right mind wishes to kill people by dropping bombs on them, the best any of us can sanely hope for is that every resource used in the construction of these bombers will be wasted. The alternative is that the bombers will be used for their designated purpose, which is to destroy. What cultural rootstock would put its resources into yielding such fruit as this? What cultural consciousness would engender such choices?

A couple of thousand years ago, Jesus of Nazareth said, "By their fruits shall ye know them." Not by their words. Not by their stated intent. By the actual produce of their labor. Corporations that consistently kill in the name of production, and governments that use the full power of the state to back them up. Pesticides. Dewatered rivers. Silicosis. B-2 bombers. Nuclear weapons delivery systems. What do the existence of these artifacts say about our culture? We study paintings on the walls of the Lascaux caves and ask ourselves

PRODUCTION

what those artifacts say about the culture that created them. We study masks of indigenous peoples of Central America to learn about their cultures. We fully recognize that the music of Jimi Hendrix provides a clue to the cultural texture of Britain and America in the 1960s. Is it so great a leap to ask what clues the stories of Union Carbide and other corporations reveal about the inner workings of our culture?

The cultural consciousness in which we find ourselves immersed is creating artifacts and institutions that are destroying life on this planet. They are destroying cultures, uprooting and eliminating ways of life. They are ripping apart communities. They are taking the lives of individuals, quickly, by killing them, and, slowly, by eliminating any alternative to the wage economy.

There is a difference between putting on a white robe and calling someone a nigger, then castrating and lynching him, and sitting behind a desk, calling someone a worker, then profiting from his labor and poisoning him. But there are clearly more similarities than we care to think about. Or than we care to think about clearly.

■   ■   ■

I called Kevin Bales—probably the world's foremost authority on modern slavery. I'd wanted to talk to him ever since I'd read his book, *Disposable People*, which deals with the fact that there are more slaves living today than came over on the Middle Passage. I asked him to define modern slavery.

"In many ways," he said, "it's exactly the same as slavery two or three hundred years ago. It's still slavery in the sense that people are controlled by violence, allowed no free will, not paid, and are economically exploited. That definition applies whether you're talking about ancient Greece, Mississippi in 1850, or Los Angeles in 2000."

Although Bales has spent a lot of time in the States, he still has a clean British accent. He continued, "Slavery is different, too, of

THE CULTURE OF MAKE BELIEVE

course, in the same way life is different now than it was in ancient Greece or antebellum Mississippi. We live in a global economy, and nowadays slavery is more globalized than ever. Also it tends at least sometimes to be more temporary—slavery for a more limited amount of time, as opposed to slavery over generations. Perhaps most importantly, there are now a lot more people who are enslaved—there is now an absolute glut of human slaves on the market—meaning that slaves have become very, very cheap, far cheaper than they've ever been in human history."

I asked him to define slavery.

He said, "I like Orlando Patterson's definition having to do with what he calls the 'social death' of the slave: Slavery is the permanent, violent domination of alienated and dishonored people." Bales hesitated a moment before he continued, "I think, however, that this definition, and the power relationship between slaveholders and slaves, can be broken into three components. The first is social, and involves the use or threat of violence by the slaveholder to control the slave. The second is psychological, and has to do with convincing slaves to perceive their slavery as actually being in their own best interests. The third is cultural, and has to do with transforming force into a right of the powerful and obedience into a duty of the powerless, which, as Rousseau would have put it, ensures that the powerful maintain continual ownership. This latter means of course that the coercive power of the slaveholder is and always has been tied intimately to the coercive power of the state. The former can't exist for long without the latter. All that said, my own definition, the simplest one and the one I use most often, is that a slave is anyone held by violence or the threat of violence, paid nothing, and economically exploited."

I commented that he had used the word *slaveholder* as opposed to *slave owner*.

He responded, "In the past, slavery entailed one person legally owning another. But modern slavery is different. Slavery in terms of ownership is illegal everywhere, and there exists in the world no more *legal* ownership of human beings. But there still exist many

PRODUCTION

many millions of people who are controlled and economically exploited by violence. This nonownership turns out in many cases to be in the interest of slaveholders, who now have all the benefits of ownership without the obligations and legalities."

I thought of the words of proslavery philosopher John Henry Hammond: "In all countries where the denseness of the population has reduced it to a matter of perfect certainty, that labor can be obtained, whenever wanted, and that the laborer can be forced, by sheer necessity, to hire for the smallest pittance that will keep soul and body together, and rags upon his back while in actual employment—dependent at all other times on alms or poor rates—in all such countries it is found cheaper to pay this pittance, than to clothe, feed, nurse, support through childhood, and pension in old age, a race of slaves." I thought also of Hammond's conclusion, that "if I could cultivate my lands on these terms, I would, without a word, resign my slaves, provided they could be properly disposed of." Finally, it occurred to me, talking to Kevin Bales, that slavery didn't disappear in the United States or elsewhere because we suddenly became less racist, or less exploitative, or more enlightened, or more humane, or for any of the other reasons I was taught in school. It didn't disappear because of the efforts of abolitionists, or even because of the Civil War. Slavery didn't disappear at all. It merely changed form, and did so because the newer form better serves the high priests of our theocracy: the producers.

I asked, "What's the relationship between globalization and slavery?"

He said that slavery was one of the first proto-globalized industries: "The Middle Passage, for example, tied together three continents—Africa, Europe, and the Americas—and the profits made around that triangle shifted back and forth among these continents. It was very internationalist. But in the past, once slavery was in place, the slaves themselves and the products of their labor often remained local. Although slave-produced cotton was exported

THE CULTURE OF MAKE BELIEVE

from the U.S., and slave-produced sugar was exported from Brazil and the Caribbean, to provide two examples among many, slaves often produced foods and other products for local markets. Today it's far more likely that the output of slaves feeds into the global market. For example, we know that there is a significant slave input in the cocoa plantations of West Africa. Now, chocolate is eaten all over the planet. Maybe forty percent of the world's chocolate is tainted with slavery. Steel, sugar, tobacco products, jewelry, the list goes on and on. There are so many products tainted with slavery, and these products move so smoothly around the globe, that the global economy has smoothed the way to move slavery around the planet as well."

I commented, "It sounds like everyone—or at least everyone in the industrialized world—probably has slave products at home."

He agreed. "A lot of people would be surprised to learn there's a very good chance they've got something in their homes that's got a link to a slave. One of the difficulties in being sure, however, is that because the global market in commodities is like a money-laundering machine, slavery can be very difficult to trace. Cocoa coming out of West Africa and entering the world cocoa commodity market, for example, almost immediately loses its label, in the sense that if you're a buyer for Hershey's or another chocolate corporation, you don't say, 'I'd like to buy six tons of Ghanian cocoa.' You just say you want so many tons of cocoa. When the cocoa is delivered at your factory, you can't actually tell whether this is Ghanaian cocoa, which might be free of slavery, or cocoa from the Ivory Coast, which has lots of slavery in it. So you pass the slave-tainted product on without knowing, and the consumers buy it without knowing.

"That's one thing I mean," he continued, "when I talk about the globalization of slavery. But I mean something else as well. It used to be that slavery tended to be virtually unique in every culture: The form of slavery you found in Pakistan wasn't the same as what you

PRODUCTION

found in Thailand. But since the Second World War, slavery in different countries has become more and more alike. We're seeing a new, global form of slavery."

∎ ∎ ∎

Our culture has made us all slaves to an idea, an idea that takes precedence over everything, over our own lives and the lives of others. And slavery to an idea is far more dangerous than slavery to a human, because we do not even know that we are slaves. We pass through our days with the freedom of a dog who never reaches the end of its leash, certain that what we see is all of reality, all there ever was, all there ever will be, all that is possible. Having enslaved ourselves to this idea, we then enslave others, passing on the knowledge of how to be a slave from father to son, father to daughter, mother to son, mother to daughter, sibling to sibling, teacher to student, owner to laborer, boss to employee, slave to slave.

It's not easy to remove this leash we're not wearing, to break this leash that doesn't exist. How could I be a slave when I live in the land of the free? I choose my jobs, I choose where I live, I choose how I spend my time. I am not enslaved to industrial mass production. I am not enslaved to the perception of others as objects to be exploited. I am not enslaved to anything. I am a free man, and nothing you can say will convince me otherwise.

∎ ∎ ∎

"The kind of slavery most Americans hold in their minds is of course slavery as it was in the United States before the Civil War," Kevin Bales said to me. "That kind of slavery had very expensive slaves. Today slaves are cheap, for a couple of reasons. The first is the population explosion, and the second is the pushing of large numbers of people in the Third World into economic and social vulnerability. This means there are a lot more potential slaves out

there. Now, factor in the third leg of the stool—with the first being sheer numbers of people, the second being that a lot of them are vulnerable, and the third being the ability to enforce slavery through violence, usually done by or with the approval of corrupt police or governmental officials—and you can see how slaveholders can harvest so many slaves."

I had never before heard the word harvest used to describe the capture of human beings.

"I'm not sure what the average price of a slave is in the world today," he continued, "but it can't be more than fifty or sixty dollars. That's obviously a significant change compared to the $50,000 you'd have paid for a slave in 1850. And the low prices slaveholders put out for slaves influences how the slaves are treated. If you pay a hundred dollars for someone, that person is disposable. In gold-mining towns in the Amazon, a young girl might cost one hundred and fifty dollars. She's been recruited to work in offices there, but then is beaten, raped, and put out to prostitution. She can be sold up to ten times a night, and can bring in ten thousand dollars per month. The only expenses are payments to the police and a pittance for food. And if the girl is a troublemaker, or if she runs away, or if she gets sick, it's easy enough to get rid of her and replace her with someone else. It's not uncommon in some of these villages for people to wake up in the morning and see the body of a young girl floating by on the river. Nobody bothers to bury them. The slaveholders throw the girls' bodies in the river to be eaten by the fish. Antonia Pinta described what happened to an eleven-year-old girl who refused to have sex with a miner: He cut off her head with a machete, then drove around in his speedboat, showing off her head to the other miners, who shouted their approval."

For a moment, neither of us spoke.

Finally, he continued, "One of the reasons modern slavery is so pernicious is that people are so cheap that they're not even seen as a capital investment: You don't have to take care of them, you just have to use them, use them hard, use them up, and throw them away. In

PRODUCTION

this way people have become completely disposable tools for making money, an input to the productive process, in the same way you buy a box of plastic ballpoint pens."

■   ■   ■

It's not possible to keep a society together using only violence and threats of violence: People who perceive themselves as having nothing left to lose are far more likely to resist than those whose privileges (or promised privileges, or perceived privileges) can be revoked for improper behavior. This is true even in prison, and is the reason for policies of "time off for good behavior," where, for example, for every day served without incident, an inmate may get an extra day removed from the sentence. Prison administrators long ago discovered that inmates facing hopelessly long sentences had no compelling reason to follow prison regulations.

This pairing of carrots and sticks works as well outside prison walls as it does inside of them. One of the carrots underlying American order is the belief that with enough diligence, perseverance, pluck, and luck, you, too, can strike it rich. Anyone can. The next Bill Gates, we're told, is even now a teenager foregoing dates and basketball games, so he can tinker on his computer and eventually invent the Next Big Thing.

The Horatio Alger tale is an extraordinary piece of propaganda, for a number of reasons, undoubtedly the foremost of which has to do precisely with what the fable doesn't talk about. One of the first rules of effective propaganda is that if you can get people to sign on to your assumptions, you can, without a break in your logic, lead them wherever you want. This was true, for example, of Hitler, about whom it was said that "from insane premises to monstrous conclusions Hitler was relentlessly logical." If you accept Hitler's premise that the "holiest human right and . . . obligation" is "to see to it that the blood is preserved pure and, by preserving the best humanity, to create the possibility of a nobler development of these beings," and, if further, you accept his assertion that "the Jew" is an "eternal blood-

THE CULTURE OF MAKE BELIEVE

sucker," a "vampire," a "maggot in a rotting corpse" who destroys cultures, then it's easy to allow yourself to become convinced that it's not unreasonable—in fact, imperative—to rid yourself of these bloodsuckers by any means possible.

The best propaganda leaves its assumptions unstated, glides quickly past them to sweep up the audience in the argument itself, until, before the audience knows it, they're agreeing to and participating in assembly-line mass murder, or in enslaving and killing the planet. What was true in the 1930s and 1940s is certainly true today, as we blithely accept the internal logic of the stories we've been handed without questioning the insane premises that lead in our own case, too, to monstrous conclusions and even more monstrous actions.

PRODUCTION

THE FAILURE OF THE GREAT PROMISE, ASIDE FROM INDUSTRIALISM'S ESSENTIAL ECONOMIC CONTRADICTIONS, WAS BUILT INTO THE INDUSTRIAL SYSTEM BY ITS TWO MAIN PSYCHOLOGICAL PREMISES: (1) THAT THE AIM OF LIFE IS HAPPINESS, THAT IS, MAXIMUM PLEASURE, DEFINED AS THE SATISFACTION OF ANY DESIRE OR SUBJECTIVE NEED A PERSON MAY FEEL (RADICAL HEDONISM); (2) THAT EGOTISM, SELFISHNESS, AND GREED, AS THE SYSTEM NEEDS TO GENERATE THEM IN ORDER TO FUNCTION, LEAD TO HARMONY AND PEACE.

ERICH FROMM

FALSE
CONTRACTS

In 1999, Dina Chan gave a speech to the First National Congress on Gender and Development in Phnom Penh. She is a member of the Sex Workers Union of Cambodia. Here is part of what she said: "I came here today as a woman, a Khmer woman. I came here today to tell you my story, in the hope that after you listen to me you can understand my situation and the situation of thousands of Khmer women and other women around the world. It is very difficult for me to come here to speak to you; but I am doing this because I want you to listen, to me the real person; and I want you to remember me and what I say to you today when you are in your offices talking about policies and strategies that affect me and my sisters.

"I want you to remember we are not 'problems,' we are not animals, we are not viruses, we are not garbage. We are flesh, skin and bones, we have a heart, we are a sister to someone, a daughter, a granddaughter. We are people, we are women and we want to be treated with respect, dignity and we want rights like the rest of you enjoy. I was trafficked. I was raped, beaten, and forced to accept men. I was humiliated and forced to be an object so men, yes, men, could take their pleasure. I brought profit to many and brought pleasure to others. And for myself I brought shame, pain and humiliation."

I've read her speech many times, and each time I think about the relationship between economics and hatred, and what it means—what it must feel like—to live in a society where more atrocities are committed in the name of economics than even in the name of hate, where a hatred, a contempt, a disdain, a disregard for all life undergirds our economics, where a woman can be forced into a situation where she brings profit to many and pleasure to others, and shame, pain, and humiliation to herself. I asked earlier what sort of people could create a god who supports slavery, and I ask, each time I read Dina Chan's testimony, what sort of people could create an economics so hateful as this.

Later in her speech, she said, "I come from a poor family; they sent me to study at a cultural school in Phnom Penh. . . . One night a man followed me when I was on my way home and raped me. I was only 17 years of age. You cannot imagine how I felt and what impact this had on me. But after that, I was lured to becoming a sex worker under false pretenses."

Every time I read her speech I think also about false contracts, about how our culture has always been based on them. We are promised always so much, yet, in the end, there are always profits for those who told us these stories, some strange sense of pleasure, perhaps, for others, and, for all of us, the shame, pain, and humiliation of living in a culture that values money over life. Now, I would not presume to know much about Dina Chan's experience. I am not sug-

FALSE CONTRACTS

gesting that I or anyone else who has not lived her life can even begin to imagine what she has been through, nor the courage and strength she has been forced to demonstrate. I am merely remarking on a pattern. Dina Chan is not the only one who has been given a false contract. There are the people of the Third World—the colonies—who are promised better lives if their homelands industrialize, if they enter the world economy. There are indigenous peoples who are promised the same. This morning I read that civilization has just contacted a previously "undiscovered" tribe of indigenous people in Brazil. I wonder what contracts they will be offered, and how long they—the contracts, and the people—will last. I think about the Indians who greeted explorers and settlers with open arms. The Indians who signed treaties. The indentured servants whose terms of enslavement seemed to end only and always in death. And, later, the settlers themselves, who more often than not found themselves defrauded of their money and their lives by corporate spokespeople who told them not to worry about the barrenness of the land they had just bought, that rain would surely follow the plow, or who, to entice peasants from around the world into buying otherwise worthless land, equated, in one example, the climate of Montana to "the mildness of Southern Ohio." Wave after wave of immigrants arrived in the United States, and wave after wave found themselves despised, exploited, worked to death. The average life span of Irish immigrants in the nineteenth century was six years. The average migrant farmworker in the United States today dies at forty-nine. But wave after wave of immigrants accepted the premises of the American Dream, and so fought other immigrants, who fought them back, fought native poor whites, who fought them back, fought Chinese and free blacks, who often dared not fight them back for fear of raising a fury of a sort only the powerless can feel toward those who have even less power, fought all of these for the opportunity to break their backs enriching those in power.

Those in power, too, have signed contracts just as false, basing their lives on the mistaken belief that power or money or physical comfort equates with safety or security, or "harmony and peace." Perhaps they live their whole lives so deluded, perhaps they die never knowing what could have been, where they could have gone, who they could have become, had they thrown off the chains they did not know they were wearing, the chains they cannot admit exist, the chains they will kill to keep hidden from their own view. But their ignorance does not belie the truth that humans were not meant to live this way, that one man's pleasure or profit based on another person's pain or degradation is pleasure or profit only for those who have objectified not only others but themselves, as well, only for those who have cut not only others but themselves into little pieces. When I make love with another, do I make love with my penis only? Is that the only part of me involved? Is that all I am? Or is there more to me than that? Does lovemaking involve my thighs, my belly, the back of my neck, the insides of my elbows? Is *that* all I am? Or is there more to me than that? Does making love involve my mind, my heart, my history, my future, my cares, my fears, as well? Now is *that* all sexuality is? Or is there more to it than that? Does it involve, as well, that intersection between me and all I am and my partner and all she is? Is there more to sex than simply that rising feeling in the belly before orgasm? And who is to say that sex is any different than any other part of our lives? Who is to say how much richness I rob myself of by interacting only economically with those around me? And, worse, how much does it hurt me to take my pleasure from one who is unwilling, or who is hurt, or degraded, in that pleasuring? How does it hurt me to redefine myself as one who feels no connection, who chains myself to one definition of myself while denying emphatically and in action those chains of relatedness that in all reality bind each of us to every other? How much does it impoverish me to live in a society where, by mutual and unsound agreement, we all seem to value something as intangible and unreal as money more than we value something so tangible, so real, so necessary as a beating heart, a willing body, and a contented and happy and self-assured and self-

FALSE CONTRACTS

possessed person? How can we value money more than relationships, more than life?

What can we say, also, about the technologies that are supposed to make our lives easier but instead endanger our own lives? Is this not, too, a false contract foisted upon us by those who believe in these technologies and that we have also foisted upon ourselves? The culture in question here has been on this continent for less than five hundred years, and it has rendered a good portion of the water undrinkable. We are in the process of rendering the air unbreathable: For those with pollution-induced asthma, cancer, or any other such diseases, we already have. We sign on the dotted line for aluminum cans and find that salmon are stolen in the bargain. We take jobs in the forest and the forests are destroyed. We turn on the lights and find that we have been handed poisons that last a thousand human lifetimes. How is it possible to make human and humane choices—choices that benefit ourselves and others as human beings—when, each time we sign a contract, we find ourselves further enslaved?

Having been tricked into signing a contract binding her to the man who became her owner, her *maebon*, her pimp, Dina Chan was locked into a pig slaughter cell and gang raped. In the morning she heard the pigs screaming as they were being pushed into their pens. She said, "I knew what that feeling was like: I was no better than the pigs to these men; and they could have killed me. Something inside me did die, and I will never be the same. I am twenty-four years old and my life has been like this since 1993. . . . I know starvation, I know slavery, I know being forced to work all day. But I also know physical violation and torture every day, I know discrimination and hatred from my country people, I know not being wanted and accepted from my society, the society that put me in this condition. I know fear, I feel it every day, even now that I dare speak my life is in danger.

"Some of you think I'm bad because I choose to remain a sex worker," she said later. "My answer to those people is I think your society, my society, my motherland Cambodia, is bad because it does-

THE CULTURE OF MAKE BELIEVE

n't give girls like me choices; choices I see are better for me. I think it is bad that my country allows men to rape young women like me and my sisters and go unpunished. I think it is bad that my society lets men seek and demand the services of women like me. I think it is criminal that we are enslaved to make money for the powerful. I think it is bad that my family are so poor and getting poorer because they cannot survive as farmers with little resources which are getting smaller because more powerful people move them off their land. I think it is bad the police treat me and my sisters like we are criminals but those who exploit us and take our dignity, our money and sometimes our lives live in freedom, enjoying their lives with their families. Because why? Because they have a powerful relative, because they have money."

Who determines that money is more valuable than life? Who determines that those with money are more powerful? What is money, in the end? It is paper. It is metal. It cannot be eaten. The paper can be burned for heat. But it is nothing. It is nothing except what we make of it. It is nothing except what we pretend it to be.

"Is this right? Is this justice? My sisters and I do not create the demand, we are the objects; the demand comes from the men, the men come to us. We are cheated, deceived, trafficked, humiliated and tortured. Why? Because men want us and we bring money to the powerful. But we are the powerless."

It all boils down to whether you believe in the possibility and desirability of fully mutual, fully engaged relationships. It all boils down to whether and when you feel it is in your best interest to perceive and treat others on their own terms, rather than as objects, as means to ends, and whether you are socially rewarded for doing so. It finally becomes a question of whether we can perceive others. It boils down to our ability to tell the difference between others and objects.

"You give us AIDS; when we are no longer profitable you leave us to die, but we do not die in peace: you point your finger and you blame us. You, the development organizations, give us condoms and teach us all the time about AIDS. We do not want your words, we do not want your judgment, we do not want you to tell us what is better

FALSE CONTRACTS

for us. We know about AIDS; we watch our sisters die from the disease.

"Ask us if we have the power to demand condom use from our clients. Look at me: You see a woman, but my boss sees dollars. An extra payment to my boss and the client does not wear a condom. If I protest I receive a beating. If I die tomorrow no one cares: There are many other girls who will be tricked and trafficked like me, because we feed many people.

"I do not want to go to your shelter and learn to sew so you can get me work in a factory," she concluded." This is not what I want. If I tell you that you will call me a prostitute. But those words are easy for you because you have easy solutions to difficult problems you do not understand, and you do not understand because you do not listen."

■ ■ ■

There is a difference between that which is natural and that which is not. I have heard people—usually, but not always, those with an antienvironmental ax to grind—suggest that because humans are natural that everything humans do or create is natural. Chainsaws are natural. Nuclear bombs are natural. Our economics is natural. Sex slavery is natural. Asphalt is natural. Cars are natural. Polluted water is natural. A devastated world is natural. A devastated psyche is natural. Unbridled exploitation is natural. Pure objectification is natural. This is, of course, nonsense. We are embedded in the natural world. We evolved as social creatures in this natural world. We require clean water to drink, or we die. We require clean air to breathe, or we die. We require food, or we die. We require love, affection, social contact in order to become our full selves. It is part of our evolutionary legacy as social creatures. Anything that helps us to understand all of this is natural: Any ritual, artifact, process, action is natural, to the degree that it reinforces our understanding of our embeddedness in the natural world, and any ritual, artifact, process, action is unnatural, to the degree that it does not.

We can make the same distinction for our humanity. We are

human creatures. Those humans around us are human creatures. These are undeniable statements. Those around us are not resources. They are not there to be used. They have lives as valuable to them as ours are to us. These are undeniable statements. Any ritual, artifact, process, action is human and humane, to the degree that it reinforces our perception of ourselves and those around us as human beings, and any ritual, artifact, process, action is unnatural, to the degree that it hinders that perception. Our economics is inhuman and it is inhumane: It hinders—or more precisely renders impossible—our perception of others as humans. It is possible to have an economics which is not inhuman but human and humane. It would be a face-to-face, nonindustrial economy. Our war is inhuman and inhumane, as it springs from the same mind- and heart-set as our economics, and is predicated on the same preconceptions. It is possible to have a war that is human and humane. It would be a face-to-face, nonindustrial war. Our hate is inhuman and inhumane. It does not see the other as an individual but as an object, insofar as the other is seen at all. It is possible to have a hate that is human and humane: I can hate another because of who he or she is: This hatred is, as true for everything else, face-to-face. And, as Dina Chan makes clear, as the millions of hits at porn sites make clear, as the one woman out of four who is raped in our culture makes clear, as the 565,000 American children who are killed or injured by their parents or guardians each year make clear, as the wretched state of so many relationships—romantic and otherwise—makes clear, love itself is inhuman and inhumane. It is possible to have a love that is humane, and that is human.

We each of us go through our days making choice upon choice. Each day, several times each day, each time she pleases a man for pay, Dina Chan makes a very reasonable choice within the strict constraints of her personal (and social) history. We, too, make reasonable choices among the limited options before us. What will it take, however, for each of us to begin rejecting the inhuman options offered by an inhumane system and begin to live like human beings?

■   ■   ■

FALSE CONTRACTS

The fundamental premise of Horatio Alger stories is that it's a good thing to strike it rich. Left unexamined, and, certainly, unanswered, are messy questions about the origins of anyone's wealth, and of the inevitability of one person's wealth being based not only on another person's poverty but on the impoverishment of the planet. At least nineteenth-century slave owners sometimes had the grace and honesty to admit that their wealth was based on the misery of others. That is more than I can say for us.

Even if we presume that wealth does not cause a concomitant and much broader poverty, rags-to-riches tales ignore the fact that the primary means by which people become wealthy in our culture is through inheritance, with the secondary means being government subsidies. One could argue that both of these lag far behind theft as a form of enrichment: theft of land from indigenous peoples, theft of habitat from nonhumans, theft of habitat from future humans, and so on. But the point, as it relates to this study, is that the tale strongly suggests that if you don't strike it rich, if your American Dream turns into a nightmare of overtime, delayed (at least) gratification, and quiet desperation (assuming no hunger, degradation, and early death), it's your own damn fault. You're too lazy, too stupid, or you just didn't follow the rules quite carefully enough. Or, maybe, you weren't the right color.

■   ■   ■

Today I saw a bumper sticker today that said, "Religion is what keeps the poor from murdering the rich." I think that's right, but it's also only part of the story. I think that the judicial system is also what keeps the poor from murdering the rich. And the police. And what we are taught in school keeps the poor from murdering the rich. The stories we are taught at home from infancy are what keeps the poor from murdering the rich. The belief that it is acceptable to be rich is what keeps the poor from murdering the rich. The desire to be like them keeps the poor from murdering the rich. None of this, of course, keeps the rich from murdering the poor.

After seeing the bumper sticker, I came home, and started looking for something. I didn't know what it was, but only that I would know it when I found it. I began pulling books off the shelves, scanning pages. And then I saw it. It was a quote from historian Howard Zinn: "[Civil disobedience] is not our problem. Our problem is civil obedience. Our problem is that numbers of people all over the world have obeyed the dictates of the leaders of their government and have gone to war, and millions have been killed because of this obedience. . . . Our problem is that people are obedient all over the world in the face of poverty and starvation and stupidity, and war, and cruelty. Our problem is that people are obedient while the jails are full of petty thieves, and all the while the grand thieves are running the country. That's our problem."

FALSE CONTRACTS

AT ALL STAGES OF THE HOLOCAUST, THEREFORE, THE VICTIMS WERE *CONFRONTED* WITH A CHOICE (AT LEAST SUB-JECTIVELY—EVEN WHEN OBJEC-TIVELY THE CHOICE DID NOT EXIST ANY MORE . . .). THEY COULD NOT CHOOSE BETWEEN GOOD AND BAD SITUATIONS, BUT THEY COULD AT LEAST CHOOSE BETWEEN GREATER AND LESSER EVIL. MOST IM-PORTANTLY, THEY COULD DI-VERT SOME BLOWS FROM THEMSELVES BY STRESSING, AND MANIFESTING, THEIR ENTITLE-MENT TO AN EXEMPTION OR TO A SPECIAL TREATMENT. IN OTHER WORDS, THEY HAD SOMETHING TO SAVE. TO MAKE THEIR VIC-TIMS' BEHAVIOR PREDICTABLE AND HENCE MANI- PULABLE AND CONTROLLABLE, THE NAZIS HAD TO INDUCE THEM TO ACT

COMP

in the "rational mode"; to achieve that effect, they had to make the victims believe that there was indeed something to save, and that there were clear rules as to how one should go about saving it. To believe that, the victims had to be convinced that the treatment of the group as a whole would not be uniform, that the lot of individual members would be diversified, and in each case dependent on individual merit. The victims had to think, in other words, that their conduct did matter; and that their plight could be at least in part influenced by what they were about to do.

ZIGMUND BAUMAN

ITION

YEARS AGO I ENCOUNTERED AN ESSAY with the provocative title *Irish as Nigger*, and later discovered that many books have been written about the choice faced by Irish immigrants upon arriving to America. Poor, despised, having a long history of resistance to British exploitation, they seemed natural allies to other exploited groups, notably people of color. But that wasn't to be. Instead of attempting to bring down the system under which one person's wealth was based on another person's life, the Irish in America decided instead to try to join the upper, or, at least, middle classes. They decided, in effect, to become white, or maybe I should say White, following the path trod before them by essentially every group of white immigrants, and, to a lesser degree, some people of color. Even when they had no hope of fitting into the privileged class, they made sure at the very least to not be associated with the most oppressed class, using the color of their skin as a means of consoling themselves: *Things could be worse: At least I'm not black (or yellow or red).* They did this even when they had to (wage) slave their lives away, receiving in return only that one iota of privilege. How and why that happened (and happens) is an intriguing and frustrating question. There are always far more of the exploited than those who materially benefit from that exploitation, yet, time and again, those ostensibly in charge get everyone else to not too strenuously rock the boat, to go along as if the divine right of kings really is divine. It so often seems that, far more important than bringing down those in power (which might also cost us whatever privilege we currently enjoy), is staying in good favor with them. It's better to be a house servant than a field hand.

This dynamic plays out daily in our lives. Each of us faces, moment by moment, the choice faced by Ham, and for the most part we side with his brothers. Just today I had two opportunities to note this dynamic within the environmental community. The first was on the radio. I was being interviewed by Amy Goodman for the program Democracy Now, about the Animal and Earth Liberation Fronts, which are underground organizations (or, more precisely, underground international movements, since they're organized along the principle of leaderless cells, where people act out of similar passions and beliefs but not under orders from a central leadership) that use sabotage (destruction of property) in defense of animals and the wild. The ALF is known primarily for liberating animals from vivisection labs and fur farms, but also trashes fast-food restaurants, meat trucks, and the like. The ELF exploded onto the scene a couple of years ago by torching part of a ski resort at Vail, Colorado (because the resort was expanding into roadless territory, some of the state's sparse lynx habitat), in what was the single largest act of economic sabotage in this country's peacetime history, before the attack on the World Trade Center in New York. Damage was estimated at twelve million dollars. ALF and ELF activities have cost corporations thirty-seven million dollars and counting. The FBI (sorry for the alphabet soup: as long as I'm at it, maybe I should try to bring into this discussion the IRS, BATF, and IRA, as well as the IWW) has called the ELF and ALF

COMPETITION

America's biggest domestic terrorist threat, despite the fact that they've never killed or injured anyone (with the exception of some vivisectionists who had their fingers cut by razor blades in envelopes sent by a splinter group of the ALF, called, the Justice Department: The ALF disavows the actions of the Justice Department). Both the ELF and ALF take great care to harm no human or nonhuman life. That the ELF and ALF can be considered terrorist organizations whose members are hunted by state police, while corporations that routinely poison and kill human beings are protected by these same police (and, more broadly, that most of us unthinkingly accept this reality) is yet more evidence to my mind of the continued deification of the process of production, making members of the ELF and ALF in a sense not so much terrorists as blasphemers. I was joined on the program by David Barbarash, a spokesperson for the ALF who has done time for liberating cats that were to be experimented on, Alicia Littletree, an Earth First!er, and John Stauffer, an activist from Vail who unsuccessfully opposed, through legal means, the expansion of the ski resort.

David and I spoke strongly in favor of the activities of the ALF and ELF. I said it's crucial for each of us to realize that the government (I almost wrote "our government") is a government of occupation, not of inhabitation. If our enemy *du jour*, al Qaeda (or is today's special Iraq, the FARC, or ELN? Maybe North Korea) invaded the United States and began to place a large minority of black males into concentration camps, there would be more rioting in the streets than there already is (as I write this, a curfew has been imposed on the streets of Cincinnati, to stifle unrest that began when a cop shot another unarmed black man). If a Vichy-style government poisoned as many Americans as do the CEOs of chemical corporations, Molotov cocktails would be the drink of the day, and high school honors students would take out bridges (although I have to admit that as I edit this (it's a few days later) tear gas hangs heavy over Quebec, as protesters riot against the FTAA). If strange creatures from outer space changed our climate and began to systematically dismantle the ecological infrastructure of the planet, you can bet we'd all put on our camo fatigues (you *do* own camo fatigues, don't you?), head to the woods, and start popping off rounds at the bad guys, never stopping, as they say, till they pried our guns from our cold, dead fingers. So long as we follow the rules of those in power, I said, those in power will win. It's like Lewis Mumford said. "This is one of those times when only the dreamers will turn out to be practical men" (or women). David talked about the nuts and bolts of the ALF and ELF, and about government repression: The millions of dollars (he's Canadian, so we're talking two-thirds as many millions of dollars American: Even when it comes to repression, you get less for your money in Canada) and thousands of person-hours that the Royal Canadian Mounted Police have put into keeping him under surveillance and attempting to entrap him.

Both Littletree and Stauffer were strongly opposed to the actions of the ALF and ELF. Littletree suggested that ELF actions might be, not the result of activists, but, instead, provocateurs and others who wish to discredit Earth First!, which she insisted has a "long history of being falsely associated with property destruction." Stauffer said that torching the ski resort destroyed discourse surrounding the expansion, and turned the community against him and other above ground activists. "I have to live here," he said, adding that the owner of the resort lives just up the road from his parents.

Barbarash corrected Littletree about Earth First! and property destruction. "I don't think it serves anyone to paint our movement as something that it's not. I've been involved in Earth First! since the early 1980s, and from the beginning we've destroyed property. For Alicia Littletree to say property destruction and Earth First! are not synonymous is not correct. It's part of our history."

I corrected Stauffer: "The arson brought tremendous national attention to the issue then, and it continues to do so. If it weren't for the ELF action, you wouldn't be on the radio right now discussing it."

Another of Stauffer's complaints was that property destruction upsets police, and increases the likelihood of police violence. He cited the WTO riots in Seattle, where police fired tear gas and rubber bullets at chanting, sign-holding, nonviolent, nonresisting protesters,

COMPETITION

and scores of black-clad anarchists broke windows of corporate chain stores. Stauffer blamed police violence on the anarchists. Goodman pointed out that Stauffer was wrong: Police began shooting at protesters long before windows were broken. I commented that we cannot allow the actions of the police to predetermine for us our own actions. To do so, I wish I would have added, is to capitulate all tactics, save those deemed acceptable to those in power. And of course those in power will deem acceptable only those forms of protest they also deem ineffective. To do otherwise would go against everything they stand for, and how they rule.

There are two other things I wish I would have said. The first has to do with discourse, and how discourse really isn't the point anyway: It doesn't matter how we talk about the expansion of the ski resort, nor how we build careers opposing it. The important question is: Should the buildings be there, or not? If not, we should remove them. The second thing I wish I would have said ties back to the decision of the Irish to become White, and the decision by Shem and Japheth to cover their father. Both Littletree and Stauffer were worried about their reputations. They were worried about what those in power might think of them. After all, they have to live in the same town—on the same street—as those in power. And we all need to get along, don't we?

So long as we worry about what Noah will think about us, we'll never be able to see him naked and vulnerable. So long as we worry about getting along with those in power, we'll never change the system.

The second example of worrying about what those in power will think hits closer to home. One of the ranchers I mentioned from the Fish and Game meeting has recently been writing lots of letters to the editor on a range of antienvironmental topics. His name is Richard McNamara. One of his recent kicks has been to prevent local schools from having activities associated with Earth Day. He trots out the arguments against Earth Day we've all heard before (no, silly, not the ones about how Earth Day is a corporate greenwash, and an opportunity for us all to feel good about ourselves as the planet burns: He trots out the *other* arguments): Earth Day is pagan, and thus anti-Christian, and thus anti-American; Earth Day is a holy day for the religion of Deep Ecology (I'm not making this up), and thus needs to be eliminated because of the separation of church and state; all Earth Day activities must be based on solid science, and have verifiable results (whatever that means). He brought out a new reason, too, one that surprised me: Earth Day is a celebration of Stalin's birthday, he said. Never mind that Earth Day is April 22, and Stalin was born December 21. I think he meant Lenin, who, it ends up, was born on the twenty-second, but if you've seen one commie, you've seen them all. Just for the record, Earth Day is April 22 because it's John Muir's birthday, but now that I think about it, he might have been a little pink, too, or, as they say, a watermelon: green on the outside, but red through and through. All of this I found more strange than worthy of response, even though the school board took his request under a somewhat confused advisement—confused because the district as a whole already doesn't sponsor any Earth Day events, nor do most teachers—and ended up appointing McNamara to an environmental studies committee of the school board, which he promptly renamed "outdoor studies." But then, perhaps acting out that need to reveal while concealing, McNamara crossed a line that let me know I needed to respond. In letters to the editor about the controversy at Lake Earl he compared government attempts to purchase land to which he holds title to the theft of Indian lands. Karen (the activist, not the hairdresser) and I got together to write a letter commenting on the irony of this, especially considering that McNamara's namesake forefather was an organizer of the Yontocket massacre. After laying out the history, we wrote, "We suppose McNamara may say this is ancient history. But while he didn't fire the gun, he benefits directly from the bullets, from the crimes. It is on these crimes that the fortunes of many of this county's finest are based. It's ludicrous for McNamara to compare the supposed 'taking' of 'his' land to taking land from indigenous people. For McNamara's comparison to be accurate, he would have to have been pulled from his church and murdered. His son would have to have been thrown into a fire. His wife

COMPETITION

would have to have been killed or forced into prostitution, as many whites did to the original inhabitants of California. Everything he holds sacred would have been destroyed."

We concluded, "It is inexcusably arrogant for McNamara to call the land here his own, when first, his title to land is based on murder and theft, and second, the 'pioneer families' who are so proud of calling this land theirs have only been here for four or five generations. That's a pittance compared to the two hundred generations or more that the Tolowa have called this their home, during which they learned how to live with what the land gives willingly. In order for the debate over Lake Earl, or over any land-use questions in this county, to be grounded in any sort of reality that makes sense, we must use as our starting point the fact that all of us who are not descendants of the original people of this land cannot lay claim to it as our own. We need to remember that we are all walking on stolen ground."

Early on the morning the letter was printed, my phone rang. A male voice demanded: "Did you write the letter in today's paper?"

Not wanting to be cursed before breakfast, I countered, "Who's this?"

He asked again, and so did I. We continued the dance until I flinched, then prepared myself for the blast. But he said, "My mother was born here, and so was I. I've been waiting all that time for someone to say this out loud. I just want to thank you."

I thanked him.

He said, "When I was a child I used to fantasize that if I'd been here a couple of generations earlier I would have run guns to the Indians." He rang off.

Also, that day, Karen said a man approached her in a gas station parking lot and gave her a high five. One of her friends at the tribe said someone was copying the letter, posting it on bulletin boards, and handing it to all the people she talked to. But here's the point: Although many environmentalists were strongly in favor of the letter and were happy it was published, it disappointed many others, made some nervous, and even angered some. The reason they gave for

THE CULTURE OF MAKE BELIEVE

their disappointment or anger was pragmatic: McNamara's planning a clear-cut next to the lake, and some environmentalists are attempting to purchase this land. "You'll just piss him off," they said. "Now he'll never sell to us." Tactically, they may be right. But I doubt it, and, in any case, it's the same old story of appeasement (can you say *Munich Pact?*): We need to let those in power, even when they're manifestly unreasonable, determine the terms of the debate. Why did it take so long for someone to state the obvious, that McNamara (and, in fact, each of us whites) is living on stolen property? And once stated, why are so many so quick to step away?

Part of the reason, I think, is that nobody likes to be hated. It's not fun to be disliked (just as I'm sure the same is true, from McNamara's perspective, but the truth is that whether we talk about it or not, his fortune *is* based on murder and theft), and if you tell people that what they're doing is wrong and exploitative, they're probably not going to like you. If you're able to put a dent in their ability to exploit, they're probably, as I mentioned earlier, going to hate you. And if you make a big enough dent, they're going to kill you.

All of this brings us back to the Irish. Pretend you have a choice. Pretend you are a son or daughter of Noah. Pretend you are a son or daughter of Ireland. Pretend you saw brothers and sisters die of starvation in the potato famine of the 1840s, or, rather, you saw them die, not so much of starvation as exportation: At the same time that a million Irish men, women, and children died between 1845 and 1850—their corpses lying in fields, with streets, according to a contemporary observer, "black with funeral processions"—Ireland was, as a colony of England, exporting grain. You come to North America on one of the appropriately named "coffin ships." Perhaps you're among the 427 passengers aboard the *Agnes*, bound for Grosse Isle, in Canada. Perhaps some of your children are among the 277 dead on the trip or in the fifteen-day quarantine. You feared the rest would die crammed on the steamer to Montreal. Your children did not, but half of the remaining immigrants did. Or, perhaps, you land in similarly straitened conditions in the United States. In either case,

COMPETITION

you're now ready—sorrowfully, because of the losses you've already suffered—to get on with this better life you've been promised.

Pretend you have a choice. You are a son or daughter of Ireland. You know the history. You know that the Council of Armagh in 1177 prohibited Irish trade in English slaves. You heard both your mother and father boast (with only slight exaggeration) that in seven centuries no slave had set foot on Irish soil. Abolitionism flows in your veins, not only because it is part of what Ireland has always stood for, but because you have experienced in your own body the British "policy of extermination," as Lord Clarendon, viceroy in Ireland, called it. You have experienced what Arthur Young observed in 1780, that "A landlord in Ireland can scarcely invent an order which a servant, labourer, or cottier dares to refuse. . . . Disrespect, or anything tending towards sauciness, he may punish with his cane or his horsewhip with the most perfect security. A poor man would have his bones broken if he offered to lift a hand in his own defense." You have overheard landlords speaking one to another that "many of their cottiers would think themselves honored to have their wives and daughters sent for to the bed of their master," and you have experienced the simultaneous shame and honor that marks this degree and form of servitude. Even before the famine, you knew that Ireland was, as Frenchman Duvergier de Hauranne wrote, "two nations," the conquerors and the conquered: "There is nothing between the master and the slave, between the cabin and the palace. There is nothing between all the luxuries of existence and the last degree of human wretchedness." You have experienced that wretchedness, and your response to it now is *No, thank you.* Your response to it for your children—those still alive—is *No, thank you.* Your decision to seek a better life came with the Poor Law Act of 1847, which stipulated that no peasant who owned more than a quarter-acre of land would be eligible for relief. Because access to land means the possibility of self-sufficiency, and denial of that access means denial of that possibility, the purpose of this law was to place the conquered even more at the mercy of the conquerors. To this, you said, *No, thank you.* You left.

THE CULTURE OF MAKE BELIEVE

And now here you are. And you're hungry. Your sons and daughters are hungry. You have no more access to land here in the States than you did in Ireland. You've never heard of John Henry Hammond, and couldn't care less about the land-ownership conditions under which he would, without a word, resign his slaves (providing, of course, that he could properly dispose of them) but you know in your bones the meaning of his highbrow language about population denseness forcing people "to hire for the smallest pittance that will keep soul and body together, and rags upon his back while in actual employment." It means if you and your children are to survive, you need a job. You're not the only person who knows this. You compete with German immigrants for jobs. You compete with Italian immigrants, Ukranian immigrants, Scandinavian immigrants, Slavic immigrants. You compete with people from other parts of Ireland. You compete with blacks, and you compete with Chinese. Your children are hungry.

This isn't a game. This isn't political theory. This is not about purchasing "comforts and elegancies." It's about food. Lives depend on your paycheck. This is true whether you are father or mother, sick or healthy, blind or sighted. You need the money.

Fuck abolitionism. Fuck revolution. Fuck working-class solidarity. If my life and the lives of my children are involved, I'm going to use every advantage I can. If I happen to have white skin, and happen to be in the middle of an economic, governmental, social, and psychological system in which white skin conveys to me any number of advantages, and if my children are hungry—remember the six-year average life span of Irish immigrants—would I not be even a little tempted to do everything in my power to emphasize the differences between myself and those who are not white? And once this habit has been established, once I'm no longer quite so hungry, would it not be possible for me to maintain that privilege just long enough for me to get a taste, just a taste, of those comforts? And how about some elegancies? Nowadays, baby doesn't so much need food as she needs new shoes. Nice ones. And a car. And a vacation home. Political

COMPETITION

power wouldn't hurt either. Of course, by this time, it has become a game, for those, at least, a little on the inside. But for those on the outside, it remains life and death. This is one of the ways our system propagates itself, by depriving people of the option of self-sufficiency, forcing them into competition with others with whom they should by all reason be in solidarity, then reifying this competition, turning it into racial and other hatreds that mask the real sources of the people's misery, then capturing these people with promises of material goods if only they will not look at those they are exploiting, not look at the exploitation at all.

Pretend you have a choice. You are a lawyer, facing what the philosopher Neil Evernden might call the lawyer's dilemma. You are defending a client. In this imaginary place where you live, one set of laws applies to people who are black, and an other, far more lenient, set of laws applies to people who have even 1 percent of whiteness in their genealogy. Your client happens to be, so far as you can tell, black. What do you do? Do you rail against the injustices of this system, and then console your client's family on the day of the execution? Or do you do your damnedest to find (or make up) at least one white ancestor in your client's lineage? Doing the former may, of course, someday help bring down the unjust system, and doing the latter may save your client's life; it will also certainly reinforce the injustices that currently stand.

It didn't take long for the Irish to turn White. When they arrived, they were, in their own words, "thought nothing of more than *dogs* . . . despised and kicked about." But before long it could be said of the Irish "that some of these people would shoot a black man with as little regard to moral consequences as they would a wild hog." Before long the Irish had been able to kick black stevedores off the docks of New York City, all the while proclaiming, as atop the banner the exclusively Irish Longshoremen's United Benevolent Society carried each year in the St. Patrick's Day Parade, "We know no distinction but that of merit." As always, the fine print revealed something else: The Society's goal was to make sure that "work upon the docks . . . shall be attended to solely and absolutely by members of the 'Longshoremen's Association,' and such white laborers as they see fit to permit upon the premises."

Blacks were caught in an impossible situation. If they attempted to find work somewhere, whites, including, notably, the Irish, would attack them, or at best go on strike against them. Frederick Douglass, who was by trade a caulker, attempted to find work, and was told that "every white man would leave the ship in her unfinished condition if I struck a blow at my trade against her." This was not unique, but, rather, almost universal. Free blacks were driven from their positions as artisans, clerks, drivers. In his book, *How the Irish Became White*, Noel Ignatiev describes the plight of the free blacks: "Black workers, already being driven out of artisanal trades by prejudice, and squeezed out of service trades and common labor by competition, could find no refuge in the manufacturing area, and hence were pushed down below the waged proletariat, into the ranks of the destitute self-employed: ragpickers, bootblacks, chimneysweeps, sawyers, fish and oyster mongers, washerwomen, and hucksters of various kinds." In time nearly the only jobs open to blacks were those made available when whites went on strike. But then the whites attacked them as strikebreakers. During strikes in 1852, 1855, 1862, and 1863, to continue the example of the docks, Irish longshoremen fought black workers who were brought in to replace them (after the Irish already forced the blacks from the docks).

Oftentimes, whites sought out places where blacks worked, and terrorized them away. For example, a primarily Irish mob attacked the black employees of a tobacco factory in Brooklyn, forcing mainly women and children to the upper stories, then setting fire to the first floor. Whites allowed the factory to reopen only when the factory owner promised to lay off the blacks and hire Irish instead.

It didn't take long for the Irish to begin attacking blacks, even outside of workplaces, with a fierceness presaging the Night Riders of the KKK. Writing at the time of the Civil War, Sydney G. Fisher noted, "The Irish hate the Negroes, not merely because they compete with them in labor, but because they are near to them in social rank. Therefore, the Irish favor slavery in the South, and for the same

COMPETITION

reason the [rest of] the laboring class of whites support it—it gratifies their pride by the existence of a class below them." Sure, the Irish fought bravely in the Civil War, but their reasons for fighting might be summed up by a bit of doggerel from the time:

I found, most gladly, no secession;
But hatred strong of abolition,
A willingness to fight with vigor
For loyal rights, but not the nigger.

Describing the attitude of "ninety-nine soldiers out of one hundred," one soldier put it even more bluntly, if less poetically: "They say they came out here to fight for the Union, and not for a pack of —— niggers." In 1863, the newspaper of the Catholic archdiocese of New York suggested, "Since fight we must, may it not be necessary yet to fight for the liberty of the white man rather than the freedom of the Negro?"

Many of the urban poor took up this challenge, and, so, later that summer, as Lee's army of northern Virginia melted back home after the battle of Gettysburg, merely a hundred and some miles away, New York City erupted in the most extreme urban violence this country has ever experienced. The catalyst was the law conscripting men for military service, which contained a provision allowing anyone who'd been drafted to buy his way out for three hundred dollars, an amount unimaginable to the working poor, but petty cash to the rich. It's easy to see why the poor rebelled. While they were fighting and dying far from home, people like the financier J. P. Morgan, who at war's start had quickly developed fainting spells in proportion to the number of recruiting stations popping up around the city, simply bought their way out of the army. Seventy-three thousand and five hundred well off males did this, including the financiers Jay Gould, James Fisk, William Vanderbilt, John D. Rockefeller, Andrew Carnegie, Philip Armour, and Andrew Mellon. The sentiment behind the provision was stated succinctly in a letter from Judge

Thomas Mellon to his son, who, until receiving the letter, had been suffering an unfortunate case of scruples: "In time you will understand and believe that a man may be a patriot without risking his own life or sacrificing his health. There are plenty of other lives less valuable." Of course, the provision was no anomaly: Of all the major nineteenth-century financiers, only one—Daniel Drew—ever directly participated in, as opposed to profited from, a war (the War of 1812), and even his participation came before his wealth. The same pattern clearly holds today. Witness the percentage of people killed in the Vietnam War who were poor and/or nonwhite. Witness the 1996 Republican vice-presidential candidate, the extremely promilitary Jack Kemp, who was given a medical discharge from the military (ostensibly because of a bad shoulder), but went on to play professional football as a quarterback for the better part of a decade. None of this is surprising, in the least, since the central purpose of politics (and economics) within this or any other destructive culture is the enrichment of the rulers through the sacrifice of lives less valuable than their own.

I'm not suggesting that Morgan and other financiers didn't involve themselves in the war effort, for many did. In 1857, for example, army inspection officers had condemned a large number of Hall carbines as obsolete and dangerous (they blew off the thumbs of people who fired them). These guns were stored in New York City until 1861, when a man by the name of Arthur Eastman purchased five thousand of them (for which the government originally paid $17.50) at $3.50 each. Because Eastman had no money, he approached Simon Stevens, former secretary to powerful Congressman Thaddeus Stevens (no relation). Stevens, certain he would be able to use his political connections to unload the weapons, agreed to buy the guns for $12.50 a piece. Because Stevens also had no money, he approached Morgan, who promptly loaned him the cash. Stevens turned around and sold the weapons to his old friend General John C. Fremont, who agreed to have the government pay Morgan $22.00 each, as well as the costs of rifling. After the guns were rifled, though, still useless,

COMPETITION

they were transported directly from the federal warehouse to Fremont's headquarters. Despite the fact that such profiteering was commonplace (Fremont's quartermaster alone was convicted of twenty-one cases of corruption), this was simply too much, and after a congressional investigation the government refused to pay the speculators "their" money. The speculators sued, and, while the court recognized that Fremont had no authority to purchase the arms, it compromised by agreeing to pay the speculators $13.31 per carbine. This worked out to a profit of $49,000 for the thirty-eight days the men held title to the government-stored guns. The financiers refused the compromise, sued the government again, and collected an additional $58,175. Historians have not concerned themselves as to whether those injured by the defective guns received any compensation.

The fact that the guns blew off the thumbs of their users is mentioned in Gustavus Myers's important *History of the Great American Fortunes*, where he cites as evidence of their malfunction the report of a congressional committee investigation. Most of Morgan's biographers, who would charitably be classified as *fawning*, at best, ignore evidence of the condition of the guns and, at worst, lie, saying, for example, that the guns were "perfectly serviceable but old-fashioned." Further, many of these biographers stretch other truths to try to make readers believe Morgan was a perfectly innocent party who happened to provide money for, and who happened then to secure much of the profit from, this sale. The fact that more writers fawn over Morgan than attack him, much less try to stop him or his modern equivalents, is precisely the point, and has to do with the deification of production and producers: Evil done in the name of production must be overlooked, and, in fact, most often ends up, as in this case, being rewarded. So long as we as a culture continue to reward—and, in fact, celebrate—destructive and immoral behavior, destructive and immoral behavior will continue, and will continue to be celebrated. More specifically, as it relates to Morgan, the deification of producers, and the inhumanity of the economics that is central to our way of living, so long as we as a culture continue to morally, ethically, legally, and causally divorce financiers from the results of their investments, financiers will continue to fund immoral and destructive activities.

This was not Morgan's only contribution to the war effort. His firm actively bought and sold U.S. bonds, which rose and fell in relation to Union victories and defeats in the field. Deaths corresponded directly to profits in this speculation, and, to maximize profits per death, Morgan installed a private telegraph wire in his office, over which he received up-to-the-minute accounts from General Grant's private telegrapher and others. Morgan, who often knew the results of battles before President Lincoln did, cabled information to his father in London, who added to his fortune by quickly purchasing or selling Union bonds. This was not the only way Morgan profited at the direct expense of the American public; he also manipulated the gold market in what amounted to another act of treason. The federal government financed the war primarily by borrowing money. This caused inflation, so the government began issuing "greenbacks," dollars not backed by gold or silver. Because of the fear that, if the United States lost the war, the greenbacks (as well as government bonds) would be worthless, the price of gold went up whenever the North lost a battle, and down whenever it won. At the same time, the United States became a major purchaser of gold in order to maintain its credit line abroad and to pay interest on bonds. Because speculation in gold damaged the government's already tenuous credit, the public raised an outcry over this form of trading. To protect the fiction of Wall Street patriotism, financiers simply moved the gold trade to an office on a different street. There, it became a tradition to sing "Dixie" over the sounds of trading whenever the Confederacy won a battle (as at Chancellorsville, where an estimated 28,300 human beings became casualties) and to sing "John Brown's Body" when the federals were victorious (as at Gettysburg, where an estimated 54,800 human beings became casualties). Not content with betting on lives as they would the turn of a card, Morgan and a partner realized that, if they could create a crisis, they could influence the price of gold. They began to secretly buy up gold on credit. Then,

COMPETITION

on October 10, 1863, they announced they were shipping more than one million dollars worth—a large share of this nation's available gold—to London. The price surged, the partners dumped their gold, and they made a quick $160,000, far more than a soldier would have earned in a thousand years. Congress responded to Wall Street gold speculation by passing an ineffectual law, ostensibly prohibiting private gold-trading, but which didn't do much of anything. The law was repealed after a lobbying group, of which Morgan was secretary, denounced the prohibition as "utter lawlessness on the part of Congress." The response by Abraham Lincoln was to say, "What do you think of those fellows in Wall Street who are gambling in gold at such a time as this? For my part I wish every one of them had his devilish head shot off." But no actions were taken. Morgan did not have his "devilish head shot off," which is less than we can say for many of the soldiers on whose deaths he wagered. He wasn't arrested, censured, or even drafted into the army. Instead, he continued to accumulate wealth, and, presumably, continued to sing "Dixie" or "John Brown's Body" at the proper times. Elsewhere in the country, soldiers whose lives were less valuable than Morgan's continued to die, of gunshot wounds, of influenza, of dysentery, of hunger.

It was against all of this that the poor Irish of New York rebelled in the summer of 1863. On July 11, more than a thousand names were drawn from barrels at conscription offices in New York, revealing some of those who would be sent to fight and, possibly, die. The next day newspapers carried lists containing these names as well as, as fate would have it, the first of the casualty lists from the Battle of Gettysburg. On the morning of the thirteenth, as officers pulled more names from a barrel in a draft office in a heavily Irish part of town, someone threw a paving stone through the front window. Then came a barrage, followed by a storm of angry men, who beat the superintendent half to death. Clerks and officers fled. The men, now numbering into the several thousands, set the offices on fire, and soon the whole block was ablaze. Instead of putting out the fire, volunteer firemen, angry that their jobs did not secure them an exemption from the draft, joined in the rioting. The mobs moved through the area, beating any expensively dressed person they saw, shouting, "There goes a three hundred dollar man." They seized an armory, burned three police stations, and began to move toward the wealthier parts of town.

Then, as seems so often to happen, the angry mob did not take their fury to the houses of Morgan, Rockefeller, Vanderbilt, Gould, Cooke, or any of the other more valuable men, but instead began attacking blacks. They substituted the word *nigger* for *three hundred dollar man*, and turned to screaming "burn the niggers' nest" as they torched a black orphanage. They hanged blacks, burned them, trampled them to death, hacked at their bodies, pulled their bodies down the street by their genitals. They marked the houses of black families with stones, to come back later. Federal troops were called in, and fought see-saw battles with the rioters. Estimates of the number of dead run from a little over a hundred to the low thousands. The casualties consisted almost exclusively of the poor.

It did not take long after immersion in our particular system of competition for the oppressed to become the oppressors, the hated to become the hateful. It did not take long for the Irish in this country to become White.

COMPETITION

THE DISTANCE WE FEEL FROM OUR ACTIONS IS PRO-
PORTIONATE TO OUR IGNORANCE OF THEM; OUR IGNORANCE,
IN TURN, IS LARGELY A MEASURE OF THE LENGTH OF THE CHAIN
OF INTERMEDIARIES BETWEEN OURSELVES AND OUR ACTS....

AS CONSCIOUSNESS OF THE CONTEXT DROPS OUT, THE
ACTIONS BECOME MOTIONS WITHOUT CONSEQUENCE. WITH
THE CONSEQUENCE OUT OF VIEW, PEOPLE CAN BE PARTIES TO
THE MOST ABHORRENT ACTS WITHOUT EVER RAISING THE QUES-
TION OF THEIR OWN ROLE AND RESPONSIBILITY. WAGE EARN-
ERS WHO INSERT THE FUSE IN BOMBS CAN THEN VIEW THEIR
ACTIVITY AS BUT A SERIES OF REPETITIVE MOTIONS PERFORMED
FOR A LIVING. RAILROAD WORKERS WHO TAKE TRAINLOADS
OF PRISONERS TO EXTERMINATION CAMPS CAN THINK OF THEM-
SELVES AS SIMPLY PROVIDING TRANSPORTATION....

DIST

THE REMARKABLE THING IS THAT WE ARE NOT UNABLE TO REC-OGNIZE WRONG ACTS OR GROSS INJUSTICES WHEN WE SEE THEM. WHAT AMAZES US IS HOW THEY COULD HAVE COME ABOUT WHEN EACH OF US DID NONE BUT HARMLESS ACTS. WE LOOK FOR SOMEONE TO BLAME THEN, FOR CONSPIRACIES THAT MIGHT EXPLAIN THE HORRORS WE ALL ABHOR. IT IS DIF-FICULT TO ACCEPT THAT OFTEN THERE IS NO PERSON AND NO GROUP THAT PLANNED OR CAUSED IT ALL. IT IS EVEN MORE DIFFICULT TO SEE HOW OUR ACTIONS, THROUGH THEIR RE-MOTE EFFECTS, CONTRIBUTED TO CAUSING MISERY. IT IS NO COP-OUT TO THINK ONESELF BLAMELESS AND CONDEMN SO-CIETY. IT IS THE NATURAL RESULT OF LARGE-SCALE MEDIATION WHICH INEVITABLY LEADS TO MONSTROUS IGNORANCE.

JOHN LACHS

NCE

IT IS POSSIBLE TO KILL A MILLION PEOPLE without personally shedding a drop of blood. It is possible to destroy a culture without being aware of its existence. It is possible to commit genocide or ecocide from the comfort of one's living room. Presumably, the people who profit from the manufacture of ozone-depleting substances are fine and upstanding men and women. Presumably, the people who profit from the manufacture of weapons of mass destruction are well-respected within their communities. Most of the horrors we are forced to live with have been caused by respectable— even great—men who themselves most often have clean hands. Warren Anderson, responsible for so many deaths in Bhopal, killed not a single Indian. The owners of Carbide who ordered the expansion of the Hawk's Nest Tunnel killed not a single black man. Thomas Jefferson killed no Indians (the same cannot be said for

Andrew Jackson). If you are a god you can kill from afar, and if you kill from afar you can maintain in your own mind the objectivity necessary to believe that those you are killing are objects, or, better, you can think of them not at all.

In 1839, Francis J. Grund wrote, "When, in one of our Atlantic cities, it is once known that a man is rich, that 'he is very rich,' that he is 'amazingly rich,' that he is 'one of the richest men in the country,' that he is 'worth a million of dollars' . . . the whole vocabulary of praise is exhausted; and the individual in question is as effectually canonized as the best Catholic saint."

Probably one of the most important saints in the American canon, and certainly one of the most destructive, is J. P. Morgan, first as a human being, and then immortalized as a corporation.

J. P. Morgan, also called Pierpont, was by most accounts a well-respected man. Called by some "Morgan the Magnificent," others counted him among the "lords of creation." His external devotion to his family (which did not include fidelity to his wife) was second only to his devotion to acquiring money and, especially, power. He was deeply religious. A patron of the arts, he secured the world's greatest private collection of the time.

Morgan was also responsible for the deaths of millions of human beings on several continents. He killed not a single one of them. He probably hated none of them. He made financial decisions that guaranteed those deaths as surely as if he had put a bullet into each of their brains.

J. Pierpont Morgan acquired his wealth the way nearly all of the wealthy do—he inherited it. His family fortune began six generations earlier, as Pierpont's ancestor, Miles Morgan, first purchased and then "justly won by the sword in defensive warfare," as van Riebeeck would have put it, land from local Indians. Morgan farmed the land, and, by the 1680s, became one of Springfield, Massachusetts' richest settlers, which is to say one of its most respected. His descendants, more than one hundred within three generations, multiplied the fortune apace with their reproductive proclivities, until, by 1847, Joseph Morgan III, Pierpont's grandfather, left behind an estate of more

DISTANCE

than a million dollars (only $102,000 of which was reported to government officials). Joseph also left a legacy of business and political acumen, having begun a bank, the Aetna Insurance Company, and relationships with Andrew Jackson, Henry Clay, and John Calhoun. Junius Morgan, Pierpont's father, soon took $600,000 of his inheritance to Boston and became a member of that city's largest mercantile house, which operated, as Pierpont's biographer Ron Chernow delicately puts it, "on a global scale, exporting and financing cotton and other goods carried by clipper ship from Boston harbor." Although Junius's hands were clean, involvement in the cotton trade inescapably involved him in the trade of slaves.

The oftentimes physical and psychic distance between financier and the activities which are financed in no way lessens their mutually reinforcing relationship. This must be understood if one is to fully apprehend the inhumanity of our culture. Most people do not cut down forests, pollute rivers, force indigenous peoples off their land, and commit genocide, or exploit workers out of a conscious sense of hatefulness (conscious being the operant word); they do it for money. Money fuels economic activities, and, at the same time, is the reward for participation in a culturally valued enterprise, causally linking financier to activity; without venture capital there can be no capitalist venture, and without monetary reward no venture capital will be provided. Another way to say this is that slavery would not have been viable without loans from bankers like Junius Morgan, and, while Junius never once wielded the whip, he undeniably, and from a distance, benefited from the lashings. It's very simple: Our culture allows, even encourages (demands would probably be the best word) someone to profit—to gain power, material possessions, or prestige—at the expense of another's misery.

The incentive for bankers to profit from human misery is well established—holding, in Chernow's words, "an honored place in their mythology,"—and is perhaps best manifested by the boast of a member of the Rothschild house, "When the streets of Paris are running with blood, I buy."

THE CULTURE OF MAKE BELIEVE

Morgan's ability to make money came to the attention of George Peabody, founder of one of London's largest merchant banks, who, in 1854, made him a partner. This could not have happened at a better time for Morgan, who quickly learned, as another Morgan biographer puts it, once again oh so delicately, "to appreciate the close link that existed between merchant banks and world politics." Another way to say this is that Morgan's entry into the partnership came at a propitious time for him because England, France, Turkey, and Sardinia were at war with Russia, which increased the demand for American cotton and grains, which increased the demand for financial services, which increased the profits for Morgan, Peabody, and others like them.

The Crimean War ended in 1856—after some five hundred thousand people had died—leading to hard times for George Peabody and Company. The company had invested heavily in American firms during the wartime boom, and as business dried up, so did the company's funds. The bank was in danger of going out of business until Peabody called on his old friend, Governor Thomson Hankey, Jr., of the Bank of England, who agreed to use public funds to bail out the bank.

The American Civil War, beginning in 1861, created the opportunities for gross profits described just a few pages ago.

Had the activities of Morgan been confined to merely swindling money and blowing the thumbs off people he never met, most of us probably wouldn't have heard of him. But Morgan was aiming much higher: His goal was to control most of this country's economy, and much of the world's. He succeeded.

Although the Civil War, with its immense opportunities for profit, ended in 1865, within a few years, Morgan embroiled himself in a highly profitable war of another type, a war for control of publicly funded railroads. His first skirmish, which in many ways formed a template for later, larger actions, was his takeover of the Albany & Susquehanna. This line, the construction of which had been funded by local and state grants and characterized by the corruption in-

DISTANCE

evitably attendant on these operations, connected the coal regions of Pennsylvania with three trunk lines in New York State. Within months of the railroad's completion, two groups of speculators—neither of which had invested a dime in building the road—were fighting to control it.

One group was headed by Joseph Ramsey, the founder of the railroad. The other was led by Jay Gould, owner of many railroads, including the Erie, one of the trunk lines fed by the Albany & Susquehanna. About the Erie, a diarist noted in 1868, "Another accident on the Erie. Scores of people smashed, burned to death, or maimed for life. We shall never travel safely until some pious, wealthy and much beloved railroad director has been hanged for murder, with a conductor on each side of him." Neither Gould nor any other owner or director was ever charged with murder. Instead, they continued to amass wealth and power through means that would have caused less valuable citizens to be removed from society. Gould was known for having bought judges at the municipal, state, and federal levels, legislators at the state and federal levels, a member of President Grant's family (Grant's brother-in-law, A. R. Corbin, who cost Gould two million in gold bonds) and at least one of Grant's appointees. He was nothing if not brazen: Arrested as he made his way to the New York state house with $500,000 in his satchel, he was out of jail within days and had "assiduously cultivated a thorough understanding between himself and the legislature." Gould later said it would be as difficult to remember the number of bribes he gave "as it would be to recall the number of freight cars sent over the Erie Railroad from day to day." He had as a partner in this Jim Fisk, who had made his pile during the Civil War, selling the government shoddy blankets, uniforms, and paper shoes. Fisk's admitted pricing strategy was, "You can sell anything to the government at almost any price you've got the guts to ask."

An investigation into Civil War contracting concluded "that contractors had decided that 'the country, as a whole, is a fair subject for plunder.' Fred A. Shannon, in *The Organization and Administration of the Union Army, 1861–1865*, wrote that army contractors handled at least a billion dollars of government money during the war, and, by conservative estimate, kept half of it."

Gould began surreptitiously buying shares in the Albany & Susquehanna. On discovering this, Ramsey issued and purchased enough stock (on credit) to maintain a majority. Gould countered by summoning his "pet judge" to the apartment of Fisk's mistress in the middle of the night, where the judge issued an order replacing Ramsey with Fisk on the board. Ramsey then had his own judge reinstate him. Having temporarily exhausted judicial opportunities, each side hired an army, and the two armies proceeded to tear up tracks, drink, attack each other with guns and knives, drink, ram locomotives together, and drink. Up to twelve thousand men faced off over this publicly funded railroad. Finally, the governor threatened to call in the militia.

At first, it seemed the two sides, neither of which was tied to the region's communities, had come to a stand-off. But along the way, Ramsey had made a near-fatal mistake. His purchase of so much stock left him with no money to bribe legislators.

A friend of Ramsey's suggested a way out: Ramsey should contact Pierpont Morgan, who was, he said, a cousin of former New York governor and U.S. senator Ed Morgan, and a good man with a lot of spunk and a lot of money. Ramsey approached Pierpont, who agreed to take over. Morgan immediately bought six thousand shares of stock, then called a shareholders meeting. When Jim Fisk attempted to attend, Pierpont punched him in the nose and threw him down the stairs, where a Morgan hireling, dressed in a police uniform, "arrested" him. The shareholders voted Morgan vice president and called a directors meeting, at which they unanimously voted to lease the railroad to the Delaware and Hudson Canal Company, which was friendly to Morgan. To guarantee it stayed friendly, one of the conditions of the lease was that Morgan be made director of the merged companies.

So far as railroad battles go, this one was no big deal. But it was important, in that it marked the real entry of Morgan into that lucrative field, and because it reveals the tactic Morgan was to use for the rest of his life, the provision of financial backing for an endeavor

DISTANCE

in exchange for control of the company. Using this method, Morgan gained eventual control of more than half this country's corporate economy. This level of control has had disastrous consequences for the majority.

Through the 1870s, Morgan continued to gain wealth, esteem, and power. In 1870, while millions of men, women, and children received less than a dollar a day for working sixteen hours, he got by on $75,000 per year. By 1882, this had risen to a half-million. The plaudits burgeoned as well. In 1873, Morgan was merely accorded "universal respect," according to *The New York Times*. By the early 1880s, it was said that Morgan had been "chosen by circumstance and inheritance as the heir of North America." His political status grew apace. Back in the early 1870s, he'd been forced to rely on the friendship between his partner Tony Drexel and President Grant (as well as pressure from newspapers owned by Drexel) to procure from the government a 50 percent stake in a monopoly to sell government bonds. By the late 1870s, it was Morgan who had the upper hand: When Congress refused to allocate money for soldiers who were "solving the Indian problem," Morgan said it was his "obvious and sacred duty" to float the cash until the government appropriated funding. The War Department agreed, and so Morgan temporarily bankrolled the killing of Indians in the North- and Southwest, as well as the killing of union organizers and teenage strikers closer to home. In addition to full repayment by the government, Morgan's fee for fulfilling his "sacred duty" was to charge the soldiers about one-twelfth of their pay to cash their checks.

In the 1870s, most Americans suffered through this country's worst depression up to that time, precipitated by the failure of the Northern Pacific Railroad Company. The suffering of the railroad investors would make unbelievably maudlin fiction. One man sent Jay Cooke, the primary financier for the railroad; a letter saying, "At the request of Eliza ———, a poor blind woman who holds a $500 Northern Pacific bond . . . I write to state to you this bond is all her earthly wealth, and the loss of it will oblige her to go to the poor house. I thought perhaps you could do something for her in her destitution. . . . She is without father, mother, sister or brother, and what she made she had by honest labor. She told me . . . that if she could only see to work she would not care." Another letter: "I wish you would try and make up the money that you owe me, three hundred and sixty dollars ($360). I worked twenty-eight years to get that little sum together. I have to support an insane husband and I am a poor woman. You told me and my little girl when we went to the bank to get out our money that all was safe, and if anything happened to the bank you would let us know. Did you do it? My number is 1127 Vine Street. I shall look for the money, for of course it is a little bill to you which you could pay out of your private purse and make us comfortable." Mr. Cooke did not suffer so greatly. He maintained an interest in Northern Pacific, as well as many other companies, and, soon enough, became a partner in a Utah mine that brought him, from this one enterprise alone, $80,000 a year.

It wasn't just investors in Cooke's railroad who suffered. Across the whole nation, business declined 32 percent, and hundreds of thousands of workers were forced out of their jobs. In 1874, ninety thousand workers in New York City, nearly half of them women, had to sleep in police stations. By 1877, even *The New York Times* noted that because of poverty and pollution "there will be a thousand deaths of infants per week in the city."

Pierpont didn't suffer, though: He turned the economy's collapse into a seven-figure profit, telling his father, "I don't believe there is another concern in the country [that] can begin to show such a result."

In 1877, massive strikes broke out across the country. In Martinsburg, West Virginia. In Baltimore, Maryland (where half the National Guardsmen quit in disgust after a bloody battle that left ten strikers, including young boys, dead). In Pittsburgh (where corporate and governmental officials, after learning the local militia wouldn't kill their fellows, called in the militia from Philadelphia, and where twenty-six people, mostly bystanders, were later killed: "The sight presented after the soldiers ceased firing was sickening. Old men and boys . . . lay writhing in the agonies of death, while numbers of children were killed outright"). In Harrisburg, Pennsylvania (where the

DISTANCE

militia gave up their guns and shook hands with strikers). In Chicago, Illinois (where twenty-one men and boys were killed by police and Morgan-paid soldiers: "The sound of clubs falling on skulls was sickening for the first minute, until one grew accustomed to it. A rioter dropped at every whack, it seemed, for the ground was covered with them"). In St. Louis (where, saying, "The people are rising up in their might and declaring they will no longer submit to being oppressed by unproductive capitalists," blacks and whites set aside their differences to shut down the city in a general strike). In New York City (where militia fraternized with workers, but police did not; after a peaceful gathering closed, with the words, "Whatever we poor men may not have, we have free speech, and no one can take it from us," police charged, clubs flailing).

Apart from profit derived from doing his "obvious and sacred duty," the strikes didn't matter much to Morgan. The poor continued to be poor, and continued to live in their "infant slaughter houses" where children were "damned rather than born."

In 1879, William Vanderbilt, the country's richest man, approached Morgan and asked him to rescue the New York Central Railroad from the American public. William's father, Cornelius, had died two years earlier, leaving his son with $100 million, an 87 percent share of the ownership in the railroad, and a host of legislators no longer on the take. Tired of poor, expensive, and dangerous rail service, the public began clamoring for action. Congress and the New York State legislature, made vague attempts to tax railroad profits, which, to that time, had not been taxed. William Vanderbilt's first response to public outrage (this explicitly directed at the cancellation of a popular express train) was, "The public be damned; I'm working for my stockholders. If the public want the train why don't they pay for it." Note that the public had paid for the train through extensive grants. Note, also, that since he owned 87 percent of the stock, he was merely saying that he was working for himself (as opposed to working for the greater good of the community), which is of course the prime manifestation of a destructive culture. His second response was to cut railroad workers' wages by

10 percent. His third was to secretly convince New York's governor to send troops to quell the ensuing riots. His fourth was to tell a reporter, "A public sentiment is growing up opposed to the control of such a great property by a single man or a single family. It says we rule by might. We certainly have control of the property by right." His fifth was to ask Morgan for help in preventing the taxes from being implemented.

Morgan agreed, then sold 250,000 shares of Vanderbilt's New York Central stock—quietly, so as to not cause a panic—removing Vanderbilt as majority owner. For his services, Pierpont received three million dollars, as much as the seamstress I mentioned earlier in this book (the one who said, "Sometimes in my haste I get my finger caught and the needle goes right through it") would have made in 12,785 years. In addition, and far more importantly, Morgan was made director of the company. By maintaining proxy votes of shares he had sold, Morgan gained effective control over the railroad. Although control of the railroad became no less concentrated, having merely shifted from Vanderbilt to Morgan, legislators backed off from their threat to impose taxes.

The next ten years were to see this oft-repeated pattern, as Morgan set out, in his words, to secure "harmony among the trunk lines." The question of legality was not important to him; when a counsel said of a Morgan action, "I don't think you can do that legally," Morgan replied, "I don't know as I want a lawyer to tell me what I cannot do. I hire him to tell me how to do what I want to do." The West Shore Railroad, the Pennsylvania, the South Pennsylvania, the Philadelphia and Reading. Each of these and more fell under his control. Others were brought together under "Gentlemen's Agreements" brokered by Morgan—at Morgan's house—which fixed the hauling prices of parallel lines. After one of his "Gentlemen's Meetings" he told a reporter, "Think of it—all the competing traffic of the roads west of Chicago and Saint Louis placed in the control of about 30 men!" His goal was to reduce that number to one.

■   ■   ■

DISTANCE

A salient feature—probably the most salient feature—of our culture is a near absolute intolerance for and hatred of diversity. Oh, I'm not talking about a phony diversity where we put up with people with different color skin or different sexual orientations (so long as the people are still White) though often we do not put up even with these variations. I'm not talking about putting up with little black boys, so long as they wear expensive shoes made by little brown girls hired on the cheap by female managers wearing men's clothing and bumping their heads on glass ceilings of corporations overseen by white males for the purposes of making profits for themselves and their shareholders. Nor am I talking about homosexual males (or females) working as engineers for these same companies. I'm not even talking about literate white males railing against their own privilege. All of this is tolerated. None of it is diversity.

So complete is our inculcation in this tradition of intolerance for and hatred of diversity that at this point any sort of real diversity has become almost unimaginable. Real diversity is a flock of passenger pigeons so large it darkened the sky for days at a time, and it is polar bears in Maine. Diversity is wood bison in Pennsylvania, and an ancient forest in New York City. Diversity is the capacity for a community of humans to confront trees, or fish, or human beings with no thought of how to best use them, how to turn them to profit. Diversity is a life lived with no concern for production, but, instead, lived with attention paid to the particular moments that pass, one by one, each bringing new beauties and carrying us at the same time that much closer to death. Diversity is entire communities integrated so fully into particular landscapes that the landscapes become more complex, more alive, more themselves, because of the presence of the communities. Diversity is water in rivers that is clean enough to drink. Diversity is an undammed river flowing from mountain to sea, turning no turbines. It is the rank smell of salmon decomposing to feed the forest and to feed the salmon's own children. Diversity is an abundance of wild cultures, each unimaginably different from all others, each grounded in its particular place. Diversity is complex languages and relationships derived from specific localities, in no way standardized across terrain. Diversity is communities, and individuals within communities, determining their own fates, dependent only on each other and on the land, neither beholden to, nor controlled by, distant entities or institutions. Diversity is dances for the hunt, dances for the spring rains, dances bundling your community together, dances for helping the dead make their passage to the next place.

Diversity is life being life, life branching toward the beauty of this particular leaf on this particular tree, this particular ant struggling to carry this particular piece of food. Diversity is life living for its own ends, with no consideration of instrumentality. Diversity is a hundred thousand simultaneous dances weaving seamlessly, no partner controlling any other. Diversity is the uncontrolled and uncontrollable flowing of human and nonhuman life, the abundance of human and nonhuman variation. Diversity is the capacity to perceive others in myriad ways, all of which are dependent not on preconception but on circumstance. If we cannot perceive others in a diversity of ways, we will destroy the diversity we cannot perceive. It has been so long since we perceived the world in diverse ways that we no longer perceive it as being possible. Our deification of production has blinded us to all ways of perceiving others, other than as means to ends. Not only does this lead ineluctably to perceiving these others with contempt, and hatred when they resist, but if you perceive the ancient forests of what is now New York City only as so many dollar bills, soon enough you will not have ancient forests, but instead New York City. Increasingly, we truncate our perception of that which cannot be controlled or used, then use what we can and destroy what we cannot.

■　　　■　　　■

In a nutshell, our culture's real response to diversity is this: Nothing shall be deliberately or unthinkingly allowed to detract from the central movement of our culture, toward monolithic control, toward production—which, after all, is nothing but the turning of the living

DISTANCE

(forests) into the dead (two-by-fours), the living (mountains) into the dead (aluminum cans)—toward the annihilation of all that is different. In other words, it calls for the annihilation of life. Production is the manifestation in the physical world of the psychic process of objectification. It is the turning of the subject (a cow, for example) into the object (profit on the hoof, as agribusinessmen say). To do so, necessarily kills the subject, first inside the objectifier's experience, and then in the physical world.

Production, however, is not the end point. Production, deified as it has become, is not the god who stands behind the god. The god who stands behind the god is annihilation. Where does our production lead us? Psychic death. Emotional death. Physical death. And, as should be increasingly clear to anyone paying any attention whatsoever, it is leading us ever more quickly toward the death of every living being.

■　　　■　　　■

The winners in Morgan's process of monopolization were the large owners, of course. The losers included the American public, which had financed these railroads to the tune of $700 million in cash as well as the gift of public lands large enough to comfortably contain all of France; passengers, who saw their fares soar and their safety concerns ignored; and small companies, which were driven out of business by higher freight costs while monopolists like Carnegie and Rockefeller enjoyed rebates. For workers, as they found themselves less able to bargain for higher wages, shorter hours, or safer conditions, the effects of "Morganization" were written in blood. Over the next eighteen years, between 1889 and 1907, the percentage of railroad employees annually killed or injured increased from 3.1 (22,000 out of 704,743) to 5.5 (92,178 out of 1,672,074). Between 1888 and 1907, 53,046 railroad workers were killed, and more than 800,000 were crippled for life.

Although Morgan's apotheosis was by this time near complete—he and his partners had become known as Pierpontifex Maximus and his Apostles, or, sometimes, Jupiter Morgan and his Ganymedes—there was still more wealth and power to be accumulated. Through the 1890s, Morgan brought under his control the Northern Pacific, with its millions of acres of grant lands, the Great Northern, the Erie, the Baltimore and Ohio, the Hocking Valley, the Mobile and Ohio, the Atchison, Topeka, and Santa Fe, the Lehigh Valley, the Central of Georgia, thirty-five small lines collectively known as the Southern Railway complex, and many more. He wanted to possess them all. By 1898, Morgan controlled 33,000 miles—one-sixth of the nation's total. "Morgan's roads," as they were called, annually brought in over $300 million, equal to one-half of the entire receipts of the U.S. government. By 1902, the mileage controlled by Morgan had increased to 55,000.

Still, he wanted more. He formed a monopoly over steel production through U.S. Steel. He controlled vast coal reserves. He controlled a communications monopoly, through American Telegraph and Telephone, a mining monopoly, through International Nickel, an electric monopoly, through General Electric, an insurance monopoly, through the Equitable Life Assurance Society, a financial monopoly, through his Bankers Trust (a congressional committee determined that the Trust, controlled by Morgan and a couple of others, held "341 directorships in 112 corporations having aggregate resources or capitalization of $22,245,000,000"), a monopoly on farm equipment, through International Harvester, which controlled 85 percent of the market and about which a partner said to Morgan, "The new company is to be organized by us; its name chosen by us; the state in which it shall be incorporated is left to us; the Board of Directors, the Officers, and the whole outfit left to us—nobody has any right to question in any way any choice we make." He tried to set up a shipping monopoly across the North Atlantic, and attempted to extend his steel monopoly to Germany. He controlled the customs houses of numerous Latin American nations, and was set up by Theodore Roosevelt as the sole financial agent—"Roosevelt's bagman"—for the newly created "Republic" of Panama. His involvement with Anglo-American, the South African gold monopoly

DISTANCE

described in the discussion of apartheid, was the reason for *American* in that company's name. A Morgan director wrote his wife from the Far East, "We've got our control and we've arranged it so that we can practically dictate the terms of China's currency reform. When you think of holding the whip hand in formulating the first real sound financial basis for a country of 400 million, it's quite a proposition." In England, vendors took to selling novelty licenses supposedly signed by Morgan for the right of one person to stay on earth.

▪   ▪   ▪

The inevitable result of our social and economic system is monopoly: centralized ownership, unified control, monolithic power. The last six thousand years have seen a grinding away at diversity: biological, cultural, theological, economic. One crop, one culture, one god, one owner—these are manifestations of a cultural urge to simplify complexity and thus increase control. Whether the crop is corn in Iowa or trees in Idaho, whether the god is Yahweh, Christ, or production, the result is inevitably deforestation and mass extinction, genocide, "Christianity or death," and a global marketplace in which billions of identical consumers purchase billions of identical cans of Coca-Cola ("the real thing"). Such are the fruits of our culture. Even a cursory examination of ecology, psychology, economics, and history reveals a relentless tightening of human and nonhuman experience, leading monotonously toward the eradication of all that is different, toward stasis, toward death.

Under this imperative, it is no wonder that we have in our midst feeble and not so feeble organizations based on the objectification of others: the KKK turning blacks into niggers; the judicial system turning blacks into inmates; the corporations turning blacks, whites, reds, yellows, and any other color you can imagine into laborers and consumers. All of these organizations—and the many others that are all reifications of our cultural imperatives—fall somewhere along the continuum that runs from the overt hatred acted out in the ritualized violence of lynchings, to the supercilious contempt inherent in wear-

THE CULTURE
OF MAKE
BELIEVE

ing a uniform that carries with it the full power of the state, as well as blinkered knowledge of the moral rightness of one's actions, to the depersonalized finality of ledgers and bank statements. Frankly, among these three, give me the former: it's much easier to fight.

When land ownership—and, by extension, economic wealth—is concentrated, there can be no democracy. Ultimately, there can be no life, save that which is regulated, controlled, overseen, regimented by those who control the land. Those who hold title or license to land have the right, backed by the power of the centralized state and, more importantly, by the bonds of cultural convention, to choose how that land will be used. They have the capability, by force of arms and force of conscience, to prevent others from living on it, farming it, or otherwise using it to enjoy their rights to liberty, the pursuit of happiness, and, ultimately, to life. If you deny people access to land, you deny them life independent of you; without access to the raw materials for self-provision of food, clothing, and shelter they must become the consumers of your products and the tenants of your houses, apartments, tenements, hutments, or slums. To pay for their necessities of life, they must go to work for you, they must sell you, as John Hammond Henry stated so clearly, the hours of their lives.

Those who hold title or license to land control the landscape itself. They determine whether or not buffalo will be killed, passenger pigeons eradicated, mountains hollowed out, hillsides denuded. But this power is exclusively destructive: They can kill seventy million buffalo and billions of passenger pigeons, yet they cannot create a single blade of grass, no matter the protestations and Frankenstein's Monsters of genetic engineering. Collectively, and acting through the mechanisms of the current economic system, those who control the land will determine whether the world remains habitable for human beings and other large species. Current levels of technology give them the capacity to destroy human life. It remains to be seen whether the cultural urge to simplify complexity—to convert, for example, the billowing web of relationships that is a living forest to board feet, to dollars, and ultimately to increased power over the lives of other human beings—is stronger than the urge to survive.

DISTANCE

THE LIMITED LIABILITY

CORPORATION IS

THE GREATEST

SINGLE INVENTION

OF MODERN TIMES.

NICHOLAS MURRAY BUTLER,

PRESIDENT OF

COLUMBIA UNIVERSITY

CORPORATIONS,
COPS,
AND HUNGRY
GHOSTS

THE CONTROL MORGAN EXERCISED is of course not possible without the assistance of many governments, not only directly, by killing or imprisoning those who oppose this concentration of wealth and power, but, more often, by passing and interpreting laws in ways favorable to monopolies, as well as failing to implement otherwise unfavorable laws drafted explicitly to soothe public opinion. Legislation, in 1887, creating the Interstate Commerce Commission, is an example of the latter. Born of public outrage over control of their lives by the wealthy, the law, as passed, was cosmetic, giving verbiage to the public while leaving control to monopolists: Rate-fixing was made illegal, but (and this was the entire point of the bill) no way was created to enforce the law. It was, as one congressman said, "A bill that no one wants . . . and everybody will vote for." Or, as U.S. attorney general Richard Olney put it, in an 1892 letter to his friend, Charles E. Perkins, president of the Chicago, Burlington & Quincy Railroad, "The [Interstate Commerce] Commission, as its functions have now been limited by the courts, is, or can be made of great use to the railroads. It satisfies the popular clamor for a government supervision of railroads, at the same time that the supervision is almost entirely nominal. Further, the older such a commission gets to be, the more inclined it will be found to take the business and railroad view of things. It thus becomes a sort of barrier between railroad corporations and the people and a sort of protection against hasty and crude legislation hostile to railroad interests. . . . The part of wisdom is not to destroy the Commission but to utilize it." The primary difference between then and now is Olney's candor.

The much-vaunted "trust-busting" by Theodore Roosevelt is another example. The truth is that two of J. P. Morgan's men—Judge Elbert Gary, chair of U.S. Steel, and George Perkins, a Morgan partner who later campaigned for Roosevelt—came to a general understanding with Roosevelt by which they agreed to cooperate in any government investigation in exchange for a guarantee of their companies' legality. As economist and historian Ferdinand Lundberg later made clear, Roosevelt "enjoyed political life only by virtue of J.P. Morgan's pleasure"; after Roosevelt filed an ultimately meaningless suit against Morgan's Northern Securities monopoly, Morgan was clearly affronted by this breach of trust and etiquette, and said to the President, "If we have done anything wrong, send your man to my man and they can fix it up."

Late in Morgan's life, a reporter put it such: "Mr. Morgan appeared to be convinced—at least that is the impression he gave—that there is no power in the state or Federal government competent to pass a set of laws that will stop much criticized practices that are common in the business world."

Morgan was correct in his conviction. He used these "much criticized practices" as well as anyone. He was no stranger to bribes, as when his associate, Charles Mellen, gave legislators over a million dollars to lubricate one minor business deal. Nor was he a stranger to strong-arm tactics, especially against employees, as, when "orders came down from the New York Office of the United States Steel Corporation . . . to line up their employees for the Penrose Candidates for the legislature. . . . They were told that their first duties were to the Corporation. They must, accordingly, break any or all promises and work for Penrose, because the United States Steel needed him in the Senate." But, most often, Morgan relied on cooperative and long-standing relationships with "the marionettes still figuring in Congress," as a writer for *Cosmopolitan* called them, who were "in place simply to carry out the orders of the world's real rulers—those who control the concentrated portion of the world's money supply." Once again, the primary difference between then and now is candor: Imagine a *Cosmopolitan* writer these days having the temerity to say such a thing (perhaps in the same issue where you get to "VOTE These Dudes NUDE: Here's your chance to strip a totally hot guy down to his birthday suit," cinched between the *Cosmopolitan* Quickie ("Make him woo you a little before letting him get lucky. Like dogs, boys enjoy a chase") and His Moan Zones ("Learn to touch and tempt him all over with these passion pointers")). They've come a long way, baby.

During and after the presidency of Ulysses S. Grant, Grant often came by Morgan's office (or his partner Drexel's) to share a cigar. Later, Morgan shared a mistress with England's King Edward VII. Presidents from Grant to Taft closely consulted Morgan on personal and professional matters (and, since that time, have continued to consult the representatives of Morgan's corporate creations); when Morgan made an 1895 trip to Washington, D.C., only to be told that President Cleveland (with whom Morgan regularly shared a smoke) would not see him, he stated, "I have come down to see the president, and I am going to stay here until I see him." Cleveland acquiesced, and during their meeting the next day, the president (against the explicit directions of Congress) turned over to Morgan the exclusive right to sell $62 million in bonds for at least one hundred and four dollars each and to keep everything over as profit; when the ink was dry on the contract, Morgan and his syndicate sold the whole lot within twenty-two minutes for up to $120 each, clearing a cool $8 million to $18 million.

Morgan's ownership of the country lasted from president to president: Soon after Taft's inauguration, Morgan partner George

Perkins wrote Pierpont: "Acting on suggestions made solely by me 2 weeks ago Franklin MacVeigh Chicago has been selected for Secretary of the Treasury. Wickersham will be Attorney General and other places are filled to our entire satisfaction."

■   ■   ■

I sometimes wince when I hear people—even longtime activists—complain that corporations are taking over "our" government, as though the government was ever ours in the first place, and as though corporations and governments are actually separable, as opposed to functionally separate components of the same machine.

Although at times governments openly appropriate wealth from communities, that's generally not their primary function. They usually act as facilitators and overseers for the corporations that directly exploit and export the resource bases of communities. They act as a force of conscience, creating laws and inculcating people to believe that to follow those laws is good and that to break them is evil, or, at the very least, antisocial.

This is not, of course, to say that there are no reasonable laws. Of course there are. Strictures against murder, for example, are generally good things. But as we would see, time and again, in the daily workings of our culture, were our acculturation not so complete, many laws are written, enforced, and, most importantly, perceived in such a way as to hold no one accountable for some types of murder. The same is generally true for ecocide, and for genocide, especially against people of color. The same is effectively true, also, for many crimes against women and children. The same cannot be said for affronts against the property of the wealthy.

■   ■   ■

Last year I talked to Christian Parenti, author of the book *Lockdown America*, about what he calls our "incipient police state." He said, "We need to always remember that while the police do everything

CORPORATIONS, COPS, AND HUNGRY GHOSTS

from getting kittens out of trees and enhancing public safety to killing strikers and framing radicals, the social control function has always been at the heart of what they do, even though most of what they do is not that."

It's an interesting contradiction. While I certainly know about the use of police violence against those who blaspheme against production, I also know that when, a few years ago, I got burgled, the first thing I did was call the cops. Not that, in this case, it did any good. I mentioned this to Christian.

He said, "Most of us would do that. But the fact remains that it's an important distinction to see, that while most of what the police do is mundane sort of pseudo-public safety functions, the heart of what they do, the most important social function, is to intervene at times of political crisis against rebels and to prevent such rebellion, too."

He's right. We needn't go far to discover what happens to people who attempt to oppose the deification of production, that is, who attempt to drive the moneylenders from the temple: Picture a couple of big pieces of wood, a half-dozen nails, and a holiday having to do with chocolate bunnies and painted eggs. Recall also that the single-minded pursuit of production was—and, if we are honest with ourselves, is—an explicit reason for the eradication of indigenous peoples everywhere.

Imagine—and please try not to laugh too hard at the absurdity of this visualization—how our lives would be different if police used guns not to put down strikers but to force owners to terms. Picture the police in Seattle shooting rubber bullets and tear gas (at point-blank range) at the CEOs of corporations and at politicians who are in essence committing treason by subverting U.S. sovereignty to transnational corporations through such mechanisms as the World Trade Organization and the various so-called free-trade agreements. Imagine a SWAT team breaking down the door to Warren Anderson's house, or imagine them swooping down upon him while he's playing out the back nine.

■   ■   ■

THE CULTURE OF MAKE BELIEVE

Several years ago I did some research on Rocky Flats, in Colorado, where Rockwell International designed and built plutonium triggers for nuclear bombs. Plutonium is one of the most dangerous materials known. The best estimate for plutonium's LD-50, or the dosage at which 50 percent of the victims die, is around ten nanograms. Plutonium metal is extremely combustible, and will combust spontaneously. This happened in 1969, at Rocky Flats, causing the United States's most expensive fire to the time, measured in monetary cost of equipment destroyed. More than 90 percent of the plutonium aerosols produced in that fire were of respirable size, "ideal for entering the lungs and lodging there."

The prevailing winds along the Front Range of Colorado's Rocky Mountains are from west to east. The winds blow through mountain canyons onto the plains, past Boulder, past Lousiville and Lafayette, past Broomfield, and into Denver. Sometimes, usually in the winter, but occasionally at other times of the year, winds exceed one hundred miles per hour, breaking windows, tearing off roofs, lifting picnic tables, and, of course, carrying all kinds of dust.

In the early 1950s, the military decided to build a nuclear weapons plant on a plateau, called Rocky Flats, just west of Denver. The decision was greeted jubilantly by the corporate press: The *Denver Post*'s front-page banner headline read: "There is Good News Today: $45 million A-Plant Near Denver." The newspaper did not mention the presumably not-so-good news that this "A-Plant" was to be built directly upwind of the majority of the *Post*'s readers.

Nor was the public informed of the full monetary cost to construct the Rocky Flats Nuclear Weapons Plant, which was not $45 million but instead closer to $240 million (never mind the full costs of operation, including decommissioning, clean-up, health care, and so on, which are inestimable). Nor was the public told that the plant, which was to be run by Dow Chemical, would routinely handle tons of plutonium.

The first major fire at Rocky Flats occurred in 1957, as some of the plutonium "skulls" in Building 771 spontaneously combusted. Although the area was supposed to have been designed to be fire-

CORPORATIONS, COPS, AND HUNGRY GHOSTS

proof, flames quickly jumped out of control. Soon, plutonium filters on the smokestacks combusted, sending a black cloud three hundred feet into the air. When carbon dioxide failed to quench the flames, firefighters decided to use water. Their decision was a reluctant one, both because they knew water would destroy equipment costing millions of dollars and because the vaporized water might carry even more plutonium toward Denver. At no time during the thirteen-hour fire did plant officials warn police, schools, health departments, or elected officials. There were no plans for evacuation, and local ranchers were not notified.

Between fourteen and twenty kilograms—equaling the potential for seven hundred billion cases of cancer—are estimated to have burned directly in the fire. This is in addition to the plutonium contained in the smokestack filters, which also burned. The filters, which had never been changed in the four years the building had been operating, were estimated to have captured thirteen grams of plutonium each day, meaning it is possible that as much as 250 kilograms of plutonium was blown toward Denver that day. An actual release only one-tenth this size would still have been enough to give each of the 1.4 million people in the Denver metropolitan area a radiation dose one million times the "permissible lung burden." In addition, the thirty thousand gallons of water used to put out the fire escaped, to irradiate local streams, the water table, and municipal water sources.

That was not the only time Rocky Flats burned; for its first twenty years, the plant averaged ten fires per year, in addition to explosions, radioactive spills, and other contamination incidents. Such was the course of normal operations. On May 11, 1969, buildings 776 and 777 erupted into flames. This time the radioactive smoke was so thick that firefighters were "forced to crawl out along exit lines painted on the floor." Eventually, the fire came under control, but only after a metric ton of plutonium had burned.

The accidental fires were not the only form of radioactive release from the plant. Thousands of drums filled with plutonium-contaminated oil were routinely stored in fields near Rocky Flats. More than a thousand of these were burned in the open air, as, first, Dow, and,

later, Rockwell (which took over operations in 1975) ordered "routine intentional burnings." Other barrels were simply buried. Faced with the possibility of exposure, one plant official suggested telling the public that the radioactive hills created by burying these wastes were actually Indian burial mounds. Barrels, neither burned nor buried, were left to corrode and leak. As Melinda Cassan, part of a Colorado governor's council on Rocky Flats, stated, "It turned out they leaked about eleven curies [about 176 kilograms] of plutonium into the ground. If properly distributed, it would be a lethal dose to every human being on the planet." Rockwell took to routinely disposing hazardous and radioactive wastes by calling them "irrigation" and spraying them continuously, even in winter, onto fields surrounding the plant. Testimony before a grand jury revealed that "Rockwell's spray irrigation practices resulted in sheet runoff of the sprayed effluent into Woman Creek and Walnut Creek." The wastes "ultimately . . . flowed downstream to municipal water."

The surrounding landscape is hot. One mile east of the plant, radiation levels are four hundred times higher than they would be from fallout alone, and just outside the fence, levels are fifteen hundred times higher than would be expected. Such radiation levels are bound to cause mutations. Lloyd Mixon, a farmer who lived his whole life in Broomfield, six miles from Rocky Flats, told of a hairless calf born with a body full of a watery substance and a liver "three times normal." He told of another calf born dead whose tissue tested similar to cows experimentally dosed with radiation. He told of pigs born with "nose and mouth twisted, where they're not able to nurse," and "with eyes that were not like they're supposed to be." He told of "chickens with no eyes," and "beaks like needles," and of chickens whose "legs have been so badly twisted and turned that they were unable to kick out of the shell. We had a chicken hatch with the brains right on top of his head." He and his neighbors have seen infertile pheasants, and they've seen "lambs born with the guts, or the insides hanging out. [Some would] be alive." They've seen kid goats born with growths on them, geese who suddenly stiffen up and die, and too many dogs who die of cancer. They've had years where every colt is born blind, and

CORPORATIONS, COPS, AND HUNGRY GHOSTS

other years where colts are stillborn or deformed. They speak of a general loss of wildlife.

Humans, too, have suffered and died. The congenital malformation rate near Rocky Flats is more than 40 percent higher than the state average. The former director of the Health Department of Jefferson County, where Rocky Flats is located, studied cancer rates for the region. He divided the downwind area into four zones—closest to farthest—and found, after correcting for age, race, sex, and ethnicity, that male cancer rates in the zone closest to the plant were 24 percent higher than in the zone farthest away. Female cancer rates were 10 percent higher. Lung cancer and leukemia rates are approximately doubled.

From the beginning, the response by company and government officials has been to avoid safety measures and to lie. After the 1959 fire, which released between twenty and two hundred and fifty kilograms of plutonium, Atomic Energy Commission (AEC) reports stated that there had been "no spread of radioactive contamination of any consequence." The manager of the AEC office at Rocky Flats mirrored this line, allowing, however, that "possibly" some radiation, once again, of "no consequence," had escaped.

After the 1969 fire, the story was the same. Rocky Flats officials insisted none of the metric ton of plutonium which had burned left the building, and refused to allow any outside investigation. Further, the AEC originally estimated damage at $3 million; actual monetary costs were closer to $45 million. When, in the 1970s, AEC and Colorado Department of Health officials discovered that lawns in Denver tested above danger levels for plutonium, they raised those levels by a factor of ten. And when, in the early 1980s, a Department of Energy epidemiologist found that too many workers at Rocky Flats were dying of certain types of cancer, Rockwell management and DOE officials "attempted to make it difficult for us to get those findings published. Since that time, the DOE has not allowed any more studies of plutonium workers anywhere."

Safety conditions inside the plant were abysmal. During the more than two years it took hundreds of employees to clean up the

radioactive mess from the 1969 fire, at least one janitor who refused to work with the radioactive materials was fired. An engineer who discovered that the duct work in many of the buildings was contaminated with "all the crud of the ages," with "pounds" of "radioactive material" (he found sixty-two pounds in just one building) was fired for making this discovery. Later, a plant technician received an even stronger lesson about what happens to people who talk about safety: "I was working with an experimental product. This product made me very ill. And I later found out these symptoms were radiation sickness. I had really odd big bruises on my body that you could touch and they didn't hurt. All the hair on my arms fell out. I was nauseated. I was vomiting. I had diarrhea for three weeks. I had this incredible, terrible rash on my skin. It was the most painful thing I've ever felt in my life, like the worst sunburn you have ever had." When she complained, she was given even more dangerous assignments and told, "We don't care what you have to do back there. We need four or five more products this week." She determined to give testimony before a grand jury about the dangerous conditions inside Rocky Flats. One morning, two weeks before she was to testify, her supervisors called her in at 3:30 with an assignment to work in an unfamiliar room. She put on her protective suit, pulled new plastic gloves from the box, and put her arms into one of the boxes containing plutonium. One of the gloves had a pinhole in it, and radioactive fireash sprayed into her face. In her words, "My face, my respirator, my hair, my hands, my sleeves, everything was hot." Two other employees began laughing and pointing at her. One said, "That's what you get for making waves."

Over the years, heavily armed security guards have kept trespassers out of Rocky Flats, including investigating scientists, citizens, agents of the Environmental Protection Agency, and the Colorado Department of Health. When EPA and Department of Health officials requested information on conditions inside the plant, they were told it was none of their business. As Melinda Cassan made clear, the reason for keeping regulators out is simple: "They couldn't get a permit to operate it legally. That's true with most of the functions at

CORPORATIONS, COPS, AND HUNGRY GHOSTS

Rocky Flats. And unfortunately it's true with the weapons complex generally. If these facilities had to get hazardous waste permits for everything that they did, they wouldn't do it. Department of Energy [which had taken over from the AEC as regulatory agency] understood that. Rockwell, the operator, understood that. That's the reason that we had these environmental battles, is because the plant can't operate in compliance with the law."

Now, here's the point, as it relates to the function of the police in our culture. In 1989, after a two-year investigation, seventy-five FBI agents raided Rocky Flats, where they spent the next nine days gathering 960 boxes of evidence. Although this may seem a huge raid, a comparison with another case may point out, once again, the priorities of our culture: More than a hundred FBI agents were assigned to investigate the Unabomber, and, when the primary suspect, Theodore Kaczynski, was arrested, federal agents searched his one-room shack for several weeks. To push this contrast further, the grand jury in the Rocky Flats case was *disallowed* from handing out indictments, although they wanted to, and when they went public with the information they had gained, the judge threatened to prosecute them. None of the people who irradiated Denver were ever indicted, much less served time. Ted Kaczynski is serving life without parole. The point is that the three people murdered by the Unabomber were not killed in the service of centralized power—the murders did not manifest the desire of the culture as a whole (and especially its leaders)—and therefore they were punished. Because the murders committed by Rockwell, the Department of Energy, and so on, do serve to further centralize power, so-called attempts to bring accountability were, and are, nominal.

■   ■   ■

J. Pierpont Morgan died in 1913. He had been, according to his own estimation, no mere mortal. Toward the end, Morgan testified before Congress that he had been ordained by "Providence" to take care of the financial and industrial, not to mention political, well-being of the country. A reporter for the *New York World* summarized Morgan's testimony: "The underlying argument in the testimony of J. Pierpont Morgan before the Money Trust Investigation Committee today was to establish his belief that his group of financiers rules the commerce of America by something akin to *divine right*."

The belief that wealth is divinely ordained is nearly ubiquitous among the rich (and, even more pathetically, among many of the poor). John D. Rockefeller, for example, stated, "I believe the power to make money is a gift of God . . . to be developed and used to the best of our ability for the good of mankind. Having been endowed with the gift I possess, I believe it is my duty to make money and still more money, and to use the money I make for the good of my fellow man according to the dictates of my conscience." There was no reason for him to mention the relationship between his "gift of God," and his use of child labor or his devastation of communities. It probably did not occur to him: Within a culture like ours, all things—children, men, women, communities, land, plants, animals—belong by right to those who have the "gifts" to seize them. This right is the endowment of an all-knowing God who, as we can all clearly see, has everyone's interests at heart. As George F. Baer, president of the Philadelphia and Reading, stated, "The rights and interests of the laboring man will be protected and cared for by the Christian men to whom God has given control of the property rights of the country."

It is not only the rich themselves who preach the gospel of divine wealth. The famous Henry Ward Beecher, who accepted money from the Northern Pacific Railroad Company to preach the good railroad's virtues, once said, "God has intended the great to be great and the little to be little." Low wages were not a problem to the workingman, he said, because "the man who cannot live on bread and water is not fit to live." History does not record his own dinner menus. The immensely popular nineteenth-century Baptist minister, Russell H. Conwell, was even more vociferous, traveling the country, giving a lecture, entitled, "Success was an outward sign of inward grace." He told his flock, "I say that you ought to get rich, and it is your duty to get rich. . . . [T]o make money honestly is to preach the

CORPORATIONS, COPS, AND HUNGRY GHOSTS

gospel. . . . The men who get rich may be the most honest men you find in the community." When asked whether he sympathized with the poor, he replied, "To sympathize with a man whom God has punished for his sins, thus to help him when God would still continue a just punishment, is to do wrong, no doubt about it, and we do that more than we help those who are deserving. While we should sympathize with God's poor—that is, those who cannot help themselves—let us remember there is not a poor person in the United States who was not made poor by his own shortcomings, or by the shortcomings of some one else. It is all wrong to be poor, anyhow."

■   ■   ■

Reading accounts of people who suffered under Morgan's control, and more generally those who have suffered under the domination of our economic system, I'm struck, time and again, by the juxtaposition of our culture's ugliness with the will and beauty of those who survive. The children who toiled so Morgan could profit were the ones who deserved praise, or, more importantly, a relief other than death.

While researching and writing this book, it has not always been possible to forever keep the tears away. So that Morgan and other owners could profit, children as young as seven worked in coal mines: "Crouched over the chutes, the boys sit hour after hour picking out the pieces of slate and other refuse from the coal as it rushes past the washers. From the cramped position they have to assume, most of them become more or less deformed. . . . The coal is hard, and accidents to the hands, such as cut, broken, or crushed fingers, are common among the boys. Sometimes there is a worse accident: a terrified shriek is heard, and a boy is mangled and torn in the machinery, or disappears in the chute to be picked out later smothered and dead. Clouds of dust fill the beakers and are inhaled by the boys, laying the foundations for asthma and miners' consumption." Of immigrants who worked in Morgan's steel mills, it was written that "the waste of

439

life and limb is great, and if it all fell upon the native born a cry would long since have gone up which would have stayed the slaughter."

Yet no cry was officially tolerated, and so the slaughter continued. About their families it was written, "One-third of all who die in Pittsburgh, die without having anything to say about it. That is, they die under five years of age. One-fourth of all who die, die without having anything to say about anything. That is, they die under one year of age. Most of these deaths are preventable, being the outcome of conditions which, humanly speaking, have no right to exist." Yet, under these conditions, which, "humanly speaking, have no right to exist," some people still carry on.

They still carry on.

■　　　■　　　■

Morgan having been named while alive "The Savior of the Nation," there was not much room for the hyperbole to continue its expansion. But at least it maintained its bloated state. After his death, Morgan was called by Pope Pius X, "a great and good man." According to a London paper, he had been "a towering constructive force," and "a generous benefactor." The New York Stock Exchange hailed him as "a constructive genius . . . devoted . . . to the whole wide field of philanthropy and humanity. The whole world has lost a wise counselor and a helpful friend." *The New York Tribune* said, "He left great riches, but he also left a good name more priceless than great riches."

He also left a corporation that bore his name.

Although corporations will undoubtedly determine whether humans survive—or, rather, whether we humans can stop them will determine whether humans survive—we don't talk about them much. We especially don't talk about what they are.

Corporations are entities that we pretend are real, that have been defined (and, institutionally, define themselves) to person status by claiming, in essence, to be a body, a living body (remember that *incorporate* comes from the Latin *in*, in, and *corporare*, to form

CORPORATIONS, COPS, AND HUNGRY GHOSTS

into a body, from *corpus*, a body). Corporations are the "embodiment," the reification, of a single idea—that of amassing wealth. To that end, they have been "granted perpetual life and diversified ownership, each part of which has limited liability for the debts and other liabilities of the firm." This limited liability means that each owner is not liable for the actions of the corporation. Investors can only lose the amount of money invested, and are not held in any way accountable if the company commits genocide, ecocide, murder, or any other crime. Who, then, is held accountable? The officers? Even when a corporate officer is held liable, the corporation and its stockholders, once again, are not. WMX (which used to be called Waste Management, until that name acquired too foul a reputation), for example, is the largest garbage collection and recycling company in the world. It is responsible for the largest toxic dump in the United States, and has located toxic dumps in minority neighborhoods across the country. It was cited six hundred times by the Environmental Protection Agency in the 1980s, and, between 1983 and 1988, faced eighteen grand juries. Yet, even though the corporation has been sued, convicted, and fined for numerous environmental, price-fixing, bribery, and antitrust violations, paying $46 million in fines for bribery and illegal waste handling alone between 1980 and 1988, and even though some executive officers have gone to jail, the company still has contracts with thousands of cities in forty-eight states and nineteen countries. Through the 1980s, WMX's sales increased from $773 million to $6 billion. The point is that on the extremely rare occasion that an executive goes to jail, nothing happens to the company—to the machine which has as its sole function the amassing of wealth.

Limited liability means more than profits, however, and it means more than toxic waste dumps in minority neighborhoods. It is more than the mere institutionalization of irresponsibility. It is an explicit acknowledgment that it's impossible to amass great wealth without externalizing costs. If costs were not being externalized, there would be no need to limit liability.

Corporations are a legal device that came into use during the eighteenth and nineteenth centuries to deal with the myriad limits exceeded by our culture's social and economic system: The railroads and other early corporations were too big and too technological to be built or insured by the incorporators' investments alone; when corporations failed, or caused gross public damage, as they often did, the incorporators did not have the wealth to cover the damage. No one did. Thus, a limit was placed on the investors' liability, on the amount of damage for which they could be held liable. Because of limited liability, corporations have allowed several generations of owners to economically, psychologically, and legally ignore the limits of toxics, fisheries depletion, debt, and so on that have been transgressed by the workings of our economic system.

By now, we should have learned. To expect corporations to function differently than they do is to engage in magical thinking. We may as well expect a clock to cook, a car to give birth, or a gun to plant flowers. The specific and explicit function of for-profit corporations is to amass wealth. The function is not to guarantee that children are raised in environments free of toxic chemicals, nor to respect the autonomy or existence of indigenous peoples, nor to protect the vocational or personal integrity of workers, nor to design safe modes of transportation, nor to support life on this planet. Nor is the function to serve communities. It never has been and never will be. To expect corporations to do anything other than amass wealth is to ignore our culture's system of rewards, to ignore everything we know about behavior modification: We reward those investing in or running corporations for what they do, and so we can expect them to do it again. To expect corporations to do otherwise is delusional. Corporations are institutions created explicitly to separate humans from the effects of their actions, making them, by definition, inhuman and inhumane. To the degree that we desire to live in a human and humane world—and, really, to the degree that we wish to survive—corporations need to be eliminated.

CORPORATIONS, COPS, AND HUNGRY GHOSTS

It would be easy to blame corporations for most of the world's ills. This, however, would not be helpful, because corporations are mere tools for governance and for the transfer of wealth from communities to the governors, the latest in a series of tools running back six thousand years to when civilization originated "in conquest abroad and repression at home."

To provide a clarifying example, although the world's forests might receive a brief reprieve were Weyerhaeuser's corporate charter revoked, we must remember that our culture was deforesting the world long before Weyerhaeuser—either the corporation or its founder, Frederick—was conceived.

Corporations don't cause destruction; they are tools to facilitate it, legalize it, rationalize it, make it respectable. Another word for "the externalization of costs," for "limited liability," is theft. But this is a special breed of theft, where even the victim is left feeling that a legitimate and just transaction has taken place; the victim may be frustrated, but is more likely to be jealous than outraged. As we have seen repeatedly in this country's elections, the victim will defend the thief's property rights, and will also spend the rest of his or her life trying to earn back the stolen goods. Political rhetoritician Edmund Burke laid out, presumably with a straight face, the responsibilities of the properly encultured, the mental and emotional states in which the poor must be maintained if they are to keep themselves at labor and not rebel against the rich: "They must respect that property of which they cannot partake. They must labor to obtain what by labor can be obtained; and when they find, as they commonly do, the success disproportioned to the endeavor, they must be taught their consolation in the final proportions of eternal justice."

But, perhaps, this is going too far. Perhaps, by changing the language, by moving away from the academic—"the privatization of profits and the externalization of costs"—to the vulgar—"theft"—I run the risk of offending. I imperil my credibility.

That is precisely the point, and precisely the strength of the corporation as a tool for privatizing profits and externalizing costs, for theft, and murder. The transaction is legitimate. The crime com-

plete. It is acceptable. It is legal. And, of course, it is still theft. And it is still murder.

But labels aren't so important; no matter what we call it, poison is still poison, death is still death, and industrial civilization is still causing the greatest mass extinction in the history of the planet.

■   ■   ■

A corporation is a "creature of the law," as Chief Justice Marshall observed in 1819, a creation of the state. When a government charters a corporation, it is setting in motion, according to Marshall, "a perpetual succession of individuals [who] are capable of acting for the promotion of the particular object, like one immortal being. . . ." Since corporations are "immortal," and since they are created solely to amass wealth, they become the institutionalization of dissatisfaction, the economic manifestation of the Buddhist notion of "hungry ghosts," spirits who roam the earth, always eating, never sated. The forest activist Jim Britell commented on this, and his statement applies not only to the timber industry executives he describes but to the culture as a whole: "In the writings and speeches of clear-cutters and deforesters, you can see and hear an intense hunger to find forests to cut. At the same time, the last few years have broken all records in the amount of forests cut down. What we are seeing is a simultaneity of poverty and richness, a special kind of insatiable hunger where the more you possess the more deprived you feel. This is the emotion that dominates and pervades the realm of the hungry ghosts. The physical representation of this state is the image of a being with a gigantic belly, a very thin neck and a tiny mouth. No matter how much the hungry ghost eats, its stomach can never be filled."

What this means is that corporations and those who run them cannot stop exploiting resources and amassing wealth until they have. . . . I cannot finish this sentence, because the truth is that they can never stop; like cancer, they can only continue to expand until they kill their host.

CORPORATIONS, COPS, AND HUNGRY GHOSTS

THE POINT TO BE GRASPED HAS BEEN STARING

WESTERN CIVILIZATION IN THE FACE FOR THE LAST HALF

CENTURY: NAMELY, THAT A PREDOMINANTLY MEGA-

TECHNIC ECONOMY CAN BE KEPT IN PROFITABLE

OPERATION ONLY BY SYSTEMATIC AND CONSTANT EXPAN-

SION. INSTEAD OF A BALANCED ECONOMY, DEDICATED

TO THE ENHANCEMENT OF LIFE, MEGATECHNICS DE-

MANDS LIMITLESS EXPANSION ON A COLOSSAL SCALE

A FEAT THAT ONLY WAR OR MOCK-WAR-ROCKET

BUILDING AND SPACE EXPLORATION-CAN SUPPLY.

LEWIS MUMFORD

WAR

WE MAY AS WELL ADMIT that war is the best possible thing for our economy. Wars bring us out of depressions, and the outbreak of peace often begins them. Speaking of things monetary—the *lingua franca* of our "money talks" theocracy—war is the best possible thing not only for the economy but for those who run it. It allows them to speak of the creation of jobs while increasing their fortunes. It allows them to speak of patriotism while sacrificing lives less valuable than their own. It brings about an urgency—a frenzy, even—that allows the rationalization of massive public expenditures, inevitably translating to private subsidy without even the illusion of public benefit. It allows them to further centralize political and economic power under the guise of efficiency and national security. It allows them to imprison or execute those who oppose this centralization, with no fear of repercussion. It allows them to praise themselves and others like them for giving voice to an urge to destroy. It allows them to invent, deploy, and use no end of nightmarish devices. It allows them to kill, or, rather, give orders, so others must kill, with no fear of public censure. It allows them to pull off the mask of public appeasement and more fully concentrate and exercise their power, or, more precisely, their power to destroy.

All of this comes at the expense of those whose lives are less valuable, and, most directly, at the expense of those who die, or kill, in the trenches. As Ferdinand Lundberg stated about World War I, and this holds true for any war, "The question which strikes at the heart of the war situation like a dagger is not, Who caused the war? . . . The revealing question is, Who profited by the war, pocketed the profit, and defends the profit?"

The answer, of course, is always the wealthy. Between April 6, 1917, when the United States declared war, and October 31, 1919, when the last U.S. troops returned home, the federal government spent on World War I more than $35 billion of the public's money; between 1914 and the end of the war, the national debt grew from $967 million to $24 billion. Net corporate profits were $38 billion between January 1, 1916, and July 1921, when wartime industrial activity finally ceased. More than two-thirds of these profits went to companies associated with the Morgan-controlled Bankers Trust.

Just as the Crimean War came at a propitious time for Pierpont's father, so World War I came at a propitious time for his son Jack. In 1914, the House of Morgan was teetering, in great measure because of problems associated with the New York, New Haven and Hartford Railroad (called the New Haven Line). While the New Haven Line resembled many of Morgan's other operations, with its blatant disregard for community interest, fiscal sanity, the free market, and the semblance of legality, the manipulation of the New Haven differed from others in that here Morgan became too greedy even for his own monetary security. Along with Charles Mellon, Pierpont had planned to take over every form of transportation in New England: every railroad, steamship line, even every electric trolley. Through the creation of hundreds of dummy corporations, "some headed by

WAR

mystified clerks who were periodically called in and told to sign contracts," Morgan and Company bilked stockholders and the public of between $60 million and $90 million. *The New York World* noted, "Thousands of men are in jail for offenses against society which are picayunish in comparison with this stupendous achievement in respectable robbery." But neither Pierpont nor his son Jack went to jail. Neither was convicted of any crime, or even indicted. Both were deified.

■   ■   ■

The relationship between economics and hatred is far deeper and more formative than what I've said earlier, that any hatred felt long enough and deeply enough feels like economics, tradition, religion, what have you. There's more to it than that. First, because our economics (and our society) is based on competition, it breeds hatred, insecurity, and fear. In *A Language Older Than Words*, I discussed how the anthropologist Ruth Benedict tried to figure out why some cultures are fundamentally peaceful and others are not, why women and children are treated well in some cultures and in others they are not, and why some cultures are cooperative and others are competitive. She found one simple rule that covered all of these. It has to do with our need as social creatures for esteem. In what she termed good, or synergistic, cultures, selfishness and altruism are merged by granting esteem to those who are generous. Cultures that reward behavior benefiting the group as a whole (and specifically that siphon wealth constantly from rich to poor) while not allowing behavior that harms the group as a whole are peaceful, respectful of women and children, and cooperative. Individual members are secure. If, on the other hand, your culture grants esteem to those who are acquisitive, that is, if your culture rewards behavior that benefits the individual at the expense of the whole (and if your culture funnels wealth from poor to rich), your culture will be warlike, abusive toward women and children, and competitive. Individuals will be insecure. She also found that members of the cultures with the former characteristics are, unsurprisingly, for the most part, happy. Members of the cultures with the latter characteristics are, just as unsurprisingly, not. Valium, anyone?

It's worse than this, actually. Because our economics (and our society) is so based on abstraction, that is, the rewards of our economic system are in dollars, which are nothing but numbers that we as a society all tend to agree are worth something, and not on tangible goods, the acquistiveness that our culture rewards can never be sated. Like hungry ghosts, we eat the world, but it's never enough. We can accumulate more than we need, more, even, than we can ever use, but because there's no limit to how high numbers can go in a bank account, those who accumulate continue to be rewarded for accumulating ever more.

Because competition is so central to our culture, because acquisition is so deeply rewarded, because this cultural urge to acquire is insatiable, and because this acquisition is inevitably based on the exploitation of others, there can be no limit to how thoroughly our culture will exploit others, both human and nonhuman. And because increasing competition leads so easily and obviously, when our lives are at stake, to increasing hatred of our competitors (as well as hatred of those who resist our exploitation), there can be no limit as to the depth and breadth of our culturally induced hatred, both of our direct peers and of those from whom we wish to steal.

But it is even worse than this. As discussed earlier in this book, another of the central movements of our culture—along with movement toward monolithic control—has been toward increasing abstraction, that is, away from the particular, away from Buber's joining of will and grace, and toward perceiving others as Its, objects, numbers, resources to be used, or, as Kevin Bales said of modern slaves, to be used hard, used up, and thrown away. Thus there can be no limit, then, also to the abstraction of our hate, that is, to the increasing emotional and physical distance over which we can and do destroy, to the veils we place between ourselves and those others we may no longer consider as existing.

■　　　■　　　■

WAR

Pierpont died, and Jack presided over the collapse of the New Haven. It was simply not possible to run a railroad while bleeding it so thoroughly. Just as the 1873 collapse of the Northern Pacific had taken down Jay Cooke's empire, so did the collapse of the New Haven threaten the House of Morgan.

Fortunately for Jack, and for the companies he controlled, World War I broke out in Europe. Immediately after the first shots, Morgan partner Harry Davison cabled the news to Morgan partner Tom Lamont, on vacation, and added, "Probably could do little if you were here the only point being that is filled with extra ordinary interest and of course great possibilitys." Capitalizing on the "possibilitys," within two weeks the company asked President Wilson if he would object to Morgan making a loan to the French. At first, Wilson stated that loans by American companies to participants would make United States neutrality difficult. But when bankers asked again, having substituted the word *credit* for *loan,* and having developed a salable rationale—extending credits to foreign governments would allow those governments to buy American goods— Wilson immediately assented, at first, to the extension of credits, and, later, to the granting of loans, with their lessened restrictions.

Soon, J. P. Morgan and Company suggested to the British and French governments that they name Morgan essentially the sole purchasing agent for what in time became $3 billion worth of war materials. This arrangement netted the company $30 million in commissions. But the real money was still to come.

Unsurprisingly, Morgan directed the contracts—and profits—to the corporations controlled by Morgan's Bankers Trust. Revenues at Du Pont went from $25 million in 1914 to $131 million in 1915. Unfilled orders at Bethlehem Steel went from $25 million at the end of 1913 to $175 million by the end of 1915. Between 1914 and 1916 profits at United States Steel jumped from $23 million to $271 million. Profits of Morgan-Guggenheim Utah Copper Company doubled in the first two years of the war. The same is true for International Harvester. And so on. And so on. Stock Exchange prices sextupled between 1914 and 1916. War is the best possible thing for our economy.

The company began issuing massive loans to the belligerents, and partner Tom Lamont spoke glowingly of the possibilities for profit and increased power to American financial institutions if, in his words, "the war continues long enough." He said, "Since the war began we have loaned direct to foreign governments something over two hundred million dollars. Yet this is a comparatively small sum. Shall we become lenders upon a really stupendous scale to these foreign governments?" The answer would be yes, he said, "if the war continues long enough to encourage us."

At the same time Tom Lamont was articulating the abstract monetary rewards that would accrue "if the war lasts long enough to encourage us," people were dying in Europe: "Men had lost arms and legs, brains oozed out of shattered skulls, and lungs protruded from riven chests; many had lost their faces and were, I should think, unrecognizable to their friends. . . . One poor chap had lost his nose and most of his face, and we were obliged to take off an arm, the other hand, and extract two bullets like shark's teeth from his thigh." While Lamont spoke of becoming "lenders on a really stupendous scale," a frontline nurse spoke of other, more tangible topics: "I pushed the clothes back and saw a pulp, a mere mass of smashed body from the ribs downwards; the stomach and abdomen were completely crushed and his left leg was hanging to the pulped body by only a few shreds of flesh. . . . The soldier's dull eyes were looking at me and his lips moved, but no words came. What it cost me to turn away without aiding him, I cannot describe, but we could not waste time and material on hopeless cases, and there were so many others waiting." At the same time that Jack Morgan, having fully internalized Thomas Mellon's advice that a man may "be a patriot without risking his own life or sacrificing his health," served at home—either his fifty-seven-room home on two hundred and fifty acres near Long Island (twelve bedrooms, twenty-five bathrooms, eighteen marble fireplaces, sixteen-car garage, and gymnasium), or his "unexpectedly light and spa-

WAR

cious" home in New York City (forty-five rooms, twenty-two fire-places, and a dozen bathrooms")—others were being killed far away from family, home, and any friendly face: "Those who could walk, got up and followed us; running, hopping, limping, by our sides. The badly crippled crawled after us; all begging, beseeching us not to abandon them in their need. And, on the road, there were others, many others; some of them lying down in the dust, exhausted. They, too, called after us. They held on to us; praying us to stop with them. We had to wrench our skirts from their clinging hands."

The House of Morgan, as is true for other banks, had already profited from the Crimean War, the American Civil War, the Franco-Prussian War, the Spanish-American War, the Boer War. Wars without end. But this is all too much. The numbers flit before my eyes, as incomprehensibly horrifying to me as the motivations of those who profit: The Marne: 1.9 million casualties ("Wherever I looked, right or left, there were dead and wounded, quivering in convulsions, groaning terribly, blood oozing from fresh wounds"). Ypres: 230,000 casualties ("We have seen too many horrible things all at once, and the smell of the smoking ruins, the lowing of the deserted cattle and the rattle of machine-gun fire makes a very strong impression on us, barely twenty years old as we are. . . . We certainly did not want this war!"). Galicia: perhaps a half-million ("In every direction from each shell hole is strewn the fragments of blue cloth of the Austrian uniform, torn into shreds and ribbons by the force of the explosive; and all about the field are still bits of arms, a leg in a boot, or some other ghastly token of soldiers, true to discipline, hanging on to a position that was alive with bursting shells and flying shrapnel."). Tannenberg, Masurian Lakes, Lodz, Aisne.

During the next year, a syndicate headed by J. P. Morgan and Company floated loans worth $620 million to the British and French. The year after that, they loaned out another $600 million.

Of course, it was not only Morgan that profited from the war: A German banker told the American ambassador that "the Germans were sick of the war; that the Krupp's and other big industries were making great sums of money, and were prolonging the war by insisting upon the annexation of Belgium." He stated also that Prussian landowners favored continuing the war, "because of the fact that they were getting four or five times the money for their products, while their work was being done by prisoners."

Gallipoli: 500,000. The Carpathians: 1.6 million. Verdun: 1.6 million. The Somme: 1.2 million. Artois. Champagne. Loos. Only for so long can I read these names, these numbers, these stories, and then I turn away. Because I can. As I think about the man whose leg hung by shreds, I know that although it's a disturbing image I'll carry with me, probably for life, the story remains abstract, as abstract in some ways as Lamont's talk of lending and Morgan's immense fortune. None of these are real. The pulped mass of flesh that one day earlier had been his abdomen: that is real. I can close the book in which I encountered the story. I can turn off the computer and quit my work. I can go to sleep. Tomorrow I can awaken, and I can walk to get my mail. Lamont and Morgan, too, could get up and start their days. Their lives were insulated from the very real effects of decisions they made on the abstract criteria of monetary gain and loss. The lives of others are never so insulated. For this man, it was the end of his leg, his body, and, ultimately, his life. Each name, each simple battlefield, signifies the end, the sudden cutting off of so many millions of stories, so many millions of moments, so many millions of opportunities for love. So many millions of living beings mown down for profit.

During the winter of 1915–1916, a few German soldiers put a plank above their trench on which they had written, in big letters, "The English are fools." The plank was immediately splintered by rifle fire. Another plank went up: "The French are fools." This, too, was immediately splintered. Up went a third plank. "We're all fools. Let's all go home." But they could not go home. They would have been shot as deserters, traitors, nonpatriots.

By early 1917 the Allies owed American bankers and their clients $1.5 billion dollars, and had reached the limit of their credit. On the battlefield, their armies had nearly been brought to their knees. One soldier, who was to die the next year, wrote his sister, "Dear child,

WAR

there is no more to say; we have lost almost all there was to lose and what have we gained? Truly as you say has patriotism worn very very threadbare." The czarist government in Russia collapsed in March.

This was all very bad news for Morgan and Company. If the Allies went under, the loans would be only so much paper. Jack Morgan would be ruined—albeit still very rich—reduced to only his personal fortune. American politicians knew that bad news for Morgan meant bad news for the U.S. government. This knowledge was articulated by Walter Hines Page, American ambassador to England, who wrote President Wilson: "I think the pressure of this approaching crisis has gone beyond the ability of the Morgan Financial Agency for the British and French Governments. . . . If we should go to war with Germany, the greatest help we could give the Allies would be such a credit. . . . Unless we go to war with Germany, our Government, of course, cannot make such a direct grant of credit. . . ." Page pointed out, correctly enough, that the alternative to war was the collapse of the Allies, and with them the House of Morgan, and with it the domestic economy.

Four weeks later, President Wilson asked Congress for a declaration of war. (I know we've all been told that the United States went to war because the Germans sank the *Lusitania*, but that this ship's sinking was mere public justification for the carnage is shown by the fact that the government had for six months prior been secretly preparing for war.) Congress agreed.

Jack Morgan was jubilant.

■　　　■　　　■

The U.S. government used the war as an excuse to break radical unions and to eliminate socialists as a political force in the United States. One of the primary ways it did this was through something called the Espionage Act of 1917, which did not have so much to do with espionage as providing legal basis on which to prosecute those who spoke out against the war. But the law's title revealed while it concealed. The word *espionage* comes from the French *espionnage*, traceable back to *espionner*, to spy, from *espion*, spy, from Old Italian *spione*, from *spia*, of German origin, akin to Old High German *spehon*, to spy. Looking up *spy* reveals that *spehon* is akin to Latin *specere*, to look at, from the Greek *skeptesthai* and *skopein*, to watch, look at, consider. Which takes us, of course, back to Noah. Those prosecuted under the Espionage Act of 1917—and nearly two thousand were— had seen those in power as they were, in all their naked power, and they had spoken out against them: given witness.

Because the war was wildly unpopular—in the first six weeks after the United States declared war only 73,000 men volunteered (out of a million that the government said it needed)—Congress overwhelmingly voted to institute a draft. Socialist antiwar meetings drew huge crowds, for example, five, ten, and twenty thousand farmers at meetings in Minnesota to protest the draft, the war, and profiteering. Numbers voting Socialist Party increased tenfold.

In response, Congress passed the Espionage Act, which prohibited anyone from obstructing the draft, including the act of speaking out against it (this law, by the way, is still in effect). A test case (in which someone distributed pamphlets stating that the Conscription Act—which the pamphleteer called "a monstrous deed against humanity in the interests of the financiers of Wall Street"—violated the Constitution's Thirteenth Amendment provision against involuntary servitude, and suggested that people who were drafted assert their right not to go) soon found its way to the Supreme Court, which ruled unanimously that the Espionage Act was constitutional. You may have heard of this ruling, because Oliver Wendell Holmes delivered here his most famous line: "The most stringent protection of free speech would not protect a man falsely shouting fire in a theatre and causing a panic. . . . The question in every case is whether the words are used in such circumstances and are of such a nature as to create a clear and present danger that they will bring about the substantive evils that Congress has a right to prevent." On one level Holmes was, of course, being disingenuous, straining his eyes hard to the right so as not to see that which was in front of his face. In no reasonable way can urging people to avoid a war they do not see as being

WAR

in their best interest (to the degree that civilized wars ever are) be likened to shouting fire in a crowded theater. The historian Howard Zinn compares it more accurately to someone standing outside a theater telling people not to enter, because they will be burned alive by the fire inside. But there is another level on which Holmes is bull's-eye accurate: Consider again his next sentence: "The question in every case is whether the words are used in such circumstances and are of such a nature as to create a clear and present danger that they will bring about the substantive evils that Congress has a right to prevent." From the perspective of one who worships at the altar of production, what would constitute a clear and present danger? What sorts of actions would Congress—sort of a production priesthood—consider evil? And what would they consider it their right to prevent? Let me put this another way: What is the substantive difference between Oliver Wendell Holmes's statement, and Noah cursing Ham?

The prosecutions were as absurd as one would expect. People were prosecuted for saying that a referendum should have preceded a declaration of war, and they were prosecuted for saying that war was contrary to the teachings of Christ (this absurdity makes sense only if you remember that our God is a god of production, meaning his son must be a Christ of War). They were punished for criticizing the Red Cross or the Y.M.C.A. It was considered a crime to discourage women from knitting, by the remark, "No soldier ever sees these socks." A woman was sentenced to ten years in prison for saying to another woman, "I am for the people and the government is for the profiteers," because, according to the judge in the case, what is said to mothers, sisters, and girlfriends may lessen men's enthusiasm for war. A man was convicted of attending a meeting at which a speaker attacked conscription: Because he applauded, and gave twenty-five cents, and though he left when the meeting was half over, he was sentenced to a year in jail. The obvious question becomes: How long would he have been forced to serve had he stayed till the end? There was a case where strangers came to a man's house saying they'd run out of gasoline. The man invited them to dinner, during which they argued about the war. His guests turned him in, and he was imprisoned. Because an elderly farmer said to a young man "that the war was for the big bugs in Wall street; that it was all foolishness to send our boys over there to get killed by the thousands, all for the sake of Wall Street; that he should not go to war until he had to," he was sentenced to five years in prison. A German American who did not buy war bonds was visited in his house by a committee wanting to know why not: He courteously replied he did not wish either side to win the war, and for this he was arrested. During an argument about the war, a South Dakota farmer said, "If I were of conscription age and had no dependents and were drafted, I would refuse to serve." He was sentenced to a year and a day in Leavenworth federal penitentiary. Robert Goldstein was prosecuted for making a film about the American Revolution—called *The Spirit of '76*—which in one scene depicted British soldiers bayoneting women and children and carrying away girls. He finished the film before the United States declared war. Because, the judge said, the film tended to "question the good faith of our ally, Great Britain," the film was seized, the company thrown into bankruptcy, and Goldstein was sentenced, in a case entitled *U.S. v. Spirit of '76*, to ten years in prison. The judge gave a reason: "No man should be permitted, by deliberate act, or even unthinkingly, to do that which will in any way detract from the efforts which the United States is putting forth or serve to postpone for a single moment the early coming of the day when the success of our arms shall be a fact."

The Espionage Act criminalized singing the third verse of the national anthem. There are rumors that singing the third verse of the Star Spangled Banner was decriminalized in 1997, but the third verse is conspicuous by its absence from official government Web sites such as the West Point Web site and the National Park Service official Fort McHenry Web site.

A man was sentenced to fifteen years in prison for circulating a pamphlet suggesting voters not reelect a congressman who voted for conscription. "There is no better way," the judge said in this case, "of unsettling the confidence of the people and stirring their souls against the war than to paint it as a war of capitalism, organized by

WAR

capitalists and for capitalists, and painting the officers of the government as representing the willing tools of Wall Street. There is no better way."

The socialist Kate Richards O'Hare was sentenced to five years in prison for saying that "the women of the United States were nothing more nor less than brood sows, to raise children to get into the army and be made into fertilizer." The radical union, Industrial Workers of the World, was broken, as the Espionage Act was used to put away more than a hundred IWW leaders for up to twenty years in prison. One of the IWW leaders told the court, "You ask me why the IWW is not patriotic to the United States. If you were a bum without a blanket; if you had left your wife and kids when you went west for a job, and had never located them since; if your job had never kept you long enough in a place to qualify you to vote; if you slept in a lousy, sour bunkhouse, and ate food just as rotten as they could give you and get by with it; if deputy sheriffs shot your cooking cans full of holes and spilled your grub on the ground; if your wages were lowered on you when the bosses thought they had you down; if there was one law for Ford, Suhr, and Mooney [three IWW organizers], and another for Harry Thaw [an heir to a fortune who not only got away with the rape and beating of his fiance and later wife, and the murder of another of her suitors (who had also raped her), but became extremely popular]; if every person who represented law and order and the nation beat you up, railroaded you to jail, and the good Christian people cheered and told them to go to it, how in hell do you expect a man to be patriotic? This war is a business man's war and we don't see why we should go out and get shot in order to save the lovely state of affairs we now enjoy." Eugene V. Debs was prosecuted for saying, "Wars thoughout history have been waged for conquest and plunder. . . . And that is war in a nutshell. The master class has always declared wars; the subject class has always fought the battles." Before he was sentenced, Debs said, "Years ago I recognized my kinship with all living beings, and I made up my mind that I was not one bit better than the meanest on earth. I said then, and I say now, that while there is a lower class, I am in it; while there is a criminal

THE CULTURE OF MAKE BELIEVE

element, I am of it; while there is a soul in prison, I am not free." The judge was unmoved, and before sentencing Debs to ten years in prison, attacked him as one "who would strike the sword from the hand of this nation while she is engaged in defending herself against a foreign and brutal power."

•   •   •

The first loan made by the American government—$400 million of American taxpayers' money—went directly to J. P. Morgan and Company to pay British debts. Of the $9.4 billion lent by the United States to the British and French, those governments received exactly none of it. Every penny went to the owners of American industries. And although the British and French governments eventually paid off all debts owed to American capitalists, they defaulted on every loan to American taxpayers. "In short," as Lundberg stated, "the war debt created by the American government amounted simply to money transferred from the people of the country to the richest families, who owned the banks and industries."

The war debt did, however, allow the slaughter to continue.

Now that the United States had officially entered the war, members of the Bankers Trust could more fully manifest their patriotism. President Wilson put Bernard Baruch—who got his start years earlier with J. P. Morgan and still ran associated companies—in charge of the War Industries Board, which spent public funds at the rate of $10 billion per year. Baruch stacked the Board with Daniel Willard, president of the Morgan-controlled Baltimore and Ohio, Walter S. Gifford, vice president of Morgan-controlled AT&T, Alexander Legge of Morgan-controlled International Harvester, Elbert Gary, chair of Morgan-controlled United States Steel, and other magnates, Morgan-associated and not. John D. Ryan, president of Morgan-associated Amalgamated Copper, was an assistant secretary of war. Morgan employee Edward Stettinius became surveyor-general of supplies for the United States Army. Russell Leffingwell, who was soon to be a Morgan partner, was assistant secretary of the treasury.

Leffingwell appointed Morgan partner Dwight Morrow director of the National War Savings Committee for New Jersey. And so on. That the Bankers Trust ran the war effort, doing everything but dying, is shown clearly in a letter by Secretary of the Interior Franklin Lane: "The President ought to send for Schwab [of Morgan's Bethlehem Steel] and hand him a treasury warrant for a billion dollars and set him to work building ships, with no government inspectors or supervisors or accountants or auditors or other red tape to bother him. Let the President just put it up to Schwab's patriotism and put Schwab on his honor. Nothing more is needed. Schwab will do the job."

Morgan partner Davison was placed in charge of the Red Cross, and filled the organization with Morgan associates. The purpose of the Red Cross in Italy was to keep the reluctant Italians in the war. Its purpose in Russia, functioning explicitly as a political arm of the War Department, was to do the same to the Russians. The Morgan partners gave food and public money to anti-German elements and withheld them from pro-German or radical elements. They carried on espionage. They paid $1 million to the Russian Congress to make certain Kerensky stayed in power, and that Russia stayed in the war. The Red Cross—which up until doing this research I had, evidently foolishly, presumed a humanitarian organization—played no small part in the actions that led to the downfall of the Kerensky government and ultimately to the Russian Civil War, with its Bolshevik victory.

The war continued. By the end, ten million human beings were dead and another thirty million were wounded. Millions more were homeless.

The industrial economy of the United States did well by the war, sustaining the trajectory already mentioned. Two brief examples show the trend: Revenues for DuPont continued its rise from $131 million in 1915 to $329 million in 1919, and profits for Standard Oil of Indiana (owned by Rockefeller) went from $6.6 million in 1916 to $43 million in 1918.

Not all this money was derived from wartime suffering. Much was derived from theft of public funds, generally with government assistance (insofar as any distinction between government and industry can be said to be meaningful). After the war a congressional investigating committee found that "the plan was . . . that the copper industry, [for example,] as well as other producing industries should be so centralized that it could be dominated and controlled by one man or a very small number of men, and that this control . . . was the paramount influence toward price-fixing and price control, and is one of the causes of high-priced commodities at this time. The plan of the Government was to centralize all industries irrespective of the results that might ultimately follow." Copper, costing eight to twelve cents per pound, was sold to the government at twenty-six cents per pound. Airplanes form another example. Even though the public paid more than $1 billion for combat airplanes, none were delivered. A third example: Morgan-associated Baruch placed orders with Morgan-controlled Bethlehem Steel for nearly a billion dollars worth of shells that were never delivered. No convictions emerged from this pattern of fraud. It sometimes seems as though it would be simpler for all involved if we just followed the advice of Senator Norris of the time, who said after yet another acquittal of an industrialist on charges of corruption (not involved in the war), "We ought to pass a law that no man worth $100,000,000 should be tried for a crime."

THE MORE HIGHLY ORGANIZED THE POWER STRUCTURE

BECOMES, THE FEWER NON-CONFORMING FACTORS CAN

BE ADMITTED, AND THE MORE OPEN THE WHOLE SYSTEM

IS TO BREAKDOWNS FROM MECHANICAL DEFECTS

AND NATURAL ACCIDENTS—BUT EVEN MORE FROM THE

COUNTER- ASSAULTS OF THOSE CLASSES AND GROUPS

THAT ARE EXCLUDED FROM THE SYSTEM OR PARTLY

DEPRIVED OF ITS BOASTED BENEFITS.

LEWIS MUMFORD

RESISTANCE

WE ALL NEED TO RECOGNIZE that there can be only one sort of relationship between civilization and those who oppose the deification of production, or war, or ever-increasing concentrations of wealth or power, or who oppose the systematic eradication of diversity, all of which are different ways of saying the same thing. Or, more precisely, we all need to recognize that there can be only one sort of relationship between our society and those who effectively oppose these things. The end of the war didn't mean the end of hatred toward those who opposed the war, or those who opposed unbridled capital, for the war merely provided an excuse for the hatred that undergirds our economics to become manifest in the torn bodies in Europe; in the jubilation of those who not only found themselves financially rewarded by the "possibilitys" afforded by this carnage, but who furthered the destruction—consciously or unconsciously, it doesn't really matter—to increase personal fortunes. The war only emphasized our culture's day-to-day practice of imprisoning or ostracizing those who oppose the One True Way. The use of war abroad as an excuse to ratchet up repression at home was a modern twining of the twin facets of civilization. But war wasn't strictly necessary to an increase in repression, because, sooner or later, an excuse will make itself apparent. There will always be the uppity black who refuses to be whipped, or who looks a white woman in the eye (or who runs from a policeman, or who reaches for his wallet), or perhaps *looks* like a black man who *might* have looked a white woman in the eye (or who might run from a policeman, or who might reach for his wallet). Perhaps he is simply black. There were the mineworkers in Colorado who struck against low pay, dangerous conditions, and "feudal domination of their lives in towns completely controlled by the mining companies" after one of their organizers was murdered. Because they struck—there's that excuse—they found themselves machine-gunned, and found their families burned to death by National Guardsmen sent out by the governor (called, by a Rockefeller mine manager, "our little cowboy governor"). There are the Indians who were hated, on the excuse that they expected Whites to abide by treaties the Indians had been forced to sign. The excuse to be hated could be opposition to a war you do not believe in. It could be opposition to the corporate theocracy.

I recently gave a talk in Eugene, Oregon. It was a benefit for the Earth Liberation Prisoners Support Network, which provides books and other help for people imprisoned for animal liberations or sabotage against those companies that deforest or otherwise harm the planet. It was a wonderful audience, probably eighty or a hundred mainly young people, nearly all frontline activists.

The event was organized by a certain someone who gives me great hope. His name is Brenton, and he is seventeen. He has read more anarchist literature than I have, and has a far better grasp of our predicament than I did when I was twice his age. When I was seventeen (hell, when I was twenty-two) I was still trying to figure out whether Canadian bacon really does go with pineapple, yet, he's already making great movement toward, as he calls it, the Luddite Revolution. I learned from someone else that because he was suspected of trashing a Nike sign, police in Eugene busted into his house and held his parents under

RESISTANCE

automatic weapons for more than seven hours. They took his computer, as well as other personal possessions, and they effectively destroyed his mother's business. Brenton came to the event with his father. His father's pride in his son was palpable.

Before and after the event, a few people talked to me about police violence in Eugene. "It's really bad," one of them said. "We're getting kicked around. Some people have been beaten up, and quite a few have been pepper-sprayed."

I remembered an incident I'd read about, a few years ago, in which Eugene police lifted the skirts of women who were protesting deforestation and applied concentrated pepper to the women's genitals.

Another person said, voice redolent with irony, "You know it's bad when they even bust down the doors of white people."

"Welcome to the future," another said.

Ever since those conversations, I've kept thinking of a line by W.E.B. DuBois, that "It is no longer simply the merchant prince, or the aristocratic monopoly, or even the employing class, that is exploiting the world: it is the nation, a new democratic nation composed of united capital and labor." In the United States, and I would say also within the so-called elite of the colonies, people still face the same situation as the Irish: whether or not to become White, or, one could say, American. Even dark-skinned people increasingly have the option of becoming Whites, as did my mother's neighbor in Spokane. And lighter-skinned people, too, sometimes have the option of becoming not-White, by opposing the united goals of America, by refusing to stand with the aristocratic monopoly, and by standing, instead, with the exploited. I'm not suggesting, by the way, that these categories of lighter and darker skinned are in any sense truly miscible within our culture. It seems pretty clear that with notable exceptions—Colin Powell, Henry Cisneros, Ben Nighthorse Campbell, and Clarence Thomas come to mind—most darker-skinned people can aspire to be no Whiter than maybe a sallow bronze, a kind of second-class Whites. Remember my mother's neighbor in Spokane still sometimes looked to the ground when speaking to a man whose skin was lighter. And as for these white peo-

THE CULTURE OF MAKE BELIEVE

ple who decide not to be White, the fact remains that they were able to choose in the first place, which means, unless they've crossed some sort of Rubicon, they can always choose to return, which is more of a choice than has been generally offered to those whose poor choice of skin color (and sometimes poor choice of parental economic status) has caused them to begin on the outside. Another way to put this is that those who are born into Whiteness—I almost wrote *born White*, but then stopped myself because of course one must be *trained* to be White—must actively do something dramatic in order to be hated, while those born of colors other than the fleshiest shades of flesh tones (defined in my dictionary as "the usual color of a white person's skin; yellowish pink") can be hated simply for the color of their skin, and must do something dramatic in order to reach even the outermost of the inner circles.

There were many blacks lynched during the late 1910s and early 1920s, a large percentage of whom were lynched for no real reason other than the color of their skin. There were always excuses. There was Private William Little, beaten to death by a white mob because, on his return from the war, he refused to take off his uniform and walk home in his underwear. There was George Holden, who was shot, beaten, tied to a tree, and riddled with bullets for writing with clear penmanship an insulting note to a white woman, even though, it ends up, Holden was illiterate. There was Lloyd Clay, roasted to death by a mob of eight hundred to a thousand men and women because they believed someone had tried to rape a white teenager earlier in the evening. The truth was that one of Miss Lulu Belle Bishop's relatives had heard her (consensual white) lover sneaking out the window, and Miss Bishop had concocted the story so as to not get into trouble. When the mob settled on Clay, both she and her father pleaded for them not to kill him, but the mob had their excuse, and so the man burned. Sixty-five-year-old Berry Washington was lynched because he shot the white man who had just raped his sixteen-year-old daughter. Cleveland Butler was shot in the face and killed because he resembled another black man some Whites wanted to kill. Ten thousand men, women, and children from Omaha broke

RESISTANCE

Will Brown out of jail and hanged him because they believed (incorrectly) that he had assaulted a white child.

If you're white, on the other hand, you've got to commit an act of blasphemy to receive this treatment. The mob in Omaha also beat to death the (white) mayor because he tried to stop them, showing that even the Whitest of the White can find themselves suddenly deprived of their Whiteness if they step away from hatred.

Or there are the cases of Frank Little, and Wesley Everest. They were Wobbly organizers, that is, members of the IWW. The union was radical, militant, staunchly anticapitalist and antiwar. It had been founded as a movement to bring the entire working class of the world into one revolutionary organization. At the founding meeting, Bill Haywood, who was to become one of its most famous members, began by calling the meeting to order, then bellowing, "The aims and objects of this organization shall be to put the working class in possession of the economic power, the means of life, in control of the machinery of production and distribution, without regard to capitalist masters." The preamble to the union's constitution begins, "The working class and the employing class have nothing in common. There can be no peace so long as hunger and want are found among millions of working people and the few, who make up the employing class, have all the good things of life. Between these two classes a struggle must go on until the workers of the world organize as a class, take possession of the earth and the machinery of production, and abolish the wage system." I disagree with the notion that taking possession of the earth is a good idea or even possible, and that by suggesting that seizing the machinery of production (as opposed to doing away with production altogether) will rid us of class struggle the Wobblies show that despite their oftentimes astute analysis, they, too, maintained a blind spot concerning the primacy of production. The belief runs deep.

"We find that the centering of the management of industries into fewer and fewer hands makes the trade unions unable to cope with the ever growing power of the employing class," the preamble continues. "The trade unions foster a state of affairs which allows one set of workers to be pitted against another set of workers in the same industry, thereby helping defeat one another in wage wars. Moreover, the trade unions aid the employing class to mislead the workers into the belief that the working class have interests in common with their employers. These conditions can be changed and the interest of the working class upheld only by an organization formed in such a way that all its members in any one industry, or in all industries, if necessary, cease work whenever a strike or lockout is on in any department thereof, thus making an injury to one an injury to all. Instead of the conservative motto, 'A fair day's wages for a fair day's work,' we must inscribe on our banner the revolutionary watchword, 'Abolition of the wage system.'" The union, which soon represented more than a hundred thousand workers, was one of the very few at the time to encourage members of all races and ethnicities to join. For example, when Haywood found himself speaking to a group of white timber workers in Louisiana, he asked them to violate state laws prohibiting mixed meetings by inviting black workers to join them. Women were not only welcome in the IWW, they were encouraged to play central roles (you may have heard, for example, of the famous IWW "Rebel Girl," Elizabeth Gurley Flynn, who was already making speeches at seventeen).

The long-term goal of the IWW was to take over industries, and have workers profit from their own labor. In the shorter run, they simply wanted to keep workers out of bondage. Chattel slavery was by this time long since illegal in the United States, but so long as the poor did not have full access to land and so long as rules for relationships between employers and laborers were made and enforced by the rich, there were always ways for the rich to obtain the free labor of the dispossessed. In Spokane, Washing-ton, for example, as an IWW organizer wrote, "Over three thousand men were hired through employment sharks for one camp of the Somers Lumber Co. (Great Northern) last winter to maintain a force of fifty men. As soon as a man had worked long enough to pay the shark's fee, the hospital dollar, poll tax, and a few other grafts, he was discharged to make room for more other slaves, so that the fleecing process could continue. These different fees are split, or cut up with the bosses. In most cases these fees consumed the time of several days' labor, when the men were then discharged and

RESISTANCE

paid off with checks ranging from 5 cents and upwards. The victim of the shark in the most cases gets his check cashed at the first saloon, and takes a little stimulation. Why not? What is life to these men? What is there in life for them? The strong, barbed-wire whiskey makes things look bright for a while. Then the weary tramp goes to town with his bed on his back. Back to Spokane, the slave market of the Inland Empire. He hears the IWW speakers on the street. The glad tidings of a great revolutionary union. An injury to one is an injury to all. Workers of the world, unite, you have nothing to lose but your bed on your back. You have a world to gain. Labor produces all wealth, and those who produce it are tramps and hoboes. This gets to him. He will go through hell for such a union with such principles. He has gone through hell in Spokane, and has given his last cent. He is soon coming back, and then again and again if necessary, until the truth can be told on the streets."

The response by authorities in Spokane—and this pattern was, unsurprisingly, repeated in town after town—was to pass laws prohibiting political speechmaking on the streets (although Spokane, and other cities, made exceptions for the speech of those more valuable, as when President William Howard Taft delivered a two-hour speech (written for him by the Chamber of Commerce) on the streets of Spokane). Consequently, thousands of Wobblies hopped freight trains to come give speeches, sometimes simply stepping onto soap boxes to recite the Declaration of Independence. Hundreds were arrested, beaten, jailed. Many died in jail because of the intentionally inhuman conditions. Still more Wobblies poured in to speak in favor of the poor. One man from Oregon sent the following note: "A demonstration meeting was just held in Sheep Camp No. 1, there being three present, a herder and two dogs. The following resolutions were adopted: Resolved, that we send $10.00 for the free speech fight in Spokane. Yours for liberty, Thomas J. Anderson. P.S. Stay with it. I'm coming."

All of this is to say that the IWW was strongly anti-White, which is to say that it was very much hated.

Corporate newspapers responded to, expressed, and fueled this

THE CULTURE OF MAKE BELIEVE

hatred. *The Los Angeles Times* stated, "During a visit of the Industrial Workers of the World they will be accorded a night and day guard of honor composed of citizens armed with rifles. The Coroner will be in attendance at his office every day." *The Fresno Herald* stated that "a whipping post and a cat-o-nine tails well seasoned by being soaked in salt water is none too harsh a treatment" for Wobblies. *The San Diego Evening Tribune* got right to the point, in purple prose that would have done Hitler proud on both literary and vituperative counts: "Hanging is none too good for them, and they would be much better dead; for they are absolutely useless to the human economy; they are the waste material of creation and should be drained off into the sewer of oblivion and there to rot in cold obstruction like any other excrement." A California representative made clear the reason for the hatred: The Wobblies were no longer White, and failure to eradicate them would cause everyone to become like they are (not a bad thought, really), to become "like the aborigines of darkest Africa, without law or any sense of justice or human rights, as are the beasts which inhabit its jungles."

On occasion, different opinions of Wobblies or treatment of them slipped past the linotypes of the mainstream presses, as when *The San Diego Sun* reported, "Murderers, highwaymen, cut-throats of the blackest type, porch-climbers, burglars, wife-beaters and all kinds of criminals in jail in the past have been treated like royalty in comparison to the manner in which the street speakers are being handled." But these opinions—and even simple facts—were quickly suppressed, either by the internalized necessity of newspapermen fulfilling their social function as boosters for capitalism, or, when self-censorship failed, by outright violence, as in the case of *The San Diego Herald*, which presented the Wobblies' side of the story until someone destroyed their type forms, then kidnapped and attempted to murder the editor. A gun to the head often works wonders on the editorial stance, not only of that newspaper, but of other publications with editors who wish to see tomorrow.

The day after the *Herald*'s editor was kidnapped, the *Evening Tribune* laid out clearly what free speech means in a culture based on

RESISTANCE

R. D. Laing's three rules of a dysfunctional family: "If there are any citizens of San Diego who sympathize with these anarchists, they should rid the city of their presence. They are not wanted here, and if they go so far as to insist upon the 'free speech' of anarchy and disloyalty, they will not be tolerated. This is San Diego's ultimatum: We claim the right to defend ourselves against these confessed outlaws, and we claim the right to choose our weapons of defense." My dictionary's first definition of *loyal* is "faithful to the constituted authority of one's country." What this means is that you may say anything you like, so long as it's faithful to the dictates of those in power, that is, so long as it pleases them (or at least does not displease them too much). In other words, you may say anything you like, so long as it's faithful neither to humanity nor reality. If you displease those in power, they claim the right to choose their weapons of defense. Before you dismiss this as the ravings of one cranky newspaper editor, remember the Espionage Act of 1917, the thousands of blacks lynched for their perceived insolence, the Indians whose mere existence is enough to cause those in power to "choose our weapons of defense," the Filipinos whose resistance caused—*allowed* is a better word, although both impart too much responsibility to the Filipinos for the atrocities done to them, when the truth is that the atrocities were well-nigh inevitable—Whites to put into action the "burn and kill the natives" policies (also known as "benevolent assimiliation") under which, as a general stated, "the more you kill and burn the better you will please me."

In town after town, Wobblies received the same treatment they received in Spokane, or worse. Citizens lined up to help firemen and policemen turn water hoses on them. Wobblies had hot tar applied to them. They were forced to participate in humiliating and painful rituals, sacraments to patriotism and production: "The first thing on the program was to kiss the flag. 'You son of a B——, Come on Kiss it, G—Damn You.' As he said it I was hit with a wagon spoke all over, when you had kissed the flag you were told to run the gauntlet. 50 men being on each side and each man being armed with a gun and a club and some had long whips. When I started to run the gauntlet the men were ready for action, they were in high spirits from booze. I got about 30 feet when I was suddenly struck across the knee. I felt the wagon spoke sink in splitting my knee. I reeled over. As I was lying there I saw other fellow workers running the gauntlet. Some were bleeding freely from cracked heads, others were knocked down to be made to get up to run again. Some tried to break the line only to be beaten back. It was the most cowardly and inhuman cracking of heads I ever witnessed." Wobblies were kidnapped, imprisoned (both with and without judicial stamps of imprimatur), had their meager belongings stolen or destroyed. They were dragged behind cars. They were hanged by their necks until dead. They were killed.

Frank Little was a Wobbly organizer lynched in Montana. He'd been there to support a strike of the United Metal Mine Workers for higher wages and better safety standards. The strike had begun in response to a fire in one of the mines that had killed about 160 workers—human beings. The death toll had been so high because, in violation of state law, the company had built solid concrete bulkheads without providing manholes. A witness testified that he "viewed several of the charred corpses at the morgue in Butte, and that their fingers were worn to the second joint, showing a protruding bone, the result of the men having clawed at the granite doors which were locked."

As I read about the role of newspapers in this strike, and the role played by journalists in general in our culture, I keep thinking about Nazi newspaperman Julius Streicher, and I keep hearing in my head the words of the Nuremberg prosecuter, who said, "It may be that this defendant is less directly involved in the physical commission of crimes against Jews. The submission of the prosecution is that his crime is no less the worse for that reason." Substitute any other human group you would like for *Jews*. Indians. Filipinos. Chinese. Irish. Wobblies. Anarchists. Subsitute the nonhuman world. Salmon. Mountains. Spotted owls. The prosecuter continued, "No government in the world . . . could have embarked upon and put into effect a policy of mass extermination without having a people who would back them and support them." This was true in the case of the Nazis, and it is true in our own case. "It was to the task of educating people,

RESISTANCE

producing murderers, educating and poisoning them with hate, that Streicher set himself." Modern propaganda serves the same function. "In the early days he was preaching persecution. As persecution took place he preached extermination and annihilation. . . . [T]hese crimes . . . could never have happened had it not been for him and for those like him. Without him, the Kaltenbrunners, the Himmlers . . . would have had nobody to carry out their orders." I'm reminded of the words of one journalist writing about the gauntlet Wobblies were forced to run in San Diego: "Thus did San Diego, having given its money to mark the historic highway [El Camino Real] with the symbols of love and charity, teach patriotism and reverence for the law to the travelers thereon."

At a later trial of I.W.W. members in Chicago (on something not related to the strike in Montana), an attorney for the Wobblies questioned a reporter for the *Butte Evening Post*:

Q: What is the attitude of your paper on the labor issue in Butte? Did it support the strikers during the recent strike?

A: Oh, no, sir, no.

Q: Who reported the fire in the Speculator Mine?

A: There were three or four of us. I was up there.

Q: Did you report that there were concrete bulk heads in that mine with no manholes and it trapped the men and were responsible for their deaths, to the number of about two hundred?

A: No, sir.

Q: You did not?

A: No, I did not.

Q: Were you there when the bodies of those miners were brought out?

A: I was there part of the time.

Q: You never colored anything you wrote to fit what you understood to be the policy of the paper?

A: I might have colored things. I might have toned
down things, and I did repeatedly.

At three in the morning of August 1, several men seized Frank Little from his boardinghouse. He had already been beaten many times, already been imprisoned many times. But this time they tied him to the bumper of their car and dragged him through the streets until his kneecaps were scraped off. Then they hanged him from a railroad trestle.

That same reporter was asked by the same attorney in the same trial:

Q: Did you ever try to find out who the occupants
of that car [behind which Frank Little was
dragged] were?

A: No, sir.

Q: If I give you the names will you publish them?

A: No, sir.

Q: You won't?

A: No, sir.

Q: If I give you the name of the boy that drove that
car, will you publish it in your paper? . . .

A: No!

In November of 1916, about 250 Wobblies left Seattle on a steamer for Everett, Washington, in support of a long shingle weavers' strike and free speech fight. Wobblies attempting to open halls there had been beaten and run out of town. These unarmed Wobblies were met at the docks by about the same number of armed citizens recruited by timber companies and deputized under the leadership of the local sheriff, and when the steamer tied down, the citizens opened fire. Wobblies who leapt off the boat became easy targets—as had the Indians at Lake Earl—for people, posted in warehouses, who shot at them each time they came up for breath. The bodies of five Wobblies were recovered, and maybe a dozen more washed out to sea. Two cit-

RESISTANCE

izens were killed in their own crossfire, and scores of people—both Wobblies and deputies—were injured. In a move that anyone who has ever opposed the full power of the state will understand, the Wobblies were arrested, beaten, and otherwise tortured. Seventy-seven of them were indicted for the murder of one of the deputies. None of the deputies were indicted for murders of Wobblies or the murder of their own. In this case, the Wobblies were acquitted.

This brings us to Wesley Everest. The Wobblies had set up a meeting hall in Centralia, Washington. They were beaten and run out of town in the same way they had been in so many other places. They were tarred and feathered (one fellow in Washington who'd been so threatened opened a pillow and placed it on his window with a note saying he'd not be intimidated, and if they came for him he'd supply his own feathers). They opened the hall again. Business leaders and patriots determined again to throw them out. On Armistice Day, in 1919, members of the American Legion and other groups, including the Elks and the Boy Scouts, marched on the Wobbly headquarters. Many in town, even across the state, knew what was going to happen. As far away as Tacoma, the *News Tribune* had editorialized that "At Centralia a committee of citizens has been formed that takes the mind back to the old days of vigilance committees of the West, which did so much to force law-abiding citizenship upon certain lawless elements. . . . Its object is to combat IWW activities in that city and the surrounding country. It invites to membership all citizens who favor the enforcement of law and order. . . . It is high time for the people who do believe in the lawful and orderly conduct of affairs to take the upper hand. . . . Every city and town might, with profit, follow Centralia's example." Leading the way in converting law and order into profit, the Legionnaires publicly bought rope for the activities of the day. The mob arrived at their destination, and shouting, "Let's go! At 'em, boys!" they rushed the hall. But this time the Wobblies fought back. They'd brought guns, and began firing. Out of hundreds of halls that had been raided over the previous two years, this was the first time the Wobblies had fired in return (they often used sabotage, and although they *had* at times used violence, as in

Pennsylvania, when they told the *militia* that they would kill one militia member for every striker killed, they had never used violence to defend their halls). Three of the attackers crumpled, and the mass of men recoiled. But soon they surged forward again, and took the hall. There they captured six Wobblies and took them to the jail. The seventh, Wesley Everest, having already emptied his pistol into the crowd, took off out the back door. Another crowd had gathered behind, but he broke through, and scaled a fence. "Don't follow me and I won't shoot," he shouted, reloading as he ran. They followed. Finally he slowed, then turned and fired. When he'd emptied his gun, he began to run again, once again loading on the fly. Again he turned to fire, and again he continued. People in the mob returned his fire. Finally, he reached the river, and splashed in. It seemed for a moment he would swim to the comparative safety of the other side, then he stopped, and came back to face the mob, a quizzical smile on his face. He said, "If there are 'bulls' in the crowd, I'll submit to arrest; otherwise lay off of me." The crowd moved in. He fired, killing the nephew of the timber baron who had instigated the whole thing in the first place. His gun jammed and he threw it away. He attempted to fight with his fists, but was overpowered. Men fought with one another for the opportunity to strike him. A businessman pulled strips of flesh from his face. Someone knocked out his teeth with a gun barrel. Someone else pulled out the rope, and Everest said, "You haven't got the guts to lynch a man in the daytime."

He was right.

They took him to the jail, where the other Wobblies had also been taken, and threw him to the floor. After dark, they returned. The policeman assigned to guard the jail said, "Don't shoot, men; here is your man." Everest weakly rose to meet them, and, as they approached, the last thing he said to the other Wobblies was, "Tell the boys I died for my class."

They threw him on the backseat floor of a car and drove him through the night toward a bridge over the Chehalis River. On the way, it is said that he struck feebly at one of his captors, so they tied his arms. Then, and this is not just said but known, someone unfolded a

RESISTANCE

razor, pulled down his pants, and castrated him. They took him to the middle of the bridge, and attached a rope to his neck. As they tried to throw him off, he clutched at one of the timbers, holding on by his fingertips. A businessman stomped on them, and Everest fell. The rope whistled, then jerked. He moaned. They hauled him back up, attached a longer rope, and threw him over again. Then a third hanging with a still longer rope. They did not mind the waste of rope: This would make for more souvenirs. They played the headlights of their cars over the body as they used it for target practice. Then they brought it back to the jail. The coronor later stated that Wesley Everest had broken out of jail, gone to the Chehalis, tied a rope around his neck, and jumped off. Finding the rope too short, he'd climbed up and done it twice more, till he broke his neck, and then shot himself full of holes. Some in Centralia thought the joke funny.

The Centralia newspaper wasted no time before praising the action: "The episode of last night is but the natural result of a red-handed revolutionist getting his just desserts without loss of time or the painfully slow process of law. . . . The apparent infringement of the law last night was the essence of law and order."

None of the mob was indicted for anything associated with this violence. Several of the Wobblies were convicted of murder, and sentenced to twenty-five to forty years in prison.

■   ■   ■

Earlier, I cited, as an example of my own racism, the fact that I merely stepped away from a group of white teenagers clustered around a pickup. Had they been black, I wrote, I may have walked down a different street. But now I'm thinking about the attention I've given to Wesley Everest, Frank Little, and others of the lighter-skinned non-Whites. Why does Everest warrant six paragraphs, while Private William Little receives only one sentence, and Lloyd Clay three? Are not their stories just as real, their lives as precious? Sure, I've devoted more space overall to lynchings of darker-skinned people than of the lighter skinned, but hundreds of times more

THE CULTURE OF MAKE BELIEVE

darker-skinned people have been lynched. Have I devoted hundreds of times more space?

I've been thinking about this a lot. Maybe the reason is that the research is easier. Whole books have been written on the Centralia Massacre, and I first heard of Wesley Everest's last words to his chums—"Tell the boys I died for my class"—many years ago. On the other hand, I never heard of Lloyd Clay until maybe a month ago, and an Alta Vista search reveals only two pages referencing him (there are several referencing others of the same name, of course), one of which lists African-American victims of lynching sorted by name, while the other, an associated site, sorts them by date of death. The second is called "The Lynching Calender: African-Americans Who Died in Racial Violence in the United States by Month of Death, 1865-1965." Lloyd Clay's date is May 14, and he receives one phrase in the middle: "Hardy Grady, lynched Effingham Co, Georgia, May 14, 1884; David Cotton, lynched Rosebud, Texas, May 14, 1897; Henry Williams, lynched Rosebud, Texas, May 14, 1897; Sabe Stewart, lynched Rosebud, Texas, May 14, 1897; 2 unidentified black men, lynched Brooksville, Florida May 14, 1900; William Willis, lynched Grovetown, Georgia, May 14, 1900; William Womack, lynched Eastman, Georgia May 14, 1906; "Dock" McLane, lynched Ashdown, Arkansas, May 14, 1910; Lloyd Clay, lynched Vicksburg, Mississippi, May 14, 1919; N/A West, lynched Longwood, Florida, May 14, 1925." Every day is like this. A Google search reveals a couple of passing references to Clay, and one transcription of a 1919 article from a radical Chicago newspaper: "What the best white citizens here termed the most glorious celebrations held in the city for many years occurred Wednesday, May 14th, when innocent Lloyd Clay, age 23, was lynched and burned on the public highways by men, women and school children. Over 1,000 persons' voices rent the air with yells similar to that of cannibals when Clay was dragged down Farmer Street to the 'gallows tree.' Clay made no outcry as his body bumped over rocks in the street and as knives and pistol shots perforated his naked form. He had been accused of entering the room of Miss Hattie Hudson [the other account I read of this, in an article several

RESISTANCE

days previous, in a different newspaper, had her name as Lulu Belle Bishop], a white woman. Sheriff Scott stood idly by and puffed vigorously on a cigar as the bloodthirsty throng massacred their helpless victim. His mother requested that the charred body be given to her, but there was nothing left of it after the fire had parched it to a crisp and souvenirs were distributed to children, who yelled incessantly, 'Mother, get me a piece of the nigger's finger.'"

It continues, "When Clay was brought before Miss Hudson, she was unable to identify him and said she did not want the innocent blood upon her hands. 'Innocent blood, hell,' yelled a voice in the crowd: 'Say, yes, he's the nigger,' came from hundreds of throats. Fearing bodily harm might be done her should she fail to accede to the demands of the mad mob, with a response hardly audible she said, 'I think he is the man.' This answer was sufficient. Clay was immediately felled by a blow from the handle of a double shotgun. The mob fell upon Clay . . . and dragged him toward North First Street. Three men climbed an elm tree directly in front of the residence of Mrs. Ida M. Keefe (white) and when a stout rope came into view the mob went wild. During this period little children were smearing kerosene upon the naked form of Clay. His head was pinned beneath a man's heel and a woman, taking advantage of the opportunity, saturated his hair with gasoline. A match was applied and Clay was lifted into the air. This increased the excitement. Clay lifted his arms, placed his palms together in an attitude of prayer, but made no sound. Shouts, howls and the screech of motor horns made a deafening noise as Clay was strung beneath the elm tree. The dainty hands of young girls, who will represent the future mothers of Vicksburg, Miss., were seen with guns pointed at the victim, eager for a chance to be a party in furthering this gruesome method of cannibalism. A bullet said to have come from a revolver in the hands of a woman crashed into the brain of Charles Lanbookes (white), an onlooker, as he stood on the lawn of Mrs. Ida Keefe watching the charred body of Clay dangle from the tree. He will die. Benny Stafford (white), said to be a member of the mob, was wounded in the chin by a stray bullet. He will recover. The body of Clay, blistered and distorted, was permitted to hang."

THE CULTURE OF MAKE BELIEVE

I don't think my original inclination to devote more space to Everest than Clay came about just because more information is available on Everest: I could easily have substituted descriptions of the hatred manifested toward Denmark Vesey or Nat Turner for that toward Little or Everest. I think there's something deeper. Sure, I'm making different points here, having to do with how lighter-skinned people, too, can be hated if they remind the majority of us of that which we're all trying so desperately to forget: that our system is inhuman and unnecessary. But the fact remains that even in writing a book about how our culture perceives certain others, including people whose skin happens to not be so flesh-colored, not as humans but as objects, my descriptions of darker-skinned people are, it seems, at least, sometimes, less personal, and I may present them less as subjective human beings than I do people whose skin happens to be the color defined as flesh. I'm not alone in this. Even after reading the article from the Chicago newspaper—presumably written by someone who wanted the lynchings to end—I still know nothing about Lloyd Clay except how he died, and that he had a mother. At least in accounts of Everest's death, we learn something of his struggles, and, through them, something about the man behind the name, rather than simply learning (a tad unbelievably, I would have thought, until I read of a black man who sang "Nearer my God to thee" as a crowd of Whites burned him) that Clay held his hands as if in prayer as he was immolated.

I thought for a while about shortening the section on Everest, or on going back to add more details to the lives of some of the African Americans whose deaths I describe (presuming these details could be found; a dubious presumption, considering that we don't even know the names of many of the murdered; nor did the murderers, and, I guess, that's the point), but decided in an attempt at transparency to not do that. I want to attempt to make visible as much of our translucent hatred as I can, and revealing my own blind spots seems as good a way to do that as any.

RESISTANCE

MAYBE WE MADE A MISTAKE IN TRYING TO MAINTAIN INDIAN CULTURES. MAYBE WE SHOULD NOT HAVE HUMORED THEM IN THAT, WANTING TO STAY IN THAT PRIMITIVE LIFE STYLE. MAYBE WE SHOULD HAVE SAID: NO, COME JOIN US. BE CITIZENS ALONG WITH THE REST OF US.

RONALD REAGAN

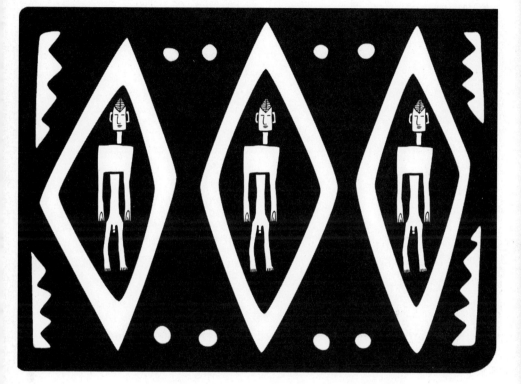

EXPANDING
THE FRONTIER

THE LETTER TO THE EDITOR Karen and I wrote about Richard McNamara, comparing himself to slaughtered Indians, has ignited a delightful little firestorm in the local newspaper. I've heard that lots of people now turn to that page the first thing every morning to catch the latest salvos in the big debate. The other day I walked into the post office, and my favorite clerk waved and called out, "Thataway to stir it up!" Over the past three weeks, probably a dozen letters have been printed on the subject, expressing opinions, ranging from the suggestion that the D.A. file murder charges against McNamara and other ranchers living on stolen land, to simple gratitude to us for writing and the paper for publishing the original letter, to one stating that, because Indians weren't creative enough to invent Western technologies, they're better off now than before they met our civilizing influence, to one calling every opinion, except McNamara's, boring, to a couple of letters I found frankly incomprehensible (the local paper shows extraordinary and admirable openness in printing all letters it receives, the downside being that at least some letters (on all topics, not just this one) reveal little save the damaging effects of heavy drug use on the cerebral cortex (I still remember an incomprehensible letter to the editor I saw years ago in a different paper with the headline "One toke over the line")). McNamara responded, as did his mother, as did his father. I'm waiting for a letter from his son.

But there's one letter in particular I've been thinking about. It was a second letter written by the fellow who'd suggested Indians weren't creative enough to invent backhoes, chainsaws, and other instruments of civilization. He asked why we were carping on something that happened 150 years ago, then suggested his own answer: Sure, whites did some nasty stuff a long time ago, but the reason Karen and I dredged up this ancient history is that we simply couldn't find any more-recent examples of white atrocities. His bottom line was that things have improved on every racial front.

And, of course, he's right. We don't see many lynchings now in the United States. Even in cases where a black man murders a white man, mobs allow the state to do the imprisoning or executing, instead of taking the law into their own hands. And while interracial dating used to be an offense punishable by death, by now most everyone I know has dated at least one person of a different color than her or his own. And people have more free speech rights now than before, do they not? Schools are integrated, black people don't have to sit in the backs of buses, and they can eat at restaurants with the white folks. For the most part, whites no longer slaughter them, at least in the United States.

Surely it's true that the central movement of civilization is "a new world of individual rights, an ever-expanding circle of liberty," as newspaper columnist Charles Krauthammer recently put it. First the men of Israel were the Chosen People. Or, from the perspective of male Mesopotamians, *they* were the Chosen Ones. Then the Greeks,

EXPANDING THE FRONTIER

then the Romans, then Europe. Wasn't all of this historical movement an expansion of the rights of those on the inside, a circle of liberty always expanding to include new groups of people, albeit, nearly always by force? Fast-forward to the United States. Have not blacks been enfranchised, and women, too (never mind that we get to choose between two factions of the same corporate priesthood)? Is not anyone now eligible to become the next Bill Gates, the next Colin Powell?

Here is what I know. I know that in Vietnam, the United States killed upward of three million brown people—people who had based their constitution on that of the United States—because they wanted self-determination, they wanted freedom from colonial exploitation. I know that persons who killed brown noncombatants from the air (at great physical distance) and from the ground (face-to-face, but from an equal emotional distance) in Vietnam have parlayed those actions into successful Senate careers and into serious runs at the presidency. I know that in the 1980s U.S.-backed troops in Guatemala killed ten thousand brown people per year, and systematically dispossessed one million of the nation's four million Indians. I know that we can tell that same story a hundred times in a hundred places in Central and South America, in Africa, in Asia. I know that in the last year before he was deposed, the U.S.-backed dictator in Iran killed more than thirty thousand brown people—as many as he dared—and that in 1992 the United States killed between 250,000 and 500,000 Iraqi brown people—mainly civilians—in the "blood for oil" Gulf War. I know that eighteen thousand brown people a month, half of whom are under five years old, die in Iraq because of U.S. sanctions. Week after week I hear of union organizers or indigenous peoples—or merely brown people who *might* be union organizers or indigenous peoples, or who might *know* union organizers or indigenous peoples—who are beheaded, killed by gunshot wounds, killed by chainsaws, killed by machetes, by U.S.-backed death squads in Colombia. Three thousand trade unionists have been murdered in Colombia in the past fifteen years: To achieve an equivalent per capita death rate in the United States,

21,000 union members would have had to die. I know that for hundreds of years brown people in North America have been driven off their land and their land has been defoliated by unnatural fire and by hand. I know that in the 1960s and 1970s brown people in Vietnam were driven off their land and their land was defoliated by Agent Orange, and I know that today in Colombia brown people are driven off their land and their land is defoliated by Roundup and Cosmoflux. I know that on the home front, the rate at which women are raped remains at full throttle—or, if this is not full throttle, then God help us all—and I know that the same is true for the rate at which children are beaten.

Yes, black men may date white women, and white men may date black women. Black men may date white men, and black women may date white women. The same is true for other races. But I know also that nearly a third of all black men in this country are under criminal justice supervision.

And I know that a strong case can be made (and has been made by writer, academic, and activist Robert Perkinson) that today's prisons evolved not so much out of the penitentiaries of the Northeast, where most historians mark their genesis, but out of the slave camps of the antebellum South. One reason, he argues, that the South had the "military tradition" that so helped it at the beginning of the Civil War was because of the antislave militias white men were forced to participate in to police the black population, doing many of the same things policemen do now: walking their "beats," stopping black people; demanding to see papers, ransacking homes looking, for contraband. Seeing this continuity, the incarceration rates for black males suddenly makes sense.

I know that the IWW free speech fights are over, and now we can say anything we want. But I know that journalists in Colombia who speak out against corporations die, and I know that journalists in the United States who do the same lose their jobs. And I know that when citizens today gather to speak out against corporations, they are met not by gauntlets of drunken citizens with wheel spokes, but by rows of gauntleted policemen with batons, tear gas, pepper spray, rubber

EXPANDING THE FRONTIER

bullets, fire hoses, and prisons at their disposal. I think I'll take my chances with the drunkard and his wheel spoke.

Things have changed. Yet things are the same. The face of power has changed. It has changed, at least in part, for reasons of economy. Just as it's cheaper to hire workers at starvation wages and dump them when you're through than it is to own them as chattel, it is cheaper—once you've been able to so domesticate the people so that not only will they no longer rebel but they will no longer perceive your control as unjust and will in fact attempt to join you as one of the owners of others—to keep people in line through the iron cages of rhetoric—through internalized violence—than through outright violence. It's Diamond's line again: At the frontier you have conquest, and at home you have repression. Or we can again think of DuBois, and his observation that even before the First World War, the United States had gained the capacity to exploit the entire world.

All of this is simply to say that as people become consumed by the system, once they cease resisting it and become a part of it (that is, once they cease to be human and begin to identify with the in-human, machine logic of the religion of production), they begin to be, and must be, treated differently by those who are even more fully consumed. What is seen by Krauthammer as an ever-expanding circle of liberty I would see as an ever-expanding circle of the living dead, the consumers of the living, of those who can be granted a certain form of liberty because they can be trusted to no longer resist.

■   ■   ■

The Ku Klux Klan reared its head again in the late 1910s and early 1920s, fueled by the runaway success of the movie *The Birth of a Nation* and as a backlash against the power of the Socialist movement. Just as the first KKK was fertilized by the hatred engendered by the loss of slave labor, this time it was fueled by the worldwide rise of dis-satisfaction with capitalism.

Prior to World War I, tremendous strikes shook Europe. The years 1913 and 1914 saw immense strikes all across Russia. Austria-Hungary was on the verge of civil war. Revolutionary movements and radical unions were on the ascent in Germany, France, Italy. We've already discussed Wobblies and Socialists in the United States. In England, even George V acknowledged the unrest, when he said, in the summer of 1914, just before the war, "The cry of civil war is on the lips of the most responsible and sober-minded of my people." Things had to explode.

The questions became—as the questions always become—how would things explode, and at whom would this explosion be directed? There is almost no better way to destroy hope than through a long and pointless war. And it worked. Most unions and left-wing parties backed the war, and those that didn't—like the Wobblies in the United States—the state simply destroyed. After the war, not many people had the heart anymore to pursue revolution, and those who did, like Mussolini or the Bolsheviks, were not true revolutionaries in terms of overturning the social order, but, instead, opportunists who turned power vacuums to their own advantage.

But the shunting of rage does not make it disappear, any more than studious avoidance by Luborsky's subjects (or any of us) changes things we find objectionable or threatening (as opposed to merely changing perception). Instead, as with Irish immigrants in America, the rage merely finds more convenient—less powerful—targets.

Just as the original incarnation of the Ku Klux Klan had its genesis in kids wanting to "start a club of some kind," the early-twentieth-century version was refounded by someone who simply could not get enough of fraternal organizations. William Joseph Simmons belonged to two different churches, and was a member of the Masons, Knights Templars, Knights of Pythias, the Odd Fellows, and eight other lodges. At one point, he'd been a circuit-riding preacher, but, more recently, he was a promoter of the organization Woodmen of the World. Years before, in a drunken stupor, he'd seen a vision of ghostly riders racing across the night sky, with the surface of the

EXPANDING THE FRONTIER

moon becoming a relief map of the United States. Simmons had fallen to his knees and begged God to tell him what this meant, but God didn't answer, until years later, after he (Simmons) had been run over by a car. Confined to bed for three months, the image raced again and again through his mind as the riders had raced across the sky. He read old Klan literature, and determined to re-form the Klan. He became obsessed with the letters *KL*. The new Klan constitution, he decided, would be called the *Kloran*. Two Klan members talking would be a klonversation. A chapter of the Klan would be called a *klavern*. And so on.

Simmons lived in Georgia, an ostensibly dry state that nonetheless allowed men to keep as much liquor as they wanted in private lockers in special clubs. He first conceptualized the Klan as a "locker club," but this idea foundered when he asked a city clerk for input on the name. The clerk thought Ku Klux Klan wouldn't cut it, because everyone in Atlanta, it seemed, wanted to be a Badger, Panther, or Buffalo: "They all want to be animals," the clerk replied.

There rested the KKK until *The Birth of a Nation* came to town. Several months prior to the arrival of the movie, a fourteen-year-old girl, by the name of Mary Phagan, had been raped and murdered in the basement of the pencil factory where she worked (the horror of her rape and murder is mentioned in every account I've seen about her: the horror of children working in pencil factories is not). Her employer, a Jew, from New York, by the name of Leo M. Frank, was falsely convicted (of her murder, not her employment), and sentenced to death. After much pressure from civil liberties groups, the governor of Georgia commuted Frank's sentence to life in prison. Decent white men across Georgia were outraged. Former U.S. representative Thomas E. Watson—who had already written, about Phagan, in language that would have made Hitler purple with envy, "Our Little Girl—ours by the Eternal God—has been pursued to a hideous death and bloody grave by this filthy perverted Jew of New York," and had stated that, like niggers, Jews have "a ravenous appetite for the forbidden fruit"—called on his fellow (white, non-

Jewish) citizens to "RISE! PEOPLE OF GEORGIA!" He wrote that "another Ku Klux Klan may have to be organized to restore home rule." Four days later, twenty-five men, including a Methodist minister, calling themselves the Knights of Mary Phagan, abducted Frank from a prison farm, took him to Phagan's hometown, and hanged him. All of this excitement caused Simmons to rethink the Klan. No longer would it simply be a club for men to come and drink, but instead it would be, as he soon called it, "The World's Greatest Secret, Social, Patriotic, Fraternal, Beneficiary Order." It was clear, as always, who would be the beneficiaries of this Beneficiary Order. Fortunately for Simmons, *The Birth of a Nation* came to town, to extraordinary reviews, such as this one in the *Atlanta Constitution*: "Never before, perhaps, has an Atlanta audience so freely given vent to its emotions and appreciation. . . . Cheer after cheer burst forth from the audience. . . . It makes you forget decorum and forces a cry into your throat. . . . It makes you actually live through the greatest period of suffering and trial that this country has ever known." By *suffering and trial*, the reviewer meant whites being victimized by having their entitlement threatened. The message resonated. The KKK burgeoned.

The KKK closely allied itself to the war effort, harassing prostitutes working near military bases, threatening people who did not hew to the prowar line, and attacking laborers "infested with the IWW spirit." The beliefs of the Ku Klux Klan were straightforward. New recruits had to swear that they were "Native Born" and that they believed in:

> The Tenets of the Christian Religion
> White Supremacy
> Protection of our Pure American Womanhood
> Preventing unwarranted strikes by Foreign Labor
>   Agitators
> Upholding the Constitution of the United States
> The Sovereignty of our State Rights
> Promotion of Pure Americanism

The Klan continued to grow after the war, but was nearly bank-rupt, and would have gone so, had Simmons not come into contact with one of the progenitors of the nascent public relations industry. Edward Young Clarke, whose brother was managing editor of the *Atlanta Constitution*, ran the Southern Publicity Association, and saw dollar signs written all over the Klan. Clarke convinced Simmons to allow the Southern Publicity Association to be the Klan's sole mar-keting agent, and, soon enough, turned it into the granddaddy of all multilevel marketing plans, a Ponzi scheme tapping a nearly unlim-ited reservoir of uncertainty, fear, bigotry, and hatred. He hired what he called King Kleagles to oversee recruitment in each state. Recruitment, called kleagling, was handled by Kleagles, who went door to door selling memberships in the Klan for ten dollars each (called *klecktokens*). The Kleagle kept four dollars from each recruit, and passed the other six to his King. The King kept a dollar, and so on, up the scale.

This is where hate came in. In order to sell memberships, the Kleagles were told to appeal to the fears of targeted communities. Kleagles in communities where a lot of recent immigrants lived em-phasized that the Klan "stood for 100 percent Americanism and would never allow the country to be taken over by a pack of radical hyphens." Where union activities threatened the status quo, Kleagles asserted the Klan's position against "alien-inspired strikers." Where Negroes might be getting a little out of hand, Kleagles only had to remind their target audience that the Klan had always known how to deal with niggers. As historian John Higham put it, "Never before had a single society gathered up so many hatreds or given vent to an inwardness so thoroughgoing."

The Klan no longer burgeoned, but exploded. In less than a year, eleven hundred Kleagles were canvassing the country, and, in fifteen months, the Klan had almost one hundred thousand members. As Clarke told Simmons, "I have never seen anything equal to the clamor throughout the nation for the Klan."

Klan violence grew apace with its numbers. Some violence was associated with elections, with robed Klan members intimidating blacks, Jews, Catholics, socialists, and others into not voting. Some violence was associated with sex, with Klansmen beating, flogging, or castrating those they deemed guilty of ravenously hungering after the forbidden fruit of Protestant white women. Nearly all of this violence was associated with entitlement, whether political, sexual, economic, or otherwise social. Nearly all had to do with maintaining the current social hierarchy. In 1921, the *New York World* published a major exposé of the Klan, complete with detailed descriptions of more than one hundred Klan outrages. The exposé was syndicated to eighteen major newspapers, and prompted a congressional investigation. The investigation was a rousing success—for the Klan. People liked what they heard. They liked what the Klan represented. Noted newspaperman H. L. Mencken remarked that "Not a single solitary sound reason has yet been advanced for putting the Ku Klux Klan out of business. If the Klan is against the Jews, so are half of the good hotels of the Republic and three-quarters of the good clubs. If the Klan is against the foreign-born or the hyphenated citizen, so is the National Institute of Arts and Letters. If the Klan is against the Negro, so are all of the states south of the Mason-Dixon line. If the Klan is for damnation and persecution, so is the Methodist Church. . . . If the Klan uses the mails for shaking down suckers, so does the Red Cross. If the Klan constitutes itself a censor of private morals, so does the Congress of the United States. If the Klan lynches a Moor for raping someone's daughter, so would you or I." (It is significant, by the way, that journalist Mencken mentioned the rape of a (presumably) white woman by a "Moor," and not the other way around: The rape of a member of the elite class by the nonelite was and is considered an outrage; whereas, if the roles are reversed, the action is generally considered not even newsworthy.) This is in a country where President Wilson had stated that "hyphenated Americans . . . have poured the poison of disloyalty into the very arteries of our national life," and, further, that "such creatures of passion, disloyalty and anarchy must be crushed out." This is a country where the attorney general, A. Mitchell Palmer had also said of the foreign born, "Out of the sly

EXPANDING THE FRONTIER

and crafty eyes of many of them leap cupidity, cruelty, insanity and crime; from their lopsided faces, sloping brows, and misshapen features may be recognized the unmistakable criminal type." Of communists, Palmer had said, "Each and every adherent of this movement is a potential murderer or a potential thief who deserves no consideration."

In the aftermath of the exposé and the investigation, Klan membership went up by another order of magnitude, to over a million members. As Simmons remarked, "Congress gave us the best advertising we ever got. Congress *made* us." By 1923, at least seventy-five U.S. representatives owed their seats to the Klan, and the Klan had been able to sweep anti-Klan governors from at least two states, and cow the rest of them (except one) into silence. That same year in Georgia the Klan counted as its members the governor, Supreme Court chief justice, attorney general, and so on. Indeed, the president of the United States, Warren G. Harding, was sworn in as a member of the Ku Klux Klan in the Green Room of the White House, using the White House Bible for the oath. In appreciation of the efforts of those who swore him in, Harding gave them War Department license plates, allowing them to run red lights anywhere in the country.

As always, it would be a mistake to believe the Klan consisted of the feebleminded, of uneducated bigots, of angry young men (although, at least as regards Harding, a case could be made for the former). In one study in Georgia, 92 percent of Klan members were married, and more than two-thirds had children. Only 15 percent could be considered "semi-skilled," "mill workers," or "unskilled," with about 10 percent being "major proprietor," "professional," or "semi-professional," and the vast majority being "petty-proprietor & managerial," "low white-collar," and "skilled trades," the single-largest category being "low white-collar," followed closely by "petty-proprietor & managerial." Many clergy cooperated closely with the Klan, or were Klan members themselves. By 1924, thirty thousand ministers were enrolled in the Klan. The point is that, what was true in the 1860s, that the Klan consisted of "the real leaders of the

Southern communities," was true as well in the 1920s, except that we can remove the word *Southern*. The Klan virtually took over Colorado and Indiana, for example. As one journalist wrote, "Outside business, the Ku Klux Klan has become the most vigorous, active and effective organization in American life." American business culture and the Klan have far more in common than we would normally like to think.

So it's natural that Klan violence wasn't prosecuted. An Atlanta attorney later stated, "Everybody in the courthouse belonged to the Klan, virtually every judge, the prosecuting officers . . . all the police and the mayor and the councilmen." The governor of Georgia was even more direct: "If anybody gets an indictment against a Klansman or a Klan itself . . . I am going to write out a pardon immediately."

■　　　■　　　■

The same is true today, only the names and battlefields have changed. I have been struck, as I've researched and written this book, by the continuities that run through our history. Oh, we're proud that the Klan no longer runs state legislatures, and the current president (feebleminded though he may be) did not take an oath to the Klan, using the White House Bible. But, if we're honest with ourselves, we'll recognize that the Seven Noble Truths of the KKK still hold sway in mainstream American politics. *The Tenets of the Christian Religion.* Imagine today a politician in the United States announcing that, as American Indian writer Vine Deloria has said, "Much of Western science must go, all of Western religion should go, and if we are in any way successful in ridding ourselves of these burdens, we will find that we can fundamentally change government so that it will function more sensibly and enable us to solve our problems." I believe the technical term for assailing any of the Western religions—Christianity, Science, or Production—is *political suicide.* Now, *White Supremacy:* Certainly the rhetoric of white supremacy has been relegated to the corners of our consciousness,

EXPANDING THE FRONTIER

but, if we look past rhetoric to the reality of who owns what in this country, and who imprisons whom, we'll see the degree to which the policies of white supremacy continue to be realized. Further, if we capitalize *White*, to signify a worldview based on exploitation of all human and nonhuman others, of a civilization based on conquest abroad and repression at home, on industrial production, then, even the rhetoric of White supremacy reigns supreme. *Protection of our Pure American Womanhood:* Fights over women's reproductive freedom make clear that, to this day, the purity of American women must be protected, even against their own desires. *Preventing unwarranted strikes by Foreign Labor Agitators:* I have only some initials to say: NAFTA; GATT; WTO; IMF. Strike, the CEOs and politicians say, and instead of bringing foreign workers into the factory, we'll simply move the factory to the foreign workers. And if the foreign workers strike, so will death squads. *Upholding the Constitution of the United States:* To attack the United States Constitution would be as politically suicidal as it would be to attack Christianity. Just two days ago I delivered a commencement speech at a community college in the Bay Area. The ceremony, I learned about an hour before it started, was to open with the national anthem. Because the government of the United States is clearly a government of occupation, and not inhabitation (I can hear the whispers already: *blasphemy*) I had vowed years ago that I would no longer stand for The Star Spangled Banner. Having not been to any sporting events since I made that vow, I'd not had the opportunity to practice this form of meditative sitting. For about fifteen seconds, I weighed whether I should or shouldn't stand, before deciding not to embarrass the student who sponsored my speech nor to unnecessarily, and with little gain, flummox the school administrators (this decision was made in great measure on my understanding that the purpose of the gathering was neither me nor my politics, nor even an earth being destroyed by the minute, but, rather, the celebration of the very real accomplishments of these students—many of whom are economically disadvantaged, to say the least, and many of whom were the

first in their families to earn college degrees—all of which is to say I decided my political statement could wait). I did not want, in this case, to wreck their evening. Were I a better singer, I might have belted out the banned, third, verse. Similarly, imagine a major political figure refusing to stand for the national anthem. What would be ruined in this case would be his career. *The Sovereignty of our State Rights:* Now, as then, sovereignty of communities, states, and nations is selective, to the degree that it supports production. When it is in the interests of production to promote communal, state, or national sovereignty, such is promoted. When communal, state, or national sovereignty impedes production, sovereignty is generally ignored. Just today, for example, I learned that the U.S. Supreme Court recently, and unanimously, struck down a Massachusetts law that restricted state purchases from companies doing business in the military dictatorship in Burma. *Promotion of Pure Americanism:* If we believe that, as former General Motors president Charles Erwin Wilson said, "What is good for the country is good for General Motors, and what's good for General Motors is good for the country," then, pure Americanism continues to be promoted. Even if we choose a less rigorous definition, to oppose "pure Americanism," whatever the hell we may choose it to stand for, is to invite disrepute.

I've been thinking also about the line by the Atlanta attorney about how everyone in the courthouse belonged to the Klan. Let's substitute one word, and revisit his sentence: "Everybody in the courthouse belonged to the corporations, virtually every judge, the prosecuting officers . . . all the police and the mayor and the councilmen." And now the words of the governor: "If anybody gets an indictment against a corporate officer or a corporation itself . . . I am going to write out a pardon immediately." It's all too similar. The biggest difference that I can see is that the stranglehold has gotten even tighter.

■   ■   ■

EXPANDING THE FRONTIER

Redwoods cannot stand alone. Roots burrow through the soil, reaching out to each other, to intertwine, to hold up these tallest of trees, so they may stand together. If you listen carefully enough, you can hear them speak. They groan and creak, and whisper in the wind. Some squeal like kittens, or sing songs eerie as those of whales. The bark is soft and spongy, inviting touch. The trees themselves are huge, as big around as ten or twelve people stretching fingertip to fingertip, and far taller than any building should ever be. They sometimes create their own weather, with small clouds forming far below their crowns.

The big ones have been cut. There are pockets, still, of ancient trees, but once, not even that long ago, there was no such thing as old growth redwoods. There was merely home. No one could have conceived of something so absurd as cutting them all down. Once, the rivers were full of salmon. Once, humans lived here in dynamic equilibrium with their surroundings. No longer.

I live in redwood country. As I write these words—in this moment—sheriffs, fish and game officers (whose job, ostensibly, is to protect wildlife, but whose real job is to protect, you guessed it, industrial production), and employees of the Pacific Lumber Company (*goons* is the technical term) are chasing people through the trees (mainly old growth douglas fir) a couple of hundred miles south of here, on the Mattole River. The people being chased are attempting to prevent these trees from being cut. The cuts violate environmental laws, but that makes no difference to the sheriffs, fish and game officers, and goons. The only thing that matters is that the trees be cut, and that opposition to this activity be eradicated. Activists have been chased down cliffsides, they have been lied to, they have been sentenced to long jail terms. A couple of days ago, a nineteen-year-old activist was charged with eight felony counts of child endangerment and eight misdemeanor counts of contributing to the delinquency of a minor. His crime? With parental permission, he brought a bunch of seventeen-year-old volunteers up from the Bay Area to participate in defending the forest. The Humboldt

County sheriff alleged the kids faced "potential bodily harm" in the forest.

For once, the sheriff is right. Loggers threatened to burn alive at least one of the teenagers, who had climbed a tree. Police assaulted others of them with pepper spray. No charges were filed against loggers, police, or the corporation they work for. Of course. The mother of one of the teenagers said, "Any danger he was in was from the loggers, the police department and the Fish and Game Department. I think they came home more courageous, angry at what's going on in the world."

A couple of years ago an activist by the name of David Chain was killed by a logger. The logger, working for Pacific Lumber, felled a tree on the protesting Chain.

The logger was videotaped just an hour before, hurling curses and threats at the protesters: "Get the fuck out of here! You've got me hot enough now to fuck! . . . Get outta here! Otherwise I'll fuckin', I'll make sure I got a tree comin' this way! . . . Ohhhhh, fuck! I wish I had my fuckin' pistol! I guess I'm gonna just start packin' that motherfucker in here. 'Cause I can only be nice so fuckin' long. Go get my saw, I'm gonna start fallin' into this fuckin' draw!" He soon began revving up his saw, shouting, "Fuck! Yee-Hoo!"

I later spoke to a friend whose ex-husband used to be a faller. She said, "Fallers can drop trees on a dime. If you can't drop it precisely where you choose, you don't last long in the woods. This sounds like murder."

Of course, the media (including so-called National Public Radio), Pacific Lumber, and the Humboldt County Sheriff's Department all went into high gear to present the murder as Chain's fault, and to present the company as the real victim.

I first heard about the murder on public radio. I don't normally listen, because I don't like being lied to. But this time I happened to be listening, and the journalists did not disappoint: First, they announced, incorrectly, that Chain had been killed not by a tree the logger cut, but by another tree knocked over in a domino effect.

EXPANDING THE FRONTIER

Second, after a brief and moving statement by a tearful Earth First!er, the journalist asked three basic questions. They were: 1) Members of Earth First! are aware that their activities are dangerous, aren't they? And isn't it true that this activist was engaged in an especially dangerous form of activism? 2) Of course the logger didn't do this on purpose, did he? (Evidently, the statement "I'll make sure I got a tree comin' this way!" was not strong enough proof of intent, nor was his wish for a "fuckin' pistol") 3) In the aftermath of this death, how is Earth First! going to change its tactics so this won't happen again?

I almost drove off the road.

The response by Pacific Lumber was equally predictable. John Campbell, president and CEO of Pacific Lumber, vehemently denied his loggers knew protesters were in the area. The predictability of this lie is the exact reason Earth First!ers brought the videotape recorder. Later, Pacific Lumber released a press statement which had as its primary purpose the same goal as the questioning by the journalist: to shift responsibility for the death onto the victim: "It is a tragedy that this young man lost his life," Campbell said. "And this was a shattering experience for our work crews, who labored for more than three hours yesterday to free Mr. Chain's body. Clearly, it is time for these groups to stop putting their members in harm's way."

Under California law, the logger should have been charged with, at the very least, second-degree murder. If a person recognizes that an action will likely cause a substantial danger to another, and proceeds with a conscious disregard for this danger, so causing another's death, that person has, under the doctrine of "implied malice aforethought," committed second-degree murder.

Not only the logger would be held accountable under a just system. If others, including the man's employers, suggested he intimidate activists by felling trees close to them, these employers and supervisors, too, are guilty of second-degree murder. Even a cursory examination of Pacific Lumber's treatment of those protesting their often illegal cutting practices reveals a consistent pattern of harrassment and endangerment against protesters. This is not the first time

THE CULTURE OF MAKE BELIEVE

a tree has been felled near an activist: It is merely the first time an activist has been killed. Loggers for Pacific Lumber continue to fall trees near tree sitters. The law is clear in what should happen to these lawbreakers.

The law, however, is of little importance to those in power, except insofar as it may be used to further their own ends: After all, they are the ones who write and implement the rules, and why should they write, or, more importantly, implement rules that are not to their own advantage? A primary purpose of sheriff's departments, as has been shown time and again, is to protect production, and to assist corporations when citizens get far enough out of line to even slightly impede companies' processes of turning the living into the dead. This particular department gained international notoriety the year before, when they daubed concentrated liquid pepper directly onto the eyeballs of nonviolent environmental protesters locked down in the office of a congressman deeply beholden to big timber corporations. That the department did so is not unusual: What is unusual is that they were proud enough of their work to videotape themselves doing it (to show they were following proper procedure). Their behavior in Chain's case is as expected as the words of the journalist, and as the words and actions of Georgia's Klan governor. The logger who killed Chain was treated not as a suspect but as a star witness. He went along with police to the "accident scene" (the police never called it a crime scene—only an environmentalist was killed, which means no crime was committed—just as the police never called the murder of Lloyd Clay a crime, nor that of Wesley Everest, and just as the courts in Georgia, for example, prosecuted precisely *one* lynching in the eighty years after the Civil War). He was not arrested, and, to my knowledge, that possibility never occurred to the investigators. Something that did occur to the investigators was to use Chain's death as an opportunity to gain more information about the protesters: A detective sent a note to an Earth First! organizer, requesting "access to records or individuals who are involved in the training of the activists. . . ." Contrast this to the investigation

EXPANDING THE FRONTIER

of the crime itself, which was nominal: No official investigation team even inspected the scene of the death until ten days after the crime.

In the meantime, the sheriff's department did not prohibit employees of Pacific Lumber from continuing to cut at the site, and left any potential destruction of evidence entirely up to the discretion of the corporation and its employees. In response, Earth First!ers set up a blockade to keep Pacific Lumber out.

At last, the sheriffs had a crime they chose to deal with: Between forty and sixty officers conducted a military-style dawn raid on sleeping protestors. Activists who got up were forced back to the ground. Warned by the sounds below, some of the activists at blockades closer to the murder site were able to lock themselves to logging equipment. One of the young women was heard screaming "pepper spray" shortly after authorities reached her. She had been locked down high on a cable yarder boom. The boom was lowered, and officers then held her head back and poured liquid pepper spray over her face from a cup. A second woman was doused the same way.

Pepper spray is available in concentrations of 1, 3, and 10 percent. The Humboldt County Sheriff's Department purchases the largest containers available of the highest concentrate sold.

That night, the protesters re-formed their barricades, and the next morning the sheriffs were back. This time the protesters were ready, and locked themselves down. The sheriffs wasted no time, immediately pulling out the pepper spray. Officers strung a large tarp, in an attempt to keep observers from witnessing their actions, but the tarp didn't prevent people from hearing the screams of the young women being doused with pepper concentrate. Police applied pepper-soaked gauze to the activist Carrie "Liz" McKee. When she refused to unlock, the gauze was wrung out directly onto her eyes. When, still, she refused, again the police applied the concentrate. Pepper was applied a third time, and she began to vomit from the pain. Still, she refused to submit, and police cut her loose.

The company's logging license had been revoked the year before, after being cited for more than two hundred rule violations (given the routine capture of regulatory agencies by the industries they purport to oversee, the issuance of more than two hundred citations implies a nearly unimaginable number of violations). But, of course, this did not hinder operations, because the corporation was then issued a conditional operating permit, similar to probation, which provided that the company could continue to cut, so long as it obeyed the rules. Citations issued at the site of Chain's death the day after the murder (Chain and others had been asking loggers to stop until the California Department of Forestry arrived, because, among other things, the loggers were cutting too close to marbled murrelet nesting sites) did not force Pacific Lumber to stop cutting. Why would the California Department of Forestry halt Pacific Lumber?

I don't know which hurts most: the murder itself; the ongoing murder of the ancient redwoods that Chain was trying to protect; the ongoing murder of the planet of which the murder of the ancient redwoods is but one manifestation; or the willful stupidity of all of us, myself included, who continue to participate in a system that rewards those who produce—that is, those who convert the living to the dead—and kills or tortures those who resist.

I'll tell you something else that hurts. The knowledge that what these light-skinned environmentalists experienced, horrible as it may be, is almost nothing, compared to the routine treatment by our culture of those who are not only not White, but also not white.

John Campbell, president and CEO of Pacific Lumber, said, "Clearly, it is time for these groups to stop putting their members in harm's way." Clearly, he is right. It is time that we begin to take care of ourselves, and to take care of our human and nonhuman neighbors. It is time we begin to dismantle this entire system of oppression, and the institutions, such as Pacific Lumber, the KKK, or the sheriffs departments, that are its primary engines and manifestations, that are putting all of us—human and nonhuman alike—in harm's way.

EXPANDING THE FRONTIER

■   ■   ■

There are a couple of points to be made through all of this. The first is that, as with the Klan of the nineteenth century, the Klan of the early twentieth century was a true grassroots organization, with numbers and influence that can only be the envy of those of us who don't support, but oppose, the injustices on which our system is based. The KKK tapped, and taps, a vein in our culture, a vein of rage that waits always to explode.

But there is a deeper point to be made, as well, about the framing conditions in our culture that not only make this rage inevitable, but make inevitable, too, the turning of this rage onto inappropriate targets. We have discussed already how rage and hatred are two of the inescapable outcomes of basing one's culture so thoroughly on competition. We have discussed also the absurd lengths to which we will go to not perceive those things that threaten our worldview, that threaten the bases of our society. We have not yet, however, put them fully together.

The militias of the 1990s up to the present in rural America have long encouraged, frustrated, and confused me. The encouragement has come because they give voice to the rage, sorrow, and terror that so many of us feel: As John Keeble said of the Ku Klux Klan ("Hate groups state openly that they're racist and afraid. We're all racist, and we're all afraid. It's just that most of us are afraid to admit it") so too we're all outraged (or should be), yet most of us simply put down our heads and get through the day. And these groups have frustrated me because—like the Irish in America—so often they turn the rage to the wrong sources. I talked once with a family farmer who said, "Cargill [a huge agricorporation] gives me two choices: Either I can cut my own throat or they'll do it for me." Although this particular farmer was very clearly out for revolution against the corporate theocracy, so often the rage gets expressed not toward these hungry ghosts and those who run them but toward, for example, an alleged International Zionist Conspiracy, or a cabal of Jewish bankers (never mind that the Morgans, who actually did control a good portion of the global economy, were bigoted against Jews, with Jack Morgan stating approvingly of Hitler, "Except for his attitude toward the Jews, which I consider wholesome, the new Dictator of Germany seems to me very much like the old Kaiser"), or environmentalists, Indians, or Mexicans. Any group but the real one. Just two days ago, I was supposed to catch a flight out of Crescent City (the airport, interestingly enough, is named McNamara Field) to do that commencement I mentioned, but heavy fog caused the flight to be canceled. The airline paid for four of us to share a taxi to catch a flight out of McKinleyville, some hour and a half south. The ride was interesting. My companions were an elderly woman and three elderly men, including the driver. As you might guess, given the mix, there were a lot more answers in the air than questions. I paid close attention, and with the exception of myself and the woman, no one asked a single question about anything. But here's the point. All four of us males—myself definitely included—expressed anger at "the way things are." For example, we all—including even the woman—had a good time complaining about the shenanigans by California's electrical suppliers. We all agreed that these huge corporations have created all sorts of dummy companies to which they sell electricity back and forth, before finally selling that electricity at grossly inflated prices to consumers. We also agreed that these same corporations have artificially created shortages in order to demand additional taxpayer subsidies or to get out of contracts they now deem unfavorable. And we all knew, too, that Pacific Gas and Electric, one of the biggest suppliers, had shuttled billions of dollars to a parent company in some other state, then declared bankruptcy (leaving, among others, many of the families supposedly represented in the Oscar-winning movie *Erin Brockovich* in the lurch: Julia Roberts, Albert Finney, and Steven Soderbergh may have gotten their payoffs, but many of the families with leukemia, cancer, and Crohn's disease are simply SOL). And we knew also that the day before declaring bankruptcy, PG&E had given its executives tens of millions in bonuses, with tens of millions more pour-

EXPANDING THE FRONTIER

ing in during the weeks after. One person in the taxi said, "If you or I transferred funds to a relative, then declared bankruptcy, we'd both be in prison." We all agreed. Then another said, "You know what the problem is?" Even though a question mark comes at the end of that sentence, it didn't count properly as a question, since he fully expected no one to answer, and made sure to answer his own question before anyone had the chance, anyway. His response, and this is the point of the story, was, "Government interference." The other two men agreed. The woman looked out the window at the redwoods slipping by. I'm reasonably certain that by *government interference* the three men didn't mean government interference with citizen outrage, either by legislators, administrators, and judges providing legal screens for these activities, or by the use of police to keep us from simply stringing up these corporate executives. (How many lynchings have you heard of, by the way, where the victim was a wealthy white male, head of a corporation?) That they meant none of this was verified by the next thing one of them said: "And it's those damn environmental regulations." In the soliloquy that followed he also somehow inculpated Indians in the energy crisis, but the drive didn't last long enough for him to get around to Mexicans, blacks, or Jews.

This happens all the time. Too many gang kids kill too many gang kids in the ghetto, shooting down mirror images of themselves. Too many small family farmers hate too many environmentalists, and too many environmentalists hate too many small family farmers. (This is not to say we shouldn't be particular: I work with many family farmers, but I won't work with McNamara). Cops shoot anti-globalization protesters with whom they ultimately have more in common than they do with the institutions they are protecting. And they do the same with poor black males.

Why? The answer, I think, has to do with Noah, Luborsky, and Laing.

Our culture's deep foundation of competition creates waves of rage and hatred. Not only does this anger get misdirected because it's easier to express it against the powerless, and not only because

THE CULTURE OF MAKE BELIEVE

we are routinely pitted against others of the powerless, but, most especially, because, if we were to focus on the real sources of that rage and hatred, we would soon find ourselves questioning our very identities. Because so many of us have identified ourselves so deeply as civilized, as producers, consumers, workers, engineers, bakers, writers, soldiers, policemen, teachers, we have forgotten that first we are human beings. And what is that? We have no idea. To identify so deeply with the system of production that permeates the deepest recesses of our bodies, just like dioxin from manufacturing, like radiation from fallout, like heavy metals from mining, is to identify with the founding processes of civilization: conquest and repression. To recognize that our lives are based on these processes would—if we reject instead of embrace them—set us adrift in unknown territory. Who would I be and how would I live if I were not a part of this system?

If we were to truly turn our rage and hatred—not envy, where we wish to take the place of those in power, but rage and hatred, where we wish to destroy their base of power—toward the right targets, we would find ourselves questioning the basis upon which anyone holds power over anyone else. We would find ourselves questioning the basis for our own privilege. We would find ourselves suddenly no longer on the inside, no longer White, but now—light-skinned or dark, deepest ebony, to subtlest russet, to the most translucent pink—hated by those who were still White, and, far more importantly, searching for a new worldview to replace that into which we were formerly indoctrinated. Our identity would be shaken, then shattered. That's all scary as hell. Which is why we don't do it. Which is why, just as those who find nudity objectionable could not see the breast in the photograph, we, too, cannot even see that which is threatening to us. Truly, if we identify with the culture, to hate the thing causing us pain—the culture—would be to hate ourselves. This is too much.

This is why Sitting Bull could make the speech he did at the Golden Spike ceremony for Northern Pacific: "I hate you. I hate you. I hate all the white people. You are thieves and liars. You have

EXPANDING THE FRONTIER

taken away our land and made us outcasts, so I hate you." Because Sitting Bull's identity was not based on being White—civilized—he could, with no major psychological distress, recognize the real source of his misery: whites, or, rather, Whites. To do so did not alter his perception of who and what he was in relationship to his family, his community, the larger social nexus of which he was a part, and, ultimately, the land. It was a simple statement of fact. Because he did not identify himself as White, he did not have to *not* see the source of his misery.

Conversely, this is why the soldier could not translate Sitting Bull's speech accurately, but, instead, had to scuttle backward to cover up his father's nakedness. Of course. To do otherwise would be to question his identity, and, in the end, to blow apart his world.

The story of Sitting Bull happens also inside of each of us every day, or, at least, inside those of us who feel rage and hate, which I'd wager is most of us, in that we all feel the loss—at some level even more deeply than our identification with the system of production, even more deeply than the dioxin, radiation, heavy metals, as deep inside of us as it is possible to be—of having had our humanity sacrificed on the altar of production, of having been forced into competition with all others with whom we should be cooperating, of having been coerced into believing that coercion is natural or inevitable, of having signed a Faustian contract—*the* Faustian contract—giving up happiness and connection for power. Inside of us—once again, deep, deep inside of us—we daily give Sitting Bull's speech, hating the system, hating what it does to others, hating what it does to ourselves. And then, somewhere on the way to the surface, the speech gets translated from our native tongue into English, into the "friendly, courteous speech" that has been prepared for us, and that we now prepare for ourselves. And so we give that courteous speech, and we laugh, and we smile, never perhaps noticing how closely a smile sometimes resembles a grimace. And what about the rage? It gets shunted, turned anywhere but at the source. And when it emerges, we smile. We smile as we lynch the black men, and we smile as we shoot them down. We smile as we shoot the photographs of women legs spread, and we smile as we look at them on our computers. We smile as we deforest the land and vacuum the oceans. We smile, we smile, we smile, never able to see the source of our hatred, never seeing even that the hate exists.

EXPANDING THE FRONTIER

THE OPPRESSED SUFFER
FROM THE DUALITY WHICH
HAS ESTABLISHED ITSELF IN
THEIR INNERMOST BEING.
THEY DISCOVER THAT WITH-
OUT FREEDOM THEY CANNOT
EXIST AUTHENTICALLY. YET,
ALTHOUGH THEY DESIRE
AUTHENTIC EXISTENCE, THEY
FEAR IT. THEY ARE AT ONE AND
THE SAME TIME THEMSELVES
AND THE OPPRESSOR
WHOSE CONSCIOUSNESS
THEY HAVE INTERNALIZED.

PAULO FREIRE

THE VIEW FROM
THE INSIDE

FROM THE PERSPECTIVE of the already metabolized, there would be, let's say, four classes of people, each of which must, if the system is to perpetuate itself, be treated far differently from each other. The first is the rulers, those whose job it is these days to appear very much like human beings as they serve the inhuman ends of the maximization of production, to smile as they convert the living to the dead, first psychically, and then in the physical world. Smiles have not always been part of their job description. At one point, not even that long ago, autocrats were simply autocrats—think of Stalin, for example—but that type of enforcement is expensive, only resorted to when ideology is insufficient to allow contempt to remain contempt and not turn over into outright hatred. Another way to say this is that this form of governance is most necessary when the mass of people have not been sufficiently metabolized—*worked over* would be another way to put it—to not resist, to cause them to give up hope of another way of being, or, best of all, to believe that no other way of being has ever existed. Naked force is the form of governance typically perpetrated at the frontier (and the frontier need not be far from home, if even the homebound exploited have been insufficiently inculcated) where straightforward conquest is the order of the day. Naked force is especially necessary where land is plentiful, meaning that, self-sufficiency is feasible, meaning that, human beings are human beings, meaning it will take a sword or gun to compel them to work for you. Naked force on the part of the governors is not so necessary where land (and self-sufficiency) are more scarce, or when people have come to believe that title to land is more than a convenient (for those who hold title) legal fiction.

Far more efficient for repression is what we've got in the United States, where the second class, the majority of those who labor so the decent white men may enjoy the comforts and elegancies of life, have bought into the system of repression, to the point where they no longer see themselves as repressed. They have by this point become self-regulating, not wanting to seem deviant, pathological, a blight on society. Within our culture there are tremendous pressures on people to be "high-functioning," to be "productive," to "realize their potential." When I finished my degree in physics, which I did not enjoy, then bailed partway through a graduate degree in economics, which I enjoyed just as little, and took up beekeeping, the father of one of my friends decried the waste of my potential. Never mind that I was happy. When he later learned I was a writer, he was mollified. At least I was, in his worldview, producing.

Another way to say all of this is that those in power—and, remember, those in power are not really the point, because they, too, are serving an ideology, and are essentially as replaceable as any of the rest of us in this mass-produced machine culture—have no need to hate us or to do us violence, because we are not resisting, and, in-

THE VIEW FROM INSIDE

deed, are helping them along. If you don't believe me, step far enough out of line, and we'll talk again, maybe in one of my creative writing classes.

This internalization of the goals and motivations and modes of perceiving and experiencing of those whose emphasis is on production, the civilized, the decent white men, means that we live under a tyranny more absolute and more dangerous than that of any dictator who has ever lived. It is the tyranny of an internalized and eventually self-imposed idea, or a cluster of ideas, that take precedence over everything.

I talked to George Ritzer about the cluster of ideas governing production in the modern world, which is to say governing the modern world, which is to say dehumanizing humans and destroying the *real* world. He calls these ideas *McDonaldization*, after the fast-food restaurant that has come to stand for so much of what is wrong with our culture, and he has written of these ideas not as something new, but, rather, "the culmination of a series of rationalization processes that have been accumulating throughout the twentieth century."

I asked him what *McDonaldization* is.

He said, "It's the process by which the principles of the fast-food restaurant—efficiency, predictability, calculability, and control through nonhuman technology—are coming to affect more and more sectors of society in more and more parts of the world."

He took them one at a time.

"Efficiency. The fast-food model offers, or at least appears to offer, an efficient way to get from being hungry to being full. You drive up, grab a meal, and go. Workers, too, are supposed to be efficient, following steps in predesigned processes overseen by managers. Even the fact that McDonald's sells hamburgers has to do with efficiency: Ray Kroc toyed with alternatives before settling on burgers as his main product. Hot dogs, for example, were too complicated, because they come in too many varieties. And there's only one way to cook a burger: grill it. A central means of increasing efficiency is the limitation of choice.

"Predictability. McDonald's and other McDonaldized systems certainly offer that: For all intents and purposes, an Egg McMuffin in New York will be the same as an Egg McMuffin in Chicago. Customers can expect no surprises, either pleasant or particularly unpleasant. Workers, too, behave in predictable ways. Many McDonaldized systems have actual scripts for their workers to follow. Customers, too, end up behaving in predictable ways.

"Calculability. The emphasis is on the quantifiable—size of portions, cost, time of delivery—as opposed to quality. This, too, carries over to the workers, who are judged generally on how quickly they accomplish specific tasks, and not on the quality of their work.

"Control through nonhuman technology. Because the greatest source of uncertainty, unpredictability, and inefficiency in any rationalizing system is people—those who work in it or those served by it—strong efforts have to be made to control both customers and employees. Customers are controlled through the entire process: Lines, limited menus, uncomfortable seats all lead diners to do what management wants them to do—eat quickly and leave. And, of course, wherever possible, these systems substitute nonhuman technologies for human workers, all in the service of cutting costs, and in the service of predictability: A worker might leave off the pickles or special sauce, or put too few or too many french fries in a bag; it's much better to get a machine to do it."

As he spoke, I was thinking not just of McDonald's, but of how these processes are central to our whole culture.

"These principles have been in existence and have been employed widely for many years or decades, perhaps even centuries," he continued. "Many of them can be traced to ancient history. Others are traced more directly to early capitalism. Certainly if you look just at the twentieth century, you have Henry Ford and the automobile assembly line, which was an effort to produce automobiles in a highly rational way: How do you produce automobiles most efficiently? How do you produce predictable automobiles, so they're exactly the same, time after time after time? How do you employ

THE VIEW FROM INSIDE

more and more nonhuman technologies? In fact the assembly line *was* the new nonhuman technology. How do you come to increasingly emphasize the quantifiable in the production process?"

The quantifiable. Such a simple word. Quantity. A number. A digit equal to all other digits. Not equivalent. Not similar. Not sharing a few qualities. Equal. The same.

The emphasis on the quantifiable, on predictability, is important because no living thing is the same as any other living thing. Nothing in nature is the same as anything else in nature. No person is the same as any other person. Only machines are supposed to be the same. And people who have been trained to be machines. To emphasize the quantifiable is to emphasize the routine, the repeatable, the machinelike. It is to deemphasize the spontaneous, the living. To emphasize the quantifiable is to emphasize the inhuman. It is to deemphasize the human.

"At the same time Ford was implementing these dimensions of McDonaldization or rationalization into the automobile industry assembly line, Frederick W. Taylor was articulating his famous notion of scientific management: How do you study workers and then routinize and systematize what they do so that workers operate in an efficient, predictable, calculable kind of way? How do you play with technologies to achieve those ends?"

He paused a moment, then continued, "The point is that McDonald's didn't really create anything new. Instead it took a series of principles that were quite widely disseminated in society, especially in the realm of production, and began to apply them to the realm of consumption. *That* was the real McDonald's revolution."

I told him it horrifies me that anyone would think that routinizing work—or consumption, or anything else—is a good thing. It has always made me sad to see an older person working at McDonald's, or, more recently, Wal-Mart. Any place like that. When I was younger, I thought this had to do with seeing an older person working at all, but, in my twenties, I realized I never feel this way when I see an old farmer. My sorrow, it came clear to me, has to do with the machinelike quality of the work. It's bad enough

THE CULTURE OF MAKE BELIEVE

when kids are forced to be cogs, but it breaks my heart when it's someone who's sixty.

Ritzer responded, "I think the key issue here is creativity. The notion you're operating with—and the notion we typically operate with—is that work should involve creativity. Cooking should involve creativity. Even consumption should involve creativity. But what Ford and Taylor did in the work world, what Ray Kroc did in McDonald's, and what is broadly done now in the world of consumption, is to limit—if not totally eliminate—creativity. No creativity is required of the person who works on an automobile assembly line. No creativity is required of the person who works behind the counter at McDonald's."

No creativity is required of the slave, I thought.

He was still speaking. "It seems to me that what's bothersome to you, especially about older people, is this attempt to limit their creativity, to constrain them, to force them to operate the way the system wants them to operate, and also to operate—and this is built into all these systems—with only a small portion of their capacities. I mean, the guy who puts the hubcap on the car every thirty seconds as the car goes by can obviously do a lot more than that, but the owners of automobile assembly lines say, in action if not in words, 'You are in effect just an extension of the machine, an automaton, and we simply want you to use that one aspect of all of your capacities to do that single job.' The same thing applies to the people who work behind the counters at fast-food restaurants, whether they're old or young. They're greatly limited in terms of the range of their full capacities that they're permitted to use on the job. In fact, people who try to be creative on the job are likely to get fired, because they are, from the point of view of the system, more likely to mess things up. That leads to one of the irrationalities of all this rationality: The system—a nonliving thing, an idea, even—has priority over living beings, over individual workers. The same constraints apply to the consumer. Picture this: You walk into McDonald's, and say, 'I'd like a Big Mac, but I want it cooked rare, and I'd like the tomatoes in quarters instead of slices.' The system will break down.

THE VIEW FROM INSIDE

It cannot, will not, accommodate even that level of creativity on the part of the consumer."

·   ·   ·

Our current system of production cannot survive creativity. It cannot survive life being life. It cannot survive humans being humans. It cannot survive each of us simply being who we are. In order for civilization to continue, we must each be tweaked, torn, our psyches twisted to conform to a social reality based on exploitation, or, failing that, our bodies broken, burned, hanged from trees as warnings to others who may otherwise be tempted to refuse to become one of those living dead who value property and production over life. The system cannot survive without each of us sacrificing our humanity and our lives to the goal and the god of production, wasting our lives in quiet desperation, or for those beyond the frontier—the non-White, or even those like the Irish immigrants who wished to be White even to their premature dying gasp—slaving away lives to a grave that may sometimes be a welcome rest after a time of too much toil. The system of production cannot survive if we so much as perceive the diversity that surrounds us, much less experience it, and much less if we shake off our identification with our Whiteness and identify instead with living individuals. For our system of production is, despite its awful momentum, extraordinarily fragile. All it would take to bring it to a halt is creativity, *persistent* creativity.

By *creativity* I do not mean the sort of feeble and febrile cleverness rewarded by our culture, where people beat a path to the door of someone who builds a better mouse- or mantrap—A more efficient way to convert the living to the dead—although, within our mind-set, that sort of cleverness is the kind of mock creativity most often rewarded. But, instead, by creativity, I mean a remembering and realizing—making real—the full range of human possibilities in the service of creation and life. What I'm suggesting is a refusal to have one's own particularity dulled or denied, or, rather, a refusal to hand it over in exchange for mass-produced commodities—the so-called comforts and elegancies—for which we sell our birthrights as living, feeling, empathic human beings.

Forget the rulers. The system of production could not long survive if those of us who are White—light-skinned or no—renounced our Whiteness and reclaimed our ability to perceive ourselves and others as individuals worthy of respect and consideration.

Of course, it's not so easy. If enough of us renounce our Whiteness so that the ability of the remaining Whites to exploit us is threatened, some of us—many of us—will be killed, often spectacularly, in an attempt to terrorize the rest of us back into docility.

■   ■   ■

The Klan of the 1920s was severely damaged by the actions of one woman, who refused to submit. After the congressional investigations, the Klan continued to grow. By 1924, it had four million members. It controlled several states, most notably, for this story, Indiana, where a full 10 percent of the state's residents were Klan members. The Grand Dragon of that state, David Curtis Stephenson, called, by most, Steve, had declared, "I did not sell the Klan in Indiana on hatreds—that is not my way. I sold the Klan on Americanism, on reform." That is to say, the Klan represented what we would now recognize as the so-called Christian right. Indeed, even more so than in other states, nearly every fundamentalist minister in the state helped to spread the gospel of the Klan. Two of the Klan's most popular marching songs were "Onward Christian Soldiers" (marching off to war) and "Give Me That Old Time Religion." Then, as now, rhetoric aside, the Klan was virulently anti-everything-but-old-time-Americanism. According to the Klan, for example, Catholics were going to take over the state. The sewer system beneath Notre Dame was filled with guns and explosives, ready for the coup. The pope himself was planning to move the Vatican to Indiana. This rumor was taken seriously enough that, at one point, nearly fifteen hundred

THE VIEW FROM INSIDE

Klansmen—having been told the day before to "Watch the trains!" because the pope "may even be on the northbound train tomorrow! He may!"—stormed the northbound *Monon* in an attempt to lynch the pope. The only passenger was a corset salesman, who was finally able to convince the Klansmen that not even the pope would carry so many corsets.

Soon enough, the Klan took over governance of Indiana, as it had taken over governance of other states. A journalist called the Klan "the most effective political organization the country has ever seen." (The journalist was evidently unaware of corporations and political parties, but, his point stands, and still stands today, as we think again of the Christian right.) In 1924, the Klan controlled the governor, the mayor of Indianapolis and his entire city council, the majority of both the House and Senate, mayors, sheriffs, and complete school boards.

Now, to the woman. Her name was Madge Oberholtzer, and, at twenty-eight, she lived with her parents, just a few blocks from where Steve lived. They met at the inaugural banquet for the new governor, and Steve immediately took a shine to her (feeling, perhaps, the same way that James Glover had felt on seeing Spokane Falls: enchanted, overwhelmed with the beauty and grandeur of everything he saw, lying just as nature had made it, with nothing to mar its virgin glory, and, so, determining that he would possess it). It must be said, by the way, that although Steve and the Klansmen represented themselves as chaste and sober, even setting up an organization called the Horsethief Detectives that would indiscriminately stop and search men and women for liquor, causing in one seventeen-month period more than three thousand prohibition cases to be brought to trial, the reality was far different. Oftentimes the Detectives themselves would down the confiscated alcohol, and it was noted that at Steve's parties, alcohol "flowed as freely as water." So did sex; chastity was never much in evidence at these get-togethers.

Madge did not reciprocate Steve's feelings. Her job, however, as manager of the state-sponsored Young People's Reading Club, was about to be terminated as a result of a bill being debated in the

House. Steve had the bill killed in committee. Grateful, Madge went to Steve's house for dinner, then later to a party (which Steve cleaned up for her benefit).

Then, one night, Madge came home from work to learn that Steve had been calling for her all day. She called back, and learned Steve urgently wanted to see her, and would send along his driver, a man named Gentry. Madge never returned home that night, and didn't arrive until two days later, when a strange man knocked on her parents' door, then carried her in. He said she'd been in a terrible car accident, then left. A doctor was sent for, and when he arrived he checked her for broken bones. There were none. He did, however, find bruises all over her body, including some the size of dinner plates on her hip and buttock. He also found places where her skin had been forcibly torn off. Her cheek and breast were ripped open. Part of her genitals had been pulled off. She knew she was dying, and told the story of what had happened.

When she'd arrived at Steve's, he'd been drinking with a body-guard. She realized no one else was in the house, and said she wanted to go home. But the three men (Steve, the bodyguard, and Gentry, who was also a bodyguard) forced her to drink with them. Unused to alcohol, she became ill. She again insisted she wanted to go home. Steve told her he loved her more than anyone he'd ever loved, and said she was going to Chicago with him. His bags were packed, and each of the men carried pistols. The bodyguard dropped them off at the station, and Steve, Madge, and Gentry shared a drawing room. When Gentry climbed into the top berth, Steve tore Madge's dress from her, then forced her onto the lower berth. He undressed, then pinned her there. She screamed.

What followed was the prototypical act of civilization. Mistaking hatred for affection, Steve consumed the subject-turned-object he professed to love. I do not mean this figuratively, drawing a veil over the act of rape by using the word *consumption*. In Madge's words: "He chewed me all over my body, bit my neck and face, chewed my tongue, chewed my breasts until they bled, my back, my legs, my ankles, and mutilated me all over my body." She passed out, not to

THE VIEW FROM INSIDE

awaken till the next morning, when the train had stopped, still in Indiana. For obvious reasons, Steve decided not to transport her across the state line. She asked him to shoot her. He put the gun to her ribs, but didn't pull the trigger. He registered them at a hotel, then went to sleep. She put the gun to his head, but, in an act unfortunately all too prototypical for the response all of us have to civilization, could not pull the trigger herself. This failure of nerve cost her her life.

I suppose she could have gone along with the plans that had been made for her by one who was rich and powerful. So many of us do. But, instead, when Steve awoke, she asked if she could go to buy a hat—anything to get out of the room—and, while she was at the store, snuck off to buy mercuric chloride tablets. Back in the room, she poisoned herself, hoping Steve would take her to the hospital, where she could tell the police what had happened. He said he would take her, but only if she registered as his wife. She refused. They drove her back to her hometown, with her vomiting in the backseat the whole way. She begged to see a doctor. They would not take her. "I'll have the law on you," she cried.

"I am the law," he responded.

They got home that evening, but, because Madge's mother was on the porch, and Steve did not want to be seen, they drove on by. At Steve's house, he told her she would stay there till she married him, and then, and this is the last thing he told her, in words again all too emblematic of what we are told daily by the culture, "You must forget this, Madge. What's done is done."

The next morning, she was taken home, where she had witnessed what had happened and, soon after, died.

Steve was found guilty of second-degree murder, then sentenced to life imprisonment. He wasn't too worried, counting, as he did, upon a gubernatorial pardon. The pardon, however, wasn't forthcoming, and here is how the Klan suffered for it. Already the Klan in Indiana had shrunk to one-twentieth of its former size, in part because many had fled in disgust at this maltreatment of a (Protestant white) woman. But when Steve had put people in power, he'd kept a paper trail of written IOUs, e.g., "In return for the political support of D.C. Stephenson, in the event I am elected Mayor of Indianapolis, Indiana, I promise not to appoint any person as a member of the board of public works without they first have the endorsement of D.C. Stephenson." Many Indiana politicians went to prison. Another congressional investigation followed. This time it cost the Klan popularity, perhaps because it focused on the purchase of political influence by a noncorporate organization, as opposed to the previous investigation's focus, on atrocities committed against those not White.

Of course, Madge's resistance to marrying Steve did not by itself bring down the Klan. There were other factors, too, among them the Scopes Monkey Trial, which allowed evolution to be taught in schools. Failing to ban the teaching of evolution, the Klan decided to lobby, at least, for the inclusion of creationism as an alternative. It is a measure of the degree to which Klan values have been incorporated into mainstream politics that in the 1920s this Klan solution "came to nothing," whereas now it is pushed by some of the most powerful politicians in the country.

But the main reason for the Klan's downfall was, I think, an economic boom in the mid-twenties. Because, on a finite planet, all economic activity must be a zero-sum game, and, because, within our culture economic production at base consists of the exploitation of human and nonhuman resources (this book, for example, could not be printed except at the expense of the trees whose bodies went, presumably unwillingly, into its production), another way to say that one group's or country's economy undergoes a boom is to simply state that they are more successful than normal, exploiting some other group of humans or nonhumans. The United States had, by this time, of course, begun to fully come into its own as an imperial power outside its borders (in addition to the internal imperialism, especially characterizing Manifest Destiny and race-based slavery, but which continues also to this day, through corporate exploitation of American citizens and depletion of resources), with colonies ringing the planet from Africa to South

America to Asia, and with American-based corporations exploiting resources worldwide. The point is that the expanding wave of hate had moved outward. Remember, contempt rolls over into outright hatred generally when entitlement either is at the point of first being emplaced (conquest), or when it is threatened. When an empire is rolling along—when an economy booms—the mass of metabolized citizens inside the borders of Whiteness will find no real reason to form or join hate groups. Contempt will serve them just fine. The KKK flourished when the end of World War I brought the soldiers home to find jobs that no longer existed when the wartime economy ceased, and folded with the end of the recession. The fact that Germany's post–World War I depression lasted much longer than that in the United States goes a long way toward explaining how the Klan—so much stronger than the National Socialists in the mid-1920s, and banging essentially the same drum—fizzled, while the Nazis did not.

Although the 1920s version of the Klan came down, the news regarding this is not so sanguine as it may seem. It's crucial to the personal part of the story that Madge was white (and probably White). Many books about the Klan in the 1920s mention Madge Oberholtzer, as do quite a few Web sites (many of which attack her character instead of Steve's, and point out that many contemporary newspapers did the same), but, at the same time that she was wasting away at home, a black man was lynched in Waverly, Virginia. I've seen him referenced in precisely zero books, and a two-hour search of the Web brought me only one phrase about him: "1 unidentified black man lynched Waverly Virginia March 20 1925." This man was murdered as surely as she, but we will never know his name, his loves, his fears, nor even the reason for his death, which might have been that he committed some heinous outrage, or it might have been that he made love to a white woman, or that he simply walked next to her, or that he did not sell his land to white men for less than its value, or that he did not work for them for free. It may have been that he attempted to prevent a white man from consuming a woman he loved. We will never know how he died, nor his last thoughts. And his death did not bring down the Klan. His death was not even particularly noticed by history.

The second reason I'm not very sanguine about the way the Klan dwindled in the 1920s has to do with the public's outrage over the IOUs that Steve kept, and the role this played in the Klan's downfall. It is a measure of the degree to which we are blind to the power of corporations—and to the needs of production—that this sort of quid pro quo between politicians and businesspeople is not only routine but inevitably fails to raise the sort of outrage necessary to bring down these institutions. This was true, as we've seen, in the days of Morgan, and it's true today. To provide two examples, probably unnecessary, since our acceptance of the tight working relationship between industry and government is so complete, current vice president Dick Cheney worked [*sic*] for five years as the CEO of Halliburton Company, a huge oil services firm. In addition to his regular salary, when Cheney decided to retire from one form of service to the firm and attempted to be elected to another, as vice president, the company gave him a $33.7 million retirement gift. Then, in August 2000, the company gave him another $7.6 million in stock options he was not entitled to receive. Out of the kindness of its corporate heart, the company also gave him a further $26.1 million in stock options. The gifts are, of course, already affecting policy. In contradistinction to those who sold their favors to the Klan, Cheney will probably not go to prison. Closer to home, just today I read in the newspaper that before his last election, California's energy czar, who is presiding over the fiasco we all had so much fun discussing in the taxi, received nearly $100,000 from the corporations he is now supposed to oversee. Politicians come cheaper in California than in D.C., even though in both places they can be bought off the shelf, with no need to special-order.

Another reason I don't see the downfall of the Klan in the 1920s as a sign for hope is that, as was true for the end of chattel slavery in the United States, it had more to do with shifts in economic conditions than any fundamental change in the hate-inducing competition and exploitation on which our culture is based. So

THE VIEW FROM INSIDE

long as these framing conditions do not change, we can expect only that hate will change its manifestations to keep up with the times, not that it will wither. Indeed, as I've already mentioned, most of the goals of the KKK of the 1920s have at the very least survived to inform the Christian right of today, and, more realistically, to shape the mainstream of American politics. Further, the KKK survives to this day and will survive into the foreseeable future, renewing itself during economic downturns and other times of social adjustment, always there to channel rage onto those even more powerless than the Klan members themselves. This happened in the 1940s through 1960s, as blacks were, to some slight degree, brought into the fold of Americanism (as the frontier of overt exploitation moved beyond them to the rest of the world, as DuBois seemed to be suggesting). And it happened again from the 1970s to the present, as real wages for American workers have fallen now for three decades, as feds and agricorporations have destroyed the farm economy in the heartland of this country, and as factories have moved overseas. As writer, filmmaker, and activist Michael Moore put it, the Michigan militia are the unemployed arm of the United Auto Workers. As the American economy continues to decay, or, rather, as conditions for American citizens continue to decay (in the modern American version of a statement by a Brazilian general about conditions in that country: "The economy is doing very well. The people, very badly") I've no doubt that formalized hate groups will continue to articulate and act out a rage at this erosion of entitlement. And who could blame them? It's not very fun to have one's standard of living reduced or threatened, one's opportunities diminished or foreclosed. It's simply true that the lifestyle of Americans cannot continue indefinitely on a finite planet. We will feel the pinch as ecological systems collapse (though, of course, the rich will suffer little, and few of us even at the fringes of Whiteness will suffer with the same finality as those who—human and nonhuman alike—are starving to death at this moment because of our cultural imperatives, and the consequent processes of ongoing ecological collapse). That pinch will make many of us unhappy. It will cause many of us to lash out at those we perceive as causing the pain. Unfortunately, we will, more likely than not, lash out against the wrong targets. It is also simply true that Americans have very real reasons to be outraged by the ways that distant institutions—corporate and governmental, insofar as real distinctions exist between them—increasingly control their lives. This outrage will be expressed, whether against the self, through various forms of internalized violence, or against others, through a violence that, once again, unfortunately, will almost undoubtedly target those even more miserable than they are.

Today, night riders do not often wear white robes as they visit the homes of uppity blacks in the American South, nor do they pull these blacks out of their homes and hang them. Instead, an equivalent force can be found wearing U.S.-made camo fatigues, shooting union leaders and uppity Indians with U.S.-made guns in Colombia. They can be found beating union organizers at factories owned by U.S.-based corporations in Mexico. They shoot indigenous peoples in Nigeria who resist despoliation of their land by oil companies. With U.S. assistance and U.S. weapons (or, sometimes, corporate assistance and corporate weapons), they form death squads and kill uppity non-Whites in Central and South America, in Africa, in Southeast Asia, in the Pacific, in Oceania. Between five hundred thousand and a million people were murdered at CIA urging and with CIA assistance just in Indonesia during the late 1960s. Why? Because the Indonesians did not vote the way the CIA—and this was no rogue CIA, but, instead, represented the corporate and governmental interests of the United States—wanted them to. Similar stories can be told in the Congo, Guatemala, Iran, Chile. Anywhere in the world that people do not vote the way the U.S. government and the corporations it serves want them to. The KKK of the 1860s had as its purpose the intimidation of the exploited into not exercising political, social, or economic autonomy. Death squads today—U.S.-backed and -funded death squads—have precisely this same function. The only reason this doesn't happen so much at home is because we've been tamed.

THE VIEW FROM INSIDE

Or, is it true that it doesn't happen at home? Perhaps, now, instead of members of the KKK wearing white robes while they teach people of color to stay in their place, those whose job it is to keep the rabble in line wear the blue or green or black of police uniforms. Why should the Klan bother to break down the doors of African Americans when SWAT teams will do it far more efficiently, and at taxpayer expense?

Imagine this. You're in Fresno, California. You are a person of color. It's past midnight, and you step onto your porch for one last breath of cool evening air before bed. You see some of your neighbors outside of their homes, too. You smile and wave, but you don't think they see you. In any case they don't respond. Then you think you see a slight movement in the shadows. Another movement confirms the first. In the distance, you hear the sound of a helicopter, and you think, "Oh, Lord, not again." The chopper roars up, and a spotlight turns the scene into day. You see dozens of white men in formation, wearing combat boots and black body armor, carrying submachine guns. You pray they're not coming for you.

Then, it starts. Flash-bang grenades are thrown, German shepherds unleashed. White men shout, "Get down! Get the fuck down!" They shoot your neighbor's dog. Bam. Bam. Bam. Three shots to the chest. An armored personnel carrier wheels around the corner, and more armored men jump out. You start to move back into your home, when one of the men sees you. He shouts, "Stay where you are, motherfucker! Don't fucking move!" You do what the man says. You know that he's got the guns, and you know that he is the law. You treat him with a deference that your grandfathers and grandmothers understood, a deference that has permeated to your bones. You do not look him in the eye. You call him sir. You do not want him to take you away.

You are in Tacoma, Washington. You are a person of color. It's past midnight, and you step onto your porch for one last breath of cool evening air before bed. You see those same movements, see them confirmed, hear those same choppers, see the same uniforms. You, too, pray they're not coming for you.

THE CULTURE OF MAKE BELIEVE

You're in Compton, California, Chapel Hill, North Carolina, or New York City. You are a person of color standing outside your home. You see the dazzle and hear the explosions of the flash-bang grenades, smell the tear gas, your eyes water from the pepper, and you ask yourself, "Is this America?"

You answer your own question: Yes, it is.

THE VIEW FROM INSIDE

AS THE GENERATIONS PASS THEY GROW WORSE.

A TIME WILL COME WHEN THEY HAVE GROWN SO

WICKED THAT THEY WILL WORSHIP POWER; MIGHT

WILL BE RIGHT TO THEM AND REVERENCE FOR THE

GOOD WILL CEASE TO BE. AT LAST, WHEN NO MAN IS

ANGRY ANY MORE AT WRONGDOING OR FEELS SHAME

IN THE PRESENCE OF THE MISERABLE, ZEUS WILL DE-

STROY THEM TOO. AND YET EVEN THEN SOMETHING MIGHT

BE DONE, IF ONLY THE COMMON PEOPLE WOULD RISE

AND PUT DOWN RULERS THAT OPPRESS THEM.

GREEK MYTH ON THE IRON AGE

THE CLOSING
OF THE IRON
CAGE

THIS BRINGS US TO THE THIRD CLASS OF PEOPLE, and how they must be treated by the system. If class one is the rulers, and class two is the laborers, that is, the people who've bought into (I mean this literally) the system, the third class is those who either do not buy into the system or who are unable to. They are the ones with nothing to lose. They are the ones radical criminologist Steven Spritzer calls "social dynamite." They are the ones who feel they're owed more by the system or who believe the system must be destroyed, the ones with the potential to do something about it, the ones who could possibly resist, organized or alone. They are the ones who, in the 1870s, would have refused to let themselves be whipped, and because of that would have been hanged. After World War I, they might have refused to take off their uniforms, and for that they might have been beaten to death. They're the ones who see through the myth of egalitarianism, see through the myths of social mobility and opportunity. They are the ones who, like Ham, see the social structure for what it is.

How do you deal with them? Christian Parenti put it well. "Controlling them requires both a defensive policy of containment and aggressive policy of direct attack and active destabilization. They are contained and crushed, confined to the ghetto, demoralized and pilloried in warehouse public schools, demonized by a lurid media, sent to prison, and at times dispatched by lethal injection or police bullets. This is the class—or more accurately the caste, because they are increasingly people of color—which must be constantly undermined, divided, intimidated, attacked, discredited, and ultimately kept in check with what Fanon called the 'language of naked force.'"

Those in power have always known that the way to win battles, as Confederate general Nathan Bedford Forrest put it, is to "Get there first with the most." This is no less true in battles for the mind as it is in battles for physical territory. It's far more efficient to repress people before they begin to exercise any sort of political freedom, before they begin to even perceive the system might be unfair, than it is to wait until the deferred dream explodes. What this means today is that it's far more efficient—expensive as incarceration might be—to lock up poor people (or non-Whites) before they have a chance to become politically active, or revolutionary. By the time they gain any sort of full political awareness (and many of my students in prison are among the most politically astute people I've ever met) they're already locked away, in some cases for the rest of their lives.

Let me put all of this a different way. For some people, the system uses carrots and a propaganda based on inclusivity and a belief in rights: I like my computer, my stereo and CD collection, my shelves full of books. I like going to my mom's and watching baseball games on her television. I like my inalienable rights to the property where I

THE CLOSING OF THE IRON CAGE

live. And if I owned property somewhere else, even if I never saw it, why, I'd like my inalienable rights over that, as well.

For others, the system uses force, and a propaganda based on terror. If group one is kept in line through inane and insane luxuries, and by a propaganda that, at one time, told them they ruled by the divine right of kings, but now tells them they rule by the divine right of money (or because *that's just the way things are*), and group two is kept in line through propaganda tying self-worth to industrial productivity (which means tying identity to the very system that exploits them), as well as the provision of enough comforts and elegancies to keep them in the game, then group three is kept in line through the use of force, and, more importantly, by the spectacle of terror. You don't need to see many of your neighbors castrated, burned to death, or hanged before you decide that you might just be better off not voting, and that, the next time you sell your crops, it would probably be a good idea to take whatever the white man offers. Similarly, you don't need to see many of your people's villages burned before you realize your best chance to live free might be to accept whatever treaty the white man offers for you to give up the land where your ancestors have lived since the beginning of the world, and move west, away from him, his guns, and his torches. And you needn't see many of your neighbors pulled from their beds and sent to prison, some for the rest of their lives (*three strikes, boy, and you're out*) before you decide that McDonald's just might be your kind of place to work, indeed, it might even be, you say with more of a grimace than a smile, a hap-hap-happy place.

∎   ∎   ∎

I asked George Ritzer what's wrong with rationalization, in the sense that he uses the term.

"The short answer," he said, "is that rational systems carry with them a series of irrational consequences. In some senses those irrational consequences are the opposite of the basic principles, so what's supposed to be an efficient system often ends up being quite inefficient. You drive ten miles and wait in line in order to get fast food. If you include driving time it would often be much quicker to cook a meal at home than to pile in a car, drive to McDonald's, and wait in line."

Efficiency. One of the chief rationales used by the civilized to buttress the killing of indigenous peoples and the stealing of their land has always been to say that the indigenous are inefficient in their use of land. Indeed, they have often been accused of not using the land at all. In the Supreme Court decision, where he stated that "discovery gave title . . . which title might be consummated by possession," John Marshall also remarked that to "leave them [Indians] in possession of their country, was to leave the country a wilderness." The irony of us perceiving our economic and social system as efficient as we systematically poison ourselves and destroy our land base has never escaped me. The question becomes: efficient at what? The answer of course leads us back to the question of precisely what happens in the process of industrial production.

"There's a broader sense of irrationality of rationality," he said, "which comes down, I think most importantly, to dehumanization. These are dehumanizing or antihuman kinds of settings. And another of the irrationalities of rationality is what I call, following Max Weber, the disenchantment of the world. The magic, the mystery, the religious qualities of the world, are progressively challenged in a progressively rationalized world, and so for Weber and for me progressive rationalization brings with it disenchantment, desacralization, whatever you want to call it. Our science and our bureaucratic social organizations have gradually and systematically stripped the natural world both of its magical properties and of its capacity for meaning."

We have also stripped magic and meaning from ourselves, I thought.

"Or perhaps they've stripped us of our capacity to perceive the magic and meaning that inheres."

I thought about the consequences of this stripping away of meaning. It's another form of that objectification I've been trying to get at in this book, a turning of everyone in the world from a You to an It. It seems to me that this stripping away can lead only to one end: the

THE CLOSING OF THE IRON CAGE

eradication of life. To psychologically convert the living to the dead through this process of rationalization is the big step. Revving the chainsaw, tearing off the mountaintop, pulling the gun's trigger, dropping the crystals of Zyklon B: these, then, become mere technical activities, forming only the final parts of the equation. I asked how all this happens.

"We can take the elements of rationalization again one by one. Efficiency leaves no room for the enchanted. Anything that's magical, mysterious, fantastic, dreamy, is apt to be inefficient. Furthermore, enchanted systems are often complex, and involve highly convoluted means to whatever ends are involved. And they may very well have no obvious ends at all. By definition, efficient systems don't allow meanderings. Thus, designers of efficient systems try to eliminate as many of the preconditions for enchantment as possible."

I thought again of life, which has no obvious end, except the process of enjoying this particular moment in this particular place, and the joy of meandering. I'm in no hurry to reach the end point of my life, nor to wish away any of the time in between. I don't want to live efficiently, nor cause others to. I want to live broadly, deeply, richly, with resonance, in full enjoyment of my own particular life.

"We can make essentially the same arguments for calculability. How do you quantify the enchanted? Since it cannot be readily quantified, it's at best ignored, and quite often eliminated when encountered at all.

"No characteristic of rationalization is more inimical to enchantment than predictability. All of these enchanted experiences of magic, fantasy, or dream are almost by definition unpredictable. As for the other characteristics of rationalized systems, control and nonhuman technologies are absolutely inimical to any feeling of enchantment. Fantasy, dreams, and so on cannot be subjected to external controls; indeed, autonomy is much of what gives them their enchanted quality."

We looked at each other across the coffee table in his living room. I sat in a comfortable chair. He sat on an overstuffed couch. Outside, the day was warm, with just a touch of November crispness.

THE CULTURE OF MAKE BELIEVE

The leaves on the trees and on the ground were yellow, and they blew in the wind. "And having disenchanted the world," I said, "or our perception of the world, our system then offers us a sort of ironic reenchantment, a simulated reenchantment. . . ."

"That's what it is," he said.

I thought of the spectacles created by our culture that dazzle us day by day. I thought of Juvenal's line about bread and circuses, that "the people, who once had the power to grant . . . everything, now holds itself back and anxiously desires only two things: bread and circuses. 'I hear many men are going to die [in the arena].' 'No doubt. The furnace is huge. . . .'" I thought about R. D. Laing's rules of a dysfunctional family or culture, and how we talk about everything but those things that matter most. I thought about O. J., Lewinski, March Madness, Super Bowls, electoral horse races, the stock market, celebrity marriages (Quick: name six celebs and their marital status; now, name six different plants that live within fifty feet of where you are at this particular moment; now, name six different species that live in your region which have been harmed by civilization; now, give the indigenous name for the place you live.) I thought of so many ways we keep ourselves distracted from the particularity of our lives.

We have a need for enchantment that is as deep and devoted as our need for food and water. Having blinded ourselves to the world's enchantment, we have filled that gap—that was previously filled with relationships—with what Ritzer calls "cathedrals of consumption," which are enchanted enough to dazzle us, yet, at the same time, designed along rational lines. In other words, they are under control, and as such can be used as a means of control.

He said, "I was just in Milan, Italy, where I walked through the Galleria Victorio Emanuele. It's an old-fashioned arcade built in the 1880s, a beautiful structure. In the very center of the arcade, as you would expect (at least these days), there's a McDonald's. And as you exit the arcade, there's a magnificent duomo—a cathedral, a huge church, the ultimate in sacred enchantment. Then directly across the square is another McDonald's. This all led me to reflect: These are *all* means of

THE CLOSING OF THE IRON CAGE

consumption, means to allow people to consume things. . . ."

I thought he meant the consumption of hamburgers on one hand and of religious services on the other. I said I thought there's a difference between McDonald's and a cathedral.

He shook his head. "They're all cathedrals of consumption. It's just that what's being consumed varies. Cathedrals were constructed along highly rationalized lines."

"I'm no fan of Christianity," I said, "but I'm still a little bit uncomfortable lumping . . ."

"Think of Notre Dame."

"Even as a post-Christian," I insisted, "I still feel a sense of awe in a big cathedral. I don't feel the same sense of awe I feel in the natural world, but I still feel *something*."

"That's precisely the point," he said. "All of these human-made settings are designed to create that sense of awe. They're designed to be spectacular. Designed to be awesome. The strip in Las Vegas is in its way awesome, and the major casinos are awesome. They're spectacular. That's what draws people to them. That's what all the cathedrals of consumption share. . . ."

I still wasn't getting it. I said, "When you say cathedrals of consumption, you're including Notre Dame?"

"Yes. The starting point for all of this is the question: How do you draw people? You get people to come by creating a structure which overwhelms them, which wows them, which causes them to throw up their hands and say, 'This is extraordinary and I'm coming back again and again and again.'"

I got it. It's part of the false contract we've signed. What keeps us coming back to civilization? What keeps us from rebelling? What keeps us from murdering our masters in their sleep, and returning to the egalitarian lives we lived throughout so much of human existence? Think about this: The music in grocery stores is chosen to pull consumers through the store. The seats at fast-food restaurants are uncomfortable, not just because those who own corporations don't want to spend money on them, but because they don't want customers to linger. Artificially created settings are designed to accomplish specific purposes. This is true whether we're talking about fast-food restaurants, capitol buildings, or cathedrals. It's true whether the structures we're talking about are physical or social. What do our rationalized social structures draw us to do? How do they enchant us, mesmerize us, draw us in? What magic do they offer if we give up our understanding—and realization—of our relatedness to all other beings? To what larger enchantments do they blind us? And to what ends to they lead us?

Years ago, I was driving in North Idaho, which is beautiful, with my friend, Roianne. We saw a church that had been started and then abandoned, and Roianne said, "It's a good thing they stopped building. How could someone even *think* about building a house of worship that would exclude all this beauty?"

I said to George, "Why should they come to your church, or to your shopping mall, if they have beauty in their own backyards?"

"No human-made spectacle approximates the natural spectacle. But the real attraction of these human-made spectacles is that you can build them the way you want in order to do what you want to people. So a cathedral—and cathedrals really aren't the point here, but instead stand in for so much of our culture—is built in a certain way. . . ."

"To make you feel puny," I said.

"To make you feel puny."

"That's very bad."

"If you bristle at external control over your life, yes, it's very bad. But from the perspective of those in power . . ."

■   ■   ■

I asked Ritzer about something he calls "the code," and quoted something he'd written: "The desire to eat Chicken McNuggets has been manufactured, like all other needs, by the code, the economic system. . . . We do not eat what we need, but what the code tells us we should eat. The code produces our needs (if they can still be called needs when they are manufactured externally)."

THE CLOSING OF THE IRON CAGE

He said, "The code, in the deeper and more subtle sense, is a hidden set of rules that allows us to understand and interpret things in our society. To talk about the code is to get at control at a far deeper level than the control exercised in the design and functioning of a shopping mall or fast-food restaurant, because those latter are a much more structured kind of control. We are controlled at many levels. There's layer after layer of control, and we're unaware of most of them."

Neither of us said anything for a moment. I shifted in my chair.

"We go through life making choices," he said, "but those choices have oftentimes been tightly constrained. Where do you want to go eat? Well, our choices have been limited. What do you want to eat there? Once again, our choices have been limited. And the differences between our various choices are for the most part superficial. Do you want a Taco Bell burrito, or a Big Mac?"

I told him I didn't see how this relates to a code.

He responded, "How have we learned to associate fast-food restaurants with being fast? How have we come to associate them with being fun? How have we come to associate Disney World with fun? How have we come to associate Las Vegas with fun? How did these interpretations get put onto these places and the activities that go on there? We go to these places, and we feel things, and we interpret those feelings, but we may not understand why we have those feelings, nor how we interpret these feelings. Nonetheless, we all interpret things pretty much the same because we all have the same code."

I asked what the code is.

"It's a series of rules and laws that allow us to understand each other. Language, for example. We all possess language, and understand the rules of language which allow us to communicate with each other. But the more general code is the code of behavior. We may not be conscious of that code of behavior, but we know that when we do certain things we'll be in accord with the code, and when we do other kinds of things we won't be in accord with the code. On the simplest level, in some cultures it is acceptable to eat with your mouth open

THE CULTURE OF MAKE BELIEVE

and to smack your lips as you eat. In other cultures that's frowned upon. How do people know this? They're acculturated into the code. Smacking your lips may not be a big deal, but it illustrates the degree to which unspoken codes govern our behavior."

I extrapolated from lip smacking to other examples of the code. I considered the primacy of production, and I considered white antipathy toward people of color. I thought about pornography, and the lenses (psychological and photographic) through which so many men perceive so many women. I thought about the lenses through which so many women perceive themselves. Anorexia. Bulimia. I thought of the billboard I saw in Southern California for breast implants. All of these spring from, and reinforce, the code.

I remembered something I'd learned years ago that taught me much about the power and longevity of social strictures. Many of our swear words—*shit, piss, fuck,* for example—have their origins in the language of the Anglo-Saxons. How did they come to be considered unacceptable in polite society? The words are just sounds; there's nothing inherently noxious about them, and they were perfectly acceptable to Anglo-Saxons. Well, in 1066, William the Conqueror and his troops invaded England from Normandy and beat the shit—in terms of language—out of the Anglo-Saxons. Before then the Anglo-Saxons had been the ruling class. Now, Normans—whose language derived from Latinate roots—were the rulers. Suddenly, if you said words that a year before had been perfectly acceptable, you were considered to be of the lower class. The upper class no longer shat, they defecated. They no longer pissed, they urinated. They no longer fucked, they had intercourse. To use those Anglo-Saxon words would betray one's low class. The point? More than nine hundred and forty years later and several thousand miles away, these words—*shit, piss, fuck*—still carry the weight of the code.

I came back to the conversation in time to hear Ritzer say, "The most powerful system is that which leads people to take hold of their own leashes. That is, the system under which people do what is expected of them without any external control being exerted over them."

THE CLOSING OF THE IRON CAGE

"And," I added, "without any perception on their own part that they're . . ."

". . . being controlled. Less powerful systems are those that have to marshal various kinds of resources—especially police and military—in order to control people. The more visible the mechanisms of control—the more visible the police and military—the less powerful is your society."

Another silence.

He continued. "I'm not talking about a conspiracy here. Instead it's simply a system of rewards. There are a limited number of things that any system rewards, and that people within a system—any kind of system—want. When we talk about our economic system, we're talking about people wanting profit, and more deeply, we're talking about control and power. Now, having control and power as goals—and as requirements—leads to the creation of a series of systems, all of which are set up to maximize profitability, power, and control. When we find ourselves either working with those systems or trapped inside of them, we consciously or unconsciously work to achieve that kind of profitability or control. But even when we're not in those kinds of systems, we may or may not become conscious of the fact that those systems are still exercising that power and control over us."

I said, "It seems to me that the problem isn't that there is a code, as such. All cultures must have codes. All communication involves codes. The question, it seems, always comes down to who benefits."

He answered, "You can't address that question without addressing capitalism."

I mentally substituted the word *civilization*.

"It's clear that, especially with the increasing elimination of alternatives, capitalism is rigged in favor of the haves. We have by some definitions the most successful economic system in the world's history, yet it is a system which benefits a relatively small number of people. The great majority of the people in the world benefit little or nothing by this."

"Far from benefitting," I said, "many are killed."

THE CULTURE OF MAKE BELIEVE

"And just in the United States," he said, "a small number of people have grown incredibly wealthy in this great economic expansion of the 1990s while the vast majority have gained little or nothing. So, who gains from all of this? The people in power, the people who control these systems, the people who own blocks of shares in these systems: they gain. It's part of our mythology in this country—part of our code, if you will—that what is good for capitalism is good for the country."

I continued throughout to substitute *civilization* for *capitalism*, and *the people* for *the country*.

Ritzer is not very optimistic. "The problem is that we have a multitude of parallel processes of rationalization and McDonaldization. In consequence, it's much harder—and getting harder all the time—to tell who the enemy is. And even when we do identify an enemy, it doesn't necessarily do us much good. For example, I think that increasingly around the world McDonald's is seen as an enemy, so anytime anybody wants to protest something, they choose a McDonald's. In Prague, during the protests surrounding the WTO, people trashed McDonald's. And there's that French farmer, Jose Bove, who wanted to protest American power. What target did he choose? McDonald's. When the Serbs wanted to protest American bombings, they trashed a McDonald's. Now, it may be at some point that this kind of opposition will succeed in putting McDonald's out of business. But that will be of no major consequence, because there's Burger King, and Taco Bell, and Kentucky Fried Chicken. Even if you take out all the fast-food restaurants, there still exist many other rationalized systems. And you can't attack them all, because they're not part of one system in any but the lowest common denominator sense. It's a multiheaded hydra, and much more difficult to deal with, for example, than a Hitler. Instead of us being in one big iron cage— the 'iron cage of rationality,' as Weber put it—we're in a bunch of tiny ones, an archipelago of cages, and we move from one to another throughout our lives."

The wind picked up outside, and leaves skittered across his sunny back porch.

THE CLOSING OF THE IRON CAGE

"The problem isn't just the organization called McDonald's. The principles of rationalization are subterranean; they burrow into every sector of our lives, and although they operate in much the same way they may not all *seem* the same. This makes it much more difficult to attack, and in fact leads me to be pretty pessimistic about our future." He paused a long while, before finally saying, "To be honest, I think we'd have much more to be optimistic about if we simply faced a Stalin or a Hitler. At least then we'd know whom to fight."

■   ■   ■

I think the question of knowing whom to fight is only a difficult one for those of us on the inside, that is, in classes one or two, the rulers or the laborers: the Whites. For those on the outside, the targets are, if Sitting Bull's words are any indication, much clearer. The enemy is the whole damn system.

■   ■   ■

Throughout the 1920s and 1930s the United States governments (both nominal and *de facto*, political and corporate) strongly supported Mussolini's Fascist regime in Italy. On the day of Mussolini's coup, which ended Italian democracy, the American ambassador wrote his father, "We are having a fine young revolution here. No danger. Plenty of enthusiasm. We all enjoy it." Fascism was praised by the ambassador as a growing, vibrant party willing to take action against the country's enemies, which included not only socialists, communists, and anarchists (that these would be considered enemies of the people we can take as a given) but also republicans. The ambassador recognized that government by the Fascists meant a dictatorship, but justified the end of democracy by saying that "People like the Italians . . . hunger for strong leadership and enjoy . . . being dramatically governed." As fascist repression became more obvious, the embassy noted with approval that "there has not been a single strike in the whole of Italy" since the end of democracy. President

Hoover's secretary of state Henry Stimson later recalled Mussolini as "a sound and useful leader," and Franklin Roosevelt called him "that admirable Italian gentleman."

J. P. Morgan and Company, controllers of a good portion of the *de facto* government, were even more enthusiastic about Mussolini. Having been in Italy during the coup, Jack Morgan commented, "We had the great satisfaction of seeing Mr. Mussolini's Revolution." Judge Elbert Gary of Morgan-controlled United States Steel thought that perhaps "we, too, need a man like Mussolini." Long after Mussolini's terrorism—including the murder of children—became undeniable, Morgan and Company continued to loan the Fascists hundreds of millions of dollars and to otherwise support the regime. Partner Thomas Lamont became, to use his word, a "missionary" for fascism. Lamont sent a letter through a mutual friend, giving the dictator lessons in public relations: "If Mr. Mussolini declares that parliamentary government is at an end in Italy such a declaration comes as a shock to Anglo-Saxons. If, on the contrary, Mr. Mussolini had explained that the old forms of parliamentary government in Italy had proved futile and had led to inefficient government and chaos; therefore they had to be temporarily suspended and generally reformed, then Anglo-Saxons would understand. Again, when Mr. Mussolini announces that the mayors of interior cities will be appointed by the Fascista government, Anglo-Saxons jump to the natural conclusion that such a step means that the interior cities are to be deprived of all local self-government. If, at the time of such announcement, Mr. Mussolini had explained that in most cases the mayors of the interior cities were simply the appointees and tools of local deputies, and were conducting the affairs of the municipalities so badly, that, for the time being, the central government had to intervene, then again such an explanation would have seemed reasonable." Lamont arranged favorable editorials in newspapers, and protested against reporters who were, in his words, "antifascist." He established an American press service for Italy. As Mussolini was in the process of invading Ethiopia, where Fascist troops killed a half-million people, Lamont stated that the dictator "should be presented to the public not as a warrior or in warlike attitudes, but in pastoral, agricultural, friendly, domestic and peaceful attitudes." He then drafted Mussolini's press release, in which with unintended accuracy he compared the Fascist use of mustard gas against unarmed Africans to prior events in the United States, "where just a half century or more ago the vast resources of Western America were developed by American emigrants."

Comforting though it may be, it would be entirely inappropriate to cling to the false hope that Lamont and the corporations he worked for were aberrations, in part because, as shown above, Lamont's views mirror those held by much of the ruling class (and the metabolized working class). Further, his views were directly in line with the fundamental movement of civilization: that of centralization of power. Lamont was perceptive enough to comprehend, though certainly not aware enough to articulate, that fascism is the alpha as well as the omega of civilization, that civilization begins with the totalitarian impulse and accelerates toward that ultimate goal. Finally, the monumental power Lamont wielded guaranteed him a position in the center of the stream of history: In 1937, Ferdinand Lundberg wrote that Lamont "has exercised more power for twenty years in the western hemisphere, has put into effect more final decisions from which there has been no appeal, than any other person. Lamont, in short, has been the First Consul *de facto* in the invisible Directory of postwar high finance and politics, a man consulted by presidents, prime ministers, governors of central banks."

Mussolini was not the only dictator with whom Lamont carried on close relations. After Mexican president Carranza was murdered (having himself already murdered the revolutionary, Emiliano Zapata), and General Álvaro Obregón rose to power, a reporter said of Lamont, "He is not the man behind the throne, he is the man on the throne." Under Lamont's tutelage, Obregón gave powerful voice to revolutionary ideals while undercutting land reforms brought about by the previous decade's popular revolutions. Lamont was later followed as "the man on the throne" by Morgan partner Dwight Morrow, who as ambassador to Mexico became "self-appointed overlord of Mexico's finances." In this capacity he devised the notion of "perpetual concessions," whereby American oil companies regained control of Mexican oil wells, which constitutionally belonged only to the Mexican people. To make up lost revenue, Morrow wanted to cut the Mexican budget by "eliminating the courthouse entirely, cutting 2.5 million off the education appropriation, one million pesos off the public health, 2.5 million pesos off statistics and some 4 million pesos off communications."

Morrow later continued these austerity programs in the United States. As a senator during the depression, he voted against food relief, unemployment relief, and the veterans' bonus bill, saying, "There is something about too much prosperity that ruins the fiber of the people." Evidently not so concerned about the fiber of his own class, he consistently voted for Morgan-controlled monopolies, and for large naval appropriations.

Lamont performed many of the same services for Japanese fascists as he did for Italian. By the mid-1920s, the House of Morgan had made itself the primary banker for Japan, a country which, like Morgan and Company, had profited by the bloodshed of World War I: Selling ships and supplies to the Allies had multiplied its gold reserves one hundred times. When, in 1931, Japan invaded Manchuria, the House of Morgan fully supported the move, in part because, as Morgan family historian (and outright toady: I think *courtier* is the polite term) Ron Chernow notes, "no business came from China." Soon after the invasion, the Japanese finance minister issued a statement in which he called the takeover "self-defense," and compared it, once again with unintended accuracy, to U.S. actions in Panama. The press release concluded by stating that "the Japanese Government and people entertain the friendliest feelings towards the Chinese. They are probably more anxious than any other nation of the earth could possibly be, to maintain friendly relations with the Chinese." It should come as no surprise that this press release was written not by Japan's finance minister, but instead by Morgan's Tom Lamont. It should also come as no surprise that Lamont arranged additional publicity for the statement. A third nonsurprise is the adamant nature of Morgan's support, with partner and former assistant secretary of the treasury Russell Leffingwell, for example, stating, "It is grotesque for the League [of Nations] or for America to interfere on the side of Chinese raiders and revolutionaries . . . and against the side of Japan, who in pursuance of her treaty rights has been keeping order in Manchuria and maintaining the only safe-asylum open to the fear-ridden Chinese." I'm not certain the more than 35 million Chinese who were eventually killed or wounded (all but 3.3 million were civilians) by Japan ("A large number of young men who were arrested, together with those who had been captured earlier, were sent outside of the city to be massacred, from several thousand to tens of thousands at a time. In most cases, the captives were shot by machine guns, and those who were still alive were bayoneted individually. In some cases, the Japanese poured gasoline onto the captives and burned them alive"), or the hundreds of thousands of women raped in a systematic program of terror, would have agreed with Mr. Leffingwell's assessment that the invading Japanese were maintaining a "safe-asylum."

By now, most of us are aware that similar relationships existed between fascist Germany and U.S. businesspeople. Many heads of corporations—in the United States, Germany, and elsewhere—were enamored of Hitler because he was good for business. "We stand for the maintenance of private property," he reassured them. "We shall protect free enterprise as the most expedient, or rather the sole possible economic order." William Randolph Hearst struck a deal with Hitler to guarantee favorable coverage of the fascists in Hearst-run newspapers. Because Alcoa (Aluminum Company of America) had a cartel agreement with notorious German manufacturer I.G. Farben, Alcoa denied the United States aluminum it needed to prosecute World War II, causing Secretary of the Interior Harold Ickes to state, "If America loses this war, it can thank the Aluminum Corporation of America." DuPont's interests in the Nazis were not merely fiscal. Irenee du Pont, the most powerful member of the family, was, to use the words of biographer and historian Charles Higham, "obsessed" with the principles of Hitler: "He keenly followed the career of the future Fuhrer in the 1920s, and on September 7, 1926, in a speech to the American Chemical Society, he advocated a race of supermen, to be achieved by injecting special drugs into them in boyhood to make their characters to order." Irenee was, it seems, a bit ahead of his time. On the home front, DuPont used General Motors money (GM was controlled by DuPont) to finance something called the Black Legion, sort of a KKK with black, instead of white, robes, that did much the same thing as the KKK: firebomb union halls and kill union organizers and African Americans. General Motors supplied trucks for Hitler's war machine (as did Ford), and Standard Oil (now Exxon) supplied gas and rubber, often at terms better than those supplied to the United States. International Telephone and Telegraph, according to Higham, built "switchboards, telephones, alarm gongs, buoys, air raid warning devices, radar equipment, and thirty thousand fuses per month for artillery shells used to kill British and American troops. . . . Without this supply of crucial materials, it would have been impossible for the German air force to kill American and British troops, for the German army to fight the Allies in Africa, Italy, France, and Germany, for England to have been bombed, or for Allied ships to have been attacked at sea." ITT owned nearly a third of the Focke-Wulf company, maker of the devastating FW190 fighter airplane. After the war, ITT sued and received compensation from the American public for wartime damage done to Focke-Wulf plants. GM and Ford received similar reparations.

■   ■   ■

It should come as no surprise that corporations supported fascist regimes in the 1930s and 1940s. They do the same today. Recall the words of the Shell Nigeria spokesperson I mentioned early on: "For a commercial company trying to make investments, you need a stable environment; dictatorships can give you that." Of course, the United States has put in power dictators the world over, to create and maintain business-friendly climates and to eliminate, wherever possible, resistance to the expropriation—theft—of resources.

THE CLOSING OF THE IRON CAGE

·   ·   ·

I've seen (and participated in) a fair amount of debate as to whether the U.S. government qualifies in a strict sense as fascist. One respectable dictionary defines fascism as "a one-party system of government in which the individual is subordinated to the state and control is maintained by military force, secret police, rigid censorship, and governmental regimentation of business and finance." The United States seems to me, under this definition, borderline fascist, or complex fascist, or good P.R. fascist. First, does the hegemony of the Democrats and Republicans (Republicrats, as they're sometimes called) constitute a one-party system? They're two faces of the same corporate party. Even the Nazis had competition among factions within the party. Second, by subordination of the individual to the state, do we mean subordination to the nominal government ("Ask not what your country can do for you. . ."), or do we mean subordination to that interlinked machinery of government and industry, the governmental/industrial complex? Or, do we mean, saying effectively the same as this latter, subordination to production? Next, is state control maintained by military force and secret police? I'm not sure whether the stronger case for these is made by pointing out that the U.S. military consumes more than 50 percent of the discretionary budget of the nominal government, by listing nations overthrown by the United States to support industry, or by talking about suppression by violence of dissenting voices at home or abroad. Now, does rigid censorship include the self-censorship of a dysfunctional family, or only externally imposed censorship? If the latter, does it include only imposition at gunpoint, or, also, imposition by pink slip, and by ownership of the means of spreading (and spinning) information? The press in this country is capitalist, that's all there is to it. The major media outlets are owned by capitalists, run by capitalists, edited and censored by capitalists, in the interests of capitalists. And what if the system uses censorship by ownership at home, and censorship by violence abroad? Does all of this make the United States fascist?

THE CULTURE OF MAKE BELIEVE

Here's another definition I've seen: Fascism is the conjoining of industry and government into one unit to facilitate the extraction of resources from an often unwilling public. And another: Fascism is a corporate state where business, labor, and government meet in tripartite bodies, with labor as a subordinate in the trio, having lost its right to strike. No less an authority than Mussolini stated that "Fascism should more appropriately be called Corporatism because it is a merger of State and corporate power." And, finally, a definition from the Communist Georgi Dimitrov, who beat the Nazis in court on the charge of conspiring to start the Reichstag fire in 1933: Fascism is the open terrorist rule of the most reactionary, chauvinist, militarist sectors of finance capital or the financial oligarchy. (Note that after World War II, Dimitrov became dictator of Bulgaria, where, revealing that, within the larger stream of industrial civilization, these definitions almost invariably get fuzzy, he himself oversaw "the open terrorist rule of the most reactionary, chauvinist, militarist sectors of" the Communist Party, in association with capital and industry for the benefit of the Communist Party oligarchy.)

Ultimately, though, as always, these are all just words, and what's at stake here moves far beyond words, far beyond linguistic arguments about the definitions of various types of governments. What's at stake moves beyond even the question that started this book for me, which was: How do you define a hate group? What's at stake also moves far beyond such important questions as who gets how much in our capitalist society. What's at stake here goes to the heart of our civilization. What's at stake is life itself. To fully understand that, we have to talk about how our culture treats the fourth class, those who are inconvenient, who are unnecessary, those who are in the way.

THE CLOSING OF THE IRON CAGE

THEY COULD BEAT

A PERSON TO DEATH,

AND THEY WERE

ABSOLUTELY NORMAL

WHILE THEY WERE

DOING IT

THAT I CAN'T

UNDERSTAND.

A FORMER POLISH
CONCENTRATION
CAMP SURVIVOR

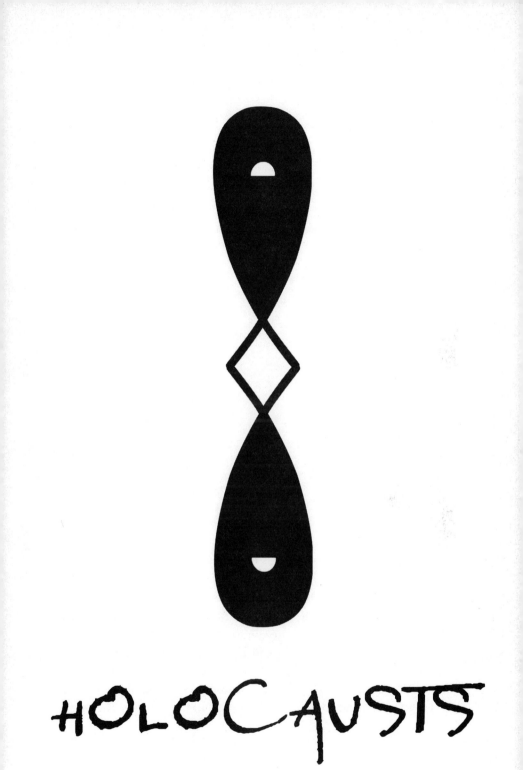

HOLOCAUSTS

WHEN I WAS, MAYBE, THIRTEEN, I decided that each night before I went to sleep I would read ten pages of some book that would have been too big or difficult for me to otherwise read. I did this every night for the next twenty years, when for some reason I stopped (if memory serves, it was in a vain attempt to actually get a life). I recently began this tradition again. In those two decades I made it through some extraordinary books: *The Decline and Fall of the Roman Empire*; most of Solzhenitsyn; a lot of Foucault; *Decline of the West*; *Lee's Lieutenants* and a four-volume biography of Robert E. Lee; the complete Brothers Grimm and Hans Christian Andersen; most of Joseph Campbell; the complete Sherlock Holmes; *The History of German Resistance 1933–1945*; other history books and books on the lives of painters; and so on. But through all of these books, the one I remember most is the first, *The Rise and Fall of the Third Reich*. Some twenty-seven years later I still remember that it weighed in at 1,481 pages, or one hundred and forty-eight days. And, from this book, there is one long passage that has stayed with me all this time, that I've held in front of me through all these years, as I have devoted my life to understanding this culture and to stopping its ubiquitous destructiveness. I've held it in front of me, particularly as I've written this book, attempting to understand the hatred and atrocities that dog us wherever we go, attempting to understand how a near-implacable hatred causes us to with machinelike regularity abandon our humanity and substitute in its place a compulsion to turn the living into the dead. There are many things I can easily understand. I can easily understand rage or hatred toward an individual. I can understand striking out in frustration. I can even understand killing in cold fury. But the regularity with which our culture has fired the villages of Indians and captured the children of Africans, has denuded hillsides and destroyed rivers, has systematically devoured so much of the world, took me aback, as a child, and takes me aback, today.

The image I remember from so long ago was the sworn affadavit by a German engineer that was read into the record at the Nuremberg trials. I do not know why this image stuck out so much; it was of, as William Shirer, author of *Rise and Fall*, put it, "a relatively minor mass execution" on the Eastern Front, nothing more than five thousand people. In the larger picture of World War II, that's not really so many at all. And in the scheme of civilization, it's the merest drop of blood in an ever-expanding ocean.

Here is what the engineer said: "My foreman and I went directly to the pits. I heard rifle shots in quick succession from behind one of the earth mounds. The people who had got off the trucks—men, women and children of all ages—had to undress upon order of an S.S. man, who carried a riding or dog whip. They had to put down their clothes in fixed places, sorted according to shoes, top clothing, and underclothing. I saw a heap of shoes of about 800 or 1,000 pairs, great piles of under-linen and clothing.

HOLOCAUSTS

"Without screaming or weeping, these people undressed, stood around in family groups, kissed each other, said farewells and waited for a sign from another S.S. man, who stood near the pit, also with a whip in his hand. During the fifteen minutes that I stood near the pit I heard no complaint or plea for mercy. . . .

"An old woman with snow-white hair was holding a one-year-old child in her arms and singing to it and tickling it. The child was cooing with delight. The parents were looking on with tears in their eyes. The father was holding the hand of a boy about 10 years old and speaking to him softly: the boy was fighting his tears. The father pointed to the sky, stroked his head and seemed to explain something to him.

"At that moment the S.S. man at the pit shouted something to his comrade. The latter counted off about twenty persons and instructed them to go behind the earth mound. . . . I well remember a girl, slim with black hair, who, as she passed close to me, pointed to herself and said, 'twenty-three years old.'

"I walked around the mound and found myself confronted by a tremendous grave. People were closely wedged together and lying on top of each other so that only their heads were visible. Nearly all had blood running over their shoulders from their heads. Some of the people were still moving. Some were lifting their arms and turning their heads to show that they were still alive. The pit was nearly two-thirds full. I estimated that it contained about a thousand people. I looked for the man who did the shooting. He was an S.S. man who sat at the narrow edge of the pit, his feet dangling into the pit. He had a tommy gun on his knees, and was smoking a cigarette.

"The people, completely naked, went down some steps and clambered over the heads of the people lying there to the place where the S.S. man directed them. They lay down in front of the dead or wounded people; some caressed those who were still alive and spoke to them in a low voice. Then I heard a series of shots. I looked into the pit and saw that the bodies were twitching or the heads lying already motionless on top of the bodies that lay beneath them. Blood was running from their necks.

"The next batch was approaching already. They went down into the pit, lined themselves up against the previous victims and were shot."

∎   ∎   ∎

By now, most of us have read or heard a great deal about the Holocaust, how and why it happened, its human costs, its horrors. We've seen the pictures of the skeletal figures of concentration camp survivors, and seen the black-and-white footage of their limp and loose bodies being thrown into pits or onto the backs of trucks to be taken away for disposal. We've seen the deep eye sockets and protruding cheekbones of the dead, and of the living. We've seen the faces of those who soon would be dead. The small boy in Warsaw, hands raised. The man in the Ukraine, kneeling at the edge of a pit where below we can see bodies; behind him stands a man in a uniform holding a pistol, tiny in his hand, yet still large enough to kill. The piles of glasses, or shoes, the bales of clothing, hair. The soap or lamp shades made of fat or skin. The assembly lines where slaves were worked to death, and the assembly lines where death was not merely the primary product but the only one.

We know that Jews were not the only people killed by Germans in assembly lines, but also Russians, Poles, Slavs, Romani, Jehovah's Witnesses, homosexuals, intellectuals (at least those who opposed the regime), the disabled, members of the resistance. And we know that Hitler again and again watched films of those who plotted against him hanging, nude. *Hang him using piano wire until he's almost dead, then release the pressure. Revive him, and do it again. And again. And again.*

We know also that Germany was not the only country to participate (odd word, *participate*, so neutral, so bureaucratic), but, that, Hungary, too, did its share, and Rumania, and Poland, and, toward the end, Italy. We know that banks in Switzerland profited from the murder of Jews, and that the Vatican did not oppose the killings. *Actively* did not oppose the killings. Time and again both the United

HOLOCAUSTS

States and Britain ducked chances to stop or slow the genocide. Indeed, a 1943 U.S. State Department memo gave the reason the United States was not willing to accept Germany's offer to deport all German Jews to the United States: "There are grave objections to a direct approach to the German Government to request the release to us of these people. . . . [It would be] impossible for us to take them. The net result would be the transfer of odium from the German to the Allied Governments." And we know that, after the war, the United States recruited many of the architects and technocrats responsible for the killing to work for the CIA, and we know that the Vatican helped the U.S. government smuggle these people—these nasty-ass motherfuckers, if ever there were any—out of justice's way.

We can probably detail the deep, broad, and absurd European tradition of hatred of Jews that has manifested in myriad ways, from the pogroms of Russia, to the Dreyfuss affair, to, especially, the Holocaust itself. We know that, in fact, as sociologist, philosopher, and scholar of the Holocaust Zygmunt Bauman put it, "before the Nazi ascent to power, and long after the entrenchment of their rule over Germany, German popular anti-semitism came a poor second to Jew-hatred in quite a few other European countries." Indeed, Germany had long been known as a relatively safe haven from the persecution Jews suffered elsewhere. We could outline the arguments used across Europe to jusify exploiting or eradicating Jews, for example, the scientific, ranging from quack phrenologists quick to provide scientific proof that Jews, like Africans (or anyone, really, but Aryans) were inferior to the scientists and their patrons, to the mainstream of the scientific community itself. Historian of science Robert Proctor painstakingly researched the relationship between Nazis and the scientific community, and found that, contrary to popular opinion, scientists were not dragged off to conduct horrid experiments on unwilling subjects under fear for their own lives. Not only is it true that "many of the social and intellectual foundations [for the anti-Jewish programs] were laid down long before the rise of Hitler to power," but that mainstream scientists "played an active, even lead-

THE CULTURE OF MAKE BELIEVE

ing role in the initiation, administration, and execution of the Nazi racial programmes." Undoubtedly, the scientists' greatest contribution to the Holocaust, however—and, in our larger case, to the destruction of the planet—is a rigid, nonsensical, absurd, and, in fact, evil insistence on the more or less absolute divorce of ethics—values—from science.

Then there was the religious argument, that Jews had killed Christ, never mind that: a) the actual killing was done by Romans; b) Jesus was a Jew; and c) it happened (if it happened at all) a hell of a long time ago. More reasonably, yet, less often stated, is the understanding that hatred of Jews emerged from Christianity defining itself as having broken away from the Jewish tradition, meaning, as Bauman put it, "Christianity could theorize its own existence only as an on-going opposition to the Jews. Continuing Jewish stubbornness bore evidence that the Christian mission remained as yet unfinished. Jewish admission of error, surrender to Christian truth, and perhaps a future massive conversion, served as the model of Christianity's ultimate triumph." In other words, Jews were to be given the same choice as other non-Christians: Christianity or death. Yet another way to say this is that Jews have been long hated because they continue to commit the unpardonable sin of not allowing themselves to be fully assimilated. As was true with the Chinese in America, this indigestibility is intolerable. Alternatively, I've heard hatred of Jews characterized as a result of long-standing resentment over the fact that they were really the first to saddle us with monotheism. "What we must recapture to mind, nakedly as we can," writes George Steiner, "is the singularity, the brain-hammering strangeness, of the monotheistic idea. Historians of religion tell us that the emergence of the concept of the Mosaic God is a unique fact in human experience, that a genuinely comparable notion sprang up at no other place or time. The abruptness of the Mosaic revelation, the finality of the creed at Sinai, tore up the human psyche by its most ancient roots. The break has never really knit. The demands made of the mind are, like God's name, unspeakable. Brain and conscience are commanded to vest belief, obedience, love in an abstraction purer, more inacces-

HOLOCAUSTS

sible to ordinary sense than the highest of mathematics." Nietzsche, by the way, would have agreed, for he called monotheism "the most monstrous of all human errors."

And there was the economic argument that we hear even today, with stories of cabals of Jewish bankers plotting their control of the most intimate aspects of our lives. Oddly enough, Jews were and are hated not only for their alleged participation in the international conspiracy of supercapitalist bankers, but also for their alleged participation in the international conspiracy of Bolshevists. This seeming contradiction has to do with the traditional role of many Jews in Europe as small businesspeople and "middle men" between the gentry and the poor, hired by the rich for such unpopular public functions as rent collection. Consequently, they were despised, or looked down upon, by the aristocracy, but, at the same time, because they formed a shield between the very rich and the poor, they were resented by this latter class. The rich often despise the poor, and the poor often hate the rich, but the Jews of much of Europe found themselves in the unenviable position of being hated by both, or, as Bauman put it, they became "objects of two mutually opposed and contradictory class antagonisms." Translated into plain English: They were screwed.

A major reason for the eruption of this hatred in Germany, as opposed to another European country, was how grievously Germans suffered after World War I, having been forced by the Allies to sign a devastating and humiliating treaty at its conclusion (we should note, however, that it was less devastating and humiliating than the treaty the Germans forced the Russians to sign a year earlier), calling for, among other things, their effective disarmament. A couple of years later, the Allies presented the Germans with a bill for reparations: a whopping 132 billion marks, or 33 billion dollars. One of the ways the German government paid this debt was by simply printing money. The mark began to fall: Within three months the exchange rate was four hundred to the dollar, six months after that, it was seven thousand to the dollar, a month later, eighteen thousand to the dollar, and ten months after that (when Hitler made his first attempt to

seize power), it was at a billion per dollar. Soon enough, it became trillions. What this meant in fiscal terms is that life savings of the middle and lower classes were wiped out virtually overnight. Once again, I'm sure we've all seen pictures or read descriptions of people carrying satchels of cash to the store to buy their daily bread. And, as always, the rich got the best of it: All through 1921, as the economy collapsed, the government lowered taxes on the rich. The collapse of the German economy made conditions right for scapegoats, for existing contempt to ripen into hatred.

And, of course, it did. Against the Jews, against the Slavs, against anyone but the real sources of their misery. Hitler articulated this rage, and captured the hearts of enough Germans to become an overwhelmingly popular leader. The Nazis, as had been true of the KKK (and the Republicans and Democrats) in the United States, became a hugely powerful political party. Hitler and the Nazis had two goals, as articulated by Hitler, which were "to make secure and to preserve the racial community and to enlarge it. It was therefore a question of space [*lebensraum*, or, living space]." The Germans, as Hitler put it, echoing American leaders from the Founding Fathers till today, had "the right to a greater living space than other peoples." He said, "The history of all ages—the Roman Empire and the British Empire—had proved that expansion could only be carried out by breaking down resistance. . . . There had never . . . been spaces without a master, and there were none today; the attacker always comes up against a possesser."

The parallels between Hitler's language and actions, and those of Americans, is more than coincidental. Hitler stated explicitly that "Neither Spain nor Britain should be models of German expansion, but the Nordics of North America, who had ruthlessly pushed aside an inferior race to win for themselves soil and territory for the future." We don't even have to take Hitler's word for American motivations. Theodore Roosevelt put it succinctly when he wrote, "Of course our whole national history has been one of expansion." He concluded the essay where he made that admission—if you can call a boast an admission—by stating "that the barbarians recede or are

HOLOCAUSTS

conquered, with the attendant fact that whether peace follows their retrogression or conquest is due solely to the power of the mighty civilized races which have not lost the fighting instinct, and which by their expansion are gradually bringing peace to the red wastes where the barbarian peoples of this world hold sway."

But the correspondence between American genocide of the nineteenth century and German genocide of the twentieth is by no means one to one. Hitler had a huge advantage: the bureaucratic nature of modern industrial society. As Bauman notes, "Rage and fury are pitiably primitive and inefficient as tools of mass annihilation. They normally peter out before the job is done. One cannot build grand designs on them." This is true whether we're talking about the destruction of the European Jews, the population of Iraq, the great runs of salmon, the Amazonian rain forests, or the lives and hearts and hopes of the vast majority of human beings. In an essay entitled "Destroying the Innocent with a Clear Conscience: A Sociopsychology of the Holocaust," John Sabini and Mary Silver commented that "Thorough, comprehensive, exhaustive murder required [I would say *requires*] the replacement of the mob with a bureaucracy, the replacement of shared rage with obedience to authority. The requisite bureaucracy would be effective whether manned by extreme or tepid anti-Semites, considerably broadening the pool of potential recruits; it would govern the actions of its members not by arousing passions but by organizing routines; it would only make distinctions it was required to make, not those its members might be moved to make, say, between children and adults, scholar and thief, innocent and guilty; it would be responsive to the will of the ultimate authority through a hierarchy of responsibility—whatever that will might be."

This bureaucracy represents the near-absolute conversion of human beings into machines. It represents the triumph of our society over our humanity.

■   ■   ■

There is a fourth group, who are not rulers to be rewarded; nor laborers to be placated, nor an excess pool of labor to drive wages down, nor, even, slaves to be harvested (and I'm putting these three only for now in the same category because, from the perspective of production, what is wanted from each is the same—their labor); nor potential revolutionaries to be terrorized, put away, or killed. These are people (and nonhumans, indeed, most of the nonhuman world) who are simply in the way, and who must be eliminated if we are going to get on about our business of production. They needn't necessarily be hated, although that can sometimes be helpful—as Nazis sometimes hated Jews, as Whites sometimes hated Indians—because it can make their killing that much more palatable (although too much hatred *can* interfere with the smooth functioning of a bureaucracy). These are people who are living on land that you want. These are people who have no skills that you wish to harvest. These are not people you particularly want to exploit. These are people you wish would disappear. These are the Hittites, Girgashites, Amorites, Canaanites, Perizzites, Hivites, Jebusites. These are the barbarians of northern Greece. These are the citizens of the island of Melos, who wanted to remain nonaligned in the war between Athens and Sparta, but who shared the island with pine trees the Athenians wanted to kill to make into masts—the best in all the Adriatic—so the Athenians starved the citizens of Melos, negotiated in bad faith—finally saying, "This is a world in which the powerful do as they will, and the weak suffer as they must"—then came in to kill the men and relocate the women and children before repopulating the island with their own. These are the Sabines, Franks, Celts, Picts, and anyone else whose land was wanted by the insatiable Romans. These are the Arawaks, Pontiacs, Pequots, Cherokee, Lakota. These are the Hawai'ians, and the Aborigines. These are the Khoikhoi, Xhosa, and San. These are the Jews, Romani, Poles, Slavs, Russians. These are the Palestinians. These are the U'Wa, who have threatened to commit mass suicide if Occidental Petroleum drills on their land (of course, if Occi could spin it right, this would serve the corporation well).

HOLOCAUSTS

The fourth group consists also of those who remind us of the flaws of our system. These are the homeless, whom we hide away beneath freeway overpasses so we do not have to see them defecate on the sidewalks of our theme-park cities, thus breaking our enchantment, reminding us that wealth comes always at the direct cost of poverty. These are the addicts who manifest in their flesh and in their corroded veins the numbness that has become our birthright as civilized—separate, isolated—shells that once were human beings. These are, in a sense, all of us, to the degree that we've given up hope that humans can live any other way. These people, who remind us of the flaws of our system—the "social junk," as Spritzer called them, or, perhaps, more kindly, the social wreckage—must be swept away from our sight, just as those whose land we covet must be swept away from the land that God gave to us, if only we will take it. Or, they must be killed. Or, they can starve. It doesn't really matter.

The logic is inescapable. When you see the world through the lense of utilitarianism—*how can these others be used?*—you will use what or whom you can. And what or whom you can't? It doesn't matter. If they're not in your way, they can survive for now. If they are, well, they'll just have to go.

■   ■   ■

I think often of a conversation I had several years ago with a friend who's a longtime environmental activist. She's Jewish. She'd been down to visit her parents in Florida, and, while there, had gone to a theater to see *Schindler's List*. It had been a disturbing experience for her, she'd said, because, afterward, "All these blue-haired old Jewish ladies came out shaking their fists and saying, 'Never again!'" When she'd said this to me, my friend had made a quick, almost reflexive motion with her head, as though trying to clear her brain from some grave confusion, or clear her mouth from some bitter taste. She'd said, "Don't they realize it's ongoing?"

"They've probably never heard of the U'Wa," I said.

"The U'Wa?" she replied. "Except for the football team they've

probably never even heard of the Seminoles, and they're living on Seminole land."

By pretending that the Holocaust (capital *H* to distinguish it from all the others) is Unique (capital *U*, because, of course, every holocaust is unique) we get to isolate it, pretend it was an aberration, a single incomprehensible act of unparalleled evil committed by a nation inexplicably in the thrall of a monstrously and, somehow, charismatically insane individual. We get to pretend that it was not an inevitable consequence of a way of perceiving others and of being in the world.

I used to wonder at the vehemence—even violence—with which some people insist that the Holocaust is Unique. There's an obvious answer, which is that Jews—as a whole—are White. They're civilized. They believe in Production. They even have flesh-colored skin. All of which is to say that they're people, as opposed to the others whom we kill—the indigenous of Africa, Europe, Asia, the Americas, Oceania, and the islands, as well as the poor the world over (and, most especially, the nonhumans)—who do not worship Production, and who therefore are not people in the fullest sense, and who, therefore, under the rules of civilized intercourse, can be eradicated with impunity. So, of course, there would be a tremendous sense of betrayal. We are, in a sense, killing our own. Brother killing brother. Brother killing sister.

There's more to it than this, though. It's crucial to the perpetuation of our culture that we perceive the Holocaust as Unique. This accomplishes much the same thing as pretending the KKK was not a true grassroots organization, and as pretending the essential cessation of lynchings in the United States manifested a collective racial epiphany. It allows meaningful analysis to stop, or, better, to lead us away from ourselves, so we can spend endless years dissecting some distant other—*What if Hitler had been successful at painting? Did he contract syphilis from a Jewish woman?*—we can blame for this otherwise unfathomable series of atrocities. This shunting of attention is necessary if we're going to continue to live the way we do. *Don't look. Don't see. Don't tell.* To pretend the Holocaust is Unique is to allow us

HOLOCAUSTS

to not question our own way of living, to not question our own innocence. It allows us to pretend we share no motivations with the perpetrators, pretend we share no cultural imperatives, no code. It allows us, one and all, to be good Germans in the larger ongoing holocaust of the planet and of its inhabitants. It allows us to continue to be decent White men. It allows us to remain civilized. It allows us to avoid being cursed by Noah, our patriarch. It allows us not to have to walk alone and afraid into the wilderness.

■　　　■　　　　■

Look again at photographs of the Holocaust. This time focus not on the victims but the killers. What do you see? Do you see maniacs gibbering for blood, gobbets of flesh and splinters of bone jutting from their leering mouths? Not particularly. You probably see soldiers, not much different from soldiers the world over, not much different from the soldiers who rode with Custer, or those who flew over Baghdad. Young men with short haircuts, guns in their hands or in their belts, wearing what look in the black-and-white photgraphs to be monochromatic uniforms. They're just kids. They've been trained to kill, but they're kids nonetheless. Sociologists Kren and Rappoport summed up current thinking on the subject: "By conventional clinical criteria no more than 10 percent of the S.S. could be considered 'abnormal.' This observation fits the general trend of testimony by survivors indicating that in most of the camps, there was usually one, or at most a few, S.S. men known for their intense outbursts of sadistic cruelty." They conclude, "Our judgement is that the overwhelming majority of S.S. men, leaders as well as rank and file, would have easily passed all the psychiatric tests ordinarily given to American army recruits or Kansas City policemen."

Now, look at the photos of those who planned the killings, rarely using words so indelicate as *murder, atrocity, hate.* They look far more bureaucratic than demonic. Indeed, they *are* more bureaucratic than demonic. The department within S.S. headquarters in charge of eradicating Jews was officially designated as the Section of

Administration and Economy (analogous, perhaps, to the U.S. bureaucracy in charge of deforesting public lands being a part of the Department of Agriculture). The Germans were neither lying nor obfuscating. As Bauman notes, "Except for the moral repulsiveness of its goal (or, to be precise, the gigantic scale of the moral odium), the activity did not differ in any formal sense (the only sense that can be expressed in the language of bureaucracy) from all other organized activities designed, monitored, and supervised by 'ordinary' administrative and economic sections."

Here is the way a technical expert described improvements in the mobile killing vans used by the *Einsatzgruppen*. I trust readers can see past the awkward writing style to the intent. The technician wrote that a shorter, fully loaded truck would be able to operate much more quickly. A shortening of the rear compartment would not disadvantageously affect the weight balance, overloading the front axle, he wrote, "because actually a correction in the weight distribution takes place automatically through the fact that the cargo [that is, the people to be killed] in the struggle toward the back door during the operation always is preponderately located there." Because the connecting pipe [where carbon monoxide was introduced] was quickly rusted through by "fluids" [that is, by blood, vomit, piss, and liquid shit], the gas should be introduced from above, not below. To facilitate cleaning, the technician suggested that an eight- to twelve-inch hole should be made in the floor and provided with a cover that can be opened from outside. The floor should be slightly inclined, and the cover equipped with a small sieve. Thus all "fluids" would flow to the middle, the "thin fluids" would exit during operation, and "thicker filth" could be hosed out afterward. The disposal of corpses was a huge technical problem, causing significant competition among firms vying for the lucrative market. One firm made the following recommendation: "For putting the bodies into the furnace, we suggest simply a metal fork moving on cylinders. Each furnace will have an oven measuring only 600 millimeters in breadth and 450 millimeters in height, as coffins will not be used. For transporting the corpses from the storage points to the furnaces we suggest using light

HOLOCAUSTS

carts on wheels, and we enclose diagrams of these drawn to scale." Another company pointed to its excellent furnaces at Dachau and Lublin, which, it said, had given "full satisfaction in practice," then continued, "Following our verbal discussion regarding the delivery of equipment of simple construction for the burning of bodies, we are submitting plans for our perfected cremation ovens which operate with coal and have hitherto given full satisfaction. We suggest two crematoria furnaces for the building planned, but we advise you to make further inquiries to make sure that two ovens will be sufficient for your requirements. We guarantee the effectiveness of the cremation ovens as well as their durability, the use of the best material and our faultless workmanship." Sometimes, ashes from the crematoria were sold as fertilizer. One company constructed an electrically heated tank for making soap, with a recipe of "12 pounds of human fat, 10 quarts of water, and 8 ounces to a pound of caustic soda . . . all boiled for two or three hours and then cooled." The conversion of the living to the dead has been converted from a moral, human, question into a technical problem to be solved, and, if at all possible, profited from.

"Precision, speed, unambiguity, knowledge of the files, continuity, discretion, unity, strict subordination, reduction of friction and of material and personal costs—these are raised to the optimum point in the strictly bureaucratic administration," wrote Max Weber, presciently, it would seem, except that he was not writing of death camps but the production process in general, whether the product is soap from the flesh of Jews, fish sticks from the flesh of cod, or two-by-fours from the flesh of trees. He continues, "Bureaucratization offers above all the optimum possibility of carrying through the principle of specializing administrative functions according to purely objective considerations. . . . The 'objective' discharge of business primarily means a discharge of business according to *calculable rules* and 'without regard for persons.'"

The point is this: When those in power set social goals aimed at increasing that power (this includes maximizing revenue, since, in our society, money translates to power, and includes maximizing pro-

THE CULTURE OF MAKE BELIEVE

duction for the same reason), and when the rest of us do not question these goals too deeply but merely attempt as smoothly as possible to make our own minuscule contributions to the goals of our
society, the culture will smoothly commit atrocities seemingly without end. This is true whether our contributions consist of making
certain that shifting cargos do not stress front axles, increasing the efficiency of oil extraction from beneath the ground, or writing books
that earn profits for bookstore chains or publishing conglomerates.
The smooth functioning of bureaucratic society requires we each do
our part.

■   ■   ■

In front of the gas chambers and crematoria were well-kept lawns
and flower gardens. Often, as those who were about to die arrived,
they would hear light music, played by an orchestra of "young and
pretty girls all dressed in white blouses and navy-blue skirts." The
men, women, and children were told to undress, so they could be
given showers. They were told, most often pleasantly, to move into
the room where they would soon die. As Bauman observes, "rational
people will go quietly, meekly, joyously into a gas chamber, if only
they are allowed to believe it is a bathroom."

Once the doors were locked, behind them, a sergeant would give
the order to drop the crystals: "All right, give 'em something to chew
on." Soon, but too late, the people would realize that they had signed
their final false contract, and, at last they would fight for their lives,
stampeding toward the doors that were sealed behind them, where
"they piled up in one blue clammy blood-splattered pyramid, claw-
ing and mauling each other even in death."

■   ■   ■

By this point, the pyramid of blue and bloodied bodies is really beside the point. The men who dropped the crystals, or who oversaw
the use of Jews to clean up the thick and thin fluids and fire the bod-

HOLOCAUSTS

ies, did not make up the bulk of the killers. Most of the killers worked at regular jobs, just like you and me. The preeminent historian of the Holocaust, Raul Hilberg, commented, "It must be kept in mind that most of the participants [of genocide] did not fire rifles at Jewish children or pour gas into gas chambers. . . . Most bureaucrats composed memoranda, drew up blueprints, talked on the telephone, and participated in conferences. They could destroy a whole people by sitting at their desk."

■   ■   ■

Of course, there is a world of difference between them and us. The Nazis were killing human beings, for crying out loud, while we're merely killing the planet (and, of course, killing humans along the way, but even these people are only, to use the U.S. military's term, collateral damage). And the Nazis set out to *eradicate* the Jews, Romani, and so on, while all the deaths we cause are just accidental (time and again) by-products of our economic system, right?

A few months ago I got into a rather sharp conversation with an old friend. We went to a restaurant that had on the walls many photographs of lumberjacks standing smiling in front of the stumps of ancient redwoods they had just felled, trees half as old, themselves, as all of civilization. The trees were big enough to beggar belief, and only 150 years ago they ran from here all down the coast. I said, "Someday, soon, I hope, people will look at these photos with the same disgust with which we now look at photos of grinning soldiers celebrating the Holocaust."

She took offense. "I don't think you want to compare killing trees to killing humans."

"It's all the same imperative," I said.

Her voice grew tense, and I could tell my original assertion had made her angry. "It's not the same at all."

I wanted to tell her that the key word in the mass murder of the trees and the mass murder of the humans is *mass*. In both cases the killing is made inevitable by a utilitarian worldview that blinds us to

relationship and makes it impossible to perceive the other as an individual, whether the other is a Jew, Indian, woman, or tree. In both cases—the Holocaust and industrial forestry—the killing was or is demanded not for any personal, that is, human, reason, but rather by abstract ideologies, and the valuing of those ideologies over life. In both cases the killing has been made feasible, rational, necessary by a bigotry that holds us separate from and superior to these others, whomever these others may be, and thus entitled to take these others' lives for no good personal animal reasons. You could argue that at least by killing trees—whom we certainly consider to have less rights to live on this land than we—we're able to harvest wood that can be converted to cash, and also turn unproductive—from an economic perspective—native growth into productive tree farms. I would respond that by killing those they deemed subhumans, Germans were able to harvest gold, glasses, shoes, soap, and hair that could be converted to cash, and were able to gain *lebensraum* that Germans would soon put to good use. The biggest, and, really, the only fundamental, difference between the nightmares is that, insofar as the one killing the planet, we're still on the inside. We still consider ourselves the master race, or species.

■   ■   ■

The assembly-line mass murder of the Holocaust is production stripped of the veneer of economics. It is the very essence of production. It took the living and converted them to the dead. That's what our culture does. It was efficient, it was calculable, it was predictable, and it was controlled through nonhuman technologies. And it was also, as well as being grossly immoral, incredibly stupid. Even from the perspective of pure acquisitiveness and land hunger, it was self-defeating. As German troops froze and starved on the Eastern Front, valuable railroad cars were used instead to move cargos that fed crematoria. The Nazis performed economic analyses showing that feeding slaves just a bit more increased their productivity, more than enough to offset the extra cost of feed. Yet, they were starved.

HOLOCAUSTS

Similarly, slaughtering Russians was foolish. Many Ukranians and Russians greeted the Wehrmacht with kisses, open arms, and flowers, happy to be out from under the tyranny of Stalinism. The Germans quickly began murdering noncombatants to make room for the Germans who would move in after the war, or because they were told to, or because the Russians were inferior, or for any of the reasons given for these slaughters since the beginning of civilization's wars of extermination. And so Russian noncombatants fought back. They blew up trains, they killed German officers, they picked off individual soldiers. They hurt the Germans. For all their vaunted rationality, the Germans weren't so very rational, were they?

Of course, we're different now. We have rational reasons for the killings. There's no silly talk of master races and *lebensraum*. Instead, the economy is run along strictly rationalist lines. If something makes money, we do it, and if it doesn't, we don't (ignore for a moment that to divorce economics from morals and humanity is as evil as it is to do the same for science). But the U.S. economy costs at least five times as much as it's worth. Total annual U.S. corporate profits are about $500 billion, while the direct costs of the activities from which these profits derive are more than $2.5 trillion. These include $51 billion in direct subsidies and $53 billion in tax breaks, $274.7 billion lost because of deaths from workplace cancer, $225.9 billion lost because of the health costs of stationary source air pollution, and so on. This is to speak only of calculable costs, since other values—such as a living planet—do not, because they're not calculable, exist. The fact remains, however, that it is manifestly stupid to destroy your landbase, regardless of the abstract financial reward or esteem you may gain. Yet, our culture spends more to build and maintain commercial fishing vessels than the fiscal value of the fish caught. The same is true for the destruction of forests. In the United States, the Forest Service last year not atypically lost $407 million on its timber sale program, or about $779 per acre deforested. Or, take aluminum, to give a more detailed example of how these subsidies actually work. Aluminum is central to the modern economy. Its strength, durability, conductivity, and lightness of weight make it ideal for use not only in

pop cans and silicon chips, but especially in airplanes, automobiles, ships, railroads and other vehicles. It is commonly used in electrical wire.

Without massive public subsidies, the aluminum industry would cease to exist. These subsidies take the form of governmental funding of infrastructure necessary to the industry, military purchases, below-cost energy sales, and, of course, the human misery and human (and nonhuman) lives destroyed by the industry.

Because war is a big consumer of aluminum, during World War II the federal government built much of this nation's aluminum-smelting capacity, and financed even more through grants and vast low-interest loans. After the war, private aluminum corporations such as Alcoa retained full use of these smelters, despite their spotty record of assisting the U.S. war effort. They never repaid the public for the construction of the smelters.

The military continues to be a large purchaser of aluminum, contracting for 93 percent of this nation's shipbuilding and 66 percent of its aircraft. This demand creates much of the market for this metal.

It takes nearly twenty times more energy to extract aluminum from ore and process it than it does for iron. Currently, it takes between fourteen and twenty-five kilowatt-hours to smelt one kilogram of aluminum. Consequently, governments all over the world have subsidized electricity sales to huge aluminum companies, tying the price of electricity to the worldwide price of aluminum. Right now it takes about two to five dollars' worth of electricity to produce a single pound of aluminum, which then sells for about $.70. In the Pacific Northwest, aluminum smelters consume one-third of the region's cheap electricity—cheap because the hydropower dams were built at taxpayer expense decades ago. Of course, you could argue that these smelters create jobs—which is a feeble and foolish argument that could have been made as well for the producers of Zyklon B—but if you divide the number of jobs in the aluminum industry in the United States by the size of the subsidy, you discover that taxpayers pay $135,000 to $150,000 per employee: We'd all be better off

HOLOCAUSTS

handing the money directly to individuals, giving them sledgehammers and dynamite, and pointing them toward the nearest dam.

The energy subsidies extend far beyond below-cost energy sales: Aluminum is the prime, if not sole, reason for the construction of a large percentage of dams worldwide. These dams are often built over the strenuous objections of the people who will be displaced. In the 1950s, for example, British Columbia gave Alcan the rights to the Nechako River, a tributary of the Fraser River, for hydroelectricity, to build the world's largest aluminum smelter. The Cheslatta peoples were relocated from the area flooded by the dam's three hundred-mile reservoir. In 1988, Alcan announced it would divert even more water (it already takes 30 to 70 percent of the Nechako River's flow) in a second phase of the project. The Canadian government exempted the project from environmental assessment requirements. In 1995, after years of challenges by indigenous peoples, environmentalists, and government scientists, the Kemano Completion Project was canceled by British Columbia. While receiving these subsidies, Alcan owes $888 million in deferred taxes.

Uganda, Central Africa, Indonesia, Papua New Guinea, Borneo, Sarawak. In each of these nonindustrialized nations, dams, ports, roads, and railways have been built with public money to benefit transnational aluminum companies such as Alcoa, Reynolds, and Kaiser (purchased in 1988 by Maxaam (the company deforesting where I live) with money gained through the Savings and Loan scandal). Locals who object are overruled, whether they are indigenous peoples forcibly relocated or killed, or the head of the Brazilian environmental agency IBAMA, who was fired after she refused to allow Alcoa to clear-cut the Saraca-Taquera National Forest where a bauxite mine was to be located. This suggests yet another way the aluminum industry is subsidized: The forced removal of people from their homelands often requires the use of the military, again paid for with public money. Here's my question: If the land is to be taken for use by an aluminum corporation, does this qualify as *lebensraum*?

Large as these subsidies—below-cost electricity and military purchases and protection—are, they're trivial, compared to the

largest public offering to the aluminum industry, which is paid not so much in dollars as in lives and misery. One typical example should suffice. In the 1950s and 1960s, the World Bank financed the giant Akosombo Dam on the Volta River, in Ghana. The explicit purpose of the dam was and is to generate electricity for the huge Valco aluminum plant, owned by the American companies Maxxam and Reynolds. The factory, which receives tax breaks as well as below-cost energy, does not smelt local ore: Valco smelts imported alumina which has been previously refined in Louisiana from Jamaican bauxite. The dam, which flooded 8,500 square kilometers (5 percent of the country), destroyed seven hundred and forty villages and displaced eighty thousand people. The poor, who do not even receive electricity from the dam, now suffer in tremendous numbers from endemic onchocerciasis (river blindness, which affects a hundred thousand people, rendering seventy thousand of them totally sightless), and from schistosomiasis (eighty thousand people have been permanently disabled by this parasitic waterborne disease carried by two species of snail that are now the most common molluscs in the Volta reservoir).

Here in the Pacific Northwest, dams are causing the extinction of the greatest runs of salmon on the planet. During runs, one hundred thousand salmon, weighing up to one hundred pounds a piece, ascended the Columbia River *every day*. Now, sixty-seven of one hundred and ninety-two Pacific salmon populations are already extinct, and another seventy-six are at risk. The primary cause of extinction for these fish is that dams block their journeys to and from the ocean.

The oil and gas industries, mining, banks, agricorporations, hospitals, pharmaceuticals, operas (Seattle, which doesn't have enough money to house all of its residents, and which periodically breaks up homeless tent cities and shanty towns, is building a new concert hall, with Seattle taxpayers contributing $18.5 million toward purchasing the land and office building, $12.5 million for construction and site preparation, $14.7 million to build a new parking garage, and $500,000 in city management costs, for a total of $18,480 per seat), none of these industries could exist without massive influxes of

HOLOCAUSTS

money. In other words, none of them make even *fiscal* sense. This is to not to speak of the fact that they are killing the planet. I guess for all our vaunted rationality, we're really not so rational at all, are we?

. . .

At least 97 percent of the native forest in the contiguous United States has been cut down. Estimates suggest half of the Amazon will be gone within the next twenty years. Nearly all major fisheries worldwide are depleted. The climate is changing.

What has been the engine for all of this destruction? What has been the fuel? What have been the mechanisms by which it has been, and continues to be, accomplished?

. . .

As I write this, U.S. military support to Colombia is increasing. It is no coincidence that as this military support increases, death squads (another name, perhaps, for the night riders of the KKK, and for the *Einsatzgruppen* of the S.S.) flourish. Nor is it a coincidence that oil accounts for 35 percent of Colombia's exports, that Colombia is Latin America's fifth-largest oil exporter, and that it sends 85 percent of its crude oil to the United States. Oh, and did I mention the Venezuelan oil pipelines that flow near the Colombia border?

. . .

Last fall I interviewed Ramsey Clark, attorney general under Lyndon Johnson, and now a strong opponent of U.S. imperialism. I began by quoting a line from the federal government's Defense Planning Guide of 1992, that "the first objective [of U.S. foreign policy] is to prevent the reemergence of a new rival . . . with the U.S. convincing potential competitors that they need not aspire to a greater goal or a more aggressive posture to defend their legitimate interests."

He responded, "Our foreign policy has been a disaster since long

before that Planning Guide, and for a lot longer than we want to believe. We can go all the way back to the arrogance of the Monroe Doctrine, when the United States said, 'This hemisphere is ours,' ignoring all the other people who lived here, too. For a part of this century there were some restraints on our ability for arbitrary action—what you might call the inhibitions of the Cold War—but with the collapse of the Soviet Union we've had a headier sense of what we could do and get away with. Our overriding purpose has been from the beginning—and continues to be—world domination, that is, to build and maintain the capacity to coerce everybody else on the planet, nonviolently if possible, violently if necessary, and once in a while just for kicks. But the purpose of our foreign policy is not to be ringmaster just for the sake of putting the rest of the world through hoops. The purpose is to dominate for the exploitation of resources. And insofar as anyone gets in the way of our domination, they must be eliminated, or at the very least shown the error of their ways.

"But no matter how inhumane are the military aspects of our foreign policy, the trade aspects are even worse. Simply put, U.S. trade policies are driven by the exploitation of poor people the world over. Vietnam is a good example of both the military and economic inhumanity. Vietnam is a government and a people that we have punished mercilessly, just because they want freedom. The Vietnamese people had to fight for thirty years to achieve freedom, first fighting the French from 1945 to after Dien Bien Phu, and then the United States till 1975. I used to be criticized for saying the Vietnamese lost two million casualties, but I've noticed people say three million now without much criticism. And yet that was nothing compared to the effects of twenty years of sanctions, from 1975 to 1995, which brought a people down—a people who were invincible when they were threatened by physical force on their own land—to such dire poverty that they were taking open boats in stormy seas, drowning, to get someplace no one in his right mind would want to be: in a refugee camp in Hong Kong or someplace like that. They went simply because they saw no future anymore.

HOLOCAUSTS

"I went up north in Vietnam in 1971, during the summer the U.S. was trying to destroy the dikes through bombing. The United States government figured if it could destroy Vietnam's capacity for irrigation, it could starve them down."

"Which in itself," I said, "is a war crime."

"Sure," he replied. "Article 58, I think it is, covers the destruction of facilities essential to civilian life support. But since when does international law stop the U.S. government, except when it comes to something like the WTO, where it's to the advantage of the owners of capital for the government to follow the law?

"The U.S. figured if the Vietnamese couldn't control water they couldn't grow rice, and if they couldn't grow rice they couldn't feed themselves. At that time they were producing about five tons of rice to the hectare, which is extremely productive. The economy was based on the women. The men were living in holes in the South, with a bag of rice, a bag of ammunition, and a rifle, and that was about it. Some had been down there for years. And we were still bombing them mercilessly, and inflicting heavy casualties on them. But they survived.

"The sanctions, on the other hand, brought them down below Mozambique, which at that time was considered the poorest country in the world, with a per capita income of about eighty dollars per year. All of that reflects a policy that is totally materialistic, and enforced by violence, the threat of violence, and economic coercion."

"Of course the people of Vietnam," I said, "and Indians, and the people of Irian Jaya, and in fact most of the people in the world would certainly agree that U.S. foreign policy has been a disaster. But do you think most Americans would agree with that?"

"Sadly, I don't think most Americans would have an opinion about our foreign policy, which may be just as well, because I don't think most of them would have the basis for an opinion: They've been anesthetized about the meaning of a foreign policy to the degree that for the most part they're entirely unconcerned. I don't think they think about our foreign policy. But worse than that, when they do think about it, it's in terms of the demonization of evil ene-

mies, and propagandizing the goodness of our capacity for violence. When the Gulf War started, you could almost feel a reverence. We had what I called at the time a forty-two-day running commercial for militarism. In the United States everybody was glued to CNN and a few other stations, and whenever you'd see a Tomahawk cruise missile taking off from a navy vessel somewhere in the Gulf, you'd feel like standing up and shouting, 'Hooray for America, God Bless America.' But that missile was going to hit a market in Basra or someplace, destroy three hundred food stalls, and kill forty-two very poor people. And we will call that something good."

We looked at each other for a moment, before I looked away.

He continued, "It's very difficult to debate military spending in this country today, which is unbelievable when you think about it. Our military spending is absolutely, certifiably insane."

He told me about the Trident nuclear submarines I mentioned earlier in the book, each one capable of taking out 408 cities spanning half the globe.

"It's an unthinkable machine. What mind would conceive of constructing such a machine? What human justification could there ever be for its existence? What would be the meaning of daring to use it? Why would you have it?

"Our foreign policy is based on the use of our military might as an enforcer, exactly as Teddy Roosevelt said—damning Africans by saying it's an old African proverb—that we should walk softly but carry a big stick. What does that mean? It means, 'Do what I say or I'll smash your head in. I won't make a lot of noise about it; I'll just do it.' When you think about it, you realize that war has been the dominant experience of every generation of Americans."

I asked how many times the United States has invaded Latin America in the last two hundred years.

"It depends on who counts," he said, "but just in the twentieth century it was undoubtedly almost once per year. Off the top of my head I could count probably seventy."

"And of course it was the same in the nineteenth century."

"We sent the word out pretty early. We had to worry about the

HOLOCAUSTS

British and the Spanish for a long time, but we were determined to make it our hemisphere while at the same time certainly not satisfying ourselves to just this side of the world."

I asked how we maintain our image of ourselves as God's gift to the world, as the great bastion of democracy, the country that exports democracy to the world.

"But we're not a democracy," he insisted. "It's a terrible misunderstanding and a slander to the idea of democracy to call us that. We're a plutocracy in the Aristotelian sense. We're a government of wealth. Wealth has its way. The concentration of wealth and the division between rich and poor is unequaled anywhere. And think about whom we praise. The people we admire most are the wealthy, the Rockefellers and Morgans, the Bill Gateses and the Donald Trumps. Would any moral person accumulate a billion dollars when there are ten million infants dying of starvation every year? Is that the best you can find to do with your time?"

I told him I remembered seeing numbers back in 1990 that summed up for me this government's priorities. For what the world spent on the military every 2.5 hours that year, smallpox was eliminated back in the 1970s. And for the price of a single B-1 bomber, about $285 million, the government could provide basic immunization treatments, such as shots for chicken pox, diptheria, and measles, to the roughly 575,000,000 children in the world who lack them, thus saving 2.5 million lives annually.

He shook his head. "Those comparisons have a powerful illustrative impact, but they imply that if the money weren't spent on bombers it would be put to good use. The fact is that if the B-1 or B-2 were canceled, we still wouldn't spend the money on vaccinations, because that's not a part of our vision. It wouldn't serve the trade interests of the United States to vaccinate all those children. So it won't happen."

"What, then, is the vision?"

"Central to our foreign policy has been to actively work to deprive governments and peoples of the independence that comes from self-sufficiency in the production of food. I've believed for many

years that a country that can't produce the basic requirements for its own people, and particularly the most basic—food, water—can never really be free.

"Egypt is a great example of that. Can you imagine what sanctions would do to Cairo? You've got twelve million people living there, ten million of them in real poverty. If the United States put sanctions on Egypt, Cairo would be bedlam in ninety days. The people couldn't survive. Mubarak, the president of Egypt, is an American surrogate dictator. A military man, with a background in the air force. But you have to ask, what choice does he really have? Where can he go? Egypt is the second-largest aid recipient in the world, after Israel. They have been for a long time. Suppose he thumbed his nose at the United States. The United States would impose sanctions, and Mubarak and those around him would be dead. There would be rebellion in the streets. The people would have no choice. The same is true of the other Arab countries. They may think they've got wealth because of their oil, but Iraq has oil, and it hasn't helped them through the period of the sanctions. The sanctions have forced impoverishment on a people who had a quality of life that was by far the best in the region. They had universal health care with free medical services. They had a good educational system. Now they're dying at a rate of about eighteen thousand per month as a direct result of sanctions imposed by the United States in the name of the Security Council."

"Why Iraq?"

"Iran was the U.S. surrogate in the region, but when our man the Shah fell—he'd been imposed by the United States in a coup against Iran's democratically-elected government—Iraq began to emerge as too powerful. And, fatally for Iraq, it wasn't reliable as our new surrogate. So we had to take them out. First we bombed Iraq, a hundred and ten thousand aerial sorties in forty-two days: an average of one every thirty seconds. Eighty-eight thousand five hundred tons of bombs—these are Pentagon figures—which destroyed the infrastructure, to use a cruel word for life-support systems. Take water. We hit reservoirs, dams, pumping stations, pipelines, and purifica-

HOLOCAUSTS

tion plants. Some other people and I drove into Iraq at the end of the second week of the war, and there was no running water anywhere. People were drinking water out of the Tigris and Euphrates rivers.

"The war showed for the first time that you could destroy a country without setting foot on it. Our total casualties, according to the Pentagon, were one hundred and fifty-seven. By Yugoslavia's time we were able to inflict severe casualties, especially on the civilian population, with no losses at all. We lost one Stealth bomber, but we didn't lose the crew. They were saved. No losses. No casualties. Never set foot on the place. Didn't have to. Crippled it. Bombed it as long as they could stand it. Continued to bomb it."

I remembered Stanley Diamond's line about civilized humans killing at a distance, and I thought about how far removed we are—each and every one of us—from who we really are.

"But just as with Vietnam the sanctions have been infinitely more damaging, causing ten or fifteen times the numbers of casualties. They've killed more than a million and a half people."

That's more than a quarter of the Jews killed in the Holocaust, I thought. *We are very, very good Germans.* I recalled a conversation I'd had with a friend in which I'd expressed puzzlement about American ignorance and apathy concerning the killings in Iraq. She looked at me in surprise, and said, "But Derrick, of course we don't care. The ones who are dying are brown." I think it's more than that, though. We can recognize and allow ourselves to be horrified by the atrocities of the Holocaust because it's safely over: There's nothing we can do right now to stop it.

Clark continued, "More than half have been children under five, because children are more vulnerable than most segments of society. Particularly in your first year you're more susceptible to disease and to malnutrition, and to malnutrition of the mother. Many of the mothers are malnourished enough that they cannot give milk. They try to give some of the children of these mothers sugar water so they can make it, but because the United States destroyed the infrastructure, the water is contaminated. Within forty-eight hours the child is dead. That child could have been saved by a rehydration tablet that

costs less than a penny, but it's not available because of the sanctions. This is in a country that before the U.S. bombing and the sanctions produced fifteen percent of its own pharmaceuticals, but now can't even get the raw materials.

"The worst thing about the sanctions, aside from the human suffering, is that they show the will of power to force impoverishment on a whole population."

Another silence while we looked at each other.

Finally, he said, "The great question of the twenty-first century will be that of the relationship between the rich and the poor, and of triage among those who are not only expendable, but who are now even undesirable. We've got thirty percent of the labor force unemployed and unemployable, and with technology we don't need them. Why, then, from the perspective of capital, and from the perspective of U.S. foreign policy, should we support them? Why worry about AIDS in Africa? Why worry about hunger and malnutrition in Bangladesh or Somalia?"

I shook my head. "Let me know if I've got this right: From the perspective of those in power, it's only desirable to keep the poor alive insofar as they're useful, and the poor are useful only as labor, and as an excess pool of labor to drive wages down. Beyond that. . . ."

"It's hard for me to see how we will find meaningful and desirable employment for the mass of the population in the face of the degradation of ecological capacities of the planet, and in the face of technology's capacity to produce more than is needed. If society doesn't need the labor, and if you don't have skills, what are you worth to a society that won't bother to vaccinate your children? Or provide food for starving infants?"

Unnecessary people. Not merely disposable, as Kevin Bales talked about, but unnecessary. Undesirable. Excess. Inconvenient. I pictured rows of people stacked like logs, each one—including a slim twenty-three-year old who moments before had pointed to herself—with a single neat hole at the base of the skull. I recalled that members of mobile killing units had been traumatized by killing so many people face-to-face. And so had come trucks with hoses from exhaust

HOLOCAUSTS

pipes to sealed beds, and then permanent gas chambers, sanitized, psychically safe, just drop in a few crystals, close the ventilators, and it's done. Now it's even easier. Push a button, or watch your victims on video screens, like so many chaingunners or imps or cyber-demons in *Doom2*. Or easier yet, set in motion economic policies that kill as surely as a bullet to the brain, then sit back and watch your bank account grow.

Clark said, "In 1900, half of the labor force in the United States was involved in agriculture. Now it's probably less than five percent. In 1900, eighty percent of the labor force in China was involved in trying to feed people. When that comes down to ten percent, what are those other people going to do? We don't want them educated: All of our education is being reoriented toward some form of economic productivity, with most of it not in production per se, because we can't produce that much. Instead it's in services."

How much, I wondered, of the work that any of us do—myself included—is actually useful. I remembered how much I enjoyed being a beekeeper, because at least then when I finished the year I had something that someone could eat, something necessary to survival. How much of what any of us do helps us to be human and humane beings, and how much simply makes work, gives us something to do?

■　　　　■　　　　■

One of the most powerful unions in this state is the California Correctional Peace Officers Union. It was a strong supporter of the state's current governor, Gray Davis, and of the state's former governor, Pete Wilson, contributing heavily to their electoral campaigns. It was the second-largest contributor to the campaign for California's three strikes law, which calls for mandatory life imprisonment for anyone convicted of a third offense, which has been as little as stealing a slice of pizza (the third strike for one of my students was to steal a bicycle from someone's garage). In exchange for political support,

the union wants, reasonably enough, higher wages and more jobs. In this case more jobs means more prisons, which means more prisoners, a 400 percent increase in the last fifteen years. But the union is reaching even higher. A few years ago, it issued a study, called, "Affordable Prisons," proposing that California build "mega-prisons," each holding up to twenty thousand prisoners—human beings, mainly those whose skin happens to not be the color of flesh—and that legislators pass a law that would forever bypass voter approval for prison bonds. How many people are spending years—years that will never come back—in prison because the union is, rationally enough, wanting job security for its members?

■   ■   ■

I want to tell you two things I learned last night. Do you remember the benefit I did for the Earth Liberation Prisoners Support Network? It was, partly, for the network, in general, and, partly, for two people specifically, who go by the names Critter and Free. They'd been accused (accurately, it ends up) of torching a sports utility vehicle at a dealership. By the time I did the benefit, Critter had already plea-bargained, and been sentenced to sixty-six months. Even presuming that anyone should be punished and not celebrated for destroying an SUV, that seemed pretty steep. Last night, I heard Free had been found guilty, and was sentenced to twenty-two years in prison. You can supply your own example of people who have committed grievous crimes who have received a far less severe punishment.

The other thing I learned has to do with the latest round of protests against globalization. Already there have been protests in Seattle, Prague, Berne, and many other cities around the world. These protests have often turned violent, as police have shot tear gas and rubber bullets at protestors, and have beaten them with clubs. Well, the violence just got ratcheted up: In Sweden, police fired live bullets at protestors, wounding nineteen, one critically, and, in

HOLOCAUSTS

Switzerland, a protester was killed.

I guess we know that things are bad when the police start shooting live rounds at other whites (and in Sweden and Switzerland, no less).

▪   ▪   ▪

I suddenly remembered a conversation I'd read about, years ago, between George McGovern and Robert Anderson, the president of Rockwell International. McGovern asked Anderson if he wouldn't rather build mass transit systems than B-1 bombers. Anderson said he would, but they both knew there was no chance Congress would give money for that. I talked to Clark about it.

"They're absolutely right. Capital in the United States would never accept that shift in priorities, for many reasons. The first is that the military is a means of international domination, and anything that threatens that domination will not be allowed to happen. The second is that capital requires continuing ever-expanding demand, and mass transit shrinks demand. Capital requires the continuous creation of new demand for capital-intensive activity from which the owners can reap enormous profits. It does not matter if those activities are detrimental to living beings or communities. For example, those in power seem to have an unlimited imagination for conjuring new excuses to throw money at the military. I was saddened by the almost pathetic naïveté of the people of this country some ten years ago when we were talking about reaping a peace dividend."

"Which, of course, we never hear about anymore."

"But people believed there would be a peace dividend! They said, 'Finally, free at last! Thank God Almighty! Now at last we can do some of the things we've always wanted to do. Now that we don't have that B-1 bomber we can vaccinate children and save millions of lives.' Which you could. But we don't.

"We have to come to grips with the fact that we've been consistently sold a bill of goods that has caused people to believe they've been heroic when they've done terrible things in the name of their country through military actions. I mean, how many of those pilots

who bombed Vietnam, even the ones who became prisoners, ever asked themselves, 'I wonder what it was like being a Vietnamese when I was coming over and dropping those bombs.'"

"I kept thinking about that," I said, "when John McCain used his prisoner of war status to gain political currency, and how I never heard anyone publicly confront him about killing civilians."

"I've never heard him wonder whether it was possible that bombing those poor people wasn't the right thing to do," Clark said. He continued, slowly, "Colin Powell seems to be a compelling figure. It took a lot of luck for him to get where he got. But he was asked during the Gulf War how many Iraqis he thought the United States had killed. And his response was, and this is a direct quote, 'Frankly, that's a number that doesn't interest me very much.' Now, aside from international law—which requires all participants in war to count their enemy dead, and identify their names and religions so that their families can be notified and so they can be buried according to their faith—that is an extraordinarily inhumane statement. It doesn't matter. I'm not interested in how many were killed. And then you see a fellow like our former drug czar, Barry McCaffrey, coming in and attacking defenseless withdrawing Iraqi troops, and causing his command to kill several thousand people just like that." He snapped his finger. "That's a war crime of the first magnitude, and yet they are rewarded; they're heroes for it. They stand up as presidential candidates, and it may be one of their best draws."

■   ■   ■

Hitler was ahead of his time. Social conditions weren't yet ripe for a government to fully realize the elimination of diversity toward which he aimed. Simply put, his—or any—corporate-governmental state had not yet achieved the sort of power necessary to emplace and maintain that purity of control. This is true for power relative to other corporate states; it's true for power relative to human beings, and it's true for power relative to the natural world.

So far as the former goes, we need to remember that Hitler was-

HOLOCAUSTS

n't defeated by Jews or members of resistance organizations; he was defeated by other imperial powers, the Soviet Union, Britain, and the United States. Had the Wehrmacht not foundered on the Russian winter and been repulsed by Russian troops, our stories of the time after Dachau would now read much differently. And, certainly, these other powers didn't stop the Nazis because of that nation's mistreatment of Jews, Romani, and so on. Indeed, each has its own august tradition of similarly unabated ruthlessness. At base, these nations stopped the German government because they didn't want it to control resources they themselves controlled or coveted.

So far as the second, control over people, imagine if Hitler had been able to broadcast his message twenty-four hours per day into people's homes, and if people had willingly tuned in to these broadcasts hour after hour, day after day. Imagine the effectiveness of his propaganda if teleplays could have insinuated his form of casting and fate into the lives of his subjects from infancy to senescence. I think we do ourselves a disservice if we look at old clips of Hitler strutting, yelling, and gesticulating, and wonder how the hell anyone came under his spell. First, consider who chose those clips: the victors, who as always have an interest in making their enemies look ludicrous. But, more importantly, that wasn't even the Nazis' main form of propaganda. Joseph Goebbels, party propaganda chief for the National Socialists, was clear that rather than having the media inculcate people with heavy-handed political messages, it was much better to give them lots of light entertainment. Goebbels also believed that propaganda worked best when it put forth the illusion of diversity, but had a numbing sameness—a purity—to the underlying ideological message.

For those whom light entertainment failed to convince, technology was also not sufficiently advanced to allow such strict governmental control of individuals as Hitler would, perhaps, have liked. Sure, his state police force was reasonably efficient for its day, but, not only did the Nazis have no satellite surveillance systems, they didn't even have satellites. And the forensic sciences were in their early stages. It would not have been possible to track, identify, or ap-

prehend antisocial individuals through computer-matching of finger-prints or facial scans. I'm sure by now you've heard that every person who attended the 2001 Super Bowl had her or his face surreptitiously scanned; these images were cross-checked with computer images, to identify lawbreakers. And now Sacramento's airport has begun scanning the face of every passenger. Hitler had no worldwide network of computers (named *Echelon* or not) capable of intercepting three *billion* phone or E-mail (*What's E-mail?* I can hear Adolf ask) messages per day, sifting through approximately 90 percent of all transmissions. Hitler not only did not have what we would consider computers, but he also did not have the capacity to capture computer signals, such as keystrokes or images, from monitors through walls or from other buildings. He did not have the capacity to point special types of cameras at people and perform strip searches, or even body cavity searches. Amateur that he was, Hitler did not even have a national system of social security numbers, which, in the words of United States secretary of state Colin Powell, "allows us to monitor, track down and capture an American citizen." None of this he had. Scientists used such unreliable means as phrenology to identify potential miscreants, having no knowledge of the human genome. And, Hitler would not even have recognized the word *genotype*, much less been able to create genetically altered diseases to target specific races.

So far as destruction of the natural world, Hitler's vegetarianism and pseudo-paganism have long been used as fodder for *ad hominem* attacks on animal rights activists and environmentalists: if Hitler was a vegetarian, the slur goes, then all vegetarians must somehow be Nazis. Well, chainsaws were developed under the Nazi regime, but I don't see anyone conflating Hitler with Weyerhaeuser (although, now that I think about it, they *are* both German). Hitler had no more connection to wild nature than any other civilized human being. The fundamental metaphor of National Socialism as it related to the world around it was the garden, not the wild forest. One of the most important Nazi ideologists, R. W. Darré, made clear the relationship between gardening and genocide: "He who leaves the plants in a garden to themselves will soon find to his surprise that the garden is

HOLOCAUSTS

overgrown by weeds and that even the basic character of the plants has changed. If therefore the garden is to remain the breeding ground for the plants, if, in other words, it is to lift itself above the harsh rule of natural forces, then the forming will of a gardener is necessary, a gardener who, by providing suitable conditions for growing, or by keeping harmful influences away, or by both together, carefully tends what needs tending, and ruthlessly eliminates the weeds which would deprive the better plants of nutrition, air, light, and sun. . . . Thus we are facing the realization that questions of breeding are not trivial for political thought, but that they have to be at the center of all considerations, and that their answers must follow from the spiritual, from the ideological attitude of a people. We must even assert that a people can only reach spiritual and moral equilibrium if a well-conceived breeding plan stands at the very *center* of its culture."

We still believe in the metaphor of the garden. There are useful species, off of which we can turn a buck, and, there are species in the way. Likewise, there are useful people—those who are instrumental, productive—and, there are those who clutter up land we could otherwise use. Now, though, the metaphor and reality of the garden has moved to its next stage, coinciding with the movement of our society. No longer do we as a whole weed by hand, which is far too inefficient. Now we have massive monocultural fields of plants genetically altered for resistance to Monsanto's Roundup™ herbicide. The reasoning has progressed, the control has gotten tighter, the act of killing more abstract, the diversity diminished.

It is significant that oftentimes when Europeans searched for Indian gardens to destroy, they could not readily tell what was garden and what was forest (not that, ultimately, this stopped the Europeans, as, in time, they destroyed them both). To not see the world in strictly utilitarian terms is not to cease having preferences. It is merely to see that—and sometimes how—things (or, rather, beings) fit together, how they move in short and long patterns of rhythm and consequence. And it is to attempt to fit oneself into those patterns, taking care to not upset the sometimes delicate balance that

THE CULTURE OF MAKE BELIEVE

must remain between those one considers friends and those one considers honored enemies. Hitler did not understand this, and, for the most part, neither do we.

But there is a difference between Hitler and us. Hitler did not have the capacity to irradiate the planet, nor to poison it (organochloride pesticides and herbicides came into common usage after World War II (and in fact were in many ways by-products of the gas warfare programs of World War I): prior to that, *every* farm was organic). He didn't have the capacity to change the planet's climate. He did not have at his disposal a standing army designed to fight two major wars in disparate parts of the globe at the same time. The Wehrmacht couldn't even handle two *fronts*. The economy had not become so integrated, so *rationalized*—in other words, it had not lost so much of its diversity—as to be under the control of so few people who could kill millions of human beings—hell, who could kill the whole planet—by the merest extension of economic pressure.

In his analysis of the social effects of information technologies, Joseph Weizenbaum wrote, "Germany implemented the 'final solution' of its 'Jewish Problem' as a textbook exercise in instrumental reasoning. Humanity briefly shuddered when it could no longer avert its gaze from what had happened, when the photographs taken by the killers themselves began to circulate, and when the pitiful survivors re-emerged into the light. But in the end it made no difference. The same logic, the same cold and ruthless application of calculating reason, slaughtered at least as many people during the next twenty years as had fallen victim to the technicians of the thousand-year Reich. We have learned nothing."

■　　　■　　　■

In her classic work, *Eichmann in Jerusalem*, Hannah Arendt articulated the central question of the Holocaust, and indeed of civilization, which is "how to overcome. . . the animal pity by which all normal men are affected in the presence of physical suffering." How, indeed? There is, at this point, though, I think, a far more important

HOLOCAUSTS

question: Having removed ourselves so far from our beginnings, how do we get back?

．　　　．　　　．

Unless it is stopped, the dominant culture will kill everything on the planet, or, at least, everything it can.

Each holocaust is unique. The destruction of European Jewry did not look like the destruction of the American Indians. It could not, because the technologies involved were not the same, the targets were not the same, and the perpetrators were not the same. They shared motivations and certain aspects of their socialization, to be sure, but they were not the same. Similarly, the slaughter of Armenians (and Kurds) by Turks did not (and does not) look like the slaughter of Vietnamese by Americans. And, just as similarly, the holocausts of the twenty-first century will not, and do not already, look like the great holocausts of the twentieth. They cannot, because our society has progressed.

And every holocaust looks different, depending on the class to which the observer belongs. The Holocaust looked far different to high-ranking Nazi officials and to executives of large corporations— both of whose primary social concerns would have been how to max- imize production and control, that is, how to most effectively exploit human and nonhuman resources—than it did to good Germans, whose primary concerns were as varied as the people themselves but probably included doing their own jobs—immoral as those jobs may have been from an outside perspective—as well as possible; may have included feelings of relief that those in power were finally doing something about the "Jewish Problem"; and certainly included doing whatever they could to not notice the greasy smoke from the crema- toria (constructed with the best materials and faultless workmanship). The Holocaust, then, also looked different to good Germans than it did to those who resisted, whose main concerns may have been how to bring down the system. And, it looked different to those who re- sisted than it did to those who were considered *untermenschen*, whose

main concerns may have been staying alive, or, failing that, dying with dignity.

Manifest Destiny looked different to Indians than it did to J. P. Morgan. American slavery looked different to slaves than it did to those whose comforts and elegancies were based on slavery, and than it did to those for whom free black labor drove down their wages.

What will the great holocausts of the twenty-first century look like? It depends on where you stand. Look around.

If you're in group one, the decent White men, your postmodern holocausts will be, at most, barely visible, and, at least, a price you're willing to pay, as Madame Albright said about killing Iraqi children. The holocausts will probably share similarities with other holocausts, as you attempt to maximize production—to "grow the economy," as you might say—and, as when necessary, you attempt to eradicate dissent. This means the holocaust will look like a booming economy beset by shifting problems that somehow always keep you from ever reaching the Promised Land, whatever that might be. The holocaust will look like numbers on ledgers. It will look like technical problems to be solved, whether those problems are increasing your access to necessary resources, dealing with global warming, calming unrest on the streets, or figuring out what to do about too many unproductive people on land you know you could be put to better use. The holocaust will look like houses with gates, limousines with bulletproof glass, and a military budget that can never stop increasing (just yesterday I read that President Bush the Second wants to increase the military budget another $18 billion, to $343.5 billion (not including classified budgets as well as bookkeeping shenanigans such as not including interest on military-related debt, the inclusion of which would boost the total to about $640 billion): Note that for about $4.6 billion—as much as the U.S. military spends on a three-day weekend—sanitary water could be provided for every human being who lacks it; but, of course, sanitary water for human beings has never been the point, or we would never have destroyed our water supplies in the first place). The holocaust will feel like economics. It will feel like progress. It will feel like technologi-

HOLOCAUSTS

cal innovation. It will feel like civilization. It will feel like the way things are.

If you're in the second group, you will continue to be co-opted into supporting the system that does not serve you well. Perhaps, the holocaust will look like a new car. Perhaps it will look like eating a bar of chocolate. Perhaps it will look like lending your talents to a major corporation—or, more broadly, toward economic production—so you can make a better life for your children. Perhaps it will look like working as an engineer for Shell or on an assembly line for General Motors. Maybe it will look like basing a person's value on her or his employability or productivity. Perhaps it will look like anger at Mexicans or Pakistanis or Algerians or Hmong who compete with you for jobs, and who, of course, because they don't live like fully human beings, can afford to work for less. Perhaps it will look like outrage at environmentalists who want to save some damn suckerfish, even (or especially) if it impinges on your property rights, or if it takes water you need to irrigate, to make the desert bloom, to make the desert productive. Maybe it will feel like continuing to do a job that you hate—and that requires so little of your humanity—because, no matter how you try, you never can seem to catch up. Maybe it will feel like being tired at the end of the day, and just wanting to sit and watch some television. Such is how it was during the Third Reich, as when Goebbels said, "The broadcasting programmes need to be put together in such a way that while they still cater for sophisticated tastes, they are also pleasing and accessible to less demanding listeners. . . . They should offer an intelligent and psychologically skillful blend of what is informative, stimulating, relaxing, and entertaining. Of these, relaxation deserves special care . . . giving them a right to recuperate and refresh themselves during the few hours when they are off work." Such is how it is now in Mexico, where Emilio Azcarraga, the billionaire head of the Mexican media giant Televisa, which has close ties to the largest U.S. media firms, says, "Mexico is a country of a modest, very fucked class, which will never stop being fucked. Television has the obligation to bring diversion to these people and remove them from their sad reality and difficult fu-

ture." I leave it to American readers to decide the degree to which this holds true in the United States. As for me, I'm going to go watch *Who Wants to Be A Millionaire?*

If you're in the subsection of the third group, who might some day resist but don't know where to put your rage, the holocaust might look like armed robbery, auto theft, assault. It might look like joining a gang. It might look like needle tracks down the insides of your arms, and might smell like the bitter, vinegary stench of tar heroin. Or maybe it smells minty strong, like menthol, like the sweet smell of crack brought into your neighborhood at the behest of the CIA. Or maybe not. Maybe it's the unmistakable smell of the inside of a cop car, and a vision through that rear window of a little girl eating an ice cream cone, with the knowledge that never in your life will you see this sight again. Maybe it looks like Pelican Bay, or Marion, or San Quentin, or Leavenworth. Or maybe it feels like a bullet in the back of the head, and leaves you lying on the streets of New York City, Cincinnati, Seattle, Oakland, Los Angeles, Atlanta, Baltimore, Washington D.C.

If you're a member of the subsection of group three, already working against the centralization of power, against the system, then, maybe, from your perspective, the holocaust looks like rows of black-clad armored policemen, and it smells like tear gas. Maybe it looks like lobbying a Congress you know has never served you. Maybe it looks like the destruction of place after wild place, and feels like an impotence sharp as a broken leg. Maybe it looks like staring down the barrel of an American-made gun in the hands of a Colombian man wearing American-made camo fatigues, and knowing that your life is over.

For those of the fourth class, the simply extra, maybe it looks like the view from just outside the chain link fence surrounding a chemical refinery, and maybe it smells like Cancer Alley. Maybe it looks like children with leukemia, children with cancer of the spine, children with birth defects. Maybe it feels like the grinding ache of hunger that has been your closest companion since you were born. Maybe it looks like the death of your daughter from starvation, and

HOLOCAUSTS

the death of your son from diphtheria, measles, or chicken pox. Maybe it feels like death from dehydration, when a tablet costing less than a penny could have saved your life. Or maybe it feels like nothing. Maybe it sounds like nothing, looks like nothing: What does it feel like to be struck by a missile in the middle of the night, a missile traveling faster than the speed of sound, a missile launched a thousand miles away?

Maybe it feels like salmon battering themselves against dams, monkeys locked in steel cages, polar bears starving on a dwindling ice cap, hogs confined in crates so small they cannot stand, trees falling to the chainsaw, rivers poisoned, whales deafened by sonic blasts from Navy experiments. Maybe it feels like the crack of tibia under the unforgiving jaws of a leghold trap.

Maybe it looks like the destruction of the planet's life support systems. Maybe it looks like the final conversion of the living to the dead.

As much as I cannot help but see the similarities between prisons and concentration camps, it seems to me a grave error to count on Zyklon-B–dispensing showers to mark the new holocaust. Perhaps the new holocaust is dioxin in polar bear fat, metam sodium in the Smith River. Perhaps it comes in the form of decreasing numbers of corporations controlling increasing portions of our food supply, until, as now, three huge corporations control more than 80 percent of the beef market, and seven corporations control more than 90 percent of the grain market. Perhaps it comes in the form of these corporations, and the governments which provide the muscle for them, deciding who eats and who does not. Perhaps it comes in the form of so much starvation that we cannot count the dead. Perhaps it comes in the form of all of these, and in many others I could not name even if I were able to predict.

But, this I know. The pattern has been of increasing efficiency in the destruction, and increasing abstraction. Andrew Jackson himself took the "sculps" of the Indians he murdered. Heinrich Himmler nearly fainted when a hundred Jews were shot in front of him, which was surely one reason for the increased use of gas. Now, of course, it

can all be done by economics.

And, this I know, too. No matter what form it takes, most of us will not notice it. Those who notice will pay too little attention. We will follow the rules layed down by Noah and his remaining sons and we will walk backward to not see our father's nakedness. It does not matter how great the cost to others nor even to ourselves, we will soldier on. We will, ourselves, walk quietly, meekly, into whatever form the gas chambers take, if only we are allowed to believe they are bathrooms.

HOLOCAUSTS

WHEN I LOOK AT HISTORY,

I AM A PESSIMIST...

BUT WHEN I LOOK AT

PREHISTORY, I AM

AN OPTIMIST.

J. C. SMUTS

COMING HOME

SOMETIMES, WHEN I'VE SPENT TOO MANY HOURS crying over sources, or when my eyes have grown fuzzy from too much time spent staring at the screen, trying to fashion the next sentence, I'll turn off the computer and step outside. Cats roll in the sunshine, and dogs run toward me to put their heads on my lap. Through and behind the panting of dogs I hear birdsongs in the thick trees that surround my home. The birds call back and forth to each other, and each time I hear them—just as, each night, when I hear frogs sing outside my windows—I know that I am listening to the most beautiful sounds in the world. Earlier today, I walked to the creek where last winter I saw coho salmon spawning, and I saw hundreds of tiny fish, silver with small dots, the next generation, for now, still surviving. When I returned, I sat again, outside, and I watched the cats, patted the heads of the dogs, listened to the bird-songs, and knew that I had everything any human being could ever want.

■   ■   ■

For years now—since I was thirteen—I've kept thinking about that slim dark-haired woman, the one about to be shot, and how she pointed to herself and told her age. She was, I believe, bringing home to the man watching, in as succinct a way as possible, that she was a unique human being. She was alive, with a past, with a present, and until, then, a future.

■   ■   ■

This book began as an exploration of hate in the Western world, and it ends, really, with the end of life on the planet. The problem, as near as I can see it, is the valuing of the abstract over the particular: of production over life; of economic (and other) systems over living beings, be they humans, or rivers, or polar bears; of our preconceptions of what niggers or Chinese or Irish dogs are supposed to be, instead of this black man, this Chinese woman, this Irish man, complete with his or her own cultural and personal histories, with desires and hopes and fears; of photographs of women over the women themselves, of the bodies of women over their whole beings, bodies and minds and hearts and sorrows and joys; of truncated conceptions of our own capacities, based on what we have been allowed to express over who we really are. The problem is, simply, that of seeing ourselves and others as instruments to be used, instead of people to be enjoyed in relationship.

COMING HOME

What I propose as a "solution" to this problem of the ascendancy of abstraction is a return to the particular. I support an anti-system to promote a falling in love with the particular. To love this particular tree, that particular person, this glint of sunlight off this dragonfly wing, and, insofar as is possible, to perceive each of those around us as subjects. This is not a simple plea for us to all just get along. I'm not suggesting we replace abstract hate with a love just as abstract. That's pointless, absurd, meaningless, and, in the end, impossible. I am not an abstract being. I have fingers, flesh, bones. I love this person. I do not love that person. Nor am I suggesting we simply step away from violence. I'm suggesting that there is a difference—all the difference in the world, really—between real fights between real people—even when real blood is spilled—and killings based on preconceptions. What I'm suggesting is a return to our humanity.

If we are to do that, the first thing we must do is to see the inhumanity of our current system for what it is, and we must speak about it. If the first rule of a dysfunctional family or society is *Don't*, the first rule of a functioning society is *Do*. Talk about it. Speak out, like Ham, Noah's curses be damned.

Of course, it's not so easy. It's all very fine for me to say how much joy it brings me to listen to birdsong, but my enjoyment, or anyone else's, is irrelevant to the suffering of others, to the degree that it does not compel me to shut down the source of the other's misery. Having fallen in love with our own lives, and the lives of those around us—even our honored enemies (though not McNamara and his likes who, by their actions, show themselves to be willing to exploit)—the next step is to get rid of our whole inhumane system, to quit valuing production over life, and to physically stop those who do. The next step is to bring down that which originated in conquest abroad and repression at home. The next step is a planet liberated from the destruction; the next step is the end of civilization.

THE CULTURE OF MAKE BELIEVE

Get rid of civilization? I can hear you say. *That's your solution?* The hatred that characterizes so much of our system—the hatred I've described and analyzed in this book—is not a product of biology. People are not fundamentally hateful. Our hate is not a result of several billion years of natural selection. It's a result of the framing conditions under which each of us are raised. It's a result of the unquestioned assumptions that inform us. If we want to stop the hate, we need to get rid of the framing conditions. Until we do that, we're bound to fail. So, yes, that is precisely my solution, we need to get rid of civilization.

Maybe that seems absurd, to you. It doesn't, to me. It just seems like a lot of work, done by a lot of people in a lot of places in a lot of different ways. But I'll tell you something that does seem absurd to me: the possibility of allowing this inhumane system to continue.

■   ■   ■

How do we bring down civilization? I cannot tell you. There are as many ways as there are people. The answers are particular, growing from particular people in particular circumstances in particular places. But I know that the first and, perhaps, most important step is to see civilization for what it is, to take into our bodies the enormity of what it has already cost us, and to learn that this realization did not kill us, that we are stronger than the pain, stronger, even, than this long and awful history of exploitation. Having realized that, we will now be ready for the technical task of dismantling all that we, as a culture, have become. And though they—the ones who still gain their identity from the system—may hate us all and try, like Noah, to curse and to enslave us, they will never be able to succeed entirely, because, beneath it all, our humanity runs far deeper than any mere socialization. We must never forget that.

COMING HOME

■   ■   ■

Once upon a time human beings lived here. They sat by the stream, and they laughed. They slept. They had sex. They caught salmon. They ate them. They quarreled with their neighbors. Sometimes, they even fought. Their children lived here, and their children's children, and so on, forever, eating the children of the salmon, quarreling with the children of the neighbors, fighting the children of the neighbors, celebrating with the children of the neighbors, marrying the children of the neighbors, and having children with the children of the neighbors. They lived, and slept, in the sun, and felt the sun on their faces in the morning. At night, when they were tired, they went to sleep, and the next morning, they got up, and they sat by the stream, and they laughed. This is how human beings lived.

■   ■   ■

The biblical story of Noah and Ham ends with the cursing of Ham, and his perpetual enslavement. Exit, stage left, and on with the play. *Of course* that's how the story would end, because it was told by the successors to Noah. But I envision another ending to this story, one that tells of events from Ham's perspective.

Ashamed, impoverished, stripped of everything he once thought of as his birthright, Ham leaves the only way of living he has ever known. He trudges through forests—for the region had yet to be deforested—and he weeps, for days. He misses his home. He misses his father.

Ham knows that he can never go back: Seeing his father in all his nakedness has caused something inside him to shift.

In time, Ham begins to walk easier. He meets other groups of people who live in ways he has not known; lives that barely seem possible. "Your father made you a slave," they say. "But what is a slave? We do not know that word." Ham lives among these people. It does not take long before he feels something he has never felt before: a happy, fecund sense of freedom.

In this version of the story, Ham never returns to his former home, and soon cannot imagine what could have held him there in the first place.

COMING HOME

ACKNOWLEDGMENTS

MY FOREMOST DEBT OF GRATITUDE is as always to the land where I live, and to those others who also call this home. The trees, frogs, fish, birds, beetles, bears, spiders, slugs, rabbits, fungi, grasses, berries, bushes, and so many others. Stars and moon, pond and stream, waves, wind, raindrops, rocks, and soil. You inform and inspire me. You teach me how to be a human being.

I owe a debt also to past and present victims of civilization. The Arawaks, Khoikhoi, Pontiacs, Xhosa, Dani, coho, chum, steelhead, silverspot butterfly, wood bison, grizzly bears, great blue whales, red-legged frogs. All these and many more, individually and collectively. Every human who has ever slaved away her or his life to provide comforts and elegancies for another. Every nonhuman who has done the same. The debt I owe you is not so much gratitude, though there is that, as it is sorrow. I include in this apology the trees whose processed flesh made this book. More so, however, even than a debt of sorrow, I owe you all the promise that I will not forget. This I give.

I am grateful to all of those who, singly or collectively, have resisted civilization. Jesus, Diogenes, Spartacus. Ambiorix, Vercingentorix, Boudicea. The Eburones, Usipetes, Tencteri, Morini, Icene. John Logan, Sitting Bull, Crazy Horse, Tupac Amaru. The Xhosa. Siyolo. The San, Dani, Lakota. Gabriel Prosser, Francois Dominique Toussaint L'Overture, Denmark Vesey. Harriet Tubman. Nanny (and the other Maroons). Thomas Münzer. Ned Ludd. Nestor Makhno. All these and so many more—those with names we know, and those whose names we never will. I am grateful, also, to those nonhumans who have actively or passively, singly or collectively, resisted the onslaught of civilization. All of this resistance has, too, taught me what it means to be a human being.

I am thankful for my mother, Mary Jensen, who has, among many other things, taught me by example the meaning of grace under adversity.

Many others helped with the book. I could never find a better editor and publisher than Beau Friedlander. Lisa Chase is right behind him in her editorial capacity. Julie Burke is simply the best book designer in the world. I thank Ramsey Clark, Richard Drinnon, George Gerbner, Kevin Bales, George Draffan, John Keeble, John Osborn, George Ritzer, and John Zerzan, whose conversations helped me find my way. George Draffan also helped me write some parts of this book as part of our Endgame project. And I thank Sy Safransky, Andrew Snee, and the others at *The Sun* for giving me the opportunity to conduct these interviews. I am grateful to Bridget Kinsella for giving me her support, her ear, her heart, and her talent, all of which (except the ear) are immense; to Roianne Ahn, for her ability to know herself, to know others, and to know me; to Laiman Mai, for her wisdom, depth, and cheer; to Melanie Adcock, for her courage and intelligence; to Val Galante, for her friendship, patience, and assistance; to Becca, for being everything I could hope for in a big sister; to Frances Moore Lappé, for her wonderful work and even more wonderful friendship; to Karen Rath, for the quality of her heart, and for her work in defense of the old ones.

And finally, I am thankful to my Muse and Dreamgiver, from whom the words and ideas flow and without whom this book would not have been possible.

UNCOVERING

■

"Monsters exist. . . ." is from Levi, 394.

The KKK "is not a hate group, but we are a LOVE group. . . . " is from http://www.kukluxklan.org/doesthe.htm.

"It may be that this defendant. . . ." is from IMT, volume v, p 118.

Hate crime statistics are from Hate, 8.

"To this day, the federal government admits that 33 percent. . . ." is cited at Churchill, 58.

"discovery gave title. . . ." is from Johnson v. M'Intosh, 14.

"However extravagant. . . ." is from Johnson v. M'Intosh, 22.

"Conquest gives a title. . . ." is from Johnson v. M'Intosh, 22.

UTILITY

■

"What an abundance. . . ." is from de Kiewiet, 96.

"been in the region for nearly two million years. . . ." is from Mostert, 24.

"justly won by the sword. . . ." is from Moodie, part I, 205.

"You may no longer be naked. . . ." is from Reader's Digest, 133–136.

"Thus were enacted the first of the infamous Pass Laws of apartheid. . . ." is cited at Wheatcroft, 55; and at Worger, 114.

"enjoined to impress upon the native mind. . . ." is from Ransome, 66, 67.

"modern South African gold mining really began. . . ." is from Innes, 45.

"Is there any way short of compulsion. . . ." is cited at Johnstone, 29.

"To make him an entirely free agent. . . ." is cited at Johnstone, 35.

"the government (made up of the mine owners and others like them) passed poll, hut, and even dog taxes. . . ." is from Frontline, Feb. 1, 1994.

"remove these poor children out of their state of sloth. . . ." is from Mintner, 24; and Reader's Digest, 206.

"The bill became popularly known as the Every-Man-to-Wallop-His-Own-Nigger Bill" is from Wheatcroft, 148.

"Additional Masters and Servants Laws prohibited Africans from breaking their contracts. . . ." is from Mintner, 24.

"death rates in the mines ran between 8 and 10 percent per year. . . ." is from Innes, 74.

"a policy that would establish once and for all. . . ." is cited at Johnstone, 27.

"Although blacks make up only twelve and a half percent of the population of this country" is from National Criminal Justice Commission Key Findings.

"they account for more than 45 percent. . . ." is from Bureau of Justice, table 1.8.

"The United States imprisons black men more than six times more frequently than it does whites" is from Kupers, 94.

"four times more than South Africa did during apartheid" is from Minnesota.

"Over 30 percent of this nation's African American males. . . ." to the end of the paragraph is all from Kupers, 94.

NOTES

"every day in the United States, at least four to six people die because they encountered police" is from Deadliest Day.

"each year Congress fails to provide funding" is from Rights For All, chapter three, page three.

The accounts of those murdered by police are from Stolen Lives.

"rates for male rape inside prison run between 9 and 20 percent" is from Kupers, 137.

"14 percent of that prison's population had been sexually assaulted there" is from Wooden and Parker, 116.

"(9 percent of the heterosexuals and forty-one percent of the homosexuals had been sexually assaulted)" is from Wooden and Parker, 99.

"22 percent of those who responded indicated they'd been forced to have sexual contact" is from Struckman-Johnson, 67.

"The level is high enough to have caused a Court of Appeals in 1988 to label it a 'national disgrace'" is from *Martin v. White*, 1.

"Few aspects of incarceration are more horrifying. . . ." is cited at Dunbaugh.

"a prison rape researcher found that 15 percent of the cases involved. . . ." is from Buffum, 105.

"Most studies suggest that about 25 percent of women. . . ." is from Russell, 35.

"the extraordinary 'Hate Directory,' which monitors even such obscure sites as. . . ." is from Hate Directory.

"Included are Internet sites. . . ." is from Hate Directory.

INVISIBILITY

■

"The truth is replaced by silence. . . ." is from Edwards, 82.

The KKK spread "with inconceivable rapidity. . . ." is from The History of the

Original Ku Klux Klan.

"Murders of Negroes are so common. . . ." is cited at Wade, 79.

"at least 2000 people. . . ." is cited at Arjet.

"The white men of the South were aroused. . . ." is from Wilson, Volume V, 58.

"to start something to break this monotony. . . ." is from Davis, Susan, 6.

"purely social. . . ." is from Lester, 22.

"There is no intention or desire. . . ." is cited at Wade, 49.

"Were all the Ku-Klux arrested. . . ." is cited at Wade, 57.

"They are going to arrest us all and execute us for Shell" is from Flames of Shell.

"Shell operations still impossible. . . ." is from Lean.

"For a commercial company to make investments. . . ." is from Flames of Shell.

"Human life does not mean much. . . ." is from Flames of Shell.

"Rule A: Don't. . . ." is cited at Edwards, 81.

"20,000 Mexican children. . . ." is from Chomsky.

"One hundred to eight hundred thousand Thai girls and boys. . . ." comes from a number of sources. UNICEF provides the lower-end estimate, the Centre for the Protection of Children's Rights the higher. For the high-end source, see Vachs, among many others.

"If you can suck it. . . ." is from Hechler.

"1.5 to 2 million child prostitutes in India" is from Robinson.

"those in Bombay. . . ." is from Lukas.

"Five hundred thousand child prostitutes work in Brazil" is from Vachs.

"a child of thirty-five pounds. . . ." is from Dimenstein.

NOTES

"There are two hundred thousand child prostitutes in or from Nepal. . . ." is from Raymond.

"Between a hundred thousand and three hundred thousand children work the sex trade in the United States" is from Lukas.

"One study of U.S. survivors of prostitution. . . ." is from Raymond

"On average, a child prostitute services. . . ." is from Robinson.

"At least a million new girls per year. . . ." is from Galeano, 17.

"A half-million children die every year. . . ." is from Edwards, Burning, 141.

"This latter has been called. . . ." is from Edwards, Burning, 141.

"This is not counting. . . ." is from Centers for Disease Control.

". . . unless we happen to be in the Philippines. . . ." is from Lukas.

"There is no difference between being raped. . . ." is from Galeano, 70.

". . . have fun, make mischief. . . ." is cited at Wade, 34.

The description of the May 1866, assault on blacks in Memphis is from Wade, 24.

"just out of wanton cruelty. . . ." is cited at Wade, 18.

Other examples from that paragraph are from Wade, 19.

"The number of outrages. . . ." is cited at Wade, 71.

"Conservative figures put the number of Klan murders. . . ." is from Sterling, 393.

"I have listened with unmixed horror. . . ." is cited at Wade, 102.

"by force and terror. . . ." is from Simon, 66.

"killing and whipping and crowding out men from the ballot boxes. . . ." is cited at Wade, 62.

"One vote, one life" is from Kennedy, 151.

THE CULTURE OF MAKE BELIEVE

"called themselves members of the White League. . . ." is from Wade, 110.

"Go to the polls tomorrow. . . ." is from Kennedy, 150.

"How many windows in the White House" is from Kennedy, 156.

"poll taxes" is from Kennedy, 150.

"A constitutional convention in Mississippi in 1890. . . ." is from Wade, 113.

"The number of black voters in Louisiana dropped. . . ." is from Kennedy, 150.

"only 110 out of 16,533. . . ." is from Kennedy, 154.

"vulgar, offensive term. . . ." is from Webster's.

"They called them *Afer.* . . ." is from Hamilton.

"Does the name derive. . . ." is from Bernal, II, 96.

"The root, however. . . ." is from Hamilton.

"Another possibility. . . ." is from Dictionary.

"The first use of the word *negro.* . . ." is from Hamilton

"How fair a thing it would be. . . ." is from Zurara, 40.

"By 1555. . . ." is from Hamilton.

"expenditure in human life. . . ." is from Freyre, 178.

"The spelling and pronunciation of *negro* and *nigger.* . . ." is from Hamilton.

"by 1808, when the United States made illegal. . . ." is from Thomas, 552.

"a late customer and a minor purchaser" is from Rawley, 428–429.

"This was true in the time of Noah. . . ." is from Genesis 9:25.

"Sarai dealt harshly with her" is from Genesis 16:6.

"Abraham's wife, who was also, by the way, his half-sister" is from Genesis 20:12.

NOTES

"Thornton Stringfellow, whose works were commonly considered 'vastly the best'. . . ." is from Faust, 138.

"If God had commissioned. . . ." is from Faust, 142.

"Return to thy mistress. . . ." is from Genesis 16:9.

"The Bible even regulated—as opposed to banning outright—the killing of slaves. . . ." is from Exodus 21:21, with a contrast to Exodus 21:12.

"If the death did not take place for a day or two. . . ." and "must hold God in abhorrence" are from Faust, 153.

"Jesus would fail to prohibit. . . ." is from Faust, 155.

"be subject to *your* masters with all fear. . . ." is from 1 Peter 2:18.

"When ye do well, and suffer *for it*. . . ." is from 1 Peter 2:20.

"It is worthy of remark. . . ." is from Faust, 158–159.

"with fear and trembling" is from Ephesians 6:5. The runaway slave whom Paul returned to his master was Philemon.

"helps set the record straight" is from Ashcroft.

"Neither Jesus nor the apostles. . . ." is from FAIR.

"American slavery is not only not a sin. . . ." is from Faust, 175.

"President Dew has shown. . . ." is from Faust, 81.

"It was slavery that first made possible. . . ." is from Engels, 668.

"Let it be remembered. . . ." is from Faust, 126.

"Indeed, the oldest extant legal documents. . . ." is from Oppenheim, 282.

"Planned scarcity and the recurrent threat of starvation. . . ." is from Mumford, 108.

"Athens contained more slaves. . . ." is from Thomas, 26.

"Humanity is divided into two. . . ." is from Thomas, 28.

"The use of slaves was *the* customary way. . . ." is from Thomas, 26.

"By the end of the Republic. . . ." is from Thomas, 26.

"A half-million new captives. . . ." is from Thomas, 26.

"Servitude is the condition of civilization" is from Faust, 95.

"In order to rationalize our military-industrial complex. . . ." is from Laing, 57–58.

CONTEMPT

■

"Even a woman is good. . . ." is from Aristotle's *Poetics*, 1454a.

"Slavery as we know it began. . . ." is from Bales, 197.

POWER

■

"Was there ever any domination. . . ." is from Mill, 13.

"Between nine and sixteen million human beings. . . ." is from Rawley, 428–429.

"Yearly mortality rates varied from 3 to 10 percent. . . ." is from Rawley, 167.

"The shortest journeys lasted. . . ." is from Thomas, 411.

"Conditions for the 'migration,' as most scholars call it. . . ." see, for example, Rawley, and Klein.

"Thus we can read that on at least one ship, the *Brookes*. . . ." is from Rawley, 283.

"The confined air, rendered noxious. . . ." is from Dow, 160.

"The constant motion of the ship. . . ." is from Dow, 162.

NOTES

"Those slaves who found no opportunity. . . ." is from Dow, 159.

"There is a marked difference. . . ." is from Faust, 206.

"The head of the Negro. . . ." is from Faust, 223.

"There is in the animal kingdom. . . ." is from Faust, 223.

"those of carnivorous animals" is from Faust, 223.

"nerves coming off the brain" and "animals where the senses and sensual faculties predominate" are from Faust, 223.

"Now it will be seen from this hasty sketch. . . ." is from Faust, 224.

"the Mongol, the Malay, the Indian and Negro" is from Faust, 233.

"One truth is clear, WHATEVER IS, IS RIGHT" is from Faust, 238.

Voltaire, Hume, Serres, and Aggasiz from Galeano, 62.

"as when tenants were to 'belong to the said office for ever'" cited at Gray, 316.

"until then most . . . 'just enough money to live on'" is from Wolf, 32; and Petulla, 27–28.

"The Englishman William Eddis described. . . ." can be seen, for example, at Burton, 253–274.

"Generally speaking, they groan beneath a burden. . . ." is from Eddis, 38.

"slaves 'are used with more barbarous cruelty. . . .'" is cited at Hoffman, 91.

"In some colonies, one-third to one-half. . . ." is from Bridenbaugh, 123.

"In others, 80 percent. . . ." is from Van der Zee, 41.

"Political prisoners 'were sold at auction. . . .'" is cited at Hoffman, 13.

"In 1701, citizens in England protested. . . ." is cited at Hoffman, 11.

"At the request of the Virginia Company. . . ." is from Johnson, 139.

"Press gangs in the hire of local merchants. . . ." is from Van der Zee, 210.

"In the colonies, mortality rates. . . ." is from Hoffman, 52; and cited at Hoffman, 73.

"The definition of dissidents included. . . ." is from Novack, 142; and cited at Hoffman, 62.

"Concerning the younge [Irish] women. . . ." is cited at Hoffman, 62.

"In 1655, four teenagers. . . ." is cited at Hoffman, 65.

"Ten thousand poor people. . . ." is cited at Hoffman, 77.

"Between 1609 and the early 1800s. . . ." is from Hoffman, 46.

"the African attempting to escape Portuguese slavers. . . ." is cited at Thomas, 57.

". . . the frontispiece of a book which is a military photograph. . . ." is from Flint, 205; Wheatcroft, 208; Kanfer, 146.

PROPERTY

■

"Government has no other end. . . ." cited at Draffan.

"The South is fulfilling. . . ." is from Fitzhugh, 340.

"Cotton is king. . . ." is from Fitzhugh, 341.

"Religion, the comforts and elegancies of life. . . ." is from Faust, 91.

"What is the essential character. . . ." is from Faust, 112.

"Where a man is compelled. . . ." is from Faust, 112.

"Is not the condition. . . ." is from Faust, 113.

"feel indignity more acutely. . . ." is from Faust, 113.

NOTES

"It is a fallacy to suppose that ours is *unpaid labor*. . . ." is from Faust, 184.

"In 1850, an average field laborer cost. . . ." is from Bales, 16.

"Besides the first cost of the slave. . . ." is from Faust, 184.

"Modern studies suggest that slavery was, in fact, not all that profitable. . . ." is from Bales, 16.

"In all countries where the denseness of the population. . . ." is from Faust, 184.

"If I could cultivate my lands on these terms. . . ." is from Faust, 184.

"Little boys for small flues" is from Smith, Sydney, 131.

"But an early-nineteenth-century investigation. . . ." is from Hoffman, 34.

"They were all either orphans or indigents. . . ." is from Hoffman, 34.

"the smaller the child, the better the price" is cited at Hoffman, 34.

Chimney sweeps malnourishment and tumors described at Butlin, 1–6, 66–71; and cited at Lappé, 21–22.

"Crippling injuries and deformities were common" is from Smith, Sydney, 132.

"they were often sent to clean even hot flues. . . ." is from Smith, Syndey, 131; 132.

"had straw lit beneath. . . ." is from Hoffman, 33.

"Forced screaming and sobbing. . . ." is from Battiscombe, 126

"In 1828, Joseph Glass. . . ." is from Phillips, 34.

"We take it for granted. . . ." is from Dew, 195.

"Let us suppose a state of society. . . ." is from Faust, 92.

"Dew threw out a figure of $100 million. . . ." is from Dew, 195.

"The Fourteenth Amendment . . . has been used far more often. . . ." is from Zinn, 255.

"could not be carried into execution without great injury to property" is from Smith, Sydney, 136.

"Smith said this after listing. . . ." is from Smith, Sydney, 131–136.

"It was quite right to throw out the bill. . . ." is from Smith, Sydney, 136.

"Influential economist David Ricardo consistently. . . ." is from Inglis, 166.

"My macroeconomics textbook listed Ricardo. . . ." is from Froyen, 36.

PHILANTHROPY

■

"Love and violence. . . ." is from Laing, 56.

"How are we to weigh the pains. . . ." is from Faust, 90.

"If there are sordid. . . ." is from Faust, 112.

"The people along this coast. . . ." is from Raven-Hart, *Before*, 47.

"Beasts in the skins of men. . . ." is from Cope, 32.

"the most hideous folk. . . ." is from Raven-Hart, *Cape*, vol. 1, 146.

"truly they more resemble. . . ." is from Raven-Hart, *Cape*, vol. 1, 85.

"has done more to elevate. . . ." is from Faust, 116.

"Can there be a doubt. . . ." is from Faust, 116.

"slavery educates, refines, and moralizes. . . ." is from Faust, 293.

"We have already seen that the principle of idleness. . . ." is from Faust, 74.

"In dealing with a negro. . . ." is from Faust, 60.

"Slaves are perpetual children" is from Faust, 99.

"To protect the weak. . . ." is from Faust, 293.

NOTES

"One does not hate so long as one despises" is cited at *AVA*, 11/1/00, 3.

"My dictionary defines *entitle* as. . . ." is from Webster's.

"My dictionary defines *despise* as. . . ." is also from Webster's.

GIVING BACK THE LAND

■

"Ask of me, and I shall give thee. . . ." is from Psalms 2:8.

The account that Karen read was in Norton, 54–57.

"Where today are the Pequot?" is from Brown, 1.

The list of extirpated of reduced tribes is from Brown, 7.

"My intention is now to attack. . . ." is from Reader's Digest, 103.

"The only way of getting rid of them. . . ." is from Mostert, 389.

"shall in future be called. . . ." is from Reader's Digest, 103.

"with great guns, and small guns. . . ." is from Stockenstrom, vol. 1, 279–280.

"You gallop in. . . ." is from Smith, 729.

Definition of the crime of Genocide is from United Nations 1948.

"approximately three thousand involuntary or coerced sterilizations. . . ." is from England.

"Just between you and me, shouldn't the World Bank. . . ." is from Vallette.

"The problem with the arguments. . . ." is from Vallette.

"Your reasoning is perfectly logical but totally insane. . . ." is from Vallette.

"incredible vitality and joy that I experienced in the villages. . . ." is from Norberg-Hodge, 134.

Dene quotes about television are from Mander, 108–109, 110–111, 112.

BEGINNING TO SEE

■

"Christophe was growing a new skin. . . ." is from Rolland, 233.

The material about Luborsky is from Edwards, 79.

"the poor and laboring classes of your own race. . . ." cited at Hammond, 136.

"Went into the pit. . . ." cited at Hammond, 136.

"Instances occur in which children. . . ." cited at Hammond, 136.

"The reports suggested that British women and children. . . ." is from Hammond, 137.

"In 1900 the government estimated that more than 750,000. . . ." is from Meltzer, 53.

"dragging out a life of slavery and wretchedness" is from Hoffman, 31; the speaker is Charles Douglass of the New England Association of Farmers, Mechanics and Other Working Men.

"The figure of 750,000 probably underestimated. . . ." is from Meltzer.

"The most beautiful sight that we see. . . ." is from Meltzer, 64.

"The average life of the children. . . ." is from Markham, Lindsey, and Creel, 47.

The material about Leykis is from Leykis.

REDEMPTION AND FAILURE

■

"There are three thousand miles of wilderness. . . ." is cited at Drinnon, 4.

NOTES

"Cods are so thick. . . ." is cited at Mowat, 168.

"a creature with which the whole country abounds. . . ." is cited at Mowat, 118.

"so great an abundance of all kinds. . . ." is cited at Mowat, 29.

"The tropical idyll of the accounts of Columbus and Peter Martyr. . . ." is from Sauer, 69.

"swam out to receive us. . . ." is cited at Brandon, 60.

"as freely and familiarly came. . . ." is cited at Brandon, 60.

"religion rather than business. . . ." is from Brandon, 60.

"welcomed the visitors, and the Indians gave freely. . . ." is from Morgan, 39.

"the Indians . . . could have done the English in. . . ." is from Morgan, 40.

"The only good Indians I ever saw were dead" is cited at Connell, 179.

"I will say nothing. . . ." is cited at Connell, 180.

"After which more than a hundred Cheyenne scalps. . . ." is from Connell, 179.

He seemed to believe. . . ." is from Connell, 181.

"While Sheridan made final. . . ." is from Utley, 149.

Description of Custer's approach to Washita is from Connell, 182.

"put their cold lips. . . ." is from Custer, E, 38.

"At last the inspiring strains. . . ." is cited at Connell, 183.

"Indian warriors dashed from. . . ." is from Utley, 151.

"behind which they could sell their lives dearly. . . ." is from Custer, E, 40.

"I dismounted. . . ." is cited at Connell, 187.

Custer's casualty report, and lies, from Connell, 191 and 187.

"875 horses and mules. . . ." is from Custer, E, 40.

THE CULTURE OF MAKE BELIEVE

"They burned all this" is from Utley, 151.

"a 'one piece dress,' adorned. . . ." is cited at Connell, 189.

Account of the slaughter of the horses is from on Utley, 151; and Connell, 189.

"The strategy was merciless and effective. . . ." is from Connell, 189.

"It was pathetic. . . ." is from Bourke, 281.

"soldiers hearts. . . ." is from Custer, E, 38.

Custer shooting the dogs is from Connell, 197.

Black Kettle's death is from Connell, 189–190.

What happened to Black Kettle's bones is from Connell, 193.

"A squaw rose. . . ." is cited at Connell, 199–200.

"In the midst of conflict. . . ." is from Keim, 119.

"Of course you have heard. . . ." is cited at Connell, 201.

The description of Custer's sex captive is from Connell, 200; and Custer, G, 415.

"Custer's wasichus wiped out. . . ." is from Connell, 200.

"The black-haired Jew-boy. . . ." is a combination of the translations from Davidson, 48, and Hitler, 325.

"There must be a punitive expedition. . . ." is from IMT, XII, 811-D, 358.

"After the extension of the war. . . ." is cited at Davidson, 540.

"plutocrats, democrats, and Jews started this war. . . ." is cited at Davidson, 540.

"You must realize the Jews. . . ." is from IMT, XXXVIII, 013-M, 122.

"The Jew always lives. . . ." is from IMT, XXXVIII, 004-M, 112-113.

NOTES

"A Jewish plot caused the explosion of the zeppelin. . . ." is from Davidson, 44–45.

"This is no matter of harmless style. . . ." is cited at Davidson, 45.

"Henry Ford claimed. . . ." is from Davidson, 42.

"aroused by the very instinct of self-preservation. . . ." is from Wilson, vol. 5.58.

"is rapidly organizing wherever the insolent negro. . . ." is cited at Wade, 47.

"Indians, the enemies of our race. . . ." is cited at Connell, 180.

"the law of the land, and must not be questioned" is from Johnson v. M'Intosh.

"The 13. we passed by water to Aquascococke. . . ." is from Roanoke, 191.

"Forasmuch as the wearing of long haire. . . ." is cited at Drinnon, 26.

"sin against God and man," is cited at Drinnon, 43.

"the Dregs and Lees. . . ." is cited at Drinnon, 40.

"our soldiers received and entertained. . . ." is cited at Drinnon, 41.

"laughed his Enemies. . . ." is from Mason, 9–10.

"Indians are known to conduct their Wars. . . . is cited at Drinnon, 70.

"What infinite pains. . . ." is from Adams, X, 361–362.

"that barbarous and hellish power. . . ." is from Paine, 49.

"to lay waste all the. . . ." is from Fitzpatrick, XV, 189–192.

"from the hips downward. . . ." is from Schmalz, 99.

"to this day, when that name. . . ." is cited at Stannard, 120.

"necessary to secure ourselves. . . . is from Lipscomb and Bergh, XIV, 24: Jefferson's December 6, 1813, letter to Baron von Humboldt.

"the possession of that country. . . ." is from Lipscomb and Bergh, XIII, 161:

Jefferson's June 11, 1812, letter to John Adams.

The citation for the Declaration of Independence is, surprisingly enough, the Declaration of Independence.

"In reality, the White Man. . . ." is from Thayer, II, 250.

"The first Spaniards to start fighting. . . ." is from Sahagún, 76–77.

"To launch a deceitful. . . ." is from Clendinnen, 70.

"So important was the notion of fair testing. . . ." is from Clendinnen, 78.

"We are minded to live at Peace. . . ." is from Budd, 33.

The account of the slaughter of the Indians at Gnadenhutten is from Schmalz, 99–100.

"feeble manner . . . did hardly deserve the Name of *Fighting*" is from Mason, 19.

"having shott away most of ther arrows" is from Spelman, cxiv.

"they might fight seven yeares. . . ." is from Underhill, 40.

"fight is more for pastime. . . ." is from Underhill, 41.

"Their Warres are farre lesse bloudy. . . ." is from Williams, 188–189.

"ordinarily spared the women and children of their adversaries" is from Hirsch, 1191.

"Many indigenous cultures, such as the Zuñi Pueblo. . . ." is from Fromm, 168.

"The most common Dani way of coping with conflict. . . ." is from Heider, 93.

"Everyone is attired differently. . . ." is from Heider, 101.

"the most perfect freedom. . . ." is from Axtell, 327.

"It was not uncommon for Indian war parties. . . ." is from Hirsch, 1190.

"It was easy to imagine they were something like battlefield commanders. . . ." is from Heider, 104.

NOTES

"came not neere one another, but shot remote. . . ." is from Underhill, 41.

"If the sole aim of war. . . ." is from Heider, 105.

"full of excitement. . . ." is from Heider, 104.

"although two of them never really got going" is from Heider, 97.

"Nobody died in the battles. . . ." is from Heider, 97.

"Death rates from war. . . ." is from Heider, 114.

"In 1966 a group of Dani made a dawn attack. . . ." is from Heider, 114.

"120,000 tons of mine tailings dumped each day. . . ." is cited at Draffan.

"in the fourteenth-century at least 486 men, women, and children were killed. . . ." is from Gregg, et al., 287.

"His wars were seldom bloody. . . ." is cited at Drinnon, 137.

"warfare among traditional indigenous peoples was, as anthropologist Stanley Diamond noted, 'a kind of play'" is from Diamond, 157.

"The loss of a warrior was a serious event. . . ." cited at Drinnon.

The account of Ruth Benedict's conversation with Mission Indians about war is from Benedict, 28–29.

"Among the plains tribes. . . ." is from Grinnell, 296–297.

"No matter what the occasion. . . ." is from Diamond, 157.

"twist in the usual upshot of 'squaw chasing' came one day. . . ." is from Drinnon, xxiix-xxix.

"This is far Worse. . . ." is from Collins, 15.

"Bad as the savages are. . . ." is from Stone, vol. 1, 404.

"This is principally owing to a natural inappetency. . . ." is from Drimmer, 13.

"I have been in the midst of those roaring Lyons. . . ." is from Rowlandson, in Lincoln, 161.

THE CULTURE OF MAKE BELIEVE

"Some women, who had been delivered up. . . ." is from Drimmer, 14.

FLESH

■

"We need pray for no higher heaven. . . ." is from Thoreau, 382.

LaDuke's "honored enemy" is from LaDuke, 6.
"Civilization originates in conquest abroad. . . ." is from Diamond, 1.
"Our moral syntax has no predicate. . . ." is from Diamond, 165.
"We exterminated the American Indians. . . ." is cited at Drinnon, 314.
"Filipinos were routinely tortured. . . ." is from Drinnon, 316.
"A man is thrown down on his back. . . ." is cited at Drinnon, 320.
"a policy that will create in the minds of all the people a burning desire. . . ." is cited at Drinnon, 325.
"American General, J. Franklin Bell (who had used similar tactics against the Lakota)" is from Drinnon, 324.
"for the purpose of thoroughly searching. . . ." is cited in Drinnon.
"General Smith, who also had previously used. . . ." is from Drinnon, 324.
"I want no prisoners. . . ." is from DIL, VII, 187.
"Humanity is divided into two. . . ." is from Aristotle, Politics, Book I.
"Ask of me, and I shall give thee. . . ." is from Psalms 2:8.
"Savages pride themselves. . . ." is from Harmon, 43.
"recognition of their uniqueness. . . ." is from Diamond, 154–155.
"The execution of the negro. . . ." is from Ginzburg, 133–134.
"People are ready to run wild. . . ." is cited at Drinnon, xxv.

SEEING THINGS

■

"It is difficult to believe that such widespread violence. . . ." is from Johnson, 146.

The description of the Inuit game of doused lights is from Freuchen, 92.

Where I say, "Far better scholars and theoreticians than I have articulated the dangers of pornography. . . ." I was thinking, for example, of MacKinnon.

"the economic cost of global warming. . . ." is from Sims, Andrew.

NOTES

"A basic misunderstanding of our global governors. . . ." is from Sims, Andrew.

"Lynch the Wrong Negro. . . ." is from the *Chicago Tribune*, November 22, 1895.

"A mob willfully and knowingly hanged. . . ." is from *The New York Times*, June 11, 1900.

"Two Blacks Strung Up. . . ." is cited at Ginzburg, 32.

"Tennessee Colored Woman Lynched. . . ." is from the *New York Tribune*, March 17, 1901.

"The coroner is of the opinion. . . ." is cited at Ginzburg, 39.

"It is possible that in the search for Richard Young. . . ." is cited at Ginzburg, 44.

The article "Two Rookies Kill Fellow Cop Making Arrest" is in the bibliography under Brazil.

"From what I read about the incident at the firehouse. . . ." is from *AVA*, July 11, 2001, 2.

"I simply cannot understand the uproar. . . ." is from *AVA*, July 11, 2001, 2.

"*all* symbolic representation by definition contributes to alienation." See, for example, Zerzan.

"One cannot live in the pure present. . . ." is from Buber, 85.

"I contemplate a tree. . . ." is from Buber, 57–59.

"I-You can only be spoken with one's whole being. . . ." is from Buber, 54.

"And in all seriousness of truth, listen. . . ." is from Buber, 85.

"find it strange that we, the Christians, work. . . ." is from Raven-Hart, *Cape of Good Hope*, vol. 1, 147.

THE OTHER SIDE OF DARKNESS

■

"From a certain point onward. . . ." is cited at Hardin, 224.

THE CULTURE OF MAKE BELIEVE

"There is a point at which everything becomes simple. . . ." Hammarskj?ld, 66.

"the growers used 170,120 pounds of dry chemicals. . . ." is from PURS.

"also called Terro-gas," is from PIP.

"But chloropicrin, also used alone, has its own problems. . . ." is from ACGIH, 299–300.

"They used 20,193 pounds of copper sulfate. . . ." is from PURS.

"they used 23,691 gallons of Metam Sodium" is from PURS.

"Metam Sodium, which has been shown to be toxic. . . ." is from Birch, 637–645.

"spill on the Sacramento River in 1991. . . ." is from Brett, 1247–1256.

"The growers . . . also used many other chemicals. . . ." is from PURS.

"If the population of the world. . . ." is from Population.

"Could it not be contrived to send the *Small Pox*. . . ." is from Parkman, vol. 2, 44–45.

"the Spanish method. . . ." is from Parkman, vol. 2, 44–45.

"the last of the lashes. . . ." is from Galeano, *Wind*, 21.

"by constitutional means, using the proper channels. . . ." is from Galeano, *Wind*, 22.

"As for the Black Admiral himself. . . ." is from Galeano, *Wind*, 22.

"if we are ever constrained to lift the hatchet. . . ." is from Lipscomb and Bergh, vol. 11, August 28, 1807, 345.

"I have on all occasions preserved the sculps [*sic*] of my killed" is from Bassett, I, 465.

"personally supervised the mutilation of the bodies. . . ." is from Takaki, 96; and Halbert, 276–277.

"that paper. . . called a treaty. . . ." is from Mooney, 126–127.

NOTES

Casualties for the Trail of Tears is from Stannard, 124.

Death rate of Jews in Germany, Hungary, and Rumania between 1939 and 1945 is from Hilberg, III, 1201–1220.

Information about Powell's trial for crimes against humanity can be found in Clark.

"In direct refutation of this portrayal. . . ." is from Parry.

Information about the *Atlantic Dawn* is from Jones, 8.

CRIMINALS

∎

"The thief who is in prison. . . ." is cited at Draffan, Endgame.

"'put in work' during riots. . . ." is from Parenti, 195.

"The La Nuestra Familia . . . was established. . . ." is from Florida.

"getting high and getting over" is from Florida.

"They [Nazi Low Riders] hate blacks. . . ." is from Golab, 28.

"Although the Black Guerrilla Family was founded. . . ." is from Florida.

The paragraph about gang validation is from Parenti, 194; and Talamantez.

"Inmates dramatically outnumber guards. . . ." is from Wood.

"If you're an officer and you've gotta supervise two hundred people. . . ." is from Parenti.

Visiting conditions for the SHU are from Parenti, 207.

"And still others go insane. . . ." is from Parenti, 207.

The execution of the two former members of the Mexican Mafia are from Parenti, 197.

The number of murders in 1998 is from UCR, Table 5.1.

The number of deaths from cancer is from Epstein, 327.

"Of those 450,000 cancer deaths per year. . . ." is from Epstein, 111.

The number of Americans killed by asbestos each year is from Epstein, 54.

"The average armed robber nets about $250" is from Mokhiber, 16.

"The average prison sentence for bank robbery is 9.4 years" is from Waldman, 134.

The cost of the criminal collapse of the Savings and Loan industry is from Waldman, 4.

"Those few who were found guilty received average sentences of 1.9 years" is from Waldman, 134.

The costs for faulty goods, monopolistic practices, and other similar violations is from Mokhiber, 15.

"The median incarceration was six months. . . ." is from Department of Justice 1993, 53.

"The greater the degree of social relationship. . . ." is from Herman, 72.

"The gold standard study for prevalence of childhood sexual abuse. . . ." is from Russell, *Secret*, 10.

"Because World War II interrupted global shipping. . . ." is from McCoy, 18.

"after World War II the CIA allied itself with the Corsican underground. . . ." is from McCoy, 46–47.

"Over the past twenty years, the CIA has moved. . . ." is from McCoy, 492.

Jesus talked about not worrying about the mote in your brother's eye while there's a beam in yours at Matthew 7:3.

The argument that slavers actually saved the lives of Africans is at Donnan, II, 570.

The argument that the battles were fought to supply the slavers is cited at Thomas, 374.

NOTES

The account of the lynching of Henry Lowry is cited at Ginzburg, 143–146.

KILLERS

■

"The greatest evil is not now done. . . ." is from Lewis, v.

"even more people die each year from respiratory illness stemming from auto-related airborne toxins. . . ." is from Eight million.

"who have designed and put in place our nuclear weapons programs, for which every American . . . has been forced to pay more than $21,000" is from Schwartz, 6.

"Of a hundred major crimes, fifty are reported to the police. . . ." is cited at Mitford, 272–273.

"Does not the law-abiding citizen. . . ." is from Mitford, 272.

"Because in this story the bodies were disposed of quickly. . . ." is from Everest, 79.

"Crematorium and cemetery records suggest. . . ." is from Kurzman, 131–132.

"We didn't even have enough space to keep the corpses. . . ." is from Everest, 15.

"To find Bhopal after the toxic release. . . ." is from Everest, 15.

"victims of the Bhopal tragedy could be fairly and adequately compensated. . . ." is from Union Carbide, 2.

"They were dead, every one of them. . . ." is from Weir, 167.

"I was rendered unconscious by the gas. . . ." is from Weir, 170.

"There was Habib Ali. . . ." is from Kurzman, 57.

"There were people who ran. . . ." is from Kurzman.

"There was twelve-year-old Sunil Kumar Rajput. . . ." is from Kurzman, 58.

THE CULTURE OF MAKE BELIEVE

"There were Munnibai Balkishensingh and V. K. Sharma. . . ." is from Kurzman 66–67; and Morehouse and Subramaniam, 27.

"There was Sajda Bano. . . ." is from Kurzman, 67.

"There was Ajeeza Bi. . . ." is from Just Cause, 17.

"human power was cut in half. . . ." is from Kurzman, 40–41.

"technical manuals were never translated. . . ." is from Kurzman, 42.

"the plant's fire truck was unusable. . . ." is from Just Cause, 7.

"If odor or eye irritation. . . ." is from Everest, 164.

"MIC can't be smelled. . . ." is from Morehouse and Subramaniam, 29.

"Our technology just can't go wrong. . . ." is from Dembo, Morehouse, and Wykle, 94.

"A company official finally arrived. . . ." is from Everest, 14.

"is highly toxic by both the peroral and skin penetration. . . ." is from Morehouse and Subramaniam, 41.

"shouldn't be permitted to make poison for which there is no antidote" is from Kurzman, 149.

"The United States alone suffers at least. . . ." is from Too Close.

"This is not the only compound. . . ." is from Everest, 77.

"when victims began streaming into a Bhopal hospital. . . ." is from Everest, 53.

"Dr. Loya's mother later died. . . ." is from Kurzman, 102.

"Our safety measures are the best in the country. . . ." is from Everest, 15.

"If I say that 'I'm carrying a deadly thing in my pocket. . . .'" is from Everest, 52.

"That first day all 155 autopsies. . . ." is from Everest, 67.

NOTES

"In response to a request from Bhopal, Dr. Bipin Avashia. . . ." is from Kurzman, 100.

"The corporate press in the United States. . . ." is from Everest, 75.

"only lifting it in April of the next year. . . ." is from the *Wall Street Journal*, April 1, 1985; and *The New York Times*, April 10, 1985.

"The Indian government also denied cyanide's role. . . ." is from Shrivastava, 59; and Kurzman, 101.

"as well as a study by the Indian Council of Medical Research. . . ." is from Kurzman, 149–150.

"Public pressure eventually caused the government. . . ." is from Kurzman, 190, 150.

"perhaps the most appalling use of force by police. . . ." is from Kurzman, 153.

"were playing into the hands of the vested interests. . . ." is cited at Kurzman, 192.

"blaming lung damage on preexisting tuberculosis" is from Dembo, Morehouse, and Wykle.

"denying the leak's long-term health effects" is from Kurzman, 192.

"blaming 'the cultural background or the basic educational level of Bhopal citizens" is cited at Everest, 19.

"a (nonexistent) group of 'Indian extremists, which calls itself. . . .'" is from Everest, 140.

"claiming that the effects of the gas leak. . . ." is from Everest, 107.

"You can't run a nine- or ten-billion dollar corporation all out of Danbury" is from The *New York Times*, March 21, 1985.

"The company did nothing that either caused. . . ." is from *The New York Times*, April 25, 1985.

"I know the two governments are in close touch. . . ." is from Everest, 147.

"And besides the misinformation. . . ." is from Everest, 147.
The account of Anderson's "jailing" is from Kurzman, 124.

"During the first months after the disaster, Union Carbide spent on relief. . . ."
is from Morehouse and Subramaniam, 46.

The amounts given to survivors as of June of 1985 is from Everest, 152.

Estimates of Bhopal's economic losses alone is from Morehouse and
Subramaniam, 61.

"Indeed, the practical impossibility of American courts and juries. . . ." is from
Everest, 155.

"the courts of the United States would soon be overwhelmed. . . ." is from
Everest, 154.

"the plaintiffs are illiterate. . . ." is from Everest, 155.

"hundreds of thousands of surivors of Bhopal wait even today for compensation" is from Aravinda, 49.

"Since the gas I have not been able. . . ." is from Just Cause, 5.

"My father could not do any work. . . ." is from Just Cause, 10.

"I believe that even if we have to starve. . . ." is from Just Cause, 11.

"Neither brilliant nor stupid. . . ." is from Lifton, 4–5.

"the German industrialists who had robbed. . . ." is from Conot, 517.

THE COST OF POWER

■

"Thou shalt have no other Gods before Me" is from Exodus 20:3.

"Modern mass society creates the modern mass soldier. . . ." is from Diamond,
158–159.

NOTES

"I will do marvels, such as have not been done. . . ." is from Exodus 34: 10–11.

"the Chosen People had to promise never to 'make a covenant. . . .'" is from Exodus 34: 11–16.

"I will deliver the inhabitants of the land. . . ." is from Exodus 23: 31–33.

For other examples of this same message of God giving power in exchange for disallowing relationships, see, for example, Deuteronomy 7 or Joshua 23.

TRANQUILLITY AND FELICITY

■

"This is God's country. . . ." is from Connell, 241.

"In 1864, the United States Congress created the Northern Pacific Railroad Company. . . ." is from 13 Stat 366.

For a thorough exploration of the Northern Pacific land grant, its effects on the forests and communities of the Pacific Northwest, and what we can do to redress those wrongs, written by three extraordinarily cool guys, see Jensen.

"the United States shall extinguish. . . ." is from 13 Stat. 366, Section 2.

Indians "rightly saw in it [the railroad] a force that would bring about the destruction of the buffalo. . . ." is cited at Utley, 242.

"General William Tecumseh Sherman saw this also. . . ." is from Utley, 242.

"could not abide Indians who wanted to live as Indians" is from Brown, 1978, 199.

"Should those wandering Sioux. . . ." is cited at Brown, 1978, 199–200.

"By holding an interior point. . . ." is cited at Utley, 244.

"One ostensible reason for the presence of federal troops. . . ." is from Utley, 244.

"If some [miners] go over the Boundary. . . ." is cited at Utley, 247.

"fifteen thousand miners moved in by the next winter," is cited at Utley, 247. "The true policy, in my judgment, is to send troops against them. . . ." is cited at Utley, 247.

The fates of Crazy Horse and Sitting Bull are from Josephy, 289–309.

"Thirty thousand square miles were taken from the Blackfoot, Arikaris, and Gros Ventre. . . ." is from Brown, 1978, 257–258.

"Land was taken as well from the Cheyenne, Crow, Flathead, Yakama, and so on" is from Cotroneo, 377, 378, 385.

"I hate you. . . ." is from Glaspell, 188.

"I can't eat or sleep in peace til I kill a god-damned digger. . . ." is cited at Norton, 96–96.

"Andrew Jackson called Indians 'savage dogs' is from Takaki, 103.

"attempts to eradicate or dispossess them would be futile. . . ." is from Bassett, vol. 5, 512.

"without knowing first where her den and whelps were" is from Takaki, 102.

"We do not want the Filipinos. We want the Philippines. . . ." is from Norton, 127.

"Toward the aborgines of this country no one can indulge a more friendly feeling than myself. . . ." is from Richardson, vol. 2, 520–521.

"They [traditional Indians] have disappeared from the face of the earth. . . ." is from Bassett, I, 494.

In 1831, Alexis de Tocqueville found it remarkable. . . ." is from de Toqueville, vol. 1, 355.

ASSIMILATION

∎

"If the worker and his boss. . . ." is from Marcuse.

"conquest abroad and repression at home" is from Diamond, 1.

"It should be the earnest and paramount. . . ." is from McKinley.

The stories of the first Chinese in the Americas is from Steiner, 3, 4.

"A few Chinese came to the Americas over the next couple thousand years. . . ." is from Steiner, 94.

"But the real influx of Chinese. . . ." is from Steiner, 112.

"Chinamen are heavy in the pack. . . ." is cited at Steiner, 110–115.

"Emancipation has spoiled the negro. . . ." is cited at Loewen, 22.

"If God in His providence. . . ." is from Commons, vol. 9, 81.

"The owners of the Central Pacific Railroad asked them to do the impossible. . . ." is from Steiner, 134.

"Frozen corpses, still standing upright. . . ." is from Takaki, 230.

"The strike was immediately denounced in newspapers. . . ." is from Takaki, 230.

"Stranded in the Sierra Nevadas. . . ." is from Takaki, 230–231.

"Give me enough Swedes and whiskey. . . ." is from Schwantes, 133.

"By 1870 some twenty thousand pounds of bones. . . ." is from Lai, 57.

"inhabitants of another planet. . . ." is cited at Gyory, 224.

"In 1886, more than 85 percent of the farm workers. . . ." is from Steiner, 144–145.

"The Chinese built the levees. . . ." is from Steiner, 146.

"The Chinese layed the foundation of the West Coast fishing industry" is from Steiner, 148.

"Jack Cade, the English reformer, wished all mankind. . . ." is from Faust, 66–67.

THE CULTURE OF MAKE BELIEVE

"It is the common fate of the indolent. . . ." is from Davis, 105.

"Eternal vigilance is the price of liberty" is from Evans.

The figure for military spending standing at 51.3 percent of the U.S. federal discretionary budget is from CDI. I have seen figures much higher than this, as high as 90 percent (see, for example, Vidal).

The ad for the porcelain eagel is Lanezes, just in case you're wondering.

The editorial cartoon from 1880 was reprinted at Gyory, 144.

"Every reason that exists against the toleration of free blacks. . . ." is cited at Takaki, 217.

"No matter how good a Chinaman may be. . . ." is cited at Miller, 185.

"leprosy of the Chinese curse" is from Miller, 198.

"Even if I just peeled potatoes there. . . ." is from Yung, 20.

The story of Lalu Nathoy/Polly Bemis is in McCunn.

The percentage of Chinese women who were prostitutes, and their being confined to cribs four-by-six feet, is from Yung, 18.

"*Lookee* two bits. . . ." is from Longstreet, 163.

"the man's head fell off. . . ." is from Steiner, 174.

"On a single night in 1871 in Los Angeles. . . ." is from Steiner, 174.

"It was a sad and painful sight. . . ." is cited at Steiner, 175.

"stood by, shouting loudly. . . ." is from Steiner, 175.

"We don't mind hearing of a Chinaman being killed. . . ." is from Steiner, 176.

"the homes of a free, happy, people. . . ." is cited at Gyory, 224–225.

The Supreme Court case acquitting the white killer is from California Supreme Court, *The People v Hall*, Oct 1, 1854.

NOTES

"Because the killing of a nonperson. . . ." is from Steiner, 176.

The Chinese Exclusion Act of 1882 was 22 Stat. 58.

The 1892 law was 27 Stat. 25.

The 1902 law was 32 Stat. 136.

The 1904 law was 33 Stat. 428.

The 1924 law was 43 Stat 153.

The 1943 law was 57 Stat. 600.

The 1965 law was 79 Stat. 911.

"And perhaps most horrifying to many Americans. . . ." is from Steiner, 130.

"These people are an indigestible element. . . ." is from Steiner, 179.

"people like Professor Henry Pratt Fairchild. . . ." is from Eugenics.

"a slimy brown mass of glop" is from Canon.

"the habitat of the Nordish race. . . ." is from McCulloch.

"The word *slave* comes from the word *Slav*. . . ." is from Dictionary; and Meltzer, 1993, 3.

"To expect our leaders to adhere to basic standards of rationality. . . ." is from Edwards, 1998, 110.

THE IMPOSSIBILITY OF FORGETTING

■

"Observance of customs. . . ." is from Jung, xviii.

"I believe that the memories are still there. . . ." is from Highfield Pearson; and Raimondo.

The BMO information is from BMO.

THE CULTURE OF MAKE BELIEVE

PRODUCTION

■

"Of the approximately 1,213 men. . . ." is from Cherniak, 168, 169.

"By 1911, twenty years before work commenced. . . ." is from Cherniak, 38.

"This means that while few South African miners. . . ." is from Cherniak, 173.

"that a private corporation could buy parts. . . ." is from Cherniak, 14.

"If a colored man was sick. . . ." is cited at Cherniak, 27.

"At least one of the white foremen routinely carried a baseball bat. . . ." is from Cherniak, 28.

"I have heard quite a few times that they used pick handles. . . ." is cited at Cherniak, 32.

". . . often at gunpoint and even before the dust had settled. . . ." is from Kurzman, 92.

". . . neither Union Carbide, New Kanawha Power Company, nor Rinehart and Dennis ever measured dust levels. . . ." is from Cherniak, 39.

"most of the drilling was 'dry'" is cited at Cherniak, 48.

"Nor was water (or even ventilation) used to suppress dust from explosions" is from Cherniak, 48, 31.

"so thick that one could not identify anybody. . . ." is cited at Cherniak, 46.

"At shift's end dust concealed. . . ." is from Cherniak, 46.

"dust marked their tracks. . . ." is from Cherniak, 62.

"Lambie inspected the tunnel and wrote a letter. . . ." is from Cherniak, 50–51.

"I wouldn't give $2.50 for all the niggers on the job" is from Kurzman, 92.

NOTES

"Like a tale from the story of Aladdin's lamp. . . ." is from the *Fayette Tribune*, 3 June 1931.

"Union Carbide expanded the diameter. . . ." is from Tyler, 50; and the *Fayette Tribune*, 6 May 1931.

"To prevent public alarm. . . ." is from the *Fayette Tribune*, 20 May, 1931.

"Union Carbide more firmly exerted its formidable influence over editorial policies of local newspapers" is from Cherniak, 53–54.

"the great deal of comments about town regarding the unusually large number of deaths. . . ." is from the *Fayette Journal*, 18 Feb. 1931.

"A reader might wonder. . . ." is from Cherniak, 52.

"their prescription for what they called 'tunnelitis' was that miners. . . ." is from Cherniak, 36.

"Rinehart and Dennis surreptitiously. . . ." is from Cherniak, 59.

"When it got so a worker couldn't make it at all. . . ." is cited at Cherniak, 95–96.

"five physicians also spoke in favor of the plaintiff. . . ." is from Cherniak, 60.

"Six days after his testimony, Lambie began a new business. . . ." is from *Charleston Gazette*, 16 April 1933.

"I think the payment of that money. . . ." is cited at Cherniak, 63.

"the convergent acts or decisions of powerful corporate entities. . . ." is from Cherniak, 73.

"I knew I was going to kill these niggers. . . ." is from Grossman.

The story of Joe Harding is from Moore.

"Even a partial cleanup of the chemical and radioactive pollution left at Oak Ridge. . . ." is from Just Cause, 14.

"By the 1970s the company's plant at Alloy. . . ." is from Dembo, Morehouse, and Wykle, 56.

"after a cloud of gas escaped a Union Carbide plant, drifted into a mall. . . ." is from Morehouse and Subramaniam, 95–96.

"I think that, if we had a release of [the perfume] Arpege. . . ." is from the *Charleston Gazette*, March 9, 1986.

"relatively affluent city for East Tennessee, populated by scientists. . . ." is from *The New York Times*, 26 May, 1983.

"female workers who married or became pregnant were fired as well" is from Dembo, Morehouse, and Wykle, 78.

"By their fruits shall ye know them" is from Matthew 7:20.

"there are more slaves living today than came over on the Middle Passage" is from Bales, 9.

"In all countries where the denseness of the population. . . ." is from Faust, 184.

"if I could cultivate my lands on these terms. . . ." is from Faust, 184.

"from insane premises to monstrous conclusions. . . ." is from McRandle, 125.

the "holiest human right and . . . obligation" is "to see to it that the blood is preserved pure. . . ." is from Hitler, 402.

"the Jew" is an "eternal bloodsucker. . . ." is from Lifton, 16.

FALSE CONTRACTS

■

"The failure of the Great Promise. . . ." is from Fromm, *To Have or to Be*, 3.

Dina Chan's speech is given in whole at Bales, 2000, 117–120.

"I read that civilization has just contacted. . . ." is from AP.

The equating of the climate of Montana to "the mildness of Southern Ohio" is from Smalley, 174.

NOTES

"The average life span of Irish immigrants. . . ." is from Miller, Kerby, 319.

"the one woman out of four who is raped" is from Herman, 30.

"565,000 American children who are killed or injured. . . ." is from Centers for Disease Control.

"[Civil disobedience] is not our problem. . . ." is from Zinn, *Failure*, 45.

COMPETITION

■

"At all stages of the Holocaust. . . ." is from Bauman, 130.

"This is one of those times when only the dreamers. . . ." is cited at *AVA*, 4/11/01, 2.

streets "black with funeral processions" is from Greeley, 39.

"Ireland was, as a colony of England, exporting grain" is from Greeley, 35.

"You come to North America on one of the appropriately named 'coffin ships'" is from Greeley, 37.

"half of the remaining immigrants did" is from Greeley, 38.

"in seven centuries no slave had set foot on Irish soil" is from Ignatiev, 7. See also his footnote on this.

"the British 'policy of extermination,' as Lord Clarendon. . . ." is from Greeley, 35.

"A landlord in Ireland can scarcely invent an order. . . ." is from Costigan, 94.

"many of their cottiers would think themselves honored. . . ." is from Costigan, 94.

"There is nothing between the master and the slave. . . ." is from Greeley, 35.

"the Poor Law Act of 1847, which stipulated. . . ." is from Greeley, 35.

"Neil Evernden might call the lawyer's dilemma" is from Evernden, 12–13. "thought nothing of more than *dogs*. . . ." is from Miller, Kerby, 318.

"that some of these people would shoot a black man. . . ." is from Burn, xiv.

Information about the Irish Longshoremen's United Benevolent Society and the St. Patrick's Day Parade is from Ignatiev, 120–121.

"every white man would leave the ship. . . ." is from Douglass, 211.

"Black workers, already being driven out. . . ." is from Ignatiev, 115.

"During strikes in 1852, 1855, 1862, and 1863. . . ." is from Ignatiev, 120.

"a primarily Irish mob attacked the black employees of a tobacco factory. . . ." is from Ignatiev, 119.

"The Irish hate the Negroes. . . ." is from Fisher, 439.

"I found, most gladly, no secession. . . ." is from Ignatiev, 166.

"They say they came out here to fight for the Union. . . ." is from Ignatiev, 88.

"Since fight we must. . . ." is from Ignatiev, 88.

"J. P. Morgan, who at war's start had quickly developed fainting spells. . . ." is from Wheeler, 78.

"In time you will understand and believe that a man may be a patriot. . . ." is from Collins, 216.

"of all the major nineteenth-century financiers, only one. . . ." is from Wheeler, 95.

"they blew off the thumbs of people who fired them" is from Myers, 550.

The story about Morgan profiting from the carbines is woven together from Carosso, 92–94; Hoyt, 99–103; Chernow, 21–22; and Myers, 549–552.

"perfectly serviceable but old-fashioned" is from Hoyt, 99.

"Morgan, who often knew the results of battles. . . ." is from Chernow, 13; and Winkler 62.

"the price of gold went up whenever the North lost a battle. . . ." is from Hoyt, 107–108.

NOTES

"it became a tradition to sing 'Dixie'. . . ." is from Wheeler, 78.

"The price surged, the partners dumped. . . ." is from Hoyt, 108–109.

"The response by Congress to Wall Street gold speculation. . . ." is from Winkler, 63; Sinclair, 24; and Jackson, 75.

"What do you think of those fellows in Wall Street who are gambling in gold. . . ." is from Sobel, 33.

"Instead of putting out the fire. . . ." is from Swogger.

"They seized an armory, burned three police stations" is from Irby.

"Estimates of the number of dead. . . ." is from Swogger; and Irby.

DISTANCE

■

"The distance we feel from our actions. . . ." is from Lachs, 13.

"As consciousness of the context drops out. . . ." is from Lachs, 57.

"The remarkable thing is that. . . ." is from Lachs, 58.

"When, in one of our Atlantic cities. . . ." is from Grund, 91.

"he secured the world's greatest private collection of the time" is from Canfield, 162.

"Morgan farmed the land, and by the 1680s. . . ." is from Hoyt, 9–11.

"Joseph Morgan III, Pierpont's grandfather, left behind an estate. . . ." is from Hoyt, 46–47.

"on a global scale, exporting and financing cotton. . . ." is from Chernow, 19.

"an honored place in their mythology" is from Chernow, 13.

"When the streets of Paris are running with blood, I buy" is cited at Chernow, 13.

"to appreciate the close link that existed between merchant banks and world politics" is from Carosso, 47.

"The bank was in danger of going out of business until Peabody. . . ." is from Hoyt, 57–58.

"Another accident on the Erie. . . ." is from Holbrook, 34–35.

"Grant's brother-in-law, A. R. Corbin. . . ." is from is from Gold Panic Investigation, House Report No. 31, Forty-first Congress, Second Session, 1870: 157.

"and at least one of Grant's appointees" is from Wheeler, 103.

"assiduously cultivated a thorough understanding. . . ." is from Myers, 411.

"as it would be to recall the number of freight cars . . . ." is from Myers, 415.

"Jim Fisk, who had made his pile during the Civil War. . . ." is from Wheeler, 99.

"You can sell anything to the government. . . ." is from Miller, Nathan, 147.

"army contractors handled at least a billion dollars of government money. . . ." is from Nagles, 200.

"Gould countered by summoning his 'pet judge'" is from Chernow, 31.

"to the apartment of Fisk's mistress in the middle of the night. . . ." is from Myers, 414–415.

"Up to twelve thousand men faced off. . . ." is from Sinclair, 31.

"His purchase of so much stock left him. . . ." is from Sinclair, 31.

"he got by on $75,000 per year" is from Chernow, 32.

"By 1882 this had risen to a half-million" is from Chernow, 46.

"In 1873, Morgan was merely accorded 'universal respect'" is cited at Carosso, 122.

"chosen by circumstance and inheritance as the heir of North America" is cited at Winkler, 89.

NOTES

"obvious and sacred duty" is cited at Wheeler, 146.

"Morgan temporarily bankrolled the killing of Indians in the North- and Southwest, as well as the killing of union organizers and teenage strikers closer to home" is from Zinn, 241.

"charge the soldiers about one-twelfth of their pay. . . ." is from Wheeler, 146.

The accounts of the suffering of those poor who invested in railroads is from Oberholtzer, 516–517.

Mr. Cooke . . . soon enough became a partner in a Utah mine. . . ." is from Oberholtzer, 525.

"Across the whole nation, business declined 32 percent is from Sobel, 192.

"hundreds of thousands of workers were forced out of their jobs" is from Smalley, 199.

"In 1874, ninety thousand workers in New York City. . . ." is from Zinn, 238.

"there will be a thousand deaths of infants per week in the city" is cited at Zinn, 240.

"I don't believe there is another concern in the country. . . ." is from Carosso, 181.

"The sound of clubs falling on skulls. . . ." is from Bruce, 245.

"The people are rising up. . . ." is from Bruce, 276.

General information on those strikes is from Bruce, 281; and Zinn, 240–246.

"leaving his son with $100 million, an 87 percent ownership in the railroad" is from Chernow, 42.

"and a host of legislators no longer on the take" is from Sinclair, 52.

"Congress and the New York State legislature. . . ." is from Jackson, 119.

"A public sentiment is growing up opposed to the control. . . ." is from Jackson, 119.

"I don't know as I want a lawyer. . . ." is from Tarbell, 81.

THE CULTURE OF MAKE BELIEVE

"Think of it—all the competing traffic. . . ." is from Wheeler, 180.

"the American public, which had financed these railroads to the tune. . . ." is from Wheeler, 149.

"the percentage of railroad employees annually killed. . . ." is from Myers, 562–563.

"Through the 1890s Morgan brought under his control the Northern Pacific. . . ." is from Winkler, 131; Jennings, 184; Wheeler, 188; Myers, 578.

"'Morgan's roads' annually brought in over \$300 million. . . ." is from Winkler, 130.

"By 1902 the mileage controlled by Morgan. . . ." is from Moody, 107.

"an electric monopoly through General Electric" is from Moscowitz, 650.

"the Trust held '341 directorships in 112 corporations having aggregate resources or capitalization of \$22,245,000,000'" is from Lundberg, 104–105.

"The new company is to be organized by us. . . ." is from Chernow, 109.

"Roosevelt's bagman" is from Sinclair, 169.

"We've got our control and we've arranged it so that we can practically dictate the terms of China's currency reform. . . ." is from Croly, 395.

"In England, vendors took to selling novelty licenses. . . ." is from Sinclair, 148.

CORPORATIONS, COPS, AND HUNGRY GHOSTS

■

"The limited liability corporation is the greatest. . . ." is from Endgame.

"A bill that no one wants. . . ." is from Josephson, 306.

"The [Interstate Commerce] Commission, as its functions have now been limited by the courts, is, or can be made of great use, to the railroads. . . ." is from

Fellmeth, xiv–xv.

"two of J. P. Morgan's men . . . came to a general understanding with Roosevelt. . . ." is from Wiebe, 194.

"Roosevelt 'enjoyed political life only by virtue of J. P. Morgan's pleasure'" is from Lundberg, 61.

"If we have done anything wrong. . . ." is from Pringle, 180.

"Mr. Morgan appeared to be convinced. . . ." is from Chapman, 41.

"Charles Mellen gave legislators. . . ." is from Chernow, 176.

"orders came down from the New York Office of the United States Steel Corporation. . . ." is from Fitch, 230.

"the marionettes still figuring in Congress. . . ." is from Walker.

The modern *Cosmo* articles are from Cosmo.

"Morgan shared a mistress with England's King Edward VII" is from Chernow, 115.

The story of Morgan insisting on seeing Cleveland, and Cleveland giving him the exclusive right to sell the bonds is from Chernow, 77; and Myers, 579.

"Acting on suggestions made solely by me. . . ." is from Chernow, 130.

"ideal for entering the lungs and lodging there" is from Edwards, Gordon.

"There is Good News Today: $45 million A-Plant Near Denver" is from the *Denver Post*, 23 March, 1951.

"Nor was the public informed of the full monetary cost to construct the Rocky Flats Nuclear Weapons Plant. . . ." is from Wasserman and Solomon, 168.

The account of the 1957 fire is from Wasserman and Solomon, 168–169.

"it is possible that as much as 250 kilograms of plutonium was blown toward Denver that day" is from Wasserman and Solomon, 169.

"enough to give each of the 1.4 million people. . . ." is from Wasserman and Solomon, 169.

THE CULTURE OF MAKE BELIEVE

"the plant averaged ten fires per year" is from Abas, 17.

"forced to crawl out along exit lines painted on the floor" is from Rapoport, 40.

"only after a metric ton of plutonium had burned" is from Frontline, Secrets.

"routine intentional burnings" is from Frontline, Secrets.

"Indian burial mounds" is from Frontline, Secrets.

"It turned out they leaked about eleven curies. . . ." is from Frontline, Secrets.

"Rockwell's spray irrigation practices. . . ." is from Frontline, Secrets.

"levels are 1500 times higher. . . ." Frontline, Secrets.

The accounts of deformed nonhuman animals are from Wasserman and Solomon, 173–174.

Rates for human health problems are from Wasserman and Solomon, 174–175.

"The manager of the AEC office at Rocky Flats mirrored this line. . . ." is from *Denver Post*, September 12, 1957.

"Rockwell management and DOE officials 'attempted to make it difficult for us to get those findings published. . . . .'" is from Frontline, Secrets.

"at least one regular janitor who refused to work. . . ." is from Wasserman and Solomon, 171.

The account of the intentional irradiation of someone who spoke out is from Frontline, Secrets.

"They coudn't get a permit to operate it legally. . . ." is from Frontline, Secrets.

"his group of financiers rules the commerce of America by something akin to *divine right*" is from Chapman, 41.

"I believe the power to make money is a gift of God. . . ." is from Josephson, 325.

"The rights and interests of the laboring man will be protected. . . ." is from Josephson, 374.

NOTES

"the man who cannot live on bread and water is not fit to live" is from Burbank, 11.

"children as young as seven worked in coal mines" is from Ireland, 35.

"Crouched over the chutes, the boys sit hour after hour. . . ." is from Spargo, 163–164.

"the waste of life and limb is great. . . ." is from Myers, 618.

"One-third of all who die in Pittsburgh. . . ." is from Myers, 618.

"Morgan having been named while alive 'The Savior of the Nation'" is from Myers, 619.

Morgan's posthumous praise is from Myers, 634–636.

Information on the crimes of WMX is from Draffan, WMX.

"in conquest abroad and repression at home" is from Diamond, 1.

"They must respect that property of which they cannot partake. . . ." is from Burke, 374.

"a perpetual succession of individuals [who] are capable of acting for the promotion of the particular object, like one immortal being. . . ." is from Trustees of Dartmouth College v. Woodward, 1819.

"In the writings and speeches of clear-cutters and deforesters. . . ." is from Britell.

WAR

■

"The point to be grasped. . . ." is from Mumford, *Myth*, 348.

"The question which strikes at the heart of the war. . . ." is from Lundberg, 134.

Paragraph about net corporate profits during World War I is from Lundberg, 134; and Harbaugh, 320.

"Along with Charles Mellon, Pierpont had planned. . . ." is from Chernow, 174.

"some headed by mystified clerks. . . ." is from Chernow, 175.

"Morgan and Company bilked stockholders. . . ." is from Myers, 639.

"Thousands of men are in jail. . . ." is from Lundberg, 136.

For the Ruth Benedict materials, see Maslow, 199–211.

"Probably could do little if you were here. . . ." is from Chernow, 185.

"Revenues at Du Pont. . . ." is from Lundberg, 143.

Information about Bethlehem Steel is from Lundberg, 143.

Information about profits at United States Steel, Morgan-Guggenheim Utah Copper Company, and International Harvester, are from Lundberg, especially 496–500.

"Stock Exchange Prices sextupled between 1914 and 1916" is from Lundberg, 143.

"Since the war began we have loaned. . . ." is from Lamont, 109–110.

"Men had lost arms and legs. . . ." is from Gilbert, 150.

"I pushed the clothes back and saw a pulp. . . ." is from Gilbert, 154–155.

Description of Jack Morgan's Long Island home is from Chernow, 170; and *The New York Times*, 11 August, 1950.

Description of Jack Morgan's home in New York City is from Chernow, 112.

"Those who could walk. . . ." is from Gilbert, 155.

Casualty counts from World War I generally derived from Harbottle.

"Wherever I looked, right or left. . . ." is from Gilbert, 58.

"We have seen too many horrible things. . . ." is from Gilbert, 93.

NOTES

"In every direction from each shell hole. . . ." is from Gilbert, 103.

"a German banker told the American ambassador. . . ." is from Gilbert, 212.

"During the winter of 1915–1916, a few German soldiers put a plank. . . ." is from Gilbert, 218.

"Dear child, there is no more to say. . . ." is from Gilbert, 325.

"I think the pressure of this approaching crisis has gone beyond the ability of the Morgan Financial Agency. . . ." is from Lundberg, 141.

"the government had for six months prior. . . ." is from Lundberg, 144.

"Jack Morgan was jubilant" is from Chernow, 202.

"The number of those prosecuted under the Espionage Act of 1917 is from Chafee, 52n.

"only seventy-three thousand men volunteered (out of a million that the government said it needed)" is from Zinn, 355.

"five, ten, and twenty thousand farmers at meetings. . . ." is from Zinn, 355.

"this law, by the way, is still in effect" is from Zinn, 357.

"violated the Constitution's Thirteenth Amendment provision against involuntary servitude. . . ." is from Zinn, 356.

"The most stringent protection of free speech would not protect a man falsely shouting fire in a theatre. . . ." is from Schenk v. United States U.S. 47 (1919).

"The historian Howard Zinn compares it more accurately. . . ." is from Zinn, 357.

"No soldier ever sees these socks" is from Chafee, 51.

"I am for the people and the government is for the profiteers. . . ." is from Chafee, 52.

"because he applauded. . . ." is from Peterson and Fite, 36.

"the war was for the big bugs in Wall street. . . ." is from Peterson and Fite, 36.

"A German-American who did not buy war bonds. . . ." is from Chafee, 54.

"the film was seized. . . ." is from Zinn, 362; and Chafee, 55.

"No man should be permitted, by deliberate act. . . ." is cited at Chafee, 35.

"the third verse is conspicuous. . . ." is from Star Spangled Banner.

"circulating a pamphlet suggesting voters not reelect a congressman who voted for conscription" is from Chafee, 56.

"There is no better way of unsettling the confidence. . . ." is from Chafee, 57.

"the women of the United States were nothing more nor less than brood sows. . . ." is from Zinn, 363.

"You ask me why the IWW is not patriotic. . . ." is from Zinn, 364.

"Wars thoughout history have been waged for conquest and plunder. . . ." is from Zinn, 358.

"Years ago I recognized my kinship with all living beings. . . ." is from Zinn, 359.

"who would strike the sword from the hand of this nation. . . ." is from Zinn, 359.

"went directly to J. P. Morgan and Company to pay British debts" is from Lundberg, 141.

"In short, the war debt created. . . ." is from Lundberg, 142.

Bankers Trust control of US war effort, and "The President ought to send for Schwab and hand him a treasury warrant. . . ." is from Lundberg, 145–146.

The role of the Red Cross in prolonging World War I is from Lundberg, 147.

"ten million human beings were dead and another thirty million. . . ." is from Schmitt, 296.

"the plan was . . . that the copper industry . . . should be so centralized. . . ." is from Lundberg, 190.

"Copper, costing eight to twelve cents per pound. . . ." is from Lundberg, 192.

NOTES

"the public paid more than $1 billion for combat airplanes. . . ." is from Lundberg, 194.

"Morgan-associated Baruch placed orders with Morgan-controlled Bethlehem Steel. . . ." is from Lundberg, 199.

"We ought to pass a law that no man worth. . . ." is from Lundberg, 189.

RESISTANCE

■

"The more highly organized the power structure becomes. . . ." is from Mumford, *Myth*, 348–349.

"feudal domination of their lives. . . ." is from Zinn, 347.

"our little cowboy governor" is from Zinn, 347.

"It is no longer simply the merchant prince. . . ." is from DuBois, 709.

"There was Private William Little. . . ." is from Ginzburg, 118.

"There was George Holden. . . ." is from Ginzburg, 118–119.

There was Lloyd Clay. . . ." is from Ginzburg, 120–121.

"Sixty-five-year-old Berry Washington. . . ." is from Ginzburg, 125.

"Cleveland Butler was shot. . . ." is from Ginzburg, 122–123.

"Ten thousand men, women, and children from Omaha. . . ." is from Ginzburg, 126–129.

"The mob in Omaha also beat to death the (white) mayor. . . ." is from Ginzburg, 125.

"The aims and objects of this organization shall be to put the working class in possession. . . ." is from Adamic, 93.

The preamble of the IWW constitution is from IWW.

"when Haywood found himself speaking to a group of white timber workers in

Louisiana. . . ." is from DeCaux, 67.

"Over three thousand men were hired. . . ." is from Heslewood, 711.

"President William Howard Taft delivered a two-hour speech. . . ." is from Heslewood, 710.

"A demonstration meeting was just held in Sheep Camp No. 1. . . ." is from Heslewood, 712.

"During a visit of the Industrial Workers of the World they will be accorded. . . ." is from Townsend.

"a whipping post and a cat-o-nine tails. . . ." is from Foner, 186.

"Hanging is none too good for them. . . ." is from Townsend, 34.

"like the aborigines of darkest Africa. . . ." is from Townsend, 34.

"Murderers, highwaymen, cut-throats. . . ." is from Townsend, 26–27.

"someone destroyed their type forms. . . ." is from Townsend, 25.

"If there are any citizens of San Diego who sympathize. . . ." is from Townsend, 50.

"the more you kill and burn the better you will please me" is cited at Drinnon, 327–328.

"The first thing on the program was to kiss the flag. . . ." is from Dubofsky, 192; and Foner, 188–189.

"viewed several of the charred corpses at the morgue in Butte. . . ." is from Peterson and Fite, 57.

The words of the prosecutor at Nuremberg are from IMT, volume v, p 118

"Thus did San Diego, having given its money. . . ." is from Dubofsky, 192.

"Q: What is the attitude of your paper on the labor issue in Butte. . . ." is from Peterson and Fite, 59.

The paragraph about Frank Little's kidnapping and murder is from Delaney and Rice, 111.

NOTES

"Q: Did you ever try to find out who the occupants of that car. . . ." is from Peterson and Fite, 59.

That the Wobblies were unarmed at Everett is from Adamic, 101.

The rest of the story of the Everett massacre is from Townsend, 73–74.

"opened a pillow and placed it on his window. . . ." is from Chaplin, 29.

Participants in the Centralia Armistice Day parade are from Levin, 51.

"At Centralia a committee of citizens has been formed that takes the mind back to the old days of vigilance. . . ." is from Chaplin, 58.

The fact that they bought rope is from Chaplin, 63–64.

The threat by Wobblies to kill one militia member for every striker killed is from Adamic, 96.

The fact that they had never used violence to defend their halls is from Chapel, 67.

The account of Everest's capture and murder is mainly from Chaplin, 70–79.

"The episode of last night is but the natural result. . . ." is from Copeland, 55.

"The Lynching Calender: African-Americans Who Died in Racial Violence in the United States by Month of Death, 1865-1965" is from Lynching Calender.

"What the best white citizens here termed the most glorious celebrations. . . ." is from Vicksburg.

EXPANDING THE FRONTIER

∎

"Maybe we made a mistake in trying to maintain Indian cultures. . . ." is from Drinnon, xiii.

"a new world of individual rights, an ever expanding circle of liberty. . . ." is from Salaita, 19.

"The cry of civil war is on the lips of the most responsible. . . ." is cited at Steiner, Zara, 153.

THE CULTURE OF MAKE BELIEVE

The discussion of the class origins of World War I owes much to Zerzan, 128–149.

"start a club of some kind" is from Davis, Susan, 16-21; and Lester, 21–22, 54, 56–57.

"Simmons had fallen to his knees and begged God. . . ." is from Wade, 141.

"Two Klan members talking would be a *klonversation*" is from Wade, 142.

"they all want to be animals" is from Greene, 240.

"Our Little Girl—ours by the Eternal God—has been pursued. . . ." is from Wade, 146.

"another Ku Klux Klan may have to be organized to restore home rule" is from MacLean, 12.

"The World's Greatest Secret. . . ." is from Wade, 146.

"Never before, perhaps, has an Atlanta audience so freely given vent. . . ." is from Wade, 147.

"infested with the IWW spirit" is from Wade, 149.

The seven noble truths of the KKK are from Wade, 150.

The mechanics of selling the KKK is from Wade, 154.

"stood for 100 percent Americanism. . . ." is from Wade, 156.

"alien-inspired strikers" is from Wade, 155.

"Never before had a single society gathered up so many hatreds. . . ." is from Higham, 289.

"In less than a year, eleven hundred Kleagles. . . ." is from Wade, 155.

"in fifteen months the Klan had almost one hundred thousand members" is from Wade, 157.

"I have never seen anything equal to the clamor. . . ." is from Jackson, Kenneth, 10.

NOTES

The Mencken quote ("Not a single solitary sound reason has yet been advanced for putting the Ku Klux Klan out of business. . . .") is from MacLean, 19.

"hyphenated Americans . . . have poured the poison of disloyalty. . . ." is from Gambino, 109.

"Out of the sly and crafty eyes of many of them. . . ." is from Coben, 198.

"Each and every adherent of this movement is a potential murderer. . . ." is from Avrich, 173.

"Congress gave us the best advertising we ever got. . . ." is from Wade, 166.

"By 1923, at least seventy-five U.S. Representatives. . . ." is from MacLean, 18.

"the Klan had been able to sweep anti-Klan governors. . . ." is from MacLean, 18.

"in Georgia the Klan counted as its members. . . ." is from Maclean, 17.

Warren G. Harding was sworn in as a member of the Ku Klux Klan. . . ." is from Wade, 165.

"92 percent of Klan members were married. . . ." is from MacLean, 10.

Categories of workers within the Klan is from MacLean, 55–56.

"thirty thousand ministers were enrolled in the Klan. . . ." is from MacLean, 8.

"the real leaders of the Southern communities" is from Wilson, vol. v, 58.

"the Ku Klux Klan has become the most vigorous. . . ." is from MacLean, 10.

"Everybody in the courthouse belonged to the Klan. . . ." is from Kuhn, 314.

"If anybody gets an indictment against a Klansman. . . ." is from MacLean, facing page 143.

"Much of Western science must go. . . ." is from Deloria, 3.

"the United States Supreme Court recently, and unanimously, struck down a Massachusetts law. . . ." is from Crosby v. National Foreign Trade Council.

"Police assaulted others of them with pepper spray" is from Taylor, 4.

"Except for his attitude toward the Jews, which I consider wholesome. . . ." is from Chernow, 394.

"I hate you. I hate you. I hate all the white people. . . ." is from Glaspell, 188.

THE VIEW FROM INSIDE

■

"The oppressed suffer from the duality. . . ." is from Freire, 32.

"By 1924 it [the Klan] had four million members" is from Wade, 253.

"a full 10 percent of the state's residents were Klan members" is from Wade, 218.

"I did not sell the Klan in Indiana on hatreds. . . ." is from Moore, Samuel, 517.

"nearly every fundamentalist minister in the state. . . ." is from Wade, 223.

"Two of the Klan's most popular marching songs. . . ." is from Wade, 218.

The story of the Klansmen and the corset salesman is from Wade, 226–227.

"In 1924, the Klan controlled the governor. . . ." is from Wade, 237.

The story of the Horsethief Detectives is from Wade, 225.

"chastity was never much in evidence at these get-togethers" is from Wade, 228.

"He chewed me all over my body. . . ." is from Wade, 241.

The Madge Oberholtzer story is found in Wade, 239–245, among many other places.

"In return for the political support of. . . ." is from Wade, 246.

"in the 1920s this Klan solution "came to nothing" is from Wade, 249.

NOTES

"1 unidentified black man lynched Waverly Virginia March 20 1925" is from The Lynching Calender.

"Out of the kindness of its corporate heart. . . ." is from Monkerud, 9.

"the economy is doing very well. The people, very badly" is from Galeano, *Century*, 218.

THE CLOSING OF THE IRON CAGE

■

"As the generations pass they grow worse. . . ." is from Fromm, *Anatomy*, xvii.

"Controlling them requires both a defensive policy. . . ." is from Parenti, 46.

"leave them [Indians] in possession of their country, was to leave the country a wilderness" is from Johnson v. M'Intosh, 14.

"the people, who once had the power to grant. . . ." is from Juvenal, Fourth Satire.

"We are having a fine young revolution here. No danger. . . ." is from Schmitz, 36.

That the ambassador included republicans in his enemies of the people is from Schmitz, 52.

"People like the Italians. . . ." is from Schmitz, 52.

"there has not been a single strike in the whole of Italy. . . ." is from Schmitz, 71.

"a sound and useful leader" is from Stimson, 270.

"that admirable Italian gentleman" is from Schmitz, 139.

"We had the great satisfaction of seeing. . . ." is from Forbes, 125.

"we, too, need a man like Mussolini" is from Schmitz, 70.

"Partner Thomas Lamont became, to use his word, a 'missionary' for fascism" is from Chernow, 283.

"If Mr. Mussolini declares that parliamentary government. . . ." is from Chernow, 281–282.

"should be presented to the public not as a warrior. . . ." is from Chernow, 403.

"where just a half-century or more ago the vast resources. . . ." is from Chernow, 406.

Lamont "has exercised more power for twenty years. . . ." is from Lundberg, 33.

"He is not the man behind the throne. . . ." is from Chernow, 239.

Dwight Morrow, as "self-appointed overlord of Mexico's finances" is from Chernow, 298.

"In this capacity he devised the notion of 'perpetual concessions'. . . ." is from Chernow, 296.

"eliminating the courthouse entirely. . . ." is from Chernow, 298.

"There is something about too much prosperity. . . ." is from Davis, Kenneth, 290.

"selling ships and supplies to the Allies. . . ." is from Chernow, 233.

"no business came from China" is from Chernow, 338.

"the Japanese Government and people entertain the friendliest. . . ." is from Chernow, 340.

"It is grotesque for the League. . . ." is from Chernow, 341.

"A large number of young men who were arrested. . . ." is from Basic.

"He keenly followed the career of the future Fuhrer. . . ." is from Higham, Charles, 162.

"firebomb union halls and kill union organizers. . . ." is from Higham, Charles, 165.

"switchboards, telephones, alarm gongs, buoys. . . ." is from Higham, Charles, 99.

"After the war, ITT sued. . . ." is from Sampson, 47.

NOTES

"For a commercial company trying. . . ." is from Flames of Shell.

HOLOCAUSTS

■

"They could beat a person to death. . . ." is from cited at Gruen, xiii.

The account by the engineer in *The Rise and Fall of the Third Reich* is from Shirer, 1252–1253.

"*Hang him using piano wire.* . . ." is from Hoffman, Peter, 721, note 42.

"Time and again both the United States and Britain ducked chances to stop or slow the genocide" is from, Morse, among others.

"There are grave objections. . . ." is from Wyman, 189.

For an account of the U.S. recruitment of Nazi war criminals, see, for example, Simpson.

"German popular anti-semitism came a poor second. . . ." is from Bauman, 31.

"Indeed, Germany had long been known as a relatively safe haven. . . ." is from Bauman, 31

"many of the social and intellectual foundations. . . ." is from Proctor, 4.

"mainstream scientists 'played an active. . . .'" is from Proctor, 6.

"Christianity could theorize its own existence only. . . ." is from Bauman, 38.

"What we must recapture to mind, nakedly as we can. . . ." is from Steiner, George, 37.

"the most monstrous of all human errors" is from Steiner, George, 38.

"objects of two mutually opposed and contradictory class antagonisms" is from Bauman, 42.

The description of the treaty that the Germans had to sign after World War I is from Shirer, 89–91.

THE CULTURE OF MAKE BELIEVE

"A couple of years later, the Allies presented the Germans with a bill for reparations. . . ." is from Shirer, 81.

The rate of German inflation is from Shirer, 81, 95.

"to make secure and to preserve the racial community. . . ." is from Shirer, 418–419.

"the right to a greater living space than other peoples" is from Shirer, 419.

"The history of all ages. . . ." is from Shirer, 419.

"Hitler stated explicitly that neither Spain. . . ." is from Rich, 8.

"Of course our whole national history. . . ." is from Roosevelt, 34, 38.

"Rage and fury are pitiably primitive. . . ." is from Bauman, 90.

"Thorough, comprehensive, exhaustive murder required. . . ." is from Sabini, 330.

"By conventional clinical criteria. . . ." is from Kren, 64.

"Our judgement is that the overwhelming majority of S.S. men. . . ." is from Kren, 70.

"Except for the moral repulsiveness. . . ." is from Bauman, 14.

The description of improvements in the mobile killing vans is from Browning, 64–65.

"For putting the bodies into the furnace. . . ." is from IMT, vol. vii, 585.

"Following our verbal discussion. . . ." is from Shirer, 1265.

"12 pounds of human fat. . . ." is from Shirer, 1264.

"Precision, speed, unambiguity. . . ." is from Gerth, 215.

"young and pretty girls all dressed. . . ." is from Shirer, 1262–1263.

"rational people will go quietly. . . ." is from Bauman, 203.

NOTES

"All right, give 'em something to chew on" is from Shirer, 1263.

"they piled up in one blue clammy. . . ." is from Reitlinger, 160.

"It must be kept in mind that most of the participants did not fire rifles. . . ." is from Hilberg, III, 1024.

"Total annual U.S. corporate profits are about $500 billion. . . ." is from Draffan, Endgame.

"These include $51 billion in direct subsidies. . . ." is from Estes, 177–178.

"Right now it takes about two to five dollars worth of electricity to produce a single pound of aluminum. . . ." is from St. Clair, 5.

The story of Alcan and the Nechako River is from Ryan, John C, 42–44, 48–49.

The story of the Akosombo Dam on the Volta is from Hancock, 140.

"oil accounts for 35 percent of Colombia's exports. . . ." is from Hull.

"For what the world spent on the military every 2.5 hours. . . ." is from Dunnigan, 373.

"Goebbels also believed that propaganda worked best when it put forth the illusion of diversity. . . ." is from Jensen, McChesney.

The information on Echelon is from Echelon Watch.

"allows us to monitor, track down and capture an American citizen" is from Fox News Sunday, 6/17/01.

"He who leaves the plants in a garden to themselves. . . ." is from Darré, 115.

"Germany implemented the 'final solution'. . . ." is from Weizenbaum, 256.

"how to overcome. . . the animal pity. . . ." is from Arendt, 106.

"just yesterday I read that President Bush wants to increase the military budget. . . ." is from Fram. Of course, now that the U.S. is attacking Afghanistan, the military has even more of a blank check than normal.

"sanitary water could be provided for every human being who lacks it" is from Dunnigan, 373.

THE CULTURE OF MAKE BELIEVE

"The broadcasting programmes need to be put together. . . ." is from Hitler's Airwaves.

"Mexico is a country of a modest, very fucked class. . . ." is from McChesney.

"Heinrich Himmler nearly fainted. . . ." is from Shirer, 1259.

COMING HOME

■

When I look at history. . . ." is cited at cited at Fromm, *Anatomy*, xvii.

I got the line about "the possibility of allowing this inhumane system to continue" being more absurd than bringing down civilization from a conversation with John Zerzan. Zerzan, personal.

NOTES

BIBLIOGRAPHY

13 Stat. 366

22 Stat. 58

27 Stat. 25

32 Stat. 136

33 Stat. 428

43 Stat. 153

57 Stat. 600

79 Stat. 111

Abas, Bryan, "The Jury That Wouldn't Stay Quiet," *Covert Action Quarterly*, Winter 1993-1994 (number 47).

ACGIH = American Conference of Governmental Industrial Hygenists, 1992, *Documentation of Threshold Limit Values and Biological Exposure Indices*, Sixth edition Cincinnati, pp 299–300.

Adamic, Louis, *Dynamite: A Century of Class Violence in America, 1830-1930*, Rebel Press, London, 1984.

Adams, Charles Francis, ed, *The Works of John Adams, Second President of the United States*, Little, Brown, Boston, 1856, vol. 10.

AP = "Brazilians Meet New Amazon Tribe," AP, Rio de Janeiro, April 8, 2001, 19:27 est.

Arendt, Hannah, *Eichmann in Jerusalem: A Report on the Banality of Evil*, Penguin, New York, 1984.

Ashcroft, John, "Partisan Conversation: Senator John Ashcroft: Missouri's Champion of States' Rights and Traditional Southern Values," *Southern*

BiBLioGRAPHY

Partisan (Second Quarter/1998), p 28.

AVA, *Anderson Valley Advertiser,* 11/1/00.

AVA, *Anderson Valley Advertiser,* 4/11/01.

AVA, *Anderson Valley Advertiser,* 7/11/01.

Aravinda, L.S., "People's Knowledge in a Paperless Society: Organizing against the Narmada Dam," *Z Magazine,* January 2001, 49.

Avrich, Paul, *Sacco and Vanzetti: The Anarchist Background,* Princeton University Press, Princeton, 1991.

Axtell, James, *The Invasion Within: The Contest of Cultures in Colonial North America,* Oxford University Press, New York, 1985.

Bales, Kevin, *Disposable People: New Slavery in the Global Economy,* University of California Press, Berkeley, 1999.

Bales, Kevin, *New Slavery,* ABC-CLIO, Santa Barbara, 2000.

Bassett, John Spencer, ed, *Correspondence of Andrew Jackson,* Kraus Reprint, New York, 1979, vol. 1, vol. 5.

Battiscombe, Georgina, *Shaftsbury: The Great Reformer, 1801-1885,* Houghton Mifflin, 1975.

Bauman, Zygmunt, *Modernity and the Holocaust,* Cornell University Press, Ithaca, 1989.

Benedict, Ruth, *Patterns of Culture,* Mentor Books, New York, 1934.

Bernal, Martin, *Black Athena: The Afroasiatic Roots of Classical Civilization,* vol. 2, Rutgers University Press, 1991.

Berry, Mary Frances, and John W Blassingame, *Long Memory: The Black Experience in America,* New York, Oxford University Press, 1982.

Birch, "Effects of metam sodium on developing *Xenopus laevis* embryos: Minimum concretration, biological stability, and degradative products," *Arch. Environ. Contam. Toxicol.* 15: 637–645

Bourke, John G, *On the Border With Crook*, Charles Scribner's Sons, New York, 1891.

Brandon, William, *New Worlds for Old: Reports from the New World and their effect on the development of social thought in Europe, 1500–1800*, Ohio University Press, Athens, 1986.

Brazil, Eric, Matthew Yi, and Jonathan Curiel, "Two Rookies Kill Fellow Cop Making Arrest," *San Francisco Chronicle*, Saturday, January 13, 2001, p 1.

Brett et. al, "Impact of a major soil fumigant spill on the plankonic ecosystem of Shasta Lake, California," 1995 *Can.J. Fish. Aquat. Sci.*, 52, 1247–1256

Bridenbaugh, Carl and Roberta, *No Peace Beyond the Line: The English in the Caribbean, 1624-1690*, Oxford University Press, New York, 1972.

Britell, Jim, "A Hungry Ghost Story," *Forest Watch*, Sept. 1991.

Brown, Dee, *Bury My Heart At Wounded Knee*, Holt, Rinehart & Winston, New York, 1970.

Brown, Dee, 1978, *Hear That Lonesome Whistle Blow: Railroads in the West*, Bantam Books, New York, 1978.

Browning, Christopher R., *Fateful Months: Essays on the Emergence of the Final Solution*, Holmes & Meier, New York, 1985.

Brownmiller, Susan, *Against Our Will: Men, Women, and Rape*, Simon and Schuster, New York, 1975.

Bruce, Robert V., *1877: Year of Violence*, The Bobbs-Merrill Company, New York, 1877.

Bryce, Robert and Susan A. Brackett. "Culture Clash: Controversy at the Grasberg Mine I Insia," *Clementine: The Journal of Responsible Mineral Development* (Mineral Policy Center, Washington), Spring/Summer 1996, 10–13.

Buber, Martin, *I and Thou*, translated and with an introduction by Walter Kaufmann, Charles Scribner's Sons, New York, 1970.

Budd, Thomas, *Good Order Established in Pennsylvania & New Jersey in America*, London, 1685.

BiBLiOGRaPHY

Buffu, Peter C, "Racial Factors in Prison Homosexuality," in Scacco, Anthony M., Jr. *Male Rape: A Casebook of Sexual Aggressions*, AMS Press: New York, 1982.

Burbank, David T., *Reign of the Rabble: The St. Louis General Strike of 1877*, Augustus M. Kelley, New York, 1966.

Bureau of Justice Statistics, *Correctional Populations in the United States, 1997*, November 2000, NCJ 177613.

Burke, Edmund, *Reflections on the Revolution in France*, in The Harvard Classics Edition (*On Taste, On the Sublime and the Beautiful, Reflections on the French Revolution*, and *A Letter to a Noble Lord*), edited by Charles W. Eliot, P. F. Collier & Son, New York, 1937.

Burn, James, D, *Three Years Among the Working Classes in the United States During the War*, Smith, Elder And Co., London, 1865.

Burton, Thomas, *Parliamentary Diary: 1656-59*, vol. 4. Henry Colburn, London, 1828.

Butlin, H J, "Three lectures on cancer of the scrotum in chimney sweeps and others," *British Medical Journal*, July 2, 1892, pp 1–6; July 9, 1892, pp 66–71; June 25, 1892, pp 1341–1346.

California Constitution, Article XIX, Sections 1–4
California Supreme Court, The People v Hall, October 1, 1954.

Canfield, Cass, *The Incredible Pierpont Morgan: Financier and Art Collector*, Harper and Row, New York, 1974.

Carosso, Vincent P., *The Morgans: Private International Bankers, 1854-1913*, Harvard University Press, Cambridge, 1987.

Centers for Disease Control, Third National Incidence Study of Child Abuse and Neglect.

Chafee, Zechariah, Jr, *Free Speech in the United States*, Harvard University Press, Cambridge, 1942.

Chaplin, Ralph, *The Centralia Conspiracy*, in the collection, *The Centralia Case: Three Views of the Armistice Day Tragedy at Centralia, Washington, November 11, 1919*, Da Capo Press, New York, 1971.

Chapman, Charles C., *The Development of American Business and Banking*

Thought, 1913–1936, Longmans, Green, and Co., New York, 1936.

Charleston Gazette, 16 April 1933.

Charleston Gazette, 9 March 1986.

Cherniak, Martin, *The Hawk's Nest Incident: America's Worst Industrial Disaster*, Yale University Press, New Haven, 1986.
Chernow, Ron, *The House of Morgan: An American Banking Dynasty and the Rise of Modern Finance*, The Atlantic Monthly Press, New York, 1990.

Chicago Tribune, 22 November 1895.

Churchill, Ward, *Struggle For The Land: Indigenous Resistance to Genocide, Ecocide, and Expropriation in Contemporary North America*, Common Courage, Monroe, 1993.

Chomsky, Noam, "The Victors: Part I, *Z Magazine*, September 1990.

Clark, Ramsey, *The Fire This Time: U.S. War Crimes in the Gulf*, Thunder's Mouth Press, New York, 1994.

Clendinnen, Inge, "Fierce and Unnatural Cruelty': Cortes and the Conquest of Mexico," *Representations*, 33, (1991).

Coben, Stanley, *A. Mitchell Palmer: Politician*, Columbia University Press, New York, 1963.

Coggins and Wilkinson, *Federal Public Land and Resources Law*, 2nd edition, Mineola, NY: Foundation Press, 1987.

Collins, Frederick L., *Money Town: The Story of Manhattan Toe: that Golden Mile which lies between the Battery and the Fields*, G.P. Putnam's Sons, New York, 1946.

Collins, Varnum Lansing, ed, *A Brief Narative of the Ravages of the British and Hessians at Princeton in 1776-1777*, The University Library, Princeton, 1906.

Commons, John R, et al., eds, *A Documentary History of American Industrial Society*, Russell & Russell, New York, 1958, vol. 9.

Connell, Evan S, *Son of the Morning Star*, North Point Press, San Francisco, 1984.

BiBLiOGRApHY

Conot, Robert E, *Justice At Nuremberg*, Carrol & Graf, New York, 1983.

Cope, John *King of the Hottentots*, Howard Timmins, Cape Town, 1967.

Copeland, Tom, *The Centralia Tragedy of 1919: Elmer Smith and the Wobblies*, University of Washington Press, Seattle, 1993.

Costigan, Giovanni, *A History of Modern Ireland, With a Sketch of Earlier Times*, Pegasus, New York, 1969.

Cotroneo, Ross Ralph, *The History of the Northern Pacific Land Grant, 1900-1952*, Ph.D. dissertation, University of Idaho, 1966. Reprinted in 1967 by Arno Press, New York.

Croly, Herbert, *Willard Straight*, Macmillan, New York, 1924.

Crosby v. National Foreign Trade Council

Custer, Elizabeth B, *Following the Guidon*, Harper & Brothers, New York, 1890.

Custer, George Armstrong, *My Life on the Plains*, University of Nebraska Press, Lincoln, 1966.

Davidson, Eugene, *The Trial of the Germans*, Collier Books, NY, 1966.

Davis, Kenneth S., *The Hero: Charles A. Lindbergh and the American Dream*, Doubleday, Garden City, New York, 1959.

Davis, Susan Lawrence, *Authentic History: Ku Klux Klan, 1865-1877*, American Library Service, New York, 1924.

Davis, Thomas, *The speeches of the Right Honourable John Philpot Curran*, James Duffy, Wellington Quay, Dublin, 1871.

DeCaux, Len, *The Living Spirit of the Wobblies*, International Publishers, New York, 1978.

Declaration of Independence.

de Kiewiet, C. W., *A History of South Africa: Social and Economic*, The Clarendon Press, Oxford, 1941.

Delaney, Edward, and M. T. Rice, *The Bloodstained Trail: A History of Militant Labor in the United States*, The Industrial Worker, Seattle, 1927.

Deloria, Vine, Jr., *Red Earth, White Lies: Native Americans and the Myth of Scientific Fact*, Fulcrum Press, Golden, CO, 1997.

Dembo, David, Morehouse, Ward, and Wyckle, Lucinda, *Abuse of Power: Social Performance of Multinational Corporations*, The Apex Press, New York, 1990.
Dew, Thomas Roderick, "Abolition of Negro Slavery," *American Quarterly Review*, XII (1832), 189–265.

Diamond, Stanley, *In Search of the Primitive*, Transaction Publishers, New Brunswick, 1993.

Dictionary of Word Origins, National Textbook Company, Lincoln, 1991.

DIL = John Bassett Moore, *A Digest of International Law* (Washington: Government Printing Office, 1906), VII, 187.

Donnan, Elizabeth, *Documents Illustrative of the Slave Trade to America*, vol. 2, Octagon Books, New York, 1965.

Douglass, Frederick, *Life and Times of Frederick Douglass: Written by Himself*, Citadel Press, Secaucus, 1983.

Dow, Geoge Francis, *Slave Ships and Slaving*, Cornell Maritime Press, Cambridge, 1968.

Drimmer, Frederick, ed, *Captured by the Indians: Fifteen firsthand accounts, 1750–1870*, Dover, New York, 1985.

Drinnon, Richard, *Facing West: The Metaphysics of Indian-Hating & Empire-Building*, University of Oklahoma Press, Norman, 1997

Dubofsky, Melvin, *We Shall Be All: A History of the Industrial Workers of the World*, Chicago, 1969.

DuBois, W. E. Burghardt, "The African Roots of War," *Atlantic Monthly*, May 1915.

Dunnigan, James F., and Nofi, Albert A., *Dirty Little Secrets: Military Information You're Not Supposed to Know*, Morrow, New York, 1990.

Eddis, William, *Letters From America*, edited by Aubrey C. Land, The Belknap Press of Harvard University Press, Cambridge, 1969.

Edwards, David, *Burning All Illusions*, South End Press, Boston, 1996

BiBLioGRAPHY

Edwards, David, *The Compassionate Revolution: Radical Politics and Buddhism*, Green Books, Devon, 1998

Edwards, Gordon, "Plutonium Anyone?" *Ploughshares Monitor*, Spring 1995.

Eight Million = "Eight Million May Die from Air Pollution by 2020," *Earth First! Journal*, November–December 2001, 19.

Engels, Frederick, *Herr Eugen Dühring's Revolution in Science [Anti-Dühring]*, Cooperative Publishing Society of Foreign Workers in the U.S.S.R., Moscow, 1934

Epstein, Samuel S, *The Politics of Cancer Revisited*, East Ridge Press, Fremont Center, 1998

Estes, Ralph, *Tyranny of the Bottom Line: Why Corporations Make Good People Do Bad Things*, Berrett-Koehler Publishers, San Francisco, 1996.

Evans, Bergen, editor, *The Dictionary of Quotations: Collected and Arranged with Coments by Bergen Evans*, Delacorte Press, New York, 1968.

Evernden, Neil, *The Natural Alien: Humankind and the Environment*, University of Toronto Press, Toronto, 1985.

Everest, Larry, *Behind the Poison Cloud: Union Carbide's Bhopal Massacre*, Banner Press, Chicago, 1986.

FAIR= Fairness & Accuracy in Reporting, Media Advisory, January 12, 2001.

Faust, Drew Gilpin, *The Ideology of Slavery*, Louisiana State University Press, Baton Rouge, 1981.

Fayette Journal, 18 Feb. 1931

Fayette Tribune, 6 May 1931

Fayette Tribune, 20 May 1931

Fayette Tribune, 3 June 1931

Fellmeth, Robert, *The Interstate Commerce Omission, the Public Interest and the ICC*, Grossman Publishers, New York, 1970.

Fisher, Sidney George, *A Philadelphia Perspective: The Diary of Sidney George*

Fisher, 1834-1871, Nicholas B. Wainwright, ed, The Historical Society of Pennsylvania, Philadelphia, 1967.

Fitch, John, *The Steel Workers*, "The Pittsburgh Survey," Russell Sage Foundation/Charities Publication Committee, New York, 1910.

Fitzpatrick, John C, ed, *The Writings of George Washington from the original manuscript sources, 1745–1799; prepared under the direction of the United States George Washington bicentennial commission and published by authority of Congress*, Government Printing Office, 1931–44, vol. 15, 189–193.

Fitzhugh, George, "Southern Thought," *De Bow's Review*, XXIII (1857) 338–50.

Flint, John, *Cecil Rhodes*, Boston, Little, Brown & Co., 1974.

Foner, Phillip S, *A History of the Labor Movement in the United States: Volume IV: The Industrial Workers of the World, 1905-1917*, International Publishers, New York, 1965.

Forbes, John Douglas, *J.P. Morgan, Jr., 1867-1943*. University Press of Virginia, Charlottesville, 1981.

Foreman, Grant, *Indian Removal: The emigration of the five civilized tribes of Indians*, University of Oklahoma Press, Norman, 1953,

Fox News Sunday, 6/17/01.

Fram, Alan, Associated Press, "Hefty rise in defense budget: Bush to ask for 10% increase of $18 billion," *San Francisco Chronicle*, June 23, 2001, A3.

Freire, Paulo, translated by Myra Bergman Ramos, *Pedagogy of the Oppressed*, Herder and Herder, New York, 1971.

Frontline, "Secrets of a Bomb Factory," 10/26/93.

Frontline: The Diamond Empire, February 1, 1994.

Freuchen, Peter, *Famous Book of the Eskimos*, Fawcett, New York, 1961.

Freyre, Gilberto, *The Masters and the Slaves*, tr. by Samuel Putnam, Alfred A. Knopf, New York, 1963.

Fromm, Erich, *The Anatomy of Human Destructiveness*, Holt, Rinehart &

Winston, New York, 1973.

Fromm, Erich, *To Have or to Be?* Harper & Row, New York, 1976.

Froyen, Richard T, *Macroeconomics: Theories and Policies*, MacMillan, New York, 1983.

Galeano, Eduardo, *Upside Down*, Metropolitan Books, translated by Mark Fried, New York, 2000.

Galeano, Eduardo, *Century of the Wind*, Pantheon Books, translated by Cedric Belfrage, New York, 1988

Gambino, Richard, *Blood of my Blood: The Dilemma of the Italian-Americans*, Doubleday, Garden City, 1974.

Gerth, H. H., and C. Wright Mills, *From Max Weber: Essays in Sociology*, Oxford University Press, New York, 1958.

Gilbert, Martin, *The First World War: A Complete History*, Henry Holt and Company, New York, 1994.

Ginzburg, Ralph, *100 Years of Lynchings*, Black Classic Press, Baltimore, 1962, 1988.

Glaspell, Kate Eldridge, "Incidents in the Life of a Pioneer," *North Dakota Historical Quarterly*, 1941, 187-188.

Golab, Jan, "The Color of Hate: Supremacy Movements in Los Angeles, California, *Los Angeles Magazine*, November, 1999, p 28.

Gold Panic Investigation, House Report No. 31, Forty-first Congress, Second Session, 1870: 157

Gorczyk, in the Foreword to the *Overview/Manual for Jail/Prison Administrators and Staff* of the *Prisoner Rape Education Project*, Brandon, VT: Safer Society Press, 1993.

Gray, Lewis Cecil, assisted by Esther Katherin Thompson, *History of Agriculture in the Southern United States to 1860*, vol. 1, Peter Smith, New York, 1941.

Greeley, Andrew M, *That Most Distressful Nation: The Taming of the American Irish*, Quadrangle Books, Chicago, 1972.

Gregg, John B., Larry J. Zimmerman, James P. Steele, Helen Ferwerda, and Pauline S. Gregg 1981 Ante-Mortem Osteopathology at Crow Creek. *Plains Anthropologist* 26(94):287–300.

Greene, Ward, "Notes for a History of the Klan," *American Mercury*, 5, June 1925, p 240.

Grinnell, George Bird, "Coup and Scalp Among the Plains Indians," *American Anthropologist*, vol. 12, 1910.

Grossman, Karl, "Of Toxic Racism and Environmental Justice," *E Magazine*, vol. 3, Number 3, May/June 1992.

Gruen, Arno, *The Insanity of Normality: Realism as Sickness: Toward Understanding Human Destructiveness*, Grove Weidenfeld, New York, 1992.

Grund, Francis J., *Aristocracy in America*, Peter Smith, Gloucester, 1968.

Gyory, Andrew, *Closing the Gate: Race, Politics, and the Chinese Exclusion Act*, University of North Carolina Press, Chapel Hill, 1998.

Halbert, Henry S., and T. H. Ball, *The Creek War of 1813 and 1815 [i.e. 1814]*, University of Alabama Press, Tuscaloosa, 1895.

Hammarsköld, Dag, *Markings*, Alfred A Knopf, New York, 1964.

Hammond, James Henry, *Two Letters on Slavery in the United States, Addressed to Thomas Clarkson, Esq*, (Allen, McCarter & Co, Columbia, 1845).

Hancock, *Lords of Poverty: The Power, Prestige, and Corruption of the Intrernational Aid Business*, Atlantic Monthly Press, New York, 1989.

Harbaugh, William H., *Lawyer's Lawyer: The Life of John W. Davis*, Oxford University Press, New York, 1973.

Harbottle, Thomas, revised and updated by George Bruce, *Dictionary of Battles, from 743 B.C. to the Present*, Stein and Day, New York, 1975.

Hardin, Jesse Wolf, *Kindred Spirits: Sacred Earth Wisdom*, Granite Publishing, Columbus, 2001.

Harmon, Daniel Williams, *Sixteen Years in the Indian Country: The Journal of Daniel Williams Harmon, 1800-1816*, edited by W. Kaye Lamb, Macmillan, Toronto, 1957.

BiBLioGRApHy

Harper, William, *Anniversary Oration. South Carolina Society for the Advancement of Learning* (Washington, DC: Duff Green, 1836)

Hate Crime Statistics, 1998, Federal Bureau of Investigation.

Heider, Karl, *Grand Valley Dani: Peaceful Warriors*, Second Edition, Holt, Rinehart & Winston, San Francisco, 1991.

Herman, Judith, *Trauma and Recovery*, Basic Books, New York, 1992.

Heslewood, Fred W, "Barbarous Spokane, *International Socialist Review*, vol. 10, no. 8 (February, 1910), p 705–713.

Higham, Charles, *Trading With the Enemy: An Expose of the Nazi-American Money Plot 1933-1949*, Delecorte Press, New York, 1983.

Higham, John, *Strangers in the Land: Patterns of American Nativism, 1860–1925*, Rutgers University Press, New Brunswick, 1988.

Hilberg, Raul, *Destruction of the European Jews*, Revised and Definitive Edition, Holmes & Meier, NY, 1985.

Hirsch, Adam J, "The Collision of Military Cultures in Seventeenth Century New England," *Journal of American History*, 74, 1988.

Hitler, Adolf, *Mein Kampf*, translated by Ralph Mannheim, Houghton Mifflin, Boston, 1943.

Hoffman, Michael A., II, *They Were White and They Were Slaves: The Untold History of the Enslavement of Whites in Early America*, Wiswell Ruffin House, Dresden, New York, 1991.

Hoffman, Peter, *The History of the German Resistance 1933–1945*, MIT Press, Cambridge, 1977.

Holbrook, Stewart H. , *The Age of Moguls*, Doubleday & Co, Garden City, New York, 1954.

Hoyt, Edwin P. Jr, *The House of Morgan*, Dodd, Mead & Company, New York, 1966.

Hull, C Bryson, "Foreign Investment Up in Colombian Oilfields," Reuters, June 13, 2001.

IMT = *Trial of the Major War Criminals before the International Military Tribunal, Nuremberg, 14 November 1945–10 October 1946* (Nuremberg, 1947–1949).

Inglis, Brian, *Poverty and the Industrial Revolution*, Hodder and Stoughton, London, 1971.

Innes, Duncan, *Anglo American and the Rise of Modern South Africa*, New York: Monthly Review Press, 1984.

Ireland, Tom, *Child Labor As a Relic of the Dark Ages*, G.P. Putnam's Sons, New York, 1937.

Jackson, Kenneth T., *The Ku Klux Klan in the City, 1915-1930*, Oxford University Press, New York, 1967

Jackson, Stanley, *J.P. Morgan: A Biography*, Stein and Day, New York, 1983.

Jenkins, Roy, *Asquith: Portrait of a Man and an Era*, Chilmark Press, New York, 1964.

Jennings, Walter Wilson, *20 Giants of American Business: Biographical Sketches in Economic History*, Exposition Press, New York, 1953.

Jensen, Derrick, George Draffan, and John Osborn, *Railroads and Clearcuts: Legacy of Congress's 1864 Northern Pacific Railroad Land Grant*, Inland Empire Public Lands Council, Spokane, 1995.

Jensen, McChesney = Jensen, Derrick, "Free Press For Sale: How Corporations Have Bought The First Amendment: An Interview With Robert McChesney," *The Sun*, September, 2000.

Johnson v. M'Intosh, 21 U.S. 543; 1823 U.S. LEXIS 293; 5 L. Ed. 681; 8 Wheat.

Johnson, Allan Griswold, "On the Prevalence of Rape in the United States," *Signs: Journal of Women in Culture and Society*, Volume 6, No 1 (Autumn 1980), 145.

Johnson, Robert C., "The Transportation of Vagrant Children From London to Virginia, 1618-1622," Reinmuth, Howard S. Jr., *Early Stuart Studies: Essays in Honor of David Harris Willson*, University of Minnesota Press, Minneapolis, 1970.

Johnstone, Frederick A., *Class, Race, and Gold: A study of class relations and racial*

discrimination in South Africa, Routledge & Kegan Paul, Boston, 1976.

Jones, Helen, "Sea Food: Say Good-bye to the Fish," *Anderson Valley Advertiser*, January 31, 2001.

Josephson, Matthew, *The Robber Barons: The Great American Capitalists, 1861 - 1901*, Harcourt Brace, 1934.

Josephy, Alvin M., Jr, *The Patriot Chiefs: A Chronicle of American Indian Resistance*, New York: Viking Press, 1969.

Jung, Carl, *Introduction*, in Wickes, Frances G., *Inner World Of Childhood: A Study in Analytical Psychology*, Appleton-Century, New York, 1966.

Just Cause, Vol I, No. 2, November 1994, "Bhopal 10 Year Commemoration," A Publication of Communities Concerned About Corporations, New York.

Juvenal, *Fourth Satire*

Kanfer, Stefan, *The Last Empire, De Beers, Diamonds, and the World*, New York, Farrar Straus, Giroux, 1993.

Keim, De B. Randolph, *Sheridan's Troopers on the Borders: A Winter Campaign on the Plains*, Claxton, Remsen, & Heffelfinger, Philadelphia, 1870.

Kennedy, Stetson, *Jim Crow Guide to the USA*, (London, Lawrence & Wishart, 1959).

Klein, Herbert S, *The Middle Passage: Comparative Studies in the Atlantic Slave Trade*, Princeton University Press, Princeton, 1978.

Kren, George M., and Leon Rappoport, *The Holocaust and the Crisis of Human Behavior*, Holmes & Meier, New York, 1980.

Kuhn, Clifford M., Harlon E Joye, and E Bernard West, *Living Atlanta: An Oral History of the City, 1914-1918*, University of Georgia Press, Athens, 1990.

Kupers, Terry, *Prison Madness*, Jossey-Bass, San Francisco, 1999.

Kurzman, Dan, A. Killing Wind, Inside Union Carbide and the Bhopal Catastrophe, McGraw-Hill, New York, 1987.

Lachs, John, *Responsibility and the Individual in Modern Society*, The Harvester Press, Brighton, 1981.

685

LaDuke, Winona, *Last Standing Woman*, Voyageur Press, Stillwater, Minnesota, 1997.

Lai, H.M., and P.P Choy, *History of the Chinese in America: Outlines*, Chinese-American Studies Planning Group, Chinatown, San Francisco, 1973. Originally publihed by the authors, 1972. Distributed by Everybody's Bookstore, 840 Kearny Street, San Francisco, California, 94108.

Laing, R. D., *The Politics of Experience*, Ballantine, New York, 1967.

Lamont, Thomas W., "The Effect of the War on America's Financial Position," *Annals of the Academy of Political Science*, vol. 60, July 1915, 106–112.

Lappé, Marc, *Chemical Deception: The Toxic Threat To Health and the Environment*, Sierra Club Books, San Francisco, 1991.

Lester, J.C., and D.L. Wilson, *Ku Klux Klan: Its Origin, Growth, and Disbandment, with an Introduction and Notes by Walter L Fleming* (1905; reprint NY: Da Capo Press, 1973).

Levi, Primo, *The Reawakening*, in, *Survival in Auschwitz* and *The Reawakening: Two Memoirs*, translated by Stuart Woolf (afterward, translated by Ruth Feldman), Summit Books, New York, 1986.

Lewis, C. S., *The Screwtape Letters; & Screwtape Proposes a Toast*, The Macmillon Company, New York, 1961.

Lifton, Robert Jay, *The Nazi Doctors: Medical Killing and the Psychology of Genocide*, Basic Books, New York 1986.

Lincoln, Charles H, *Narratives of the Indian Wars, 1675-1699*, Charles Scribner's Sons, New York, 1913.

Lipscomb, Andrew A., and Bergh, Albert Ellery, ed, *The Writings of Thomas Jefferson*, Definitive Edition, Thomas Jefferson Memorial Association, Washington, 1905. vol. 11, 13.

Loewen, James W, *The Mississippi Chinese: Between Black and White*, Harvard University Press, Cambridge, 1971.

Longstreet, Stephen, *The Wilder Shore: A Gala Social History of San Francisco's Sinners and Spenders, 1894-1906*, Doubleday, Garden City, 1968.

Lukas, Ellen, *Children For Sale: The Stockholm Congress Against the Commercial*

Exploitation of Children.

Lundberg, Ferdinand, *America's 60 Families*, The Vanguard Press, New York, 1937.

MacKinnon, Catherine, *Toward A Feminist Theory of the State*, Harvard, Cambridge, 1989.

MacLean, Nancy, *Behind the Mask of Chivalry: The Making of the Second Ku Klux Klan*, Oxford University Press, New York, 1994.

Mander, Jerry, *In The Absence of the Sacred: The Failure of Technology and the Survival of the Indian Nations*, Sierra Club Books, San Francisco, 1991.

Marcuse, Herbert, *One Dimensional Man*, Beacon Press, Boston, 1992.

Markham, Edwin, Benjamin B. Lindsey, and George Creel, *Children in Bondage*, Arno, New York, 1969.

Martin v. White, 742 F.2d 469, 470 (8CT,1984)

Maslow, Abraham H, *The Farther Reaches of Human Nature*, The Viking Press, New York, 1971.

Mason, John, *A Brief History of the Pequot War*, Kneeland & Green, Boston, 1736. The version I looked at was from University Microfilms, Inc, Ann Arbor.

Matthew 7:3. The bible, silly.

Matthew 7:20.

McChesney, Robert, "Springtime for Goebbels," *Z Magazine*, December, 1997.

McCoy, Alfred W., *The Politics of Heroin: CIA Complicity in the Global Drug Trade*, Lawrence Hill Books, Chicago, 1991.

McCunn, Ruthanne Lum, *Thousand Pieces of Gold*, Design Enterprises, San Francisco, 1981.

McKinley, William, "Benevolent Assimilation Proclamation," December 21, 1898.

McRandle, James H, *The Track of the Wolf: Essays on National Socialism and Its Leader, Adolf Hitler*, Northwestern University Press, Evanston, 1965.

687

Meltzer, Milton, *Cheap Raw Material: How Our Youngest Workers Are Exploited and Abused*, Viking, New York, 1994.

Meltzer, Milton, *Slavery: A World History*, Da Capo Press, New York, 1993.

Mill, John Stuart, *On The Subjection of Women*, introduction by Wendell Robert Carr, The MIT Press, Cambridge, 1970.

Miller, Kerby, *Emigrants and Exiles: Ireland and the Irish Exodus to North America*, Oxford University Press, New York, 1985.

Miller, Nathan, *Stealing From America: A History of Corruption from Jamestown to Reagan*, Paragon House, New York, 1992.

Miller, Stuart Creighton, *The Unwelcome Immigrant: The American Image of the Chinese, 1785-1882*, University of California Press, Berkeley, 1969.

Mintner, William, *King Solomon's Mines Revisited: Western Interests and the Burdened History of Southern Africa*, New York, Basic Books, 1986.

Mokhiber, Russell, *Corporate Crime and Violence*, Sierra Club Books, San Francisco, 1988.

Monkerud, Don, "Follow the Money to Understand Oil Policy," *Anderson Valley Advertiser*, May 23, 2001, page 9.

Moodie, Donald, *The Record, or a Series of Official Papers Relative to the Condition and Treatment of the Native Tribes of South Africa*, A.A. Balkema Reprint, Amsterdam, 1960.

Moody, John, *The Truth About Trusts: A Description and Analysis of the American Trust Movement*, Moody Publishing Company, New York, 1904.

Mooney, James, *Myths of the Cherokee*, Scholarly Press, St Claire Shores, (House of Representatives, 56th Congress, 2d Session, Document 539, Nineteenth Annual Report, Bureau of American Ethnology, Part 1, p 126.

Moore, Samuel, "How the Kleagles Collected the Cash," *Independent*, 113, 13 December, 1924, p 517.

Moore, Taylor G, "Joe Harding's death list: The growing toll of workers in the uranium enrichment industry," *The Progressive*, January, 1980.

Morehouse, Ward, and Subramaniam, *The Bhopal Tragedy: What Really*

Happened and What It Means for American Workers and Communities at Risk: A Report for the Citizens Commission on Bhopal, Council on International and Public Affairs, New York, 1986.

Morgan, Edmund S., *American Slavery, American Freedom: The Ordeal of Colonial Virginia*, W.W. Norton and Company, New York, 1975.

Mores, Arthur D., *While Six Million Died: A Chronicle of American Apathy*, Ace, New York, 1967.

Moskowitz, Milton, Robert Levering, and Michael Katz, *Everybody's Business: A Field Guide to the 400 Leading Companies*, Doubleday Currency, New York, 1990.

Mostert, Noël, *Frontiers: The Epic of South Africa's Creation and the Tragedy of the Xhosa People*, Alfred A. Knopf, New York, 1992.

Mumford, Lewis, *The City in History: Its Origins, Its Transformations, and Its Prospects*, Harcourt, Brace & Word, New York, 1961.

Mumford, Lewis, *The Myth of the Machine, Volume II: The Pentagon of Power*, Harcourt Brace Jovanovich, New York, 1970.

Myers, Gustavus, *History of the Great American Forttunes*, The Modern Library, New York, 1937.

Nagles, James F. A History of Government Contracting. Washington DC: George Washington University, 1992,

R. W. Darré, "Marriage Laws and the Principles of Breeding, *Nazi Ideology Before 1933: A Documentation*, translated by Barbara Hiller and Leila J. Gupp, University of Texas Press, Austin, 1978.

The New York Times, June 11, 1900, "An Innocent Man Lynched."

The New York Times, August 11, 1950, "Morgan Mansion Will Be Restyled." .

The New York Times, May 26, 1983.

The New York Times, March 15, 1985.

The New York Times, March 21 1985.

The New York Times, April 10, 1985.

THE CULTURE OF MAKE BELIEVE

The New York Times, April 25, 1985.

The New York Times, October 21, 1987.

New York Tribune, March 17, 1901, "Tennessee Colored Woman Lynched."

Norberg-Hodge, Helena, *Ancient Futures: Listening to Ladakh*, Sierra Club Books, San Francisco, 1991.

Norton, Jack, *Genocide in Northwestern California: When Our Worlds Cried*, Indian Historian Press, San Francisco, 1979.

Nott, Josiah C, *Two Lectures on the Natural History of the Caucasian and Negro Races*, (Mobile: Dade and Thompson, 1844)

Novack, George, "Slavery in Colonial America," from Novack, George, ed, *America's Revolutionary Heritage*, Pathfinder Press, New York, 1976.

Oberholtzer, Ellis P., *Jay Cooke: financier of the Civil War*, George Jacobs and Co. 2 vols, Philadelphia: 1907.

Oppenheim, A. Leo, *Ancient Mesopotamia: A Portrait of a Dead Civilization*, University of Chicago Press, Chicago, 1964.

Paine, Thomas, *Common Sense*, 1776, in *Common Sense, The Rights of Man, and Other Essential Writings of Thomas Paine*, New American Library, New York, 1969.

Parenti, Christian, *Lockdown America: Police and Prisons in the Age of Crisis*, Verso, New York, 1999.

Parkman, Francis, *The Conspiracy of Pontiac And the Indian War After the Conquest of Canada*, Volume 2, Little, Brown, and Company, Boston, 1898.

Peterson, H. C., and Gilbert C Fite, *Opponents of War, 1917-1918*, University of Wisconsin Press, Madison, 1957.

Petulla, Joseph M., *American Environmental History: The Exploitation and Conservation of Natural Resources*, San Francisco: Boyd & Fraser, 1977.

Phillips, George L, *England's Climbing-Boys: A History of the Long Struggle to Abolish Child Labor in Chimney-Sweeping*, Harvard Graduate School of Business Administration, Baker Library, Boston, 1949.

BIBLIOGRAPHY

PIP = Pesticide Information Profile, Cornell University, June 1996. .

Pringle, Henry F., *Theodore Roosevelt: A Biography*, Harcourt, Brace, New York, 1956.

Proctor, Robert N, *Racial Hygiene: Medicine Under the Nazis*, Harvard University Press, Cambridge, 1988.

PURS = Del Norte County Department of Agriculture Pesticide Use Reports, 1999.

Quinn, David B., *Roanoke Voyages 1584-1590*, Volume I, (London, 1955, 2nd ser., CIV, CV.

Ransome, S. *The Engineer in South Africa*, E.P. Dutton, New York, 1903.

Rapoport, *The Great American Bomb Machine*, E.P. Dutton, New York, 1971. .

Raven-Hart, Major R., *Before Van Riebeeck: Callers at South Africa from 1488 to 1652*, C. Struik, Cape Town, 1967.

Raven-Hart, Major R, *Cape of Good Hope, 1662-1702: the First Fifty Years*, Volume 1, A. A. Balkema, Cape Town, 1971.

Rawley, James A, *The Transatlantic Slave Trade: A History*, WW Norton, NY, 1981.

Reader's Digest Illustrated History of South Africa: The Real Story, Reader's Digest Association, Pleasantville, 1988.

Reitlinger, Gerald, *The Final Solution: The Attempt to Exterminate the Jews of Europe, 1939-1945*, Second Revised and Augmented Edition, Thomas Yoseloff, New York, 1961.

Rich, Norman, *Hitler's War Aims: Ideology, the Nazi State, and the Course of Expansion*, Norton, New York, 1973.

Richardson, James D., *A Compilation of the Messages and Papers of the Presidents 1789-1897*, vol. 2, published by Authority of Congress, 1900. Jackson's Second Annual Message.

Richmond *Religious Herald*, February 25, 1841, "A Brief Examination of Scripture Testimony on the Institution of Slavery. Republished by the Congressional Globe Office, 1850.

Rolland, Romain, *Jean Christophe*, Avon, New York, 1969.

Roosevelt, Theodore, *The Strenuous Life: Essays and Addresses*, Scholarly Press, St. Clair Shores, 1970.

Root, Deborah, *Cannibal Culture: Art, Appropriation, and the Commodification of Difference*, Westview Press, Boulder, 1996.

Rowlandson, Mary, *Narrative of the Captivity of Mrs. Mary Rowlandson*, (1682), collected in Lincoln.

Russell, Diana E. H., *Sexual Exploitation: Rape, Child Sexual Abuse, and Sexual Harassment*, Sage, Beverly Hills, 1984.

Russell, Secret = Russell, Diana E. H., *The Secret Trauma: Incest in the Lives of Girls and Women*, Basic Books, New York, 1986.

Ryan, John C., *Hazardous Handouts: Taxpayer Subsidies to Environmental Degradation*, Northwest Environment Watch, Seattle, p. 42–44, 48–49.

Sabini, John P., and Maury Silver, "Destroying the Innocent with a Clear Conscience: A Sociopsychology of the Holocaust," in *Survivors, Victims, and Perpetrators: Essays in the Nazi Holocaust*, ed. Joel E Dimsdale, Hemisphere Publishing, Washington, 1980.

Sahagún, Bernardino de, *Conquest of New Spain*, 1585 revision, translated by Howard F. Cline, edited and with an introduction by S.L. Cline, University of Utah Press, Salt Lake City, 1989.

St Clair, Jeffrey, and Alexander Cockburn, "Power, Profits and Salmon," *Anderson Valley Advertiser*, June 6, 2001, page 5.

Salaita, Steven Nasr, ". . . Invisible, With Liberty and Justice for All: Thoughts on the Elections," *Z Magazine*, December, 2000, 16–20

Sampson, Anthony, *The Sovereign State of ITT*, Stein and Day, New York, 1973.

Sauer, Carl Ortwin, *The Early Spanish Main*, University of California Press, Berkeley, 1966.

Schenk v. United States U.S. 47 (1919)

Schmalz, Peter S., *The Ojibwa of Southern Ontario*, University of Toronto Press, Toronto, 1991.

BIBLIOGRAPHY

Schmitt, Bernadotte E., and Harold C. Vedeler, *The World in the Crucible, 1914-1919*, Harper & Row, New York, 1984.

Schmitz, David, *The United States and Fascist Italy, 1922-1940*, University of North Carolina Press, Chapel Hill, 1988.

Schwantes, Carlos, *Railroad Signatures Across the Pacific Northwest*, University of Washington, Seattle, 1993.

Schwartz, Stephen I., editor, *Atomic Audit: The Costs and Consequences of U.S. Nuclear Weapons Since 1940*, The Brookings Institution, Washington, 1998.

Shirer, William, *The Rise and Fall of the Third Reich: A History of Nazi Germany*, Fawcett Crest, Greenwich, 1970.

Paul Shrivastava, *Bhopal, Anatomy of a Crisis*, Second Edition, Paul Chapman Publishing, London, 1992.

Simpson, Christopher, *Blowback: The First Full Account of America's Recruitment of Nazis, and its Disastrous Effect on our Domestic and Foreign Policy*, Weidenfeld & Nicolson, New York, 1988.

Sims, Andrew, "Globalisation: Time to say a daily prayer for the global economy," *The Independent*, United Kingdom, December 12, 2000.

Simon, John Y., ed, *The Papers of Ulysses S. Grant, Volume 23, February 1–December 31*, 1872, Southern Illinois University Press, Carbondale, 1967.

Sinclair, Andrew, *Corsair: The Life of J.Pierpont Morgan*, Little, Brown and Company, Boston, 1981.

Smalley, Eugene Virgil, *History of the Northern Pacific Railroad*, G.P. Putnam's Sons, New York, 1883, Arno Press (NY), 1975 reprint.

Smith, Harry, *The Autobiography of Lieutenant General Sir Harry Smith* (one volume edition), edited by G. C. Moore Smith, John Murray, London, 1902.

Smith, Sydney, *Works of The Reverend Sydney Smith: Three Volumes Complete in One*, D. Appleton and Company, New York, 1867.

Sobel, Robert, *The Curbstone Brokers: The Origins of the American Stock Exchange*, Macmillan, New York, 1970.

Spargo, John, *The Bitter Cry of the Children*, Chicago, Quadrangle, 1968.

693

Spelman, Henry, "Relation of Virginea" (London, 1613), in Arber and Bradley, eds, *Travels and Works of John Smith, Volume One*, Burth Franklin, New York, 1967.

Stannard, David, *American Holocaust: Columbus and the Conquest of the New World*, Oxford University Press, New York 1992.

Steiner, George, *In Bluebeard's Castle: Some Notes Towards the Redefinition of Culture*, Yale University Press, New Haven, 1971.

Steiner, Stan, *Fusang: The Chinese Who Built America*, Harper & Row, New York, 1979.

Steiner, Zara, *Britain and the Origins of the First World War*, St Martin's Press, New York, 1977.

Sterling, Dorothy, *The Trouble They Seen: Black People Tell the Story of Reconstruction*, Doubleday, Garden City, 1976.

Stimson, Henry L., and McGeorge Bundy, *On Active Service in Peace and War*, Harper & Brothers, New York, 1947.

Stockenstrom, Andries, *The Autobiography of the Late Sir Andries Stockenstrom, Bart.*, edited by C.W. Hutton, Cape Town, 1887, Struik Reprint, Cape Town, 2 vols., 1964

Stolen Lives: Killed By Law Enforcement, second edition, Stolen Lives Project, New York, 1999.

Stone, William L, *Life of Joseph Brant—Thayendanegea, Including the Indian Wars of the American Revolution*, vol. 1, Alexander V. Blake, New York, 1838.

Struckman-Johnson, Cindy, et al, "Sexual Coercion Reported by Men and Women, *The Journal of Sex Research*, vol. 33, no. 1, 1996.

Takaki, Ronald T., Iron Cages: Race and Culture in Nineteenth-Century America, Alfred A. Knopf, 1979.

Tarbell, Ida M., *The Life of Elbert H. Gary: The Story of Steel*, D. Appleton & Co., New York, 1925.

Taylor, Ellen, "The Protester's Mother," *Anderson Valley Advertiser*, June 6, 2001, page 4.

BIBLIOGRAPHY

Thomas, Hugh, *The Slave Trade: The Story of the Atlantic Slave Trade, 1440–1870*, Simon & Schuster, New York, 1997.

Thayer, William Roscoe, *The Life and Letters of John Hay*, vol. 2, Houghton Mifflin, Boston, 1915.

Thoreau, Henry David, *The Illustrated: A Week on the Concord and Merrimack Rivers: with photographs from the Gleason Collection*, text edited by Carl F. Hovde, William L Howarth, and Elizabeth Hall Witherell, Princeton University Press, Princeton, 1983.

Tocqueville, Alexis de, *Democracy in America*, Toqueville, Vol 1, Alfred A Knopf, New York, 1966.

Todorov, Tzvetan, *Facing the Extreme: Moral Life in the Concentration Camps*, Metropolitan Books, New York, 1996.

Townsend, John Clendenin, *Running the Gauntlet: Cultural Sources of Violence Against the IWW.*, Garland Publishing, New York, 1986.

Turner, Frederick, *Beyond Geography: The Western Spirit Against the Wilderness*, Rutgers, New Brunswick, 1992.

Tyler, A, "Dust to Dust," *Washington Monthly*, January, 1975, 50.

Underhill, John, *Newes from America, or A New and Experimentall Discoverie of New England*, London, 1638, Da Capo Press, New York, 1971.

Union Carbide Annual Report, 1984.

Union Carbide Annual Report, 1994.

United Nations Convention on the Prevention and Punishment of the Crime of Genocide, 1948.

United States, *Riot at Memphis*, 39 Cong., 1 sess., House Exec Doc no 122 1866): 1–3.

Utley, Robert M., *Frontier Regulars: The United States Army and the Indian, 1866-1891*, Macmillan Publishing Company, New York, 1973.

Vallette, Jim, "The Tragic Rise of Lawrence Summers," *Eat The State*, May 19, 1999.

695

Van der Zee, John, *Bound Over: Indentured Servitude and the American Conscience*, Simon and Schuster, New York, 1985.

Wade, Wyn Craig, *The Fiery Cross: The Ku Klux Klan in America*, Simon and Schuster, New York, 1987.

Waldman, Michael, *Who Robbed America: A Citizen's Guide to the Savings & Loan Scandal*, Random House, New York, 1990.

Walker, John Brisben, "The World's Greatest Revolution," *Cosmopolitan*, April 1, 1901, 677–680.

Wall Street Journal, April 1, 1985.

Wasserman, Harvey, and Norman Solomon, with Robert Alvarez and Eleanor Waters, *Killing Our Own: The Disaster of America's Experience with Atomic Radiation*, Delta, New York, 1982.

Webster's New Twentieth Century Dictionary of the English Language Unabridged, Second Edition, Simon and Schuster, NY, 1979.

Weir, David, *The Bhopal Syndrome, Pesticides, Environment, and Health*, Sierra Club Books, San Francisco, 1987.

Weizenbaum, Joseph, *Computer Power and Human Reason: From Judgment to Calculation*, W.H. Freeman, San Francisco, 1976.

Wheatcroft, Geoffrey, *The Randlords: South Africa's Robber Barons and the Mines that Forged a Nation*, New York, Simon & Schuster, 1985.

Wheeler, George, *Pierpont Morgan and Friends: The Anatomy of a Myth*, Prentice-Hall, Englewood Cliffs, New Jersey, 1973.

Wiebe, Robert H., *The Search for Order, 1877-1920*, Hill and Wang, New York, 1966.

Williams, Roger, *A Key Into the Language of America*, 1643, reprinted by Gryphon Books, Ann Arbor, 1971.

Wilson, Woodrow, *A History of the American People*, vol. 5, Harper & Brothers, New York, 1901.

Winkler, John K., *Morgan the Magnificent: The Life of J. Pierpont Morgan (1837–1913)*, Garden City Publishing, Garden City, 1930.

Wolf, Peter, *Land in America: Its Value, Use, and Control,* New York: Pantheon Books, 1981.

Wood, Daniel B., "To Keep Peace, prisons allow race to rule," *Christian Science Monitor,* September 16, 1997.

Wooden, Wayne, and Parker, Jay, *Men Behind Bars: Sexual Exploitation in Prison,* Plenum Press, New York, 1982.

Worger, William, lecture, "Incarceration and Industrialization: Changes in Punishment in Late Nineteenth Century South Africa, delivered Stanford University, January 29, 1987.

Wyman, David S., *The Abandonment of the Jews: American and the Holocaust, 1941–1945,* Pantheon, New York, 1984.

Yung, Judy, *Chinese Women of America: A Pictorial History,* University of Washington Press, Seattle, 1986.

Zerzan, John, *Elements of Refusal,* Left Bank Books, Seattle, 1988.

Zerzan, personal = I am endebted to John Zerzan for this excellent line. It's his, and I've merely stolen it.

Zinn, Howard, *A People's History of the United States,* Harper Perennial, New York, 1980.

Zinn, Howard, *Failure to Quit: Reflections of an Optimistic Historian,* Common Courage Press, Monroe, 1993.

Zurara (Azuzara), Gomes Eannes De, *The Chronicle of the Discovery and Conquest of Guinea,* Eng tr. ed Beazley, Charles Raymond, and Prestage, Edgar, Hakluyt Socity, 1st Ser, vol 95 (London, 1896 and 1899). Version I looked at: Burt Franklin, Publisher, NY.

INTERNET:

Arjet, Robert, History of the Ku Klux Klan, The First Era: http://hatewatch.org/klan/1st_era.html, visited December 2, 2000

Basic = Basic Facts on the Nanjing Massacre and the Tokyo War Crimes Trial, pamphlet published by New Jersey Hong Kong Network, P.O. Box 18, Bound Brooks, NJ 08805. http://ww4.cnd.org/njmassacre/nj.html site visited June 8, 2001

BMO = Behavior Modification Operations, http://www.milinfoserv.net/BMO.htm Site visited March 26, 2001

Bureau of Justice, Correctional Populations in the United States, 1997 November 2000, NCJ 177613, U.S. Department of Justice Office of Justice Programs, http://www.ojp.usdoj.gov/bjs/pub/ascii/cpus97.txt visited December 2, 2000

Canon, Scott, "Leader Defends Conservative Group Against Charges of Racism," *The Kansas City Star*, Jan 24, 1999, http://about.ferris.edu/isar/Institut/CCC/KCstar.htm Site visited March 11, 2001

CDI = Military Spending Clock by CDI (Center for Defense Information), http://www.cdi.org/msc/clock.html visited March 7, 2001

Cosmo = Cosmopolitan Magazine's web page. http://www.cosmomag.com/?rn site visited April 23, 2001

The Deadliest Day, http://www.sonomacountyfreepress.org/police/deadliest-day.html visited December 2, 2000.

Department of Justice, 1993 = Bureau of Justice Statistics, Compendium of Federal Justice Statistics, 1993, http://www.ojp.usdoj.gov/bjs/pub/pdf/cfjs93.pdf site visited February 13, 2001

Dimenstein, Gilberto, "Little Girls of the Night," http://pangaea.org/street_children/latin/brzpros.htm, visited December 3, 2000

Donaldson, Stephen, Rape of Incarcerated Americans: A Preliminary Statistical Look, Seventh Edition, July, 1995, http://www.spr.org/docs/stats.html visited December 2, 2000

Draffan, George, Corporate Profiles Compiled by George Draffan, Public Information Network, PO Box 95316, Seattle WA 98145-2316 USA, http://endgame.org/ then look under corporate profiles, Freeport McMoRan. Visited February 7, 2001

BiBLioGRAPHY

Draffan, George, WMX, both personal communications with George, and his Corporate Profiles Compiled by George Draffan, Public Information Network, PO Box 95316, Seattle WA 98145-2316 USA, http://endgame.org/ then look under corporate profiles, WMX. Visited April 28, 2001

Draffan, George, Endgame. http://endgame.org/endgame.html Site visited June 16, 2001

Dunbaugh, Frank, "Argument," http://www.igc.apc.org/spr/docs/farmer/argument.html visited December 2, 2000

Echelon Watch, "Answers to Frequently Asked Questions (FAQ) About Echelon," http://www.aclu.org/echelonwatch/faq.html#3 visited June 23, 2001

England, Charles R, "A Look at the Indian Health Service Policy of Sterilization, 1972-1976. http://www.dickshovel.com/IHSSterPol.html visited November 26, 2000

Eugenics = American Eugenics Society List of Officers http://www.africa2000.com/ENDX/aeoff.htm site visited March 11, 2001

The Flames of Shell: http://www.thirdworldtraveler.com/Boycotts/Flames_Shell.html visited December 2, 2000

Florida: Major Prison Gangs: Gang and Security Threat Group Awareness, Florida Department of Corrections. http://www.dc.state.fl.us/pub/gangs/prison.html site visited February 9, 2001

http://www.kukluxklan.org/doesthe.htm, with "does the" referring to the first two words of the page's title, "Does the Klan Hate Negroes." From the official webpage of the Knights of the Ku Klux Klan National Party Headquarters.

Hamilton, Alison B, *Nigger Please*, http://parallel.park.uga.edu/distance/texts/hamilton.html

Hate Directory: http://www.bcpl.net/~rfrankli/hatedir.htm visited December 2, 2000

Hechler, David, Child Sex Tourism,
ftp://members.aol.com/hechler/tourism.html visited December 3, 2000

Highfield, Roger, "Scientists unlock the secrets of selective amnesia," *Telegraph*,
3/15/01
http://www.telegraph.co.uk/et?ac=002484462443787&rtmo=QwemLS0R&atm
o=tttttttd&pg=/et/01/3/15/wmem15.html
visited March 18, 2001

History of the Original Ku Klux Klan, http://kukluxklan.org/whenan.htm, visited December 2, 2000

Hitler's Airwaves, http://cmsu2.cmsu.edu/~sms21640/airwaves.html, site visited
June 24, 2001

Irby, Richard E, Jr, The New York City Draft Riots,
http://www.geocities.com/Athens/Acropolis/2691/nycdr.html
Site visited April 19, 2001

IWW = Preamble and Constitution of the Industrial Workers of the World.
Found on the internet, at the site:
http://digital.library.arizona.edu/bisbee/docs/018.php
site visited May 3, 2001

Lanezes = http://www.lanezes.com/myron/usa.htm
Site visited March 7, 2001

Lean, Geoffrey, "Shell 'paid Nigerian Military'"
http://www.greenpeace.org/~comms/ken/opay001.html visited December 2,
2000

Leykis, Tom, from The Tom Leykis Show, December 27, 1999. The transcript
came from Media Watch http://www.mediawatch.com, by way of Charlotte
Watson

The Lynching Calender: African-Americans Who Died in Racial Violence in
the United States by Month of Death, 1865-1965.
http://www.geocities.com/Colosseum/Base/8507/Calendar1.htm
site visited May 5, 2001; June 1, 2001

McCulloch, Richard, "The Nordish Crisis,"
http://www.racialcompact.com/nordishcrisis.html#anchor221023
Site visited March 12, 2001

BIBLIOGRAPHY

Minnesota State Public Defender: Sources: South Africa's incarceration rates compared to the U.S.
http://www.pubdef.state.mn.us/homepages/statepd/south_africa.htm
Visited December 2, 2000

National Criminal Justice Commission Key Findings,
http://www.igc.apc.org/ncia/KEY.HTML, visited December 2, 2000

Parry, Robert, and Norman Solomon, "Behind Colin Powell's Legend: My Lai," The Consortium, http://www.consortiumnews.com/archive/colin3.html, visited February 7, 2001

Pearson, Helen, "Some Choose to Lose Memory," *Nature Science Update*, March 15, 2001, http://www.nature.com/nsu/010315/010315-10.html
Visited March 18, 2001

Population = [www.census.gov/ipc/www/world.html]

Raimondo, Justin, "Selective Amnesia: The Epidemic," Antiwar.com: Behind the Headlines, 3/16/01, http://128.121.216.19/justin/justincol.html, site visited March 18, 2001

Raymond, Janice, Legitimating Prostitution as Sex Work, December 1998, Coalition Against Trafficking in Women,
http://www.uri.edu/artsci/wms/hughes/catw/legit.htm, December 3, 2000

Reid, John Alden (Park Ranger—interpreter-historian at Horseshoe Bend National Military Park), "The 'Carnage was Dreadful:' The Battle of the Horseshoe, March 27, 1814,"
http://homepages.rootsweb.com/~cmamcrk4/crkwr8.html
Site visited March 1, 2001

Rights For All, Amnesty International
http://www.rightsforall-usa.org/info/report/ro3.htm

Robinson, Laurie Nicole, "The Globalization of Female Child Prostitution: A Call For Reintegration and Recovery Measures Via Article 39 of the United Nations Convention on the Rights of the Child," *Indiana Journal of Global Legal Studies*, Fall 1997: Volume 5, Issue 1. Online version visited at:
http://www.law.indiana.edu/glsj/vol5/no1/robinson.html visited December 3, 2000
Site renamed: http://ijgls.indiana.edu/archive/05/01/robinson.shtml#6 visited December 20, 2001

Star Spangled Banner,
http://www.geocities.com/Athens/Acropolis/2691/fsk.html
Site visited June 21, 2001

Swogger, Michael J, "Federal Conscription and the New York Draft Riots of 1863," http://www.i5ive.com/article.cfm/381/23843
Site visited April 19, 2001

Talamantez, Luis, "California Prisoner Challenges Torture," *North Coast Xpress*, Fall 99, http://thunder.sonic.net/~doretk/Issues/99-09%20FALL/calif.html
Visited February 10, 2001

Too Close = Too Close For Comfort
http://www.pirg.org/reports/enviro/home98/page2.htm
Site visited July 7, 2001

Uniform Crime Report, 1999, Section Five, on the murder rate, is available at http://www.fbi.gov/ucr/Cius_99/99crime/99cius5.pdf site visited February 12, 2001

Vachs, Andrew, Stop Child Sex Tourism, http://night-flight.com/dbt/
Visited December 3, 2000

Vicksburg= *The Chicago Defender*, Chicago, Illinois, May 24, 1919 online at http://www.lib.uchicago.edu/ecuip/diglib/social/chi1919/aline/a5/lynch.html
Site visited May 5, 2001.

BIBLIOGRAPHY

DERRICK JENSEN is the author of the award-winning books *A Language Older Than Words* and *Listening to the Land*. He writes for *The New York Times Magazine*, *Audubon*, and *The Sun*. Jensen lives near the ocean and among the redwoods in Crescent City, California, where he works to improve habitat for the coho salmon who swim upstream near his home, and for the California red-legged frogs who sing nightly outside his windows. He teaches creative writing at Pelican Bay State Prison.